Over the past forty y ... ity of Chicago have won more than one-tl ... pline and have been major influences on ... nomics presents the first collective attempt ... to chart the rise and development of the Chicago School during the decades that followed the Second World War. Drawing on new research in published and archival sources, contributors examine the people, institutions, and ideas that established the foundations for the success of Chicago economics and thereby positioned it as a powerful and controversial force in American political and intellectual life.

Robert Van Horn is assistant professor of economics at the University of Rhode Island. He received his Ph.D. in economics from the University of Notre Dame in 2007 and was a postdoctoral associate at the Center for the History of Political Economy at Duke University in 2008–2009. His published work on the history of the Chicago School comprises two chapters in Philip Mirowski and Dieter Plehwe's *The Road from Mont Pèlerin: The Making of the Neoliberal Thought Collective* (2009) and two articles in Ross Emmett's *The Elgar Companion to the Chicago School of Economics* (2010). He has also published in *History of Political Economy, Journal of the History of Economic Thought, Research in the History of Economic Thought and Methodology*, and *Social Studies of Science*.

Philip Mirowski is Carl Koch professor of economics and the history and philosophy of science at the University of Notre Dame. His areas of specialization are in the history and philosophy of economics and the politics and economics of knowledge, with subsidiary areas in evolutionary computational economics, the economics of science and technological change, science studies, and the history of the natural sciences. His most recent books include *The Effortless Economy of Science* (2004, winner of the Ludwig Fleck Prize from the Society for the Social Studies of Science), *Machine Dreams* (Cambridge University Press, 2002), and *ScienceMart* (2011), and he edited *Agreement on Demand* (2006), *Science Bought and Sold* (2001), and *The Road from Mont Pèlerin* (2009). His book, *More Heat than Light* (Cambridge University Press, 1989), has been translated into French (2001). He has been the recipient of fellowships from the Fulbright program and New York University and was elected visiting Fellow at All Souls' College Oxford. He was elected president of the History of Economics Society for 2011.

Thomas A. Stapleford is associate professor in the program of liberal studies at the University of Notre Dame, where he also teaches in the graduate program in the history and philosophy of science. Trained as a historian, his research focuses on the history of the social sciences, especially economics and the mind sciences. His dissertation, revised and published as *The Cost of Living in America: A Political History of Economic Statistics, 1880–2000* (Cambridge University Press, 2009), won the Joseph Dorfman Best Dissertation Award from the History of Economics Society in 2004. He was a visiting scholar at the American Academy of Arts and Sciences in Cambridge, Mass., in 2008–2009, and has published articles on the history of economic statistics and American political economy in a variety of journals.

HISTORICAL PERSPECTIVES ON MODERN ECONOMICS

General Editor: Craufurd D. Goodwin, Duke University

This series contains original works that challenge and enlighten historians of economics. For the profession as a whole, it promotes better understanding of the origin and content of modern economics.

Other books in the series:

Arie Arnon, *Monetary Theory and Policy from Hume and Smith to Wicksell*
William J. Barber, *Designs within Disorder: Franklin D. Roosevelt, the Economists, and the Shaping of American Economic Policy, 1933–1945*
From New Era to New Deal: Herbert Hoover, the Economists, and American Economic Policy, 1921–1933
Filippo Cesarano, *Monetary Theory and Bretton Woods: The Construction of an International Monetary Order*
Timothy Davis, *Ricardo's Macroeconomics: Money, Trade Cycles, and Growth*
Jerry Evensky, *Adam Smith's Moral Philosophy: A Historical and Contemporary Perspective on Markets, Law, Ethics, and Culture*
M. June Flanders, *International Monetary Economics, 1870–1960: Between the Classical and the New Classical*
J. Daniel Hammond, *Theory and Measurement: Causality Issues in Milton Friedman's Monetary Economics*
Samuel Hollander, *The Economics of Karl Marx*
Samuel Hollander, *Friedrich Engels and Marxian Political Economy*
Lars Jonung (ed.), *The Stockholm School of Economics Revisited*
Kim Kyun, *Equilibrium Business Cycle Theory in Historical Perspective*
Gerald M. Koot, *English Historical Economics, 1870–1926: The Rise of Economic History and Mercantilism*
David Laidler, *Fabricating the Keynesian Revolution: Studies of the Inter-War Literature on Money, the Cycle, and Unemployment*
Odd Langholm, *The Legacy of Scholasticism in Economic Thought: Antecedents of Choice and Power*
Robert Leonard, *Von Neumann, Morgenstern, and the Creation of Game Theory: From Chess to Social Science, 1900–1960*
Harro Maas, *William Stanley Jevons and the Making of Modern Economics*
Philip Mirowski, *More Heat Than Light: Economics as Social Physics, Physics as Nature's Economics*
Philip Mirowski (ed.), *Nature Images in Economic Thought: "Markets Read in Tooth and Claw"*

(continued after index)

Building Chicago Economics

New Perspectives on the History of America's Most Powerful Economics Program

Edited by

ROBERT VAN HORN
University of Rhode Island

PHILIP MIROWSKI
University of Notre Dame

THOMAS A. STAPLEFORD
University of Notre Dame

CAMBRIDGE
UNIVERSITY PRESS

CAMBRIDGE UNIVERSITY PRESS
Cambridge, New York, Melbourne, Madrid, Cape Town,
Singapore, São Paulo, Delhi, Mexico City

Cambridge University Press
The Edinburgh Building, Cambridge CB2 8RU, UK

Published in the United States of America by Cambridge University Press, New York

www.cambridge.org
Information on this title: www.cambridge.org/9781107616431

First published 2011
Reprinted 2012
First paperback edition 2013

A catalogue record for this publication is available from the British Library

Library of Congress Cataloguing in Publication Data

Building Chicago economics : new perspectives on the history of America's
most powerful economics program / edited by Robert Van Horn, Philip
Mirowski, Thomas A. Stapleford.
p. cm. – (Historical perspectives on modern economics)
Includes bibliographical references and index.
ISBN 978-1-107-01341-4
1. Chicago school of economics – History – 20th century. 2. Free enterprise – History – 20th
century. 3. Friedman, Milton, 1912–2006. I. Van Horn, Robert, 1978– II. Mirowski, Philip, 1951–
III. Stapleford, Thomas A., 1974– IV. Title. V. Series.
HB98.3.B85 2011
330.15′53–dc22 2011010559

ISBN 978-1-107-61643-1 Paperback

Contents

Figures and Tables

Figures

Tables

Contributors

Jamie Peck is the Canada Research Chair in Urban & Regional Political Economy and professor of geography at the University of British Columbia, Canada. The recipient of Guggenheim and Harkness fellowships, Peck was previously professor of geography and sociology at the University of Wisconsin-Madison and professor of geography at the University of Manchester, UK. His principal publications include *Work-Place* (1996), *Workfare States* (2001), *Contesting Neoliberalism: Urban Frontiers* (coedited with Helga Leitner and Eric Sheppard, 2007), *Politics and Practice in Economic Geography* (coedited with Adam Tickell, Eric Sheppard, and Trevor Barnes, 2007), and *Constructions of Neoliberal Reason* (2010).

Thomas A. Stapleford is associate professor in the Program of Liberal Studies at the University of Notre Dame, where he also teaches in the graduate program in the history and philosophy of science. He is the author of *The Cost of Living in America: A Political History of Economic Statistics* (Cambridge University Press, 2009) and has published related articles on economic statistics in *Labor: Studies in the Working-Class History of the Americas*, *Labor History*, *The Journal of American History*, and *Science in Context*.

J. Daniel Hammond is Hultquist family professor at Wake Forest University. He is the author of *Theory and Measurement: Causality Issues in Milton Friedman's Monetary Economics* (Cambridge University Press, 1996) and editor, with Claire H. Hammond, of *Making Chicago Price Theory: Friedman-Stigler Correspondence, 1945–1957* (2006).

Paul Burnett is currently visiting assistant professor of science and technology studies at St. Thomas University in New Brunswick, Canada, where he is writing a book on Theodore W. Schultz and agricultural economics as a policy science in the Cold-War United States.

Ross B. Emmett is professor of political economy and political theory & constitutional democracy, James Madison College, Michigan State University. He is the author of *Frank Knight and the Chicago School in American Economics* (2009) and has edited three collections relevant to the Chicago School: *The Elgar Companion to the Chicago School of Economics* (2010); *The Chicago Tradition in Economics, 1892–1945* (8 vols., 2001); and *Selected Essays of Frank H. Knight* (2 vols., 1999). He is also the lead editor of the research annual, *Research in the History of Economic Thought and Methodology.*

Edward Nik-Khah is associate professor of economics at Roanoke College, Virginia. His research on auction theory, "A Tale of Two Auctions" (*Journal of Institutional Economics*, 2008), won him the K. William Kapp prize for best article from the European Association for Evolutionary Political Economy. Along with Philip Mirowski, he has critiqued the actor-network notion of "performativity" in Donald MacKenzie, Fabian Muniesa, and Lucia Siu's *Do Economists Make Markets?* (2007) and in Trevor Pinch and Richard Swedberg's *Living in a Material World* (2008). His research on George Stigler has appeared in Ross B. Emmett's *The Elgar Companion to the Chicago School of Economics* (2010). His current research examines the role of the Chicago School in reformulating pharmaceutical regulation.

Steven G. Medema is professor of economics and director of the University Honors and Leadership Program at the University of Colorado Denver. Professor Medema received his Ph.D. in economics from Michigan State University in 1989. Professor Medema has published more than eighty books, refereed articles, and book chapters. His articles have appeared in outlets including *Journal of Public Economics*, *Journal of Economic Perspectives*, *Economica*, *History of Political Economy*, *Journal of the History of Economic Thought*, and *Economics and Philosophy*. He is author or coauthor of *The Hesitant Hand: Self-Interest, Market, and State in the History of Modern Economics* (2010), *Ronald H. Coase*, and *Economics and the Law: From Posner to Post Modernism*, and the editor of *Lionel Robbins, A History of Economic Thought: The LSE Lectures*. Professor Medema served as editor of the *Journal of the History of Economic Thought* from 1999–2008 and is currently president elect of the History of Economics Society.

Robert Van Horn is assistant professor of economics at the University of Rhode Island. Professor Van Horn received his Ph.D. in economics from the University of Notre Dame in 2007, and he was a postdoctoral associate at the Center for the History of Political Economy at Duke University 2008–2009. His recently published work on the Chicago School comprises two chapters in Philip Mirowski and Dieter Plehwe's *The Road from Mont Pèlerin: Making of the Neoliberal Thought Collective* (2009) and two articles in Ross B. Emmett's the *Elgar Companion to the Chicago School of Economics* (2010). He has also published in *History of Political Economy, Journal of the History of Economic Thought, Research in the History of Economic Thought and Methodology*, and *Social Studies of Science*.

Matthias Klaes is professor of commerce at Keele University. He was the founding director of the Stirling Centre for Economic Methodology, and served as managing editor of the *Journal of Economic Methodology* for five years. Having published widely on the history of transaction costs, historiography, and the social framing of individual choice, his current research interests focus on economic narrative, semantic ambiguity of scientific terms, and conceptual history.

Jack Vromen is currently professor of philosophy (with a focus on philosophy of economics) at Erasmus University Rotterdam. He also is the academic director of EIPE (Erasmus Institute for Philosophy and Economics). His main research interest is in evolution and economics.

Philip Mirowski is Carl Koch Chair of economics and the history and philosophy of science, and fellow of the Reilly Center, University of Notre Dame. He works at the intersection of science studies, the history of science and of economics, the philosophy of science, and the development of non-neoclassical economic theory, such as computational and evolutionary approaches to formal models of markets. Lately, he has become increasingly interested in the political theory that underpins orthodox economic research and the various epistemic presumptions it requires. He is author of *Machine Dreams* (2002), *The Effortless Economy of Science?* (2004), *More Heat than Light* (1989), *ScienceMart* (2011), and the forthcoming *Never Let a Dire Crisis Go to Waste*. His book *Effortless Economy* was awarded the Fleck Prize of the Society for the Social Studies of Science in 2006. A symposium on his ideas in *Journal of Economic Behavior and Organization* (2007) discussed an alternative future for microeconomic theory. His most recent visiting professorships have been at All Soul's College Oxford and CNRS-Cachan in Paris.

Bruce Caldwell is research professor of economics and the director of the Center for the History of Political Economy at Duke University. He is the general editor of *The Collected Works of F. A. Hayek* and the author of *Hayek's Challenge: An Intellectual History of F. A. Hayek*.

Béatrice Cherrier received her Ph.D. from the University of Paris X Nanterre, France, in 2008. She is a member of EconomiX-Cachan. In 2009–2010, she worked as a postdoctoral associate at the Center for the History of Political Economy at Duke University.

Blueprints

Robert Van Horn, Philip Mirowski, and Thomas A. Stapleford

When the University of Chicago announced in May 2008 that it was establishing the Milton Friedman Institute for Research in Economics (MFI), it provoked an intense campus debate that soon spread to the national media. More than one hundred tenured faculty members signed a petition protesting the university's plans, while economists and other scholars unaffiliated with Chicago argued about the propriety of the university's actions in an atmosphere fraught with emotion.[1]

Official descriptions of the MFI emphasize generic objectives (e.g., "creating a highly collaborative intellectual environment") that would seem to belie such controversy.[2] Like other interdisciplinary research institutes, the MFI will serve as a venue where visiting scholars and postdoctoral fellows can collaborate and debate with university faculty – in this case, members of the University of Chicago Law School, the Department of Economics, and the Booth School of Business. Furthermore, the MFI will strive to educate the general public about economic research through lectures, conferences, and online publications.

Hostile reactions to the MFI, of course, owed less to these general features than to its funding structure and its connection to Milton Friedman, whose vocal advocacy of neoliberal economic policies has made him a polarizing figure. (When Friedman was selected for the Nobel Prize in economics, for example, two other Nobel laureates – George Wald and Linus

1 See Patricia Cohen, "On Chicago Campus, Milton Friedman's Legacy of Controversy Continues," *New York Times*, July 12, 2008, p. 9, subsection B; Marshall Sahlins, "Institute Will Give the U. of Chicago a Bad Name." *Chronicle of Higher Education*, Aug. 18, 2008; Kari Lydersen, "University's Plans for Milton Friedman Institute Spark Outcry," *The Washington Post*, August 28, 2008; and David Glen, "At U. of Chicago, Dispute over Friedman Center Continues to Simmer," *Chronicle of Higher Education*, October 31, 2008.

2 Cf. the official MFI Web site: http://mfi.uchicago.edu/about/index.shtml.

Pauling – accused him of being an accessory to human rights abuses in Latin America.)[3] By naming the proposed institute after Friedman, the university appeared to be reifying, even formally supporting, its longstanding association with the so-called Chicago School of economics – a cluster of methods, economic principles, and free-market ideology promulgated primarily by Friedman and his colleagues and students. This symbolic connection was reinforced by certain statements in the initial proposal, including the declaration that proper "evaluation of economic policies" must consider "the essential role of markets," and the claim that Friedman had "demonstrated" how the "design of public policy without regard to market alternatives has adverse social consequences."[4] Moreover, the funding mechanism for the MFI raised additional questions about its intellectual independence: The university announced that it would seek $200 million in private donations to endow the institute – an extraordinary sum for a social science institute. Donors who contributed $1 million or more each would be granted membership in the Milton Friedman Society and access to a private annual conference. In light of these features, critics argued that this lavishly funded institute would serve to bolster neoliberal defenses of free-market capitalism while supporting the views of wealthy elites. Proponents denied any ideological motives for the institute, contending that the MFI would nurture high-quality economic and social research and thereby ensure a strong and long future for Chicago economics.

The public outcry over the MFI illustrates how the doctrines and legacy of the Chicago School of economics remain controversial. (Indeed, that status has been reinforced by the recent financial upheaval, as many moderate and left-wing Americans have blamed the crisis on the very kinds of deregulation and free-market policies that have long been associated with Chicago.)[5] Yet the public debate over the MFI has also revealed how little most Americans (including economists) know about the history of the Chicago School, and in turn how ill-prepared they are to analyze the ties between institutional structures, political conditions, and theoretical development in economics. Although critics of the MFI have warned that the

[3] See George Wald and Linus Pauling, "The Laureate," Letter to the Editor, *New York Times*, October 24, 1976, p. 166.

[4] The original proposal has been removed from the MFI Web site. This quotation can be found in the online petition created by the "Committee for Open Research on Economy and Society," an offshoot of the original group of faculty who protested the MFI. http://www.miltonfriedmancores.org/cores/petition/

[5] Stephen R. Strahler, "U of C Loses its Place," *Chicago Business*, Nov. 15, 2008, http://www.chicagobusiness.com/cgi-bin/news.pl?id=31838; Michael Fitzgerald, "Chicago Schooled," *University of Chicago Magazine*, 102, no. 1(2009): 32–37.

university is embarking on a novel institutional innovation, the institute actually employs elements that have been integral to the history of economics research at Chicago. Research institutes, corporate funds, cross-disciplinary ventures, recruiting young promising researchers, general public education, and business-academe relationships were all crucial to the postwar trajectory of Chicago economics. The Chicago School was not the product of the "spontaneous order" of the free market often lauded by its members; it was constructed, quite deliberately, for specific ends.

The architects of the Chicago School have been extremely successful. From 1969 to 2009, twenty-six of sixty-four Nobel Prizes in economics have been awarded to faculty members, researchers, or students of the University of Chicago's Department of Economics.[6] Equally important, many observers have tied the school to the rise of a right-wing orthodoxy in the American political scene starting in the 1980s, and politicians such as Ronald Reagan, Margaret Thatcher, and George W. Bush have been effusive in their praise of members of the school as informing their own policies (Klein 2008; Harvey 2005; Galbraith 2009; Peck this volume). Despite this prominence, however, the Chicago School has received relatively little concerted attention from historians.[7] Most popular accounts of postwar Chicago economics (such as Johan van Overtveldt 2007) rely largely on an "oral tradition" created by past members and eschew a balanced engagement with archival and secondary sources. *Building Chicago Economics* offers the first collective attempt by historians to chart the rise and development of the postwar Chicago School.

In selecting essays for this volume, we chose to focus on what might be called the "incubation period" of the postwar Chicago School (roughly 1940–1965), a time when the Chicago approach remained a minority position within the profession as a whole. The three subsequent decades witnessed the flourishing of Chicago economics, marked by a series of major publications and events including the growing popularity of Friedman's monetarism, the first publication of Eugene Fama's efficient market hypothesis (1965), the arrival of Gary Becker (1968), the spread of Chicago law and economics, and the emergence of a rational expectations approach to macroeconomics modeled on the work of Robert Lucas. Although we recognize how deeply these later developments have become associated with Chicago in the public imagination, we have nonetheless kept our attention on the leading figures of the first generation – men such as Friedman,

6 "Nobel Laureates," http://www.uchicago.edu/about/accolades/nobel/. Access date: 5/30/10.

7 Beyond this volume, see Warren Samuels (1976) and Emmett (2010).

Stigler, Director, Hayek, and Schultz – those who laid the foundation for the postwar school.

Our emphasis on the earlier period derives from two factors. First, there is already a significant body of literature documenting the later, public rise of the Chicago School, including studies of monetarism (Laidler 1999, 2006; Leeson 1998, 2000; Hirsch and deMarchi, 1990; Mehrling, 2002), the rational expectations movement (Hoover 1990, 1999; Sent 1998; Snowdon and Vane 2005), and the revolution in financial theory (Bernstein 1992; Mehrling 2005; MacKenzie 2006; Vane and Mulhearn 2009). Undoubtedly, the recent economic crisis will prompt scholars to reconsider the more triumphal aspects of some of these narratives; yet that process of reflection has only just begun. By contrast, an exciting new body of work on the first generation of postwar Chicago – often based on close studies of new archival evidence – has now reached a point of maturity. It was our goal as editors to gather some of this work together and present it in an integrated volume.

Second, it is our conviction that the early years of the postwar era provided a crucial basis for Chicago's later success. It was here – in the methodological approaches that the first generation of Chicago economists adopted, in the objectives that they set, in the institutional structures that they established, in the pedagogy that they developed – that the Chicago School was built. This conviction has led our contributors to emphasize the practice of Chicago economics, and not merely the content of its conclusions. It has also shaped the contours of the volume, leading, for example, to a greater focus on Chicago microeconomics, because even Chicago's approach to macroeconomic analysis is famously grounded in its distinctive microeconomic views. It is our belief, therefore, that this analysis of postwar Chicago economics illuminates both the past and the present, highlighting institutional structures and ideas that continue to have a profound effect on both American economics and American economic policy more than half a century later.

The Postwar Foundations of Chicago Economics

Drawing on new research into archival and published sources, *Building Chicago Economics* is simultaneously a project of excavation and reconstruction: excavation of institutional and intellectual aspects of Chicago economics that have hitherto seen little study and reconstruction of a new historical perspective on the foundations of the postwar Chicago School. In the process, our volume emphasizes four major themes.

First, the early leaders of the postwar Chicago School were not cloistered academics, but empire builders who set up or forged influential relationships with well-funded institutional organizations in order to provide vital support structures for the creation, incubation, and propagation of their ideas.[8] Several chapters in our volume explore the empire-building strategies of key figures such as Friedrich Hayek, Theodore Schultz, and George Stigler. In the process, these chapters uncover the novel institutional foundations that bolstered the later success of the Chicago program.

Second, the ideas of the postwar Chicago School did not remain unchanged over time; on the contrary, the views of its principal members sometimes underwent radical shifts. As our volume demonstrates, for example, the founders of the postwar Chicago School (including Friedman, Stigler, and Aaron Director) departed quite sharply from the classical liberalism that had animated their mentors at the university, such as Frank Knight and Henry Simons. Moreover, even during the postwar era itself, Chicago economists differed among themselves as they developed their views on economic theory and policy in response to a changing political and institutional environment.

Third, beginning at least in the 1930s, the leaders of postwar Chicago economics sought to construct an economics built for policy. Contrary to conventional wisdom, the policy applications of Chicago economics were not accidental byproducts of a research program focused primarily on the internal development of economic theory. Nor did these applications arise spontaneously from a well-established and uncontroversial theoretical core (a role often ascribed to Chicago price theory).[9] Instead, the trajectory ran in the opposite direction: Chicago economists constructed a form of economic knowledge (and a matching training program for graduate students) designed to make economics successful as an applied discipline and to allow it to colonize other domains, such as legal theory and political science.

Fourth, understanding the growth of the Chicago School requires a nuanced consideration of the relationship between political ideology and economic knowledge. Our contributors take a variety of positions on this

[8] Friedman himself attests to the importance of a well-funded institutional structure for the rise of the Chicago School: "For advocacy of capitalism to mean anything, the proponents must be able to finance their cause.... Radical movements in capitalist societies ... have typically been supported by a few wealthy individuals" (1962, 17).

[9] For historical accounts that make this error, see Johan van Overtveldt (2007), Richard Posner (1978), and – albeit to a lesser extent – Neil Duxbury (1995).

controversial question: Several of our authors tie Chicago to a broader program of neoliberalism whereas others disagree, emphasizing a wider range of epistemological commitments and convictions that proved equally or more formative than neoliberalism per se. We devote the last section of the volume to an explicit discussion of these issues, but the theme runs through many of the volume's other essays as well, giving readers a rich and complex set of perspectives through which to assess what has become the most central question for any analysis of Chicago economics.

The Layout

The opening "Orientation" by Jamie Peck provides an overview of the Chicago School from the interwar period to the Reagan era and charts the sinuous path of its development. He explains how Chicago economics moved from Simons's "A Positive Program for Laissez-Faire" (1934), which contained his notorious nationalization scheme, to Friedman's *Capitalism and Freedom* (1962), which Reagan sported on his campaign trail and which called for, contra Simons, the privatization of state-controlled industries and institutions. Amidst the "Reagan revolution" of the 1980s, the doctrinal principles and policy prescriptions of the Chicago School had their heyday in American politics.

Part I, Economics Built for Policy, examines how Chicago's most celebrated and criticized figure, Milton Friedman, understood the "scientific" nature of economic research and its relationship to public policy. Chapter 1, by Thomas A. Stapleford, explores the links between Milton Friedman and the tradition of institutional economics at the National Bureau of Economic Research, highlighting their common goal of creating a new form of economics that could have an extensive role in democratic policy making. Stapleford demonstrates that this objective entailed several other methodological commitments – including the belief that history could be a predictive science – that shaped the culture of the Chicago School and its relationship with other groups. Chapter 2, by Dan Hammond, considers why Friedman became such a controversial figure. Comparing the development of Friedman's empirical methodology and neoliberal policy positions to those of John Kenneth Galbraith and Paul Samuelson, Hammond argues that criticism of Friedman owed more to the left-wing character of American academia than to Friedman's political activism per se.

Part II turns to the institutional construction of the Chicago School. The creators of the MFI understood that influential schools of thought in economics do not simply spring forth from the head of Athena. On the contrary, thoughtful institutional design and munificent monetary contributions were prerequisites for Chicago's success in the postwar period. The chapters in this section examine three critical but understudied institutional components of the postwar Chicago School.

In Chapter 3, Paul Burnett provides the first archival-based analysis of the work of Theodore Schultz. Burnett details how Schultz, through his fundraising acumen, his careful self-fashioning, and his research network in agriculture economics, not only developed University of Chicago–based research programs in agriculture economics and economic development, but also forged an influential blueprint for postwar U.S. agriculture policy. In Chapter 4, Ross B. Emmett demonstrates that Schultz and his colleagues consciously integrated faculty research and graduate education in ways that reinforced Chicago's view of economics as an applied policy science. The requirement that graduate students participate in department "workshops" fostered a scientific environment in which the analytical tools of price theory and statistics were applied to a variety of policy issues. This system, Emmett argues, laid the foundation for the Chicago School's eventual trademark mode of economic analysis. In Chapter 5, Edward Nik-Khah examines an often overlooked pillar of the Chicago School, the Graduate School of Business (GSB). According to Nik-Khah, George Stigler used his entrepreneurial talent to reshape the research program of the GSB and buttress it with well-funded institutions that reflected and advanced his own beliefs.

The Chicago School is famous not merely for its contributions to economics per se, but for its attempt to apply economic methodology to a range of problems and disciplines outside its traditional scope, a process aptly dubbed "economics imperialism." In Part III, we take up two under studied and divergent strands of this imperial project. The first, "Law and Economics," examines a classic and widely influential imperialist expansion. The traditional story claims that Chicago economists, through the perspicacious use of an accepted price theory tradition, illuminated legal issues. In Chapter 6, Steve Medema challenges this claim by undermining one of its central assumptions, that price theory existed in a monolithic form at Chicago and that the principal Chicago economists all accepted this form. Medema claims that two different versions of price theory existed at Chicago prior to 1970, and that each version propelled a movement in Chicago law and economics, an "old" and a "new." Medema fleshes out the price theory structure on which each movement depended, claiming that old Chicago law and economics thus significantly differed from new Chicago law and economics. In Chapter 7, Robert Van Horn and Matthias

Klaes examine the Chicago School and its understanding of patent law, one area of law on which Chicago economists have exerted a considerable influence. By primarily focusing on the immediate postwar period, from 1946 through the mid-1950s, they show how Chicago economists moved from a broad hostility toward patents to a broad acceptance of patents in the course of their effort to create a more robust form of liberalism.

Imperialism, however, involves something more than conquest; it is equally characterized by colonial appropriation: the extraction of resources for use (and transformation) in the homeland. The next two chapters of Part III examine colonial appropriation by the Chicago School: the application (and great simplification) of concepts from evolutionary biology to the analysis of markets. The relationship of neoclassical economics to the natural sciences has been preoccupied with physics, which provided the original template (Mirowski 1989). However, in the case of the Chicago School, an argument can be made that biology was much more important. In Chapter 8, Jack Vromen argues that although Gordon Tullock, Gary Becker, and Jack Hirshleifer presented their "bioeconomics" as a mutually beneficial two-way transfer of ideas, concepts, and approaches between biology and economics, they were more interested in showing that the constrained maximization framework used by economists was superior to the prevailing explanatory framework in biology. In Chapter 9, Philip Mirowski claims that Hayek, Friedman, and Armen Alchian all differed on their understandings of evolution, and that this may have been part of the reason why their references to "science" took somewhat longer to catch on within the economics profession.

The relationship between political ideology and economics has been the most controversial aspect of the Chicago School's history. In Part IV, we close the volume by considering whether postwar Chicago economics can be aptly characterized as "neoliberal." In Chapter 10, Van Horn builds on his previous studies of Chicago neoliberalism by contrasting Jacob Viner's conception of concentrated power with that of postwar Chicago economists. Van Horn argues that Viner should be understood as a critic of the neoliberalism exemplified by Chicago research projects during the 1950s and 1960s, and that Viner's disagreement with his former colleagues stemmed for his adherence to classical liberalism. In Chapter 11, however, intellectual historian Bruce Caldwell challenges the classification of the Chicago School as neoliberal, focusing his attention on a recent publication from Van Horn and Mirowski (2009). Caldwell claims that this categorization is flawed and contends that Van Horn and Mirowski misconstrue the role of figures (e.g., F. A. Hayek and the Volker Fund) central to the formation of the Chicago School. In Chapter 12, Beatrice Cherrier brings a different perspective in her analysis of one of the most controversial figures in the Chicago School: Milton Friedman. Cherrier contends that the consistency between Friedman's science and politics arose from his steadfast adherence to a more fundamental "worldview" that undergirded both his methodology and his political outlook. Thus, Cherrier denies that Friedman's approach to economics was strictly a product of any political ideology (such as neoliberalism), instead tracing both to deeper, interlocking principles. Finally, Edward Nik-Khah brings the debate about neoliberalism up to the present day by examining the Milton Friedman Institute. He explores how the history of Chicago neoliberalism may be used to better understand the MFI and its surrounding controversy, thereby suggesting that the rise of Chicago neoliberalism in the postwar era continues to shape and define the development of economics at Chicago.

References

Bernstein, Peter. 1992. *Capital Ideas*. New York: Free Press.

Duxbury, Neil. 1995. *Patterns of Jurisprudence*. New York: Oxford University Press.

Emmett, Ross B., ed. 2010. *The Elgar Companion to the Chicago School of Economics*. Cheltenham: Edward Elgar.

Friedman, Milton. 1962. *Capitalism and Freedom*. Chicago: University of Chicago Press.

Galbraith, James K. 2008. *The Predator State*. New York: Free Press.

Harvey, David. 2005. *A Brief History of Neoliberalism*. Oxford: Oxford University Press.

Hirsch, Abraham and deMarchi, Neil. 1990. *Milton Friedman*. Ann Arbor: University of Michigan Press.

Hoover, Kevin. 1990. *The New Classical Macroeconomics*. Oxford: Blackwell.

1999. *The Legacy of Robert Lucas, Jr.* Cheltenham: Elgar.

Klein, Naomi. 2008. *The Shock Doctrine*. New York: Picador Press.

Laidler, David. 1999. "The Chicago Monetarist Tradition." *Journal of Economic Perspectives*.

2006. *Three lectures on Monetary Theory and Policy*. Austrian National Bank. http://www.dieaktuellezahl.oenb.at/en/img/wp128_tcm16-43013.pdf#page=19

Leeson, Robert. 1998. "The Early Patinkin-Friedman Correspondence," *Journal of the History of Economic Thought* (20):433–448.

2000. *The Eclipse of Keynesianism*. London: Palgrave.

MacKenzie, Donald. 2006. *An Engine, not a Camera*. Cambridge: MIT Press.

Mehrling, Perry. 2002. "Don Patinkin and the Origins of Postwar Monetary Orthodoxy," *The European Journal of the History of Economic Thought* (9): 161–185.

2005. *Fischer Black and the Revolutionary Idea of finance*. New York: Wiley.

Mirowski, Philip. 1989. *More Heat than Light*. New York: Cambridge University Press.

Peck, Jamie. 2008. "Remaking Laissez Faire." *Progress in Human Geography* 32(1): 3–43.

Posner, Richard. 1978. "The Chicago School of Antitrust Analysis." *University of Pennsylvania Law Review* 127: 925–48.

Samuels, Warren. 1976. *The Chicago School of Political Economy.* University Park: AFEE.

Sent, Esther-Mirjam. 1998. *The Evolving Rationality of Rational Expectations.* New York: Cambridge University Press.

Snowdon, Brian and Howard Vane. 2005. *Modern Macroeconomics: Its Origins, Development and Current State.* Cheltenham: Elgar.

Vane, Howard and Chris Mulhearn. 2009. *Harry M. Markowitz, Merton H. Miller, William F. Sharpe, Robert C. Merton and Myron S. Scholes.* Cheltenham: Elgar.

Van Horn, Robert and Philip Mirowski. 2009. "The Rise of the Chicago School of Economics and the Birth of Neoliberalism." In *The Road from Mont Pèlerin*, edited by, P. Mirowski and D. Plehwe. Cambridge, MA: Harvard University Press.

Van Overtveldt, Johan. 2007. *The Chicago School.* Chicago: Agate.

Orientation: In Search of the Chicago School

Jamie Peck

January 29, 2007, was Milton Friedman Day in Chicago. The city council's formal resolution, signed by Mayor Daley, called on "the citizens of our great city to observe this day with appropriate ceremonies and activities that honor the significant contributions that Milton Friedman has made to our nation." The renowned free-market economist, who had died a few weeks earlier, was honored at a memorial service at the University of Chicago featuring, among others, fellow Nobel laureate Gary Becker, president of the Czech Republic, Václav Klaus, and chairman emeritus of the Chicago Mercantile Exchange, Leo Melamed. As the City of Chicago's resolution summarized Friedman's contribution:

> It was here … that Friedman … synthesize[d] his theories of economics, based on the idea that government should be kept small and spending should be kept low.… Though his embrace of free-market economics was very unpopular at the time, Friedman was tireless in championing his ideas. He knew that [the] free market was the answer, not only to allowing broad prosperity, but also to enduring political freedom.… "The society that puts equality before freedom will end up with neither," Professor Friedman once wrote. "The society that puts freedom before equality will end up with a great measure of both." … Today, most nations in the world embrace the free-market precepts he espoused and popularized.… Milton Friedman's work, which began here at the University of Chicago, has served to advance America's economy … and spread the economic, political and social benefits of free-market economics throughout the world.[1]

This chapter is an abbreviated version of "Finding the Chicago School" in Jamie Peck (2010) *Constructions of Neoliberal Reason*. Oxford: Oxford University Press; by permission of Oxford University Press. Support provided by the John Simon Guggenheim Memorial Foundation and the Social Sciences and Humanities Research Council of Canada is gratefully acknowledged.

[1] City of Chicago (2006) Declaration of January 29, 2007 as 'Milton Friedman Day' in Chicago, Agreed Calendar, 90577, November 1. Accessed at www.chicityclerk.com/citycouncil/journals/.

Friedman was remembered by President George W. Bush as a "revolutionary thinker [whose] bold ideas ... serve as the foundation of many of America's most successful government reforms."[2] Portrayed in the *New York Times* as the "grandmaster of free-market economic theory and a prime force in the movement of nations to less government," Friedman was credited with building the Chicago School of economics into a "counterforce" to Keynesian hegemony and its East Coast strongholds like Harvard and MIT (Noble 2006). However, Friedman's iconoclastic contribution was not simply to mount a challenge to Keynesianism, renowned conservative economist (and former student) Samuel Brittan (2006, 13) wrote in the *Financial Times*, because in the final analysis "to some extent [he] supplanted it." Friedman had done so both as a remarkable "economic scientist" and as a skilled public intellectual, whose contributions had already been placed, by friends and foes alike, on a par with those of Keynes himself (see Galbraith 1987; Walters 1987; Warsh 1993; Hammond, this volume).

The thirty-year war that Friedman and his colleagues waged against the Keynesian intellectual occupation began in earnest in the mid-1940s, reaching its moment of vindication in the mid-1970s. The beginning of Chicago's unrivalled dominance of the Nobel Prize for economics can be dated to this moment, but more fundamentally, it also marked onset of the long-anticipated Keynesian nightmare of stagflation. In the space of a few years, Chicago transitioned from the status of a belligerent outpost of free-market dissent to one of the embryonic sites of the neoliberal project, becoming a source of unambiguous "advice" for political leaders in Chile, Britain, the United States, and elsewhere (see Yergin and Stanislaw 1998; Harvey 2005; Klein 2007). Like its Keynesian predecessor, the free-market doctrine of the Chicago School eventually achieved traction during a period of crisis, though its gestation had been a long one (Robinson 1972; Nik-Khah, this volume, Chapter 13).

Friedman himself recognized that these crisis conditions were decisive, simultaneously delegitimizing the faltering Keynesian orthodoxy while prompting an urgent search for new approaches. In this context,

> a major change in social and economic policy is preceded by a shift in the climate of intellectual opinion, itself generated, at least in part, by contemporaneous social, political, and economic circumstances. This shift may begin in one country but, if it proves lasting, ultimately spreads worldwide.... All in all, the force of ideas, propelled by the pressure of events, is no respecter of geography or ideology or party label. (Friedman and Friedman 1988, 455, 466)

[2] Accessed at http://www.friedmanfoundation.org/friedman/friedmans/statementworld.jsp.

In a wide range of accounts, from the self-congratulatory to the scathingly critical, the Chicago School of economics is designated as having a decisive role in this process of intellectual contestation and succession, first as a bastion of opposition to statism and Keynesianism, and subsequently as the birthplace of a rejuvenated form of free-market economics. In Naomi Klein's (2007, 53) rendering, the Chicago School represents the epicenter of an historic process of "capitalist Reformation," with the 1970s experiment in Chile serving as an offshore "laissez-faire laboratory" for the restoration of a purified market order. Here, the Chicago School itself is endowed with remarkable purposive capacity, with Friedman ("Dr. Shock") as the principal protagonist. Orthodox and sympathetic historiographies, in contrast, eschew the conspiratorial undertones in favor of heroic narratives of scientific contestation and transformation, culminating in the righteous defeat of flawed Keynesian formulations and the revelation of enduring economic truths. Echoing Klein, the language of crusades is often invoked (minus the connotations of blind faith and fundamentalism). Johan Van Overtveldt's (2007, 1) comprehensive history of the Hyde Park revolution, for example, begins with the observation that "Chicago is both a Mecca and a Rome for economic science," with due deference to the immaculate lineage: "If Adam Smith is the father of the dismal science called economics, then Chicago is arguably its capital."

But why *Chicago?* Friedman was, according to financier Leo Melamed, "one of Chicago's most treasured icons."[3] Yet beyond the well-attended memorial service and pulses of activity on conservative blogs and on the Web site of the Heartland Institute, the Chicago-based free-market think tank, Milton Friedman Day passed almost entirely without incident in the Windy City. That, locally, this should be a borderline nonevent is curiously fitting. Friedman always had an ambivalent relationship with the city that was his intellectual home for three decades. And like most of his colleagues, he was never entirely comfortable with the Chicago School moniker. "To economists the world over," Friedman (1974, 11) once remarked, "'Chicago' designates not a city, not even a University, but a 'school'" – an apt observation, in many ways, for a public intellectual who may have been at Chicago, but was never *of* Chicago. As he would later claim, the free-market project would probably never have been hatched had its originators been located in New York City rather than Chicago. Can this be true?

[3] Accessed at http://www.friedmanfoundation.org/friedman/friedmans/statementworld.jsp.

Roots

Milton Friedman went to Chicago in the fall of 1932 to enter graduate school, his first time west of the Delaware River. If he left Rutgers as a frustrated insurance actuary, he arrived in Chicago an economist. A talented mathematician, as an undergraduate Friedman was converted to economics by two of his instructors at Rutgers, Homer Jones and Arthur Burns, who at the time were enrolled in the graduate programs at Chicago and Columbia respectively. Burns, who went on to chair the Federal Reserve through the turbulent 1970s, would become a lifelong friend and mentor to Friedman; but it was the Iowa farm boy, Homer Jones, who introduced the impressionable young statistician to "what even then was known as the Chicago view" (Friedman and Friedman 1998, 32). Jones's advisor, Frank Knight, epitomized this view at the time, combining a passionate defense of individual freedoms with mordant skepticism (by some accounts, bordering on nihilism) with regard to government regulation and social intervention. Young Milton may have been many things, but a nihilist he was not. On the contrary, he was attracted to economics as an empirical, problem-solving science (see Stapleford, this volume):

> I graduated from college in 1932, when the United States was at the bottom of the deepest recession in its history before or since. The dominant problem of the time was economics. How to get out of the depression? How to reduce unemployment? What explained the paradox of great need on the one hand and unused resources on the other? Under the circumstances, becoming an economist seemed more relevant to the burning issues of the day than becoming an applied mathematician or an actuary. (Friedman 2004, 69–70)

At Chicago, Friedman was soon learning life-changing lessons in both in the discipline of Economics and in the daily realities of economics. He found part-time employment as a waiter – paying one meal a day, plus board – but even after securing a second job in a shoe store, he was unable to pay his own way without borrowing from family members. In the economics department, meanwhile, the mandatory, right-of-passage class in price theory, Economics 301, yielded revelations of a quite different kind. (For the significance of price theory for the later development of Chicago law and economics, see Medema this volume.) Taught by the department's other "star" professor, Jacob Viner, Econ 301 "opened up a new world" for Friedman (2004, 70), convincing him that "economic theory was a coherent, logical whole that held together, that didn't consist simply of a set of disjointed propositions." An intimidating and unforgiving teacher, who George Stigler (1988, 19) would later characterize as "the stern disciplinarian" of price theory, Viner had his students sit in alphabetically ordered rows, which placed Friedman next to Rose Director, the younger sister of one of the faculty, Aaron Director, and a research assistant of Knight's. Rose was to become Friedman's wife and lifelong collaborator. Her brother, after a period in Washington, DC, would return to Chicago as a founder of what would become known as the law and economics movement. In the same year, 1946, Friedman was appointed to a faculty position in Chicago (following spells in New York, Washington, DC, Wisconsin, and Minnesota), signifying the emergence of the Chicago School *qua* school.

Although much is often made of the long conservative tradition in Chicago economics dating back to the founding of the program in the 1890s, this was a necessary, but far from sufficient condition for the mid-1940s reboot of the Chicago School, which within a few years constituted "the strongest group of free market economists not only in the country but in the world at this time" (Friedman 1976, 23). Half a century earlier, when the department was founded, Chicago had been the "storm center" of roiling conflicts between the East Coast industrial and intellectual establishment and the upstart west. One prominent commentator adjudged "the chasm between capital and labor [to be] deeper and broader in Chicago than anywhere else in the country" (Lyman Abbott, quoted in Coats 1963, 488). Into this fray stepped the first president of the University of Chicago, William Rainey Harper, whose aggressive hiring policy was already fueling a climate of resentment and suspicion around what critics liked to call Standard Oil University. Determined to build his new university on a "grand scale," Harper recruited research stars from the Ivy League, paying high salaries but requiring them to live "the life of frontiersmen ... isolated from the rest of the country in a venture which had no past" (Shils 1991, x). This was a "new university located on the outskirts of a new city," which to some seemed to embody "all the tensions, uncertainties, and hopes of America in the new century" (Emmett 2002a, xvii). The formation of the University of Chicago as a private institution in a "new" city represented what Friedman (1974, 15) later characterized as a *tabular rasa*, because there was "no dead wood to be eliminated, no vested interests to be rooted out." Moreover, in contrast to the great public universities of the Midwest, it was free from the "inevitable entanglements with state government" (Kitch 1998, 228). As a result, Chicago became a place of robust intellectual independence, never "trucking in vulgar opinion," and riding out the political storms of the first half of the twentieth century as if securely moored in a "sheltered inland sea" (Shils 1991, xv).

Armed with deep reserves of Rockefeller money, Harper courted controversy by appointing the outspoken and doctrinaire J. Laurence Laughlin, "one of the most conservative economists in the country" (Coats 1963, 489), to chair his new department of political economy. If Laughlin's partisan reputation appeared to confirm received views of Chicago as a conservative redoubt, however, the new chair did not simply move to construct a department in his own image. Instead, he embraced the principles of robust heterodoxy and academic freedom, recruiting institutionalists like Thorstein Veblen and John Maurice Clark, among others. If there was a "school-like" economics program at the time, this was a much more fitting description of the progressive institutionalism of neighboring Wisconsin under the influence of Ely and Commons, with which Chicago was often less than favorably compared (Lampman 1993). Chicago, in contrast epitomized an early form of economic heterodoxy.

On his retirement in 1916, Laughlin's faculty line was filled by Jacob Viner, who would later be joined by Frank Knight; they would come to be regarded as the dominant intellectual forces in the department. However, if this reflected an incipient "Chicago tradition," it had more to do with a commitment to vigorous intellectual individualism than it did some programmatic or monocultural conservatism. Although Knight and Viner are sometimes credited with the distinction of cofounding the Chicago School, or even of establishing a "first" Chicago School (see Bronfenbrenner 1962; Formaini 2002; Sally 1997), they had very different personal styles and did not always see eye to eye. Viner's students never constituted a "club." In contrast, several of Knight's former students maintained "affinities" that would be crucial to the establishment of the Chicago School proper after the Second World War, even though Knight himself played little or no direct role in this (see Reder 1982). Curmudgeonly and idiosyncratic, according to his admirers, Knight believed that economics was neither an empirical nor a predictive science (Stapleford, this volume). "Knight's specialty was debunking," Friedman later recalled (quoted in Van Overtveldt 2007, 72). Libertarian and contrarian, he defended free-market capitalism not out of utopian conviction, but for want of a better arrangement for the coordination of human affairs (see Breit and Ransom 1998). Knight's (1947, 341) notion of a far-from-idealized economic actor was "less *homo sapiens*, the knower, than *homo mendax*, the liar, deceiver, hypocrite, pretender, practicer of make-believe."

Another Knight protégé, Henry Simons, joined the Chicago faculty in 1927 and fashioned critical elements of what would later be characterized as a Chicago School position, although some of its leading members would subsequently disown him. Very much "a midwest product," Simons was to develop a passion – and indeed a plan – for market-oriented reformism; but he remained relatively detached from the political world, making "few trips to the nation's capital" (Davenport 1946, 116). In a premonition of the law and economics movement destined to grow into pillar of Chicago-style neoliberalism, he also migrated between economics and the Law School, though not entirely of his own volition, honing his "positive program for laissez-faire" along the way. (For an examination of Simons's *Positive Program for Laissez Faire*, see Van Horn this volume.) A close friend of Friedrich von Hayek, Simons (1934) shaped a distinctive case for economic freedom, contra the economics of the New Dealers, against the backdrop of a 1930s economy "visibly ruined by banking and monopoly." As his colleague Aaron Director remembered, "Simons thought that doomsday was upon us" (quoted in Kitch 1983, 179), which was also reflected, as another friend recalled, in his "never too peaceful" state of mind (Davenport 1946, 119). Although Stigler (1982, 166) would posthumously enthrone Simons as the "Crown Prince of that hypothetical kingdom, the Chicago school of economics," his embrace of later-heretical positions like redistributive taxation, limited public ownership, and the restraint of private monopoly would confuse the intellectual lineage. It seems to be for this latter reason that revisionist histories of the Chicago School often marginalize or exclude Simons, with Friedman, Coase, Stigler, and others branding the man – who took his own life in 1946 at age forty-seven – as an "interventionist" (see Kitch 1983; de Long 1990). For his part, Friedman was "astounded" on rereading in the early 1980s Simons's (1934) *Positive Program for Laissez Faire*, although he conceded that its interventionist framing may have reflected the political and intellectual context of Depression-era Chicago:

> I would say that close to a majority of the social scientists and students … at Chicago … were either members of the Communist Party or very close to it.… It was an environment in which the general intellectual atmosphere was strongly prosocialist. It was strongly in favor of government going all the way to take over the whole economy.… Relative to that kind of atmosphere, [Simons's] pamphlet created a great stir because it was widely interpreted as being, if you want, reactionary. (Milton Friedman, quoted in Kitch 1983, 178–179)

Although Friedman chose not to remind the audience at the time, he himself had hardly been immune to the "general intellectual atmosphere." In fact, when Simons's intervention was published, Friedman was about to leave the "sheltered academic cloister at Chicago" to accept a posting at one of the New Deal agencies in Washington, DC – the National Resources Committee – where along with Chicago alumnus Allen Wallis he would work on long-range planning in the statistical section. "New Deal Washington was a wonderful place for a young economist," Friedman later confessed, revealing a reformist streak that he would never entirely lose. "There was a sense of excitement and achievement in the air [and we] had the feeling – or illusion – that we were at the birth of a new order" (Friedman and Friedman 1998, 55; see also Silk 1976).

Aaron Director would also later concede that Simons's interventions were styled in such a way to render them "palatable" to his left-leaning colleagues at Chicago. Just after Simons's death, Director (1948) wrote that he had been "slowly establishing himself as the head of a 'school,'" which some believe to be the first printed reference to the existence of a Chicago School of economics. Yet the economics department proper had been disinclined to tenure Simons – just at it would turn up its nose at the prospect of Hayek joining as a tenured colleague in 1950 – prompting Simons's relocation to the Law School in the mid-1930s, albeit as a professor of economics. At the time of Simons's death, much of the groundwork for the establishment of the Chicago School of economics had been laid. Friedman had just been hired away from Minnesota, although following a recruitment snafu it would take more than a decade to secure a position for Friedman's former office mate, George Stigler, back in Chicago. Nevertheless, another strategically key hire had been prosecuted more smoothly – Freidman's brother-in-law, Aaron Director, had been brought back to the Law School from the Commerce Department in Washington, DC. Friedman's old friend, Allen Wallis, also returned to Chicago to join the business school.

Plans had been afoot for some time to bring Hayek to Chicago. Simons had been the principal interlocutor in these discussions, along with the president of the university, Robert Hutchins (see Van Horn and Mirowski 2009; cf. Van Overveldt 2007). Although acknowledging the pressing need to rebuild, Hutchins was fond of boasting that he possessed "the most conservative economics department in the world" (quoted in Van Horn and Mirowski 2009, 169). Despite the availability of generous financial lubrication from a private foundation, the arch-conservative (but isolated) Volker Fund, the negotiations proved to be protracted and difficult. The economics department's refusal to provide a tenure home for Hayek doubtless brought back painful memories for Simons; neither did the department demonstrate any enthusiasm for hosting the Volker Fund's proposed Free Market (or "American Road") Project, a venture modeled on Hayek's (1944) *Road to Serfdom*. As Aaron Director – who had been identified by Simons and Hayek as the ideal leader of the project – later recalled, it was almost through a process of elimination that Chicago became the "only place" that might host such a venture, and the Law School would be the "only part of the University of Chicago that would be accommodating" (quoted in Kitch 1983, 181). (For a detailed examination of this project and its efforts, see Van Horn and Klaes, this volume.)

The Free Market Project, in fact, never did take shape in the form that Simons, Hayek, and their benefactors at the Volker Fund had envisaged. Although the implicit responsibility for the project lay with Director, his redoubtable skills as a debater and teacher were matched by a remarkable reluctance to commit to print. Nevertheless, Director occupied a galvanizing leadership role in Chicago's conservative project, working alongside Friedman as the two "main intellectual forces" shaping the attendant policy program (Stigler 1982, 170). Following Simons's suicide, Director worked tirelessly to secure Hayek's move to Chicago, culminating in the talismanic figure's arrival in 1950. This would further consolidate the transatlantic bonds that had been developing since the inaugural Mont Pèlerin Society (MPS) meeting in Switzerland in 1947. What Stigler later described as a "junket to ... save liberalism" would be Friedman's first time outside the United States, a journey that he made in the reassuring company of his brother-in-law, Aaron Director, his mentor, Frank Knight, and his former office mate, George Stigler (quoted in Friedman and Friedman 1998, 158).

Rather than reify some supposedly unbroken lineage from Laughlin through Viner and Knight, isolate a uniquely Chicagoan brand of economic theory, or anoint moments of immaculate conception in Econ 301, Van Horn and Mirowski locate the origins of the Chicago School at this politicized nexus (see also Nik-Khah, this volume, Chapter 5), underlining the mutual constitution of the MPS and the Chicago School:

> [The] establishment of the Chicago School constituted just one component of a much more elaborate transnational institutional project to reinvent a liberalism which had some prospect of challenging the socialist doctrines ascendant in the immediate postwar period.... That MPS and the Chicago School were joined at the hip from birth is verified by the fact that most of the major protagonists were present at the creation of both organizations: Director, Friedman, Wallis, and Knight. (2009, 158–159)

Viner later recalled that it was not until long after he had left the University of Chicago – in fact at a conference in 1951 – that he "began to hear rumors of a 'Chicago School' which was engaged in an organized battle for laissez faire ... against 'imperfect competition' theorizing and 'Keynesianism'" (Patinkin 1981, 266). George Stigler (1988, 148) was more emphatic: "There was no Chicago School of Economics when the Mt. Pèlerin Society first met at the end of World War II." That was to come.

Remobilization

By the time that Hayek arrived in Chicago for a sabbatical in the spring of 1946, it was clear that something was afoot. Simons had been maneuvering to construct a "project" around Hayek for some time, including a planned "raid" on Minnesota, for Stigler and Friedman (see Van Horn and Mirowski 2009). Simons was dead by the summer of 1946, but his plan was in motion. Before the year's end, the "Knight affinity group" had been reassembled in Chicago, consisting of Friedman in economics, Allen Wallis in the Graduate School of Business, and Aaron Director in the Law School – now as Simons's replacement. Securing the services of Hayek and Stigler would take several more years. Meanwhile, Knight's well-known social and leadership deficits meant that the paternal figure was neither inclined nor capable of sustaining any kind of programmatic project. Nevertheless, according to Emmett (2002b, viii), he clearly "inspired those around him to go against the odds and oppose the progressive spirit of the age." It was Friedman, most conspicuously, who would energetically grow into the leadership role.

This would be no simple takeover, however. In fact, a new source of opposition had just arrived on the scene. The Cowles Commission had established a permanent base at the University of Chicago during the war. Cowles was to become a powerhouse of the new science of econometrics, controversially favoring Walrasian approaches and general equilibrium modeling over the Marshallian approach, as interpreted by Friedman. If the increasingly intense intramural disputes between Friedman and the Cowlesmen were primarily methodological and analytical, not far beneath the surface they were also political. Cowles was "stocked with self-identified socialists," with a range of affiliations ranging "somewhere between Keynes and [Oskar] Lange politically," whereas Friedman had begun to adopt what his biographer portrayed as an "extremist libertarian position" (Ebenstein 2007, 55; see also Van Horn and Mirowski 2009, 151). Although leading members of the Cowles Commission were to remain ambivalent about Keynes and Keynesian macroeconomics during the Chicago years, their preferred forms of general equilibrium modeling would later be associated with the formalization of a distinctly American version of the "Keynesian synthesis" (Van Overvetveldt 2007, 37–39; Warsh 1993, 67; cf. Mirowski 2011).

A frequent yet pugnaciously combative attendee at Cowles seminars, Friedman became the Commission's self-appointed "hair shirt" (Friedman and Friedman 1998, 197). It was during this time that his legendary debating skills were honed, with the benefit of what were formidable adversaries.

Although relations between the Cowlesmen and the Friedman wing of the economics department were generally civil, by the late 1940s it was obvious that an "intense struggle" for intellectual and institutional dominance had been joined on both sides (Reder 1982, 10). With the assistance of an increasingly combative cohort, including Allen Wallis and Aaron Director, Friedman was ultimately "instrumental" in winning the civil war with the Cowlesmen, who eventually decamped to Yale in 1955 (see Ebenstein 2007, 57; Mirowski 2002). Friedman, who had energetically assumed the "intellectual leadership of the [ultimately dominant] faction of the department, had relished the 'intramural struggle'" (Reder 1982, 10). And when, the following year, Wallis recruited George Stigler to the "luxuriously upholstered" Walgreen Professorship of American Institutions, the Knight affinity group was duly reconsolidated, as indeed was the Chicago School itself (Stigler 1988, 157).

Rationality

Battle hardened from the tussles with the Cowlesmen, the Chicago School of the 1950s began to articulate its alternative vision in an increasingly assertive fashion. Friedman's (1951, 91) hope was that the ideological trend toward collectivism was already showing signs of maxing out, and that the time was ripe to begin to "promote the ideas that can guide the next generation of legislators." Somewhat ironically, Friedman was soon to argue – in his influential essay on methodology, published in 1953 – for a strict separation of positive ("what is") and normative ("what ought to be") modalities of economic discourse. His concern was to elaborate a methodology of "positive economics," judged according to its predictive power (rather than the "realism" of its assumptions), and "in principle independent of any particular ethical position or normative judgments" (Friedman 1953, 4). Harry Johnson (1971, 9), who for a time was the Chicago School's leading in-house rebel, later claimed that this form of positive economics was peculiarly suited not only to post-Cowles Chicago, but also to the proclivities (and limitations) of its diminutive author: Rather than pursue the goal of descriptive realism in the form of proliferating systems of general equilibrium equations, positive economics enabled Friedman and his followers to "select the crucial relationships that permit one to predict something large from something small, regardless of the intervening chain of causation … [an approach that] offered liberation to the small-scale intellectual, since it freed his mind from dependence on the large-scale research team and the large and expensive computer program."

More and less sympathetic commentators seem to agree that the positive and political faces of Chicago School economics are intricately, if not deeply and definitively, intertwined (see Coats 1960; Reder 1982; Van Horn and Mirowski 2009). In contrast to Hayek, who believed that his popular tract, *The Road to Serfdom* effectively destroyed his reputation as an academic economist, Friedman attempted to inhabit both worlds, essentially at the same time – issuing audacious and uncompromising policy advice on the one hand while fiercely protecting his reputation as an empirically oriented economist on the other (see Hammond, this volume). While noting, *en passant*, that the 1947 MPS meeting "marked the beginning of my involvement in the political process," at least in his own mind, Friedman maintained a sharp distinction between his efforts to "influence public policy" and his scientific endeavors:

> I have spoken and written about issues of public policy. In doing so, however, I have not been acting in my scientific capacity, but in my capacity as a citizen, an informed one, I hope. I believe that what I know as an economist helps me to form better judgments about some issues than I could without that knowledge. But fundamentally, my scientific work should not be judged by my activities in public policy. (Friedman 2004, 75; Friedman and Friedman 1998, 159)

These activities, however, were hardly mere diversions. Beginning in 1956, for example, Friedman played a leading role in a series of summer schools funded by the Volker Fund, which were designed to hone a set of popular arguments for "economic freedom." This represented, in effect, the long-frustrated American Road project of refitting Hayek's message for a U.S. audience. Presented to groups of "twenty to thirty young academics" and recalled as "amongst the most stimulating intellectual experiences of my life," with Rose's assistance, these lectures were gradually shaped into the bestselling book, *Capitalism and Freedom* (Friedman and Friedman 1998, 57). Although effectively shunned by the academic and journalistic establishment, the book went on to sell more than 500,000 copies and has never since gone out of print. In the book's preface, Friedman acknowledged his funders from Volker and the "incisive probing and deep interest" of the summer-school delegates, together with his current and former Chicago colleagues – Knight, Simons, Mints, Director, Hayek, and Stigler – from whom he had taken "so much … [that] what I have learned has become so much a part of my own thought that I would not know how to select points to footnote" (Friedman 2002 [1962], xvi).

Enclavization had clearly helped, in retrospect, to solidify and sharpen what Reder (1982) called the "Chicago subculture." In addition to the close intellectual affinities to which Friedman referred – and on the basis of which many laid claim to a Chicago "tradition" – this was rooted in a set of mutually reinforcing, locally institutionalized practices, including Chicago's rigorous and unforgiving graduate program and the distinctive framework for intellectual exchange developed in the department (Emmett 2002a). Chicago's graduate program simultaneously served the function of intellectual socialization (notably, at the altar of price theory symbolized by Econ 301) and Darwinian selectivity (failure was commonplace). As if to underline the role of elemental proximity, accounts of the Chicago School invariably emphasize its treasured oral tradition, the insights of sacred texts being passed, literally, between successive generations of teachers and students (see Hammond 1999; Steindl 1990). Paul Samuelson, who attended the University of Chicago as an undergraduate at just sixteen years old, once remarked that although his Jesuit upbringing eventually "wore off," the searing impact of Chicago economics never did – he felt that he had been "somewhat brainwashed" at Hyde Park (quoted in Silk 1976, 20).

Another important feature of the Chicago subculture was the intensely combative workshop system (Emmett, this volume) pioneered by Friedman, which drew equally on graduate students and senior faculty. Here, rigorously formulated knowledge claims would be subjected to searching critique, "scientific progress [achieved through] a process of creative destruction," though one strictly bounded by a locally cultivated and policed variant of a hyperrationalist economic orthodoxy – stylized as "tight prior equilibrium," or TP (Reder 1982, 19, 20). Reder's sympathetic insider account of the functioning of the TP regime invokes the notion of a locally calibrated scientific paradigm, although a less charitable reading might call attention to what sounds like a form of provincial scientific dogma:

> The paradigmatic nature of TP gives its adherents a particular perspective upon empirical evidence.... [N]ew findings are accepted far more readily if they are consistent with the theory's implications.... This posture of TP causes its adherents to distrust reports (from historians, journalists, practitioners of other social sciences, and from some economists) of behavior incompatible with the implications of economic theory.... Resistance to paradigm-disturbing evidence is paralleled by a reluctance to accept disruptive theoretical innovations. A theoretical innovator must squeeze between the rock: "if an innovation is consistent with what is known, it serves no useful purpose" and the hard place: "if inconsistent with what was previously believed, it must be wrong."... Consequently, at Chicago, a would-be theoretical innovator must be unusually self-confident and determined [while] Chicago-type innovations are "paradigm preserving" or "paradigm extending" rather than "paradigm shattering." (1982, 21–22)

A purified methodological space, circumscribed by tight intellectual and social networks, enabled Chicago to generate something large from something small, in Harry Johnson's words, and to do so from what might be called the theoretical "margins."

This shared marginality, tinged in some cases with a sense of righteous grievance, found its echo in the University of Chicago's cherished identity as an intellectual "haven," proudly tolerant of renegade stripes of opinion. On the "inside," this made for extremely close intellectual and often social ties, and a culture that Stigler once characterized as "monastic" (see Nelson 2001, 164). The microgeographies of the Hyde Park campus happened to facilitate this. "Physical geography," Harry Johnson (1977, 100) explained, made a difference: "[T]he Harvard and Yale economists were scattered among widely separated buildings, whereas the Chicago economists lived on one, the fourth, floor with a single elevator around and in which they automatically met frequently and informally." Relative isolation from the distractions of downtown further intensified the academic monoculture; Deidre McCloskey was among those who attributed the vigor of intellectual engagement to the fact there was "literally nothing else to do" on the campus (quoted in Van Overtveldt 2007, 43).

The Chicago School's theoretical and methodological proclivities therefore melded with a conducive local institutional environment to create the impetus behind what had become a formidable intellectual program, albeit one still located on the borderlands of mainstream or establishment thinking in the 1950s. Laurence Miller's assessment of the Chicago School during this time acknowledged that it was certainly "not monolithic," although he maintained that a "tendency toward a common position seems indisputable." Chicago's "polar position" within American economics was distinctive by virtue of its "unambiguous advocacy of a private-enterprise economy and limited government," because relative to the economics profession, the defining traits of the Chicagoan included the following:

> The polar position that he occupies among economists as an advocate of an individualistic market economy; the emphasis that he puts on the usefulness and relevance of neo-neoclassical economic theory; the way in which he equates the actual and the ideal market; the way in which he sees and applies economics in and to every nook and cranny of life; and the emphasis that he puts on hypothesis-testing as a neglected element in the development of positive economics. (Miller 1962, 65)

Although Chicago types remained a small minority in the profession at large, they were emboldened both by the strength of their convictions and by a fervent belief that the collectivist-interventionist tide would eventually turn. Then, the time would come for "classical" undercurrents in economic theory to reap their deserving revalidation.

No doubt, the tight prior connections of those in Chicago's inner circle were instrumental in establishing the preconditions for the postwar Chicago school, but this hard-earned reputation as an infamous intellectual outpost had yet to be converted into influence. Slowly, though, the tides were turning.

Raison d'être

Milton Friedman (2004, 72) claimed to have only narrowly avoided contracting "Potomac Fever" during his two years at the U.S. Treasury in the early 1940s, where among other things he helped devise a plan for the withholding tax. During this time, however, he had been mainly working as what he liked to call a "technical economist," his life's vocation, therefore limiting his exposure to the disease. Engagement with the worlds of policy and politics came later. Even though this "sideline" was, for him, practically a continuous one from the late 1950s onward, Friedman always insisted that such interventions were calculated acts of professional transgression:

> This policy stuff has been a strict avocation. If you really want to engage in policy activity, don't make it your vocation.... Get a job. Get a secure base of income. Otherwise, you're going to get corrupted and destroyed.... I think you'll make a mistake if you're going to spend your life as a policy wonk. I've seen some of my students who have done this. And some of them are fine, and some of them, especially those who gone to Washington and stayed, are not. (quoted in Doherty 1995, 34)

Cultivating an outsider identity, of course, suited Friedman's political message, but he would soon be drawing on – and helping to reconstruct – elite circuits of his own. Some of this required organizational innovation as well as resources. For example, Friedman was instrumental in establishing the Philadelphia Society, a sort of American branch of the MPS. The Philadelphia Society's inaugural meeting, held in Chicago in 1965, where the organization was incorporated, was described by one observer as a "conclave of the brave." Today, Philadelphia Society meetings are scheduled to coincide with the annual gathering of the Heritage Foundation's Resource Bank, the main event on the calendar for "more than 500 think tank executives, public interest lawyers, policy experts, elected officials, and activists from around the world to discuss issues, strategies, and methods for advancing free market, limited government public policies."[4]

4 See http://www.heritage.org/About/Community/resourcebank.cfm.

Friedman was also present at the rebirth of the American Enterprise Institute (AEI), which took a free-market turn in the mid-1950s under the determined leadership of incoming president, Bill Baroody, ostensibly as a counterweight to the centrist, establishment presence of the Brookings Institution (see Cockett 1995). It was as an adviser to AEI that Friedman "entered the Washington political scene" shortly thereafter (Friedman and Friedman 1998, 344). He was to provide academic stewardship for AEI's research and publication program for many years, but the offices of the think tank also enabled the ambitious economist to make contact with a cabal of ideologically motivated Republican congressmen (including Melvin Laird, Gerald Ford, and Donald Rumsfeld), whose intelligence and commitment to a programmatic agenda for the party especially "impressed" the Chicagoan (see Laird 1964). During this same period, Friedman met Senator Barry Goldwater at one of Baroody's Washington dinner parties, which were positioning AEI as the "brains trust" for the candidate who would become the standard bearer for free-market conservatives within the Republican Party (see Doherty 1995; Friedman and Friedman 1998).

Friedman later served as Goldwater's senior economic advisor, in the senator's iconoclastic but ill-fated presidential run of 1964. His prominent role on the Goldwater policy team prompted, he recalled, "disgust and dismay [from] most of my academic friends," hardly any of whom were "on our side" (Friedman 1974, 16; Friedman, quoted in Rossant 1964, 63). Called on by the *New York Times* to articulate the "Goldwater view of economics," Friedman responded comprehensively, while also gently demurring that he was no hired gun. Noting some differences between his own, more absolutist policy positions and those of the comparatively pragmatic senator, the economist nevertheless called attention to what he saw as their closely overlapping convictions:

> [Goldwater's] goal is always the same: to promote the freedom of the individual and to widen his opportunity; to stop the drift toward centralization and collectivism that has been underway in the past few decades, a drift that has not achieved its professed objectives but that has served to curtail individual freedom, to undermine individual responsibility and to weaken the moral fiber of the people.... Senator Goldwater is often depicted as a reactionary mossback who wants to turn back the clock to an earlier but vanished era.... [He] is, of course, inspired by ideas of an earlier age. So are we all.... [But as] the Senator said in accepting the Republican Presidential nomination, "We must and shall return to proven ways – not because they are old, but because they are true." (Friedman 1964, 37)

Paul Samuleson, in a characteristically erudite response, rejected what he characterized as Friedman's "Economic Libertarianism" as simply too "extreme" for mainstream American politics. In another flashback to his undergraduate days at Chicago in the 1930s, Samuelson (1964, 131, 134) confessed to having been seduced for a while by the "cold beauty" of the utopian worldview of Hayek, Mises, Simons, and Knight. But three decades later, he was no longer vulnerable to such syllogistic reasoning, with its appeal to the "semantics of freedom": The electorate should not be presented with false choices between government regulation and individual freedom because, in the modern mixed economy, they could reasonably "hope to have the best of both worlds." Manichean reasoning, however, suited Chicago's brand of Cold War economics.

During the mid-1960s, Friedman possessed a visceral sense of his location as a member of the intellectual antiestablishment. As he would later recall, Chicago was the ideal base in this respect, because he could advance contrary opinions, and even campaign for a candidate like Goldwater, "without losing the respect of either town or gown" (Friedman 1974, 16). Several degrees of separation from the dense circuits of opinion formation in the Boston-Washington corridor created the necessary space to work against the grain. Had he pursued his career in New York City, Friedman reflected, he would no doubt have been written off as a "kook." It was his visiting professorship at Columbia, in the thick of the Goldwater campaign that had afforded him

> a rare entrée into the New York intellectual community. I talked to and argued with groups from academia, from the media, from the financial community, from the foundation world.... I was appalled at what I found. There was an unbelievable degree of intellectual homogeneity, of acceptance of a standard set of views complete with cliché answers to every objection, of smug self-satisfaction of belonging to an in-group. The closest similar experience I have ever had was at Cambridge, England, and even that was a distant second [compared to] the homogeneity and provincialism of New York.... This kind of intellectual homogeneity is destructive of tolerance. It is no accident that in the New York – or more generally, the eastern – environment, divergent views take the form of cults, not schools. One of the greatest economists of all time, Ludwig von Mises ... was barely tolerated for years in a peripheral academic position at New York University.... [He] had disciples but few students because of the stultifying intellectual atmosphere of New York. (Friedman 1974, 16)

By way of evidence for his claim that Chicago stood for robust heterodoxy, Friedman cited George Stigler's earlier boast that the University of Chicago was the only institution that could have staffed a Council of Economic Advisers for *both* Johnson and Goldwater, circa 1964. "If Chicago's geographical location had an effect," Friedman reflected, it was certainly not an isolation-induced proneness to "homogenous, if offbeat views"; rather it stemmed from a robustly liberal intellectual environment, actively dismissive of "narrowness, homogeneity, and inbreeding," New York-style (Friedman 1974, 14; see also Crocker 1965).

Speaking at an annual dinner of the University's board of trustees, Friedman went on to conclude his "amateur exercise in the sociology of knowledge" by speculating that the intellectual fecundity of the various Chicago schools could be explained by the fact that

> we were established in Chicago, a new, raw city, bursting with energy, far less sophisticated than New York, but for that very reason far more tolerant of diversity, of heterodox ideas. New York looked east, to the Old World [while looking] down its nose at the New.... Chicago, like other cities this side of the Appalachians, looked west, to the frontiers.... Chicago [became] characterized by diversity in every dimension, by a willingness to experiment, to judge people by their performance rather than their origins, to judge ideas by their consequences rather than their antecedents. (1974, 16)

Chicago symbolized Friedman's relative independence, the fact that he was "firmly based in a scientific academic discipline [rather than] simply a preacher or an ideologue or an unconnected philosopher" facilitating a constructively safe distance from the suffocating intellectual and political culture of New York, which tended to transform conservatives into cultists (Milton Friedman, quoted in Doherty 1995, 37), and from Washington, where the fetid ranks of think tanks and policy wonks could not help but dilute and distort, if not derail truly pathbreaking ideas.

Revolution

The spring of 1975 marked the beginning of Chile's "silent revolution." General Augusto Pinochet – who beyond suppressing labor unions and other "subversive" elements, "knew little about economics" (Yergin and Stanislaw 2002, 239) – had set the country on a path of radical free-market reconstruction. His guide was a monetarist tome known as "the brick" – ostensibly due to its 189-page length, rather than its lack of subtlety – which had been drafted in secret during the Allende period by a group of economists at the Universidad Catolica de Chile, under the leadership of Sergio de Castro. In one of the most storied episodes in the history of neoliberalism, Pinochet effectively handed control of economic policy over to "Los Chee-Ca-Go Boys," as they became known – a group of Chicago-trained economists, led by de Castro, who would staff the key positions in his administration. In this notorious application of "shock treatment," the Chicago Boys went to war against inflation, which had spiked at 370 percent in the first year of the junta, their actions driving the economy immediately into recession, while at the same time setting about an uninhibited program of trade liberalization, tax reform, privatization, deregulation of foreign investment flows, and monetary restraint. An early move was to invite two of their Chicago professors, Arnold Harberger and Milton Friedman, for a week of seminars, public lectures, and meetings with military managers, culminating in an audience with Pinochet – all designed to bolster the credibility of the reform program. Not surprisingly, Harberger and Friedman signed off on the plan, which they might have authored by proxy. The Chicago School was about to learn a lesson in the politics of outsourcing.

Pointedly negative press commentary soon followed on the *New York Times* editorial page: Here, the Chilean visit raised "troubling questions … about the social role of academics," given the instrumental role of the "ideas of Milton Friedman … and his Chicago school" in legitimizing the junta's "draconian" program (*New York Times* 1975, 32; Lewis 1975). Although he continued stridently to defend Pinochet's economic program – later dubbing Chile "an economic miracle" in his *Newsweek* column (Friedman 1983b [1982]) – Friedman had to learn to make his way to public speaking engagements "via the kitchen":

> The protests organized by the united front [against the Friedman/Harberger Collaboration with the Chilean Junta] were annoying, especially when they included pickets marching up and down with signs in front of the apartment house in which we lived, but they were not very serious.… I never could decide whether to be more amused or more annoyed by the charge that I was running the Chilean economy from my office in Chicago. (Friedman and Friedman 1998, 404, 402, 400)

As Friedman and his supporters also insisted on pointing out, Harberger was actually the architect of the program that had brought Chilean economists to Chicago, beginning in the mid-1950s. As late as Friedman's ninetieth birthday, setting the record straight remained a priority: "I realize the 'Chicago-Boys-with-Milton' is the premise of numerous fine articles in the *New York Review of Books*," Deidre McCloskey (2003, 144) huffed, "But they and you are wrong. Milton didn't do it." It was, apparently, the entire economics department that did it.

Although supporters of Chicago School economics would later claim vindication, when Chile eventually transitioned to both economic growth and democratic rule, there has been continuing defensiveness about the fact that the first full-scale implementation of the Chicago method had occurred in the context of an authoritarian regime. For many critics, this merely confirmed the suspected relationship between political repression and the economic violence of free-market governance (see Green 1995;

Klein 2007). In the space of a few fateful months in 1975, the "image of the 'Chicago Boys' was born," Van Overtveldt (2007, 346) complains, in the form of "a group of amoral, ruthless, and antidemocratic hyper-technicians, who believed that the free-market economy was the only thing worth worrying about." Not only would the associated controversy cast a cloud over the remainder of Friedman's teaching career at Chicago, but following his award of the Nobel Prize in 1976, it brought an estimated five thousand protesters onto the streets of Stockholm. Many years later, when an interviewer put it to Friedman that Chile did, in fact, deserve "a place in history [as] the first country to put Chicago theory into practice," he sputtered, "No, no, no. Not at all. After all, Great Britain put Chicago theory into practice in the nineteenth century [and the] United States put Chicago theory into practice in the nineteenth and twentieth century. I don't believe that's right."[5]

Reaganomics

Although Friedman continued to be the public face of the Chicago School of economics, he was to become somewhat estranged from domestic politics during the 1970s. He had served on Nixon's economic advisory group, which was chaired by his mentor, Arthur Burns, but pointedly had little or nothing to do with the doomed president after he imposed price controls – "I saw him only once after that" (Milton Friedman, quoted in Doherty 1995, 33). And then came Reagan. For Friedman, at least, this represented a long-awaited sea change. He would serve on Reagan's fourteen-member Economic Policy Coordinating Committee, chaired by fellow Chicagoan George Shultz, which was tasked with engineering an advance plan for the new administration. Among the committee's recommendations was the immediate removal of price controls on oil, which was duly enacted by the incoming president. Friedman later joined the president's Economic Advisory Board, which also included Alan Greenspan, Arthur Laffer, and William Simon – a cabal that he portrayed as "independent thinkers" with a "free-market orientation," and all professional economists rather than "'yes' persons" (Friedman and Friedman 1998, 391). Fully half of the members of Reagan's economic "brains trust" had substantial Chicago connections. The president's eyes would reportedly twinkle whenever he joined this group of true believers for a working lunch. In the words one of Reagan's senior policy advisors, this was "truly the board of directors for the development of

[5] Milton Friedman interview, conducted in 2000, accessed at http://www.pbs.org/wgbh/commandingheights/hi/resources/pdf_index.html.

Reaganomics" (Anderson 1988, 267). Friedman, Anderson disclosed, was one of the president's "favorites."

The same could not be said of George Stigler. One day in late October 1982, Chicago's Mr. Micro learned that he had been awarded the Nobel Prize, securing his reputation as "the intellectual Father of Deregulation" (Stigler 1988, 87; Warsh 1993, 84). On the face of it, this was a timely shot in the arm for Chicago economics, the achievements of which in theory had been overshadowed by some very public failures in practice – notably, in the first domestic applications of monetarism and in the Chilean experiment (see Greider 1989; Malabre 1994). The United States was in the second, painful part of an unprecedented "double dip" recession, and the Republicans were facing major setbacks in the midterm elections. Seizing the opportunity for some free publicity on the eve of the vote, the White House paraded Stigler in front of the Washington press corps.

The president joked with reporters that, "Our critics are saying that the economy is on its knees, well you know something, if the economy is back on its knees, that's quite an improvement because two years ago it was flat on its back." The unemployment rate had topped 10 percent, but Reagan quipped that his administration need only take responsibility for 2.7 percent, because it had stood at 7.4 percent when he entered office. Misplaced levity aside, it was expected that the newly minted Nobel laureate would at least offer a vote of support for the administration's experiment in "supply-side economics." Yet when reporters invited Stigler to comment on Reagan's economic program, he curtly dismissed supply-side economics as "a gimmick [if not] a slogan.... Where they went too far was in claiming so much for it and saying that if we do that, that alone will take care of inflation and things like that. I don't think that was in the cards."[6] And when he went on to use the word "depression," he was practically bundled from the platform "in a manner reminiscent of vaudeville days" (Stigler 1988, 137). The liberal use of what Stigler rather proudly described as his "unruly tongue" had apparently confirmed, for both parties, this Chicagoan's long-held view that politicians and economists were breeds apart.

Stigler had long before grown skeptical of the potential for even well-intentioned reform efforts (Nik-Khah, this volume, Chapter 5). His work on the microeconomics of regulation, in particular, had extended the rational choice paradigm deep into the arena of politics itself, yielding the conclusion that policy makers should be seen as "endogenous participants in a political-economic process," whose preoccupations with the calculus of

[6] Quoted in ABC News Transcripts, *World News Tonight*, November 1, 1982.

utilitarian and electoral gain rendered them "incapable of acting on advice as to the promotion of general welfare, and unlikely to be much interested in receiving such advice" (Reder 1982, 26). These arguments had been articulated most forcefully, of course, by James Buchanan, who after working with Frank Knight in Chicago, went on to establish the Virginia school of public choice.

Although a studied cynicism concerning the prospects for constructive governmental intervention might be considered typical of the "Chicago view," a rather conspicuous exception is provided by Friedman himself, who repeatedly flew perilously close to the governmental flame. Like Stigler, Friedman had come to regard congressional testimony as a "waste of time" (Milton Friedman, quoted in *Playboy* 1973, 52), but quite unlike Stigler, Friedman did not extend this interpretation to the political process *in toto*. To the contrary, he grew increasingly preoccupied with public policy interventions, both in the popular media and as a high-level policy advisor. Friedman possessed a sense of the progressive role of reform, at least when allied to a market-oriented program and the "right ideas" (see Nelson 2001). Stigler's joke, which they shared, was that, "Milton wants to change the world. I just want to observe it."[7]

Friedman had pursued public policy objectives with increasing vigor in the second half of his career, after he relocated to the Hoover Institution, pushing *inter alia* for education vouchers, the abolition of the military draft and professional licensure, flat taxes, and the privatization of social security. These policy positions, as Reder (1982, 25–26) points out, were all broadly consistent with the Chicago School worldview – because they invoked market logics and incentives, favoring private over public systems of delivery, and voluntary provisions over mandatory requirements – but they bluntly contradicted public-choice fatalism of Stigler and Buchanan, with its principled rejection of the notion that an "economist-reformer could move the economy in a desired direction simply by persuading a beneficent ruler, constrained by prices but otherwise omnipotent, to behave appropriately." Stigler's position, in the final analysis, represented a more positive variant of positive economics than its original proponent was willing to accept, undermining the rationale for normative economics, and leaving would-be economist-reformers either with "nothing to do" or, worse still, suggesting the unpalatable conclusion that policy agitators might be in it "for their own

[7] An Interview with Milton Friedman, Podcast Transcript, Library of Economics and Liberty, Russ Roberts and Milton Friedman September 4, 2006, accessed at http://www.econlib.org/library/Columns/y2006/Friedmantranscript.html.

amusement or private advantage" (Reder 1982, 26; Nik-Khah, this volume, Chapter 5).

The full implications of this interpretation seem never to have been fully explored in Chicago, at least while Friedman was still on the faculty. At the start of the Reagan era, however, by which time Friedman had relocated to the West Coast, the mood in the economics department was somewhat paradoxically one of disengagement, if not fatalism. Reder observed in the first months of the Reagan Administration:

> [M]any of the younger Chicago economists are quite apolitical. In current lunch time discussions, the political question is at least as likely to be: "Why take the time and trouble to vote?" as it is: "For whom should one vote?" Nevertheless, the aversion to government activity built into the Chicago sub-culture remains strong.... Fortunately, affection and good sense have prevented serious intellectual disagreement from causing any breach of personal relations between Stigler and Friedman.... But despite the lack of public debate the fact of the disagreement has been well-known in Chicago for the last decade. (1982, 26)

Experience would soon temper Friedman's reforming zeal, however. Although remaining fiercely defensive of the president himself, Friedman became dismayed to find that the radical policy program advocated by Reagan's band of free-thinking economists was being diluted, delayed, and derailed. His *Newsweek* columns grew increasingly shrill, accusing the U.S. Congress and even the White House of "hypocrisy," "schizophrenia," and unprincipled backsliding (see Friedman 1983a). From their new perch in San Francisco, Milton and Rose were soon complaining about the *Tyranny of the Status Quo* (Friedman and Friedman 1984), to which the Reagan project had apparently also succumbed.

Reliberalization

The Chicago School may have achieved its paradoxical apogee in the early 1980s, the point at which both its doctrinal principles and its policy prescriptions passed – secularized and sullied, at least by Chicago standards – into the mainstream. Within a few years, one of the School's most astute chroniclers, Melvin Reder (1987, 417), was reflecting that, if "the vitality of [the Chicago] tradition is threatened," this was, ironically, more a product of "the growing acceptance of many of its key ideas than [due to] resistance to them"; what was once a highly distinctive Chicago emphasis on competition and the money supply had "become mainstream economics."

Several months before his fateful encounter with Reagan at the White House press conference, George Stigler was putting the finishing touches to his *Economist as Preacher, and Other Essays*, while also contemplating the provenance of the Chicago School. Long critical of claims that economic science might be seriously susceptible to "environmental" influences, and for that matter that economic theory might be associated with short-term influences in the earthly domains of policy and politics, Stigler nevertheless arrived at the conclusion that the "Crown Prince" of the Chicago School, Henry Simons, had been

> closely tuned to the time and place in which he lived: America in the Great Depression. It was a time for great fears and bold reforms – indeed bold reforms require great crises, and Simons frequently invoked utter catastrophe as the justification of his proposals.... The "Chicago School" has always been a phrase whose accuracy varied inversely to its content. The leading figures of the School in the 1930s were highly diverse: Knight was the great philosopher and theoretician, almost in a Marxian sense; Viner was studiously non-dogmatic on policy views; Mints was a close historical student of money, and restricted himself to that field; Simons was the utopian.... At a doctrinal level, the one specific idea that carries over to the present day in Friedman's writings is Simons' demand for a fixed rule for the conduct of monetary policy. In forming most of the present day policy views of Chicago economists, Director and Friedman have been the main intellectual forces.... Simons' central goal is as vital and irresistible today as it was forty years ago: to devise a decentralized, unpoliticized world in which personal freedom and economic efficiency find wide scope and strong defense. (1982, 170)

It was, perhaps, the futility of this premature expression of neoliberal utopianism that eventually overcame Simons – the "decentralized, unpoliticized world" would remain, for him, forever elusive. Friedman, in contrast, was always more willing to engage with the purveyors of politicized and even centralized power more or less as he found them, albeit with the option of beating occasional tactical retreats to the Social Science Research Building or the Quadrangle Club. Quite unlike Simons, Friedman was repeatedly drawn to power, only to find his relatively uncompromising ambitions frustrated. It might be said that he was substantially defined by the lived contradiction between his professional and political roles. While choosing to exaggerate the distance between Friedman and the corridors of power, Deirdre McCloskey (2003, 144) conveys a sense of this when she defensively observes, "He has in fact been notably careful about advising *any* government, including even the American one.... [He] advised Goldwater, Nixon, Reagan, but always as an outsider, never ... as a paid employee." It was, of course, his *tenure* at the University of Chicago – a system he personally opposed – that facilitated this measure of principled freedom.

Notwithstanding supply-side arguments about the power of ideas emanating from Hyde Park, it is difficult to escape the conclusion that it was the conjunctural opening provided by the stagflation crisis that ultimately established an international market for Chicago's brand of provincial economics – even though it must also acknowledged that Friedman and his colleagues had assiduously prepared for this moment, subsequently exploiting it to the full. Notwithstanding all the talk of the "power of ideas," the influence of the Chicago School essentially rose in lockstep with the misery index – a simple measure of the late-Keynesian ordeal of unemployment *plus* inflation – the historic peak of which coincided, exactly, with the presidential election of 1980. It is no coincidence that this moment of macroeconomic rupture also represented the moment of rapture for the Chicago brand of crisis theory. "Only a crisis – actual or perceived – produces real change," Friedman (1982) famously wrote at the time; yet his soberingly materialist conclusion was that changes in the climate of opinion are wrought by "experience, not by theory or philosophy."

References

Breit, William and Ransom, Roger L. 1998. *The Academic Scribblers: American Economists in Collision*, Third edition. Princeton, NJ: Princeton University Press.

Brittan, Samuel. 2006. "Iconoclastic Economist Who Put Freedom First." *Financial Times* November 17: 13.

Bronfenbrenner, Martin. 1962. "Observations on the 'Chicago School(s).'" *Journal of Political Economy* 70(1): 72–75.

Christ, Carl F. 1994. "The Cowles Commission's Contributions to Econometrics at Chicago, 1939–1955." *Journal of Economic Literature* 32(1): 30–59.

Coats, A. W. 1960. "The Politics of Political Economists: Comment." *Quarterly Journal of Economics* 74(4): 666–669.

1963. "The Origins of the 'Chicago School(s)'?" *Journal of Political Economy* 71(5): 487–493.

Cockett, Richard. 1995. *Thinking the Unthinkable: Think-tanks and the Economic Counter-Revolution, 1931–83*. London: Fontana Press.

Crocker, George N. 1965. "New Torch Burns." *San Francisco Examiner* March 7: 30.

Davenport, John. 1946. "The Testament of Henry Simons." *Fortune* 34(3): 116–119.

de Long, J. Bradford. 1990. "In Defense of Henry Simons' Standing as a Classical Liberal." *Cato Journal* 9(3): 601–618.

Director, Aaron. 1948. "Prefatory Note." In Henry C. Simons, *Economic Policy for a Free Society*. Chicago: University of Chicago Press, pp. v–vii.

Doherty, Brian. 1995. "Best of Both Worlds." *Reason* 27(2): 32–38.

Ebenstein, Lanny. 2007. *Milton Friedman: A Biography*. New York: Palgrave.

Emmett, Ross C. 2002a. "Introduction." In Ross C. Emmett, ed., *The Chicago Tradition in Economics, 1892–1945*, volume 1. New York: Routledge, xvii–xxiv.

2002b. "Introduction." In Ross C. Emmett, ed., *The Chicago Tradition in Economics, 1892–1945*, volume 7. New York: Routledge, pp. vii–x.

Formaini, Robert L. 2002. "Frank H. Knight: Origins of the Chicago School of Economics." *Economic Insights* 7(3): 1–4.

Friedman, Milton. 1951. "Nyliberalismen Og Dens Muligheter" [Neoliberalism and its Prospects], *Farmand* February 17: 89–93.

1953. *Essays in Positive Economics*. Chicago: University of Chicago Press.

1957. *A Theory of the Consumption Function*. Princeton, NJ: Princeton University Press.

1964. "The Goldwater View of Economics." *New York Times* October 11: 35–137.

1974. "Schools at Chicago." *University of Chicago Magazine* Autumn: 11–16.

1982. *Capitalism and Freedom*. Chicago: University of Chicago.

1983. *Bright Promises, Dismal Performance*. New York: Harcourt Brace Jovanovich.

1983b. [1982] Free Markets and the Generals. In Milton Friedman, *Bright Promises, Dismal Performance*. New York: Harcourt Brace Jovanovich, 391–93.

2002. [1962] *Capitalism and Freedom: Fortieth Anniversary Edition*. Chicago: University of Chicago.

2004. "Milton Friedman." In William Breit and Barry T. Hirsch (eds.) *Lives of the Laureates: Eighteen Nobel economists*. Cambridge, MA: MIT Press, 65–78.

Friedman, Milton and Friedman, Rose D. 1984. *The Tyranny of the Status Quo*. New York: Harcourt Brace Jovanovich.

1998. *Two Lucky People: Memoirs*. Chicago: Chicago University Press.

Friedman, Rose D. 1976. "Milton Friedman: Husband and colleague – (3)." *Oriental Economist* 44(7): 18–23.

Galbraith, John K. 1987 *Economics in Perspective: A Critical History*. Boston: Houghton Mifflin.

Green, Duncan. 1995. *Silent Revolution: The Rise of Market Economics in Latin America*. London: Cassell.

Greider, William. 1989. *Secrets of the Temple: How the Federal Reserve Runs the Country*. New York: Simon and Schuster.

Hammond, J. Daniel. 1999. *The Legacy of Milton Friedman as Teacher*. Northampton, MA: Edward Elgar.

Harvey, David. 2005. *A Brief History of Neoliberalism*. Oxford: Oxford University Press.

Hayek, Friedrich A. 1944. *The Road to Serfdom*. Chicago: University of Chicago Press.

Johnson, Harry G. 1971. "The Keynesian Revolution and the Monetarist Counter-revolution." *American Economic Review* 61(2): 91–106.

1977. "Cambridge as an Academic Environment in the Early 1930s: A Reconstruction from the Late 1940s." In Don Patinkin and J. Clark Leith, eds., *Keynes, Cambridge and the General Theory*. London: Macmillan, 98–114.

Kitch, Edmund W. 1983. "The Fire of Truth: A Remembrance of Law and Economics at Chicago, 1932–1970." *Journal of Law and Economics* 26(1): 163–234.

1998. "Chicago School of Law and Economics." In Peter Newman, ed., *The New Palgrave Dictionary of Economics and the Law*, volume 1. London: Macmillan, 227–233.

Klein, Naomi. 2007. *Shock Doctrine: The Rise of Disaster Capitalism*. New York: Metropolitan Books.

Knight, Frank H. 1947. *Freedom and Reform*. London: Harper.

Laird, Melvin G ., ed., 1964. *The Conservative Papers*. Chicago: Quadrangle Books.

Lampman, Robert J. 1993. *Economists at Wisconsin: 1892–1992*. Madison: University of Wisconsin Press.

Lewis, Anthony. 1975. "For Which We Stand: II." *New York Times* October 2: 38.

Malabre, Alfred L. 1994. *Lost Prophets: An Insider's History of the Modern Economists*. Boston: Harvard Business School Press.

McCloskey, Deirdre N. 2003. "Milton." *Eastern Economic Review* 29(1): 143–146.

Miller, H. Laurence. 1962. "On the 'Chicago School of Economics,'" *Journal of Political Economy* 70(1): 64–69.

Mirowski, Philip. 2002. *Machine Dreams: Economics becomes a Cyborg Science*. Cambridge: Cambridge University Press.

2011 "The Cowles Commission as an Anti-Keynesian Stronghold 1943–1954." In Pedro Duarte and Gilberto Lima, eds., *Historical Explorations in the Microfoundations of Macroeconomics*. Cambridge: Cambridge University Press.

Nelson, Robert H. 2001. *Economics as Religion: From Samulelson to Chicago and Beyond*. University Park, PA: Pennsylvania State University Press.

New York Times. 1975. "Two Years of Pinochet." *New York Times* September 21: 32.

Noble, Holcombe B. 2006. "Milton Friedman, the Champion of Free Markets, is Dead at 94." *New York Times* November 17: A1.

Patinkin, Don. 1981. *Essays on and in the Chicago Tradition*. Durham, NC: Duke University Press.

Playboy. 1973. "Playboy Interview: Milton Friedman." *Playboy* February: 51–68, 74.

Reder, Melvin W. 1982. "Chicago Economics: Permanence and Change." *Journal of Economic Literature* 20(1): 1–38.

1987. "Chicago School." In John Eatwell, Murray Milgate and Peter Newman, eds., *The New Palgrave: A Dictionary of Economics*, volume 1. London: Macmillan, 413–418.

Robinson, Joan. 1972. "The Second Crisis of Economic Theory," *American Economic Review* 62(2): 1–10.

Rossant, Murray J. 1964. "A Talk with a Goldwater Man." *New York Times* October 8: 63.

Sally, Razeen. 1997. "The Political Economy of Frank Knight: Classical liberalism from Chicago." *Constitutional Political Economy* 8(2): 123–138.

Samuelson, Paul. 1964. "The Case against Goldwater's Economics." *New York Times* October 25: 131, 134.

Shils, Edward. 1991. "Foreword." In Edward Shils, ed., *Remembering the University of Chicago*. Chicago: University of Chicago Press, ix–xxi.

Silk, Leonard. 1976. *The Economists*. New York: Basic Books.

Simons, Henry C. 1934. *A Positive Program for Laissez Faire: Some Proposals for a Liberal Economic Policy*. Public Policy Pamphlet No. 15, Chicago: University of Chicago.

Steindl, Frank G. 1990. "The 'Oral Tradition' at Chicago in the 1930s." *Journal of Political Economy* 98(2): 430–432.

Stigler, George J. 1982. *The Economist as Preacher, and Other Essays*. Chicago: University of Chicago Press.

1988. *Memoirs of an Unregulated Economist*. New York: Basic Books.

Van Horn, Robert and Mirowski, Philip. 2009. "The Rise of the Chicago School of Economics and the Birth of Neoliberalism." In Philip Mirowski and Deiter Plehwe, eds., *The Road from Mont Pèlerin: The Making of the Neoliberal Thought Collective*. Cambridge, MA: Harvard University Press, 139–178.

Van Overtveldt, Johan. 2007. *The Chicago School*. Chicago: Agate.

Walters, Alan. 1987. "Milton Friedman." In John Eatwell, Murray Milgate and Peter Newman, eds., *The New Palgrave: A Dictionary of Economics*, volume 2. London: Macmillan, 422–427.

Warsh, David. 1993. *Economic Principals*. New York: Free Press.

Yergin, Daniel and Stanislaw, Joseph. 2002. *The Commanding Heights*. New York: Touchstone.

PART ONE

ECONOMICS BUILT FOR POLICY: THE LEGACY OF MILTON FRIEDMAN

ONE

Positive Economics for Democratic Policy

Milton Friedman, Institutionalism, and the Science of History

Thomas A. Stapleford

As economics pushes on beyond "statics," it becomes less like science, and more like history.

– Sir John R. Hicks 1979, xi

Conventional wisdom would place early institutional economics and the postwar Chicago School on opposite ends of any methodological spectrum. Prominent faculty and graduates from postwar Chicago have derided institutional economics not merely as incorrect but as actually devoid of content. Thomas Sowell characterized it as "half economics, half sociology, and all mush" (Sowell 1993, 788); Ronald Coase claimed it "had nothing to pass on except a mass of descriptive material waiting for a theory, or a fire" (Coase 1984, 230); and George Stigler found it vacuous beyond "a stance of hostility to the standard theoretical tradition" (Kitch 1983, 170).

Nonetheless, recent scholarship has softened this superficially sharp contrast. In the first place, institutionalism encompassed a diverse range of approaches (Rutherford 2000), and postwar Chicago economists have been noticeably less critical of at least one prominent strand: the quantitative analysis associated with Wesley C. Mitchell, the National Bureau of Economic Research (NBER, cofounded by Mitchell), and some aspects of the Robert Brookings Graduate School (forerunner of the Brookings Institution). Stigler expressed grudging respect for Mitchell, and Milton Friedman likewise concluded that Mitchell was "not as empty of content as most of the [institutionalists]" (Kitch 1983, 170, 171). In fact, Friedman spoke quite positively about Mitchell in a lengthy posthumous assessment

I am grateful to numerous generous colleagues whose comments have greatly improved this essay, including Eric Schliesser, Dan Hammond, Roger Backhouse, Ross Emmett, and the participants at the 2010 workshop on the History of Economics as History of Science at the École normale supérieure de Cachan.

in 1950 in which he argued for viewing Mitchell as an "economic theorist" (Friedman 1950), a significant label because the most common objection to institutional economics from postwar Chicago was its alleged neglect of theory (e.g., Kitch 1983, 169–171).

This more benign view of Mitchell surely results in part from the personal connections between him and key members of the postwar Chicago School, especially Friedman. Friedman studied under both Mitchell and one of Mitchell's most prominent advisees, Arthur F. Burns; Chicago economists (including Mitchell and Stigler) worked closely with the NBER when it was directed by institutional economists (Mitchell and Burns); and interwar Chicago itself was home to a diverse range of methodological approaches, including those promoted by institutional economists (Hammond 2001; Rutherford 2010). Yet Friedman's assessment of Mitchell reflects more than respect for a former colleague and mentor: As Abraham Hirsch and Neil de Marchi have argued in detail, Friedman's own methodological outlook was quite similar to Mitchell's except for their disagreement over the empirical validity of neoclassical price theory (Hirsch and de Marchi 1990, 42–52; cf. Hammond 1996).

In this essay, I aim to reinforce the perceived ties between Friedman and the strand of institutional economics associated with Mitchell. On the most concrete level, I introduce a new and important locus for that connection: Friedman's 1935–1937 work for the U.S. National Resources Committee. More broadly, I highlight a hitherto overlooked dimension to their shared methodological perspective, namely the common goal of creating a new form of economics that could have an extensive role in democratic policy making. Briefly put, both Mitchell and Friedman believed that economics could be established as a predictive science with a broad scope capable of yielding objective claims (that is, claims that demanded universal assent from all rational observers). The source of this power would be an expanded empiricism: Theories and analytical tools would be developed from, and tested against, "real-world" data, especially statistics.

The predictive and empirical character of this scientific economics was the foundation for its political value. Because it was predictive – given appropriate variables and constraints, economists could predict outcomes for real-world policy choices – the development of economics was de facto the development of human capability to control economic behavior. Likewise, because (according to proponents) it was objective and politically neutral – resting strictly on the fit between models and facts – it could be readily assimilated into political life without subverting democratic discussion. Economists, in other words, could provide policy knowledge independent of political judgments. Crucially, both Mitchell and Friedman envisioned economists as heavily involved in policy making, where they would not serve as partisan advisers but as neutral scientists who clarified available means and predicted the outcomes of various actions. Thus the expansion of scientific economics was simultaneously the rationalization of politics.

Given this emphasis on prediction and empiricism, it should be unsurprising that both Friedman and Mitchell saw strong parallels between the physical sciences and economics (Hirsch and de Marchi 1990, 47). Just as the physical sciences provided objective, predictive theories for the behavior of nonhuman objects, so too would economics provide objective, predictive theories in the social realm. One serious glitch in this analogy, of course, was economists' general inability to isolate a phenomenon for repeated experimentation. In practice, economists collected empirical, historical data (whether from last month or last century) and then developed, refined, and tested their theories with that data. "Prediction" thus frequently reduced to "fit with historical data." Not only did this practice raise epistemological puzzles (in what sense could tests against existing data count as prediction?), it also committed adherents to a particular vision of history. If the value of economics lay in its ability to make predictions about future outcomes, and if these predictions were (in practice) extrapolations from historical analysis, then belief in the scientific character of economics implied a similar belief in the potential for scientific history. In other words, to believe in economics as defined by Mitchell and Friedman was to believe that historical analysis could yield objective predictions about future developments. In fact, economics *qua* science was the embodiment of this very kind of historical study. Thus the prediction of social behavior, the establishment of a scientific form of historical analysis, and the rationalization of politics all formed a logically connected framework that united Mitchell's strand of institutional economics with Friedman's version of Chicago economics.

Recognizing these connections helps us distinguish Friedman from many of his mentors in the interwar economics department at Chicago, notably Frank Knight. Melvin Reder (a self-described "participant-observer" of Chicago economics) has suggested that the germ of the postwar school "sprang from the affinity group of Knight's students and protégés that formed in the middle 1930s," including "Milton and Rose Director Friedman, George Stigler, Allen Wallis, Aaron Director and Henry Simons" (Reder 1982, 1, 6–7). Not only was Knight a vocal critic of institutional economics (including Mitchell's version) and a committed proponent of neoclassical price theory, but his political leanings corresponded to those of key Chicago School figures: Thus in 1947 he would join Friedman, Director, and Stigler as founding members of the Mont Pelerin Society. Yet this superficial alignment can be highly misleading, because Knight's critique of institutional economics targeted many of the same features that it shared with the postwar Chicago School: the conviction that economics could make reliable predictions about real-world problems, the belief in the scientific character of historical analysis, and the effort to rationalize politics (which Knight found both futile and dangerous). In short, whereas Knight attacked institutional economics from a largely orthogonal direction – denying its key presumptions – Friedman's critique came from within the general framework that Mitchell had already established and institutionalized in several locations, including the NBER and (as we will see) economic planning agencies within the New Deal. Thus, surprising though it may seem at first, Friedman's outlook was fundamentally much closer to Mitchell's than to Knight's.

Having grasped this connection, we are better positioned to understand the ambiguous relationship between the Chicago School and institutional economics, to understand why key members could be so clearly indebted to Mitchell's methodological outlook and yet so dismissive of the movement with which he was associated. For behind this attitude lies a natural consequence of any effort to rationalize politics through objective scientific study: If policy analysis is a matter of objective science, then opponents who use different methods to reach diametrically opposed conclusions must not only be incorrect but actually unscientific, doomed by flawed methods. In the conclusion, I suggest that this dynamic explains much of the rhetoric surrounding the Chicago School (from both critics and supporters) and also illuminates contemporary discussions of economic policy. Just as the Chicago School was the heir to Mitchell's methodological vision on the political right, so too does the political left have its parallel version, and the clash between these conceptions can involve nothing but appeals to scientific purity and charges of ideological blindness.

1.1. Wesley C. Mitchell and the Reconstruction of American Economics

One of Mitchell's more famous methodological statements was his 1924 presidential address to the American Economics Association (Mitchell 1925) in which he dismissed neoclassical theory as an unrealistic creation of armchair philosophers and outlined a new vision for economics founded on extensive empirical study. However, another essay from the same year, "The Prospect of Economics" (Mitchell 1924), is equally revealing. Here, Mitchell more explicitly discussed the motivation underlying his proposed reforms: the desire to make economic theory useful for policy.

Mitchell divided his assessment of economics into two sections: the "Past" and the "Future." Tellingly, the "Past" started not with Adam Smith, but with David Ricardo, who had constructed a systematic analysis of political economy in response to the financial crises and social unrest arising in England in the wake of the Napoleonic Wars. Thus economics, in Mitchell's depiction, began as pragmatic policy science. Yet his tale of origins also included a sinful fall that left classical political economy alienated from the political concerns that had animated it.

By the turn of the twentieth century, Mitchell lamented, "economics had settled into an academic discipline, cultivated by professors and neglected by men of action, modest in its pretensions to practical usefulness, more conspicuous for consistency and erudition than for insight, hated by few and feared by none" (Mitchell 1924, 19). This irrelevance was a direct corollary of the isolation of economic theory from applied problems:

> For many years there has been a notable difference between the way in which economists handled economic theory on the one hand and the way in which they handled such problems as transportation, public finance, tariffs, money, banking, insurance, trusts, and labor on the other hand. The monographs made little use of the theoretical treatises, and the treatises drew upon the monographs for little beyond illustration. Text books often had a theoretical part and an applied part held together by nothing more intimate than the binding. (24)

Returning economics to political relevance would require bridging this division.

According to Mitchell, blame for the bifurcation fell on Ricardo's successors, who had treated economics as a set of "hypothetical" deductive analyses that began with "certain postulates" and yielded "tendencies" within political economy. These tendencies were not predictions (in the strict sense) because they took no account of the particularities in any given case. Rather, they formed general trends that might be realized to a greater or lesser degree in any specific situation, or perhaps not realized at all.

In Mitchell's view, this approach created a double mischief. First, it rendered economic theory practically immune to empirical correction because general tendencies could not be disconfirmed by any particular evidence (Mitchell 1924, 12). Second, it left economics unable to offer concrete policy guidance. As Mitchell explained, a science of tendencies had proven inadequate for economic planning during the First World War. When economists were asked to devise production or labor policies, "it seldom sufficed to say that a given action would have consequences of a certain kind," although that was the only guidance offered by "orthodox treatises." Instead, "the important thing was to find out at least in what order of magnitude these consequences should be reckoned." Managerial decisions required calculation, not loose generalization. Accordingly, Mitchell concluded, "in proportion as economists face real problems they will strive to cast even their general theory into the quantitative mold" (Mitchell 1924, 27–28).

To move from tendencies to quantitative predictions required "objective records of mass behavior" – that is, historical statistics – which in turn would permit economics to become a "science of behavior." Rather than deduce likely actions from an analysis of imputed motives (the procedure of classical political economists), future economists would gather statistical data in order to improve "the objective validity of the account [economics] gives of economic processes." According to Mitchell, this confrontation with the empirical record would transform the very nature of economics. As economists grasped the role of institutions and "social habits" in shaping behavior, they would recognize the necessarily dynamic character of economic theory, which would make "the cumulative change of institutions" a primary component of its work (Mitchell 1924, 22–28).

Economics, therefore, was fundamentally a historical science for Mitchell, albeit a soft Hegelian – or better, a Marxist – form of history in which one studied the dynamics of historical transformation. Significantly, Mitchell believed that Marx had grasped how "the central problem of economics" lay in analyzing the "cumulative change in economic institutions," and despite the flaws in Marx's analysis, he had nonetheless revealed the "scientific possibilities" within such studies (Mitchell 1924, 18). The task for future economists was to blend Marx's attention to historical evolution with detailed empirical research, all while recognizing (contra Marx) that the possibility of altering social and institutional structures through political action implied the potential to direct that evolution down alternate paths. Ultimately, Mitchell declared, "In economics as in other sciences we desire knowledge mainly as an instrument of control," which raised "the alluring possibility of shaping the evolution of economic life to fit the developing purposes of our race" (Mitchell 1924, 25). Statistics and historical analysis would thereby make possible what Mitchell elsewhere called "a method by which we may make cumulative progress in social organization" (Mitchell 1919, 232). Economics would once again become an applied science, now built on a firmer foundation.

For Mitchell, that future looked much closer after the First World War. Not only had war mobilization revealed the weakness of orthodox theory, it had also convinced a growing number of businessmen, social scientists, government officials, and philanthropists that the nation suffered from a dearth of empirical knowledge about the economy. By the mid-1920s, Mitchell could point to a range of new organizations dedicated to "economic research," including his own postwar cocreation, the NBER (Mitchell 1924, 28–29). The NBER made quantitative research the hallmark of its work and was soon collaborating with philanthropic organizations (such as the Carnegie Corporation) and U.S. Secretary of Commerce Herbert Hoover on a variety of research projects, notably estimates of national income and research on business cycles (Hawley 1974; Alchon 1985; Barber 1985). As these projects suggest, Mitchell did not envision economics as a source for radical, abrupt social transformation. Instead, empirical investigation would allow social scientists to describe and analyze the economy as an interlocking system; to recognize tensions, pressures, imbalances, and lags; and to highlight adjustments that might ease potential economic disruption or social unrest. It was a program, in the assessment of the historian Guy Alchon, dedicated to developing a "technique of balance" (Alchon 1985) predicated on recognizing historical patterns and understanding their relevance to the present (cf. Mitchell 1927, 56–57).

Mitchell's desire to make economics more relevant to policy discussions (exemplified in practice by the NBER's choice of research topics during the 1920s and its intermittent collaboration with Hoover) necessarily raised a thorny question: What role should economists play in the political life of a democratic nation? Mitchell took this issue very seriously, and his response rested on two principles.[1] First, he drew a sharp distinction between ends and means, with social science providing only the latter. As he put it in a 1936 lecture, "It is not the business of the social sciences to say what is good and what bad; all they can do is to trace functional relationships among social processes, and so elucidate the most effective means of obtaining whatever ends we set ourselves" (Mitchell 1936, 161). Mitchell embedded that distinction in institutional structures whenever possible, most notably in his efforts to keep the NBER at arm's length from policy decisions even when consulting for government agencies. Thus when the NBER was asked to prepare a report for Herbert Hoover's Committee on Unemployment and Business Cycles in 1921, Mitchell emphasized that the bureau would not offer "recommendations concerning what ought to be done, but facts which ought to be considered by those who have the responsibility of formulating policies." The resulting volume separated the NBER's contribution from the

[1] Biddle 1998 provides the most detailed and nuanced evaluation of Mitchell's perspective on this question.

analysis written by Hoover's committee, and likewise contained a disclaimer absolving the NBER of any responsibility for the committee's policy proposals (Committee of the President's Conference on Unemployment 1923, 2, xxxiii). A similar arrangement governed the NBER's extensive work with the committee later that decade (President's Conference on Unemployment. Committee on Recent Economic Changes 1929).

To this distinction between means and ends, Mitchell wedded a strong belief in the pragmatic possibility of producing objective (universally accepted) social-scientific research, and once again, he structured the NBER to reflect this commitment. Officially, the NBER was led by a board composed of twenty-one directors associated with various academic, commercial, and labor organizations. Mitchell's description of the board emphasized its diversity, with members having "widely divergent training, experience and opinions" and collectively "represent[ing] all the important angles from which economic problems are viewed" (Committee of the President's Conference on Unemployment 1923, 1). These directors had to approve all NBER publications, and any director who disagreed with the majority vote had the right to publish a dissent in the resulting report. If the board eschewed radicals and kept itself largely to the political mainstream, its diversity was nonetheless sufficient to lend credence to the bureau's hope that its work would "carry conviction to Liberal and Conservative alike" (President's Conference on Unemployment. Committee on Recent Economic Changes 1929, xxxv).

This last statement reminds us that the pursuit of objectivity in the interwar social sciences was ultimately a political strategy: an effort to supersede the conflicts of a pluralistic society by crafting a domain of consensus that could form the basis for political action. Mitchell's assessment of the NBER's first year (1921) made the point clearly. To gather "men who represented so many and such divergent views on public policy" in hopes that they might approve extensive reports on "controverted social facts" had been "a very bold plan." Yet it had succeeded and thereby had justified Mitchell's vision: "We believe that social programs of whatever sort should rest whenever possible on objective knowledge of facts.... By putting this faith into practice we are making a contribution to the working methods of intelligent democracy" (Mitchell, quoted in Mitchell 1953, 355–356).

The phrase "intelligent democracy" hints at Mitchell's skeptical view of prior efforts at democratic social action, which, despite good intentions, had been ad hoc and often unsuccessful (cf. Mitchell 1919, 229). In this respect, his concerns matched those of many moderate and left-wing progressives, for the United States in the early twentieth century presented a difficult environment for government-led economic reforms due to its regional economic diversity and strongly federalist political structure (e.g., Graebner 1977; Berkowitz and McQuaid 1988; Gordon 1994). Would-be reformers therefore needed to craft a compelling national interest in federal regulatory activity that would draw support from well outside their own ranks. War mobilization proved one such opportunity, and many moderate and left-wing progressives entered the government during the First World War with high hopes for expanding state regulation and managerial oversight.[2] Yet the war ended too quickly, and progressive hopes were dashed by postwar conservative triumphs. By the mid-1920s, if not before, more politically savvy progressives had recast their ambitions in two directions, buttressing their proposed reforms with scholarship that could be sanctioned by a larger professional community (i.e., the pursuit of objectivity) and emphasizing how their analyses could boost general public welfare. Within political economy, statist and prolabor social scientists aimed to build coalitions with moderate businessmen by seeking data and analyses that would be acceptable to (even supported by) important constituents and by presenting reform ideas as attacks on "waste" and "inefficiency" (Eakins 1972; Purcell 1973; Wunderlin 1992; Critchlow 1993; Fink 1997).

The NBER fell squarely into this trend. The board of directors provided evidence of the bureau's political neutrality while it emphasized topics (national income, unemployment, and business cycles) deemed to be valuable to a variety of groups, including businessmen and labor activists. Naturally, the desire to pursue consensus constrained the range and tenor of NBER reports, and not surprisingly the political left grew disillusioned with the bureau over the ensuing years.[3] The split was exemplified in Robert S. Lynd's *Knowledge for What?* (1939), in which Lynd, a longtime friend of Mitchell, criticized the NBER for tacitly adopting the "folkways" of mainstream America, such as its fundamental assumption that "private, competitive business enterprise, motivated by the desire for profit" should form the basis for production and distribution (Lynd 1939, 144). Mitchell, however, remained unmoved. In his notes for a response to Lynd at the Economics Club at Columbia that same year, he discussed the "difficulty ... of getting scientific findings accepted by people whose attitudes you wish to influence." Warning that the "disturbing discordance among the opinions on

[2] Murray Rothbard provides ample documentation of this trend (of which he disapproves, of course): Rothbard 1989.

[3] More prosaically, perhaps, George Stigler (a longtime member of the NBER) later declared that "the Bureau's review procedures ... almost guaranteed dull books" (Stigler 1988, 70).

fact and policy expressed by economists" was a detriment to the effective use of social-scientific knowledge, he returned to the central concern that motivated so much of his approach to economics: "To be useful practically, scientific findings must be accepted, and in a democratic community they must be accepted by many people." That had been the rationale behind "the National Bureau's plan of organization," he reiterated, and in his own view, it had been "fairly successful" (quoted in Mitchell 1953, 566–567).

If Mitchell's general views on the ideal relationship between economics and political action had remained unchanged during the two decades following the First World War, however, his conception of the proper institutional arrangements had shifted. In the late 1920s, the NBER's informal collaboration with Herbert Hoover had been humming along smoothly and apparently profitably. The subsequent crash and depression, however, both drove Hoover from office and prompted many advocates of economic planning (including Mitchell) to break with Hoover's emphasis on voluntary public-private coordination in favor of a more centralized approach (Hawley 1974; Alchon 1985).

In 1933, Mitchell joined the political scientist Charles Merriam and President Roosevelt's uncle, Frederic Delano, as external advisors for a new federal agency: the National Planning Board. Established under the auspices of the National Recovery Administration (NRA), the board was intended to provide a comprehensive guide for federal oversight of the nation's economy, its human capital, and its natural resources. After the demise of the NRA in 1935, the board was reconstituted as the National Resources Committee (NRC), and in 1939 it was renamed the National Resources Planning Board. Much of the agency's time was devoted to supporting a mundane sort of "planning": gathering data about mineral deposits and waterways, coordinating state and local public-works projects, and producing lengthy reports on topics such as transportation, urbanization, and the economic effects of technology. However, behind this capacious data collection and seemingly endless documentation lay a clear purpose: As one observer put it, the NRC aimed "to replace private regimentation of business with public regulation" and to support "social efficiency as opposed to business and industrial efficiency" (Gruchy 1939; more generally, see Karl 1974; Clawson 1981; Reagan 2000). Nowhere was this purpose more evident and ambitious than within the NRC's Industrial Committee, which served as the clearinghouse for New Deal debates about economic planning between 1935 and 1939. The committee had its own dedicated staff for research and analysis – known as the Industrial Section – a group led by Gardiner C. Means, formerly an economist within the Department of Agriculture.

Although Mitchell left the NRC's advisory board to concentrate on his own research in the fall of 1935, the agency nonetheless retained much of his early vision. Writing about the NRC's Industrial Committee in the *American Economic Review* in 1939, Allen Gruchy argued that the agency's program could be aptly characterized by reference to two men: Mitchell and Means. Both were steeped in the "institutional" approach to economics, and both (like the NRC staff as a whole) were what Gruchy dubbed "experimental economists" who were "vitally interested in the application of their theories of economic control to the modern economic scene" (Gruchy 1939, 63). Likewise, the NRC as a whole embodied Mitchell's understanding of the proper relationship between technical expertise and democratic politics. Though the Industrial Committee (unlike the NBER) was part of the government, it would maintain a functional separation between technical advising and political decisions: Planning experts would outline possible outcomes and strategies whereas elected leaders would choose which elements to pursue and how they could be realized. The committee was led by economists and social scientists from a variety of federal departments (Agriculture, Commerce, Interior, and Labor) and reported to a board composed of three external advisers (initially Mitchell, Merriam, and Delano) plus the relevant cabinet secretaries.[4] In turn, the board (primarily through its three advisers) reported directly to the president. Despite these connections, however, the agency had no direct control over federal programs; it offered advice to the executive branch and sought to inform public discussion through its numerous reports, which (in the Industrial Committee) typically contained massive amounts of empirical data and sophisticated quantitative analysis.[5]

The NRC's Industrial Section was thus the federal counterpart to the NBER: an organization devoted to data gathering and analysis that could achieve a tighter bond between economic expertise and political action than had been possible through the ad hoc arrangements that the NBER established with Herbert Hoover in the 1920s. Here, the divorce between economic theory and applied policy that Mitchell had lamented two decades earlier would be overcome as economists prepared technical reports for government policy making. Here, too, Milton Friedman would find his first paid employment as an economist, working in an agency that valued objectivity, quantitative study, and prediction based on the analysis of historical data.

4 When the NRC was reorganized as the National Resources Planning Board in 1939, the board was reconstituted with five external members and no cabinet representatives.

5 On the structure and operation of the NRC, see Karl 1974, 226–283; Clawson 1981. The similarities to Mitchell's vision are evident: Mitchell 1936, esp. 464.

1.2. Milton Friedman and Positive Economics

In the abstract, it may seem incongruous to find Friedman joining a government agency devoted to economic planning, a puzzle that grows deeper when one understands the aims of the NRC. In practice, the Industrial Committee was a bastion for statist planning, stocked with prominent left-wing economists such as Mordecai Ezekiel, Lauchlin Currie, Leon Henderson, Isador Lubin, and Thomas Blaisdell. Gardiner Means, who led the technical division in which Friedman worked, was famous (or infamous, in some circles) for his recent report on "administered prices" (Means 1935), which blamed highly concentrated corporate control of certain industrial sectors for disrupting market price mechanisms and thereby deepening and prolonging the Depression. Not surprisingly, Means's work had drawn the ire of many corporate officials, and he would later be a central target for postwar Chicago economists such as George Stigler, Warren Nutter, and Arnold Harberger.[6]

After the demise of the NRA, the Industrial Committee became the home for federal economists seeking to establish an American version of centralized planning. Under Means's leadership, the Industrial Section coordinated a massive survey of American consumer expenditures and collected extensive data on industrial production as part of an ambitious effort at macroeconomic modeling. Using the data, the staff hoped to create a set of possible "production-consumption patterns" for each industrial sector representing "economical" use of natural resources and manpower under different economic conditions (notably different distributions of income). Having constructed these patterns (and following the NRC's functional separation between technical analysis and political action), the committee would pass the baton to the politicians, leaving elected officials to make "social or political decisions" as to which pattern was most desirable and feasible and then to enact policies to move toward that objective.[7] It was a vision for a democratically controlled, state-managed economy in which the Industrial Section would provide predictive macroeconomic models that would permit conscious choice of future economic conditions.

Few projects would seem less fitting with our familiar image of Milton Friedman. Yet placed in context, his participation in the Industrial Section

[6] For more on Gardiner Means's economic analyses and subsequent controversies, see Samuels and Medema 1990, as well as Schliesser 2010.

[7] Means to NRC, October 12, 1935, box 205, COR, Records of the National Resources Planning Board. For more on this project, see Lee 1990; Stapleford 2007.

becomes less peculiar. Friedman's undergraduate training at Rutgers (1928–1932) had a heavy dose of statistical methods and quantitative analysis courtesy of Arthur F. Burns (one of Mitchell's top students) and Homer Jones (then a doctoral student in economics at Chicago). Torn between applied mathematics and economics for graduate study, Friedman eventually chose economics, but he never lost his love for mathematical analysis: Shifting back and forth between Chicago and Columbia as a graduate student, he continued to hone his statistical skills under Henry Schultz (Chicago) and Harold Hotelling (Columbia). His work for the NRC involved highly sophisticated problems in survey methodology, sampling, and data analysis within a major study of consumer expenditures and incomes. It was thus an ideal setting for someone working at the boundaries of economics and statistics.[8]

Furthermore, Friedman's employment in the NRC was not anomalous among Chicago graduate students: He was recruited by fellow student (and future Chicago School mainstay) Allen Wallis, who had been hired earlier in 1935; Friedman's future wife, Rose Director, also worked briefly on the project, as did Erika Schoenberg (a student of Paul Douglas) and Alice Hanson Jones (another doctoral student at Chicago and the wife of Friedman's good friend and former teacher, Homer Jones).[9] The presence of so many bright young Chicago graduate students reflects both the department's strengths in quantitative analysis and the dismal academic job market for economists in the mid-1930s. The NRC's efforts to estimate production and consumption patterns promised both money and serious intellectual challenges.

Finally, through the early 1940s, Friedman was far more sympathetic to state intervention in the economy than he would later become. For example, upon learning of Friedman's engagement to Rose Director, Aaron Director good-naturedly lamented his future brother-in-law's "very strong New Deal leanings – authoritarian, to use an abusive term." Likewise, Friedman later recollected how "thoroughly Keynesian" he was until "shortly after the war." The combination of the Depression and the New Deal "attracted the best and brightest to Washington," Friedman recalled, and they were initially suffused with "the feeling – or illusion – that we were in at the birth of a new order" (Friedman and Friedman 1998, 81, 113, 60–61).

Still, Friedman's early enthusiasm for government intervention had its limits – for example, both he and Rose Director opposed the price and

[8] On Friedman's early career, see Hammond 2001.

[9] George Stigler also worked briefly for the NRC (1935–1936), but on a different project (Stigler 1988, 52–53).

wage controls of the NRA and the Agricultural Adjustment Administration (Friedman and Friedman 1998, 59) – and although he supported stimulus measures and public-works employment programs, it is doubtful that he would have agreed with Means's plans for extensive federal management of industrial production. More generally, it is unlikely that so many future members of the Chicago School would have joined the NRC had not the Industrial Committee also embodied Mitchell's commitment to pragmatic objectivity. Despite Means's desire to use NRC studies to provide a framework for centralized management of the industrial economy, the staff worked hard to cultivate allies across the political spectrum. Take, for example, the Study of Consumer Purchases, a massive survey of consumer expenditures (roughly five times larger than any previous comparable survey) and the project on which most of the Chicago students (Friedman included) were employed. Market researchers, who had begun creating a successful professional identity in the 1920s, had been clamoring for more data on consumer incomes and expenditures (Stapleford 2007), and NRC project leaders, expecting that a national government survey of family finances would attract conservative opposition, carefully courted business support. Internal proposals and public descriptions emphasized the value of the survey for analyzing the consumer market, and when critical press reports first arose in early 1936, government economists promoted the study before trade associations and select businessmen, with the result that, as Gardiner Means put it, "big associations of technical distribution experts" shifted the larger business community behind the project.[10] Whatever Means's own objectives, he had managed to position the Study of Consumer Purchases as a politically neutral, empirical study – a perfectly acceptable technical project for any young economist with a statistical bent.

Overall, the NRC's approach paralleled that of the NBER: It aimed to establish a common ground of accepted facts and analysis that could smooth the way for subsequent political action. For a government agency in a (comparatively) weak and permeable national government subject to considerable democratic oversight from a highly pluralistic and regionally diverse country, that was a necessary strategy. Of course, it had its limits:

[10] "Report of Proposed Project on Consumption of Goods and Services of American Families" (draft), September 1935, box 1, Unpublished Reports, Records of the National Resources Planning Board; minutes of the Technical Subcommittee, 14 July 1936, box 2 and "The Study of Consumer Purchases," Instructions for Editing, box 1, both in RCESP, Records of the Bureau of Labor Statistics; National Resources Committee, *Progress Report, 1936*, 48. Means to Charles Eliot, July 17, 1936, box 208, COR, Records of the National Resources Planning Board.

Few studies pleased everyone, and any complex survey required assumptions and judgments that could be (and often were) readily challenged. For example, corporate economists quickly attacked some results of the Study of Consumer Purchases (notably a claim that more than half of American families operated at a deficit), arguing that the numbers derived from flawed methodology (e.g., Tucker 1940; Tucker 1942; Tucker 1942). Nonetheless, it's fair to say that NRC reports were a great success, widely used and praised by businessmen and economists of different political outlooks (for details, see Stapleford 2007). The NRC studies, like the NBER, thus offered its participants concrete proof that it was possible to produce economic knowledge acceptable to "Liberal and Conservative alike" (to borrow the NBER's description), knowledge that at least promised to have valuable policy applications. In many ways, it was the fulfillment of Mitchell's vision for the rationalization of economic reform through quantitative, predictive, expert knowledge, and it could both attract Friedman and provide a tangible exemplar of the "positive economics" he would famously promote after the war.

Friedman worked on the Study of Consumer Purchases for two years before leaving for a post even closer to Mitchell at the NBER itself. If we step back to consider Friedman's early career, therefore, we find the following: He spent 1928–1932 taking undergraduate courses at Rutgers, where a key mentor was Mitchell's student, Arthur Burns. He then had two years of graduate study at Chicago (1932–1933; 1934–1935) and one in Mitchell's home department at Columbia (1933–1934), which was a stronghold of interwar institutional economics. From fall 1935 to fall 1937, he worked at the NRC, following that with a three-year stint at the NBER. During his time at the NBER, Friedman began a close collaboration with another institutional economist, Simon Kuznets, on a major statistical study that became the basis of Friedman's doctoral dissertation at Columbia (1946), eventually published with Kuznets as *Income from Independent Professional Practice* (1954). It seems fair to say, therefore, that the first decade of Friedman's career featured a far greater immersion in the quantitative institutional economics of Wesley Mitchell than in the economics department at Chicago (cf. Hammond 2001; 2006).

Given this background, we should not be surprised to find strong similarities between Mitchell and Friedman, and indeed there is substantial evidence of this front. Consider the treatment of economic theory and statistical investigation in a 1942 paper with Allen Wallis on "The Empirical Derivation of Indifference Functions" (Wallis and Friedman 1942). In this essay, Wallis and Friedman examined the ties (or lack thereof) between indifference functions – a fundamental concept for neoclassical theories of consumer demand[11] – and empirical studies of consumer behavior.

According to Wallis and Friedman, the basic concept of an indifference function had "proven fruitful in theoretical economics," but efforts to specify the form of such functions for actual consumers had failed (176, 175). How much this failure mattered depended on one's goals. Wallis and Friedman identified two motivations for defining actual indifference functions in quantitative terms. First, this exercise could "provide more detailed premises about the form of the function … and would thereby lead to more specific [deductive] conclusions." This goal, the authors argued, could be aided even by imperfect analyses, because just confronting the empirical record would refine ideas about the basic structure of indifference functions and important variables (188).

However, there was a deeper, second objective tied to economic control: "to obtain exact knowledge of the quantitative relation of consumer expenditures to prices and income for the purpose of predicting the effect of changes in economic conditions on the consumption of various commodities and services." For this objective, the empirical derivation of indifference functions fell far short, and Wallis and Friedman saw "little prospect of material progress" in the future (Wallis and Friedman 1942, 188). The trouble was that indifference functions were "defined for a single individual at a given time," but useful predictions dealt with many consumers and had to hold true across multiple time periods. In principle, the form of an indifference function could be expanded to include many variables that might change with time (such as income, technology, physical environment, fashion, culture, and so forth), but the resulting theory would be unwieldy and its derivation "impractical" (183–184, 187).

Fortunately, Wallis and Friedman saw another option: "the direct approach of isolating factors correlative with consumer demand and measuring the relationships." Rather than forcing empirical data to conform to the terms of neoclassical microeconomic theory, economists could study how purchases varied with specific factors such as "income, wealth, prices,

[11] These functions specify sets of commodities between which a given consumer is indifferent (e.g., a consumer might be equally happy with two apples and an orange or with one apple and two oranges). Each collection of such sets forms an indifference surface, and the indifference function also ranks all possible surfaces in order of preference. (Thus our consumer might prefer three apples and an orange over either of the previous options; three apples and an orange would thus be part of a higher, more-preferred indifference surface.) Neoclassical theory states that consumers will choose the least expensive set of commodities on the most-preferred indifference surface that they can afford.

family type, occupation, age, nationality, regional location, type of community, ownership of home and automobile, etc." (Wallis and Friedman 1942, 189). This was not raw empiricism; what the authors called "heavy theoretical artillery" would still be required to define potentially relevant variables and to answer specific questions (e.g., "How are quality differences in goods to be treated?"; 189) Rather than abandoning economic theory, Wallis and Friedman were following the path outlined by Mitchell: using statistical analysis to craft a new kind of theory that (unlike existing neoclassical microeconomics) would yield specific, real-world predictions and hence enhance conscious control over economic change.

Two more subtle aspects of this essay are also worth noting. First, although Friedman and Wallis did not explicitly mention the NRC, its projects formed the background to the paper. The Study of Consumer Purchases (on which both authors had worked) had been the first major survey explicitly designed to yield correlations between expenditures and a matrix of other variables (including income, occupation, region, family composition, and degree of urbanization). Project leaders had unabashedly (and far too optimistically) hoped to use these relationships to predict future consumption patterns after demographic and economic shifts (Stapleford 2007). In essence, therefore, Wallis and Friedman derived their vision for new research on consumer demand directly from their experience on the NRC; small surprise that it looked remarkably like Mitchell's approach.

Second, the alleged superiority of the new economics over traditional theory lay in its promise to handle temporal (historical) change. Wallis and Friedman's most substantial critique of indifference functions fell along these lines: Whereas indifference functions typically assumed stable tastes and environment, real life was a constant state of flux (Wallis and Friedman 1942, 183–187). Wallis and Friedman's solution did not avoid the problem entirely: Rather, their proposal rested on the hope that at least some of the "observed relations" between expenditures and various factors (as revealed in survey data) would be "stable through time." This presumption could be tested through "direct empirical investigation"; in other words, through predictions (189). As with Mitchell, the potential for this new economics therefore depended on the potential for scientific historical analysis: If cross-sectional data could yield correlations that were "stable through time" – if the past could predict the future – then economists could offer powerful policy tools.

Similar themes can be found in Friedman's widely cited essay on "The Methodology of Positive Economics" (1953), the bulk of which focused on distinguishing "positive economics" from "normative economics." Whereas normative economics dealt with ethics and "what ought to be," positive economics aimed "to provide a system of generalizations that can be used to make correct predictions about the consequences of any change in circumstances." Because the evaluation of knowledge in positive economics depended solely on its ability to yield accurate predictions, it "is, or can be, an 'objective' science, in precisely the same sense as any of the physical sciences" (Friedman 1953, 4).

Friedman's treatment of positive economics has attracted an enormous amount of commentary, much of it devoted to classifying and assessing the epistemology alleged to underlie the essay. (Did Friedman truly believe that the realism of assumptions employed within a theory is irrelevant to judging that theory? Was he an instrumentalist, a realist, or something else entirely?)[12] Yet, as David Teira and Jesús Zamora have argued, it can be equally informative to read the essay as Friedman's prescription for how economists can effectively and legitimately contribute to policy discussions (Serrano and Bonilla 2009).

Friedman began his discussion by quoting John Neville Keynes's tripartite division between positive economics, normative economics, and the "art" of economics (which corresponds to applied economics: "a system of rules for the attainment of a given end"; Friedman 1953, 3). Tellingly, despite Friedman's interest in policy, the art of economics quickly disappeared from his essay in favor of a dominant focus on positive and normative economics. In part, this absence reflected the genealogy of the piece: Friedman did not conceive the work through Keynes's categories; rather, he added the quotation in a later draft (Hammond 2009). Yet Friedman's inattention to the art of economics also reflected his understanding of positive economics. If positive economics was characterized by robust predictive power, it was also de facto the domain of scientific knowledge about "means" in economics. The art of economics, therefore, was only a residual, the uncharted territory that positive economics had yet to comprehend, and it would necessarily fade as positive economics expanded.[13]

Friedman fully anticipated such an expansion, albeit one that would never be entirely complete. In his categorization, the hypotheses of positive economics consisted of "a conceptual world or abstract model simpler than the 'real world'" and a "set of rules" defining when "the 'model' can be taken as an adequate representation of the 'real world'" (Friedman 1953, 24). As

[12] For a valuable recent overview of these debates, see the essays in Mäki 2009.

[13] Tellingly, Friedman concedes that there is not "one-to-one relation between policy conclusions and the conclusions of positive economics," but he attributes that divergence solely to normative economics (Friedman 1953, 5).

scientists, economists aimed "to formulate the rules explicitly in so far as possible and continually to widen the range of phenomena for which it is possible to do so," thereby extending the scope of positive economics. In practical terms, Friedman acknowledged that "there inevitably will remain room for judgment in applying the rules," because every concrete situation was unique in some respect (25). Nonetheless, both the introduction and conclusion of the essay expressed high hopes for the "progress of positive economics," that is, for the expansion of concrete predictive power and thus objective policy knowledge (e.g., 5–7, 42).

Indeed, not only would positive economics increasingly displace art, it would reveal that the scope for debate in normative economics (what ought to be) was actually quite small:

> I venture the judgment ... that currently in the Western world, and especially in the United States, differences about economic policy among disinterested citizens derive predominantly from different predictions about the economic consequences of taking action – differences that in principle can be eliminated by the progress of positive economics – rather than from fundamental differences in basic values. (Friedman 1953, 5)

Friedman continued to sound this theme over the next two decades; as he put it in 1967, "I have been much impressed ... that most differences in economic policy in the United States do not reflect differences in value judgments, but differences in positive economic analysis" (Friedman 1967, 86). Continued progress in economic science would lead to the rationalization of politics and produce the "intelligent democracy" for which Wesley Mitchell had longed.

Knowing that Friedman became a deeply polarizing figure later in his career, it may be difficult to read these statements without viewing them as either extraordinarily naïve or downright disingenuous, a smokescreen created by a consciously politicized economist seeking to hide behind a mask of alleged neutrality. (Indeed, though Friedman never abandoned his commitment to rationalization, he became less confident in its success after facing repeated controversy in his later career: Friedman and Friedman 1998, 217–219.) Yet to understand Friedman's perspective, we must recognize the extent to which he was steeped in a culture of pragmatic objectivity during the early years of his career at the NBER, the NRC, and even his wartime work for the Treasury and the Statistical Research Group at Columbia University. As I argued earlier, objectivity was not only an ideal at the NBER and NRC, it was a lived reality (if only to a limited extent), as economists and citizens of divergent political leanings agreed to sanction certain data and interpretive analyses. Friedman continued to seek and espouse such expert consensus throughout his career. From 1947 to 1949, for example, he served on a five-member subcommittee of the American Economic Association that intended to inform the "interested public" about areas in which economists had reached a "broad consensus" about the "facts, ideas, and policy" related to the pursuit of full employment and price stability (Despres, Hart et al. 1950, 503, 505). Likewise, even amid his later public persona as a libertarian economist, he continued to insist that there was much greater consensus among economists than disagreement (Friedman 1967, 86–87; Friedman 1983, 9). In this respect, it was more than mere convenience that led Friedman to produce and publish his three major pieces of economic research – *Income from Independent Professional Practice* (1954), *A Theory of the Consumption Function* (1957), and his multivolume study of monetary history with Anna J. Schwartz (1963, 1970, 1982) – under the auspices of the NBER. Each volume addressed a controversial policy issue (monopoly in the health professions, the efficacy of Keynesianism, and the power of the money supply), and in each case Friedman hoped that his work, certified by the NBER board of directors, would establish an objective basis for policy discussions (cf. Cherrier, this volume).

Of course, it is also in the details of Friedman's research (as opposed to his general methodological statements) that we find the greatest contrasts with Mitchell's institutional economics. Most obviously, Friedman's critiques of government intervention share little with the affinity for public planning and "social control" that animated much of Mitchell's work. Equally important, whereas Mitchell eschewed neoclassical theory, Friedman was a self-acknowledged disciple of the British economist Alfred Marshall, who treated neoclassical theory as an "engine for discovery" in economics.[14] Thus neoclassical price and monetary theories became analytical tools for Friedman in ways that they never were for Mitchell.

Nonetheless, we should not overstress these points and thereby overlook the shared framework that united the two men. Friedman's admiration for Marshall, for example, was shared by many American economists in the interwar years, because most (including institutional economists such as Mitchell) could find value in aspects of Marshall's eclectic and inclusive approach to economic analysis (Backhouse, Bateman et al. 2011). Marshall's interest in historical transformation, his valorization of empirical study, and his concern for policy questions were attributes shared by both Mitchell

[14] On Friedman's appropriation of Marshall, see Hammond 1996; Hoover 2009. However, one should not assume that Friedman's view of "Marshallian" economics was fully congruent with Marshall's own work; see Hirsch and de Marchi 1990, 32–40.

and Friedman. In this respect, we should not be surprised that many interwar economists saw Mitchell's own work as falling within the Marshallian tradition (Hammond 1996, 12–15).

Friedman retained far more of Marshall's price theory, but both he and Mitchell understood themselves to be making a substantial expansion of orthodox economics (which included the work of Marshall). Though Friedman accepted the full validity of neoclassical theory for analyses of hypothetical, *static* situations (where nothing changed beyond a few variables), he joined Mitchell in questioning its complete applicability to the real, *dynamic* world absent suitable testing and reformulation (Hirsch and de Marchi 1990). Such skepticism formed the root of his critique of indifference functions in the empirical study of consumer demand (discussed previously), and it shared substantial parallels with Mitchell's critique of classical political economy (with its attention to "tendencies" and imperviousness to empirical refutation). Both men sought to create a new form of economic knowledge that would remain robust and predictive in real-world applications. Both saw prediction as serving a dual purpose, ensuring that the results of economic research were objective and suitable for policy applications. Both envisioned economics as crafting a truly scientific form of historical analysis in which (for example) a monetary history of the United States over the previous century could be an objective scientific guide for future policy. Both hoped for the rationalization of politics – for the replacement of contentious debate with technical knowledge and the rise of economists as neutral experts who could offer quantitative models predicting the results of different policies. In Friedman's assessment, "the fundamental difference between Chicago" and other economics departments was not Chicago's emphasis on price theory but its attitude toward policy: "At Chicago, economics was a serious subject to be used in discussing real problems, and you could get some answers from it" (Hammond 1992, 110).

1.3. Frank Knight's Critique of Economics as a Policy Science

It is easy to overlook the radical nature of the position taken by Mitchell and Friedman. Many economists believed that economics is, or could be, an objective science. Most, if not all, thought that economic knowledge should be valuable for policy decisions. Yet Friedman and Mitchell pushed further, arguing that economics could predict outcomes for concrete, real-world problems and thus provide an objective scientific analysis of means so that policy makers could focus narrowly on ends. That view was hardly universal.

We have seen, for example, that John Neville Keynes distinguished the art of economics from economics as a positive science, and he did not anticipate the former being absorbed into the latter.[15] Nor was this view merely a nineteenth-century relic: Elsewhere in this volume, Dan Hammond demonstrates that neither John Kenneth Galbraith nor Paul Samuelson would have accepted Friedman and Mitchell's view of economics as a policy science. Galbraith called for the union of economics and political analysis not by reducing politics to economics, but by bringing it into economics itself; Samuelson valued economic theory but doubted its sufficiency for concrete policy decisions (Hammond, this volume). Yet the most useful alternative perspective to explore may be that of Frank Knight, who not only applied a keen philosophical mind to the concept of a policy science, but also served as a mentor, in the self-report of its members, to the postwar Chicago School.

Like Friedman, Knight believed economics was a positive science that was valuable for policy decisions. Furthermore, he shared Friedman's objections to government planning and was a vigorous critic of the quest for "social control" espoused by Mitchell and other moderate to left-wing progressives during the interwar years.[16] Yet despite these commonalities, Knight's perspective on the nature of economic knowledge and its political function was fundamentally opposed to that of Friedman. Ironically, in fact, the grounds for Knight's critique of institutional economics could have applied equally well to Friedman and the postwar Chicago School.

Knight made his most extensive attack on Mitchell's political agenda for economics in the very same 1924 volume that opened with Mitchell's essay on "The Prospects of Economics" (discussed earlier). For Knight, there was "a science of economics, a true, and even exact, science, which reaches laws as universal as those of mathematics and mechanics" (Knight 1924, 256). These laws, which included things like diminishing utility and diminishing returns, were "characteristics of the world ... so obvious that it is impossible to escape recognizing them and so fundamental that to think them away would necessitate creating in the imagination a different type of universe" (257). Though one might expect little of value to be deduced from such axioms, these expectations were "belied by the facts of economic science itself," as well as by an analogy with mathematics, where "a few simple axioms"

15 For Keynes, the art of political economy did involve the creation of rules defining means to various ends, but he insisted that these rules did not and could not depend on positive economics alone: Keynes 1904, 34–35, 55–83.

16 My interpretation of Knight's thought owes much to the well-grounded, nuanced analysis in Emmett 2009.

had developed into "a structure of boundless and ever-growing scope and intricacy" (258).

Economics thus followed mathematics in being a deductive, abstract science, and as such, it could never fully encapsulate working reality. Accordingly, Knight saw an equally "close analogy" with theoretical physics, where the application of theory encountered "aberrations" such as friction (Knight 1924, 259). Unlike Friedman, however, Knight doubted that economists could replicate physicists' success in binding their theoretical system closely to the operations of the material world. The trouble lay in the constant flux of crucial factors within economic theory, as effects from one process became causes in others, with the whole system in a constant state of dynamic evolution. Whereas Newtonian physicists, for example, could successfully treat mass as a stable factor in kinematic and temporal change, economists had no such luxury:

> The means of want-satisfaction and the resources used to produce them, and the technology and business organization according to which the process is carried out – all are *data*, causes, independent variables, in some regards and with reference to some time periods, and all are effects, dependent variables, in other regards and with reference to other time periods. (263)

Such deep interdependence would thwart efforts to provide systematic and exact predictions for concrete phenomena.

The problem was not unique to economics; rather it was endemic to the sciences of human behavior. Treated in the abstract, when dense loops of causality could be ignored through hypothetical analyses, the social sciences could indeed be *sciences*. However, applied to messy temporal reality – becoming in effect a form of historical study – they became subject to the very factors that had thwarted previous efforts to devise "a science, or a philosophy, of history" (249).[17] As Knight reminded his readers, few contemporary historians believed that their discipline could provide clear predictive rules.

Mitchell and Friedman (as we saw in the discussion of indifference functions) had hoped to bypass these problems through statistical analysis, developing correlations or other quantitative relationships that would be "stable through time" (to borrow Wallis and Friedman's phrase). Knight, however, argued that the mere act of quantification or the application of mathematical tools was insufficient to raise an essentially historical study to the level of objective science: "[T]he data lack the stability, classifiability and

[17] The allusion to Hegel here, of course, is telling given Mitchell's comments about Marx in his own essay for this same volume (discussed earlier).

measurability requisite to scientific treatment, and actual economic practice must... be at least as much an art based on wide general knowledge and sound judgment." Moreover, such reliance on "informed judgment" rather than "reasoning according to the canons of science" would be enhanced as the time period in question grew longer. "The movements of history," Knight concluded, "are to be 'sensed' rather than plotted and projected into the future" (Knight 1924, 264).

Exiling history from the halls of science did not render it worthless, nor were historians mere sophists. On the contrary, Knight "consider[ed] history the one subject about which no one can ever know as much as he needs to know." Nonetheless, "the usefulness of history is not in giving us rules which can be made the basis of inference and prediction; it is not in this respect a science, but rather an art." Rather than offering prediction, history's value lay in "training the judgment, giving insight into human life," all of which operated at the level of "unconscious knowledge" (249). In a similar vein, economics (and indeed economic history) held value for policy decisions, but in a different form than either Friedman or Mitchell had envisioned. Economics could enhance judgment, but not supplant it. "Common sense ... can be trained to predict and control better," Knight stated, "but that does not prove that science can predict and control better than common sense" (254).

Ultimately, for Knight economics could not be a predictive policy *science*, for the very concept of a policy science was itself unrealizable. Instead, the application of economics to concrete problems remained an art, an unsystematizable exercise of judgment. In turn, this subjectivity undercut the hopes of Mitchell, Friedman, and many other interwar economists to establish themselves as neutral experts who could resolve (or at least untangle) policy problems through strictly scientific analysis. Indeed, the ramifications were more threatening: Economists who (with good intentions or ill) offered ostensibly scientific, objective policy analysis were engaged in a dangerous act of self-deception, blinding themselves and the recipients of their advice to the true nature of such transactions.

1.4. Assessing Economics as a Policy Science

Knight, of course, had found no logical flaw in Mitchell's program; his argument was (to adopt his own terminology) a matter of judgment, an informed dissent to the proposition that economics could become a scientific form of history and hence a policy science. On the other side, as we have seen, Friedman's major 1953 essay on methodology reserved some role for "judgment" in economics and recognized that objectivity might be more of an ideal than a working reality (e.g., Friedman 1953, 25, 30). It would seem, therefore, that the clash between these two visions for economics was more a matter of emphasis, of the degree to which one highlighted subjectivity in applied economics. Likewise, one would expect that the dispute could be resolved through empirical observation: Either economics would develop into an effective objective policy science, or it would not. But the matter is not so simple.

On the one hand, since the Second World War, numerous economists have accepted something like the Mitchell/Friedman view of their discipline. As David Colander has argued, the "art of economics" became a "lost art" after 1950, with most economists implicitly adopting Friedman's largely binary classification of their field into normative ends and positive means (Colander 1992). Similarly, many of those who pursued the Mitchell/Friedman program enjoyed enormous professional success, including agricultural economists (who had their own ties to interwar institutional economics; Banzhaf 2006) and the postwar members of the Chicago School. Nor was the commitment to economics as a policy science limited to this particular lineage: Although the econometricians of the Cowles Commission adopted a very different methodological stance from Mitchell and Friedman, they also wrestled with the problem of historical change (e.g., Haavelmo 1944, 12–39) in route to crafting widely used tools for macroeconomic policy.

On the other hand, by the 1970s, concern about the actual predictive power of quantitative economic models and their applicability to concrete policy questions (especially at the macro level) had become a common theme in assessments of the field by leading economists. For example, in Wassily Leontief's 1971 presidential address to the American Economics Association, he explored a widespread "uneasiness" over "the palpable *inadequacy* of the scientific means" by which economists addressed "practical problems" (Leontief 1971, 1; for similar concerns, see Brown 1972; Worswick 1972; Hendry 1980; Leamer 1983).[18] These doubts were enhanced, of course, by the widespread failure of macroeconomic policies during that decade, and it should surprise no one to find similar skepticism in the wake of the more recent financial collapse (e.g., Krugman 2009).

The apparent contradiction between the common conviction that economics ought to be an objective policy science and the repeated evidence

[18] Some of these same questions reappear in a spring 2010 symposium in the *Journal of Economic Perspectives* inspired by Leamer's 1983 critique.

that it is not – that it rarely produces full consensus about proper means to given ends – can be reconciled in two ways. First, proponents for viewing economics as a policy science (including Mitchell and Friedman) typically did so on the basis of its potential rather that its actuality, and assessments of potential can never be refuted by failure. Nothing exemplifies that trait better than Mitchell's own career. Ironically, though Mitchell began his professional life intending to make economic theory relevant to policy, he never contributed directly to major policy debates and by the end of his career was also under attack for his inadequate theoretical foundations (e.g., Koopmans 1947). These failures (if that is the proper term) arose primarily from Mitchell's deep commitment to the pragmatic objectivity of the NBER and his own acute awareness of the inadequacy of existing empirical evidence for resolving fundamental theoretical and policy debates (e.g., Burns and Mitchell 1946, 3–10). This awareness did not, however, lessen Mitchell's conviction that economics could become an empirically based policy science; instead, it kept him focused on the data collection and basic analysis that he hoped would eventually yield greater insights (cf. Mitchell 1953, 550–568). Similarly, lamentations about the current weaknesses of applied economics frequently end with prescriptions that will, in the eyes of proponents, finally make it more of an objective science (e.g., Hendry 1980).

Whereas Mitchell confined himself to a relatively weak (in the philosophical sense) version of economic theory that could be more widely accepted, Milton Friedman evinced little of the same reticence. Not surprisingly, he had a much harder time achieving the same consensus – the pragmatic objectivity – that characterized the response to Mitchell's work. Two of Friedman's five major studies for the NBER (1954, 1963) included dissenting statements from an NBER director; more generally, his work attracted substantial controversy and criticism. Other scholars have written insightful accounts that attempt to explain why these disputes arose and why they frequently proved difficult, if not impossible, to resolve (e.g., Hirsch and de Marchi 1990, 251–269; Hammond 1996; Teira 2009; Cherrier, this volume). Yet it may be equally valuable to examine Friedman's own explanations for the lack of consensus in economics, including the critical reactions to his work, for this reveals a second resource for those committed to viewing economics as a policy science despite continued dissent: bias.

As we have seen, in his major 1953 essay on "The Methodology of Positive Economics," Friedman declared that "there will inevitably remain room for judgment" when applying economic models to the real world (Friedman 1953, 25). Several pages later, he returned to this theme, suggesting that "the background of scientists" might affect "the judgments they reach" about economic theories, and thus that "there is never certainty in science" (Friedman 1953, 30). Yet, as he explained in 1967, this practical reality "does not alter the fundamental point that, in principle, there are no value judgments in economics" (Friedman 1967, 86). Economics was, in fact, objective; it was only human beings who were flawed and limited.

For someone of Knight's persuasion, recognition of such inherent limitations might produce skepticism about Friedman's 1953 conviction that "the progress of ... positive economics" held great hope for building "consensus on 'correct' economic policy" (Friedman 1953, 6). Like Mitchell, however, Friedman took a far more optimistic view of economists' potential to overcome these constraints by a dogged commitment to objective analysis, and in his own mind he saw that potential realized. As Eric Schliesser has argued, Chicago economists such as Friedman and Stigler viewed economics as an immature science through the late 1940s, but over the next decade they became far more confident in its status as a positive science (Schliesser 2010).

Against this background, the frailty of human reason appears to have become less a warning against dogmatism than a resource for explaining dissent, especially dissent from propositions that Friedman considered to be clearly established. For example, Friedman attributed several critiques of his early work to bias or the self-interest of his antagonists (see Cherrier, this volume). He returned to this theme when reflecting on his career in 1986, suggesting that self-interest lay behind the resistance to Chicago-style free-market theories. Thus economists tended to find market imperfections (such as externalities, monopolistic practices, etc.) because these flaws "create jobs for us in the government"; Keynesianism created "wonderful opportunities for employment and influence" for its proponents; and the "unenthusiastic acceptance" of his own monetarist position reflected how it "would sharply reduce the number of jobs available for economists" (Friedman 1986, 8–9). As he explained in 1998, he had begun to doubt the possibility for rationalization in politics largely because he had "repeatedly experienced attacks on what I regarded as scientific findings by economists who seemed driven more by their values than their objective judgment" (Friedman and Friedman 1998). Self-interest and ideological blindness – not legitimate differences in judgment – blocked the acceptance of the truths of positive economics.

Friedman's colleagues at Chicago, especially the younger generation, pushed this line of argument more vociferously and followed it to its logical conclusion: If economics was a policy science and science was objective, then anyone promoting policies that conflicted with one's own "scientific findings" was clearly biased. If these opponents used methods sufficiently at variance with those promoted by one's favored colleagues and mentors, then it was easy to suggest that they had left the bounds of scientific economics entirely. From this perspective, we can understand why the Chicago School reacted so harshly to institutional economics, despite their shared general framework. Most institutional economists advocated extensive government intervention into the economy; most also ignored the neoclassical price theory that became so central to postwar Chicago (see Emmett, this volume). Accordingly, it became natural to see "lack of theory" as the critical flaw that had doomed institutional economists to false conclusions and unscientific analysis.

Similarly dogmatic attitudes toward opposing policy positions continue to pervade economists associated with the University of Chicago. Thus, to take two recent examples, in the midst of revived interest in Keynesian thought after the 2008 recession, John Cochrane described Keynesian stimulus packages as "fairy tales that have been proved false," and Luigi Zingales insisted they have "little or no empirical support" and indeed are not based on "economic principles."[19] Chicago's reputation for rhetorical excess no doubt owes much to its combative intellectual atmosphere (again, see Emmett, this volume), but it is equally a product of its strong commitment to viewing economics as an objective science for solving concrete problems: Within such a framework, prolonged disagreement naturally slides into charges that one participant or another has simply abandoned scientific analysis altogether.

Of course, because the binary positive/normative view of economics has been accepted outside of Chicago, we should expect to find similar views elsewhere. Thus accusations that crass politicization has corrupted true "scientific" approaches to political economy are common features of left-wing assessments of the Chicago School (e.g., Herman 1995; Klein 2007). More generally, a vocal group of economists continues to treat the discipline as an applied science that provides straightforward policy lessons. Reactions to the financial crash of 2008 make this clear: Although some economists emphasized the uncertainty inherent in macroeconomic analysis, others insisted that their favored policies were not only reasonable, but in fact the only empirically justifiable responses. (A parallel reading of economists'

[19] John Cochrane, quoted in Oliver Staley and Michael McKee, "Yale's Tobin Guides from Grave as Friedman is Eclipsed," February 27, 2009, Bloomberg.com; Luigi Zingales, "Closing Remarks," March 18, 2009, *The Economist* debate on "Keynesian Principles": http://www.economist.com/debate/days/view/283#con_statement_anchor

contributions to the editorial pages of the *New York Times* and the *Wall Street Journal* during 2008–2009 makes this point abundantly clear.)

As I have argued earlier, commitment to viewing economics as an objective policy science is tantamount to believing in the potential for an objective scientific history: The causal relationships that have governed human social interactions in the past must be amenable to formulation as quantified models and must be assumed to hold true in the future. Economics, when applied to a complex and dynamic world of changing institutions, social norms, legal settings, technology, values, knowledge, and political alignments, is necessarily a deeply historical enterprise. We should not be surprised, therefore, that policy debates during the recent steep recession have been accompanied by a revival of debates about the causes of the Great Depression and the effects of the New Deal (Cohen 2009). Nor, given the continued dominance of Friedman's positive/normative bifurcation, should we wonder that most of these accounts claim to have captured the true, empirically verified processes underlying the decade-long slump.

What we make of continuing dissension among economists about both the recent crisis and the proper response depends, therefore, on our ultimate view of historical analysis. One might join, say, John Cochrane or Paul Krugman in asserting that the way forward is clear and only ideological blindness prevents others from agreeing. Or one could acknowledge the uncertainty of the present state of knowledge but hold out hope, like Mitchell, that applied economics will become a positive science given enough time, proper methods, better data, and so forth. Alternatively, one could accept Knight's analysis, that both now and for the foreseeable future, the study of history (and hence applied economics) inescapably requires a substantial exercise of judgment.

Reliance on judgment does not mean that applied economics is immune to empirical reality, nor does it mean that all opinions are equal or that we are incapable of discerning between superior and inferior policy analysis. Indeed, we may have very good reason for distrusting the judgments of certain individuals. Rather, conscious reliance on judgment indicates the inadequacy of formal rules and models in the face of deep complexity and uncertainty, and hence it grants priority to experience and close familiarity with the phenomena in question. It does not free us from concern for analytical rigor; on the contrary, it makes reasoning more rigorous by recognizing the limits of formal knowledge. It does, however, force us to grapple with uncertainty, to abandon the image of economics as a policy science and accept it as a tool for training judgment, and in turn, to reconsider the functions of economists and economics in contemporary political life.

Archival References

Records of the Bureau of Labor Statistics. Record Group 257, U.S. National Archives II, College Park, Maryland.

Records of the National Resources Planning Board. Record Group 187, U.S. National Archives II, College Park, Maryland.

Published References

Alchon, Guy. 1985. *The Invisible Hand of Planning: Capitalism, Social Science, and the State in the 1920s*. Princeton: Princeton University Press.

Backhouse, Roger E., Bradley W. Bateman, and Steven G. Medema. 2011. "The Reception of Marshall in the United States." In *The Impact Alfred Marshall's Ideas: The Global Diffusion of His Work*, edited by T. Raffaelli, G. Beccatini, K. Caldari, and M. Dardi. Cheltenham: Edward Elgar.

Banzhaf, H. Spencer. 2006. "The Other Economics Department: Demand and Value Theory in Early Agricultural Economics." In *Agreement on Demand: Consumer Theory in the Twentieth Century*, edited by Philip Mirowski and D. Wade Hands. Durham: Duke University Press.

Barber, William J. 1985. *From New Era to New Deal: Herbert Hoover, the Economists, and American Economic Policy, 1921–1933*. New York: Cambridge University Press.

Berkowitz, Edward D. and Kim McQuaid. 1988. *Creating the Welfare State: The Political Economy of Twentieth-Century Reform*. New York: Praeger.

Biddle, Jeff. 1998. "Social Science and the Making of Social Policy: Wesley Mitchell's Vision." In *The Economic Mind in America: Essays in the History of American Economics*, edited by Malcolm Rutherford. New York: Routledge.

Brown, E. H. Phelps. 1972. "The Underdevelopment of Economics." *The Economic Journal* 82(325): 1–10.

Burns, Arthur F. and Wesley Clair Mitchell. 1946. *Measuring Business Cycles*. New York: National Bureau of Economic Research.

Clawson, Marion. 1981. *New Deal Planning: The National Resources Planning Board*. Baltimore: Johns Hopkins University Press.

Coase, Ronald. 1984. "The New Institutional Economics." *Zeitschrift für die Gesamte Staatswissenschaft* 140: 229–231.

Cohen, Patricia. 2009. "New Deal Revisionism: Theories Collide." *New York Times*. April 9.

Colander, David. 1992. "Retrospectives: The Lost Art of Economics." *The Journal of Economic Perspectives* 6(3): 191–198.

Committee of the President's Conference on Unemployment. 1923. *Business Cycles and Unemployment*. New York: McGraw Hill.

Critchlow, Donald T. 1993. "Think Tanks, Anti-Statism, and Democracy: The Non-Partisan Ideal and Policy Research in the United States, 1913–1987." In *The State and Social Investigation in Britain and the United States*, edited by Michael J. Lacey and Mary O. Furner. Cambridge: Woodrow Wilson Center Press and Cambridge University Press.

Despres, Emile, Albert G. Hart, et al. 1950. "The Problem of Economic Stability." *American Economic Review*. 40(4): 501–538.

Eakins, David W. 1972. "The Origins of Corporate Liberal Policy Research, 1916–1922: The Political-Economic Expert and the Decline of Public Debate." In *Building the*

Organizational Society: Essays on Associational Activities in Modern America, edited by Jerry Israel. New York: The Free Press.

Emmett, Ross B. 2009. *Frank Knight and the Chicago School in American Economics*. New York: Routledge.

Fink, Leon. 1997. *Progressive Intellectuals and the Dilemmas of Democratic Commitment*. Cambridge, MA: Harvard University Press.

Friedman, Milton. 1950. "Wesley C. Mitchell as an Economic Theorist." *The Journal of Political Economy*. 58(6): 465–493.

1953. *Essays in Positive Economics*. Chicago: University of Chicago Press.

1957. *A Theory of the Consumption Function*. Princeton: Princeton University Press.

1967. "Value Judgments in Economics." In *Human Values and Economic Policy*, edited by Sydney Hook. New York: New York University Press.

1983. *Bright Promises, Dismal Performance: An Economist's Protest*. Sun Lake, Ariz.: Thomas Horton and Daughters.

1986. "Economists and Economic Policy." *Economic Inquiry*. 24(1): 1–10.

Friedman, Milton and Rose D. Friedman. 1998. *Two Lucky People: Memoirs*. Chicago: The University of Chicago Press.

Friedman, Milton and Simon Kuznets. 1954. *Income from Independent Professional Practice*. New York: National Bureau of Economic Research.

Friedman, Milton and Anna J. Schwartz. 1963. *A Monetary History of the United States, 1867–1960*. Princeton: Princeton University Press.

1970. *Monetary Statistics of the United States: Estimates, Sources, and Methods*. New York: National Bureau of Economic Research.

1982. *Monetary Trends in the United States and the United Kingdom: Their Relation to Income, Prices, and Interest Rates, 1867–1975*. Chicago: University of Chicago Press.

Gordon, Colin. 1994. *New Deals: Business, Labor, and Politics in America, 1920–1935*. New York: Cambridge University Press.

Graebner, William. 1977. "Federalism in the Progressive Era: A Structural Interpretation of Reform." *Journal of American History*. 64(2): 331–357.

Gruchy, Allan G. 1939. "The Economics of the National Resources Committee." *American Economic Review*. 29(1): 60–73.

Haavelmo, Trygve. 1944. "The Probability Approach in Econometrics." *Econometrica*. 12(supplement): iii–115.

Hammond, J. Daniel. 1992. "An Interview with Milton Friedman on Methodology." *Research in the History of Economic Thought and Methodology*. 10: 91–118.

1996. *Theory and Measurement: Causality Issues in Milton Friedman's Monetary Economics*. New York: Cambridge University Press.

2001. "Columbia Roots of the Chicago School: The Case of Milton Friedman." American Social Science Association, New Orleans, LA, January 2001.

2006. "More Fiber Than Thread? Evidence on the Mirowski-Hands Yarn." In *Agreement on Demand: Consumer Theory in the Twentieth Century*, edited by Philip Mirowski and D. Wade Hands. Durham: Duke University Press.

2009. "Early Drafts of Friedman's Methodology Essay." In *The Methodology of Positive Economics: Reflections on the Milton Friedman Legacy*. New York: Cambridge University Press.

Hawley, Ellis W. 1974. "Herbert Hoover, the Commerce Secretariat, and the Vision of an 'Associative State', 1921–1929." *Journal of American History*. 61(1): 116–140.

Hendry, David F. 1980. "Econometrics – Alchemy or Science?" *Economica*. 47(188): 387–406.
Herman, Edward S. 1995. *Triumph of the Market: Essays on Economics, Politics, and the Media*. Boston: South End Press.
Hicks, John R. 1979. *Causality in Economics*. New York: Basic Books.
Hirsch, Abraham and Neil de Marchi. 1990. *Milton Friedman, Economics in Theory and Practice*. Ann Arbor: University of Michigan Press.
Hoover, Kevin D. 2009. "Milton Friedman's Stance: The Methodology of Causal Realism." In *The Methodology of Positive Economics: Reflections on the Milton Friedman Legacy*, edited by Uskali Mäki. New York: Cambridge University Press.
Karl, Barry D. 1974. *Charles E. Merriam and the Study of Politics*. Chicago: University of Chicago Press.
Keynes, John Neville. 1904. *The Scope and Method of Political Economy*. London: MacMillan Co.
Kitch, Edmund W. 1983. "The Fire of Truth: A Remembrance of Law and Economics at Chicago, 1932–1970." *Journal of Law and Economics*. 26(1): 163–234.
Klein, Naomi. 2007. *The Shock Doctrine: The Rise of Disaster Capitalism*. New York: Henry Holt.
Knight, Frank H. 1924. "The Limitations of Scientific Method in Economics." In *The Trend of Economics*, edited by Rexford G. Tugwell. New York: Knopf.
Koopmans, T. C. 1947. "Measurement without Theory." *Review of Economics and Statistics*. 19: 161–172.
Krugman, Paul. 2009. "How Did Economists Get It So Wrong?" *New York Times*. September 6: 36.
Leamer, Edward E. 1983. "Let's Take the Con out of Econometrics." *The American Economic Review*. 73(1): 31–43.
Lee, Frederic S. 1990. "From Multi-Industry Planning to Keynesian Planning: Gardiner Means, the American Keynesians, and National Economic Planning at the National Resources Committee." *Journal of Policy History*. 2(2): 186–212.
Leontief, Wassily. 1971. "Theoretical Assumptions and Nonobserved Facts." *The American Economic Review*. 61(1): 1–7.
Lynd, Robert S. 1939. *Knowledge for What? The Place of Social Science in American Culture*. Princeton: Princeton University Press.
Mäki, Uskali (ed). 2009. *The Methodology of Positive Economics: Reflections on the Milton Friedman Legacy*. New York: Cambridge University Press.
Means, Gardiner C. 1935. *Industrial Prices and Their Relative Inflexibility*, 74th Congress U.S. Senate Document 13, 1st sess. (Washington: Government Printing Office).
Mitchell, Lucy Sprague. 1953. *Two Lives: The Story of Wesley Clair Mitchell and Myself*. New York: Simon and Schuster.
Mitchell, Wesley C. 1919. "Statistics and Government." *Publications of the American Statistical Association*. 16(125): 223–235.
1924. "The Prospects of Economics." In *The Trend of Economics*, edited by Rexford G. Tugwell. New York: Knopf.
1925. "Quantitative Analysis in Economic Theory." *American Economic Review*. 15(1): 1–12.
1927. *Business Cycles: The Problem and Its Setting*. New York: National Bureau of Economic Research.

1936. "Intelligence and the Guidance of Economic Evolution." *Scientific Monthly*. 43(5): 450–465.

President's Conference on Unemployment. Committee on Recent Economic Changes. 1929. *Recent Economic Changes in the United States*. New York: McGraw-Hill.

Purcell, Edward A. 1973. The Crisis of Democratic Theory; Scientific Naturalism & the Problem of Value. Lexington: University Press of Kentucky.

Reagan, Patrick D. 2000. *Designing a New America: The Origins of New Deal Planning, 1890–1943*. Amherst, MA: University of Massachusetts Press.

Reder, Melvin W. 1982. "Chicago Economics: Permanence and Change." *Journal of Economic Literature*. 20: 1–38.

Rothbard, Murray N. 1989. "World War I as Fulfillment: Power and the Intellectuals." *Journal of Libertarian Studies*. 9(1): 81–125.

Rutherford, Malcolm. 2000. "Understanding Institutional Economics: 1918–1929." *Journal of the History of Economic Thought*. 22(3): 277–308.

2010. "Chicago Economics and Institutionalism." In *The Elgar Companion to the Chicago School*, edited by Ross B. Emmett: Edward Elgar.

Samuels, Warren J. and Steven G. Medema. 1990. *Gardiner C. Means, Institutionalist and Post-Keynesian*. Armonk, NY: M.E. Sharpe.

Serrano, David Teira and Jesús Bonilla Bonilla. 2009. "The Politics of Positivism: Disinterested Predictions from Interested Agents." In *The Methodology of Positive Economics: Reflections on the Milton Friedman Legacy*, edited by Uskali Mäki. New York: Cambridge University Press.

Schliesser, Eric. 2010. "Inventing Paradigms, Monopoly, Methodology, and Mythology at 'Chicago': Nutter and Stigler." Available at SSRN: http://ssrn.com/abstract=1628102.

Sowell, Thomas. 1993. "A Student's Eye View of George Stigler." *Journal of Political Economy*. 101(5): 784–792.

Stapleford, Thomas A. 2007. "Market Visions: Expenditure Surveys, Market Research, and Economic Planning in the New Deal." *Journal of American History*. 94(2): 418–444.

Stigler, George J. 1988. *Memoirs of an Unregulated Economist*. New York: Basic Books.

Teira, David. 2009. "Why Friedman's Methodology Did Not Generate Consensus among Economists." *Journal of the History of Economic Thought*. 31(2): 201–214.

Tucker, Rufus S. 1940. "The National Resources Committee's Report on Distribution of Income." *The Review of Economic Statistics*. 22(4): 165–182.

1942. "Distribution of Income in 1935–36." *Journal of the American Statistical Association*. 37(220): 489–495.

1942. "Estimates of Savings of American Families." *The Review of Economic Statistics*. 24(1): 9–21.

Wallis, W. Allen and Milton Friedman. 1942. "The Empirical Derivation of Indifference Functions." In *Studies in Mathematical Economics and Econometrics; in Memory of Henry Schultz*, edited by Oscar Lange, Francis McIntyre and Theodore O. Yntema. Chicago: University of Chicago Press.

Worswick, G. D. N. 1972. "Is Progress in Economic Science Possible?" *The Economic Journal*. 82(325): 73–86.

Wunderlin, Clarence E. 1992. *Visions of a New Industrial Order: Social Science and Labor Theory in America's Progressive Era*. New York: Columbia University Press.

TWO

Markets, Politics, and Democracy at Chicago

Taking Economics Seriously

J. Daniel Hammond

In September and October 1975, *New York Times* columnist Anthony Lewis reported on the University of Chicago pedigree of the Pinochet government's economic program. The so-called Chicago Boys, a group of Chilean alumni of the University of Chicago, had written a set of policy recommendations for Jorge Alessandri when he was a candidate in Chile's 1970 presidential election. The election was won by Salvador Allende. In October 1973, a month after the military coup led by General Augusto Pinochet, the Chicago Boys published their policy recommendations as "El Ladrillo" (The Brick). Several members of the group were subsequently appointed to positions in the government. Anthony Lewis portrayed Friedman, who had visited Chile in the spring of 1975 with Arnold Harberger, as the "guiding light" of the Pinochet economic policy, a "policy that could not be imposed on a free society" (October 2, 1975). He attributed to Friedman the idea that a growing disparity of incomes between the rich and poor is part of the mechanism by which anti-inflation policy works. Lewis asked "if the pure Chicago economic theory can be carried out in Chile only at the price of repression should its authors feel some responsibility? There are troubling questions here about the social role of academics" (October 2, 1975).

Almost immediately, protests began on the University of Chicago campus under the auspices of the "Committee against Friedman/Harberger Collaboration with the Chilean Junta." Protesters demanded that Friedman be driven out of the university. The protests and harassment lasted for the next five years, reaching a peak after the announcement that Friedman would receive the 1976 Nobel Prize. Friedman had fewer defenders among academics than one might expect given the collegiate totem of academic

Thanks for comments to Ross B. Emmett, Warren J. Samuels, and participants in the Duke University History of Political Economy Workshop.

freedom. Some balanced their defense of Friedman's rights against the gravity of the charges of giving policy advice to a repressive regime. Other academics joined the protesters. Nobel laureates George Wald and Linus Pauling wrote to the *New York Times* (October 24, 1976) accusing Friedman of being an accessory to human rights crimes. In a second letter published alongside theirs, two other Nobel laureates, David Baltimore and S. E. Luria, characterized the Nobel Prize committee's selection of Friedman as "an insult to the people of Chile, burdened by the reactionary economic measures sponsored by Professor Friedman."[1]

Friedman did not expect to stir up a hornet's nest when he accepted the invitation to Chile, not having drawn criticism for visiting Brazil, Yugoslavia, the Soviet Union, and India on prior trips. Trips in the future to China, before and after Tiananmen Square, and conversations with Zhao Ziyang and Jiang Zemin would likewise pass without protest. As he wrote in a letter of reply to an anonymous University of Chicago colleague who criticized him in the *Chicago Maroon*:

> I do not regard visiting any of them as an endorsement. I do not regard learning from their experience as immoral. I do not regard giving advice on economic policy as immoral if the conditions seem to me to be such that economic performance would contribute both to the well-being of the ordinary people and to the chance of movement toward a politically free society. (July 16, 1975, reprinted in Friedman and Friedman 1998, Appendix A)

However, in the view of many members of the academic and journalistic communities, his trip to Chile was completely different from other visits and consultations.

The Chile incident was one in a series of flare-ups that ran throughout Friedman's University of Chicago career. Chile was the most public incident and the most damaging personally. Friedman's ideas about economic policy were viewed as extreme, beyond the pale for many intellectuals. In October 1998, Friedman, who was eighty-six at the time, was slapped in the face with a pie by a twenty-seven-year-old man as he talked with a group of people at an education conference. The assailant was only four years old when Anthony Lewis denounced Friedman. Friedman was controversial throughout his University of Chicago career (Caldwell, this volume). A former student, Eugene Lerner, wrote from MIT, where he was a visitor in 1961, "If a man's importance is in proportion to the time spent denouncing him, you are

[1] The letters are reproduced in appendix A of Friedman and Friedman, *Two Lucky People* (1998). See Brender (2010) for a history of the University of Chicago Chile program and Burnett, this volume.

some fellow. I think I've heard more of you here than I have of Samuelson. Everyone here is waiting for someone to bell the cat" (September 11, 1961).

How do we explain the passion that Friedman evoked? I will make some conjectures by comparing Friedman with two other economists, John Kenneth Galbraith and Paul Samuelson. Why these two economists? Because they and Friedman were of the same age cohort. Friedman (born in 1912) is bracketed by Galbraith (1908) and Samuelson (1915). All three were honored economists, serving as president of the American Economic Association. All three wrote for audiences outside the scholarly community and developed popular followings. Yet the three followed different tracks in their scholarly work. There were also differences in their engagement with American political life. My conjecture is that their different approaches to economic scholarship, viewed against the political culture of American intellectuals in the postwar period, provide some of the keys to understanding differences in the reactions of economists and others in the academic world as well as the wider intellectual community outside academia to Friedman, Galbraith, and Samuelson (Cherrier, this volume).

We begin with Friedman. He and other members of the postwar "Chicago School" believed that economics was an empirical science. As a science, they believed that economics could provide a knowledge basis for improvements in community life. As an empirical science they believed that economists could acquire tested knowledge of the social world. They also believed that scientific economic knowledge was politically neutral. That is, economic knowledge was as neutral politically as any other scientific knowledge. Milton Friedman and others of the postwar Chicago School also held the Hayekian principle that useful information is widely dispersed. Markets harness this local information for the common good. Local information includes information about what is best for any individual. That information resides first and foremost within the individual. In the context of postwar American intellectual life, Chicago economics was radically democratic. From a slightly different perspective, one could say that Friedman embraced Adam Smith's axiom that the differences between the philosopher and street porter were to be found in institutions and their environments rather than in their selves.

The belief that economics is an empirical science extends deep into Friedman's intellectual formation. His first interests as an undergraduate at Rutgers, interests that were deepened by his graduate work at Chicago and Columbia, included mathematics and statistics. With Arthur Burns as his guide, Friedman developed an attachment to Alfred Marshall's *Principles of Economics* that lasted his entire career. He claimed Marshall as his methodological forebear in recognizing in economics "an engine for the discovery of concrete truth." According to Marshall, the economist

> must stand fast by the more laborious plan of interrogating the facts in order to learn the manner of action of causes singly and in combination, applying this knowledge to build up the organon of economic theory, and then making use of the aid of the organon in dealing with the economic side of social problems. (Marshall, 1885)

Two of Friedman's early professional associations serve well to indicate the self-image he developed as an economist. In 1937, he joined the staff of the National Bureau of Economic Research, having studied at Columbia under Wesley C. Mitchell, one of the Bureau's founders and its Director of Research, and at Rutgers under Burns, who succeeded Mitchell as Director of Research (Stapleford, this volume). The National Bureau's purpose was to serve the

> growing demand for exact and impartial determinations of facts bearing on economic, social, and industrial problems.
>
> It seeks not only to find facts and make them known, but to determine them in such a manner and under such supervision as to make its findings carry conviction to Liberal and Conservative alike. (Mitchell 1927, frontispiece)

In 1943, Friedman joined the Statistical Research Group. Although the National Bureau was strictly nonpolitical, the express purpose of the Statistical Research Group was victory over the Axis nations. So Friedman's work at the Statistical Research Group had a direct public purpose that in a global sense was political. However, in the circumstances of World War II, their purpose was not political among Americans. After Pearl Harbor, few Americans doubted that it was appropriate to marshal material resources and human intelligence to defeat the enemy.

His experience in both organizations reaffirmed for Friedman that science is empirical and that scientific research is grounded in the world of practical problems. At the National Bureau in the 1930s, he worked on estimates of income and wealth and their size distributions. This project was an outgrowth of development of national income accounts. Friedman came to the National Bureau from the National Resources Committee, where he worked on the Survey of Consumer Purchases. At the National Bureau, the National Resources Committee, and the Statistical Research Group, Friedman's tasks were development of procedures for collection and testing of data as well as actual data collection and analysis. Throughout his scientific career, Friedman never strayed far from collection, production, or analysis of data. In the postwar period, with the rise of mathematical economics, data production was not the most glamorous of activities among Friedman's fellow economists. Sometimes lost in the attention given to his and Anna J. Schwartz's *Monetary History* and *Monetary Trends* is their 600-plus-page data production, *Monetary Statistics*.

Like others of his generation, Friedman chose economics as a scholarly subject not only because it was intellectually satisfying, but also because it offered the prospect of making improvements in material life. He wrote:

> The reason I chose as I did was not only, perhaps not even primarily, the intellectual appeal of economics.... I graduated from college in 1932, when the United States was at the bottom of the deepest depression in its history before or since. The dominant problem of the time was economics. How to get out of the depression? How to reduce unemployment? What explained the paradox of great need on the one hand and unused resources on the other? Under the circumstances, becoming an economist seemed more relevant to the burning issues of the day than becoming an applied mathematician or an actuary. (1986, 82–83)

The connectedness of economic theory to practical problems was one of the features that set it apart from other intellectual disciplines. It is on this point that in the late 1940s Friedman believed that methodological Walrasians were taking economics off track. His preference for the Marshallian approach to economics was linked to its preservation of the ties between economic theory and practical problems. In a 1988 interview, Friedman responded to a question about Jacob Viner's graduate price theory course, in which he was a student in 1932:

> It had no explicit methodological content whatsoever. But there was a very strong implicit methodological content, since you came away very clearly with the feeling that you were talking about real problems. Part of the distinction is viewing economics as a branch of mathematics – as a game – as an intellectual game and exercise – as Debreu, Arrow and so on – and it's a fine thing to do. There's nothing wrong with that. After all, mathematics is a perfectly respectable intellectual activity, and so is mathematization of economics or anything else. The other part of it is viewing it (using Marshall's phrase) as an engine of analysis. And there was no doubt that Viner viewed it as an engine of analysis, and no doubt when you were in his course that you came away with the feeling that economics really had something to say about real problems and real things. In that sense it had methodological content. (Hammond 1992, 104–105)

In the same interview, he distinguished between economics at Chicago and in Cambridge, Massachusetts:

> There's no doubt that Chicago was distinctive, and has been ever since. The real distinction was not making price theory the focal point of the graduate curriculum. That isn't the real distinction at all. The fundamental distinction is treating economics as a serious subject versus treating it as a branch of mathematics, and treating it as a scientific subject as opposed to an aesthetic subject if I might put it that way.... The fundamental difference between Chicago at that time and let's say Harvard, was

that at Chicago economics was a serious subject to be used in discussing real problems, and you could get some knowledge and some answers from it. For Harvard, economics was an intellectual discipline on a par with mathematics, which was fascinating to explore, but you mustn't draw any conclusions from it. It wasn't going to enable you to solve any problems, and I think that's always been a fundamental difference between Chicago and other places. MIT more recently has been a better exemplar than Harvard. And of course there are no such things as one hundred per cent pure cases either at Chicago, or elsewhere. (Hammond 1992, 110)

In Alfred Marshall's Cambridge college room hung a portrait of a working man. Marshall is reported to have said, "I set it up above the chimney-piece of my room in college and thence forward called it my patron-saint, and devoted myself to trying to fit men like that for heaven." (Groenewegen, 130). For Friedman the purpose of economics was not so much to fit working men for heaven as to allow them to find a bit of heaven here on earth, and on their own terms. If you put Friedman's belief that economics is a practical science together with his belief in the dignity and competence of common people, you have a big piece of his ideology.[2]

It is likely that Friedman's (classical or neo) liberal commitments were cemented at the April 1947 founding meeting of the Mont Pèlerin Society. The opening discussion, at which Friedman was a speaker, was "'Free' Enterprise or Competitive Order." He also spoke in sessions on "The Future of Germany" and "Contra-Cyclical Measures: Full Employment and Monetary Reform," and he made opening remarks for the session on "Taxation, Poverty, and Income Distribution." Themes from these sessions began to appear in Friedman's publications soon after Mont Pèlerin.

Friedman's first published argument for classical liberal principals was "Neo-Liberalism and Its Prospects," published in the Norwegian journal *Farmand* in 1951. Drawing from A. V. Dicey's *Law and Public Opinion*, he argued that although the trend toward collectivist policies had not slowed, collectivist ideas were beginning to wane. Thus it was important to make the case for a new liberalism, one that he called the "competitive order." Friedman said that it was not his wish to turn back the clock to nineteenth-century laissez-faire liberalism, which "failed to see that there were some functions the price system could not perform and that unless these other functions

2 For instance, Friedman wrote in *Capitalism and Freedom*, "the heart of the liberal philosophy is a belief in the dignity of the individual, in his freedom to make the most of his capacities and opportunities according to his own lights" (1962). There is evidence that this was not simply rhetoric for Friedman in his *Newsweek* correspondence files (Milton Friedman Papers, Hoover Institution). People who wrote to him in response to his columns received thoughtful replies that reveal his presumption that readers of his columns who took the trouble to write to him deserved thoughtful consideration of their concerns.

were somehow provided for, the price system could not discharge the tasks for which it is admirably fitted" (1951, 91). Among these functions was to ensure that no one had undue economic power over others. Friedman's vision of the proper role of the state was Hayekian in emphasizing rule of law:

> There are broad powers and important responsibilities that the neo-liberal would give to the state. But the essential point is that they are all powers that are limited in scope and capable of being exercised by general rules applying to all. They are designed to permit government by law rather than by administrative order. They leave scope for the exercise of individual initiative by millions of independent economic units. (1951, 93)

The opening chapter of *Capitalism and Freedom*, on "The Relationship Between Economic Freedom and Political Freedom," was written for a symposium held at Princeton in September 1956 and published under the title "Capitalism and Freedom" (in Morley, 1958). Here we find Friedman's two-fold argument for economic freedom: that it is itself important and that it is essential as a guarantor of political freedom.

The first publication where Friedman used neo-liberal principles to inform policy analysis was "A Monetary and Fiscal Framework for Economic Stability" (1948). He did not make an argument for the principles, but assumed them:

> The basic long-run objectives, shared, I am sure, by most economists, are political freedom, economic efficiency, and substantial equality of economic power.... I believe – and at this stage agreement will be far less widespread – that all three objectives can best be realized by relying, as far as possible, on a market mechanism within a "competitive order" to organize the utilization of economic resources. (1948 in 1953, 134)

The paper spelled out proposals for a competitive order – government provision of a monetary framework operated under rule of law and use of fiscal measures to reduce inequality.

Another of Friedman's early applications of economics and neo-liberal principles to public policy was his paper on education policy in *Economics and the Public Interest* (Solo, 1955), which with revisions became chapter 6 in *Capitalism and Freedom* (1962). Friedman had a draft of this paper in 1953–1954, for he thanks three associates from his Fulbright year at Cambridge University for comments.[3] He took as his starting point the primacy of the individual:

> In what follows, I shall assume a society that takes freedom of the individual, or more realistically the family, as its ultimate objective, and seeks to further this

[3] P. T. Bauer, A. R. Prest, and H. G. Johnson.

objective by relying primarily on voluntary exchange among individuals for the organization of economic activity. In such a free private enterprise exchange economy, government's primary role is to preserve the rules of the game by enforcing contracts, preventing coercion, and keeping markets free. (1955, 123–124)

He allows for two instances of paternalistic abridgment of individual rights, for children and the insane, who are unable to care for themselves. The problem of children was generally resolved within the family, obviating the need for state paternalism. His analysis led to the familiar proposal to separate financing of education from its administration and use of vouchers in circumstances in which public financing is deemed appropriate.

In the next section of this essay, I consider Paul Samuelson and John Kenneth Galbraith, for comparison with Friedman. Following a sketch of their views of economics as a science and their politics, I will return to the question of why there was such passion in critical reactions to Friedman and his ideas.

In the same volume of autobiographical essays by Nobel laureates in which Friedman wrote of his attraction to economics because of its connection to burning issues of the day, Samuelson wrote of what attracted him to economics. He made no mention of the use of economics in solving practical problems. Like Friedman, Samuelson came of age during the Depression and developed proficiency in mathematics. However, for Samuelson, the prospect of bringing mathematics to bear on economics was more of an attraction than solution to poverty and the business cycle. Economics was a source of puzzles – exercise for the mind. He wrote in his essay on "My Evolution as an Economist":

Yes, the year 1932 was a great time to be born as an economist.[4] The sleeping beauty of political economy was waiting for the enlivening kiss of new methods, new paradigms, new hired hands, and new problems.... The year 1932 was the trough of the great depression, and from its rotten soil was belatedly begot the new subject that today we call macroeconomics. (1986, 60)

I am not suggesting that Paul Samuelson did not care about the misery of the Depression, but the significance of the Depression to him for the economics profession and his career was that it provided material and employment opportunities for economists. His thrill of discovery is captured in the following story told by Samuelson in the third person:

It is not true that PAS began life as a physicist or mathematician. Well into his undergraduate course he discerned that mathematics was to revolutionize modern

[4] Samuelson began college in 1932.

economics. Proceeding to learn mathematics, PAS still remembers how a Lagrange multiplier first swam into his ken and how, with a wild surmise, it gave him independent discovery of the Edgeworth-Stackelberg asymmetric solution for duopoly – an insight that has kept him immune to the false charms of Nash-Cournot purported solutions. (1986, 66)

That Samuelson would pose and then counter a presumption that he began life as a physicist or mathematician tells us of his self-identity. It was not as an empirical worker like Friedman, but as a pure theorist.

The day I proved that no one could be more than 60,000 standard deviations dumber than the mean, that Samuelson inequality made my day. The fact that subsequent writers have both generalized beyond it and discovered antecedents of it in earlier writings has not altered my pleasure in it. For that is the way of science, and sufficient to the day is the increment to the house of science that day brings. (1986, 73)

The reward of doing economics well, in Samuelson's view, was fame. "Scientists are as avaricious and competitive as Smithian businessmen. The coin they seek is not apples, nuts, and yachts; nor is it coin itself, or power as that term is ordinarily used. Scholars seek fame" (1986, 72).

Like Friedman, but unlike his Cambridge, Massachusetts, neighbor Samuelson, John Kenneth Galbraith did think it was important for economics to be directly applicable to social problems. After growing up on an Ontario farm, Galbraith began his career as an agricultural economist. He completed his Ph.D. at the University of California at Berkeley in 1934 and took an instructorship at Harvard, where he assisted the distinguished agricultural economist, John D. Black. Galbraith noted with pride that he and his fellow agricultural economists were practitioners of what Thorstein Veblen called exoteric learning (with little academic prestige, but practically useful) in contrast with esoteric learning (with prestige, but of little practical value).

Galbraith worked for the Office of Price Administration (OPA) fixing prices during World War II. After the war, he published *A Theory of Price Control* (1952), in which he observed that although price control had become accepted as a necessary component of wartime economic policy, there was no economic theory of price control. The task he set out in the book was to bridge the gap between prevailing theory, which was generally taken to suggest that price control could not work, and the World War II experience, which suggested that the policy had worked. In his memoir, *A Life in Our Times* (1981), Galbraith wrote of the challenge he faced when he was appointed as "price czar" in the OPA:

The job required one to envision the structure of the wartime economy in the largest terms and then to translate this into extremely specific lines of action. That, better than most economists, I could do. It also required a truly extraordinary capacity to adjust one's views and actions when the initial conception or some details were shown to be inadequate or wrong. Economics is not durable truth; it requires continuous revision and accommodation. Nearly all of its error is from those who cannot change. (1981, 125)

During a postdoctoral stay at the University of Cambridge in 1937, Galbraith attended lectures by D. H. Robertson, G. F. Shove, and J. H. Clapham (Keynes was recovering from a heart attack) and made weekly treks to the London School of Economics (LSE) for the seminars of F. A. Hayek and Lionel Robbins. He reports becoming "one of the acknowledged oracles" of Keynes's work, and that after returning to Harvard he was firmly committed to Keynesian evangelism (1981, 77, 93). Yet he also reports that the reading he did at Cambridge in 1937 convinced him that mastery of technical economic theory was of little value apart from intellectual preening:

A suitably complex exposition of some theoretical point in one of the professional journals ... serves to establish the credentials of a learned and priestly circle and to exclude the unwashed. It will rarely provide guidance on any question of practical policy, and, in fact, this is not expected. (1981, 77)

Nor did Galbraith have much truck with statistics, an attitude for which he blamed Harvard's William L. Crum:

In my adult life I have occasionally been criticized for inadequacy in statistical or econometric method. Crum is responsible; from him I early formed the impression that no figure and no calculation was really valid and that it was foolish to expose one's self by citing one. (1981, 45)

In his AEA presidential address, Galbraith made a critical attack on neo-Keynesian economics and neoclassical economics: "Neoclassical and neo-Keynesian economics, though providing unlimited opportunity for demanding refinement, has a decisive flaw. It offers no useful handle for grasping the economic problems that now beset the modern society" (1973, 2). For Galbraith the problem with both neoclassical and neo-Keynesian economics was that they removed power and politics from the picture of the economy:

In eliding power – in making economics a non-political subject – neoclassical theory, by the same process, destroys its relation with the real world. The problems of this world, moreover, are increasing both in number and in the depth of their social affliction. In consequence neoclassical and neo-Keynesian economics is relegating its players to the social sidelines where they either call no plays or urge the wrong ones. (1973, 2)

This brings us to the question of economics and politics. Recall the concern of Wesley Mitchell and the founders of the National Bureau to ensure scientific integrity by making determinations of the facts of economic, social, and industrial life in a politically impartial manner. Galbraith found economists wanting for their failure to come to terms with the reality of power and politics. "Power being so comprehensively deployed in a very large part of the total economy, there can no longer, except for reasons of game-playing or more deliberate intellectual evasion, be any separation between economics and politics" (1973, 6). Galbraith said that his point was not that economics should be absorbed into political science, for just as economists labored under the illusion that consumers control markets, political scientists were under the illusion that citizens control the state. In reality the state and thus economic policy are controlled by powerful self-serving economic interests.

Galbraith practiced what he preached; he embraced politics as a component of economics. In his AEA presidential address, he claimed that his call was not for a politically partisan economics, but for neutrality, which required an admission that the state was controlled by economic interests. Galbraith was anything but neutral in his own political economy. In his memoirs he recounts that his interest in politics began as a child in Canada when he accompanied his father to political meetings. His arrival in the United States for graduate school coincided with the campaign for the 1932 presidential election, and he quickly developed a fierce loyalty to Franklin D. Roosevelt. He secured his first job in the United States, at the Agricultural Adjustment Administration, by affirming that he was a Democrat even though he was not an American citizen. Galbraith worked as a speechwriter for Roosevelt in the 1940 campaign, the beginning of regular service to Democratic presidents and presidential candidates including Adlai Stevenson, John F. Kennedy, Eugene McCarthy, George McGovern, and Ted Kennedy. Galbraith served as Ambassador to India during the Kennedy administration. He reports that when he returned to the Harvard faculty from his post as a writer at *Fortune* magazine in 1948, there was concern at the university, "not wholly illegitimate, that I might concern myself unduly with political activity … at the expense of the students, scholarly writing and decent academic reticence" (1981, 277).[5]

Writing of the traits that qualified him for the task of setting prices at the OPA, Galbraith claimed that in addition to the ability to envision the whole structure of an economy and translate that vision into policy actions, he was able to adjust his views when circumstances changed; moreover, he

[5] The previous year Galbraith had been among the founders of Americans for Democratic Action.

had enduring confidence: "[O]ne had to believe that one's critics were ill-motivated, uninformed, unintelligent or instinctively wrong" (1981, 125). He followed this ground rule in comments about Friedman in his memoirs. For example:

> The city of Berkeley, in the days before Messrs. Jarvis and Gann and professor Milton Friedman made the spending of money on urban sanitation an infringement of personal liberty, was sparkling clean and covered with geraniums. (1981, 44)
>
> . . .
>
> Agricultural economists in those years were bitterly divided between a progressive faction led by John D. Black and a retarded faction headed by Professor George F. Warren of Cornell. (The terminology reflects Black's view.) The difference turned partly on the farm problem. Black greatly approved New Deal farm policies while Warren, anticipating the later faith of Professor Milton Friedman, thought all could be solved by the right monetary policy. (1981, 55)
>
> . . .
>
> So when monetary policy is invoked against inflation, the primary effect is on the small man, not the large corporation. The approval of the policy by the rich and powerful is thus an accurate reflection of their own self-interest. The applause by those so favored that has long been accorded Professor Milton Friedman, its most distinguished advocate, has been greatly deserved. (1981, 348)

In *The Good Society* Galbraith identified the political alignment of the rich and powerful:

> In the United States the Republican Party is avowedly on the side of the fortunate, and to the influence and wealth of the latter the Democratic Party, or many of its members, are also attracted.
>
> In the good society voice and influence cannot be confined to one part of the population. In the United States the only solution is more active political participation by a coalition of the concerned and the poor. And their instrument must be the Democratic party, for this has been its past role and the source of its past success.... Those whose primary concern is to protect their income, their capital and their business interest will always vote for the party that most strongly affirms its service to their pecuniary well-being. This is and has always been the Republicans. (1996, 141–142)

Paul Samuelson kept more distance between his professional and political life than Galbraith. Samuelson advised Adlai Stevenson, Averell Harriman, and John F. Kennedy, but served in no official political capacity. Nor did he serve in the Washington bureaucracy. "Moses-like PAS did not pass into the promised land beyond the Potomac, but as an *eminence gris* he had the fun of backing the poker hands of such magnificent Joshuas as Walter Heller, James Tobin, and Kermit Gordon at the Kennedy Council of Economic Advisers" (1986, 68). In the 1960s Samuelson's allegiance was less to Democrats than to the New Economics of the Kennedy Council of Economic Advisors (CEA). He did not portray economists on the other side as fools or knaves. However, party politics is prominent in Samuelson's *Newsweek* columns, and a reader of the columns is left with little doubt of Samuelson's party preference.

Samuelson believed that political rhetoric exaggerated the differences between the parties, but there were nonetheless important differences: "The count in November [1968] matters much. What matters is not simply whether a man has a majority of the votes, but also how large is the opposition. In our democracy we elect a team and not just a man. For this reason, party regularity, rather than being a substitute for careful thought, may instead be its consequence" (1973, 185). In a 1969 column on "The Economics of Class," he wrote:

> To a first approximation the Republican Party is the party of the affluent, and the Democratic party is the party of the underdog.... To a second approximation, money income cannot alone explain all the facts of political allegiance. Intellectuals, the world over, are the despair of their well-to-do uncles....
>
> Why is this so? ... Intellectuals tend to be liberal for the simple reason that *inequality* – if only you will *focus* on it *and think about it* – is at first blush abhorrent to most men. (1973, 186)

This theme was repeated with some regularity in Samuelson's columns during election campaigns, such as in 1976 when he wrote, "At the core, American political parties are oriented along class lines, to represent either those who have or the larger number of those who don't" (1983, 28).

Friedman's *Newsweek* readers might have inferred that he was a Republican, but there is less political party attachment in Friedman's articles than in Samuelson's. Friedman focused mostly on policies, sometimes on policy makers, relatively little on politics, but hardly ever on political parties. A recurring theme of his articles was that politics was too often the enemy of good policy, for Democrats and Republicans. For instance, writing on "The Politics of Economics" in 1978, Friedman criticized Presidents Nixon (wage and price controls) and Ford (energy policy) along with then President Carter (national health insurance) for putting political considerations ahead of sound policy. Two years earlier, he opened his piece "Rising above Principle" by charging that "President Ford's recent straddle on the picketing and energy bills was a dazzling example of the political art of rising above principle" (1983, 111). Although he was a supporter of President Reagan, Friedman did not withhold criticism when he thought politics was driving out good policy. He wrote about the congressional budget resolution for fiscal year 1981, "I am moved as a citizen and taxpayer to shout at the president and most members of Congress: 'Have you no shame?'" (1983, 119).

A frequent theme of Friedman's was that the public, that is, politicized, sector of the economy was too large. Where Galbraith and Samuelson viewed Republicans and Democrats as the party of the rich and the party of the poor respectively, Friedman viewed Republicans and Democrats as more or less the parties of the private sector and public sector. That he did not make this argument explicitly in his columns reflects his belief that all too often the distinction did not hold up in practice. Republicans aspiring to gain or keep office were as likely as Democrats to hand out favors. And "most members of Congress will do almost anything to postpone problems" (1983, 334). Friedman's strong support for the balanced budget amendment in the early 1980s was based on his belief that the ubiquity of special interests (e.g., *Tyranny of the Status Quo*, 1983) reduced to very small the chances of budgetary discipline without an external constraint on Congress. This reform was aimed at Congress, not at Democrats or Republicans.

Friedman reports in *Two Lucky People* (1998) that neither he nor Rose were active in politics until William Baroody, Sr. asked him to help draft a campaign platform for Senator Barry Goldwater in 1963. Friedman became Goldwater's economic advisor and one of his speechwriters during the presidential campaign. He signed on as adviser to Goldwater before the 1964 Republican convention, which pitted the emergent "conservative" Goldwater Republicans against the "liberal" Rockefeller Republicans. He was attracted to Goldwater not only because of his views on government policy, but also because of "Goldwater's firm adherence to basic principles, his courage in taking unpopular positions, [and] his willingness to sacrifice what seemed like political expediency to stand up for what he thought was right" (1998, 368). From the 1964 election campaign there emerged the second presidential candidate for whom Friedman retained lasting respect and admiration, Ronald Reagan.

Friedman's close friends, Arthur Burns and W. Allen Wallis, both served in the Eisenhower administration. Friedman met Vice President Nixon through an introduction from Wallis, and was impressed by Nixon's intellectual acuity. During the 1968 presidential campaign, Nixon recruited Burns as his primary economic adviser, and Burns recruited Friedman to the advisory group. As he describes the responsibility of the economic and other advisory groups, they were "not organized to promote the campaign, but rather to engage in advance planning for the administration after the election" (1998, 375). Friedman was an active supporter of two of President Nixon's policy initiatives, the move from conscription to volunteer armed forces and the family assistance program. The latter was a form of the negative income tax Friedman proposed in *Capitalism and Freedom* (1962). However he came to oppose the family assistance program in the form it ultimately took in Congress. He was also a vocal critic of the Nixon wage and price controls. Friedman sums up his view of Richard Nixon in *Two Lucky People*:

> I was a strong supporter of Nixon in 1968, less so in 1972, though I still voted for him. In retrospect, I must confess that I question whether the support was justified. Few presidents have come closer to expressing a philosophy compatible with my own; and few if any have had a higher IQ; yet performance belied the rhetoric and the ability. (1998, 387)

Friedman worked with Ronald Reagan on spending limitation initiatives for California when Reagan was governor. During Reagan's presidential campaign, Friedman helped plan economic policy for after the election, as he had for Nixon. He also served during Reagan's two terms on the Economic Policy Advisory Board, a volunteer group of twelve economists. Friedman's closing comment on Ronald Reagan in *Two Lucky People* is in contrast with his assessment of Nixon. Of Reagan he writes, "No other president in my lifetime comes close to Reagan in adherence to clearly specified principles dedicated to promoting and maintaining a free society" (1988, 396).

Samuelson, Galbraith, and Friedman – all three evaluated economic policy as scholars, but from different perspectives. For Friedman and Samuelson, identification of themselves as scientists was important. For Friedman, science was the accumulation of empirically tested knowledge. Samuelson's methodological statements indicated the same view, as for example he put it in an AEA roundtable on economic methodology, "Every science is based squarely on induction – on observation of empirical facts" (1952, 57). Yet his practice indicates that he regarded his contribution to economic science as the accumulation of mathematically tested knowledge. It is not so clear that Galbraith thought it important to be recognized as a scientist; he saw his scholarship as rising above what passed for science among economists. My contention is that the lessons Friedman learned from Wesley Mitchell and Arthur Burns and others about the nature of economic science, the primacy of empirical facts, and the importance of scholarly detachment represented by the nonpartisan creed of the National Bureau set him apart from Samuelson and Galbraith. Friedman believed that the economist as a scientist can contribute to public policy by producing tested knowledge and letting the chips fall where they may. He believed that many of the disagreements about policy were about matters of fact, and that scientific progress in economics would contribute to greater agreement about policy. To protect the sphere of economic science, Friedman regularly distinguished between his roles as an economic scientist and a public policy advocate. He wrote in *Two Lucky People*:

> Technical economics and public policy are intimately connected. Every public policy issue involves two steps: predicting the consequences of a suggested policy and evaluating those consequences as good or bad. The first step is the domain of science, the second, of values. The distinction is easy to state but it is far from easy to keep the one domain from intruding on the other. (1996, 213)

For Paul Samuelson, notwithstanding his methodological statements that science is empirical, economic science played a smaller role in formation of economic policy. This is because in practice Samuelson's economics was mathematical economics. And mathematical economics, although expressed in the language of mathematics, is not quantitative. For example, a mathematical model without values for coefficients cannot tell us how much teen unemployment is caused by the minimum wage, how much deadweight loss there is from a tariff, or how much crowding out there is with countercyclical fiscal policy. Economists see a world of policy trade-offs; something is gained from a policy, but at a cost. Only an empirically quantitative economics can yield information about the terms of policy trade-offs. The implication is that, for Samuelson, policy advocacy would have to lean less heavily on economic science as he practiced in his scholarly work and more heavily on values and information from outside his economic scholarship. For instance, in considering the role of confidence in the business cycle Samuelson described his forecasting technique:

> I am not now referring to the regressions of the computer but I am speaking now of the regressions of the mind, the intuitive forecasting which I do. The other day a colleague of mine … said to me, "Paul, how long do you think it will take before a computer will replace you?" … I thought for a moment, and as the question seemed to be asked in a mean way, I replied, "Not in a million years." (Burns and Samuelson, 1967, 92–93)

Galbraith was still less bound by the canon of economic science, empirical or mathematical, for he rejected both. Galbraith's economics is an economics of grand visions of historical processes, in particular of the rise of the organization, which renders economic theory obsolete:

> Organization, the subordination of the individual to the common purposes of a highly structured association, is a general phenomenon. For economic purposes, however, it has three relevant manifestations – in the modern corporation, the modern trade union, and the modern state. In all three of these, but especially in

the corporation and the state, organization – bureaucracy – has become the decisive source of power and the controlling influence on economic behavior. (Galbraith and McCracken, 1983, 28–29)

Economics must no longer be about markets, but about the organization. In an effusive *Newsweek* article marking publication of *The New Industrial State*, Samuelson said of Galbraith, "He does not write for his brethren within the guild. He is, par excellence, a non-economist's economist" (1973, 258). I am not sure if this statement was intended to be ironic, but it can be read that way.[6]

Samuelson also referred to Galbraith as "Sage of the Mixed Economy" (1973, 259). Mixed economy is a term that Samuelson used repeatedly. A mixed economy is not pure; it is a mixture of markets and government, of competition and monopoly. The United States does not have a laissez-faire, perfectly competitive economy. The implication of using the term mixed economy is that there are important policy questions for which a model that assumes perfect competition and no government is of little use. Samuelson placed himself in the middle ground on matters of economic policy and was inclined to play the devil's advocate. The center is exactly where Leonard Silk located Samuelson in *The Economists*:

Within the American economics establishment, I consider Paul Samuelson to be the vital center, with intellectual and moral views which themselves extend over a wide spectrum and are difficult to categorize. Nevertheless, clearly to his right is Milton Friedman, to his left John Kenneth Galbraith and Wassily Leontief. (1974, xi)

Two debates, with George Stigler on the proper role of government and with Arthur Burns on the Kennedy-Johnson wage and price guidelines, illustrate Samuelson's rhetorical use of the middle ground, both for the economy and for himself. Stigler and Samuelson spoke at Swarthmore College in early 1963. Stigler opened with the assertion that Americans' faith in the ability of government to solve problems was stronger than evidence warranted. His thesis was that those whose business it is to know what government can do in the realm of economic policy – economists – actually know very little about the success and failures of policy, for they had not pursued this knowledge. He used as an example regulation of electric utilities, a matter on which there was little dissent among economists about the role for regulation, and in which there was a long record of regulatory control. He and Claire Friedland had recently completed a study trying to answer the

[6] Samuelson honored Friedman in his column after the announcement of Friedman's Nobel Prize, referring to him as "an economist's economist." (1983, 130).

counterfactual question of how the industry would have performed in the absence of regulation (1962). Their conclusion was that regulation had had little effect on performance. Stigler gave a handful of public choice reasons for failure of government to live up to expectations, and then turned to the question of what government should do. Sketching the bare outlines of an argument, he suggested that the state should: (1) (a) prevent monopolistic mergers and dissolve existing monopolies where competition is efficient, (b) capture monopoly rents where competition is not feasible with an auction of monopoly rights, (c) leave the few remaining monopolies not subject to control alone; (2) ameliorate poverty with monetary grants and enhanced opportunities for the poor to acquire skills; (3) pay compensation for economic distress caused by government and use grants to relieve distress from other sources; and (4) punish those who commit fraud.

In his talk to the Swarthmore audience Samuelson turned the question around and asked what roles the private sector should perform. His answer was, "I believe the private economy should be left alone to do those activities which, on balance after netting out all advantages and disadvantages, it can best do" (Stigler and Samuelson, 1963, 23). He observed that logically either form of the question should lead to the same conclusion, but that in practice a certain amount of bias is inherent in posing the question one way or the other. Presuming that efficiency lay in the public sector and liberty in the private sector, he drew the conclusion that "the subject is an open one – open for debate and open to compromise. At some terms-of-trade, efficiency can be traded off against liberty (Stigler and Samuelson, 1963, 24). It is interesting that this comparison stands on its head the usual nostrum that markets provide efficiency and government fairness. Presumably Samuelson considered the public sector more effective than the private sector at providing both fairness and efficiency.

Samuelson then discussed the technical requirement for competitive optimality (no consumption externalities, constant returns to scale, perfect competition, and nondistorting lump sum transfers), and answered an imagined challenge from someone who complained that the real world does not meet these requirements. He next turned his sights on a hypothetical "one hundred per cent libertarian," who a couple pages later is identified as Milton Friedman. Samuelson commends *Capitalism and Freedom* to his audience so they can see Friedman's exposition of the notion "that it is better for one who deplores racial discrimination to try to persuade people against it than to do nothing at all – but, failing to persuade, it is better to use no democratic coercion in these matters" (Stigler and Samuelson, 1963, 34). Samuelson extends this libertarian rule against coercion to a general precept against coercion. He then demolishes it by drawing the implication that it is good to persuade someone not to gas five million humans, but not good to go beyond persuasion to prevent the atrocity. Samuelson concludes his discussion of the proper role of government: "The whole matter of proper government policy involves issues of ethics, coercion, administration, incidence, and incentives that cannot begin to be resolved by semantic analysis of such terms as 'freedom,' 'coercion,' or 'individualism'" (Stigler and Samuelson, 1963, 37).

He tells his audience that if they remember only one thing of what he has said it should be this: "There are no rules concerning the proper role of government that can be established by a priori reasoning" (Stigler and Samuelson, 1963, 37). Does this not rule out using the bulk of Samuelson's own economics to say anything about the proper role of government? He had warned his audience early in his talk that they might find his conclusion uncomfortably nihilistic, but he hoped it would be liberating.

Arthur Burns and Samuelson debated the Kennedy-Johnson wage and price guideposts at George Washington University in 1967. Burns opened with a brief history of economic conditions and policies from the late 1950s to the present. For the most part he was laudatory of both economic performance and of economic policy over the period. However, he argued that the continuation of expansionary policy in 1965 after signs of inflation appeared showed that there was much to be learned. He attributed the delay in adjusting policy to deficiencies in forecasting, insufficient data to distinguish aggregate demand deficiencies from structural problems, data deficiencies for prices and government budgets, and other such constraints. Apart from the technical limitations, Burns also blamed the Council of Economic Advisors, members of Congress, and the executive branch for placing too much emphasis on the estimated gap between actual and potential output and giving too little attention to the stage of the business cycle. He also criticized them for undervaluing price level stability and for expecting too much from wage and price guideposts.

Samuelson opened his talk with a disclaimer, saying that there were aspects of the guideposts (and other informal controls) that he admired and aspects that he did not care for. Despite the misgivings, "I shall have to be the devil's advocate in an adversary procedure designed to bring out truth and balance" (Burns and Samuelson, 1967, 43–44). Samuelson did not know the content of Burns's remarks when he prepared his. So he set out to defend the need for guideposts and other informal controls. Acknowledging economic arguments against the guideposts, Samuelson pointed out that despite economists' misgivings, all mixed economies were struggling with the problem of creeping inflation and output gaps. Furthermore:

> [W]e may with fine rhetoric or telling syllogism slay the presidential guideposts a dozen times; but still, in the opinion of the vast majority of economic experts, we shall be left with the vexing dilemma that free markets do not give us a stable consumers price index at the same time that the rate of unemployment stays down to a socially desirable minimum. (Burns and Samuelson, 1967, 45)

Samuelson used Galbraith and Friedman as examples of extreme views of guideposts. He quoted Galbraith to the effect that price controls worked during World War II and the Korean War, therefore they will work in peacetime, and Friedman saying that inflation is always and everywhere a monetary phenomenon and therefore the only way to stop inflation is by controlling money supply growth. He then played off these two positions: "I suppose it will be argued by many that Professors Galbraith and Friedman are not middle-of-the-road men" (Burns and Samuelson, 1967. 48). His response to Galbraith was that it was absurd to think that you can just hold wages and prices down. His response to Friedman was that if the Phillips curve is "bad," that is, the noninflationary rate of unemployment is too high, monetary and fiscal policy cannot remedy that problem. Improving the Phillips curve is a task for guideposts. "The guideposts and related 'incomes policies' are attempts all over the world to give us the same degree of fullness of employment with less price creep than would otherwise have been the case" (Burns and Samuelson, 1967, 57). Samuelson suggested that corporations and unions had considerable leeway in setting prices, so they could be persuaded to set them in the public interest.

Al Decker, the man who slapped Friedman with the pie in 1998 explained to reporters that he had done so because "he is the world's preeminent neoliberal economist, and that economic philosophy is responsible for the destruction of our environment, the deterioration of our social structure and has brought the world to the brink of an economic collapse" (Lite, 1998). As pointed out earlier, when Anthony Lewis accused Friedman of complicity in human rights crimes in Chile, the pie assailant was only four years old. Decker was not yet born in 1964, the year that historian Richard Hofstadter wrote of the Barry Goldwater campaign, "[W]hen, in all our history, has anyone with ideas so bizarre, so archaic, so self-confounding, so remote from basic American consensus, ever gone so far?" (1964) Nor had he been born in 1953, when after Adlai Stevenson first lost to Dwight Eisenhower in the presidential election, Arthur Schlesinger, Jr. wrote:

> Today, as a consequence of the election, the American intellectual finds himself in a situation he has not known for a generation.... For twenty years, the government of the United States, while often one which the intellectual has found confused or mistaken, has nevertheless been one which has basically understood, respected and protected intellectual purposes. Now business is in power again, and with it

will inevitably come the vulgarization which has been the almost invariable consequence of business supremacy. (1953, p. 162)

Concern that business interests were patrons and beneficiaries of the neoconservative movement persists today among historians of economics. Van Horn and Mirowski (2009) develop the thesis that the Chicago School was the creation of corporate sponsors through the Volker Fund's support of Friedrich Hayek, Aaron Director, and Milton Friedman:

Capitalism and Freedom, a crude neoliberal version of the *Road to Serfdom*, appears to have finally provided Luhnow [Harold, of the Volker Fund] with the book he had arguably paid for many times over.... Crude argumentation of this ilk [*Capitalism and Freedom*] proved wildly popular in the American arena, as evidenced by the fact that the book has never gone out of print. Friedman accomplished what Hayek never did, and what Director was apparently incapable of doing. The *Road to Serfdom* is an intricate and subtle tract compared to its confident bromides. But the major difference is that *Capitalism and Freedom* wore its own provenance on its sleeve: it was *proud* [emphasis in original] to be the work of an intellectual for hire, because all human discourse was essentially just a sequence of disguised market transactions. (2009, 166–168)

What is it that made Friedman a candidate for such opprobrium? My conjecture is that among the salient facts are these:

1. Friedman's academic career at Chicago and the development of postwar Chicago economics coincided with a period when intellectuals were most at home in the Democratic party, looking on the Republican party as representing anti-intellectualism – businessmen, bigots, and boobs. After the 1952 election, Republicans became an endangered species on university faculties and among intellectuals.
2. Although Friedman had little direct involvement with politics or Republican administrations in the 1950s, Arthur Burns and Allen Wallis both served in the Eisenhower administration. When Friedman became more involved as an advisor to politicians, it was to Republicans.
3. The academic and intellectual environment of the 1950s and 1960s that was generally hostile to market forces put academic economists in a bind. As George Stigler has argued, training in economics tends to make a person politically conservative (i.e., "in economic matters a person who wishes most economic activity to be conducted by private enterprise, and who believes that abuses of private power will usually be checked, and incitements to efficiency and progress usually provided, by the forces of competition" [1959, 524]).

4. Therefore, with their training in economics pulling in one direction and the broader intellectual culture in the other, incentives were in place for academic economists to trim their economic analysis to better fit intellectual fashion.
5. Galbraith's resolution of this conflict was not to trim, but to throw the economics out and build a new economics fully consistent with Democratic party politics.
6. Samuelson had considerable leeway to match policy judgments with political preferences, for his scholarly work in mathematical economics had only the most general implications for policy.
7. Friedman's economics was more intimately connected with policy issues and his notoriety was in part the product of intellectuals' fury that he would not trim his policy judgments to fit the prevailing intellectual and political fashions.

Although these conjectures are on the level of party politics (i.e., the smaller degree of loyalty that Friedman had to the Republican Party and elected Republicans' policies than Samuelson and Galbraith had to the Democratic Party and elected Democrats' policies) there is, I think, a more fundamental ideological divide that separated Friedman from many of his fellow economists and most academics. This can be seen in the reactions to Friedman's 1975 visit to Chile, which were discussed in the first part of this paper. Friedman was roundly condemned for visiting Chile and giving economic advice to the government, and the condemnations were fueled by something deeper than party politics.

"When Americans hear about repression in another country, about concentration camps and torture, our concern is often limited by a sense of distance from the horror." So wrote Anthony Lewis in the *New York Times* article (October 2, 1975) in which he portrayed Friedman and Arnold Harberger as the guiding lights of draconian economic policy in Chile. The letters to the editor of the *New York Times* from Nobel laureates Wald, Pauling, Baltimore, and Luria charged Friedman with culpability for the junta's human rights abuses even in his narrow role of giving technical economic advice. Noting Friedman's protestations that he profoundly disagreed with the authoritarian political system of Chile, Wald and Pauling replied: "Yes, indeed, a proper physician would treat a wounded criminal, but he must not help him to commit the crime" (1976). Baltimore and Luria responded to Friedman's letter in defense of himself: "Your disclaimers of having been a formal supporter of that regime do not remove our belief that the award of the prize evidenced a regrettable insensitivity to the significance of your association, however indirect, with the political and economic policies of the Chilean government" (1977).

There is an asymmetry between these reactions of intellectuals to human rights abuses in Chile and to abuses elsewhere, particularly in Communist countries. This asymmetry is well illustrated by an exchange between fellow economist Gerhard Tintner and Friedman. The German-American econometrician Tintner wrote to Friedman on June 16, 1975, expressing outrage that Friedman had visited Chile. He sent copies of his letter to seventeen economists. Tintner sarcastically suggested that the economics of gassing Jews might be a suitable topic for Ph.D. theses in the Chicago Economics department, which used to have among its faculty "some civilized members." He said that he assumed Friedman had a portrait of General Pinochet over his desk, and offered to provide a portrait of Hitler to accompany it.

Friedman replied to Tintner that he had traveled and lectured in many different countries, including countries with Communist governments, to which Tintner responded: "I did not know you had been to Russia and Yugoslavia. I myself tried twice without success to give lectures in East Germany." Tintner thus backed off his criticism a bit, but only a bit. He told Friedman that he still believed that he had aided and abetted a fascist government. He suggested that Friedman's trip to Chile was no more defensible than it would have been for "say Frank Knight and Paul Douglas [to] go to Berlin as 'observers' in order to assist Dr. Schacht in his economic work for Hitler."

Paul Douglas may not have gone to Berlin, but he did go to Moscow in 1927, with a group of academics, journalists, and union officials. The visitors had audiences with both Trotsky and Stalin.[7] Unlike some of his fellow travelers, Douglas was not a Communist, and he seems to have been under no illusion about the dictatorial nature of Soviet society. But he did go on the trip, and accepted the hospitality of the Soviet government.

Tintner's report to Friedman that he himself had tried without success to give lectures in East Germany was without any hint of irony. Presumably the lectures would have been on the use of econometrics for economic planning. Tintner also visited Moscow, Leningrad, and Warsaw in 1976, and although it is not clear if he lectured there on Soviet planning, he wrote about developments in mathematical economics and econometrics behind the Iron Curtain. For example, in 1967 Tintner and E.M. Fels published "Mathematical Economics in the Soviet Union" in *Communist Affairs*. Tintner later wrote (with Peter Peek): "There has been an impressive use of

[7] See Shlaes (2007), ch. 2.

linear methods in Russian and, more generally, East European economics, especially for economic planning" (1976, 367). Considering the danger that empirical economics might "degenerate into conformist endeavors," either in the East or West, Tintner and Peek concluded: "Modern methods of economic and econometric analysis are 'value-neutral,' and one can only hope that they will be used for peaceful rather than bellicose purposes" (1976, 370). This sounds very much like Milton Friedman's defense of his trip to Chile. It also suggests that for Tintner the danger of war between the United States and U.S.S.R. outweighed any concerns Tintner may have had about human rights violations of the Soviet government.

How could Gerhard Tintner be scandalized and infuriated that Friedman would travel to Chile and give economic advice and not see a parallel with his own travel to the Soviet Union and his contributions to the economics of Communist central planning? It must have been the case either that he regarded the Chilean government's treatment of citizens different in kind from the Soviet government's treatment of citizens, or that the scale of human rights abuses in Chile was greater than that in the Soviet Union. Yet Tintner made no mention of Soviet or East German human rights abuses in either of his letters to Friedman.

Joan Robinson (1968, 1969) went well beyond Tintner's study of the Communists' use of mathematical economics in central planning. After her fifth visit to China, she wrote an apology for the Cultural Revolution. Of that revolution she concluded:

> The Chinese are building up an economy of a huge country, still poor but well equipped with natural resources, and now they have committed themselves to doing so without taking any short cuts, and in a genuinely democratic manner. The Cultural Revolution makes the accusation of aggressiveness less plausible than ever. (1968, 223)

Notice that as was the case with Tintner, the issue for Robinson with regard to China and the West was whether the Chinese would act aggressively toward Western nations, not whether Westerners had a responsibility to protect the human rights of the Chinese people.

Robinson's admiration for Mao Tse-tung was close to fawning. For example:

- Mao Tse-tung has developed Marxist theory in accord with experience and common sense (1968, 214).
- The old guerrilla had not lost his cunning (219).
- As with many aspects of Mao's policy which seem extravagantly idealistic, there is a very practical side to the concept of a classless army (221).

- Comfortable foreigners, however sympathetic, cannot know what it means when the young soldier bursting with health and energy, tells them how his little sisters were sold, during a famine, to keep the rest of the family alive, or when the well-read Party secretary tells them that his mother was a beggar. They may guess, but cannot feel, the wave of gratitude, at once intimate and exalted, that goes out to all that the name of Mao Tse-tung stands for (221).

John Kenneth Galbraith visited the Soviet Union four times between 1959 and 1984. A regular theme of his writings was that American capitalism and Soviet communism were more similar than dissimilar in their institutions and performance. A year before the Mikhail Gorbachev was elected General Secretary and the collapse of the Soviet Union began, Galbraith pronounced: "Since the Russian system functions less than perfectly, some Americans have gone on to suggest that it is in crisis – in danger of collapse. This I strongly doubt; nor, I think, is it the view of competent observers generally" (1984, 61). Galbraith expressed concern that with the Soviet people's prosperity the planners were faced with the burdens of "the incredibly diverse requirements of the modern consumer-oriented economy" (1984, 60). If the Soviet people were not as materially well-off as they were, the planners' work would be so much easier! He reported that on observing queues in shops, he suggested to his Russian hosts that it would be wise to reduce money incomes so the people would blame their inability to buy on themselves rather than on the Soviet economic system.

Galbraith also visited Communist China, reporting after a 1973 trip that "there can be no serious doubt that China is devising a highly effective economic system" (1973, 118). Using clinically sterile language, Galbraith wrote of the Cultural Revolution, "There is a hint in the thought of Mao Tse-tung that a periodic churning-up is necessary" (121). There is no mention of human rights abuses. Indeed,

> I was two days at the Ritz [Paris, on the way home from China] with no grievous sense of social guilt, no insuperable problem of culture shock, wrote the foregoing summary of the Chinese economy, dined with Colette Modiano-Gustin who once wrote a very funny book about taking a French tourist party to China and Michelle Lapatre who sells my books in France. (1973, 137–138)

Friedman was condemned for going to Chile. Tintner, Robinson, and Galbraith were not condemned for going to Russia and China. How does the Pinochet regime's human rights record stack up against that of Communist governments of Russia and China? Estimates of the number of people killed by the Pinochet government made by the National Commission for Truth and Reconciliation and the National Commission on Political Imprisonment and Torture in Chile are 3,000 or fewer. For the U.S.S.R., the number of citizens killed by their government is in the neighborhood of 20 million, and for China, 60 million.[8] As Friedman himself pointed out, the sensitivity to human rights abuses in Chile was selective. Though trivial in comparison with the abuses perpetrated by the Soviet and Chinese Communists, the Pinochet government was condemned by the American and European press and intellectuals, but the Communists received a pass and often admiration. Friedman's visit to Chile was considered unconscionable, but Tintner, Galbraith, Robinson, and Friedman returned from visits to the Soviet Union and China without any tarnish on their moral credentials. The appeal of Communism remains one of the puzzles of the intellectual and political culture of the West in the twentieth century.[9]

References

Baltimore, David, and Luria, S.E. 1977. "Letter to the Editor." *New York Times*. February 18.

Brender, Valerie. 2010. "Economic Transformations in Chile: The Formation of the Chicago Boys." *American Economist* 54 (Spring): 111–122.

Burns, Arthur F., and Samuelson, Paul A. 1967. *Full Employment, Guideposts, and Economic Stablity*. Washington: American Enterprise Institute.

Courtois, Stéphane, Werth, Nicholas, Panné, Jean-Louis, Paczkowski, Andrzej, Bartošek, Karel, and Margolin, Jean-Louis. 1999. *The Black Book of Communism*. Cambridge: Harvard University Press.

Dicey, Albert Venn. 1905. *Lectures on the Relation Between Law & Public Opinion in England During the Nineteenth Century*. London: Macmillan.

Friedman, Milton. 1948. "A Monetary and Fiscal Framework for Economic Stability." *American Economic Review* 38 (June): 245–264.

1951."Neo-Liberalism and Its Prospects." *Farmand*. No. 7, February 17.

1953. *Essays in Positive Economics*. Chicago: University of Chicago Press.

1955. "The Role of Government in Education." In Solo (ed.), pp. 123–144.

1962. *Capitalism and Freedom*. Chicago: University of Chicago Press.

1975. "Letter to Anonymous Professor." *Chicago Maroon*, July 16. In *Two Lucky People*, pp. 595–596.

1983. *An Economist's Protest*. Glen Ridge, NJ: Thomas Horton and Daughters.

1986. "My Evolution as an Economist." In *Lives of the Laureates: Seven Nobel Economists*, 77–92. Edited by W. Breit and R. W. Spencer, Cambridge: MIT Press.

Friedman, Milton, and Friedman, Rose D. 1984. *Tyranny of the Status Quo*. New York: Harcourt, Brace Jovanovich.

1998. *Two Lucky People: Memoirs*. Chicago: University of Chicago Press.

[8] See Courtois et al. (1999).

[9] See Revel (2000).

Friedman, Milton, and Schwartz, Anna J. 1963. *A Monetary History of the United States, 1867–1960*, Princeton: Princeton University Press for the National Bureau of Economic Research.

1970. *Monetary Statistics of the United States: Estimates, Sources, Methods*. New York: National Bureau of Economic Research.

1982. *Monetary Trends in the United States and the United Kingdom: Their Relation to Income, Prices, and Interest Rates, 1867–1975*. Chicago: University of Chicago Press.

Galbraith, John Kenneth. 1952. *A Theory of Price Control*. Cambridge: Harvard University Press.

1973. "Power and the Useful Economist," *American Economic Review* 63 (March): 1–11.

1973. *A China Passage*. Boston: Houghton Mifflin.

1981. *A Life in Our Times: Memoirs*. Boston: Houghton Mifflin Co.

1984. "Reflections: A Visit to Russia." *New Yorker*. September 3.

1996. *The Good Society: The Humane Agenda*. Boston: Houghton Mifflin.

Galbraith, John Kenneth, and McCracken, Paul W. 1983. *Reaganomics: Meaning, Means, and Ends*. New York: The Free Press.

Groenewegen, Peter. 1995. *A Soaring Eagle: Alfred Marshall, 1842–1924*. Cheltenham, UK: Edward Elgar.

Hammond, J. Daniel. 1992. "An Interview with Milton Friedman on Methodology." In *Research in the History of Economic Thought and Methodology*. 91–118. Edited by W. J. Samuels and J. Biddle, Greenwich, CT: JAI Press.

Hofstadter, Richard. 1964. "A Long View: Goldwater in History." *New York Review of Books*, October 8.

Lerner, Eugene. 1961. Letter to Milton Friedman. Correspondence. September 11. Box 29, Milton Friedman Papers, Hoover Institution, Stanford University.

Lewis, Arthur. 1975. "For Which We Stand: II." *New York Times*. October 2.

Lite, Jordan. 1998. "Nobel Prize-Winning Economist Pied by Environmentalist." Associated Press, October 10. www.sfgate.com.

Marshall, Alfred. 1925 (1885). "The Present Position of Economics," In *Memorials of Alfred Marshall*, 152–174. Edited by A.C. Pigou. London: Macmillan.

Mitchell, Wesley C. 1927. *Business Cycles: The Problem and Its Setting*. New York: National Bureau of Economic Research.

Morley, Felix. 1958. *Essays on Individuality*. Philadelphia: University of Pennsylvania Press.

Revel, Jean-François. 2009. *Last Exit to Utopia: The Survival of Socialism in a Post-Soviet Era*. New York: Encounter Books.

Robinson, Joan. 1968. "The Cultural Revolution in China." *International Affairs*. 44 (April): 214–227.

1969. *The Cultural Revolution in China*. Harmondsworth: Pelican.

Samuelson, Paul A. 1952. "Economic Theory and Mathematics – An Appraisal." *American Economic Review*. 42 (May): 56–66.

1973. *The Samuelson Sampler*. Glen Ridge, NJ: Thomas Horton and Company.

1983. *Economics from the Heart*. San Diego: Harcourt Brace Jovanovich.

1986. "My Evolution as an Economist." In *Lives of the Laureates: Seven Nobel Economists*, 59–76. Edited by W. Breit ,and R.W. Spencer, Cambridge: MIT Press.

Schlesinger, Arthur F., Jr. 1953. "The Highbrow in American Politics." *Partisan Review* 20 (No. 2): 156–165.

Shlaes, Amity. 2007. *The Forgotten Man: A New History of the Great Depression*. New York: Harper Collins.

Silk, Leonard. 1976. *The Economists*. New York: Basic Books.

Solo, Robert A. ed. 1955. *Economics and the Public Interest*. New Brunswick, NJ: Rutgers University Press.

Stigler, George J. 1959. "The Politics of Political Economists." *Quarterly Journal of Economics* 73 (November): 522–532.

Stigler, George J., and Friedland, Claire. 1962. "What Can Regulators Regulate? The Case of Electricity." *Journal of Law and Economics*, 5 (October): 1–16.

Stigler, George J., and Samuelson, Paul A. 1963. *A Dialogue on the Proper Economic Role of the State*. Selected Papers, no. 7, Chicago: University of Chicago Graduate School of Business.

Tintner, Gerhard, and Peek, Peter. 1976. "Marginalism and Linear Economics, East and West." *History of Political Economy*. 8 (3): 367–379.

Van Horn, Robert, and Mirowski, Philip. 2009. "The Rise of the Chicago School of Economics and the Birth of Neoliberalism." In *The Road From Mont Pèlerin: The Making of the Neoliberal Thought Collective* . Edited by P. Mirowski and D. Plehwe,. Cambridge, MA: Harvard University Press.

Wald, George, and Pauling, Linus. 1976. "Letter to the Editor." *New York Times*. October 14.

PART TWO

CONSTRUCTING THE INSTITUTIONAL FOUNDATIONS OF THE CHICAGO SCHOOL

THREE

The Price Is Not Right

Theodore W. Schultz, Policy Planning, and Agricultural Economics in the Cold-War United States

Paul Burnett

In the early winter of 1945, the Committee for Economic Development (CED) met to discuss the wording of their new pamphlet, "Agriculture in an Expanding Economy," with University of Chicago economist Theodore Schultz. The arguments under discussion were his and would be featured in his forthcoming book, *Agriculture in an Unstable Economy*, published with the support of the CED by McGraw-Hill. In attendance were other members of the CED Advisory Board: Sumner Slichter, a professor at the Harvard Business School, William Benton, vice president of the University of Chicago, and Beardsley Ruml, former head of the Laura Spelman Rockefeller Fund, policy advisor to FDR, and Treasurer of Macy's. Schultz attempted to put his associates at ease: They were mindful of how the mandate of their organization – the promotion of free enterprise – would fit into a discussion about heavily subsidized American agriculture.

Several of the members were unclear about Schultz's vision. According to his rationale, government planning could help those farmers on the cusp of modernizing their operations to do so, as well as help those who lacked the education and resources to take advantage of agricultural modernization to migrate to the cities. When several members questioned how this proposal might be received by the public, given that it could be construed as another move toward socialism, Schultz reduced his grand program to its lowest common denominator: "It is based on classical economics – if earnings are too low then there are too many people and some must get out." Finally, Schultz boldly stated that it was possible to plan to facilitate a relatively free market, at least given the recalcitrance of the large farm organizations: "There is a great amount of government control and a great amount of individual freedom in the farm picture at the present time. We may need more government to give the farmer greater freedom."[1]

This would seem to be an odd statement from a professor of economics from the University of Chicago, still less from one who would lead the department during its heyday in the 1950s. Was Schultz not speaking before like-minded individuals who were focused on the common task of promoting free enterprise as opposed to *more* government planning in the post–World War II era? One answer can be found in the story of Schultz's transition from Iowa State to the University of Chicago, in the efforts of the University of Chicago to build up an advanced research program in agricultural economics, in the rise of private policy planning associations on the periphery of the university during World War II, and in Schultz's cultivation of a particular kind of neoliberal agricultural economics expertise.

According to historians like Kim McQuaid and Robert M. Collins, the participants in policy associations such as the CED were corporate liberals, that is, businessmen, technocrats, or academics who believed that rational cooperation between the dominant large organizations of American society (e.g. corporations, labor unions, and farm organizations) and government was possible and desirable.[2] Lessons learned from the failure of the Chamber of Commerce's oppositional strategy during the New Deal translated to a new spirit of dialogue with government, labor, and farm groups.[3] Yet filing these particular business policy associations under corporate liberalism threatens to gloss over some important differences of the political commitments and fundamental worldviews of the members of these organizations.

Under the banner of associations such as the CED, there appeared to be at least three major approaches to policy advocacy. The first group believed that capitalism had evolved or matured into an age in which markets were at times worse distributors of resources than planned economies (public or private). We can count some of the followers of J. M. Keynes, such as Alvin Hansen, in this group.[4] Others felt that cooperation between government, business, and labor after World War II was to be a fact of life that needed to be accommodated, if not embraced. However, a third group within these organizations argued that corporations were *the* dominant organization in American life, and that their dominance was the source of American

1 TWSP, CED Advisory Board Meeting, Jan. 20, 1945, pp. 20–23, box 28, folder "CED – General Correspondence."

2 McQuaid (1987, 342–368).

3 Collins (1981, 42–47).

4 Hansen was a member of the National Planning Association.

prosperity, which in turn depended on combating the power of the newly risen labor unions and farm groups. The following story from the meetings of the CED shows that the latter group often had the dominant voice in this period. In these discussions, disagreements over policy were often about how the corporate liberal associations might be used as a cover for undermining or altering the positions of the other countervailing powers of labor unions, farm organizations, and state-run programs. In them, we can finds the seeds of a nascent neoliberal ideology and policy advocacy, which historians Philip Mirowski and Robert van Horn have defined as the belief that a market society must be actively constructed, using a strong state to roll back the power of monopolies of certain pernicious forms while guaranteeing the property rights of corporations.[5] Schultz's work for the CED can be seen as a reflection of the early strategies of this emerging neoliberal thought collective at the University of Chicago.

According to a recent history of the "The Chicago School"[6] by Johan Van Overtveldt, Schultz was but a facilitator who organized and made possible the work of others, such as Gary Becker. Overtveldt leaves the impression that Schultz's scholarly contributions were merely those for which he received his Bank of Sweden (Nobel) Prize in economics in 1979: his work on human capital and in development economics. However, Schultz had already had a vibrant career prior to the 1950s as a first-rate agricultural economist and agricultural policy adviser for both the federal government and private policy associations. Examining this prehistory of the Nobel Prize–winning Schultz helps us to situate him in relation to the Chicago School of the 1950s, and may even suggest one way of understanding what was so unique about that scholarly community.

Overtveldt commented briefly on the "splendid isolation" of the University of Chicago, its double sequestration from distractions of Washington politics or the economic powerhouses of the coastal cities and from local distractions from focused academic debate.[7] When it came to agricultural economics and development economics, however, there was nothing isolated about Schultz or the University of Chicago. Schultz was already an important node in multiple overlapping networks of powerful actors by the time he arrived in 1943. He was to prove the linchpin in the university's bid to achieve a greater role in generating relevant, policy-applicable academic

[5] Van Horn and Mirowski (2009, 158–163).

[6] Van Overtveldt (2007). Overtveldt defines the Chicago School as a group of scholars situated in the School of Business, the Law School, and the Department of economics at the University of Chicago.

[7] Van Overtveldt (Ibid., 42–44).

work during his tenure as chair of the economics department from the mid-1940s until the early 1960s. Overtveldt was right to note the importance of the University of Chicago's location, which enhanced the intellectual ferment. However, the promoters of the university and Schultz regarded the university's characteristics and location as unique assets to be capitalized upon aggressively. They did not consider Chicago to be isolated from the centers of commerce. Rather, it was Chicago's centrality to important industrial and agricultural sectors of the economy that would govern their efforts to build new institutions at the university.

Schultz can be easily placed under Overtveldt's definition of the "Chicago Tradition," a picture of a common approach to intellectual inquiry at the university. As Overtveldt argued, Chicago seemed to thrive on scholars who dissented from orthodoxy. Schultz was no exception to this tradition. However, if Schultz seemed unafraid of the potential public fallout of his farm policy proposal in the aforementioned CED meeting, his courage was partly a function of his familiarity with public controversy. A few months after he joined the CED's Research Advisory Board in March 1943, Schultz dismissed the publicity of the cotton industry as propaganda. Pointing to the gigantic accumulation of cotton stocks under government price-support programs, he reasoned that cotton could not be such a strategic crop if 11 million bales were still stacked in government warehouses. On NBC radio, he stated, "You could take all the 1943 crop and dump it in the Gulf of Mexico and you wouldn't hurt the war effort one iota."[8] That fall, he became a national symbol of academic freedom when he resigned his position as head of the Economics Department at Iowa State College. He quit because his department was under pressure from dairy interests to rewrite a pamphlet that it had published about the nutritional equivalence of margarine and butter. This "cotton controversy" and "Oleo-Margarine Affair" may have reinforced the reputation of agricultural economists among some in the national audience as "long-haired, crack brained, un-American" socialists.[9] Yet the controversies only seemed to help Schultz's career. Another private policy group, the National Planning Association, approached Schultz in the fall of 1943 to chair their Agricultural Committee, and immediately after he resigned from Iowa, the economics department at the University of Chicago secured him a position as a full professor for that fall as well.

[8] University of Chicago Round Table (1943).

[9] Senator Dan R. McGehee (Miss.) to Clinton Anderson, Sec. of Agriculture, Nov. 15, 1945, in Kirkendall (1966, 236). McGehee was referring to the economists of the Bureau of Agricultural Economics who had written unflattering reports on the racial dynamics of the Cotton South.

That he was well qualified for the professorship in the Chicago economics department is beyond dispute. However, as regards his stand for academic freedom, Schultz's move to Chicago was not so much an effort to free himself and his science from political influence as it was an exchange of one set of political environments for another. Working at a private university and for private policy associations enabled Schultz to articulate a new rationale and new techniques for agricultural subsidies – from farm welfare to state-fostered agricultural modernization and trade liberalization. A consensus builder who traded on his reputation as a fiercely independent policy intellectual, Schultz became a public figure who nevertheless represented particular agribusiness and industrial interests.

To be clear, the production of economic knowledge at Chicago was political work. It was political for the university; it was political for the corporations and foundations that paid for fellowships and research; and it was political for the scholars themselves. Indeed, some of the acrimonious rifts between leading figures of the department were about the degree to which political commitments could be balanced with what they deemed to be objective economic scholarship. Paul Douglas and Frank Knight fought bitterly in the mid-1930s over the retention of their junior lecturer Henry Simons, whose engagements as a public intellectual (a "propagandist" in Douglas's words) were weighed against his potential as a researcher.[10] Theodore Schultz was a political actor in a political world. Like many successful policy intellectuals of his day, he navigated among these various positions by couching his claims strictly in terms of objective social science.

As Thomas Stapleford has demonstrated in the first part of this volume, there was a range of opinion among experts during the 1920s and 1930s about both the nature of modern capitalism and the degree to which the state could or should assume the functions of the market. During World War II, Schultz – and a number of his colleagues in business, government, and academia – hoped to challenge more than a decade of farm policy that was predicated on some concept of "social justice" for the farmer and on the assumption that the state could successfully administer prices.[11] His move to Chicago in 1943 enabled him to develop and articulate a different though apparently paradoxical vision – government planning for a capitalist agriculture. This ambition would bring Schultz into contact with other nascent projects at the University of Chicago, namely the "Free Market Project" of revamped and revitalized neoclassical economics. Schultz's protean identity,

[10] EPUC, Paul Douglas to Frank Knight, January 5, 1935, box 41.

[11] Ezekiel and Bean (1933, 1).

so necessary to his participation in multiple communities, ultimately prevented him from remaining directly and publicly committed to espousing a new variant of liberalism, a torch that Milton Friedman would take up later in his career. Nevertheless, Schultz's careful self-fashioning and networking enabled him to transform the Chicago economics department into an engine for applied research and to outline an important blueprint for postwar agricultural and international development policies.

3.1. From Iowa State to Chicago

By the time Schultz made his case for a different kind of government intervention in agriculture, there had been almost fifteen years of federal government programs to improve the lot of the American farmers. The standard method of government intervention was to subsidize the farmer through price supports, guaranteeing a price ratio between industrial and agricultural products by buying up farm products, requiring production controls, and raising import tariffs. Each of the government's efforts had been politically controversial and fraught with logistical problems.

During the 1930s, Schultz was far from the direct heat of these national conflicts over farm policy. He was instead helping to build one of the most mathematically sophisticated and innovative research centers in his discipline. After he received his doctorate from the University of Wisconsin in 1930 under B. H. Hibbard, he was hired at Iowa State College, Hibbard's previous employer. The Iowa State Department of Economics and Sociology was unique in that it was a department of economics situated in the Division of Science rather than the customary Division of Agriculture.[12] British population geneticist R. A. Fisher was brought in during the summer of 1931 and again in 1936, nearly suffocating in the Iowa heat in the process. During the1930s, Fisher revolutionized statistical agricultural research around the world by establishing methods for analyzing and extrapolating from small samples. Other leading applied statisticians followed Fisher to Iowa State

[12] The American Farm Management Association, the first national agricultural economics institution in the country, was founded at Iowa State College in 1910. Warren (1932, 6).

Established in 1906, Iowa State's economics department was administered jointly by the Division of Industrial Science and the Division of Agricultural Engineering by 1917, and was expanded under the leadership of Chicago graduate Edwin G. Nourse during the 1920s. Nourse hired new staff to teach courses in marketing, money, and finance in addition to the farm economics curriculum. Nourse left at the end of the decade to become director of research at the Brookings Institution, after precipitating a public controversy of his own by predicting the collapse in Iowa Farm prices in the 1920s. ISUA, Arthur, box 1, Department of Economics Subject File.

the year after, including Frank Yates from the Rothamsted Experiment Station and Jerzy Neyman from University College London.

When Schultz became the Economics Department chair in 1932, he pursued a rapid expansion of the faculty and encouraged graduate students to publish in the discipline's journal of record, the *Journal of Farm Economics*.[13] Early on, Schultz developed a partnership with the Statistical Laboratory of the college, which was established 1933, and was an early advocate of Fisher's sampling methods.[14] Together, the laboratory and the economics department began to undertake research for the during the 1930s, resulting in the production of the Master Sample for U.S. agriculture,.[15]

This partnership garnered a national reputation for its policy papers and analyses of crop outlooks, commodity reports, and farm management. In fact, it was clear that the economics department at the premier private research university in the Midwest – the University of Chicago – admired the quality of the statistical work and educational standards at Iowa State College during the 1930s. Having taught at Iowa State, Henry Simons reminded his Chicago economics department that Iowa had developed a national reputation among government policy makers and farm organizations for its policy statements, as well as among other schools for the mathematical rigor of its undergraduate program.[16]

3.2. The University of Chicago Eyes the Farm Problem

Meanwhile, the University of Chicago had its own ideas about developing a center for agricultural research. It had a decidedly different constellation of patrons from that of Iowa State. Instead of the federal government, state

13 Iowa State already provided the greatest number of contributions to the Journal of any university. Yet Schultz made an even greater effort to promote submissions while he was editor from 1938 to 1941.

14 Schultz (1933, 452–475).

15 David and David (1984, 15).

16 "Their students will soon be better prepared for substantial economics training than are even those few students here who complete Math 104 105 and 106." Henry Simons to members of the Chicago economics department, July 8, 1937. EPUC, Department of Economics Records 1912–61, box 41, folder 12. Within a few short years, Schultz had researched and prepared a report on intra-hemispheric relationships and agriculture for the Carnegie Foundation. The Social Science Research Council had commissioned him to write a report on Southern educational institutions. The Farm Bureau consulted regularly with his department on matters of its policies and testimony before Congress. And of course the USDA and the Interstate Commerce Commission regularly made use of the department's economics staff.

TWSP, R.E. Buchanan and Harold Gatskill to C.E. Friley, Dec. 17,1941, box 76, folder – Schultz,TW.

extension services, or farm groups, they hoped to court private industry. During the 1920s and 1930s, many industry leaders had grown frustrated with government agricultural policy, particularly the special taxes on their operations that were used to pay for farm programs. Foundations and mushrooming private associations sought out technocrats whose experience, training, and inclinations could dovetail with those of agribusiness and perhaps dampen the interventionist enthusiasm of some government bureaucrats.

For their part, private universities also sought to enter the traditional domains of the state colleges. The University of Chicago's department of economics was situated at a private university in the largest center of agricultural commerce in the world. The university was famous for having nurtured American social science, particularly anthropology and social psychology. Although the faculty represented diverse areas of expertise and a range of political beliefs, the department was reputed to be behind the times. Indeed, in 1950 it was described as the last bastion of laissez-faire economics in the country.[17]

Although they worked in the center of an agricultural watershed, economists in the department such as Jacob Viner commented only sporadically on farm policy in the professional journal and meetings of agricultural economists. When they did, it was usually to dismiss as folly proposals to have the government raise farm income by raising prices artificially through a combination of loans, import tariffs, or mandated acreage reductions.[18] As a private institution, Chicago was not bound by the agricultural colleges' mandate of service to farmers.

The university was instead more beholden to the industrial concerns of the city – the meat packers, the farm-machinery manufacturers, and the processors and distributors of agricultural products. In 1905, the Institute of American Meat Packers was founded to promote economic research into

[17] McDonald (1950).

[18] "Nor does there appear to exist any valid appeal to noneconomic or to special economic considerations in support of the subsidization of agriculture. There is no obvious military necessity requiring an increase in American agricultural production, or even its maintenance in undiminished volume, regardless of economic costs. There is no clear case for artificial maintenance of the balance between urban and rural population ... If agriculture should appeal to the infant industry argument in support of protection to itself, it would be a valid if not courteous retort that any signs of infancy it displays pertain rather to the infancy of second childhood than of budding youth. And if agriculture is in need of alms, there are more economical and more equitable ways of distributing them than through tariff subsidies.... The sound position for the farmer to take is to disavow protection of his own products and to maintain vigorous opposition to protection for any other products" Viner (1925, 123).

the operations of the industry. Thomas E. Wilson, of the Wilson & Co. meatpackers, initially led the institute. During World War I, Wilson chaired the Packers' Committee in Washington, and it was through this experience that he reoriented the institute to address the position of the packing industry in the national economy and in world affairs. In 1923, the Institute began a relationship with the School of Business at the University of Chicago, undertaking scientific investigations of food-processing techniques. The Institute of Meat Packing at the University also provided training in economics for the employees of the packing companies.[19] Finally, the Institute served as a trade association, because one of its initial functions was to determine how to implement government regulation of the meatpacking industry such as the Food and Drug Act. Later, in the 1920s, the Institute engaged in policy advocacy, arguing against the 1920 Consent Decree, which had stemmed from antitrust action against the meat industry.

During the 1920s, university president, Max Mason, hoped to use Chicago's geographic centrality and proximity to large industrial concerns to draw research dollars and attention to the university's professoriate. The university hosted an annual Conference of Major Industries, which brought together luminaries from the world of business to discuss important matters facing each major industry. For its part, the Institute of American Meatpackers would host dinners for "pioneers of American industry" in New York, where guests of honor Henry Ford, Thomas Edison, Curtiss and Wright, George Eastman, and Harvey Firestone could be feted with clear green turtle Key West soup and broiled sirloin steak bouquettierre.[20] Whether such subtle forms of solicitation paid off in the near term is unclear. However, by the 1940s, million-dollar contracts for industrial-food and economic research were being provided to the Institute by individual companies such as Ralston-Purina, as well as smaller but considerable sums from trade groups such as the National Restaurant Association and the National Canners Association.[21]

The leaders of the University of Chicago had long wanted to make their institution a center for agricultural research of a very particular kind. As

[19] PPUC, 1925–45, box 54, folder 7. Total enrollments to Sept 1, 1927 were 688 students – 277 students in "economics of the meat packing industry," 221 in "pork industry," 77 in beef operations, 29 in manufacturing operations, 38 in accounting, 16 in science, 10 in production and marketing. Most of the students were from the large houses, Armour & Co. and Wilson & Co., but there were a couple of students each from dozens of small packing and dairy companies, fruit and vegetable associations, etc.

[20] PPUC, 1925–45, box 54, folder 7.

[21] BTSI, 1944–45.

early as 1928, a memorandum was circulated concerning the development of a "center for research in agriculture, and closely related business and industrial enterprises." However, this variant of agricultural-economic knowledge production had a completely different orientation to the farm problem and a different audience from those of the state colleges. Throughout the agricultural depression, agricultural economics, along with the rest of the sciences devoted to agriculture, was still primarily devoted to increasing farmers' production at the level of the farm. For the Chicago boosters, however, it was no longer a question of the application of scientific principles to farm production, but also to such aspects as "banking, including credit structure, marketing, taxation, and general land utilization." Such analysis required not only an economic point of view, but those of many of the other social sciences as well.

The precise provenance of the first plans for an interdisciplinary center is unclear, but several sources point to E. T. Filbey, who in the late 1920s was director of the Institute of Meat Packing.[22] He also sought to create links among disciplines, departments, industries, and state agricultural colleges to train scholars and business professionals in the larger political economy of agriculture and agribusiness in the United States. Such proposals read as if there were no government coordinating body for agricultural policy (for instance, the Bureau of Agricultural Economics) or agricultural schools (such as Iowa State) that produced economic research. In another proposal dating from the late 1920s, the institute would better prepare a few agricultural economists for their roles as bureaucratic functionaries: "It would produce trained leaders for agricultural schools, federal departments, railroad and business agricultural relations departments: it would also produce scientifically accurate reports of facts studied and popular easily understood summaries of conclusions from these facts." Only a private research university could provide an objective vantage point from which to see the farm problem as a national and international problem: "The federal department when not limited to politically expedient subjects of study has confined itself chiefly to technical production questions; the state agricultural schools stick to questions within their own state and not those including wider sections of this country and international market factors."[23]

The onset of the Depression dried up promising sources of potential corporate and foundation support, so the project lay dormant until the end of

[22] PPUC, 1925–45, RH (Hutchins) to Ralph Gwinn (J.C. Penney), June 3, 1929, box 3.

[23] PPUC, 1925–45, "Confidential memorandum for Mr. Eugene Stevens on Agricultural Project at the University of Chicago," box 3, folder 15.

the 1930s. The first chief of the Bureau of Agricultural Economics in the 1920s, Henry C. Taylor, hoped to help the university become a center for advanced research in agricultural economics in the late 1930s. Taylor was head of the Farm Foundation, which started in 1933 with an endowment from the first president of International Harvester, Alexander Legge. The foundation provided a series of generous fellowships for academic economists as well as senior economists in agribusiness to hold seminars together. Begun in 1938, its grants were suspended after 1942 for the duration. Yet during those four years, the foundation brought together likeminded agricultural economists from the business community and land-grant college system – those who sought advanced training in economic theory and statistics, and who wished to think about economic problems on a national and international scale. Taylor had ready allies at the top of the university administration. By the late 1930s, Filbey, author of the original plan ten years before, was now the acting vice president of the university and dean of faculty.[24]

In spite of the Depression, the Chicago promoters hoped that the university's advantages would be recognized by donors. In their view, the federal government and the state colleges were merely interested parties, hopelessly narrow in their purview, and as biased in their research as the railroads were in theirs. The private university, by contrast, nestled *in* the economic hive of the agricultural economy but somehow not *of* it, was uniquely positioned to produce a larger and more accurate picture of the U.S. agricultural economy, the Iowa Statistical Laboratory notwithstanding: "There are many instances of research bearing upon national policy in agriculture which may better be conducted in a private university than in any of the state institutions or in the Federal Dept. of Agriculture."[25] In one proposal, the university would be able to gain access to different groups – chain stores, packers, terminal market managers, railroads, and so on – as it was not a direct competitor of any of these other businesses.[26] This, of course, left aside the question

[24] PPUC, 1925–45, E. T. Filbey (now Acting Vice-President, U. of Chicago) to C. D. Kinsman, an unemployed agricultural engineer looking for work with what he had heard was a new agricultural economics research department at the University of Chicago, April 22, 1932, "I regret that the business depression has somewhat interfered with the development of our program in agricultural research." box 3, folder 15.

[25] EPUC, E. T. Filbey to Hutchins, March 25, 1941. Filbey was an old hand at the relationship between private foundations and research/training opportunities with the Chicago economics department. During the 1920s and 1930s, he was the director of the Institute of Meat Packing (later, the American Meat Institute), at which economists were trained for the meat industry. box 24, folder 14.

[26] PPUC,1925–45, box 3, folder 15.

of its competition with other colleges, the data-gathering and distribution functions of the federal and state governments, and, more importantly, the influence of private funding sources on their research. However, this kind of claim to objectivity was pitched at these very sources of the university's fundraising, which were made up entirely of private philanthropic foundations and corporations that intersected with the agricultural economy in one way or another.

3.3. Schultz in Chicago

Schultz's earliest association with Chicago stemmed from his teaching a summer quarter in their economics department under the auspices of one of the Farm Foundation fellowships in 1939. The Farm Foundation would provide a venue for Schultz and this group of economists well into the 1950s. He had arrived at the moment when the agricultural institute seemed to be finally taking shape. President Hutchins and Filbey seized on Schultz as the ideal candidate to lead their agricultural program. In his pitches to prospective donors, Hutchins cited a study produced by Schultz and his Iowa State colleague O. H. Brownlee, which concluded that the New Deal Agricultural Adjustment Administration was reducing the availability of feed grains and thus hurting the cattle ranchers and the packers.[27]

Early in 1941, Filbey and Hutchins approached the trustees with a proposal to hire a senior agricultural economist who could lead this Food Research Institute. By April 1941, the University of Chicago had made an offer to Schultz. For his part, Schultz wanted to establish at Chicago some form of privately funded "Rural Social Science Institute," perhaps with the support of the Farm Foundation or the Kellogg Foundation. After a series of negotiations, Schultz accepted the offer from the University of Chicago on September 3, 1943. Convinced that Iowa State had failed to protect his researchers from the machinations of the state Farm Bureau and the dairy industry, Schultz was ready to leave. Two weeks later, he resigned from Iowa State College, "to become a professor of agricultural economics at the University of Chicago," which was a substitution for a more candid letter stating, "I have lost confidence in the administration of Iowa State College."[28]

[27] PPUC, Hutchins to Filbey, Jan. 6, 1941. box 1, folder 4. The pamphlet in question was called "Data Pertaining to Crop Control in Corn, 1941."

[28] TWSP, T.W. Schultz to Finance Committee, Iowa State College, 15, Sept. 16, 1943. box 29, folder – Oleo-Margarine Affair 1943–44.

Of course, Schultz did not resign in protest from Iowa State College solely because of the Oleo-Margarine Affair.[29] However, after the twin disappointments that Iowa State could neither match his list of demands for a new research institute nor revive the morale of the department in the wake of the Oleo-Margarine Scandal, Schultz had a third waiting for him at Chicago. Efforts to find funding for a research institute had come to naught. Although Hutchins had failed to interest any of the prospective private donors,[30] Filbey encouraged Schultz to develop new links with outside institutions in addition to his former connections:

> We have, however, had no thought of giving up our general interest in the broad field of rural life and agricultural interests. Your position in the university points to the importance of your leadership in these fields with or without the Institute. I have, therefore, in all of my discussions referred to the importance of your maintaining relationships with Colleges of Agriculture and other groups and activities relating to the rural scene. This makes you something more than a Professor in the Department of Economics.[31]

Throughout the war years, the department attempted to get support through a number of philanthropists, including Fowler McCormick, the Babson Bros. Co., the General Education Board, and the Ball Foundation, without success.

The absence of a guarantee for his own research institute notwithstanding, Schultz hoped to find greater intellectual freedom at the University of Chicago. As historian Richard Kirkendall's story of the Bureau of Agricultural Economics has shown, controversies over the role of agricultural economists in designing and implementing national farm policies for the federal government could make economists' tenure in these "action agencies" brief and particularly unstable. Indeed, by the end of World War II, political protests, especially from Southern congressmen and the American Farm Bureau Federation, smothered broad-based economic policy planning in the USDA.[32] The farm interests that had long been critical of the BAE's action programs nonetheless promoted the preservation

[29] The Oleo-Margarine Affair is the standard explanation for Schultz's move to Chicago. There is, as yet, no monograph about Schultz, except for the following memorial article and Schultz's own reminiscences about his "standard puffing vita" for his Bank of Sweden Prize acceptance speech. Nerlove (1999, F730).

[30] A representative of the implement dealers had argued that, as longtime customers of the dealers, it was the land-grant colleges that deserved first crack at donations.
PPUC, 1940–46, Edwin Winter to Hutchins, July 18, 1941. box 1, folder 4.

[31] Filbey to T. W. Schultz. Sept. 1, 1943, TWSP, box 76, folder – Schultz, T. W.

[32] Kirkendall (1966, 232–33).

of state-supported commercial agriculture rather than freer international trade. Schultz's market-oriented efforts to plan for capitalism were at risk of being lumped in with the BAE's "socialistic" efforts to assist the rural poor.

Because Schultz knew his policy pronouncements were politically charged, having been excoriated in public several times, he sought shelter from such protest. Other economists of Schultz's caliber, such as Mordecai Ezekiel and Howard Tolley, had either lost government positions, continued in a far more muted career, gone to work for international organizations, or some combination of the three. Shortly after World War II, broad-based agricultural-economic policy planning moved out of the USDA's Bureau of Agricultural Economics and into private planning associations such as the Committee for Economic Development and the National Planning Association. Economists like Schultz continued to do their work in helping the federal government to sort out agricultural policy, but without the public accountability that came with working for a land-grant institution.

3.4. Schultz and the Private Planning Associations

Although the University of Chicago proper was unable to provide Schultz with the immediate institutional support he sought, several top university leaders drew Schultz into policy planning organizations at the periphery of the university that would satisfy some of his ambitions as a policy intellectual. Under the larger objective of postwar planning, a group of leaders from the University of Chicago, philanthropic foundations, and government planning bureaus established private policy associations to promote policy options for a number of sectors of government policy. This group of business leaders and agricultural economists debated the role of agriculture in an advanced industrial society. Together they hoped to forge a consensus and influence political discourse about farm policy.

The organization closest to the leaders of the University of Chicago was the Committee for Economic Development. It was formed in 1942 as part of a corporate reaction against the perceived excesses of the New Deal, and was fueled by a concern about postwar government policy. It stemmed from two projects. President Robert Hutchins and Vice President William Benton of the University of Chicago and Paul Hoffman of the Studebaker Corporation had hoped to create a think tank that would bring together leading minds in the academy and the business community.[33] Secretary

[33] Jones's plan was in part based on an earlier group that had advised FDR during the early New deal, known as the Business Advisory Council (BAC). Members of this new group

of Commerce Jesse Jones, hoping to solicit business opinion on postwar government planning, offered to assist Benton in the formation of a business policy group that would be independent of government and financed entirely by its participants.[34]

The CED putatively sought solutions to political problems by bringing together representatives of industry, labor, and agriculture to articulate and publicize government policy options thought to be beneficial to all groups. They published scholarly monographs in runs of several thousand at a time and sent free copies to senators, editors, chairwomen of clubs, and so on. The CED weighed in on specific tax policies by publishing pamphlets by the hundreds of thousands. During the war, the CED gradually developed several hundred local chapters of its organization to give it the patina of grassroots associationalism. But unlike the Chambers of Commerce, for example, the CED was an organization that initially represented only the largest corporations in the United States.

The CED claimed to step above the counterbalancing powers of the different sectors of the economy. And step above them it did, as it had minimal representation from labor or farm organizations. Notwithstanding this unbalanced representation, the CED promoted itself as the disembodied voice of sound thinking – "neither left, nor right, but responsible," its motto proclaimed. There was also a large contingent of erstwhile government planners who took up residence as trustees or advisors: Among a number of other industry leaders, bank presidents, social scientists, and university leaders were Beardsley Ruml and Gardiner Means, former economic advisors to FDR, and Chester Davis, former head of the Agricultural Adjustment Administration.

The CED was organized into committees that focused on urgent policy issues of the day, such as agricultural policy, regional development, and tax reform. However, certain ways of looking at agricultural or industrial policy were excluded from the outset. From a list of prospective experts for the agriculture committee, the note beside the name of Mordecai Ezekiel, the primary author of the first Agricultural Adjustment Act of 1933, read as follows: "considered brilliant but inflexible and committed to certain preconceptions."[35] John Kenneth Galbraith was considered for the position

shared the BAC's concern about the New Deal, and as such were primarily devoted to shaping postwar government policy. Other important CED members from the University of Chicago included its Research Director, Theodore Yntema, economist with the University of Chicago Business School, and Neil Jacoby, Secretary of the University of Chicago.

34 TWSP, Clarence Francis, Charles R. Hook, Eric A. Johnston to CED membership, July 29, 1942, box 28, folder – CED – General Correspondence.

35 TWSP, Notes on Meeting of the Research Advisory Board, January 24, 1943, box 28, folder – CED – General Correspondence.

that was eventually offered to Schultz, that of Research Director. However, CED leaders found him to be, like Ezekiel, too controversial a figure to be of use.[36]

With the onset of World War II, the CED promoted a subtle shift in the discourse about federal agricultural policy away from the more left-liberal views of Galbraith and Ezekiel. Although this new rationale retained a faith in the role of government in the administration of agricultural markets, it dispensed with the justification of farm policy in terms of economic or "social justice" that was present in the AAA of 1933. In its place, the members of the CED supported a rationale based on market mechanisms, anticipating the restoration of world trade at the end of World War II.

Although the CED had a large number of former government planners in its membership and leadership, its stated goal was to promote the virtues of the free enterprise system.[37] There were rhetorical nods to tools of state planning, however, the emphasis in its 1943 Statement of Principles was committed to rolling back the purview of the state: "The CED believes that business, labor, agriculture, and government must divest themselves of those traditions developed during an era of scarcity – traditions which tended to check expansion of production or to restrict output – and must make appropriate adjustments to the age of abundance which today's technical advances have made possible."[38]

[36] Former Office of Price Administration director John Kenneth Galbraith was present at only one CED meeting, as a guest. When William Benton was working with Ralph Flanders on possible candidates for Schultz's position as Director of Research with the CED, Galbraith's name was proposed. Before eventually deciding on Schultz, Benton noted that "Many, such as Moulton, question selecting a man so prominently identified with government. Paul Hoffman reports, and Clare Francis confirmed today at lunch, strong business antagonism throughout the country to Galbraith. Both Paul and Clare think this operates heavily to his disadvantage on the assignment for which we are considering him."

PPUC, 1945–50, William Benton to Ralph Flanders, August 6, 1942, box 15, folder 11.

[37] Collins (1981, 72).

[38] TWSP, "CED Statement of Principles, 1943–44," box 28, folder – CED Gen Correspondence, (p.27 of Statement). If we look at the policy aims of the CED that were published in the October 1944 issue of *Fortune*, one gets a better sense of what CED chronicler Karl Shriftgeisser called the "quiet" Keynesianism of the CED: It is the role of government to devise and enforce reasonably stable rules that will encourage private, voluntary enterprise.

Collective bargaining is a right, but it must not become a monopoly.

Private and public enterprise is natural in a democracy.

Prolonged depression is unnatural and government has a responsibility to use fiscal and monetary policies to mitigate downturns.

The coverage of social security, unemployment insurance, and old-age pensions should be extended.

With such a mission statement, one might assume that the agriculture committee would propose the dismantling of price supports and production adjustment for crops. After all, Schultz was well regarded for not having "certain preconceptions" such as those of Ezekiel. Some of his Chicago colleagues, such as Henry Simons, referred to Schultz as a libertarian.[39] Yet Schultz's policy proposal appeared to be an even more comprehensive plan for agriculture.

The value of Schultz's work lay in its capacity to bridge the diverse interests within the CED by attacking price supports. In his published work, Schultz argued persistently that the parity formula of high fixed price supports had failed. Parity was the explicit objective of New Deal farm policy: to raise farm prices to the purchasing-power equivalent of a base period of farm prosperity between 1910 and 1914. According to Schultz, parity had failed to promote farm welfare not only because moving millions of people out of agriculture and 45 million acres out of production had not checked the long-term decline in farm prices, but also because the policy treated a particular price as an end in itself. "Prices are not goals," Schultz wrote; "they are incentives."[40]

For Schultz, the justifications for parity, from "equality for agriculture" to the improvement of the distribution of resources, were redolent

Shriftgeisser acknowledged, however, that most CED businessmen were probably not in agreement with welfare provisions and the necessity of public enterprise. But compared with the principles of some of the more laissez-faire Chicagoans such as Viner or Simons, CED's official stance was conciliatory with respect to collective bargaining rights, public enterprise, and social welfare programs.

Shriftgeisser (1960, 69).

39 In his correspondence with Austrian economist Friedrich Hayek concerning a proposal for a "Free Market Project" at the University of Chicago, Simons described Schultz in 1945 as one among an inner circle who could be trusted to carry out the project of promoting and reflecting upon the traditions of classical liberalism over the long term.

HSP, "Memorandum on a Proposed Institute of Political Economy," p.11, box 8, folder 2.

40 Schultz (1945, chapters 2, 6, p. 256). Schultz elaborated upon this analysis a few years later in *Production and Welfare of Agriculture*. He argued that a perverse economic effect of the Agricultural Adjustment Act of the New Deal was not to raise prices through production control, but rather to increase farm efficiency through the adoption of expensive and risky new technologies and the substitution of complementary crops. Despite a mandated cut in corn acreage by 8 percent in 1937–1939, he noted that there was a 17 percent increase in production: "Finally it should be noted that as a consequence of the AAA corn program, partly because of the better rotations which were introduced as a result of crop control features and partly because of the supplementary income which farmers derived through benefit payments, more capital has been invested in soil productivity. Land has been improved. The agricultural plant in the heart of the Corn Belt has become somewhat larger than it was before the AAA programs began" Schultz (1949, 140–141).

of efforts to achieve some "monopoly gain" for the agricultural sector. To forestall this development, Schultz proposed two changes to the system of price supports. The first was for the government to establish a system of "forward prices" for agricultural products. Using the forecasting resources of the USDA, the government would set prices one season ahead to help farmers meet world demand more precisely.[41] In this manner, subsidies could vary inversely in response to long-term changes in prices on the world market.[42]

Although Schultz's proposal proved controversial in CED meetings, he argued that a forward price policy was exactly what the government had been doing in wartime with tremendous success. Forward prices could stabilize farm income and therefore encourage many farmers to risk purchasing expensive inputs to increase the productivity of their operations. Other poorer and less productive farmers, who had stayed on the land because price supports had acted as a welfare payment, would be encouraged to move to the cities to take jobs in industry. Thus, the income of more efficient producers who remained behind would be raised, while the supply of cheaper labor in the cities would be increased.[43] Finally, farmers' production decisions would be oriented toward future markets, rather than some baseline of production from before World War I.

The second part of Schultz's vision for farm subsidies was a program of counter-cyclical "compensatory payments." In a time of depression, commodity prices would be permitted to fall to world levels, and the government would pay farmers directly the difference between the world price and the "pre-depression price," or a rolling average of previous years.[44]

Lastly, this system could provide food security for the world without recourse to an internationally administered food reserve and assist in stabilizing world prices such that food shortages could be avoided in the first place. However, Schultz, who decades later would receive the Nobel Prize for his second career in development economics, recognized that such a system of direct subsidies would be devastating to farmers in poorer countries, who, much like the African American tenant farmers in the South,

[41] This is an important story in itself, the increasing success of the agricultural economics discipline generally in predicting prices for crops in the following season, a confidence that only emerged in the mid-1930s.

[42] Schultz (1943, 44).

[43] In a speech before the Farm Equipment Institute on Oct. 12, 1944, Schultz argued that the excessively cheap and abundant labor supply, "partly enforced by institutions of agriculture," was what held down farm machinery consumption. TWSP, box 17, folder – Unsorted 1944–48.

[44] Schultz (1945, 230).

would not be able to compete with mechanized, fertilized, and irrigated American production on the world market.[45]

With his policy proposals, Schultz bridged the multiple constituencies with interests in agricultural policy in the CED. More efficient production would lower prices for consumers, especially primary consumers such as processors; greater efficiency would be achieved by encouraging the purchase of farm equipment and inputs; and market-oriented supports would clear the accumulated stocks and reduce the burden on government. Contrary to the conventional portrait of Chicago economists as tireless advocates of market liberalism, Schultz articulated economic rationales for trade liberalization *within* the framework of state-supported agriculture. For Schultz, the functioning of this freer market in some sectors depended on the suspension of market forces in others.[46]

45 With modern machinery, Schultz argued, U.S. rice farming was already twenty to fifty times more productive than that of the "Oriental" rice farmer. Along with soybeans and wheat, it could easily compete even with low world prices. Although U.S. cotton production still awaited mechanization, Schultz argued that a technical revolution in the Cotton South was already in the works. But the future of countries with an insufficiently industrial and diversified economy would not be so sanguine:

"Consider, as an extreme case, a small trading country producing only wheat, with all nonlabor resources in that country specific to wheat. Let us suppose further that other wheat-growing and exporting countries introduce labor-saving technology which reduces the labor required to produce a bushel of wheat by more than one-half and thus reduces the cost of growing wheat enough to lower the world price one-third. The income per head in our hypothetical country would fall sharply unless a considerable part of the labor force were to leave agriculture, which under the conditions given, would entail migration to some other country with more diverse resources.

Trade does not in itself avert this difficulty. Better trading conditions, essential as they are to the economic health of nations, cannot keep incomes per head from declining in some countries producing such crops as wheat, cotton, sugar, oils, and fats. This will be true where the nonlabor resources are essentially specific to a particular crop, the potentials for industrialization are insufficient to absorb the excess supply of labor in agriculture, and the opportunity for people to migrate to another country is severely restricted. Cuba, Puerto Rico, and other Caribbean areas, the Danubian countries for the most part, and old Poland are countries faced with these adverse circumstances."

Schultz (1945, 149–155, 160).

46 I have not discussed the public appeal that Schultz's proposals might have had, merely its utility to a broad range of interest groups. However, Schultz's proposals did have a particular political utility at the time he made them. A letter written by Professor W. M. Drummond, economic advisor to the Progressive Conservative Party of Canada, in response to Schultz's presentation of his proposals for forward prices and compensatory payments at a conference at McGill University in June of 1944, illustrates one valence of his proposals:

"I was wondering whether you had managed to get any more copies of your most excellent paper typed. The reason I am concerned at the moment is that our Ottawa government here is just about to introduce a bill outlining its plan for establishing floor prices for farm products. When this bill is introduced it will probably be necessary or desirable for our party, which is the official opposition, to have something to say by way of opposition and perhaps, better still, to have something in the nature of an alternative to the government's

One could argue that this period during and just after World War II was the high watermark of cooperation between business, government, labor, and agriculture, that although these sectors were brought together by the exigencies of war, they were split apart afterward in the fission of peacetime prosperity. In fact, however, the CED flourished and indeed increased its influence and public profile throughout the 1950s and 1960s. The same was true of Schultz's career. Of course, neither the CED nor Schultz determined agricultural policy directly. They themselves had no illusions about that. Despite the fact that Schultz and his student and colleague D. Gale Johnson continued to promote the concept of forward prices throughout the 1940s and into the 1950s, the government never fully adopted the plan. Secretary of Agriculture Charles Brannan adopted elements of Schultz's ideas in 1949, but ran into opposition almost immediately, due in part to his failure to consult with major farm groups before publicizing the plan. Schultz distanced himself publicly from the plan, not least because it did not go far enough in that it applied the technique of direct payments only to perishable commodities.[47]

However, Schultz's basic ideas for introducing some market flexibility into the agricultural parity price-support system were widely lauded. As early as the 1948 Agriculture Act, the standard of parity was redefined as a ten-year rolling average, instead of the baseline period of 1910–1914. The Republicans enacted flexible supports into law once the tumult of the immediate postwar era and the Korean War had passed, which would vary as a percentage of this rolling average based on the world price. In fact, Schultz's neoliberal redefinition of the purpose of farm subsidies was reflected increasingly in U.S. farm policy for the rest of the century, in the advent of direct payments in the 1960s, decoupled payments in the 1996 "Freedom to Farm" Act, and in the Farm Security Act of 2002.[48] These were

own plan. Personally, I would very much like to have our members give some consideration to your suggestion for a compensatory price.... No doubt you will have read of the political swing to the C.C.F. [the Co-operative Commonwealth Federation, a socialist-populist political party] in Saskatchewan. The reaction to this development has been pronounced all over Canada. The general feeling seems to be that there is a radical spirit abroad in the land and that it will take something which at least sounds more radical than anything the old parties have yet suggested to head off the C.C.F. threat at the Federal Elections."

TWSP, W.M. Drummond to T.W. Schultz, July 3, 1944, box 17, folder – CDN J of Econ & Political Science.

47 TWSP, "Food Prices and Farm Income: An NBC Radio Discussion by George Aiken, Charles Brannan, and Theodore Schultz," Radio transcript. May 29, 1949, box 17, folder – University of Chicago Round Table; Schultz (1950, 5–8); Dean (2006). Schultz must have been chagrined when the business press gave him credit for the Brannan Plan: "Theodore Schultz (Chicago), enough of whose agricultural market theories were adopted by Brannan for them to be known jestingly as the Schultz Plan," McDonald (1950).

48 Federal Agricultural Improvement and Reform Act. Acreage reductions and "target" (read: parity) prices were to be eliminated, whereas the loan program of the Commodity

all forms of compensatory payments that would not, at least in theory, affect the price of commodities and thus permit American farm products to move on world markets. Schultz's prediction of their dire effects on markets in poorer countries has also resonated with trade conflicts today.[49]

Under the auspices of the CED, Schultz expressed a rationale that was fundamentally different from the farm policies of the New Deal and that influenced the leaders of the Farm Bureau, Congress, and debates in the press. Before he launched himself and members of the Chicago economics department into international economic development work, Schultz brought with him the service-oriented model that he developed at Iowa State. Even though the proposal for the Food Research Institute stalled, Schultz was able to use the Chicago-linked policy associations such as the CED to conduct graduate research on national and international farm policy questions outside of the land-grant system. From his brief participation in the fledgling "Free Market Project" with Chicago colleagues Aaron Director, Henry Simons, and Friedrich Hayek immediately after World War II, it is clear that Schultz's political sympathies lay closer to the CED interest in the promotion of free enterprise. But as an agricultural economist of his day, Schultz knew that he had to formulate his ideas to blend in with the convoluted farm politics of his day.

The political orientation of the CED certainly dovetailed with the intellectual climate in the Chicago department of economics at the time. It also matched economist Friedrich Hayek's objective of building a network of intellectuals at the University of Chicago who would engage in subtle critical analysis of the contemporary vogue of government planning and market intervention.[50] The point however, is that this network was a perfect reflection of Schultz's chosen role: the broker between worlds of economic thought. On the one side, there was the paradigm of state-driven capitalist

Credit Corporation would remain in place, supposedly as a transition to freer markets. The Farm Security Act of 2002 reversed this transition rather dramatically. Cf. Ruttan (1984, 549–559). Scholars such as Bill Winders have explained long-term changes in agricultural policy in terms of shifting coalitions of agricultural producers and processors, the most important being that of corn and feed grain producers and their agribusiness customers. According to Winders, this increasingly influential coalition grew to oppose price supports – and especially the production controls that accompanied them – over the course of the last half of the twentieth century. It is significant, however, that economists and the planning associations that spread their message advocated precisely this model for agricultural subsidies consistently during the third quarter of the twentieth century, and influenced directly the advocates of some of these reforms, such as Earl Butz, the Secretary of Agriculture during the Nixon and Ford administrations.

Bill Winders (2010).

[49] Schultz (1945, Chapter 11).

[50] Van Horn and Mirowski (2009).

planning whose star would wax until the end of the 1960s. On the other, there was Schultz's desire to embed price mechanisms in a state-planned agricultural economy. This vision would only be partially realized in agricultural policy over the coming decades. However, the long-run consequence for American agricultural policy and international development was that the New Deal's emphasis on farm welfare, which was limited to begin with, would eventually be replaced by a robust expansion of the American agricultural economy and an equally aggressive promotion of U.S. agricultural exports after the war.

3.5. Schultz, Chicago, and Economic Development

Although Schultz continued to write about domestic farm policy issues in the 1950s, he was ever the research entrepreneur, keen to take advantage of opportunities for research in new areas. And although the Chicago economics department had served an important constituency before the war, by training the economists of the meatpackers, Schultz brought to Chicago the systematic practice of applying economic analysis to policy problems in research contracts with new outside clients. He brought the spirit and practice of agricultural extension and service to Chicago, as well as a number of colleagues and graduate students who resigned with him from Iowa State, notably his student D. Gale Johnson and home economist Margaret Reid.

Along with this talent, Schultz brought his experience and contacts with the federal government, the land-grant system, private foundations, and industry, which resulted in his garnering large grants. Schultz then encouraged the graduate students to participate in these externally funded research projects. This infusion of capital was crucial. The department had halved its number of full professors in the years following World War II, losing Jacob Viner, Ted Yntema, Frederick Harbison, John Nef, and Oscar Lange. To make matters worse, the Cowles Commission moved to Yale in 1954, and Chicago lost one of the premier engines of econometric research in the world. Schultz's strategy was to recruit young professors to the faculty via the workshops. By the mid-1950s, Schultz's "research and instruction workshops" had become an established model that had acquired an international reputation sufficient to draw in funding totaling more than $1.4 million in support during only one academic year.[51]

[51] PPUC, 1952–60, Theodore W. Schultz, "A Program to Rebuild the Department of Economics, 1956," box 74.

Although it would be an overstatement to attribute the development of the workshop system at Chicago to any one person, it seems clear that Schultz was the linchpin in bringing about this innovation. There was no workshop program before Schultz arrived; the first workshop at Chicago was on agricultural economics. He had set up a similar forum at Iowa State for bringing graduate-student talent into contact with outside clients, in the pattern of the extension service there. In addition, Reid and Johnson conducted some of the first workshops at Chicago. Seen from this vantage point, the Chicago economics department appears as a kind of private extension service for the largest corporations and foundations in the United States, helping these clients with problems of monopoly, farm subsidies, or the nature of international economic development.

As astute observers of the academic marketplace, Schultz and his colleagues were drawn to the opportunities presented by Truman's Point Four speech in 1949. The commitment of the United States to technical cooperation with friendly nations as a bulwark against the spread of communism reinforced the orientation of the old philanthropic foundations toward international development and assistance in education and health, and set the agenda for the younger ones. Schultz seized these new opportunities and oversaw a multiyear Ford Foundation–funded project with the National Planning Association called Technical Assistance for Latin America (TALA), which probed the possibilities for developing a U.S.-style model of agricultural extension for Latin American nations.[52]

The theories of economists, however, were never easily separated from the political ground in which they grew. At times, Schultz voiced an awareness of this, as when he lamented to his colleague at the NPA about the direction of the private policy association for which he worked. He told Christian Sonne that the association had drifted away from larger "national and international problems," his preferred arenas: "In much of the work that we are doing, we have almost lost sight of the public interest and have put forward the importance of the private interests to the point that it overshadows and even biases the point of view."[53]

Agricultural economists such as Schultz were in the first rank of American development efforts abroad for a reason. As an administrative science, agricultural economics was a preestablished body of American expertise in

[52] For a thorough discussion of the evolution of neoliberalism and economic development discourse, see Plehwe (2009).

[53] TWSP, T.W. Schultz to Christian Sonne, Dec. 5, 1957, box 5, folder – NPA Agric & International, 1956–59.

technology transfer. Agricultural economists also brought with them their political experience as policy experts. Now, of course, farm management and rural sociology were also very important in U.S. technical assistance programs, but Schultz and others like him represented a particular kind of American policy intellectual among agricultural economists. As such, he understood well the larger context of his research. Schultz offered proof of the returns to investment in American education and technology at a time when developing countries were suspicious of the motives of the United States. Much of the research on economic development at Chicago during this period was designed to counter the Latin American prescriptions for autarkic national development, such as those coming from the United Nations Economic Commission for Latin America (ECLA).[54] The much-discussed "Chile Project," Chicago's experiment in teaching economics faculty at the Catholic University in Santiago, can be seen as part of this larger effort to predicate economic development on freer international trade. Rather than protectionism and import substitution, the TALA research promoted the returns to investment in scientific research on agricultural technologies. In order to effect this technology transfer, the multinational corporations and foundations that underwrote the National Planning Association and, indirectly, the TALA project, would need to continue to have access to markets in Latin America.

In these two instances, in his efforts to influence domestic farm policy and his work on economic development, Schultz injected a concern for prices as determinants of market exchange into policy discourse. In this manner, he inhabited the same sphere as the Chicago economists of the 1950s. However, Schultz did not entirely agree with figures like Friedman, who have often come to represent the Chicago School in their celebrations of the virtues of the free market. Schultz did believe that, to the extent that agriculture was on an export basis, it had to submit sooner or later to the forces and logic of international markets. Yet he also believed that the state had to be engaged in critical research and development functions, which individual farmers could not afford to undertake. Owing to his multiple constituencies – farmers, corporations, bureaucrats, and politicians – Schultz was a

[54] Prebisch (1949); United Nations (1951).

Immediately upon publication, Prebisch's pamphlet drew the harshest criticism from current and erstwhile Chicago economists such as Gottfried Haberler and Jacob Viner. Viner had been lecturing in Brazil in 1950, and warned against the Prebisch hypothesis thus: "stay with free trade; don't be wooed away from neoclassic verities by sirens promoting economic diversification; devote yourselves to agriculture and birth control." Dosman (2001, 99).

broker between groups with conflicting interests and thus could not afford to be seen as an ideologue.

Schultz's success as the chair of the economics department at Chicago was the realization of a longstanding objective of the university's leaders: to build an interdisciplinary community of scholars who would engage with the pressing issues of the day. He had a three-fold influence on the identity and activities of the Chicago department of economics. The first was that the workshop system that was so central to the identity of departments' members was shaped if not founded by Schultz. The second was that Schultz as chair made the department into an applied-research laboratory, bringing in tremendous amounts of outside funding for graduate students to do research. The third was his understanding that the purported objectivity of the researcher had political value that could be deployed strategically. One can take the standard portrait of the Chicago practitioners at face value – independent mavericks who found an oasis of tolerance for their brilliant but unconventional views.[55] However, although figures such as Schultz may have considered the truth to have been the sole metric for their labors and had taken principled stands to prove that they could not be bought or cowed, they were obviously quite aware that their economics had a political valence and that their policy advice was politically useful.

References

Archival Sources

HSP	Henry Simons Papers, Regenstein Library, University of Chicago
TWSP	Theodore W. Schultz Papers, Regenstein Library, University of Chicago
PPUC	President's Papers, Regenstein Library, University of Chicago
BTSI	Board of Trustees Subject Index, Regenstein Library, University of Chicago
EPUC	Department of Economics Papers, Regenstein Library, University of Chicago
ISUA	Iowa State University Archives

Published Sources

Arthur, I.W. "A Brief Informal Review of the Development of the Field of Economics at Iowa State, 1856–1956." Unpublished. Box 1. Department of Economics Subject File. Iowa State University Archives.

Collins, Robert M. 1981. *The Business Response to Keynes, 1929–64*. NY: Columbia University Press.

David, H.A. 1984. "Iowa State Statistical Laboratory, 1914–47." David, H.A. and H.T. David, eds. *Statistics: An Appraisal. Proceedings of the 50th Anniversary of the Iowa State Statistical Laboratory*. Ames: Iowa State University Press.

55 Van Overtveldt (2007, 30–34).

Dean, Virgil. 2006. *An Opportunity Lost: The Truman Administration and the Farm Policy Debate*. Columbia: University of Missouri Press.

Didier, Emmanuel. 2000. "De l'échantillon à la population: Sociologie de la généralisation par sondage aux États-Unis avant la seconde guerre mondiale." Ecole des Mines, Ph.D. thesis.

Dosman, Edgar. 2001. "Markets and the States in the Evolution of the Prebisch Manifesto." *CEPAL Review*, 75: 99.

Ezekiel, Mordecai and Louis Bean. 1933. *Economic Bases for the Agricultural Adjustment Act*. Washington, DC: Government Printing Office.

Kirkendall, Richard S. 1966. *Social Scientists and Farm Politics in the Age of Roosevelt*. Ames: Iowa State University Press.

McDonald, John. 1950. "The Economists." *Fortune*, December.

McQuaid, Kim. 1987. "Corporate Liberalism in the American Business Community, 1920–40," *Business History Review*, 52: 342–68.

Nerlove, Marc. 1999. "Transforming Economics: Theodore W. Schultz, 1902–1998: In Memoriam," *The Economic Journal*. 109: F730.

Plehwe, Dieter. 2009. "The Origins of the Neoliberal Economic Development Discourse." Philip Mirowski and D. Plehwe, eds. *The Road from Mont Pelerin: The Making of the Neoliberal Thought Collective*. Cambridge, MA: Harvard University Press.

Prebisch, Raul. 1949. *The Economic Development of Latin America and its Principal Problems, United Nations Publication*. NY: United Nations.

Ruttan, Vernon. 1984. "Social Science Knowledge and Institutional Change," *American Journal of Agricultural Economics*. 66: 549–559.

Schultz, Theodore W. 1933. "Testing the Significance of Mean Values Drawn from Stratified Samples," *Journal of Farm Economics*. 15: 452–475.

1943. *Redirecting Farm Policy*. New York: MacMillan.

1945. *Agriculture in an Unstable Economy*. New York: McGraw-Hill.

1949. *Production and Welfare of Agriculture*. New York: MacMillan.

1950. "That Turbulent Brannan Plan." *Farm Policy Forum*. 3: 5–8.

Shriftgeisser, Karl. 1960. *Business Comes of Age: The Story of the Committee for Economic Development and Its Impact upon the Economic Policies of the United States, 1942–1960*. NY: Harper and Brothers.

United Nations. 1951. *The ECLA/ ECE/ FAO Report on Trade Between Latin America and Europe*. New York: United Nations.

University of Chicago Round Table. 1943. "The Farmer and Victory." New York: National Broadcasting Corporation.

Van Horn, Robert and Philip Mirowski. 2009. "The Rise of the Chicago School of Economics and the Birth of Neoliberalism." P. Mirowski and D. Plehwe, eds. *The Road from Mont Pelerin: The Making of the Neoliberal Thought Collective*. Cambridge, MA: Harvard University Press.

Van Overtveldt, Johan. 2007. *The Chicago School: How the University of Chicago Assembled the Thinkers Who Revolutionized Economics and Business*. Chicago: Agate.

Viner, Jacob. 1925. "The Tariff in Relation to Agriculture." *Journal of Farm Economics*. 7: 123.

Warren, G.F. 1932. "The Origin and Development of Farm Economics in the United States." *Journal of Farm Economics*. 14: 6.

Winders, Bill. 2010. *The Politics of Food Supply: U.S. Agricultural Policy in the World Economy*. New Haven: Yale University Press, pp. 170–171.

FOUR

Sharpening Tools in the Workshop

The Workshop System and the Chicago School's Success

Ross B. Emmett

What accounts for the remarkable success of the Chicago School of Economics in the postwar period? In his recent book, *The Chicago School*, Johan van Overtveldt argues that the answer to that question has five key ingredients: "a strong work ethic, an unshakable belief in economics as a true science, academic excellence as the sole criterion for advancement, an intense debating culture focused on sharpening the critical mind, and the University of Chicago's two-dimensional [i.e., geographic and academic] isolation" (Van Overtveldt 2007). Others will argue that his answer deemphasizes some essential external ingredients in the School's success: For example, the ability of Chicago economists to put socialism on the ideological defensive has been emphasized both by those who see the School as an effective defender of classical liberalism (Friedman 1962) and those who see it as the initiator of a new rationalization of democratic capitalism – neoliberalism (Amadae 2003; Van Horn 2007). Although the argument about external-element contributors to the School's success is important, I will focus, like Overtfeldt, on its internal conditions. However, unlike Overtveldt, I will focus on the institutional infrastructure that supported that success rather than the individual brilliance of its faculty and the

Author's Note: I would like to thank Roger Backhouse, Jeff Biddle, Dan Hammond, Philippe Fontaine, Allan Hynes, Bruce Kaufman, Deirdre McCloskey, Steven Medema, David Mitch, Don Moggridge, Malcolm Rutherford, Warren Samuels, and Pedro Tiexiera for research help and comments on earlier versions of the paper. Participants in the Chicago Oral History Project are thanked for their willingness to allow me to use material from the interviews. Permission to use unpublished material from the records of the Department of Economics at The University of Chicago has been granted by the University of Chicago Library's Special Collections Research Center. The paper was presented at the "Revisiting Chicago" conference, University of Notre Dame (September 2007), the École normale supérieure de Cachan (May 2008), and the History of Economics Society meeting at York University (Toronto, June 2008).

cultural conditions – such as the work ethic, a debating culture, and common beliefs – to which Overtveldt ascribes its success. Setting aside the issue of whether Chicago's economists were naturally more brilliant than others (a claim I doubt), the cultural conditions Overtveldt attributes to the Chicago School will be seen here as the consequence of the institutional infrastructure that was built in the postwar era in the department of economics at the University of Chicago, not its cause.

T. W. Schultz, head of the Department of Economics at the University of Chicago from 1946–1962, believed that research success was not the product of a string of coincidences, but rather the result of a favorable and efficient organizational context (Teixeira 2008). Under his watch, the Chicago School built an institutional infrastructure that is often called the "workshop system." Chicago's famous workshops are often misunderstood as simply a variant of the seminars that are part of every economics department's life today; from this perspective, the fact that everyone has seminars, and that Chicago's were particularly successful, suggests that it must be the combination of the unique atmosphere of the university and the individuals involved that explain the School's success. I will argue, however, that Schultz's instinct was right: The workshop system, initiated in the late 1940s and early 1950s and built on the department's existing teaching of a set of "tools of analysis" in price and monetary theory and statistics/econometrics, created an integrated framework for research and teaching that enabled the expansion of the Chicago approach to economic science across the disciplinary spectrum (and eventually beyond). To use Kuhnian language, the workshop system provided the means for the normalization of the Chicago paradigm. The workshop system's success as a means for normalizing science is no mistake; as we will see, part of its roots lie in the attempt to design a laboratory for applied economic research. For the scientific community of economics, the ubiquitous presence of the Chicago approach is as sure a sign of its dominance as "normal science" as the number of its Nobel laureates.

The Chicago School can trace its roots back to the emphasis on price theory and the economic organization of a free enterprise economy provided by Frank H. Knight and Jacob Viner as early as the late 1920s (Emmett 2008, forthcoming). For our purposes, however, the first steps toward the institutional infrastructure built in the mid-1950s were taken in the early to mid-1940s, when Frederick Harbison initiated the Industrial Relations Center, Jacob Maschak took over as research director at the Cowles Commission, Milton Friedman was at the National Bureau of Economic Research (NBER), and the agricultural economists from Iowa

State University moved to the University of Chicago. The second section of the paper will briefly trace the development of the teaching and research infrastructure up to the departure of Cowles in the mid-1950s. The Cowles Commission departure, along with several other events in the department in the early to mid-1950s, precipitated the formal creation of the workshop system. The third and fourth sections, then, are the heart of the paper, outlining the construction of the workshop system and its initial implementation through the department's Economics Research Center during the period from the mid-1950s to the mid-1960s, and examining how it "normalized" the Chicago approach. The last section of the paper discusses briefly how the workshop system expanded across the department and reached outside to other parts of the university by the early 1980s. However, before we turn to these sections, the first section will provide some background on developments at the University of Chicago related to the design of teaching and research during the presidency of Robert Hutchins (1929–1951).

I should add a couple of warnings about the limitations of this study. First, the focus is on activity within the department of economics. By the 1950s, the Chicago School reached out to the Law School and the Graduate School of Business, and the workshop system was gradually adapted to those environments, at least as a vehicle for organizing faculty research. To make this a manageable chapter, however, I have concentrated attention on the activity in the department, which is where the workshop system was created. Second, my account relies heavily on the Records of the Department of Economics and material gleaned so far from the Chicago Oral History Project. Unfortunately, the Records of the Department of Economics for the postwar period are only beginning to become accessible, and I have interviewed only a few of the many Chicago faculty and graduate students from the postwar period. However, I expect further research will only strengthen the argument made here, providing greater detail about the operation of the workshop system and a richer account of debates within them.

4.1. Background

Since its beginnings, the University of Chicago has been at the forefront of academic reform in liberal education and graduate research. The presidency of Robert Hutchins, from 1929 to 1951, is particularly noted for efforts at the reform of undergraduate liberal education (McNeill 1991; Levine 2006), but changes in the Hutchins years also had an effect on graduate education and research. Shortly before Hutchins took office, the four graduate divisions (biological sciences, humanities, physical sciences, and social sciences) were separated from the college. By the early 1940s, the economics department no longer carried any responsibility for undergraduate instruction, and even when the Division of Social Sciences regained some control over undergraduate education in the late 1950s and early 1960s under provost and then president Edward Levi, the control was only over upper-division students. Hutchins's centralization of undergraduate education in the college, then, freed the economics department from the need to somehow reconcile the demands of undergraduate education with its mission of graduate education and research. I have previously sketched the story of the transition from the late 1920s to the early 1950s, emphasizing the role that "entrenching disciplinary competence" played in the construction of the program of graduate study (Emmett 1998). For our purposes here, the important part of my previous argument is that the department's curricular reform efforts were designed to make the work of an applied policy science a common venture for its participants, faculty, and graduate students alike. Graduate study and faculty research became integrated, with the "workshop" functioning as the infrastructure of that integration.

Hutchins's innovations followed on the heels of a decade of efforts by Chicago's social scientists to create an infrastructure to support empirical, interdisciplinary research. The construction of "Eleven Twenty-Six" – the Social Science Research Building at 1126 East 59th Street – included rooms for research groups to meet to work and hold seminars and to conduct statistical data analysis, as well as data storage facilities and several social-scientific laboratories. No undergraduate teaching was conducted in the building, and the offices of academic staff engaged in undergraduate teaching were housed elsewhere. Most of the space for statistical work was housed on the building's fourth floor, where one would also find the offices of economists Henry Schultz, Harry Millis, and Simeon Leland (Bulmer 1984). Eventually, as we will see, the Cowles Commission was also housed on the fourth floor. Empirical work by the institutionally minded economists who preceded the Chicago School at the University of Chicago was spurred by the common empirical orientation developing among Chicago economists in the 1920s (Rutherford 2008, forthcoming).

Another aspect of the department's activity during the postwar period that needs to be mentioned at the outset is its admission policy. From the late 1940s until the early 1980s (and to a certain extent even today), the department admitted to its graduate program almost anyone who expressed a serious interest in attempting economics research and could show aptitude for theoretical and quantitative analysis. Approximately seventy students per year entered the program between the early 1950s and the early

1980s. A high failure rate on the preliminary examinations was the primary mechanism of academic control over the graduate population. Rather than admitting only those who the department was certain could meet its standards, Chicago welcomed many but promoted to continued research only those who showed early aptitude in the mastery of economic theory and empirical methods required for membership in the scholarly community of an applied policy science.[1]

Finally, we should not forget the remarkable continuity and stability in the management of the department over the postwar period. In 1946, Schultz took over as department chair from Simeon Leland; he was head of the department until 1962, when Albert Rees became chair. Rees left for Princeton three years later, and Al Harberger became chair. He held the chair until the early 1980s. Thus there were three department heads in almost forty years. Yet this remarkable run was bested by the H. Gregg Lewis's record of departmental service: He served, first as the graduate student advisor and then as director of the graduate program, from 1945 to 1976. Schultz, Rees, Lewis, and Harberger were all involved in the development and expansion of the workshop model. The administrative commitment to the workshop system from the late 1940s to the early 1980s ensured the model had time to show its success.

4.2. Setting the Stage: The 1940s

In 1940, the Department of Economics at the University of Chicago looked reasonably similar to the departments at the East Coast research-oriented universities, although with only seven tenured members, it was probably smaller. Its tenured faculty members were less engaged in undergraduate teaching than faculty elsewhere, but Chester Wright, John Nef, and Paul Douglas did teach upper-division courses.[2] Small size necessitated that the department's strengths were concentrated in a few fields: economic theory (the famous triumvirate of Viner, Knight, and Oskar Lange), economic history (Wright, Nef, and Knight), labor (Paul Douglas), public finance

1 Al Harberger (2007) claims that most of the students who did not proceed on to continued research as a doctoral student did receive a Master's and that some of those did not complete the doctorate because they had to return to their home country.

2 By 1943, these courses were abandoned under Hutchins's plan for a four-year college that granted the bachelor's degree at a point equivalent to the end of the usual sophomore year. Three members of the department in 1940 were assistant professors or instructors in the college with no research or graduate instructional responsibilities: Maynard Krueger, Mary Barnett Gilson, and Gerhard E. O. Meyer.

(Leland), and international economics (Viner). The breadth of field coverage was increased by associated faculty from the professional colleges[3] and the department's assistant professors, instructors, and visiting professors.[4] Several of the assistant professors and instructors in the 1940–1941 year were destined to occupy important positions in the department's future: Harbison, Lewis, and Henry Simons. Individual faculty members pursued their personal research interests, taught graduate courses in their own research field or a related area, supervised graduate students, and gave public lectures. Doctoral students were expected to have a broad knowledge of the economics discipline[5] and would have to pass comprehensive preliminary exams in economic theory (including monetary theory) and two other fields before becoming candidates and working on a thesis. Although the University of Chicago is frequently cited, along with Johns Hopkins University, as an innovator in graduate study by its introduction of the graduate "seminar," borrowed from German universities, in 1940 the department of economics only offered such seminars in economic theory (Knight), economic history (Nef and Knight), and labor (Harbison). Thus, although the department had a unique constellation of faculty, in other regards its research and graduate study were not unusual among its peer institutions.

The Cowles Commission moved into the Social Sciences Research Building at the University of Chicago in 1939 – fourth floor, down the hall from the statistical laboratories, two flights up from the economics department. No formal connection with the department existed until 1943, when Jacob Marshak was simultaneously named director of research at the Cowles Commission and a professor in the department.[6] In 1944, the commission

[3] Hazel Kyrk from the School of Social Service Administration taught courses and supervised research in the economics of consumption; and faculty from the Graduate School of Business taught statistics, accounting, marketing, and risk-bearing.

[4] In the 1940–1941 academic year, George S. Wehrwein from the University of Wisconsin taught courses and supervised research in agricultural economics. T. W. Schultz and D. Gale Johnson did not arrive from Iowa State until 1944; more on that in the next section.

[5] Represented by course work (graduate or undergraduate) in eight areas: economic theory; statistics; accounting; economic history; money, banking, business cycles, and corporation finance; government finance; labor and personnel administration; and monopolistic industries.

[6] The previous director (1939–1942) was Theodore O. Yntema, professor in the business school. Henry Schultz had attended a Cowles Commission summer conference before his death in 1938, and his work in mathematical economics and econometrics was one of the things that attracted the commission to Chicago. H. Gregg Lewis, Jacob Mosak, and Oskar Lange – all members of the economics department in 1939 and the early 1940s – were part-time staff members of the commission prior to Marschak's arrival. See Cowles' *Economic Theory and Measurement* report (1953) for details. It is of some consequence to

is listed in the University's *Announcements*, under the Department of Economics, as a close affiliate. Much has been made of the debate between department members (especially Friedman after his arrival in 1946) and Cowles over both theory and measurement. Less obvious, but more important for our purposes, was the context within which Cowles's research and, eventually, the debates took place. Once the commission was up and running at Chicago, a permanent complement of both faculty and staff supervised the common overall research program, and several research associates (usually recent Ph.D.s or junior members of the economics department) stayed for a year or two to work on parts of the project.[7] The commission also attracted visiting professors who were guests for a year. Finally, Cowles was able to fund several fellowships each year for doctoral students in the economics department. Funding for this operation came not only from the Cowles family, but also from University and nonuniversity sources. The University's Social Science Research Committee provided funds for the research associates and helped coordinate the commission's funding from external sources, including the Rockefeller and Guggenheim foundations. The NBER also provided funding for the commission's work on a price control study (Katona 1945).

From its beginnings, Cowles had distinguished itself by its summer conferences on econometrics. With Marschak's arrival as research director, a new dimension was introduced: regular biweekly seminars with presentations by both internal and external researchers. Today's economist is so accustomed to a regular sequence of seminars that it may be useful to reiterate the unusual nature of what Cowles began for Chicago economists. Although faculty members in economics at the University of Chicago did not operate in isolation prior to the early 1940s, neither did they work in research teams on common projects similar to what had emerged in the sciences and even elsewhere in the social sciences (e.g., the NBER). Cowles began the process of moving Chicago economics toward social-scientific research as a team project. Members of the commission regularly participated in discussion of research papers prepared "in-house."[8]

the future of Chicago economics that Yntema took a leave from the university from 1944 to 1949 to work for the Committee for Economic Development, and then became a senior manager and director of the Ford Motor Company.

7 A list of all the faculty, research associates, guests, and fellows during the Chicago years is provided in Hildreth (1986), Appendix II.

8 From 1943 until the 1954–1955 academic year, the Cowles Commission ran an econometrics seminar that was the focal point of this discussion. From 1950 to 1954, Marschak also ran a seminar on "Modern Developments in Economic Theory" – obviously a counter to the Marshallian price theory taught in the required economic theory courses taught in

The discussion served as an implicit methodological control function in a manner analogous to the role that workshop discussion served later in the department. A particular "Cowles" analytical method was reinforced in the regular seminars and was characterized by four requirements: Every study should exhibit (i) a system of simultaneous equations; (ii) error terms in some of the equations to reflect randomness; (iii) use of time series; and (iv) mathematical work to make older empirical data sets suitable to Cowles-style analysis (Economics 1953). Although the results of research were frequently published in scholarly journals, the commission independently published sets of the research papers conducted under its auspices in its own papers series.

At the same time that the Cowles approach was taking hold under Marschak's direction, the Industrial Relations Center (IRC) was created by Harbison. The IRC appears to be modeled after the social-scientific research collaborations in sociology and anthropology taking place already at Eleven Twenty-Six.[9] Harbison brought together researchers in the social sciences and business to further research in industrial relations, labor economics, and personnel administration across the university. The center's home was in the economics department until the late 1940s, when it was moved to the Graduate School of Business.[10] Unlike the Cowles Commission, the IRC grew out of the institutionalist tradition in economics and collaborated with likeminded scholars in sociology and business. Like the other research teams in Eleven Twenty-Six, the IRC existed to coordinate the contributions necessary to carry out several large-scale social research projects. Where Cowles used Chicago as the hub of a growing international network of researchers, the IRC organized internal resources related to a common research project. However, despite the IRC's effort to unify research on industrial relations, in the early 1950s Harbison, Albert Rees, and H. Gregg Lewis each ran different seminars or "research" courses for graduate students in industrial relations and labor economics.[11]

the department. In 1954, Marschak ran a seminar on "Theories of Economic and Social Organization," and Gerard Debreu also taught a seminar on mathematical economics (information from University *Announcements*).

9 No history of the IRC exists, and its papers in the University of Chicago Archives are sporadic in their coverage of the center's activity. On the first decade of social science research at "Eleven Twenty-Six," see Wirth (1940).

10 Harbison was often on leave for government service and left the university officially in 1956. Albert Rees joined the center when he came to Chicago in 1947, and was its director during part of the 1950s. Rees also served as departmental chair from 1962 to 1964.

11 From 1951 to 1954, Harbison taught a seminar on Industrial Relations and the Individual Firm (a new name for the seminar in Industrial Relations that he taught from 1946 to

I would be remiss not to mention the arrival of T. W. Schultz, D. Gale Johnson, William Nichols, and Margaret Reid from Iowa State College (now University) in the mid-1940s. Iowa State had an enviable record of applied agricultural economic research during the 1930s and 1940s, largely developed under the leadership of Schultz. Schultz's arrival at Chicago in 1943 led almost immediately to three things. First, he became department chair in 1946 and led the department through the period in which the workshop system was created and extended. Second, Schultz brought several key applied economists, mostly focused on agriculture and development, to the department. His former student and colleague, Johnson, joined Schultz in 1944, Nichols arrived in 1945, and Schultz was finally able to arrange for Reid to join the Chicago department in 1951 upon the retirement of Hazel Kyrk.[12] Third, he and Johnson revitalized the Chicago tradition of applied research that had begun to disappear from the department during the early 1940s through retirements and departures. By the early 1950s, agricultural economics, with its extensions into econometrics, economic development, labor, and the study of consumption, was an essential driver of empirical and policy-oriented research within the department.

The early work of the Cowles Commission, the IRC, and the agricultural economics seminar provided opportunities to marshal the research efforts of doctoral candidates, faculty researchers, and research associates in common pursuits. The use of the word "laboratory" in Eleven Twenty-Six reflected the nature of their projects. A group of scholars, in the same or different research fields, would join together to carry out a research project. Graduate student assistants would work in a common space (the lab) on various aspects of the project, which often also required field work to gather data. The statistical laboratories provided space for the "computers," who also worked in a common space doing the calculations they were asked to carry out on mechanical devices and then checking each other's work. Until the end of the 1940s, however, these efforts remained on the fringes of the department's activity, complementary to the department's graduate study and faculty research but functionally independent of the department's mission. Further changes in both the integration of faculty and graduate student research and the graduate curriculum were required to create the unified model of study and research that the workshop system represented.

1950), Rees taught a seminar on Industrial Relations Research, and Lewis introduced Research in Labor Economics, the first version of the labor economics workshop.

[12] On the departure from Iowa State and Schultz's role as department chair there, see Wolff and Hayward (n.d.).

4.3. The Workshop System

The construction of a unified model for scientific research in economics by both graduate students and faculty required two things: the reorganization of faculty and graduate student research and a reconceptualization of the curricular requirements of graduate education. Around 1950, Gregg Lewis sketched out the problem and a vision for such a reorganization and reconceptualization in a memo to Schultz and the department: "I have been discomforted for some time," he said, "by the belief that graduate faculties of economics generally are neglecting their responsibilities for making economics an effective science and for training their students as scientific craftsmen." Both faculty and graduate students would need to learn new habits and skills and develop the "instincts of workmanship" appropriate to scientific research (quoted in Emmett 1998). Although this required more than just a reorganization, Lewis thought that an idea suggested to him by Arthur Burns[13] would provide an institutional framework for these skills and habits to be learned:

> Each professor – whether of money and banking, business cycles, public finance, or what not – will have his own laboratory. He will have one or two assistants who would share responsibility for the laboratory, and other assistants as needed. The students (doctoral candidates) in a certain subject will get their training in the laboratory, by working on some project. The individual assignments will be of limited scope, but it will be the function of the professor in charge to see that they fit together. The projects will grow out of the research program of the laboratory and will be supervised closely. (Lewis, quoted in Emmett 1998)

Lewis himself tried to implement this lab model[14] in labor economics, although with limited success because of his role as director of graduate programs. In early 1951, he wrote a letter to Schultz requesting permission to start a labor economics lab along the lines suggested in his earlier memo (H. G. Lewis to T. W. Schultz, n.d., Department of Economics Records, Box 41 Folder 1). Lewis's request was brought to the departmental meeting on April 4, 1951. The minutes of the meeting (Department of Economics Records,

[13] Arthur Burns was recruited heavily by Chicago in the early 1950s, and they were quite disappointed when he finally declined.

[14] The Burns/Lewis laboratory model was closely related to activity at the NBER, which wanted research projects that fit together, work for each research participant that could be clearly seen as part of the larger project, and a common work space where the work of research assistants could be closely supervised. Methodological uniformity was less important at the NBER (and in Chicago, at the IRC) than physical proximity and subdivided labor. Burns's conception of a laboratory reflects the NBER's emphasis.

Box 41 Folder 2) indicate that the proposal engendered a long discussion particularly focused on the use of departmental resources. The department was willing to negotiate the use of faculty time but urged outside funding for any "labs." The Ford Foundation was suggested as a possible funding source. Schultz and Lewis negotiated a compromise position: In the 1951–1952 academic year, Lewis initiated "Research in Labor Economics" – the first course listed under the department's "Special Seminars" in the University *Announcements* that did not bear the word "seminar" in its title, although informal usage (as in departmental minutes) refer to it (and several others) as "research seminars." Lewis's research course lasted three years and was followed (although not without a gap of five years) by "Research in Labor Economics and Industrial Relations," which was organized by both Lewis and Rees. Neither of these "research seminars" were quite workshops, and we do not yet know if they were funded externally.

Shortly before Lewis's first efforts, D. Gale Johnson "accidentally" introduced the first version of what we now think of as a Chicago workshop in the context of a time-saving meeting of students involved in an externally sponsored research project. Shortly before his death in 2003, Johnson described what happened to the alumni newsletter of the University's Division of the Social Sciences:

> In the late 1940s, the Rockefeller Foundation was a major supporter of our work in agricultural economics. There was a project for which I had primary responsibility on which six or seven students were involved in writing their dissertations. I was concerned with the problem of coordinating their work and meeting the objectives of the project. Instead of each student working entirely on his or her own, we decided to meet on a weekly basis. Prior to each meeting, one student would prepare a paper that was distributed to the others in advance so that they could read it and come prepared to assist the author in improving it. The paper was not presented at the meeting except by a brief summary. Nearly all of the meeting was devoted to the discussion of the presenter's research. (Johnson 2002)

Johnson goes on to say that Schultz liked what Johnson's workshop produced and started to encourage others to take up the idea. Friedman was the first formally to create a Johnson-style workshop, although the oral tradition and Schultz's memos and notes suggest that other research groups and even seminars also began to experiment with it in the early 1950s.[15]

In 1953, Friedman created the "Workshop in Money and Banking." According to Dan Hammond, Friedman started his workshop on a small

[15] Johnson's description of his workshop accords with the descriptions of the public finance, Latin American, and economic history workshops provided to me by Harberger (2002) and McCloskey (2001).

scale in 1951 (Hammond 1999a, 1999b), about the same time that Lewis was trying to start his lab. Friedman was able to initiate the workshop fully in 1953 when he received an honorarium from the Ford Commission on Money and Credit (Hammond 1989); in 1954, a three-year grant was obtained from the Rockefeller Foundation (Hammond 1999). The workshop was described in the *Announcements* for 1952 as follows:

> An experiment in combining training in research and learning of subject matter organized around a continuing investigation into monetary factors in business cycles. Students participate in this central investigation, both directly and by undertaking individual projects in the general area. Each project is directed toward the preparation of a report of publishable quality. Guidance is provided on general reading in the field, and informal seminars are held from time to time to discussion general issues or specific projects. Students are required to give full time to the workshop; they receive three credits per quarter of registration.

Gary Becker has provided us with a glimpse of the Money and Banking workshop in its early days. The graduate students who had registered in the workshop (including Becker himself) were allocated a room in the basement of the Social Science Research Building for their work,[16] and they met twice a week to discuss a paper written by either one of the participants (faculty or student) or a visiting professor. The paper for discussion was circulated ahead of time, and participants were assumed to have read it in advance. The paper presented provided a platform for discussion of theoretical, methodological, and empirical issues facing economic researchers in their current work. After the first year, the funding for the workshop was provided by the Rockefeller Foundation (Becker 1991). Between Johnson's workshop-style research project group and Friedman's workshop (late 1940s to 1955), the research half of the workshop system came to be.

The research side of the workshop system still lacked a curricular corollary. However, in 1954–1955 (the last year of the Cowles Commission's residency in Chicago), the department did unveil a significant change in its program of graduate study that paved the way for fuller implementation of the workshop system. The requirements for doctoral study in 1940 were described earlier in the paper. Students were required to have broad disciplinary knowledge and to specialize in three fields, one of which had to be economic theory, which included monetary economics. These requirements did not substantially change until 1954, although the department's field strengths had expanded to include agricultural economics and the

[16] Was the original plan to provide laboratory space? Reports from students in the 1950s suggest that common work space (for at least some of the workshops) continued at least into the early 1960s.

economics of consumption. The change initiated in 1954–1955 required students to take courses in economic theory, economic history, and statistics as part of their program of study, and to pass a set of preliminary written field examinations in price theory and monetary theory. The students would then specialize in one other field, in which they would take courses providing an economic analysis of that area of knowledge and eventually another preliminary exam. The price/money preliminaries (the "core" exams) were administered at the conclusion of the spring quarter of the first year of the doctoral program. The preliminary examination in their specialization was usually written in the second or third year of their program. Whereas the department had previously maintained high failure rates on all preliminary exams (as mentioned earlier), the core exams at the end of the first year now became the major obstacle to participation in the research program of the department. Students could and did retake the core exams after an initial failure, but the workshop system succeeded in part because the population of students working in them as research "apprentices" was much smaller than one might have estimated from the program's entering class.

The departmental description in the University *Announcements* also underwent a change in 1954 that identified how the new curricular requirements were going to be worked out over the next several years. An "introductory" statement was added, which began:

> The Department of Economics views the central problem of economic science as that of understanding the social organization of human and other scarce productive resources: principally the allocation of these resources among alternative uses by a system of exchange. The purpose of the Department is both to train economic scientists and to advance economic science.

At the end of the introductory statement, the connection between training scientists and advancing science is made: "The Department devotes a large proportion of its resources to research and research training. Some of the research is organized on a continuing basis by one or more faculty members working with associates and students in research centers and workshops." Lewis's vision of the department as a laboratory for economic science was closer to its full realization.[17]

[17] An interesting student perspective on the problems and solutions to the pre-1954 curriculum is seen in Lorne Sonley's memo to T. W. Schultz on "Improving the department of economics" (Department of Economics, University of Chicago Records, Box 41, Folder 2). Sonley, a Latin American student, argues for a first year set of courses and core exams much like what the department adopted in 1954, saying that the purpose of such a program would be "not to make economists but rather to isolate those who might become economists" (p. 4).

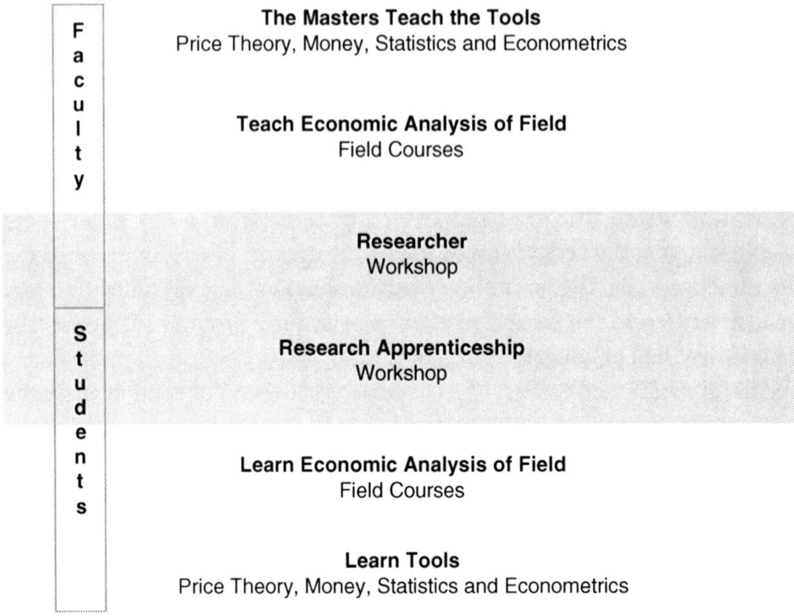

Figure 4.1. The Chicago Workshop System.

The following years saw the maturation of the workshop system. However, before passing on to its expansion across the department and, indeed, the university, we need to look more closely at the infrastructure the model provided for the department's eventual success. Figure 4.1 provides a schematic conceptualization of the model.

Students enter the diagram in Figure 4.1 at the bottom as new graduate students. Even students with significant background in economics were not excused from the core courses in price theory and money. Some perhaps grumbled about the requirement to sit through theory they had learned before, but the department thought it necessary because the core courses taught the *tools* that students would be using throughout their program. To emphasize the point, let me quote from a memo from Schultz to the department at the beginning of the fall quarter in 1957 (Department of Economics, University of Chicago Records, 1912–1961, Box 41, Folder 11):

> [T]he core courses, he indicated, provided the "tools for analysis" – not just theoretical knowledge, not ideological perspective, but tools.[18] When I asked a student who entered the program at the end of the period we are considering what students in

[18] Schultz includes statistics and econometrics as part of the tools, but the core exams were not expanded to include them until after 1980.

his generation did to pick their dissertation topic, he said that they would pour over the price theory books by Stigler (1966), Friedman (1976), and Alchian and Allen (1969) again and again trying to make the use of the tools almost second nature, and then think of ways to apply them to common issues that they had not been used on before (Thurman 2005).

The core exams examined whether a student had sufficiently mastered the use of the tools to move onto the project of applying them to a specific area of economic research. After a couple courses in the research area in addition to successful completion of the core exams, students were ready to become research apprentices. Their apprenticeship took place in the same setting that the masters and other researchers were conducting their research – the workshop. Once the workshop system spread across the department, few if any researchers, students, or faculty members were conducting their research outside the framework of the workshops.

In the Chicago workshop system, completion of a dissertation may have signaled the end of the apprenticeship and qualified one to continue conducting research and teach in a particular subfield of economics, but it did not necessarily make one a master of the discipline. Chicago operated in reverse of the way most economics departments function with regard to who teaches the entry-level theory courses. For Chicago, only the very best could help students begin to grasp intuitively the analytical power of the tools, and only they were to be trusted with teaching the core courses. Thus from the late 1920s until the early 1980s, the core price theory course was primarily taught by Viner, Knight, Friedman, Gary Becker, and Al Harberger. From 1948 to 1977, Friedman was the primary professor for the required money course.[19]

In order to facilitate the adoption of the workshop system across the department, the Economics Research Center was created in 1957. The purpose of the center was to "co-ordinate the research and research training activities of the Department" (*Announcements* 1957, p. 230). The center supported the organization and scheduling of workshops, distributed papers to workshop members, provided computer services, maintained the department's reference library, and published the research output of the workshops in the series "Studies in Economics." At its inception, the center coordinated activities for seven workshops or research groups: mathematical economics and econometrics; money and banking; labor economics and industrial relations; the newly formed Office of Agricultural Economic

[19] Friedman's service to the department in that capacity, then, almost matches Lewis's service as graduate student advisor.

Research; public finance; economics of consumption; and economic development. In his memo from September 21, 1957, Schultz also listed economic history and international trade as informal research groups. The center formally existed about ten years, until the mid-1960s, when the Center for Mathematical Studies in Business and Economics assumed some of its responsibilities, and the Center for Latin American Economic Studies became the focal point for much of the department's work in economic development. By the mid-1960s, however, there were at least a dozen workshops or research groups in operation.

How was all this workshop activity funded? The answer to that question at one moment in the department's history comes from a memo that Schultz wrote to the department in September 1956. After identifying the teaching assignments, workshops, and research groups operating during the 1956–1957 academic year, Schultz goes on to detail the department's external funding (see Table 4.1). The key participants are no surprise: Rockefeller and Ford dominate the list and provide a significant portion of the funds for the operation of the workshops and specific research projects.[20] Johnson tells us that Schultz sold the workshop idea to the Ford Foundation, which promptly started workshops at four other universities in the mid-1950s. However, the workshop system did not fit the other programs well, and Ford eventually stopped funding all workshops, including those at Chicago (Johnson 2002). Chicago's success, however, allowed it to find other funding sources to fill the gap. Schultz was also the origin of the Ford Professorships, which the Foundation also gave to the other universities that it tried the workshop model on. The professorship funded a visiting professor for a year, which allowed the department to maintain the Cowles tradition of including leading international scholars in the research activity of the department. The rest of the funds provided for specific research projects, postdoctoral fellowships, or graduate student fellowships. The fellowship funding indicated in Schultz's memo was supplemented by internal fellowships, sometimes provided by external sources. For example, in the 1956–1957 year, Yossef Attiyeh was a Falk Foundation Fellow and George Edward Schuh was a Sears, Roebuck Fellow in Agricultural Economics.[21]

[20] Resources for the Future was spun out of Ford Foundation operations.

[21] Internal fellowships also included funds from endowments by (or in honor of) Alex Hillman and Frank H. Knight. There were also fellowships provided internally from Marshall Field, the university's International House, and the university. One external source of fellowship funding not mentioned in Schultz's memo was the Canadian Social Science Research Council.

Table 4.1. *Department of Economics External Funding Sources, 1956–1957*

Grants	Total Value ($)	1956–57 Amount ($)
Ford Foundation (Ford Research Professorship)	500,000	25,000
ICA Chile Enterprise Fellowships and ERC support 3 yrs	375,000	125,000
Ford Foundation Workshop support 5 yrs	200,000	30,000
Rockefeller Foundation Money & Public finance Workshops 3 yrs (1 yr. left)	100,000	40,000
Resources for the Future 3 yrs (1 yr. left)	67,000	27,000
Russian Agriculture 2 yrs (1 yr. left)	47,000	22,000
Rockefeller Foundation consumption economics 3 yrs	45,000	15,000
Conservation Foundation 2 yrs	33,000	16,500
American Enterprise 2 yrs	17,250	8,625
National Science Foundation 2 yrs	13,000	6,500
Ford Foundation E. J. Hamilton research	12,500	8,000
Ford Foundation 3 pre-doctoral grants	10,200	10,200
Earhart Fellowships	6,000	6,000
S.S.R.C. Student Grants	5,000	5,000
Rockefeller Foundation Latin America ([Marto] Ballestreros)	5,000	5,000
Sears Roebuck Fellowships	4,000	4,000
Total	*1,439,950*	*353,825*

Notes: ICA = U.S. International Cooperation Administration; S.S.R.C. = Social Science Research Council; the Conservation Foundation existed from 1948 to 1968.

The extent to which the department's work in Chile and other Latin American countries funded the operation of all the workshops from its start may surprise some. The first year of the first multiyear contract between the department and the Universidad Católica de Chile was 1956–1957. Schultz was successful in ensuring that the contract included not only funds for student fellowships and for faculty support in Chile, but also for support of the research infrastructure at the University of Chicago. In 1959, Harberger launched both the Government Finance workshop and the Economic Development of Latin America workshop. They were merged in 1974 because most of the public finance participants were working on Latin American topics. Dozens of students from Chile, Argentina, Brazil, and other Latin American countries came through the Chicago program over the next thirty years; most stayed through the completion of their coursework, and some completed their dissertation after their return to Latin America, where they took university positions. Sebastian Edwards claims that he is the first of only a small number of Chileans who completed their dissertations in residence in Chicago (Edwards 2002).[22]

With its curricular implementation in place and the initial experimentation completed, the workshop system was firmly ensconced in the department by the late 1950s. By the mid-1960s, the departmental workshops included econometrics, industrial relations and labor economics, agricultural economics, government finance, money and banking, economic development in Latin America, industrial organization, urban studies, international economics, and economic history.

4.4. The Grindstone of Workshop Debate: Normalizing Science One Paper at a Time

So exactly what happened in a workshop? The answer to that varied by the workshop. The agricultural economics seminar and Harberger's public finance workshop were largely closed; only the faculty and graduate students involved in the project met. Members presented at various stages of their research, and discussion was focused on obstacles that the researcher/student faced and how they might be overcome (Harberger 2002; Muth 2002). Friedman's money and banking workshop was closer to what became the norm: Workshop meetings included faculty, students, and invited guests, with other department members sitting in as they pleased; papers were distributed ahead of time and everyone was expected to have done their reading. However, Friedman's workshop had the unusual practice of not allowing the paper's author to present the paper; instead, Friedman would begin by asking if there were any questions about the first page of the paper and then proceed through the entire paper page by page asking for comments. Of course, if a paper generated a lot of discussion, the page-by-page procedure would eventually be set aside as debates raged over the paper's use of the analytical tools, its methods and data, and its policy consequences.

The norm for workshop debate, however, is what David Levy (2001) refers to as "Chicago rules." The paper to be discussed is distributed ahead of time (remember, that meant mimeographs in the 1950s and 1960s!), and

22 Edwards says the only other Chilean he knows who finished in residence was his wife: Alejandra Cox Edwards.

workshop participants are expected to read it ahead of time. The paper's author (student, faculty, or visitor) knows that five minutes of uninterrupted time is provided to summarize the argument of the paper. After five minutes, questions can be asked from the floor. The quality of the paper's argument will be directly correlated with the intensity of participant discussion: You know your paper has little to offer if you are not interrupted early, and are simply allowed to proceed for forty-five minutes or so. By the 1970s, most of the workshops used this common format.

Workshop discussion and criticism regularly employed the tools that all Chicago economists had learned to use already. The regular application of these tools in workshop discussion meant that participants quickly "cut to the chase." Deirdre McCloskey (McCloskey 2001) described workshop debate as the process of "finding where the bodies were buried" in the paper. Although the intense debates in Stigler's Industrial Organization workshop and the Law and Economics workshop organized in the law school are the most notorious, and gave Chicago workshops a reputation for chewing up visitors, most workshop debate was intense without being insulting.[23] For workshop members, exposure to the regular pattern of questions asked by senior members of the workshop taught what economic research required. Week after week, paper by paper, participants saw a common format of analytical criticism and research success carried out by the active participants. The purpose of the workshop was not to commend one on a job well done, nor was it to provide a friendly environment supportive of fledgling endeavors. A scientific laboratory has a single purpose: the pursuit of truth. The Chicago workshop, in its own way, had the same goal. When asked, Harold Demsetz (2002) described the Chicago workshop in two words: "Prove it." Soon-to-be doctoral candidates heard, "Go thou and do likewise." And their participation in the workshop system over the coming years ensured that many of them would be able to do exactly that.

4.5. Expansion and Contraction

By the mid-1960s, then, the workshop system was fully developed at Chicago and was integral to almost all of the research conducted by the department. Table 4.2 provides a list of the workshops formally identified in

[23] Harold Demsetz reported that a visiting scholar once asked Stigler at the luncheon before his presentation where he should present his paper from (meaning whether he would be expected to stand at a podium or sit at a desk). Stigler's response was: "[I]n your case, you will probably want to present from underneath the desk."

Table 4.2. *Department of Economics Workshops & Research Groups, 1978, and their year of initial operation*

Agricultural Economics	1947
Labor Economics (and Industrial Relations)	1951
Money & Banking	1952
Econometrics (and Mathematical Economics)	1957
Economic Development of Latin America	1957
Economic History	1959
Industrial Organization	1960
Urban Economics	1961
International Economics	1965
Special Problems in the Economics of Education	1966
Applications of Economics	1971
Economic Theory	1974
Applied Price Theory	1978
Resource Analysis	1978

the University *Announcements* of 1978 and their initial dates of operation.[24] Yet even this list does not indicate how extensively the workshop system coordinated the research of faculty and students. Between 1960 and 1980, several other workshops were started in the department and either merged into existing workshops or dropped as faculty came and went. For example, Harberger's successful Public Finance workshop was merged into the Economic Development of Latin America workshop in 1974.[25] An Asian Economic Development workshop ran for several years in the late 1960s.

The role that the workshops played in the eventual success of the Chicago School is perhaps best illustrated by the fact that about the time that the School's influence reached its peak, the University ended up adopting the workshop system as a model for graduate research across the humanities and social sciences. In 1980, President Hanna Gray charged a Commission on Graduate Study with conducting a study of graduate education at the University of Chicago. Although declining graduate student enrollments and lengthening completion time-periods precipitated the study, the commission returned frequently to the striking dichotomy between the

[24] From observations made by different participants, one should expect that each of these came into existence informally prior to their formal recognition in the University *Announcements*.

[25] Robert Lucas was one of the products of Harberger's government finance workshop. Two books collect the production of the workshop's research: Harberger (1960) and Harberger and Bailey (1969).

students' experience of post-graduate research in the two science divisions – where students were quickly integrated into laboratories and functioned in research teams including faculty and technical staff – and the "lonely scholar" experience of most students in the humanities and social sciences divisions. Not only did the students in the sciences complete their degrees sooner, but they also reported a more satisfactory experience. Gary Becker and Stephen Stigler (son of George Stigler) were members of the commission, and the economics department's workshop system was soon circulated as a possible model for other humanities and social science research. The commission's report (known as the Baker Report because the commission's chair was Keith M. Baker, now at Stanford University) recommended the establishment of research institutes in both the humanities and social sciences divisions. Each institute would centralize the administrative functions necessary to run a large set of workshops and research seminars (Baker 1982).[26]

Today, the University's Council of Advanced Studies oversees approximately seventy workshops each year, spanning the humanities and social sciences. Each workshop functions in a manner analogous to the economics workshops. Students register to participate after completion of the first portion of their graduate program. Faculty mentoring of graduate research occurs within the context of the workshops, and participants attend regular seminars with both internal and external presenters. Economics is represented in the council, but many of the economics-related workshops, which already had a funding base from prior sources, function independently, operating today out of the Graduate School of Business, the Harris School of Public Policy, and the Law School.

4.6. Conclusion

The success of the Chicago School of Economics has been attributed to its ideological positioning, the power of its ideas, and the brilliance and strong work ethic of its leaders. The argument made here is that the adoption of the workshop system in the 1940s catalyzed Chicago's success. Am I arguing that, in the absence of the workshop system, Chicago economics would not have been successful? No. But the foundation of the School's success lies not in the power of its ideas or the brilliance of its people, but rather in

[26] Becker opposed the commission's recommendation on the grounds that no central implementation and coordination of workshops was necessary; where workshops were an efficient solution, they would arise spontaneously (Baker 1982).

the daily grind of its research workshops, which normalized the Chicago approach by coupling of the tools of price theory with empirical research to produce an applied policy science.

References

Department of Economics, University of Chicago Records, 1912–1961. University of Chicago, Special Collections Research Center.

Alchian, Armen A., and William R. Allen. 1969. *Exchange and Production: Theory in Use*. Belmont, CA: Wadsworth.

Amadae, S. M. 2003. *Rationalizing Capitalist Democracy: The Cold War Origins of Rational Choice Liberalism*. Chicago, IL: University of Chicago Press.

Baker, Keith M. 1982. Report of the Commission on Graduate Education. *University of Chicago Record*, May 3, 67–180.

Becker, Gary S. 1991. "Milton Friedman." In *Remembering the University of Chicago: Teachers, Scientists, and Scholars*, edited by E. Shils. Chicago: University of Chicago Press.

Bulmer, Martin. 1984. *The Chicago School of Sociology: Institutionalization, Diversity, and the Rise of Sociological Research*. Chicago, IL: University of Chicago Press.

Demsetz, Harold. 2002. Interview with Ross B. Emmett. Chicago Economics Oral History Project. University of California, Los Angeles, February.

Economics, Cowles Commission for Research. 1953. *Economic Theory and Measurement: A Twenty Year Research Report, 1932–1952*. Chicago: Cowles Commission for Research in Economics.

Edwards, Sebastian. 2002. Interview with Ross B. Emmett. Chicago Economics Oral History Project. University of California, Los Angeles, February.

Emmett, Ross B. 1998. "Entrenching Disciplinary Competence: The Role of General Education and Graduate Study in Chicago Economics." In *From Interwar Pluralism to Postwar Neoclassicism*, edited by M. S. Morgan and M. Rutherford. Durham: Duke University Press.

2009. "Did the Chicago School Reject Frank H. Knight? Assessing Frank Knight's Place in the Chicago Economics Tradition." In *Frank Knight & the Chicago School in American Economics*. Abingdon UK: Routledge.

Friedman, Milton. 1962. *Capitalism and Freedom*. Chicago: University of Chicago Press.

1976. *Price Theory*. Chicago, IL: Aldine.

Hammond, J. Daniel. 1989. An Interview with Milton and Rose Friedman. San Francisco, CA.

1999a. "Introduction." In *The Legacy of Milton Friedman as Teacher*, edited by J. D. Hammond. Cheltenham, UK: Edward Elgar.

1999b. "Labels and Substance: Friedman's Restatement of the Quantity Theory." *History of Political Economy* 31 (3): 449–71.

Harberger, Arnold C. 1960. *The Demand for Durable Goods*. Chicago, IL: University of Chicago Press.

2002. Interview with Ross B. Emmett. Chicago Economics Oral History Project. Los Angeles, February.

2008. *When Capital Earns a 20% Real Return, What is Left for Labor? A Glimpse into Latin American Reality*. Center for Global Development 2007 [cited May 20, 2008]. Available from http://www.sarpn.org.za/documents/d0002756/Capital_returns_CGD_Transcript_Aug2007.pdf.

Harberger, Arnold C., and Martin J. Bailey, eds. 1969. *The Taxation of Income from Capital*. Washington, DC: Brookings Institution.

Hildreth, Clifford. 1986. *The Cowles Commission in Chicago, 1939–1955*. Edited by M. Beckmann and W. Krelle. *Lecture Notes in Economics and Mathematical Systems*. Berlin: Springer-Verlag.

Johnson, D. Gale. 2002. "D. Gale Johnson Reflects." *Social Science News*, Division of the Social Sciences, University of Chicago (Autumn): 1–2.

Katona, George. 1945. *Price Control and Business: Field Studies among Producers and Distributors of Consumer Goods in the Chicago Area, 1942–44*. Bloomington, IN: Principia Press.

Levine, Donald N. 2006. *Powers of the Mind: The Reinvention of Liberal Learning in America*. Chicago, IL: University of Chicago Press.

Levy, David M. 2001. Interview with Ross B. Emmett. Chicago Economics Oral History Project. Buchanan House, George Mason University, Fairfax, June.

McCloskey, Deirdre N. 2001. Interview with Ross B. Emmett. Chicago Economics Oral History Project. Chicago, May.

McNeill, William H. 1991. *Hutchins' University: A Memoir of the University of Chicago, 1929–1950*. Chicago: University of Chicago Press.

Muth, Richard. 2002. Interview with Ross B. Emmett. Chicago Economics Oral History Project. Atlanta, January.

Rutherford, Malcolm. 2010. "Chicago Economics and Institutionalism." In *The Elgar Companion to the Chicago School of Economics*, edited by R. B. Emmett. Cheltenham, UK: Edward Elgar.

Stigler, George J. 1966. *The Theory of Price*. 3rd. ed. New York: Macmillan.

"Theodore William Schultz." In *The Elgar Companion to the Chicago School of Economics*, edited by R. B. Emmett. Cheltenham, U.K: Edward Elgar.

Thurman, Walter N. 2005. Interview with Ross B. Emmett. Chicago Economics Oral History Project. Property & Environment Research Center, Bozeman, MT, July.

Van Horn, Robert. 2007. *The Origins of the Chicago School of Law and Economics*. Department of Economics, South Bend, IN: Notre Dame University.

Van Overtveldt, Johan. 2007. *The Chicago School: How the University of Chicago Assembled the Thinkers Who Revolutionized Economics and Business*. Chicago, IL: Agate.

Wirth, Louis, ed. 1940. *ElevenTwenty-Six: A Decade of Social Science Research*. Chicago, IL: University of Chicago Press.

Wolff, Nancy, and Jim Hayward. 2007. *The Historical Development of the Department of Economics at Iowa State, 1929–1985* n.d. [cited July 22, 2007]. Available from http://www.econ.iastate.edu/department/history/EconomicsHistory1929–1985.pdf.

FIVE

George Stigler, the Graduate School of Business, and the Pillars of the Chicago School

Edward Nik-Khah

5.1. Introduction

George Stigler is universally regarded as a principal architect of the postwar Chicago School. Gary Becker (1993) recalls Stigler as "Mr. Micro" to Milton Friedman's "Mr. Macro," a crucial figure whose stature was equal to that of Friedman in the postwar Chicago School of Economics. Harold Demsetz (1993, 794) recalls Stigler as having a "penchant for defending and extending [Chicago] neoclassical price theory." Picking up on this theme, Warren Samuels (in Moss 2002, 642) has characterized Stigler as the "leader" and "principal author" of Chicago Economics, more important in some respects than even Friedman in that he sought to reformulate Chicago price theory "to absorb what hitherto had been excluded." Similarly, many credit Stigler with extending price theory to industrial organization, regulation, politics, and science (Mincer 1983; Peltzman 1993; Diamond 2005). For these reasons, one can agree with the judgment of Melvin Reder (1982, 10) that Stigler's arrival at Chicago in 1958 was "key to the development and eventual dominance" of the postwar Chicago School. Yet despite Stigler's important role at Chicago, there exists evidence that this role is not entirely understood.

Stigler's relationship to Chicago is very different than those of the other principal architects of the school. He arrived at Chicago much later than

Author's note: I am grateful to Philip Mirowski, Rob Van Horn, Bruce Caldwell, and Ross Emmett for their helpful suggestions. I would like to thank Stephen Stigler for his permission to access the George J. Stigler papers and Nancy Martin for her help with the W. Allen Wallis papers. This chapter benefited from presentation at the Rethinking the Chicago School Conference at the University of Notre Dame and the 2008 History of Economics Society Conference at York University. Archival materials from the George J. Stigler Papers and Walgreen Foundation Papers, Special Collections Research Center, Regenstein Library, University of Chicago and the W. Allen Wallis Papers, Department of Rare Books and Special Collections, Rush Rhees Library, University of Rochester quoted with permission.

Friedman and Aaron Director (who both arrived in 1946). Stigler accepted a joint appointment in the Graduate School of Business (GSB) and the economics department, but was housed in the GSB – a fact the significance of which has never been fully addressed.[1] Finally, during his stay he trained relatively few students. Whereas one often encounters celebrations of Friedman's influence as a classroom teacher (e.g., Hammond 1999), the reviews of Stigler as a teacher are mixed at best (Freedman 2003; Levy in Moss 2002; Sowell 1993). Suffice it to say that whatever Stigler's influence in the events at Chicago, it could not have operated in precisely the same fashion as that of these other figures.

This chapter will argue that Stigler's contribution to the Chicago School far exceeded authoring *The Theory of Price* and providing a model for how to write a good "Chicago style" paper in new areas. Using unexploited archival materials, this chapter will show that from his arrival at Chicago's GSB, Stigler's designated role was to be an *empire builder*. Although there exists no systematic treatment of this role, one does find in the recollections of those closest to Stigler an acknowledgment of his institution-building skills and their importance for developments at Chicago. In his memorial address to the Mont Pèlerin Society, Allen Wallis (1993, 775) recalled Stigler's "great skills as an administrator and an organizer."[2] Demsetz (1993, 806–807; 1982, 656) points out that Stigler influenced the profession, "not only through his writings … [but also through] the Industrial Organization workshop, which Stigler organized and led for many years," and by "financ[ing] the research of others." Ronald Coase (1991, 477) recalls Stigler's creation of the Center for the Study of the Economy and the State, "which has resulted in the publication of many articles by many talented economists who have had fellowships at the Center and has, in consequence had a considerable impact on the views on regulation held by economists."

There are three immediate advantages to examining the empire-building activities of Stigler. A first advantage of taking this approach is that it sheds light on some important institutions Stigler had a hand in constructing. At the GSB, Stigler was able to repurpose an unusual institution (the

[1] Craig Freedman (2003, p288n6) reports a conversation with Lester Telser in which the latter suggests that this physical separation is important to understanding Stigler's unusual relationship with the economics department. Freedman does not follow up on Telser's suggestion.

[2] Wallis continues: "…both Jacques Barzun at Columbia and Edward Levi at Chicago recognized [his administrative talents] and tried to seduce George into administrative posts." Levi offered the deanship of Chicago's GSB to Stigler upon Wallis's departure for the University of Rochester.

Walgreen Foundation) and construct another (the Center for the Study of the Economy and the State) to promote his approach to "governmental control of economic life" as well as his views about the "capacities" of democracy, with implications reaching far beyond Chicago, as noted by Coase and others. A second advantage is that it provides a perspective on aspects of his career that have been ignored or suppressed by extant accounts. Stigler, who served as president of the Mont Pèlerin Society (MPS) and often published his academic work alongside more conspicuously political tracts (work that was often presented at meetings of the MPS), has been described as a "quintessential conservative" economist (McCann and Perlman 1993, 994), an impression he did not discourage. Yet both supporters and critics of Stigler's work have struggled to reconcile his academic work with his political or ideological work. This has led some to express puzzlement about what appears to be an inconsistency between Stigler's theory about markets and his actions with respect to policy.[3] Finally, understanding Stigler's empire-building activities sheds light not only on "how the University of Chicago assembled the thinkers who revolutionized economics business," to take the subtitle of one recent journalistic account of the history of the Chicago School (Van Overtveldt 2007), but also on the goals of crucial figures at the GSB to more precisely define the nature of the "revolution" achieved there.

To provide a framework within which to consider Stigler's empire-building activities, this chapter looks to Stigler's participation in the neoliberal project of the MPS, and argues that this participation was crucial not only to the development of his ideas about politics and regulation, but also to those of economics and science. This chapter is not the first to use Stigler's participation in the MPS to explain aspects of his work. Craig Freedman (2008) has argued that Stigler's participation in the MPS project conditioned him to place ideological considerations above scientific considerations, effectively making him "a partisan" (66). Although it is true that Stigler's participation in the MPS was a crucial factor shaping his career, it is important to note that Stigler disagreed with other Chicago MPS members about matters fundamental to their approach to markets, and it is therefore misleading to characterize Stigler as a partisan.[4] Stigler's participation in the

[3] For example, whereas Stigler portrayed regulation as sought by and operated for the benefit of industries, industries opposed some of the most important regulations of the day, and in at least one case directly supported Stigler's own intellectual efforts to oppose regulation. Stigler's nuanced position on the relationship between industries' wants and regulation is examined in Section Four.

[4] In glossing the disagreement between Friedman and Stigler as pertaining only to the public role of the economist, Freedman (2008, p. 209) minimizes its significance. Section Four provides a more comprehensive explanation of the source of Friedman and Stigler's disagreement.

MPS project was crucial to the unfolding of his career, but so too were the disagreements he had with other Chicago neoliberals.

To capture the interplay between Chicago neoliberals' commitment to broad aims and their disagreement about some fundamental issues, this chapter depicts the Chicago School as being composed of three distinct "pillars," one located in the business school, one in the Law School, and one in the economics department. Each pillar buttressed the larger MPS project of promoting neoliberal views. The portrait of Stigler that emerges from this chapter is someone committed to the MPS project, but whose participation was inflected by the circumstances surrounding his location in the business school and his own beliefs about the operation of the "marketplace of ideas." This project would not only distinguish the GSB from rival business departments, but also from the economics department, with profound consequences for the Chicago School, other business schools such as Rochester's and Carnegie Mellon's, and for public policy. George Stigler is justly famous for his contributions to the Chicago School; the purpose of this chapter is to come to a better understanding of *all* the contributions for which he should be famous.

5.2. Building the "Stigler Team": The Walgreen Foundation and the Transformation of Business Education at Chicago

The Graduate School of Business (GSB) at the University of Chicago is widely regarded as one of the most important programs for the postwar development of U.S. business education. Although there is some disagreement about whether the influence of Chicago on business education should be celebrated or lamented, most agree that academic economists played a crucial role in the developments there: Some observers point out the "uncommonly close relationship" between business and economics (Schlossman, Michael, and Harold 1998, 18); others stress the "linked ecologies" between the fields (Fourcade and Khurana 2008); and others simply label the business school a "great economics department" (Van Overtveldt 2007) and thereby eliminate any distinction between the two. There are good reasons these accounts focus on the role of economists at the GSB, because to an unusual degree economists occupied positions of administrative and intellectual leadership at Chicago's GSB. Economists or those with economic training have occupied key administrative roles at the GSB (W. Allen Wallis and George Shultz as deans, and James Lorie as associate dean), and several prominent economists (including six Nobel laureates in economics) have called the GSB home.

In addition to standard channels of influence at the GSB, Chicago economists were involved in rather novel (and underappreciated) forms of alliance formation and institution building and repurposing, efforts that would have consequences for the GSB and ultimately for the entirety of U.S. business education. The central figure in these efforts was the most prominent hire that Wallis made during his tenure, his former classmate at Chicago, George Stigler.

Stigler joined the GSB in the midst of a period of revolutionary change at Chicago and across U.S. business education, a time during which traditional leaders in business education underwent radical transformation and a handful of newcomers assumed prominence. According to Augier et al. (2005, 89), "the postwar period provided an opportunity for university presidents, academically oriented business school faculty, and visionary business executives to combine with external forces to impose academic respectability on the business school community." Of these external forces, the most important was a joint effort between the military (which funded studies of optimal decision rules through the use of engineering, operations research, and economics) and the Ford Foundation (which worked to promote this form of analytical decision making to business schools). They found a program receptive to developing these types of decision techniques at the upstart Carnegie Graduate School of Industrial Administration (GSIA)[5]; Ford immediately christened this type of program the "New Look" in business education, designated Carnegie its "advanced projects laboratory," and soon thereafter held up Carnegie as a model for other business schools (Schlossman et al. 1998). Carnegie's profile increased as it maintained its relationship with the Air Force and the Office of Naval Research and undertook new projects sponsored by the Ford Foundation (Augier and Prietula 2007; Simon 1991).[6] As a result of these efforts, Carnegie developed behavioral theories of the firm, ran early experiments, examined themes from the computer, and wove all these elements into a program that emphasized the social responsibility of the corporation.[7] Emboldened by the

5 According to Judy Klein (2008, 28), "The GSIA marketed their interdisciplinary analytical decision-making approach as a contrast to the casebook approach of what they perceived as a key rival, the business school at Harvard University."

6 Major research projects undertaken during that period included the *Organization* project by Herbert Simon and James March and the *Behavioral Theory of the Firm* project by Richard Cyert and James March.

7 "It is likely that the social responsibility of the corporation and of the businessman in it will continue to bulk larger in the day-to-day life of most business firms. In contrast to any simple emphasis on short-term profit maximization, explicit interest in "the public good" as a legitimate and important goal of business behavior will continue to grow. Business will participate in a conscious fashion to an increasing extent in the social-economic process of our democratic society" (Bach, quoted in Gleeson and Schlossman 1995).

Carnegie experiment, Ford initiated a program to fund Chicago and three other "Centers of Excellence" (Harvard, Stanford, and Columbia) to serve as model programs from which practices would "trickle down" to lower-tier business schools. Ford was especially enthusiastic about the prospects for Chicago, primarily due to the naming of Wallis as dean of Chicago's Graduate School of Business (Schlossman et al. 1998).[8] Ford hoped that Chicago would, alongside Carnegie, provide a "Midwestern counterweight" to Harvard's more "clinical" (and to many, outdated) approach (Schlossman et al. 1998, 18); to that end, Ford financed Chicago's efforts to the tune of $1,375,000 – its second-largest commitment to a business program. Wallis then went on a hiring spree, luring to the GSB, among others, the Columbia economist George Stigler, in this case with the Walgreen Chair for the Study of American Institutions.

Although the hire of Stigler was celebrated at Chicago, the shift in emphasis signaled by offering the most prestigious and well-funded professorship in the business school (if not the entire university) to an economist known for his full-throated opposition to alternative theories of the firm provoked some concern at Ford: "Emphasis on the economic ingredient of the curriculum (and probably of a traditional Chicago mold particularly if George Stigler accepts the Walgreen professorship) might override the other social science elements" (Robert Gordon, quoted in Fourcade and Khurana 2008, 29). Subsequent events would reveal the prescience of this memo: In the years following Stigler's hire, the environment would become so hostile at the GSB to behavioral science as to invite comparison with the noxious dispute surrounding the Cowles Commission, eventually producing calls for the "complete elimination" of behavioral sciences from the curriculum; the economists at the GSB were a principal source of this opposition (Van Overtveldt 2007, 252–253).

With many of the changes at Chicago already under way, Stigler immediately assumed a position of leadership among GSB economists. He was already associated with Chicago through his friendships with Wallis and other luminaries, such as Milton Friedman in the economics department and Aaron Director in the Law School. Chicago economists were quite familiar with his existing body of work; by that time, the *Theory of Price* had already gone into its second edition and Chicago economics graduate students were expected to familiarize themselves with it (McDonald 2009). Stigler's control of the Walgreen Foundation bolstered his stature. The Walgreen Foundation had

[8] As was the case with Carnegie's Herbert Simon, Wallis had previously advised the Ford Foundation's behavioral science division (Augier 2000, p. 428).

been established by a grant from the drugstore magnate Charles Walgreen; upon Stigler's arrival, it was relocated from political science to the GSB, and was placed (along with the Walgreen Chair) under Stigler's control by Wallis. Because this is the first account of the role of the Walgreen Foundation in the development of the GSB, it will be necessary to discuss its founding and subsequent activities in some detail.

The Walgreen Foundation was born of a troubled time at the university: Charges of "radicalism" were regularly lodged against the faculty by prominent Chicago businessmen and national politicians and were trumpeted by William Randolph Hearst's *Chicago Herald-Examiner*.[9] Against this backdrop, Walgreen became convinced in 1935 that Chicago professors were indoctrinating his niece Lucille Norton into "communism and free love"; outraged, Walgreen demanded a public inquiry. He got his wish, but the inquiry vindicated the university of the most serious charges.[10] Walgreen eventually made a donation to the university in the amount of $550,000 as a *mea culpa*, but also to "foster greater appreciation of American life and values among University of Chicago students." The resulting Walgreen Foundation, which was constituted by these funds, was placed under the authority of Jerome Kerwin, Professor of Political Science at Chicago. Under Kerwin the foundation funded student research, supported faculty salaries, and, most prominently, initiated a lecture series that resulted in the publication of several books by such notables as Eric Vogelin and Leo Strauss. The funds were also intended to support a Walgreen Professorship, but the position went unfilled for several years. Then, in 1955, Lawrence Kimpton, now president of the university, halted the activities of the Walgreen Foundation and ordered a review of its past activities. After a few years of inactivity, Kimpton relocated the Walgreen Foundation to the GSB, at which time Wallis offered its chair to Stigler, who was named the first Walgreen Professor.

Stigler's acceptance of the "luxuriously upholstered" Walgreen Chair was celebrated by his colleagues in song (Friedman 1993, 771):

Twenty-five years for the tale to unfold
Yo-ho-ho and again there are three

[9] The account of the circumstances surrounding the establishment of the Walgreen Foundation provided in this paragraph draws from (Mayer 1993; Boyer 2002).

[10] There were, however, serious repercussions. The panel recommended forced retirement for Robert Morss Lovett, and that Frederick Schuman be censured; Robert Hutchins, president of the University of Chicago, faced a near rebellion by the trustees, who were worried that taking too strong a stand in favor of academic freedom would compromise the ability of the University to raise funds from the business community.

Walgreen was good and Kimpton was bold
Yo-ho-ho and again there are three.

The "three" were Wallis, Friedman, and Stigler, who had been friends since their graduate school days at Chicago. Although this reunion has been characterized as "key to the development and eventual dominance" of the postwar Chicago School (Reder 1982, 10), the circumstances leading to this reunion – the removal of the Walgreen Foundation from social science and its placement in business under the control of Stigler – have received little scrutiny. In recalling the events leading to the transfer of the Walgreen Foundation to Stigler's control, Wallis describes having convinced Kimpton to "transfer the Walgreen Foundation (which had been moribund) to the business school" (Wallis in Olkin 1991, 136). However, one would like to know how he convinced Kimpton to take a program designed to "foster greater appreciation of American life and values among University of Chicago students" from the social sciences division and place it in a *business program for graduate students.* An important contributing factor was that the actors in the original Walgreen drama were no longer on the scene: Kimpton replaced Robert Hutchins, who left for the Ford Foundation; and Charles Walgreen, Jr. succeeded his father, who died in 1939, as president of Walgreen's. One of Kimpton's priorities was to convince large donors that their gifts to the university would be used in accordance with their wishes (Friedman and Friedman 1998, 187). And Charles Walgreen, Jr. was not bashful about expressing his wishes. For example, in a letter addressed to Kerwin, Charles Walgreen, Jr. objected to the placement of the Nobel Peace Prize winner (and liberal intellectual) Ralph Bunche on the May 1950 program:

> Although this is most interesting and Mr. Bunche's material is very well presented, I am afraid it is somewhat far afield from the basic purposes of the Foundation – the Study of American Institutions. It would seem that a program should be inaugurated which will portray more fundamentally the American way of life.[11]

Especially noteworthy is the suggestion that "a program should be inaugurated," because presumably Walgreen felt the Walgreen Foundation was that very program. Following this note, Kerwin's activities were subjected to more oversight, and in the subsequent year Kerwin was asked to submit a report of his activities. In a 1955 letter to Kerwin, the dean of the social science division reported that Kimpton ordered a review of the Foundation's

[11] Letter from Charles Walgreen, Jr. to Jerome Kerwin, dated May 9, 1950 (WFRL Box 1, Folder: 3).

activities as a result of two "long discussions with Charles R. Walgreen" on July 22 and July 26.[12] Charles Walgreen, Jr. was therefore instrumental in the cessation of the Foundation's activities in 1955.

In addition to his disapproval over some of the Foundation's activities, Walgreen was also displeased with Chicago's failure to hire a Walgreen Professor, as Wallis recalls in an unpublished interview:

> [The Walgreen Professorship] had been set up in the Division of the Social Sciences and they never filled the job. Charlie Walgreen [Jr.] had the right of veto on the first appointment and he vetoed the people they thought up, most of whom were inappropriate, I think. So the dean of the social sciences, Mort Grodzins, said to Kimpton, "Well you know it is improper for the university to take a professorship with a string like that attached to it anyway, and we should give the money back." He was talking that up and I said to Kimpton, "Well, I don't think it was improper – he doesn't have the right to make the appointment, he just has the right to veto it. We won't appoint anybody we don't want. And if you turn it over to the business school, I'll guarantee that we'll make a first-rate appointment within a year," because Charlie Walgreen [Jr.] was beginning to holler about, "Well, if you aren't going to appoint somebody after 20 years" (which it was), "How about giving the money back?" And, so that's why we had the Walgreen Professorship. (WWRL Box 20, File Meckling Interview)

In this passage Wallis provides two remarkable revelations. First, Wallis reveals that Walgreen was directly responsible for the failure to hire a Walgreen Professor. Second, Wallis reveals that the primary reason for the relocation of the Foundation to the GSB was Wallis's willingness to accept Walgreen's participation in an academic hiring decision – a role that struck others as improper. Wallis elaborates on what his accepting Walgreen's role entailed: "[T]he key thing here was we had to have Leonard Read's approval, because that's who Charlie Walgreen was going to rely on.... And Leonard took the line, when Jim [Lorie] and I went to see him, that anybody we wanted was OK with him."[13] In light of the difficulties encountered by previous attempts to name a Walgreen Professor, the trust shown by Walgreen's advisor in Wallis's judgment might seem a bit curious. However, Read's confidence in Wallis (as well as the significance of Wallis's acceptance of Read's participation in the Walgreen Professorship decision and the agreement to

12 Letter from Chauncy Harris to Jerome Kerwin, dated July 29, 1955 (WFRL Box 1, Folder: 4).

13 Leonard Read was the founding president of the Foundation for Economic Education, a think tank devoted to arguing for "the sanctity of private property, individual liberty, the rule of law, the free market, and the moral superiority of individual choice and responsibility over coercion" (available: http://fee.org/about/a-tradition-of-freedom/). He is most widely known as the author of the essay "I, Pencil."

give the Walgreen Professorship to Stigler) becomes understandable when considered in light of an important bit of background Stigler shared with both Wallis and Read.

Stigler had enrolled in Chicago's Ph.D. program in economics in 1933, and had quickly gravitated toward his fellow students Wallis and Friedman, as well as Frank Knight and Henry Simons. Knight became Stigler's dissertation supervisor, and Stigler completed a study of production and distribution in the history of economic thought under him; Simons's *A Positive Program for Laissez Faire* deeply influenced Stigler's views on the appropriate economic role of the state, particularly on the need for robust antimonopoly policies to safeguard competition (Stigler 1988b). However, Stigler's views, along with those of Friedman and Wallis, underwent a profound transformation in the 1950's, largely as a result of his participation in the Mont Pèlerin Society (MPS).[14] Organized by Friedrich Hayek, the MPS was a group of economists, political theorists, and other intellectuals that devoted itself to reformulating liberalism as a counterblast against social welfare liberalism and socialism. The MPS turned out to be an obligatory passageway for those most heavily involved in constructing the postwar Chicago School of Economics (Van Horn and Mirowski 2009), including Hayek (who came to the University of Chicago in 1950), Stigler's classmates and friends Friedman and Wallis, and Aaron Director. Certain business intellectuals also participated – including, importantly, Leonard Read.

In the context of their shared participation in the MPS project, Stigler came to believe that monopoly behavior was "outside the logic of the [market] system," now preferring instead to conceive firm behavior as efficiency enhancing (Stigler 1963, 87–88; 1988b, 161–166). With respect to policy, Stigler revised his beliefs about the appropriate economic role of the state and now opposed an activist antitrust policy. The link between his academic work and his participation in the MPS project is evident in such works as *The Citizen and the State*, which places pieces such as "What Can Regulators Regulate?" alongside more conspicuously political tracts as "Reflections on Liberty." Wallis's own contributions would be published in his *The Overgoverned Society*.

As Stigler has since noted (1988b, 148), there was no "Chicago School" in the current sense of the term prior to the first meeting of the MPS, but in the context of that project, Stigler, Director, Friedman, Wallis, and others

[14] Rob Van Horn (Chapter 10, this volume) makes clear just how profound were the changes in Chicago's attitudes toward monopoly by viewing these changes from the perspective of Stigler's (and Friedman's, Wallis's, and Director's) teacher Jacob Viner.

set to the task of constructing one. More to the point, Wallis's offer of the Walgreen Chair to Stigler and Leonard Read's (and Walgreen's) approval of this offer should be understood in the context of their shared participation in the MPS project. Therefore, the true significance of Stigler's arrival was that it strengthened the neoliberal project within the business school.

Shortly after taking control of the Walgreen Foundation, Stigler completely revised its mission: He shed the obligation to educate undergraduate students, creatively reinterpreted its mission to promote study of the "American way of life," and announced his intention to devote the Walgreen resources to a study of the "causes and effects of governmental control over economic life."[15] He then hired a fulltime research assistant (Claire Friedland), established the famous Industrial Organization Workshop, and began to fund research he deemed relevant to the study of governmental control. Although Stigler possessed neither the administrative authority of an Allen Wallis (who served as dean of the GSB) nor the classroom authority of a Milton Friedman (who taught price theory in the economics department; Stigler taught no core courses), control of the Walgreen Foundation enabled him to build and support the activities of what Harold Demsetz has since called "the Stigler team."[16] Between 1958 and 1980, the Walgreen Foundation provided well over one hundred fellowship grants, with the vast majority over $1,000 (in unadjusted dollars) and several over $10,000 (GSRL Box 3, File: University of Chicago Walgreen Fellowship and Grants). The purposes for these fellowships ranged from stipends and tuition waivers to postdoctoral fellowships to research grants for both Chicago faculty and visitors. Recipients of support included Lester Telser, Harold Demsetz, Reuben Kessel, James Lorie, John McGee, Richard Posner, Peter Pashigian, Sam Peltzman, Gary Becker, and Robert Lucas,

[15] Letter of Stigler to Walgreen, dated December 28, 1959 (GSRL Box 13, File: Walgreen Correspondence).

[16] Letter of Harold Demsetz to Stigler, dated July 21, 1972 (GSRL Box 7, File: Demsetz #1). Walgreen was completely on board with the decision to repurpose the Foundation. In a 1959 letter to Wallis, soon after Stigler's arrival, Walgreen gushed, "The Walgreen Foundation has really increased it's [sic] stature!" Letter of Walgreen to Wallis, dated December 28, 1959 (GSRL Box 13, File: Walgreen). When Stigler reported to Walgreen in 1964 that "Chicago is consolidating its position as the leading center for the study of industrial organization and public control in the world" (letter of Stigler to Walgreen dated March 25, 1964, GSRL Box 13, File: Walgreen Correspondence), the latter raised no objection (unlike with Kerwin). During the twenty-three years Stigler controlled the Foundation, there is no evidence of Walgreen ever calling his activities into question. Stigler was therefore not being overly boastful when in a 1965 letter to Thomas Kuhn (the famous historian and philosopher of science) he wrote, "The Walgreen Foundation, c'est moi." Letter of Stigler to Thomas Kuhn, dated May 7, 1965 (GSRL Box 10, File: Kuhn).

among many others. Peltzman, Becker, and Lucas received large grants as part of an effort to recruit from other universities (Sam Peltzman from UCLA, Gary Becker from Columbia, and Robert Lucas from Carnegie).[17] Stigler built his "team" by paying his players and recruiting "free agents" with lavish "signing bonuses" (but not usually by teaching).[18]

The Walgreen Foundation also directly intervened in political debates of the day. For example, the Stigler used Walgreen Funds to underwrite a 1966 conference on government "guidelines" for prices, wages, and foreign trade and investment (Shultz and Aliber 1966), apparently for the purpose of attacking the Johnson Administration for what Stigler viewed as an unwarranted intervention into the economy. In a 1966 letter to Walgreen that provides insight into Stigler's aims for the Foundation, Stigler reported, "This was a very successful affair ... the heavy attacks on the guidelines program have had a good effect upon [Chair of the Council of Economic Advisers for the Johnson Administration] Gardner Ackley!"[19] No one at Chicago's GSB held an equivalent position.

Stigler's project on "governmental control" would have a profound influence on the GSB. Stigler himself contributed studies of the regulation of electricity and securities and of the enforcement of antitrust laws, and he financed several others (Stigler and Friedland 1962; Stigler 1964, 1966). As a result it became a shared creed at the GSB that government policies would never accomplish their publicly stated goals. Stigler's famous article, "The Economics of Information" (1961), provided a theory of how information was acquired in markets through (costly) individual search, an approach that he then used to portray advertising as an "extremely efficient" method of conveying information to the consumer – thereafter another GSB creed. Stigler also used an information-based approach to oligopoly to upbraid those who did not deduce firm behavior from the "traditional theory of profit maximizing enterprises" (1968, 39). Finally, Stigler bankrolled studies that combined various elements of these approaches, for example, by attacking government regulation on the grounds that it was a poor substitute for privately produced information (see Landau 1973).

17 Stigler was unsuccessful in luring Harold Demsetz back to Chicago from UCLA.

18 These bonuses were generous, especially for that time period: Robert Lucas received $25,000, Gary Becker received $50,000, and both grants came with no strings attached. As Claire Friedland has since noted (1993, 780), Stigler would "go to extremes of irresistible persuasion to keep a valued colleague from being tempted away by another university, or to tempt to Chicago someone he thought would be an important addition."

19 Letter of Stigler to Walgreen, dated June 20, 1966 (GSRL Box 13, File: Walgreen Correspondence).

The significance of these activities for the GSB can best be appreciated by comparing it to the Carnegie approach promoted by Ford. Carnegie stressed the development of operations research-based techniques to improve administrative decision making, conceiving the source of the businesses' problems to be the complexity of managing a modern organization. This program blended an interest in empirical studies of firm decision making, comparative studies of organizations, and various themes emerging from studies of the computer. It stressed bounded rationality and satisficing, sought to incorporate computer simulations into new theories of oligopoly, and even ran experiments (Sent 2004, 740–742; Augier, James, and Bilian 2005; Augier and Prietula 2007, 510–511). Contrariwise, Stigler's program deemed both behavioral approaches and theories of imperfect competition to be useless, and instead cast the "governmental control of economic life" as the central problem for business, whereas the house version of the "economics of information" rejected satisficing explanations. This emphasis on efficient search and regulation placed less emphasis on improving businesses' decisions than on voicing businesses' complaints[20]; Stigler was especially hostile to the idea that one should attempt to get businesses to act in the public interest.

Although it would be an exaggeration to attribute all the developments at the GSB to him alone,[21] Stigler's efforts had set the tone at the Chicago GSB, even in areas normally considered to be far outside his field of expertise. Stigler's tone setting is best exemplified by the Nobel Prize–winning financial economist Merton Miller, who has credited Stigler with "a great influence on my life ... and in bringing me to serious modern economics" (quoted in MacKenzie 2006, 40). Although Miller was originally located at Carnegie, he would eventually follow Stigler in studying the regulation of financial markets (Van Overtveldt 2007, 264–269) and in being an

[20] Or, to be more precise, the complaints that businesses *should* be making about governmental control. Stigler did not entirely trust the judgment of businesspersons, believing they had often accepted what he viewed to be an unwarranted encroachment upon "economic life." Stigler's position on the relationship between businesspersons and government control is discussed further in Section Four.

[21] In particular, Wallis also played a large role in Chicago's successful application for the Ford funds, in gaining Kimpton's approval of a significant increase in the GSB budget, and of course in the relocation of the Walgreen Foundation. But it is important to note that after accomplishing these goals Wallis was basically an absentee dean. Wallis spent 1957 at Stanford; From 1959 to 1961, Wallis took leave to serve as special assistant on economic policy to President Eisenhower; he finally left Chicago for good in 1962 to assume the presidency of the University of Rochester (Dreiser 1988, 20; Van Overtveldt 2007, 249). Wallis's early departure serves to underscore the significance of Stigler for developments at the GSB.

"activist supporter of free market solutions to economic problems." One can also point to Stigler's support for Robert Lucas, also formerly at Carnegie and a pioneer of rational expectations economics. Rational expectations economics was developed, in the view of some, to counter Simon's program of bounded rationality (Sent 1998, 8–9). Therefore, at Chicago the most immediate impact of Stigler's program was to provide an alternative to the "New Look" for the business school and to inculcate the set of attitudes toward corporations and the government he developed in the context of his participation in the MPS.

These efforts also came to matter outside Chicago and throughout U.S. business education, again, not only because of the research produced there, but also due to the methods of institution building developed at the GSB. Chicago's strategy would be replicated elsewhere: After Wallis left Chicago to assume the presidency of the University of Rochester, he oversaw the establishment of a similar effort (in this case the Center for Research in Government Policy and Business, which was placed under the care of the MPS neoliberal Karl Brunner, and which involved the extensive participation of William Meckling, another MPS member).[22] These tactics would even register an impact at the Carnegie GSIA, as Karl Brunner would organize along with fellow MPS member Allan Meltzer (then at the GSIA) the Carnegie-Rochester Conference on Public Policy. Through these complementary activities, MPS neoliberals had begun to transform U.S. business schools. Meanwhile, at Chicago Stigler would draw from additional sources of private funding to redouble his efforts.

5.3. The Center for the Study of the Economy and the State: An Applied Economics of Science

By the early 1970s, Stigler had begun to describe a project that would study the "nature" and "capacities" of the political process. Stigler was frank about his ambitions for this project, at least in his unpublished work: "Let us be candid: economists are beginning to apply their logic and analytical apparatus to the political process, and with luck will conquer much of political science!" (GSRL, Box 21, File: A Research Institute in Economics) This imperial expedition would represent a new and much more ambitious direction for Stigler's work on the government, and which called for an expanded

[22] Meckling first began developing along with Michael Jensen their theory of the firm at one of Karl Brunner's seminars on analysis and ideology in Interlaken (Fourcade and Khurana 2008, 48n30).

staff that would include Gary Becker, Richard Posner, Sam Peltzman, Peter Linneman, George Borjas, and himself. It would also necessitate an operating budget in excess of the Walgreen Foundation.

Stigler was embarking on a project to increase the scale of privately funded research at Chicago, in part as a response to changes sweeping across higher education ranging from the precarious budgetary position of leading private research universities to changing patterns of governmental support for higher education, and more locally, to the Ford Foundation's abrupt withdrawal of support for research-oriented business schools (Khurana 2007, 282–283). During the mid- to late 1960s, a conviction developed among private universities that they were in the midst of a severe financial crisis (Geiger 1993). Several prominent universities (e.g., Cornell, Princeton, Yale, Chicago) suffered operating deficits, in some cases for the first time in their histories; endowments underperformed; government support of the private universities stagnated; finally, newer sources of funding (such as the Ford Foundation) pulled back from investment in business education. These developments hit private research universities particularly hard; expert analysis concluded that the emphasis placed on graduate education had left them especially vulnerable.[23] Stigler was well aware of these challenges facing private higher education in the United States, and he actively sought to secure alternative sources of finance for his new project.[24]

[23] Stigler was deeply involved in studying the economics of private universities. A widely circulated report entitled *The Economics of the Major Private Universities*, authored by the Princeton economist (and, later, provost) William Bowen, singled out the emphasis of major private universities on graduate training and research as a major contributing factor to the cost increase, whereas the major stories on the income side were the displacement of endowment income by government grants and contracts as the largest source of income and the dramatic increase in private giving in the decade following 1955. The report was pessimistic of the long-term ability to increase incomes by private giving, warned of impending disaster if the deficits went unaddressed, and ended with a "public interest" argument for increasing government support of elite private universities. At Chicago, the Bowen report provoked university president Edward Levi to assemble a committee of the faculty to produce a report of their own. The final product was a study entitled *Private Universities and Private Giving* (GSRL Box 10, File: James Lorie). Although this report merely repeated many of the results of the Bowen report (federal funds were becoming less and less useful to private universities; the emphasis on research left them vulnerable), the Private Universities and Private Giving report arrived at an entirely different conclusion – that the "reliance [of major private universities] on federal funds must not be significantly increased," and therefore "private resources available to them must be increased" (29). It then identified foundations and corporations as the largest source of private giving to the university. George Stigler coauthored this report.

[24] In a letter dated November 9, 1969, to George Stigler, Milton Friedman observed of the circumstances of the day: "[T]he point you have made in the past comes to play. It is the temporary upheavals and uncertainties that are the real opportunities of the

Now, if we were discussing another economist, we might be safe in assuming that practical exigency would be all there is to note about the motivation for constructing a private research institute, but in the case of Stigler, recent claims urging us to consider Stigler as the progenitor of an "economics of science" immediately and irresistibly come to mind. The chief proponent of this view is Arthur Diamond (2005), who argues that the characteristic methodological feature of Stigler's work on science is its use of "basic economic theory" to generate testable hypotheses about how science behaves (637). Diamond finds in Stigler's work a commitment to the belief that scientific institutions were competitive and therefore efficient (639). For Diamond, Stigler harbored an "aversion to institutional reform" of science (641–642) and refused to draw any direct lessons for the organization of science, a conclusion that comes as something of a disappointment in light of the fact that Stigler was so deeply involved in organizing science, and because Stigler's use of the Walgreen Foundation to finance Diamond's own work (Diamond 1986) would seem to give him (Diamond) a valuable insider perspective on Stigler's views. Contrary to what Diamond maintains, Stigler had some very strong views about the performance of scientific institutions.[25] As early as 1957, Stigler participated in a discussion at the MPS meetings on "Egalitarianism and Democratisation of Education," wherein he argued for the essential incompatibility of democratic and scientific values. Instead, he called for an elite to "impose" scientific standards on both the public and the scholarly professions (GSRL Box 26, File Mont Pèlerin Society 10th Anniversary Meeting). Stigler later developed these themes pertaining to science, democracy, and markets in *The Intellectual and the Market Place* (*IMP*), whose title essay was reprinted and distributed by MPS member Ralph Harris's Institute of Economic Affairs as its

entrepreneur.... [To do nothing] throws away a temporary opportunity to strengthen the Univ. vis a vis others, to get new financial backing, etc. which would have permanent value – and by a policy that protects against the possibility that the trends are longer lived" (GSRL Box 8, Folder: Friedman, Milton 1971 and before).

Although the immediate subject of this letter was how the administration should respond to the antiwar student protests at Chicago, this letter is significant, first, because it reveals that Stigler had sought an opportunity to seek new financial backing, and second, that he had apparently for some time been considering ways to be more "entrepreneurial" in so doing. Stigler then chose to view the looming crisis as an opportunity and to launch a new program of financial backing stable enough to enable him to improve his program's standing vis-à-vis others dependent on funding from the government (and the Ford Foundation).

25 And I do mean *all* of science. For example, Stigler was active in efforts to supply arguments for the reform of clinical science (Landau 1973). This case is made in fuller detail in Nik-Khah 2010.

"Occasional Paper 1."[26] In *IMP*, Stigler complained that the government was pursuing a harmful egalitarian policy toward science:

> The basic trends of our time are strengthening the forces of diffusion of able men among institutions. The state has taxed away great private fortunes and generously supported public institutions ... the universally premier institution is becoming increasingly more unattainable. And the rules of economics make no exception for Chicago. (1963, 38)

Here Stigler revealed his belief that research should be conducted in an environment where resources are highly concentrated. Elsewhere in *IMP*, Stigler remarks on the quality of science produced in privately funded institutions: "Inquiry has been most free in the college where trustees are a group of top-quality leaders of the market place" (1963, 87). For Stigler, both politicians and *professors* should be treated as threats to intellectual freedom, largely because of their "instinctive dislike of a system of organizing economic life through the search for profits" (1963, 94). *Businesspersons*, according to Stigler, should be viewed as the staunchest defenders of academic freedom.[27] Read in light of his remarks on "Egalitarianism and Democratisation of Education," Stigler's *IMP* argument carries the implication that research must be concentrated in centers, protected from both the public and wrongheaded scholars, and financed by "leaders of the market place." Far from exhibiting aversion to "reforming" scientific institutions, *IMP* is actually calling for it: *IMP* links together Stigler's views on the economics of science with his desire to promote the "correct" views of markets, and suggests that the best way to do so is to concentrate research and seek financing for these efforts from "top-quality leaders of the market place." At this time, however, it was not clear to Stigler how this could be accomplished.

The Intellectual and the Market Place represents only the first published example of Stigler's concern with how best to organize and finance research. Relatively soon thereafter, Stigler zeroed in on the relative merit of alternative methods of concentrating research in an advisory memo for Warren Weaver of the Sloan Foundation, later published as "The Foundations

[26] In his correspondence with Stigler, Harris reports, "A good deal of interest has been aroused among some of our business friends by your talk 'The Intellectual and the Market Place.'" Harris then arranged for copies of the text to be sent to "20,000 British intellectuals." Letters of Harris to Stigler, dated June 27 and September 26, 1963 (GSRL Box 9, File Harris).

[27] Given that Stigler was almost certainly aware of the circumstances surrounding the establishment of the Walgreen Foundation, this position reveals a great deal about Stigler's views on free inquiry.

and Economics" (Stigler 1967).[28] It is necessary to carefully review this paper because it provides evidence of the further development of Stigler's approach to the economics of science, as well as insight into his aims in later proposing the private research institute.[29] In this work, Stigler judged that the large foundations (e.g., Ford), unlike government, had promoted the centralization of talent, which, recall, is a good thing. However, he was unimpressed with the administration of these foundations. Because professional administrators rely on the consensus of the discipline to determine which projects to fund, he believed they tended to reinforce intellectual fads and make research homogeneous. He therefore rejected this option. Stigler then entertained the possibility of entrusting research to "special institutes" such as the NBER (for which Stigler served as a research staff member) or Brookings:

> On the whole, the experiments with the special institutes have been worth making. The university world, with its tenure and tradition of freedom from supervision has not shown itself to be capable of organizing research teams, and so universities provide a weak organizational basis for a strong program-building scientist. Such a scientist *can* make a large impact at the head of a research institute, with its definite lines of authority resting on salary control, nontenure appointments, etc. (1967, 279)

The positive light in which Stigler casts "program-building" is particularly noteworthy because it brings to mind Demsetz's reference to the "Stigler Team" and suggests just how important was his desire to build a research team. Furthermore, it reveals Stigler's pessimism about launching his research program from within a normal academic department and his ambivalence about the performance of traditional academic institutions. Yet the history of existing research institutes indicated to Stigler that this option, too, was flawed. The institutes had received most of their support from the large foundations, making them vulnerable to the same academic-freedom problems already discussed previously. More concretely, the NBER was, in his view, "dissipating its resources in every direction," and the Brookings Institution had become "a Democratic Economists in Washington center" (GSRL Box 21, File: A Research Institute in Economics). These institutes were neither effective in promoting academic freedom nor able to benefit from the advantages of concentration, and so Stigler rejected this option as well.

[28] Stigler confirms the origin of this report in a letter to Lionel Robbins. Letter of Stigler to Robbins, dated September 30, 1965 (GSRL Box 12; Folder: Robbins, Lionel).

[29] Another reason to linger a bit on this work is that Diamond (2005, 642) mischaracterizes it as suggesting that public research "crowds out" private research.

In that same report, he took note of the "perfect swarm of smaller but by no means poverty-stricken foundations" that had recently come on the intellectual scene and was "eager to foster particular policies and viewpoints" (1967, 276–277). Stigler was almost certainly thinking of promarket foundations such as the Volker Fund and the Earhart and Relm Foundations, but also the Foundation for Economic Education (with which he and Milton Friedman had a run-in over their publication of "Roofs or Ceilings").[30] Stigler did not judge these promarket foundations to be reliable partners for his project – at least not at that time. For Stigler, the problem was not their interest in advocacy, but the unreliable judgments of the "dominant personalities" that ruled over them: "I suspect that some donors have not recognized the fact that the problem of intelligent disposal of wealth begins, not ends, with the creation of a foundation" (1967, 277). Seeking funding from foundations for the purpose of avoiding dissipation of talent would jeopardize academic freedom: The larger ones would encourage homogeneity, whereas the smaller ones were subject to the suspect judgments of nonprofessionals. Therefore, as of the writing of his "Foundations" report, Stigler was clearly persuaded of the desirability of forming a research team, but still unsettled on the best method of supporting it.

Stigler's first breakthrough would come as a result of his sponsorship (through Walgreen) of the December 1972 Conference on the Regulation of the Introduction of New Pharmaceuticals. The 1962 passage of the Kefauver-Harris Amendments to the Federal Food, Drug, and Cosmetic Act, which granted the USFDA the power to restrict advertisements and to require drug manufacturers to provide proof of drug efficacy, concerned the pharmaceutical industry and sympathetic observers; it also provided the impetus for George Stigler to organize efforts to intervene in academic debates about pharmaceutical regulation, intellectual property, and clinical science. For the 1972 conference, Stigler lined up an impressive roster of participants (Ronald Coase, Harold Demsetz, Reuben Kessel, Edmund Kitch, Sam Peltzman, Richard Posner, and Lester Telser, among others); assigned leading roles to Sam Peltzman (his Ph.D. student at Chicago and by then an economist at UCLA) and Edmund Kitch (of the Chicago Law School); and directly funded at least one of these papers.[31] Several pharmaceutical

[30] His beliefs regarding the efficacy of small pro-market foundations came from a position of knowledge, not ignorance (Blundell 2003; Davis 2004; Edwards 1999, 140; Friedman and Friedman 1998, 150–152; Silk 1976, 69–70; Sowell 1993, 789).

[31] Stigler arranged for Peltzman to receive $12,000 of support from the Walgreen Foundation. He would later gush in a letter to Peltzman, "you are the best purchase the Walgreen Foundation has yet made." Letter of Stigler to Sam Peltzman, dated November 13, 1972 (GSRL Box 3, File: Walgreen Foundation).

companies (Pfizer, Smith, Kline & French, G. D. Searle, Merck, Sharp & Dohme, and Upjohn) responded by pledging financial support for the effort (GSRL Box 3, File: Walgreen Conferences); the executive director of clinical research at Merck, Sharpe & Dohme and the executive vice president of Upjohn both participated in the conference, with the latter delivering a paper.

The most immediate result of these efforts was the publication of a volume entitled *Regulating New Drugs* (Landau 1973). This book attracted a surprising amount of attention, beginning with Milton Friedman reviewing Peltzman's contribution in his *Newsweek* column, and resulting in U.S. Senate hearings (for which Peltzman was invited to testify). Yet the true significance of these efforts went far beyond the initiation of a set of congressional hearings (they led to no major changes in law, at least in the short run). Instead, they demonstrated to Stigler the willingness of certain corporations to fund academic studies of economic policy, a practice that has by now become standard operating procedure for the pharmaceutical industry.

By 1977, Stigler had expended nearly two decades thinking through how to construct institutions to promote his view of politics and the market. The outcome of his efforts, the Center for the Study of the Economy and the State (CSES), was a response to all the problems in funding economic research that Stigler had encountered. Whatever the response to diffusion and threats to academic freedom, it would have to provide a sufficient buffer from politicians, professors, and students, realize the benefits of concentration, and invest significant authority in the hands of a strong "program-building scientist." It must offer the same program-building flexibility that prevailed at the NBER before its recent transformation, while at the same time provide a platform sufficiently independent of the grip of dominant personalities and drab professional consensus to launch a program designed to transform economics and political science. To fund this effort, Stigler courted corporations and eventually warmed to the possibility of approaching certain promarket foundations, believing he had found a way to neutralize the impact of the "dominant personalities." His solution was to seek a long-term commitment of at least ten years from the foundations and to place a program-building scientist in charge of dispensing funds. The research institute (GSRL Box 21, File: A Research Institute in Economics) would then remove most of the administrative responsibilities from the foundations, effectively neutralizing the undesirable influence of the "dominant personality." Stigler restricted his program to a size that he deemed large enough to benefit from the concentration of talent, yet small enough to enable the director to effectively supervise the activities of the other scholars. He argued for locating it at Chicago to maintain independence from the "dominant intellectual establishment of the eastern seaboard" (as noted by Peck in this volume, others at the University of Chicago had also hit upon the theme of opposition to the "East-coast establishment"). Finally, because the primary rationale for having such an institute was to "shatter the fond hopes of the scholarly professions," it was crucial that the person occupying the position of program-building director be immune to the stultifying influence of general professional opinion. Stigler reserved this role for himself.

It is almost impossible to overestimate the success of CSES. From an initial roster of six (Gary Becker, Richard Posner, Sam Peltzman, Peter Linneman, George Borjas, and Stigler), it has since expanded to house fifteen faculty and several visiting scholars (its roots in the GSB are still visible: Eleven faculty are affiliated with the business school). The CSES received early support from Proctor and Gamble – which was at that time looking to enter into the pharmaceutical industry (Petryna 2009, 61); it also received support from Amoco and Getty (GSRL Box 3, File: GSB Dean's Office Correspondence; Letter to Wallis, dated Nov. 12, 1979, GSRL Box 13, File: Wallis). In recent years, the pharmaceutical multinational Pfizer has emerged as a major source of financing. Promarket foundations have also played a crucial role. The Scaife, Lilly, and Olin Foundations provided early support. Since that time, funding has exploded: Between 1985 and 2005 the Lynde and Harry Bradley Foundation (for which Stigler would serve as a director), the John M. Olin Foundation, and the Sarah Scaife Foundation donated over $5 million to the CSES.[32] With these funds, Stigler built the CSES into one of the most important institutions in the production and promulgation of Chicago doctrine: It has yielded over two hundred working papers and has circulated these ideas through its sponsorship of conferences and publication of condensed versions of its working papers in the GSB's in-house journal, *Capital Ideas*.[33] That the resulting program is still extant in the form of the (now renamed) George J. Stigler Center for the Study of the Economy and the State stands as a monument to Stigler's success as an empire builder.

[32] This figure was taken from information accessed at www.mediatransparency.org on 7/4/2007 and 8/23/2007.

[33] A good survey of this output is provided by the volume *Chicago Studies in Political Economy* (Stigler 1988a), which also gives some idea of the relative importance of the CSES in promoting this approach. Ten contributions were funded by the CSES, four through the Walgreen Foundation, and three were authored or coauthored by Stigler himself. The CSES funded every single piece in that volume written after its establishment.

5.4. Stigler's Project in Comparative Perspective: The Three pillars of the Chicago School

The circumstances leading to the construction and ultimate success of the CSES raises one question: What could possibly motivate an economist to seek corporate and foundation funding for the purpose of launching an imperial expedition from *business* into *political science*? Casting our glance back at the initial research institute proposal offers some insight into Stigler's thinking:

> The relevance of this work to public policy will be both indirect and decisive.... [It] is intended to work its effects upon the appropriate disciplines (economics and political science) rather than directly on public opinion. The work will often shatter the fond hopes of the scholarly professions. (GSRL Box 21, File: A Research Institute in Economics)

This passage is revealing because it establishes that for Stigler the purpose of engaging in "economics imperialism" was not merely to promote a certain methodology, but ultimately to influence public policy – a motivation that remains suppressed in his published work on economics imperialism (Stigler 1984). Stigler believed that the most effective way to influence public policy is not to communicate directly to the public, but instead to act on the attitudes of economists and political scientists, or as he put it in his own inimitable way, to "shatter [their] fond hopes."

The decision to launch the CSES was motivated by a variety of considerations pertaining to regulation, politics, and science that escape the simple characterization as mere applications of Chicago price theory. In fact, one cannot begin to appreciate the relationship between the various strands of his work woven into the CSES – his imperialistic designs on political science, his wish to promote skeptical attitudes toward "governmental control," his work in the economics of science – without making reference to his participation in the MPS project. Recall that the MPS project devoted itself to developing and actively promoting promarket views as a counterblast to socialism and social welfare liberalism. The emphasis here is on "actively promoting," because the belief of the MPS that the ideal market would not develop spontaneously differed profoundly from the promarket view of classical liberalism, and carried with it an imperative to organize their efforts (Mirowski 2009). Worries about how the organization of higher education and research promotes what they regarded as incorrect views of the market formed a prominent theme within the MPS, and among MPS members Stigler was one of the most sophisticated thinkers about how to organize their activities to best promote their views about markets.

Of course, it is unsurprising that the CSES was designed to foster pro-market views: Its mission statement declares that it seeks to subject government institutions, policies, and regulations affecting the private economy to a "Chicago-style" analysis, which is defined by its "deep appreciation of the role of private markets in improving human welfare" (Stigler Center 2009).[34] Although it is certainly true that Stigler was market friendly, his program was animated by very different considerations than those of the other Chicago-style programs that held sway in other parts of the university, a point that can best be appreciated by way of contrast with other neoliberal figures central to the development of the postwar Chicago School, such as Friedrich Hayek, Milton Friedman, and Aaron Director. Although it is true that that they all harbored a "deep appreciation" for the market and they all believed that the wrong ideas about markets had assumed prominence, each held very different views about how this had come to happen and therefore about how to respond.

For Hayek the prominence of incorrect views of the market stemmed from the composition of the intellectual class, which according to him was populated mostly by people who have had no experience administering property, and therefore understand neither the working of the economic system nor the "facts of present-day life" (Hayek 1949). Because he did not think neoclassical economics was especially useful for his project, Hayek ultimately left economics. His project, originally financed by the Volker Foundation, was intended to study the legal foundations of capitalism in order to plan for competition (Van Horn and Mirowski, this volume). Hayek outsourced this project to Aaron Director, who received an appointment at the Chicago Law School.[35] This Free Market Study identified areas of law to facilitate movement toward Director's idea of the "free market." As it expanded beyond Chicago to become the "Law and Economics" movement, Director's program took on the role of convincing judges to take into account its preferred set of economic principles when reaching decisions (Van Horn 2009).

For Friedman, the problem originated with government intervention, which in his view creates a bias in favor of further government intervention. According to Friedman, the dependence of scholars on government

[34] See also the description available at http://research.chicagogsb.edu/economy/.

[35] An important component of this program is the emasculation of antitrust. The focus of this approach on attacking a set of policies, along with the relative indifference to efforts designed to convince economists, might provide some account for some critics' impression that the Chicago School's chief contribution was not to the field of industrial organization, but instead to the policy arena (Martin 2007).

(e.g., the National Science Foundation or state legislatures for those teaching at state universities) produces a "chilling effect" on academic speech directed at the activities of the government (Friedman and Friedman 1980, 68–69; Friedman 1981). Friedman's solution was to overcome this distortion by popularizing the lessons of neoclassical economics for the purpose of appealing directly to the public through his bestselling books (Friedman and Friedman 1980; Friedman 1962), his television series, and his *Newsweek* column. Friedman conceived of his role as alerting people to the costs of government intervention that are not readily apparent and are often suppressed by academicians. Friedman's popularizations of neoclassical-libertarian ideas made him the public face of the Chicago School (Reder 1982, 10), and he pursued his project from the economics department.

Because Stigler's position has proven somewhat more elusive for scholars, we shall support our reading of his proposals for how to respond to incorrect views about markets with more extensive quotation. Stigler believed he had spotted an inconsistency in Friedman's position:

> As I mentally review Milton's work, I recall no important occasion on which he has told businessmen how to behave.... Yet Milton has shown no comparable reticence in advising Congress and public on monetary policy, tariffs, schooling, minimum wages, the tax benefits of establishing a ménage without benefit of clergy, and several other subjects.... Why should businessmen – and customers and lenders and other economic agents – know and foster their own interests, but voters and political coalitions be so much in need of his and our lucid and enlightened instruction? (1975b, 312)

Here, and throughout his work on the economics of politics, Stigler posits a symmetry between the "political market" and the market for goods: People operating in both markets rationally gather information. At the heart of Stigler's position is a belief that there exists a "marketplace of ideas" and an insistence that it operates just as those other markets do:

> [T]he organizing principles of both [the marketplace and intellectual world] are the same.... Neither fraud nor coercion is within the ethics of the market system.... All real economic systems contain some monopoly, and hence some coercive power for particular individuals, but the amount and the extent of such monopoly power are usually much exaggerated.... Just as real markets have some fraud and monopoly, which impair the claims for the market place, so the intellectual world has its instances of coercion and deception, with the coercion exercised by claques and fashion. But again these deviants are outside the logic of the system. (1963, 87–88)

Stigler believed that monopoly behavior was "outside the logic of the [market] system," preferring instead to conceive firm behavior as efficiency enhancing, a position that accompanied his conversion from a

Henry Simons–inspired classical liberalism to neoliberalism.[36] His conviction about the efficient operation of the marketplace of ideas came to be expressed in a variety of ways, from his support for expanding patent protection to his enthusiasm for corporate participation in knowledge production at levels ranging from heavy involvement to outright delegation. The salutary consequences of each of these activities would be to counteract "claques and fashion" – there was therefore no basis for the concern that this knowledge would be biased. In the end, people would end up with all the information they want and need.[37] This led Stigler to conclude that efforts to popularize neoclassical economics (like Friedman's) for the purpose of changing public opinion were a waste of time:

> The large mass of the public does not find it economically worthwhile to become well acquainted with the effects of policies which have small harmful effects upon each non-beneficiary. (GSRL Box 20, File: Schools in Science)
>
> [Average people] lead useful lives, and they buy the amount of economic information that's appropriate for them to have. And they don't go home every night and say, "I wonder what Friedman wrote today that I can read." (Stigler in Hazlett 1984, 45)

Yet despite the fact that voters are held to collect the individually rational amount of information, Stigler was dubious of democracy. Democracy would neither make the best use of social science, nor was it generally a good way to organize intellectual life, as he argued during the MPS discussion on "Egalitarianism and the Democratisation of Education" mentioned previously:

> Affairs of science, and intellectual life generally, are not to be conducted on democratic procedures. One cannot establish a mathematical theorem by a vote, even a vote of mathematicians. [Therefore] an elite must emerge and instill higher standards than the public or the profession instinctively desire.
>
> The best econ[omics] in the U.S. is not the one the public would elect: a science must impose the standards of an elite upon a profession. (GSRL Box 26, File Mont Pèlerin Society 10th Anniversary Meeting)

Stigler's point is not merely that people are (rationally) ignorant; it is that their instincts are bad: "I cannot believe that any amount of economic

[36] Accounts of Stigler's career that have mistakenly attributed classical liberal views to Stigler include (Freedman 2003; McCann and Perlman 1993). Early in his career when under the influence of Henry Simons, Stigler was a classical liberal, but his views, like those of other architects of the Chicago School (Van Horn and Mirowski 2009), underwent a change as a result of his participation in the MPS project.

[37] This places the observation of Diamond (2005), that Stigler believed that scientific institutions operated efficiently, in its proper perspective.

training would wholly eliminate the instinctive dislike for a system of organizing economic life through the search for profits" (1963, 95). Stigler denied that democratic results such as the public's willingness to countenance an expansion of government regulation were an outcome of reasoned reflection, holding instead that they were the inevitable outcome of the poor instincts possessed by the vast majority of people (public and professors alike): "the best economics is not the one the public would elect." Yet rather than call for the public to rethink its views and eliminate regulation (a prospect Stigler believed to be unrealistic in most cases), Stigler sought to immunize government policy from the public, for example, by developing for regulators a set of "intelligent guides" and subjecting regulators to performance audits conducted by scientific bodies purged of their public interest attitudes (see Stigler 1975a). Therefore, Stigler's program to study the "capacities" of democracy was informed by a profoundly negative view of the instincts of the vast majority of people.

If the instincts of the public and the profession alike are untrustworthy, then it is the instincts of elites that must be promoted. For Stigler, the aim was to impose a specific kind of political reform onto the state, and the only way to accomplish the feat was to forge relations with economic elites (the "top-quality leaders of the market place" Stigler praises in *The Intellectual and the Market Place*) and make these relations more durable through skillful institution building. The related academic challenge is that the instincts of these economic elites have not generally been formulated into a set of explicit beliefs, but instead remain "latent," awaiting an "intellectual entrepreneur" who then must innovate to produce the kind of intellectual product that the elites desire (Stigler in Hazlett 1984, 48). Elites, in turn, will know a good account when they read it and will pay accordingly.[38]

Stigler's view of the well-functioning marketplace of ideas sets up for the good neoliberal program-building scientist the practical challenge of identifying and successfully courting the set of elites most likely to organize in support of political intervention. As he put it in an interview with *Reason Magazine*, "[T]he thing we can do as political advisors is to say, 'Look, the industry structure is changing.' … Whenever that's on the horizon … that's a great area to start deregulation. Because then half the industry is going to support you. You're not fighting the battle of your life just for consumers,

[38] This reading is broadly consistent with what one assumes to be a firsthand report of Stigler's position that elites always get to choose scientific merit (Diamond 2005, 640), though probably inconsistent with Diamond's personal interpretation of the significance of this position.

who tend not to be organized and not to support such efforts" (Stigler in Hazlett 1984, 45).

Recall, once again, the Pharmaceuticals project. Stigler organized the conference as a response to the complaints of a handful of pharmaceutical companies. Although these companies were invited to participate, the most important output of the conference was scholarly research designed primarily for an academic audience. Pharmaceutical companies could not usually write these studies themselves (though there were exceptions), but could always signal their desire for such accounts by agreeing to pledge money to the conference. Thereupon, this research was held out as an example of just the sort of research that should be carried out at the GSB. Finally, a much larger-scale effort was devised, also with the support of pharmaceutical companies, but also from other corporations and conservative foundations.[39] These efforts directly led to the formation of a rich network of think tanks and research institutes devoted to circulating Chicago-generated views about the economic role of the government. In the project's wake have followed sweeping changes in regulation and intellectual property, the legacy of which is evident today. As Allen Wallis (1993, 779) correctly noted during the MPS memorial service for Stigler: "[Stigler's] work continues, even expanding and strengthening, through his students, his colleagues, his readers, and several 'think tanks.'"

5.5. Conclusion

To review the previous argument, this chapter has shown that George Stigler used his control of the Walgreen Foundation and the CSES to incubate a research program on the "governmental control of economic life," which later came to encompass industrial organization, regulation, and politics. Stigler was an important figure involved in "assembling the scholars that revolutionized economics and business"; it was by successfully constructing, repurposing, and funding institutions to promote his views about markets, science, and democracy that the "revolution" was achieved. The aim of all this activity was not only to promote skeptical attitudes toward the "capacity" of democracy, but also to achieve some concrete policy changes – a set of objectives developed in the context of Stigler's participation in the

[39] Therefore, to complain that Stigler's unwillingness to engage in the same sort public advocacy as Milton Friedman amounts to "scholasticism" (Klein 2001) misses the mark. Although it is true Stigler's intended audience was usually composed of scholars, Stigler was never cloistered, and instead was always looking to forge alliances with "top-quality leaders of the market place."

MPS project. Therefore, this chapter agrees substantively with the account provided by Robert Van Horn and Philip Mirowski (2009), which emphasizes the central role of skilful institution building, nontraditional sources of private giving, and the MPS project for the developments at Chicago.

This chapter does, however, shift emphasis a bit in stressing some fundamental differences between Stigler's program at the GSB and adjacent neoliberal-oriented programs in the economics department and Law School. Although the research carried out at the GSB was "economics," it differed from the economics carried out elsewhere at Chicago, a fact that might explain the propensity of some members of the Chicago School to engage in public disputes with one another. Successful though Stigler's program might have been, not all at Chicago welcomed this success, as is evident from the spirited disputes between "card-carrying" members of the Chicago School. A good example is Deirdre McCloskey's (1998, 190) charge that George Stigler was "America's leading vulgar Marxist," a view shared by others at Chicago (Klamer and Colander 1990, 152). By distinguishing between the programs at Chicago, the "Three Pillars" depiction of the Chicago School provides an explanation of this otherwise puzzling tendency for some to view the success of Stigler's program as disadvantaging their own preferred approach. Therefore, this chapter agrees with Steve Medema (in Chapter 6 of this volume) in holding that the Chicago School is not homogeneous.

Yet to focus on the smaller internecine battles carries a danger of distracting from the big picture. To return one final time to the Pharmaceuticals example, Sam Peltzman's critical analysis of the Kefauver-Harris Amendment enjoyed a life outside academic precincts via its popularization in Milton Friedman's *Newsweek* column (Friedman 1973). This suggests that Chicago's heterogeneity might have actually helped to promote its members' shared aims. Finally, complementary institutions outside Chicago (in the case of the Pharmaceuticals example, think tanks such as the American Enterprise Institute and the Competitive Enterprise Institute) have also contributed. That having multiple pillars supporting the same edifice – or, to formulate the point in a more Stiglerian fashion, one "product" for the masses and another for the elite – may have served to strengthen Chicago is a possibility that surely merits further study.

Archival Sources

GSRL George J. Stigler Papers, Special Collections Research Center, Regenstein Library, University of Chicago

WFRL Walgreen Foundation Papers, Special Collections Research Center, Regenstein Library, University of Chicago

WWRL W. Allen Wallis Papers, Collection D.261, Department of Rare Books and Special Collections, Rush Rhees Library, University of Rochester

References

Augier, Mie. 2000. "Models of Herbert A. Simon." *Perspectives on Science* 8(4): 407–443.

Augier, Mie, March, James, and Sullivan, Bilian. 2005. "Notes on the Evolution of a Research Community: Organization Studies in Anglophone North America, 1945–2000." *Organization Science* 16(1): 85–95.

Augier, Mie, and Prietula, Michael. 2007. "Historical Roots of the A Behavioral Theory of the Firm Model at GSIA." *Organization Science* 18(3): 507–522.

Blundell, John. 2003. *Waging the War of Ideas*. London: Institute of Economic Affairs.

Becker, Gary. 1993. "George Joseph Stigler: January 17, 1911–December 1, 1991." *Journal of Political Economy* 101(5): 761–767.

Bowen, William. 1968. *The Economics of the Major Private Universities*. Berkeley: Carnegie Commission on Higher Education.

Boyer, John. 2002. "Academic Freedom and the Modern University: The Experience of the University of Chicago." *The University of Chicago Record* 37(3): 2–15.

Coase, Ronald. 1991. "George J. Stigler." In Edward Shils (ed.), *Remembering the University of Chicago*. Chicago: University of Chicago Press.

Davis, Martin. 2004. "Measuring Success in Generations." *Philanthropy Roundtable* May/June.

Demsetz, Harold. 1982. "The 1982 Nobel Prize in Economics." *Science* 218(4573): 655–657.

1993. "George J. Stigler: Midcentury Neoclassicist with a Passion to Quantify." *Journal of Political Economy* 101(5): 793–808.

Diamond, Arthur. 1986. "What is a Citation Worth?" *The Journal of Human Resources* 21(2): 200–215.

2005. "Measurement, Incentives, and Constraints in Stigler's Economics of Science." *European Journal of the History of Economic Thought* 12(4): 635–661.

Dreiser, Harry. 1988. *A Brief History: The University of Chicago, Graduate School of Business*. Chicago: Graduate School of Business.

Edwards, Lee. 1999. *The Conservative Revolution*. New York: Free Press.

Fourcade, Marion, and Khurana, Rakesh. 2008. "From Social Control to Financial Economics: The Linked Ecologies of Economics and Business in Twentieth Century America." Harvard Business School Organizational Behavioral Working Unit Working Paper No. 09–037.

Freedman, Craig. 2003. "Do Great Economists Make Great Teachers? George Stigler as a Dissertation Supervisor." *Journal of Economic Education* 34(3): 282–290.

2008. *Chicago Fundamentalism: Ideology and Methodology in Economics*. Singapore: World Scientific.

Friedland, Claire. 1993. "On Stigler and Stiglerisms." *Journal of Political Economy* 101(5): 780–783.

Friedman, Milton. 1962. *Capitalism and Freedom*. Chicago: University of Chicago Press.

1973. "Frustrating Drug Advancement." *Newsweek* January 8: 49.

1981. "An Open Letter on Grants." *Newsweek* May 18: 99.

1993. "George Stigler: A Personal Reminiscence." *Journal of Political Economy* 101(5): 768–773.

Friedman, Milton and Friedman, Rose. 1980. *Free to Choose*. New York: Harcourt Brace Jovanovich.

1998. *Two Lucky People*. Chicago: University of Chicago Press.

Geiger, Roger. 1993. *Research and Relevant Knowledge*. New York: Oxford University Press.

Gleeson, Robert and Schlossman, Steven. 1995. "George Leland Bach and the Rebirth of Graduate Management Education in the United States, 1954–1975." *Selections* 11(3): 8–37.

Hammond, J. Daniel. 1999. *The Legacy of Milton Friedman as Teacher*. Northampton, MA: Edward Elgar.

Hayek, Friedrich. 1949. "The Intellectuals and Socialism." *The University of Chicago Law Review* 16(3): 417–433.

Hazlett, Thomas. 1984. "Interview with George Stigler." *Reason* (January): 44–48.

Khurana, Rakesh. 2007. *From Higher Aims to Hired Hands*. Princeton, NJ: Princeton University Press.

Klamer, Arjo and Colander, David. 1990. *The Making of an Economist*. Boulder, CO: Westview.

Klein, Daniel. 2001. "A Plea to Economics Who Favor Liberty: Assist the Everyman." *Eastern Economic Journal* 27(2): 185–202.

Klein, Judy. 2008. "How War Grows Economics: The Modeling Nexus of Operations Research, Control Engineering, and Macroeconomic Theories of Expectations." Paper presented at HES meetings, Toronto, CA.

Landau, Richard (ed.). 1973. *Regulating New Drugs*. Chicago: University of Chicago Center for Policy Study.

MacKenzie, Donald. 2006. *An Engine, Not a Camera*. Cambridge, MA: MIT Press.

Martin, Stephen. 2007. "Remembrance of Things Past: Antitrust, Ideology, and the Development of Industrial Economics." In Vivek Ghosal and John Stennek (eds.), *The Political Economy of Antitrust*, New York: Elsevier.

Mayer, Milton. 1993. *Robert Maynard Hutchins: A Memoir*. Berkeley: University of California Press. (Available: http://ark.cdlib.org/ark:/13030/ft4w10061d/)

McCann, C.R. and Perlman, Mark. 1993. "On Thinking about George Stigler." *The Economic Journal* 103(July): 994–1014.

McCloskey, Deirdre. 1998. *The Rhetoric of Economics*. Madison, WI: University of Wisconsin Press.

McDonald, John. 2009. "Graduate Education in Economics: Microeconomics at Chicago and Yale in the 1960s." *Journal of the History of Economic Thought* 31(2): 161–180.

Mincer, Jacob. 1983. "George Stigler's Contributions to Economics." *Scandinavian Journal of Economics* 85(1): 65–75.

Mirowski, Philip. 2009. "Postface: Defining Neoliberalism." In Philip Mirowski and Dieter Plehwe (eds.), *The Road from Mont Pèlerin: The Making of the Neoliberal Thought Collective*. Cambridge, MA: Harvard University Press.

Moss, Lawrence (ed.). 2003. "George J. Stigler (1911–1991): Scholar, Father, Dissertation Advisor, Referee, Textbook Writer and Policy Analyst." *American Journal of Economics and Sociology* 61(3): 609–656.

Nik-Khah, Edward. 2010. "Getting Hooked on Drugs: The Chicago School, the Pharmaceutical Project, and the Construction of Medical Neoliberalism." Unpublished manuscript.

Olkin, Ingram. 1991. "A Conversation with W. Allen Wallis." *Statistical Science* 6(2): 121–140.

Peltzman, Sam. 1993. "George Stigler's Contribution to the Economic Analysis of Regulation." *Journal of Political Economy* 101(5): 818–832.

Petryna, Adriana. 2009. *When Experiments Travel*. Princeton, NJ: Princeton University Press.

Reder, Melvin. 1982. "Chicago Economics: Permanence and Change." *Journal of Economic Perspectives* 20(1): 1–38.

Schlossman, Steven, Sedlak, Michael, and Wechsler, Harold. 1998. "The "New Look": The Ford Foundation and the Revolution in Business Education." *Selections* 14(3): 8–28.

Sent, Esther-Mirjam. 1998. *The Evolving Rationality of Rational Expectations*. New York: Cambridge University Press.

2004. "Behavioral Economics: How Psychology Made Its (Limited) Way Back Into Economics." *History of Political Economy* 36(4): 735–760.

Shultz, George and Aliber, Robert (eds.). 1966. *Guidelines, Informal Controls, and the Market Place*. Chicago: University of Chicago Press.

Silk, Leonard. 1976. *The Economists*. New York: Basic Books.

Simon, Herbert. 1991. *Models of My Life*. New York: Basic Books.

Sowell, Thomas. 1993. "A Student's Eye View of George Stigler." *Journal of Political Economy* 101(5): 784–792.

Stigler Center. 2009. *2008–09 Annual Report*. Available: http://research.chicagobooth.edu/economy/

Stigler, George. 1961. "The Economics of Information." *Journal of Political Economy* 69(3): 213–225.

1963. *The Intellectual and the Market Place*. New York: Free Press of Glencoe.

1964. "Public Regulation of the Securities Markets." *Journal of Business* 37(2): 117–142.

1966. "The Economic Effects of the Anti-trust Laws." *Journal of Law and Economics* 9: 225–258.

1967. "The Foundation and Economics." In Warren Weaver (ed.), *U.S. Philanthropic Foundations*. New York: Harper and Row.

1968. *The Organization of Industry*. Homewood, IL: Irwin.

1975a. *The Citizen and the State*. Chicago: University of Chicago Press.

1975b. "The Intellectual and His Society." In Richard Selden (ed.), *Capitalism and Freedom: Problems and Prospects*. Charlottesville, VA: University Press of Virginia.

1984. "Economics: The Imperial Science?" *The Scandinavian Journal of Economics* 86(3): 301–313.

Stigler, George (ed.). 1988a. *Chicago Studies in Political Economy*. Chicago: University of Chicago Press.

1988b. *Memoirs of an Unregulated Economist*. New York: Basic Books.

Stigler, George and Friedland, Claire. 1962. "What Can Regulators Regulate? The Case of Electricity." *Journal of Law and Economics* 5(1): 1–16.

Van Horn, Robert. 2009. "Reinventing Monopoly and the Role of Corporations: The Chicago School of Law and Economics." In Philip Mirowski and Dieter Plehwe (eds.), *The Road from Mont Pèlerin: The Making of the Neoliberal Thought Collective*. Cambridge, MA: Harvard University Press.

Van Horn, Robert and Mirowski, Philip. 2009. "The Rise of the Chicago School of Economics and the Birth of Neoliberalism." In Philip Mirowski and Dieter Plehwe (eds.), *The Road from Mont Pèlerin: The Making of the Neoliberal Thought Collective*. Cambridge, MA: Harvard University Press.

Van Overtveldt, Johan. 2007. *The Chicago School: How the University of Chicago Assembled the Thinkers Who Revolutionized Economics and Business*. Chicago: Agate.

Wallis, W. Allen. 1993. "George J. Stigler: In Memoriam." *Journal of Political Economy* 101(5): 774–779.

PART THREE

IMPERIAL CHICAGO

SIX

Chicago Price Theory and Chicago Law and Economics

A Tale of Two Transitions

Steven G. Medema

It is common practice to equate "law and economics" with the Chicago School and Chicago law and economics with Richard Posner and the economic analysis of law. Just as common is the tendency to equate Chicago microeconomics, or price theory, with Gary Becker, George Stigler, and the hard-nosed rational choice approach that has extended the economic paradigm across the social spectrum. In fact, however, these are distinctly modern variants of what are lengthy Chicago traditions in law and economics and price theory. The Chicago price theory tradition is now more than three quarters of a century old, and the law and economics tradition is only a couple of decades younger than that. However, Chicago price theory prior to, say, the 1960s was a rather different enterprise than that of the subsequent period.[1] Likewise, law and economics at Chicago has undergone a major transformation during the same period, as pointed out by, for example, Alain Marciano (2008) and Steven Medema (1998, 2009b). To date, however, there has not been a historical explanation given for this transformation in law and economics. The position taken here is that the transformations of price theory and law and economics are linked – specifically, that the transformation of Chicago law and economics evolved out of the transformation in price theory.

Department of Economics, University of Colorado Denver, CB 181, PO Box 173364, Denver, CO 80217-3364, USA (email: steven.medema@ucdenver.edu). I have benefited tremendously from comments provided by Roger Backhouse, Ross Emmett, Dan Hammond, Alain Marciano, Deirdre McCloskey, David Mitch, Warren Samuels, and participants in the "Revisiting the Chicago School" conference at the University of Notre Dame and the Toronto-York History of Economic Thought Workshop.

[1] One can see the evolution of Chicago price theory played out in the collection of classic articles in Chicago price theory, edited by Hammond and Medema (forthcoming).

The first generation of Chicago law and economics – as reflected in the teaching and scholarship of Aaron Director, Director's students, and Ronald Coase – has its foundations in the first generation of the Chicago price theory tradition, that is, in the approach to the subject found in the price theory courses and scholarship of Frank Knight, Jacob Viner, and, later, Milton Friedman. The second generation of Chicago law and economics – the economic analysis of law – is grounded in the rational choice theory, a form of price theory quite different from the "old" Chicago version, in spite of elements of common lineage,[2] as well as a very different conception of "economics," one that involved a (then) distinctive take on Lionel Robbins's definition of the subject as "the science which studies human behaviour as a relationship between ends and scarce means which have alternative uses" (1932, 15).

This paper will attempt to bring out the distinctions between the old and the new versions of Chicago price theory, and will describe how this transition on the price theory side made possible and indeed gave rise to a significant structural shift in the form of law and economics as practiced at Chicago – from "law and economics" to the "economic analysis of law."

6.1. Price Theory at Chicago

6.1.1. *The Founding of a Tradition*

The origins of the Chicago price theory tradition can be found in the lectures and published writings of Frank Knight and Jacob Viner in the 1920s and 1930s. Together, Knight and Viner taught price theory to a generation of students, including several – Milton Friedman, George Stigler, and Aaron Director – who would go on to shape Chicago economics in the middle of the twentieth century.

Both Knight and Viner emphasized a deductive approach to economics, as opposed to the inductive approach favored by the institutional economists who were dominant in the profession in the 1920s. Knight was a theorist *qua* theorist and made no secret of his disinterest in empirical analysis. His most significant influences lay in his support for the competitive market system at a time when professional currents had moved forcefully in favor of more extensive regulation of economic activity, as well as in his conception of economics and its distinction from the "choice under scarcity" approach that was being offered by some, such as Lionel Robbins (1932) as

[2] My reference to the "first generation" here corresponds very closely to what McCloskey (1998) has called "The Good Old Chicago School." I have chosen to use terms such as "first generation," "second generation," "old," and "new" to avoid the appearance of taking sides.

the appropriate way to open up vast areas of life to economic analysis. However, Robbins's definition did not describe Knight's approach to the subject.[3] Indeed, Knight was arguing already in the mid-1920s – four decades prior to the rise of economics imperialism – that people ascribed *too broad* a role to economics and that nothing was more important than the recognition of economics' "limited place among the human interests at large" (1933, 1).[4] He believed that economics texts erred in "including virtually all intelligent behavior" under the definition of economics, and he spoke dismissively of one text that defined economics as "the science of rational activity" (1933, 1), blaming this conception of economics on the attempt by his professional colleagues to make their subject appear more scientific.

Knight thought it essential that economists use a more broad conception of man, arguing that "economizing, even in this broad sense of rational activity, or the intelligent use of given means in achieving given ends, does not include all human interests" (1933, 2). In his essay on "The Limitations of Scientific Method in Economics" (1924) Knight argued:

> From a rational or scientific point of view, all practically real problems are problems in economics. The problem of life is to utilize resources "economically," to make them go as far as possible in the production of desired results. The general theory of economics is therefore simply the rationale of life. – In so far as it has any rationale! The first question in regard to scientific economics is this question of how far life is rational, how far its problems reduce to the form of using means to achieve given ends. Now this, we shall contend, is not very far; the scientific view of life is a limited and partial view; life is at bottom an exploration in the field of values, an attempt to discover values, rather than on the basis of knowledge of them to produce and enjoy them to the greatest possible extent. We strive to "know ourselves," to find out our real wants, more than to get what we want. This fact sets a first and most sweeping limitation to the conception of economics as a science. (1924, 1)[5]

The behavioral definition of economics and the focus on individual action was, for Knight, too narrow.[6] Against this conception of the subject, Knight insisted that "Economics deals with the *social organization* of economic activity," primarily via "the price system, or free enterprise" (1933, 4). This includes "the organization of want satisfaction," and the object of the subject is to improve this organization and increase its efficiency (7–8). Knight thus put markets, as coordinating devices, rather than the individual agent,

[3] On Robbins's definition and its influence, see Backhouse and Medema (2009a). For Knight's critique of Robbins, see Knight (1934).

[4] Knight's *Economic Organization* (1933) was completed in draft form in 1924–1925 although not published until 1933.

[5] These ideas are also the subject of Knight (1922).

[6] See also Knight (1933, 1 4).

at the center of Chicago price theory. His antiempirical bent shows through here, for he considered individual freedom and competitive markets to be good in and of themselves and did not look to or engage in empirical inquiry to support or even test this.

Jacob Viner's impact on Chicago price theory came via his approach to the subject, one grounded in the demand-supply framework of Alfred Marshall's *Principles of Economics* (1890/1920). His graduate price theory lectures were practically a walking tour of Marshall's *Principles*, the text that was to dominate the teaching of price theory at Chicago for five decades. With this, he brought an empirical applications orientation that emphasized the use of price theory to analyze concrete economic problems.[7] Viner, for his part, never set out a formal definition of economics, though he is said to have quipped on more than one occasion, "Economics is what economists do."

Like Marshall, Knight and Viner did not see economics as offering virtually inviolable laws. Instead, they looked at theories as tendency statements, as when Knight said that "Economic laws, like other scientific laws, state a *tendency*, a result which *would* follow if certain conditions are present" (71). This, said Knight, applies to the marginal conditions for efficient consumption, the satisfaction of which he felt was not something that consumers do, or even "carefully strive to do." Yet he considered the equimarginal principle "valuable as stating a tendency" because it helped "to make economic behavior in the large more understandable" (77). Even the law of demand, that cornerstone of price theory, was, in the eyes of Knight, a tendency statement: People, he said, will "generally" buy less when price increases (74). Viner adopted a similar stance.[8]

6.1.2. *The Fork in the Road*

Viner left Chicago for Princeton in the mid-1940s, and Knight's influence in the department was greatly diminished by the 1950s. The second generation of Chicago price theory was dominated by their students, particularly Milton Friedman and George Stigler – each of whom, in his own way, attempted to refine and build on the framework laid out by Knight and Viner.[9] Some of this work was developed outside of Chicago proper, as

[7] By "empirical" here I do not mean "econometric"; Viner was more ambivalent about the application of statistical and econometric methods than were (eventually) his students, although not as hostile on this front as was Knight.

[8] See, e.g., Viner (1930).

[9] The Friedman-Stigler correspondence in Hammond and Hammond (2006) provides many interesting insights into the similarities and differences in Friedman's and Stigler's approaches to the subject.

Friedman did not join the Chicago faculty until 1946 (replacing Viner) and Stigler until 1958.

Friedman's approach to price theory was profoundly influenced by both Knight and Viner, although more so by the latter's emphasis on Marshall, whose *Principles* was, for Friedman, a cornerstone of price theory throughout his career.[10] Friedman's definition of economics was actually very Knightian, being "the science of how a particular society solves its economic problems" (1962, 6), although it was wedded to the increasingly dominant professional view that an "economic problem exists whenever *scarce* means are used to satisfy *alternative* ends" (6).[11] Reading Friedman's *Price Theory* from the perspective of the present, one is tempted to infer a premonition of economics imperialism when Friedman says, "This conception of an economic problem is a very general one and goes beyond matters ordinarily thought of as belonging to economics" (6). However, he then cites the allocation of leisure time as the example of this expansiveness – hardly a topic that someone even in the 1970s (to say nothing of today) would consider other than straightforwardly "economic."

The methodological approach underlying Friedman's price theory was set out very clearly in his influential essay on "The Methodology of Positive Economics" (1953). Here, Friedman argued that economic theory is a "language" or a "filing system," a conception of economic theory that for him was essentially Marshallian (coinciding with Marshall's *engine of analysis*), and the relevant aspect of which is its "usefulness" rather than its correctness (1953, 7).[12] In his classic essay on "The Marshallian Demand Curve" (1949), Friedman criticized what he considered an excessive fixation by economists on the mathematically sophisticated Walrasian general equilibrium approach and suggested that abstraction, generality, and mathematical elegance had become "ends in themselves" for too many of his professional colleagues (490). He gave general equilibrium analysis only scant attention in his graduate price theory lectures, something that Gary Becker (1991, 143) would later suggest was a shortcoming of the course. Like Viner, Friedman found in the Marshallian framework a means to understand and explain concrete facts via its relative simplicity and lack of restrictive assumptions. Yet theory was more than a language for Friedman; it was also "a body of substantive empirical propositions" that yields predictions, and this emphasis on the ability

[10] For example, Marshall's *Principles* was a centerpiece of Friedman's graduate price theory courses until his retirement in the mid-1970s.

[11] See Backhouse and Medema (2009a) on the diffusion of the scarcity definition.

[12] See also Friedman (1962, 8).

of the theory to explain and predict became a hallmark of the Chicago price-theoretic identity.[13]

Friedman's price theory, like that of Knight and Viner before him, was centered on the analysis of markets, and so was grounded in the analysis of demand rather than in a particular underlying theory of consumer behavior. As his 1953 methodology essay makes clear, Friedman was keen to separate economics from psychology, and one sees this reflected in his price theory. Both his classic article with Leonard Savage on "The Utility Analysis of Choices Involving Risk" (1948, 287–288) and his essay on "The Marshallian Demand Curve" (1949, 479) explicitly incorporate the "as if" approach to consumer theory rather than making assumptions about how individuals actually make choices.[14] Likewise, in his price theory lectures and text, Friedman traced the theory of demand and supply without grounding it in any particular theory of individual behavior.[15] Although Friedman did allow that decisions regarding what goods and services to purchase involve "a deliberate act of choice," he went only as far as to say that, in making these choices, "we shall suppose that the individual is making these decisions *as if* he were pursing and attempting to maximize a single end" (1962, 37). This characterization of the problem is present in student notes on his lectures from 1947, and it is repeated verbatim in the 1976 revision of his text (1976, 35).[16] Of course, this "as if" approach to theorizing is a centerpiece of Friedman's methodological perspective (Friedman 1953).

That Friedman's price theory was not of the hard-nosed rational choice variety is evident throughout his work. In fact, one finds no discussion of rationality in either edition of Friedman's *Price Theory* or in the recently published set of student lecture notes from his 1947 class (Johnson 1947/2008). Friedman does tip his hat, in passing, to public choice analysis in both the

[13] Friedman gives the definition of a demand curve as an example of the language/filing system and the statement that demand curves are downward sloping as substantive empirical proposition (1962, 8). On the predictive aspect, see the chapters by Stapleford, Hammond, and Cherrier in this volume.

[14] For example, Friedman and Savage (1948) depict the situation as follows: "In choosing among alternatives open to it, whether or not these alternatives involve risk, a consumer unit (generally a family, sometimes an individual) behaves *as if* (a) it had a consistent set of preferences; (b) these preferences could be completely described by a function attaching a numerical value – to be designated 'utility' – to alternatives each of which is regarded as certain; (c) its objective were to make its expected utility as large as possible" (287–288, emphasis added).

[15] Friedman's text was actually based on student lecture notes taken in the 1950s. See the preface to Friedman (1962) and the discussion in Fand (1999).

[16] The class notes are those of Glenn Johnson from Friedman's Winter 1947 price theory lectures (Johnson 1947/2008).

1962 and 1976 editions of his text, but he added nothing regarding the burgeoning rational choice–based "economics imperialism" literature in the 1976 edition, and we see there only a passing reference to Becker's work on the economics of the household and human capital.[17] Friedman's reading list is also instructive: Large chunks of Marshall's *Principles* were still required reading in Friedman's price theory course in the 1970s, whereas Becker's 1971 text, *Economic Theory*, is listed along with several other books as a recommended (but not required) supplementary reading.[18]

George Stigler did not arrive at Chicago until 1958, but he too was working away at price theory during the 1940s, and in fact authored the first commercially published text book in the Chicago price theory tradition – *The Theory of Competitive Price* (1942). Here, Stigler gave what might be called a "Robbins-plus" definition of economics, making it "the study of the principles governing the allocation of scarce means among competing ends when the objective of the allocation is to maximize the attainment of the ends" (12). Within this, Stigler identified scarcity as "the most fundamental characteristic of an economic problem" (13). What is novel here is that Stigler put maximizing behavior in his definition of economics. In contrast to his good friend Milton Friedman, who made maximizing behavior an "as if" factor, Stigler said that it is "very realistic to assume that a maximum fulfillment of needs is sought" (1942, 13).[19] Ironically, though Stigler was a student of Knight, it was Friedman who adopted the more Knightian definition, whereas Stigler moved down the Robbins road – at least for a time.

In their important paper on the stabilization of demand theory during the twentieth century, Philip Mirowski and Wade Hands (1998) argue that the Chicago tradition takes demand as the starting point and largely ignores its underpinnings. Although this depiction certainly fits Knight, Viner, and Friedman, it cannot be said to apply to Stigler (nor, as we shall see, Becker). Indeed, the chapter on demand theory in Stigler's *Theory of*

[17] The reference to Becker's work on the household deals with traditional activities being transferred in and out of the household context; human capital is mentioned in a sentence noting that it impacts labor contracts (Friedman 1976, 4, 233).

[18] See Friedman (1976, Appendix A). That Friedman saw a real difference between himself and Becker is suggested by Friedman's decision to revise his *Price Theory* when he resumed teaching the course in the 1970s following a hiatus of roughly a dozen years. Friedman could have used Becker's *Economic Theory* (1971) if he had found Becker's approach sufficiently congenial, rather than going to the effort of revising his own text. That Friedman chose the revision route is at least suggestive of a distinction in his own mind between his own preferred approach and that of Becker.

[19] Knight's influence is evident too, though, as Stigler, like Friedman, discussed the economic organization of society early on in the text.

Competitive Price takes consumer behavior as the starting point and derives demand curves from there. For Stigler, self-interested behavior was at the center of economic analysis and had been since the time of Smith, whose *Wealth of Nations* he described as "a stupendous palace erected upon the granite of self-interest" (1971, 265).[20] Stigler's perception of the centrality of self-interested behavior in Smith here led him to label Smith "the premier scholar of self-interest" (1971, 268) and to call this aspect of Smith's work "the crown jewel" of *The Wealth of Nations* (1976, 1201). Stigler even went so far as to link up Smith's approach with contemporary economics imperialism, characterizing Smith as giving us "a theorem of almost unlimited power on the behavior of man" that is "Newtonian in its universality" (1976, 1212). This "always and everywhere" gravitational allusion is not accidental, but rather reflects what Stigler saw as the pervasiveness of self-interested behavior throughout human life.[21] The fact that economists were at this time "busily extending this construct into areas of economic and social behavior to which Smith himself gave only unsystematic study is," said Stigler, "tribute to both the grandeur and the durability of his achievement" (1976, 1212).[22]

Stigler carried the Robbins definition of economics into the first edition of *The Theory of Price* (1946),[23] but, for reasons that are unclear, he altered his definition for the second edition, published in 1952, in favor of something much closer to Knight: "Economics is the study of the operation of economic organizations, and economic organizations are the social (and rarely, individual) arrangements to deal with the production and distribution of economic goods and services" (1952, 1). This last reference to "economic goods and services" is particularly interesting for our purposes and is even remarked upon by Stigler, who noted:

> It should be only a minor annoyance to the reader that we define economics in terms of economic goods and services. A more popular definition of economics – the study of the allocation of scarce means among competing ends – also requires

[20] The interesting relationship between Smith and the Chicago School is discussed in Evensky (2005) and Medema (2009a).

[21] Both Stigler and Becker see the idea of fixed tastes and preferences that influence behavior across the spectrum of human behavior evidenced in Smith. See, e.g., Stigler (1981/1982, 6) and Becker (1976, 282).

[22] This is just one of a number of examples of the use by Chicago economists of the history of ideas to lend support to their approach.

[23] *The Theory of Price* essentially reproduced *The Theory of Competitive Price*, along with several additional chapters on subjects including imperfect competition, multiple products, and capital and interest.

> the tacit introduction of "economic" before "ends" in order to exclude a vast area of which economists have no professional knowledge. (1n)

As we shall see, Stigler was later to take a somewhat different view of the necessity of this last qualification. Yet even as he adopted the more Knightian definition of the subject, Stigler continued to maintain that scarcity is the "central element of the economic problem" (1), although he seems to have believed at this stage that the scope of applications is rather narrow.

By the third edition of 1966, both the definition of economics and the footnote about "economic goods and services" had disappeared from *The Theory of Price*, and three references to Becker's work on discrimination, investment in education, and fertility offered a signal that perhaps Stigler was finding his earlier definitional discussions overly restrictive. The fourth (and final) edition, published in 1987, also eschewed definitions, although Stigler did allow that his text "presents the essentials of the theory of the allocation of resources and the determination of prices" (1987, 1); and his chapter-length Knightian discussion of the economic organization, which had been carried through every edition to that point, was replaced by a treatment of the role played by *prices* in an enterprise economy. The 1987 edition is also distinguished by the attention that it gives to economics imperialism in general and to Becker in particular. The treatment of Becker includes a full-page boxed insert (one of twenty in the book) in which Stigler notes that "Becker has done more than any other economist to enlarge the working domain of the profession" (1987, 239), and the book contains numerous references to Becker's work on discrimination, education, crime, the family, and politics. In contrast, Friedman's 1976 edition contains only the two passing references to Becker's work, and these to fairly traditional economic topics.

One of the defining aspects of Chicago price theory has been the marriage of theory and empirical work. Though Knight had no use for empirical analysis and Viner was ambivalent about the use of statistical and econometric methods in economics, this changed radically with Friedman and Stigler. Friedman (1953) made prediction the centerpiece of economic analysis in his classic essay on methodology. His undergraduate training was in statistics, and he spent World War II working with the Statistical Research Group, where he made a seminal contribution to statistical sampling processes as part of his work on optimal munitions testing methods. Friedman was also profoundly influenced by Columbia University senior colleague and National Bureau of Economic Research Director Arthur Burns (a pioneer in the statistical analysis of business cycles), with whom he worked following completion of his graduate studies at Chicago.

The theory plus testing approach was seen early on as contrasting with the "measurement without theory" approach of the institutionalists and later with the theory sans empirical work that characterized general equilibrium analysis.[24] Chicago price theorists were pioneers in the econometric testing of economic theories, and this work had a profound persuasive impact, particularly when combined with the increasing professional acceptance of Friedman's methodological dictum that the appropriate test of a theory is its ability to predict well, rather than the realism of its assumptions.

It was Stigler, though, whose research best exemplified Friedman's dictum during this period. He, too, had worked with Burns and served with the Statistical Research Group during World War II. Stigler's extensive empirical studies of the market process – in particular, on the effects of legislation and of industry structure on market outcomes – were fundamental in transforming the field of industrial organization and the economics of regulation. Stigler was able to combine the assumption of maximizing behavior with that of imperfect information to offer an explanation for how markets could generate outcomes at odds with the received view – such as the law of one price. In Stigler's hands, these were not market failures that required government intervention, as suggested by the orthodox approach; rather, they were efficient responses to economic circumstances.[25] Other empirical research supported the competitive markets model's prediction that rates of return are equalized across sectors over time and that prices are flexible rather than sticky. In contrast to Knight, who considered liberal society, and thus free markets, a good in and of itself, Friedman and Stigler took a more empirically oriented approach, arguing that the competitive market system was good because it generated better results than did alternative systems.

Though much of Stigler's work was market oriented, his move to ground the analysis of the market process in the actions of rational individual agents marked a move toward a more rational choice–based approach to price theory. His identification of scarcity as "the most fundamental characteristic of an economic problem" made it quite easy to consider virtually anything an "economic problem" – although Stigler himself was not inclined to give broad scope to economics early on. Indeed, in this and other ways Stigler can be said to have had feet in both the older and newer

[24] But the contrast with institutionalism is not as great as one might think. Stapleford's essay in the present volume presents an extensive discussion of the institutionalist influences on Friedman.

[25] One gets a greater sense for this in the discussions of Stigler presented by Schliesser and Nik-Khah in their respective chapters in this volume.

Chicago price theory camps over time. It was with Gary Becker that we see what was perhaps the most significant transition in Chicago price theory. Although more known for his forays into traditionally noneconomic disciplines, Becker's approach to price theory marked a shift toward a more overtly rational choice orientation and provided the theoretical toolkit that really made those forays possible. If Friedman and Stigler represent a fork in the Chicago price theory road, Becker went down the Stigler branch and, in the process, solidified it as the future of Chicago price theory.

6.1.3. *Rationalizing Price Theory*

Becker had taken Friedman's price theory sequence at Chicago during his graduate days and, after more than a decade at Columbia, returned to Chicago as a faculty member in 1969. In the preface to his *Economic Theory* (1971), which was based on the course that he had taught for a decade at Columbia, Becker stated that "there is only one kind of economic theory," and it applies to both market and nonmarket decisions (viii). This economic theory studies "the allocation of scarce means to satisfy competing ends," a definition that Becker unashamedly allowed was very "wide," and under which he included the "choice of a car, a marriage mate, and a religion; the allocation of resources within a family; and political decisions about how much to spend on education or on fighting a Vietnam war" (1).

Whereas Stigler had put scarcity at the center, for Becker "the basis of economics is choice" (1971, 3). From the perspective of the present, these may seem to be two sides of the same coin, but this is not inevitably the case. The study of the allocation of resources can take various forms and can be undertaken sans any specific reference to the individual choice process, as reflected in Mirowski and Hands's observation about Chicago demand theory and Friedman's tendency to focus on the market process absent any explicit underpinnings in individual behavior. Becker, however, explicitly and specifically put individual choice at the center of the subject. Two decades later, in his Nobel address, Becker gave this even greater specificity, equating the "economic … approach" with the "rational choice approach" (1993, 402).

Because most economists spend their time studying the market sector – or at least did circa 1971 – Becker allowed that his definition was too broad in terms of describing "what most economists generally do" (1).[26] His belief, though, was that "the economic principles developed for [the market] sector are relevant to all problems of choice"; this view was the "unique

[26] As such, it would seem to violate the Viner dictum that "economics is what economists do."

theme" of the course of lectures that he taught and subsequently wrote up into *Economic Theory* (1). In fact, Becker considered economic analysis "essential for understanding much of the behavior traditionally studied by sociologists, anthropologists, and other social scientists" (2). As he put it in 1976, this approach is

> applicable to all human behavior, be it behavior involving money prices or imputed shadow prices, repeated or infrequent decisions, large or minor decisions, emotional or mechanical ends, rich or poor persons, patients or therapists, businessmen or politicians, teachers or students. (1976, 8)

But it was not simply that one *could* apply economic analysis to various areas; Becker saw economics as providing a "valuable *unified framework* for understanding *all* human behavior" (1976, 14, emphasis added) and thus offered the possibility of a unified approach to doing social science (1976, 5; 1993, 403). In adopting this almost axiomatic approach to economic analysis and the view that it offered a unifying framework for doing science, Becker sounded the very themes that characterized the work of Oskar Morgenstern,[27] under whom Becker studied game theory while an undergraduate at Princeton (Becker 2007).

Gone, then, is the subject-matter approach of Knight's study of "the *social organization* of economic activity." For Becker, economics is ultimately an approach to the analysis of human behavior, one that combines the assumptions of maximizing behavior, market equilibrium, and stable preferences, using them "relentlessly and unflinchingly" to analyze human behavior under conditions of scarcity (1976, 5). From this perspective, it is not the subject matter that distinguishes economics from other social sciences – its subject matter is essentially coterminous with all of them. It is the *approach* that makes economics distinct (5).

Three provisional conclusions follow from the foregoing discussion. First, the Chicago price theory tradition is not homogeneous and, in fact, has exhibited significant heterogeneity since the early days of Knight and Viner. Second, even allowing for this heterogeneity, there is a significant distinction to be drawn between the earlier and later generations of Chicago price theory – Knight, Viner, and Friedman on the one hand and the generation from Becker onward on the other (with Stigler having a foot in each camp and more or less migrating from the former to the latter). Early Chicago price theory was grounded in demand theory and the analysis of markets. There was an underlying idea of utility maximization, but only in an "as if"

[27] See, for example, Morgenstern (1936).

sense. With Stigler and Becker, we see a move toward the analysis of individual behavior as the foundation of price theory, with the theory placed on a rational choice footing: Individuals are deemed to be rational maximizers, not necessarily of utility, but of whatever their chosen ends may be. Demand theory was sufficient to explain *prices*; a more refined behavioral grounding was necessary to explain *choices*. This move to a rational choice approach to modeling agent behavior was bound up in the axiomatic turn in the profession during the 1950s and 1960s. Third, Chicago price theory increasingly came to define economics as the analysis of choice rather than as the study of the economic organization – moving, that is, from a subject-matter definition of economics to an analytical one.[28] The move to center economics in rational choice analysis offered the prospect of accounting for a far greater variety of behaviors than did earlier approaches to consumer behavior. This, in turn, fed into the transformation of law and economics, which is the subject of the next section of the paper.

6.2. From Law and Economics to Economic Analysis of Law

Like Chicago price theory, Chicago law and economics is heterogeneous, particularly when considered historically. Its origins date to the 1930s, when the Law School instituted a four-year curriculum that included courses in economics, accounting, and other subjects outside of the traditional realm of legal training (Katz 1937).[29] In 1939, the Law School appointed its first economist, Henry Simons, a former student of Frank Knight, who taught a course entitled "Economic Analysis of Public Policy" and in doing so brought price theory into the Law School curriculum at Chicago. In 1945, Simons became the first economist granted tenure by the Law School.

Simons's integration of economics and law took the form of analyzing the impact of the legal environment on the economic system. His most significant scholarly work on this front came already in 1934 in his *Positive Program for Laissez Faire*. Here, Simons set out a blueprint for a legal/regulatory regime that would ensure the maintenance of competitive conditions in the face of increasing concentration in corporate America. His proposals ranged from nationalization to legal limits on advertising and to redefining the courts' criterion regarding the maximum firm size consistent with competition. As

[28] But whereas the approach to and underpinnings of Chicago price theory have changed significantly over time, the emphasis on the study of competitive markets has remained a virtual constant, making this an element of continuity rather than change.

[29] See, e.g., Reder (1982), Kitch (1983), Coase (1993), Hovenkamp (1995), Duxbury (1995, chapter 5), and Medema (1998).

Stigler (1988, 149) later noted, Simons's program seems "almost as harmonious with socialism as with private-enterprise capitalism," giving far more credence to the possibilities of government than one would expect from a "founder" of the Chicago law and economics tradition.

Knight's antiempirical bent was evidenced in Simons's *Positive Program*, as he provided no empirical underpinnings for his analysis and offered no evidence for the ability of the government to bring off such competition policy or for the ability of such policies to enhance the efficiency with which the economy operated. Methodologically, then, his approach was, as Coase has described it, "the very antithesis of that which was to become dominant as a result of the emergence of that new subject, law and economics" (1993, 242). It is fair to say, with Coase, that Simons had little or nothing to do with the development of that body of ideas and approach that became known as Chicago law and economics (1993, 242). His legacy, rather, came through his role in establishing economic education in the Law School and in bringing to it the individual most responsible for firmly establishing the Chicago law and economics tradition – Aaron Director.

Director arrived at the University of Chicago for his graduate training in 1927. He studied price theory under Knight and Viner and remained at Chicago as a graduate student and part-time instructor until 1934. After more than a decade spent in Washington, DC and London, Director returned to the University of Chicago in 1946 to take up a position in the Law School and head up the "Free Market Study," a project housed in the Law School and dedicated to undertaking "a study of a suitable legal and institutional framework of an effective competitive system" (Coase, 1993, 246).[30] When Simons committed suicide in the summer of 1946, Director was asked to take on his basic Law School price theory course, "Economic Analysis of Public Policy." This provided Director an initial forum for bringing the perspective he had learned from Knight and Viner into the Law School classroom.

The transition from having an economist on the Law School faculty to the establishment of a law and economics tradition at Chicago began not long after this, when Edward Levi invited Director to collaborate in the teaching of the antitrust course. Levi taught a traditional antitrust course for four days each week; Director came in on the fifth day and, using the tools of price theory, attempted to show that the traditional legal approach could

[30] Van Horn and Mirowski (2009) provide an analysis of the motivations behind and events surrounding the origins of the "Free Market Study." A contrasting perspective on certain aspects of their analysis can be found in Caldwell's chapter in the present volume.

not withstand the scrutiny of economic analysis. The basic pattern was very simple: Director would ask whether the practice in question was, in general, consistent with monopolistic profit-maximization. The answer was often negative, which meant that there had to be some sort of legitimate rationale for the supposedly anticompetitive practice in question. What price theory showed, Director argued, was that the "simple and obvious" answers were often wrong-headedly simplistic. This approach had a profound impact on students and colleagues alike, with Director's students often referring to the "conversion" they experienced in this class.[31] Indeed, even Levi himself became a partial convert.[32]

Director published little himself, but his insights made their way into the antitrust literature – and, eventually, antitrust policy – through the writings of students and colleagues on topics including predatory pricing, resale price maintenance, and tie-in sales.[33] His influence was also prominent in Stigler's view of oligopoly and antitrust policy, Richard Posner's perspective on oligopoly and cartels, and Robert Bork's influential articles on antitrust.[34] All of this coalesced in a distinctive Chicago approach to antitrust analysis, the influence of which today is inescapable in both scholarship and jurisprudence.[35]

In 1964, as Director was approaching retirement, Ronald Coase was brought to the Law School from the University of Virginia to succeed Director on the faculty and as editor of the *Journal of Law and Economics*. Prior to Coase's arrival, the Law School never had more than one economist on the faculty, although there were enough economics and law professors with sympathies for examining antitrust cases, regulatory issues, and so on through the lens of economic analysis to form a small reading group. Yet the presence of scholars such as Karl Llewellyn, a prominent Legal Realist, on the faculty managed to ensure that there was always strong resistance to expansion of the influence of price theory in the 1950s. Henry Manne has reported that the economic analysis that was in the air "infuriated" Llewellyn, particularly when students would use it in attempts to refute positions that Llewellyn would take in the classroom (Kitch 1983, 184).

31 This group included Robert H. Bork, Ward Bowman, Kenneth Dam, Edmund Kitch, Wesley J. Liebeler, John S. McGee, Henry Manne, and Bernard H. Siegan. See Kitch (1983) and Director and Levi (1951).

32 See Kitch (1983) and Director and Levi (1951).

33 See, e.g., McGee (1958), Telser (1960), Director and Levi (1951), Bowman (1957), and Burstein (1960), as well as the survey in Peltzman (2005).

34 See, e.g., Posner (1969), Bork and Bowman (1965), and Bork (1967). Van Horn (2009) provides an interesting discussion of the evolution of antitrust analysis at Chicago.

35 See, e.g., the discussion in Hovenkamp (1986).

Llewellyn even went so far as to question whether Chicago was doing a proper job of training lawyers (191).[36] Edward Levi, as dean, protected and encouraged law and economics,[37] but, as Director has pointed out, on the whole there was neither "any great resistance" to nor "any great enthusiasm for" law and economics – at least until it was proposed that a second economist be hired (Kitch 1983, 186). In fact, the status of economics in the Law School at that stage was such that Coase's initial appointment was partially in the business school.

Coase's arrival promised a measure of continuity in the legal-economic approach at the Law School. Although Coase was not trained in the Chicago brand of price theory, his approach was thoroughly Marshallian and very consonant with the Chicago view.[38] Coase had studied under Arnold Plant at the London School of Economics. Plant had done pioneering work analyzing the economic implications of rules governing patents, copyrights, and intellectual property generally,[39] and Coase's approach to the analysis of legal-economic policy issues, informed by Plant, resonated with the Chicago approach.[40] He believed that there were important lessons to be learned by examining the relationship between law and economy – by "examining cases, examining business practices, and showing that there was some sense to them, but it wasn't the sense that people had given to them before" (quoted in Kitch 1983, 193). This is the perspective that was being applied at Chicago by Director and others in the area of antitrust, and it almost certainly accounts for much of Director's interest in bringing Coase to Chicago.

This approach was expanded to the analysis of a wide range of issues in legal and regulatory policy, largely through the influence of Director and Coase as editors of the *Journal of Law and Economics*. The *Journal* was founded by Director in 1958, and its aim was "the examination of public policy issues of interest to lawyers and economists" (Coase 1993, 251).

36 Llewellyn was not inherently opposed to legal-economic analysis, but his preference was for something approximating the old institutionalist variety. See, e.g., Llewellyn (1925).

37 This after several years of serving as the foil for Director's economic critique of the received approach to antitrust analysis. See, e.g., Kitch (1983).

38 On the Marshallian aspect in Coase, see Coase (1975) and Medema (1996).

39 See Plant (1974).

40 Coase has said that "[t]here were typical 'Chicago' lessons that I didn't have to learn, and I got them through Plant" (Kitch 1983, 214). He said that Plant's most significant influence on him involved getting him to see that 'there were many problems concerning business practices to which we had no satisfactory answer' (1982a, 34; see also Coase 1986). Much of Coase's career was spend looking for these answers, and this perspective, along with Plant's approach of looking at real world problems, are reflected throughout Coase's scholarship.

Coase himself was a four-time contributor to the *Journal* prior to his arrival at Chicago, with articles on the regulation of broadcasting (1959, 1962), externalities (1960), and postal monopolies (1961) evidencing the *Journal*'s and Coase's concern with issues in legal-economic policy.[41]

The 1960s also saw the emergence of the seeds of a second strand of law and economics scholarship alongside the first. In 1957, Gary Becker had published *The Economics of Discrimination*, a book based on his University of Chicago Ph.D. dissertation that applied the model of *homo economicus* to an area beyond the standard context of economic analysis. A succession of published and unpublished papers on topics such as politics, human capital, altruism, fertility, and the allocation of time followed over the next decade. Then, in 1968, Becker's "Crime and Punishment: An Economic Approach" brought the rational maximizing agent into the legal arena. Here, Becker argued that criminals are essentially rational utility maximizers like everyone else, but the relevant constraints and opportunity sets they encounter generate maximizing outcomes that involve engaging in criminal activity. At least as important, though, was the associated implication that criminal activity, like any other labor/occupational/economic choice, is subject to alteration by scaling price incentives – that is, by altering legal rules – in one direction or the other.[42]

To give a sense for the contrast between the "old" and "new" approaches, a first-generation Chicago economics of crime and punishment might have attempted to estimate the cost of crime to society – that is, the economic impact of crime – perhaps under alternative legal regimes. Becker, in contrast, was taking the analysis in a very different direction, modeling agent behavior in response to legal rules. The subject was the criminal and his maximizing choice rather than the cost of crime to society, and the area of inquiry was the legal system rather than the economy. This work, along with the economics-informed analysis of the common law found in parts of Coase (1960) and in Yale law professor Guido Calabresi's (1961) work on torts, inspired both economists and legal scholars to examine legal behavior and legal issues through the lens of economic analysis; and it was the major impetus behind the development of a new economic analysis of legal rules and how rational individuals will respond to them.

41 To understand the origins of this work, one must really examine the greater corpus of Coase's analysis of institutions. See Medema (1994, 1996) for citations to and discussions of these various works.

42 E.g., the alteration of expected cost in the form of the product of probability of detection, probability of conviction, and monetized value of cost if convicted.

However, Becker's impact on the economic analysis of law goes well beyond his early scholarship in the field. He was the motivating force behind the establishment of a law and economics program at the National Bureau of Economic Research in 1971, the original members of which included Richard Posner, Isaac Ehrlich, and William Landes, in addition to Becker. More importantly, though, his larger efforts in the 1960s, 1970s, and 1980s to push the boundaries of economic analysis and the rational choice approach beyond the confines of traditional market activity had two important implications for the economic analysis of law. First, some of this work – for example, on drug use and addiction, marriage and divorce, adoption, and sodomy – had legal ramifications and so suggested a range of potential applications of economics to legal issues far beyond even the "new" areas of property, contracts, torts, and crime inspired by the work of Coase, Calabresi, and Becker himself. Second, the broad scope of Becker's scholarship and the research by his students and others that it stimulated progressively made the extension of the rational choice approach more like "normal science," and thus helped to create an environment in economics (and perhaps even in law) that was more receptive to the economic analysis of law than it might otherwise have been.

By the early 1970s, the idea that there could be an "economic analysis of law" had some momentum behind it. It would be hard to dispute, though, that the catalyst for the explosion of the field was the publication of Richard Posner's treatise, *Economic Analysis of Law*, in 1973. *Economic Analysis of Law* spanned virtually the entire range of law and, as Posner called it, "the legal regulation of non-market behavior" (2007, xix). It showed the possibilities of the application of economic theory to legal issues and outlined a framework for an entire field of analysis. Posner's approach to economics here bears the imprint of Stigler and Becker, as when he defined the subject as "the science of human choice in a world in which resources are limited in relation to human wants," and instructed the reader that it "explores and tests the implications of the assumption that man is a rational maximizer of his ends in life, his satisfactions – what we shall call his 'self-interest'" (1973, 1).[43] The growth of the field was further assisted by the founding, in 1972, of the *Journal of Legal Studies* (*JLS*) under Posner's editorship. The *JLS* was conceived of as a "law journal" that would "encourage the application of scientific methods to the study of the legal system" (Posner 1972, 437), and it provided an outlet for the burgeoning output in the economic analysis

[43] Posner has carried this definition of economics through several subsequent editions of the book.

of law whereas the *Journal of Law and Economics* continued (for a time) to focus on scholarship that examined issues in legal-economic policy.

Although Posner is perhaps the individual most responsible for the growth of the economic analysis of law, he actually began his law and economics career with his feet planted rather solidly in the first-generation law and economics camp.[44] Posner was working on antitrust issues as an associate professor of law at Stanford in 1968 when he sought out Aaron Director, who had an office at Stanford Law School following his retirement from Chicago, for a conversation on antitrust law.[45] This meeting and the relationship that it engendered had a significant impact on Posner's development. It was Director who taught Posner to think like a Chicago economist, introduced him to Stigler and Ronald Coase, and in this and other ways was instrumental in Posner's move to the Chicago Law School after only one year on the Stanford faculty.[46]

Posner's transformation from someone doing law and economics in the "old" way to developer of the economic analysis of law really came via the influence of Stigler and Becker, and one can see their influence in Posner's definition of economics, quoted previously. Discussions about price theory with Stigler gave Posner a set of theoretical tools that he could use to analyze legal rules. Becker's economic theory of crime and punishment suggested that price theory could be applied to a wide range of traditional legal issues, and Posner touched on most of them in his *Economic Analysis of Law*. Coase's suggestions in "The Problem of Social Cost" regarding judges' applications of economic thinking also stimulated Posner to examine whether there might be an efficiency logic underlying the development of legal rules across the common law.[47] The tools for all of this analysis were those of Chicago price theory, in its Stigler-Becker variant. The

44 On this point, see also Marciano (2006).

45 Virtually all of the dozen or so articles that Posner published from 1969 to 1971 were in the area of antitrust and related areas of regulatory policy. Posner's views on antitrust are best seen in his 1976 book, *Antitrust Law: An Economic Perspective*, a second edition of which was published in 2001.

46 Richard A. Posner, e-mail correspondence with the author, October 3, 2006, and April 25, 2007.

47 Coase said that "the courts have often recognized the economic implications of their decisions and are aware (as many economists are not) of the reciprocal nature of the [externality] problem" (1960, 19). He also suggested that when judges used terms like "reasonable" or "common or ordinary use," there seemed to be "some recognition, perhaps largely unconscious and certainly not very explicit, of the economic aspects of the questions at issue" (Coase 1960, 22). Posner has acknowledged that his "interest in using economics to try to explain legal rules stems in significant part" from this aspect of Coase's analysis in "The Problem of Social Cost." See Kitch (1983, 226).

analysis involved the application of individual decision-making calculus to agents faced with constraints imposed by legal rules, and, where relevant, the assessment of the resulting outcomes against the standard of wealth maximization.

The other major figure in the establishment of the economic analysis of law at Chicago was William Landes. Like Posner, Landes began his law and economics work in the older tradition, writing his Ph.D. thesis on employment discrimination under Becker at Columbia. His initial foray into the economic analysis of law was "An Economic Analysis of the Courts" (1974), the genesis of which was in his encounter with a news article dealing with plea bargaining. This stimulated Landes to apply the rationality postulate to parties involved in the plea-bargaining process. When he presented an early draft of the paper as a young assistant professor at the University of Chicago in 1967, senior Chicago colleague Zvi Grilliches told him that he should instead focus his energies on work that was of interest to economists. Grilliches's attitude is not surprising: Landes was, in fact, one of the first economists doing research in the economic analysis of law, and doing so as a member of an economics department faculty.

Becker played a major role in Landes's scholarly development. As Landes himself has said, "Becker opened my eyes as a student to the power of economics to illuminate social issues and has been a source of inspiration ever since" (Landes 2005, 306). Beyond this, it was Becker who suggested that Landes and Posner collaborate, and, as noted earlier, Becker brought the two of them into the NBER's law and economics program at the time of its founding in 1971. Posner and Landes have coauthored roughly three dozen books and articles in work that Landes has called "a truly joint effort." He does allow that he had "greater responsibility for the economic modeling and empirical analysis, and Posner for the law," but he is unequivocal in saying that each of them contributed to all aspects of the analysis (Landes 2005, 300). Becker also helped bring Landes back to Chicago in 1973, when he joined Coase as an economist on the law faculty.[48]

6.3. Making Connections

To this point, then, we have established that both Chicago price theory and Chicago law and economics underwent transitions during the 1960s and 1970s. Is there a connection? The answer given here is yes: The history of law and economics at Chicago reflects two different visions of the subject,

[48] Landes had left Chicago for the NBER in 1968.

derivative of two different visions of price theory and of the definition of economics.

Chicago price theory began as a theory grounded in basic Marshallian demand-supply analysis and with fairly loose grounding in a theory of individual behavior. Its domain was that body of activity considered "economic" since at least the classical period – production, consumption, and the distribution of "economic goods and services" – and that was reflected in Knight's conception of the economic organization. Early Chicago law and economics fit squarely into this framework. Director had learned his price theory from Knight and Viner and taught it in the Law School for roughly two decades. Many of those doing law and economics in the Chicago way in the late 1950s and the 1960s had learned their price theory from Director. The work of Director and his students thus reflected the same early Chicago price theory that one finds in Knight's *Economic Organization* and Friedman's *Price Theory*. It also flowed out of a subject-matter definition of economics: It was concerned with analyzing the interaction between the law and the economy, and the study of how the legal environment impacts the economic system was seen as an important and even necessary component of economic analysis. This was the law and economics of Director and Coase, and it filled the pages of the *Journal of Law and Economics* in the 1950s, 1960s, and into the 1970s.

The "new" Chicago price theory was grounded in a rational choice approach to individual behavior and was the foundation of a larger movement in which economic analysis came to be viewed not simply as the study of the economic system per se, but as an approach, method, or toolkit applicable to all areas of life in which choices are made. The logic of this extension is simple: Economics is the study of choice; if preferences are assumed to be stable – a hallmark of the "new" approach to price theory[49] – should not economics be applicable to individual decisions across the choice spectrum? The economic analysis of law was thus part – and one of the earliest manifestations – of a larger movement within economics, sometimes referred to as "economics imperialism," that saw in rational choice analysis the key to understanding the behavior of agents in all manner of "non-market" contexts. It consciously reached beyond the boundaries of economics into other fields, with a view toward influencing scholarship in *those* fields, rather than to bring back to economics insights that would contribute to the understanding of the economic system. In the case of the economic analysis of law, the focus was on the application of price theory

[49] The definitive statement here is Stigler and Becker (1977).

to agent behavior within the legal arena, and the analysis had little or nothing to do with understanding the legal bases of the economic system – that is, with Knight's "economic organization." Simply put, what we see in the move from the first generation of law and economics to the second – that is, to economic analysis of law – is a shift from the analysis of how rights influence the economic organization and its performance to the analysis of how rights impact the behavior of rational individuals with respect to law. One can see this evolution played out the pages of the *Journal of Law and Economics* from the late 1960s through the 1980s.

If the explanation for the transition in Chicago law and economics lies at least in part in the transition that took place in Chicago price theory, it remains to offer some explanation for the latter movement. Although this topic deserves its own paper, if not a book, two larger professional currents can be identified as instrumental. The application of rational choice analysis in economics did not originate at Chicago; rather, it was the result of a complex set of phenomena, including the efforts of scholars such as Kenneth Arrow and Gerard Debreu to work out the contours of general equilibrium analysis, an approach that was anathema to Friedman and Stigler, who remained wedded to a Marshallian approach against this larger professional current. However, Becker, for one, saw the rational choice model as a powerful tool for the analysis of individual behavior inside and outside of traditional market contexts, and he grafted this to the Chicago partial equilibrium framework. Stigler, too, moved increasingly in this direction.

The rational choice framework, however, also resonated with the definition of economics laid out by Robbins in his *Essay on the Nature and Significance of Economic Science*, a definition that, although a long time in gaining broad-based professional acceptance, had come to achieve wide currency by the early 1960s. But Robbins's 1932 discussion did more than lay out a definition of economics. Although the evolution of rational choice analysis across the social sciences is a complex phenomenon,[50] the license for economists to cross over into subjects traditionally noneconomic in nature, too, came via Robbins's *Essay*, at least indirectly. Rejecting the extant notion that the boundaries between "economics" and "not economics" are set by behavior that is or is not directed toward the enhancement of material welfare, Robbins argued that economics focuses on the form of behavior "imposed by the influence of scarcity" and went on to note the implications of this definition:

[50] See, e.g., Amadae (2004).

> It follows from this, therefore, that in so far as it offers this aspect, *any kind of human behaviour* falls within the scope of Economic Generalizations. We do not say that the production of potatoes is economic activity and the production of philosophy is not. We say rather that, in so far as either kind of activity involves the relinquishment of other desired alternatives, it has its economic aspect. There are *no limitations* on the subject-matter of Economic Science save this. (Robbins 1932, 16, emphasis added)

When writing "no limitations," Robbins almost certainly did not anticipate how the boundaries of economics would be stretched in the decades to come. Indeed, Gary Becker has even gone so far as to suggest that Robbins did not really believe his own definition, given that he did not discuss the extension of economics to other fields in 1932 or at any point thereafter.[51]

It took more than three decades following the publication of Robbins's *Essay* for scholars to begin seriously extending the economic paradigm (Backhouse and Medema 2009a). The practice of economics continued to reflect the "old" view that economics is the study of the economic system – the same view that characterized the first generation of Chicago law and economics – even as it assimilated the idea that it is choice under scarcity within that context that defines the scope of economic analysis. Yet it also seems clear that Robbins defined economics in a manner that naturally allowed for its extension beyond the analysis of standard market phenomena. There is certainly some tension evident in the Chicago price theory tradition between Knight's "economic organization" definition and the scarcity approach of Robbins. That having been said, the Chicago school does seem to have accepted the Robbins definition and its potentially broader implications more quickly than did the rest of the profession, with Stigler being among the first U.S. economists to use it in a textbook.[52] The gradual institutionalization of the Robbins definition meant that it was only a matter of time before economists began to broaden the scope of their analysis to areas such as law.[53] Indeed, by the Robbins definition, the analysis of legal issues falls squarely within the scope of economics. Law is unambiguously about rights, and rights by their very nature exist because of the problem of scarcity. And under the Robbins definition, phenomena with a scarcity component are, prima facie, amenable to analysis using price theory.

The discontinuity between the first and second generations of law and economics and the price theories that underpin them is also evident in the

[51] Conversation with the author, January 2007.

[52] The Cowles Commission economists, then housed at Chicago, were also quick to accept the Robbins definition. For more on this, see Backhouse and Medema (2009b).

[53] See Backhouse and Medema (2009a).

attitudes of the players themselves. Director, generally considered to be the founder of Chicago law and economics, was never interested in the extension of economic analysis to other disciplines, nor were Viner and Knight. Director was old school: His work was not concerned with expanding the boundaries of economics to include law, but with making the study of the economic system more complete by analyzing how legal rules impact economic performance. The divide is made even more explicit by Coase, who has commented directly on this issue. Coase argued that Robbins's definition "makes economics a study of human choice," which, he says, "is clearly too wide if regarded as a description of what economists do" (1978, 207). Coase finds more congenial the definitions given by Marshall in his *Principles* (1890, 1) – "a study of mankind in the ordinary business of life" – and, interestingly, by Stigler in his 1952 edition – the Knightian definition rather than the Robbins-esque one used in his 1942 and 1946 editions. Coase both objected to the rational actor model[54] and, evincing an attitude bordering on outright hostility, predicted the failure of economics imperialism because he felt that economists lacked expertise in these "outside" areas. To date, of course, his prediction has proven incorrect.[55] Even so, Coase has continued to be quite blunt in stating his indifferent feelings about the economic analysis of law. He has said that, in writing "The Problem of Social Cost," he was not interested in offering a new perspective on jurisprudence but, rather was attempting "to improve our analysis of the working of the economic system." He went on to note that "Law came into the article because, in a regime of positive transaction costs, the character of the law becomes one of the main factors determining the performance of the economy" (Coase 1993, 251).[56] Indeed, Coase has consciously distanced himself from Posner, whose "main interest is in the legal system" (Coase 1993, 251), noting that "I have no interest in lawyers or legal education" (Coase, in Kitch 1983, 192) and acknowledging that "In the development of the economic analysis of the law [i.e., the "new" law and economics] ... Posner has clearly played the major role" (Coase 1993, 251).[57]

54 For example, there is no mention or use of it in "The Problem of Social Cost."

55 Interestingly, Coase (1978, 206) also cites (approvingly) Stigler's 1952 definition of economics, which is the Knightian rather than Robbins-esque definition, and notes its connection to the traditional subject matter studied by economists.

56 Landes, too, understands the measure of discontinuity in the Chicago law and economics tradition. As he has put it, the former analyzes "the legal regulation of markets" whereas the latter "applies to tools of economics to the legal system itself" (2005, 295).

57 Robert Bork has also been critical of the economic analysis of law. Posner (1993a,b) has criticized Coase for his attitude toward the economic analysis of law.

6.4. Conclusion

There has been a propensity among economists and others to speak in terms of a homogeneous "Chicago School," or, at the very least, to describe the evolution of the School as one of continuity from generation to generation. In fact, however, the Chicago School has never been homogeneous in approach or in ideology, and the passage of time has seen at least as much change as continuity at Chicago. This is certainly true of price theory and of law and economics, each of which has loomed so large in the Chicago School's history. Although both traditions have associated with them some measure of continuity with their past, each has also been the subject of fundamental structural change. As the present chapter has attempted to show, the changes on the price theory side played a significant role in stimulating changes in Chicago law and economics.

References

Amadae, Sonja. 2004. *Rationalizing Capitalist Democracy: The Cold War Origins of Rational Choice Liberalism*. Chicago: University of Chicago Press.

Aslanbeigui, Nahid and Steven G. Medema. 1998. "Beyond the Dark Clouds: Pigou and Coase on Social Cost." *History of Political Economy* 30 (Winter): 601–625.

Backhouse, Roger E. and Steven G. Medema. 2009a. "Defining Economics: The Long Road to the Acceptance of the Robbins Definition." *Economica* 76 (October): 805–820.

2009b. "Robbins's *Essay* and the Axiomatization of Economics." *Journal of the History of Economic Thought* 31 (December): 485–499.

Becker, Gary S. 1957. *The Economics of Discrimination*. Chicago: University of Chicago Press.

1968. "Crime and Punishment: An Economic Approach." *Journal of Political Economy* 76 (March/April): 169–217.

1971. *Economic Theory*. New York: Knopf.

1991. "Milton Friedman, 1912-." In Edward Shils, ed., *Remembering the University of Chicago: Teachers, Scientists, and Scholars*. Chicago: University of Chicago Press. Reprinted in J. Daniel Hammond, ed., *The Legacy of Milton Friedman as Teacher*, volume 1. Aldershot: Edward Elgar Publishing.

1976. *The Economic Approach to Human Behavior*. Chicago: University of Chicago Press.

2007. "Introduction to the Transaction Edition." In Gary S. Becker, *Economic Theory*. New Brunswick, NJ: Transaction Publishers.

Bork, R.H. 1967. "Antitrust and Monopoly: The Goals of Antitrust Policy." *American Economic Review* 57: 242–253.

Bork, R.H. and W.S. Bowman, Jr. 1965. "The Crisis in Antitrust." *Columbia Law Review* 65: 363–376.

Bowman, W.S., Jr. 1957. "Tying Arrangements and the Leverage Problem." *Yale Law Journal* 67: 19–36.

Burstein, M.L. 1960. "The Economics of Tie-in Sales." *Review of Economics and Statistics* 42: 68–73.

Calabresi, Guido 1961. "Some Thoughts on Risk Distribution and the Law of Torts." *Yale Law Journal* 70 (March): 499–553.

Coase, Ronald H. 1959. "The Federal Communications Commission." *Journal of Law and Economics* 2 (October): 1–40.

1960. "The Problem of Social Cost." *Journal of Law and Economics* 3 (October): 1–44.

1961. "The British Post Office and the Messenger Companies." *Journal of Law and Economics* 4 (October): 12–65.

1962. "The Interdepartment Radio Advisory Committee." *Journal of Law and Economics* 5 (October): 17–47.

1975. "Marshall on Method." *Journal of Law and Economics* 18 (April): 25–31.

1978. "Economics and Contiguous Disciplines." *Journal of Legal Studies* 7 (June): 201–211.

1984. "The New Institutional Economics." *Journal of Institutional and Theoretical Economics* 140: 229–231.

1993. "Law and Economics at Chicago." *Journal of Law and Economics* 36 (April): 239–54.

Director, Aaron and Edward H. Levi. 1956. "Law and the Future: Trade Regulation." *Northwestern Law Review* 51: 281–296.

Duxbury, Neil. 1995. *Patterns of American Jurisprudence*. Oxford: Oxford University Press.

Evensky, Jerry. 2005. "'Chicago Smith' versus 'Kirkaldy Smith'." *History of Political Economy* 37 (Summer): 197–203.

Fand, David I. 1999. "Friedman's Price Theory: Economics 300 at the University of Chicago in 1947–1951." In J. Daniel Hammond, ed., *The Legacy of Milton Friedman as Teacher*, volume 1. Aldershot: Edward Elgar Publishing, pp. 9–21.

Friedman, Milton. 1949. "The Marshallian Demand Curve." *Journal of Political Economy* LVII: 463–495.

1962. *Price Theory: A Provisional Text*. Chicago: Aldine.

1976. *Price Theory*. Chicago: Aldine. Reprinted with a new introduction by Steven G. Medema. New Brunswick, NJ: Aldine-Transaction, 2007.

Friedman, Milton and L.J. Savage 1948. "The Utility Analysis of Choices Involving Risk." *Journal of Political Economy* 56 (August): 279–304.

Hammond, J. Daniel and Claire H. Hammond. 2006. *Making Chicago Price Theory: Friedman-Stigler Correspondence, 1945–1957*. London: Routledge.

Hammond, J. Daniel and Steven G. Medema, eds. Forthcoming. *Classics in Chicago Price Theory, 1920–1979*. Aldershot: Edward Elgar Publishing.

Hovenkamp, Herbert. 1986. "Chicago and its Alternatives." *Duke Law Journal* 1986 (December): 1014–1029.

1995. "Law and Economics in the United States: A Brief Historical Survey." *Cambridge Journal of Economics* 19 (April): 331–352.

Johnson, Glenn 1947/2008. "Notes from Milton Friedman's Course in Economic Theory, Economics 300A, University of Chicago, Winter Quarter 1947" (edited by Marianne Johnson and Warren J. Samuels). *Research in the History of Economic Thought and Methodology*, vol. 26-C: 63–117.

Katz, Wilbur 1937. "A Four-Year Program for Legal Education." *University of Chicago Law Review* 4 (June): 527–536.

Kitch, Edmund W. 1983. "The Fire of Truth: A Remembrance of Law and Economics at Chicago, 1932–1970." *Journal of Law and Economics* 26 (April): 163–233.

Knight, Frank H. 1922. "Ethics and the Economic Interpretation." *Quarterly Journal of Economics* 36 (May): 454–481.

1924. "The Limitations of Scientific Method in Economics." In Ross B. Emmett, ed., *Selected Essays by Frank Knight, Volume One: What is Truth in Economics?* Chicago: University of Chicago Press, 1999.

1933. *The Economic Organization.* Chicago: University of Chicago Press.

1934. "The Nature of Economic Science in Some Recent Discussions." *American Economic Review* 24(2): 225–238.

Landes, William M. 1971. "An Economic Analysis of the Courts." *Journal of Law and Economics* 14: 61–107.

2005. "The Art of Law and Economics: An Autobiographical Essay." In Francesco Parisi and Charles K. Rowley, eds., *The Origins of Law and Economics Essays by the Founding Fathers.* Cheltenham: Edward Elgar, pp. 291–308.

Llewellyn, Karl N. 1925. "The Effect of Legal Institutions upon Economics." *American Economic Review* 15 (December): 655–683.

Marciano, Alain 2006. "Public Choice, New Law and Economics and the Economic Analysis of Law." *Working Paper*, University of Reims Champagne Ardenne.

Marshall, Alfred 1920. *Principles of Economics*, 8th edition. London: Macmillan.

McCloskey, Deirdre N. 1998. "The Good Old Coase Theorem and the Good Old Chicago School: A Comment on Zerbe and Medema." In Steven G. Medema, ed., *Coasean Economics: Law and Economics and the New Institutional Economics*, Boston: Kluwer, pp. 239–248.

McGee, J.S. 1958. "Predatory Price Cutting: The Standard Oil (N.J.) Case." *Journal of Law and Economics* 1: 137–169.

Medema, Steven G. 1994. *Ronald H. Coase.* London: Macmillan.

1996. "Ronald Coase on Economics and Economic Method." *History of Economics Review* 24 (Summer): 1–22.

1998. "Wandering the Road From Pluralism to Posner: The Transformation of Law and Economics, 1920s–1970s." In Mary S. Morgan and Malcolm Rutherford, eds., *The Transformation of American Economics: From Interwar Pluralism to Postwar Neoclassicism: History of Political Economy Annual Supplement* 30: 202–24.

2007. "Introduction." In Milton Friedman, ed., *Price Theory.* New Brunswick, NJ: Aldine-Transaction.

2009a. "Adam Smith and the Chicago School." In Jeffrey Young, ed., *The Elgar Companion to Adam Smith.* Aldershot: Edward Elgar Publishing, pp. 346–357.

2009b. *The Hesitant Hand: Taming Self-Interest in the History of Economic Ideas.* Princeton: Princeton University Press.

Mercuro, Nicholas and Steven G. Medema. 2006. *Economics and the Law: From Posner to Post Modernism and Beyond*, 2nd edition. Princeton: Princeton University Press.

Mirowski, Philip and D. Wade Hands. 1998. "A Paradox of Budgets: The Postwar Stabilization of American Demand Theory." In Mary S. Morgan and Malcolm Rutherford, eds., *The Transformation of American Economics: From Interwar*

Pluralism to Postwar Neoclassicism: History of Political Economy Annual Supplement 30: 260–292.

Morgenstern, Oskar. 1936. "Logistics and the Social Sciences." Reprinted in Andrew Schotter, ed., *Selected Economic Writings of Oskar Morgenstern*. New York: New York University Press, pp. 389–404.

Plant, Sir Arnold. 1974. *Selected Economic Essays and Addresses*. London: Routledge and Kegan Paul.

Posner, Richard A. 1969. "Oligopoly and the Antitrust Laws: A Suggested Approach." *Stanford Law Review* 21: 1562–1606.

1972. "Volume One of *The Journal of Legal Studies* – An Afterword." *Journal of Legal Studies* 1 (June): 437–440.

1973. *Economic Analysis of Law*. Boston: Little, Brown and Company.

1976. *Antitrust Law: An Economic Perspective*. Chicago: University of Chicago Press. Second edition, 2001.

1981. *The Economics of Justice*. Cambridge, MA: Harvard University Press.

1987. "The Decline of Law as an Autonomous Discipline: 1962–1987." *Harvard Law Review* 100 (February): 761–780.

1993a. "The New Institutional Economics Meets Law and Economics." *Journal of Institutional and Theoretical Economics* 149 (March): 73–87.

1993b. "Ronald Coase and Methodology." *Journal of Economic Perspectives* 7 (Fall): 195–210.

2001. *Frontiers of Legal Theory*. Cambridge, MA: Harvard University Press.

2007. *Economic Analysis of Law*, 7th edition. New York: Wolters Kluwer.

Reder, Melvin W. 1982. "Chicago Economics: Permanence and Change." *Journal of Economic Literature* 20 (March): 1–38.

Robbins, Lionel. 1932. *An Essay on the Nature and Significance of Economic Science*. London: Macmillan.

Stigler, George J. 1942. *The Theory of Competitive Price*. New York: Macmillan.

1946. *The Theory of Price*. New York: Macmillan.

1952. *The Theory of Price*, revised edition. New York: Macmillan.

1966. *The Theory of Price*, 3rd edition. New York: Macmillan.

1971. "Smith's Travels on the Ship of State." *History of Political Economy* 3 (Fall): 265–77.

1976. "The Successes and Failures of Professor Smith." *Journal of Political Economy* 84 (December): 1199–1213.

1981. "The Economist as Preacher." *The Tanner Lectures on Human Values*, vol. 2 (Salt Lake City: University of Utah Press). Reprinted in *The Economist as Preacher and Other Essays*, Chicago: University of Chicago Press, 1982, pp. 3–13.

1987. *The Theory of Price*, 4th edition. New York: Macmillan.

1988. *Memoirs of an Unregulated Economist*. New York: Basic Books.

Stigler, George J. and Gary S. Becker. 1977. "De Gustibus Non Est Disputandum." *American Economic Review* 67 (March): 76–90.

Telser, L.G. 1960. "Why Should Manufacturers Want Fair Trade?" *Journal of Law and Economics* 3: 86–105.

Van Horn, Rob. 2009. "Reinventing Monopoly and the Role of Corporations." In Philip Mirowski and Dieter Plehwe, eds., *The Road From Mont Pelerin: The Making of the Neoliberal Thought Collective*. Cambridge, MA: Harvard University Press, pp. 204–237.

Van Horn, Rob and Philip Mirowski. 2009. "The Rise of the Chicago School of Economics and the Birth of Neoliberalism." In Philip Mirowski and Dieter Plehwe, eds., *The Road From Mont Pelerin: The Making of the Neoliberal Thought Collective*. Cambridge, MA: Harvard University Press, pp. 139–78.

SEVEN

Intervening in Laissez-Faire Liberalism

Chicago's Shift on Patents

Robert Van Horn and Matthias Klaes

The Chicago School is typically associated with a pro-patent position: They have defended patents on the grounds that they are vital to encourage innovation and have condemned claims that patents allow patent-holding firms to extend their monopoly power from one market to another. The Nobel Prize–winning Chicago economist, George Stigler, claimed that an inventor's financial incentive was optimum only if he had exclusive and perpetual ownership of the patent.[1] Steven Cheung, a third-generation representative of the Chicago School, observed in 1977: "In a free society an individual owns his brain, and by way of a number of different arrangements he may utilize and market the outputs of this mental resource to generate income" (Cheung 1977, 597). To Cheung, the patent system was the best way to facilitate this generation of income. In 1973, Ward Bowman, a principal proponent of the Chicago law and economics movement in the 1960s and 1970s, maintained that alleged forms of patent misuse might "actually be the most efficient use of the patent from the social as well as the private point of view. It pays monopolists as well as competitors to be efficient" (1973, 9). More recently, in 2006, Richard Epstein, a public face of Chicago law and

We would like to express our gratitude to the Center for the History of Political Economy at Duke University for research support during the early stages of this paper. We would also like to thank Craufurd Goodwin, Thomas A. Stapleford, Ross Emmett, Bruce Caldwell, Edward Nik-Khah, Dave Campbell, James Wible, and the participants of the 2009 History of Economics Society meeting for helpful comments and Philip Mirowski for directing us to some helpful archival material. Last, but not least, we would like to thank Monica Van Horn and David DeLong for helpful editorial suggestions on multiple drafts. Archival material quoted from the Mont Pèlerin Society Records, Liberaal Archief Ghent quoted with permission. Archival Material quoted from Aaron Director Papers, Regenstein Library, University of Chicago quoted with permission.

1 GSRL, undated typescript, box 23, folder: "Discussion of K. Arrow on Risk-Bearing." For more on Stigler's pro-patent position, see Nik-Khah (2010).

economics, defended the pharmaceutical industry from prospective regulations. Taking a pro-patent position, he stated, "[Pharmaceutical companies] are very heavily dependent on the patent law, [which] have allowed these firms to bring a wide variety of vital products to market" (Epstein 2006).

However, members of the Chicago School did not always take a pro-patent position. In the 1930s, the respected University of Chicago professor and self-identified classical liberal, Henry Simons, described monopoly in all its forms, including "gigantic corporations" and "other agencies of price control," as "the great enemy of democracy" because they undermined the necessary condition for democracy to flourish, namely, a competitive market.[2] In championing democracy and competitive markets, Simons displayed a broad hostility toward patents and claimed that the patent system enabled the creation and extension of monopoly power.

Simons was not alone in his position on patents. In the 1930s and 1940s, other liberal Chicago economists such as Frank Knight, European liberals such as Michael Polanyi, and government leaders in the United States displayed a broad hostility toward patents. The circumstances of the post–WW II period, however, motivated classical liberals in the United States and in Europe to reconsider their anti-patent position. They found their doctrine overall on the verge of demise and unable to serve as a countervailing intellectual force to the challenges of Keynesianism, Institutional reformism, and socialism. Led by Friedrich Hayek, liberals turned to organizing an intellectual movement, the Mont Pèlerin Society, a transnational institutional project that sought to reinvent a liberalism that had some prospect of challenging collectivist doctrines ascendant in the immediate postwar period. A crucial objective of the Mont Pèlerin Society was to understand the legal foundations necessary for effective competition – that is, how to create a competitive order. Because patent law was a significant part of the competitive order, liberals believed that examining patent law was essential to reinvigorating liberalism.

Beyond the Mont Pèlerin Society, the effort to reformulate liberalism took place at institutions based in Europe and America. In some places, such as Germany, the effort was already well under way by the time of the first Mont Pèlerin meeting. At the University of Freiburg, "Ordoliberals," such as Walter Eucken, had been creating a liberal program suited to the institutional milieu of Germany (Ptak 2009, 101–102). In America, the central base was the University of Chicago Law School. Hayek had acquired funding from a right-wing foundation, the Volker Fund, to set up a research

2 Simons (1948, 43). For evidence of Simons' classical liberal bent, see DeLong (1990).

project called the Free Market Study (1946–1952). Starting in the fall of 1946, Director, who headed the study, along with other Chicago economists and lawyers such as Edward Levi and Milton Friedman, attempted to reconstruct key liberal concepts with a primary focus on the competitive order. Consequently, they studied issues such as monopoly, antitrust law, and patent law. Because of their focus on the legal foundations of capitalism, their efforts mark the rise of postwar Chicago law and economics.

With the caveat that the development of postwar liberal thought was an international and multiinstitutional development, this chapter will focus on the Chicago School and its efforts to arrive at a more robust liberal position. More specifically, it will identify a significant change in the Chicago School's attitude toward patents. In previous work, the first author of this chapter has written about the roots of Chicago law and economics in connection with the emergence of a reconstituted liberalism at Chicago, or "Chicago neoliberalism," as it relates to industrial monopoly, concentrations of market power, and antitrust law (Van Horn 2009).[3] The second author has explored the links between the emergence of Chicago neoliberalism and the rise of neoinstitutional economics (Campbell and Klaes 2008). This chapter continues in the spirit of our earlier work and focuses on patent law, especially patent issues that relate to antitrust law. It traces the shift from the Chicago School's broad hostility toward patents and its position that patents extended monopoly power to its broad acceptance of patents and its condemnation of claims that patents extend monopoly. This chapter links this transition to the efforts of the Free Market Study and its sister project, the Antitrust Project (1952–1956); as a Chicago neoliberal position regarding industrial monopoly and large corporations emerged, a new position toward patents developed.

Chicago neoliberal claims of the Free Market Study and the Antitrust Project later played an important role in advancing the ideas of the Chicago law and economics movement in the 1960s and 1970s, especially in the area of antitrust law. However, it was not until the 1980s that these claims started to have an impact on the economic policy in the United States. Since the era of the Reagan administration, the Chicago School's take on patents and

[3] The term "neoliberalism" was coined at the Colloque Walter Lippmann in Paris in 1938. This term heralded the appearance of a new orientation toward the previous liberal tradition (Plehwe 2009), and we qualify it as "Chicago neoliberal" when the departure is associated with the work of the Chicago School. Notably, Milton Friedman later used the term "neoliberalism" self-referentially in his 1951 article, "Neoliberalism and Its Prospects." For a sophisticated treatment of the term "neoliberalism," see Mirowski (2009) and Plehwe (2009).

antitrust law has brought the Chicago law and economics much renown. In particular, the Chicago law and economics argument that a patent-holding firm, or any firm with monopoly power, cannot extend that monopoly power into another market has come to be called "The Single Monopoly Profit Theorem" in the prominent antitrust casebooks (e.g., Areeda, Kaplow, and Edlin 2004, 382–383).[4] This argument has come to be "widely accepted," according to Supreme Court Justice Breyer, by "several members of the Supreme Court."[5]

For many years, the courts held (and to some degree still do) that a patent could be used as a lever to extend monopoly power from the market of the patented product to the market of an unpatented product through the use of a tying arrangement, and thus maintained that patent tie-ins should be per se illegal.[6] In contrast, the Single Monopoly Profit Theorem states that, in general, patent tie-ins cannot extend or create monopoly power. That is, if a firm with a patent monopoly in one market ties its patented product to an unpatented product, it thereby cannot extend its monopoly power into the market of the unpatented product through the tying arrangement.

The topic of patent law is a vast and intricate one, and the forms of patent misuse are numerous.[7] For a manageable scope, this chapter will primarily focus on patent tie-ins because of the Chicago School's notable contribution to this topic, and it will focus on the Chicago School's general attitude toward patents.

Four sections follow. Section One describes the broad hostility toward patents in the 1930s and early 1940s, especially in the economic thought of Arnold Plant, Michael Polanyi, Henry Simons, and Frank Knight. Section

4 Areeda, et al. state: "[T]he 'theorem' is that a monopoly in a single market can choose to exercise its power in other markets … but that in so doing it does not earn more than one monopoly profit, it does not gain monopoly power over additional markets, and it does not increase the harm it causes society." They added, "By exercising its power in other markets … the firm may increase its profits by capturing a *larger portion* of consumers' value for the goods of its single monopoly; in other words, it may more fully capture its single monopoly profit" (383).

5 See then Judge Breyer's opinion in *Town of Concord v. Boston Edison*, 915 F.2d (1990).

6 A tying arrangement is one form of vertical integration. Tying takes place when a seller stipulates that a buyer must purchase the "tied" product in order to obtain the "tying" product, the one the buyer wants. A tying arrangement is almost always imposed by the seller on the buyer. For example, if retailer, a small business owner, runs a fishing boat business and if a manufacturer that commands monopoly in the fishing boat motor market demands that the retailer must purchase the manufacturer's motor oil in order to purchase its motors, then the manufacturer has tied its fishing motors (tying product) to its oil (tied product).

7 For a thorough overview of some of the various forms of patent misuse in the early 1950s, see Watkins and Stocking (1950).

Two turns to the opening session of the 1947 Mont Pèlerin meeting, "'Free' Enterprise or Competitive Order," and argues that when Director began his effort to reconstitute liberalism, he, like Hayek, held anti-patent views and maintained that patents enabled the creation and extension of monopoly power. Section Three traces the emergence of a pro-patent Chicago neoliberal position by focusing on the work of the Free Market Study and the Antitrust Project. The concluding section briefly explores how Ward Bowman, a representative of Chicago law and economics and a former Antitrust Project member, further developed the pro-patent position in the 1960s and 1970s and repudiated the arguments of those associated with the anti-patent consensus prior to 1950.

Part Four of this volume, Debating "Chicago Neoliberalism," sheds some light on the question of why Chicago neoliberalism developed the way it did. In this chapter, we complement this effort. We explore the effort of the Free Market Study and the Antitrust Project to reconstitute liberalism and thereby offer further evidence of the rise of Chicago neoliberalism. To do so, we trace the development of the changing position on patents, and thereby chart the Chicago School's move from its broad hostility toward patents and its claim that patents created and extended monopoly power to its broad acceptance of patents and its position that patents could not be used as a lever to create and extend monopoly power.

7.1. An Antipatent Consensus

Discussion about patents during the 1930s and 1940s was increasingly characterized by a skeptical stance and corresponding calls for corrective action. In the United States, the Temporary National Economic Committee (TNEC), a late New Deal creation, published strong anti-patent statements linking patents to the growing concentration of power in the United States economy. "New Dealers," who opposed concentrations of power in industry, believed that patents allowed for the creation and perpetuation of monopolistic strongholds. Ellis Hawley, a prominent TNEC historian, succinctly conveyed their views as follows:

> [Patent] laws, it seemed, offered the favored concern every opportunity to dig in, to fortify its position, seize the channels of distribution, and barricade the trade against any newcomer. Once entrenched, a firm could use the law to hold and expand its position. It could threaten complicated infringement suits in which the odds naturally favored the party with the greatest financial staying power. It could hem in a basic process by acquisition of patents covering all possible improvements.... And if the circumstances warranted, it could use such devices as patent pools and cross-licensing agreements to limit the business to a favored few. (1966, 368–369)

Thurman Arnold, the renowned trustbuster and New Deal proponent, played a key role advancing the New Dealers' claim that patents allowed for the extension of monopoly power (Waller 2005). During his time as head of the Antitrust Division of the Department of Justice (1938–1943), Arnold crusaded against patent abuses. He testified before Congress, broadcasted his message over public radio, and published his views in popular magazines. "Arnold railed every chance he could against the misuse of patents," wrote Spencer Waller, Arnold's biographer (2005, 98). According to Arnold, patent misuse, like other forms of monopolistic control, needed to be curbed for the free market economy to thrive.

By the 1940s, the Supreme Court had adopted a general hostility toward patents (Hovenkamp 2005, 261). Indeed, some have called the 1940s the "Dark Ages" of patents (May and Sell 2006, 139). The origins of this hostility toward patents in the Supreme Court may be traced back to the Clayton Act of 1914. Contrary to the precedent of the Court at that time, this act declared that a tying arrangement that substantially lessened competition was illegal; this act's tying provision explicitly included patented goods. Soon thereafter, the Court heard *Motion Picture Patents* (1917).[8] Motion Picture had sold movie projectors subject to the licensing restriction that only the defendant's films could be shown with them. The Court condemned the defendant's practice. It claimed that the defendant sought to monopolize the whole movie industry; the tying arrangement allowed the defendant to create a bottleneck with its movie projectors that enabled it to control exhibited films. According to Herbert Hovenkamp, "Ever since ... *Motion Picture Patents* the antitrust law of tying has been closely allied to disputes about the appropriate scope of [intellectual property] rights" (2005, 261). Two later cases refined and extended the legal reasoning of *Motion Picture*. In *Cabrice Corp. of America* (1931), Justice Brandeis articulated what has become known as the "leverage theory." Herbert Hovenkamp states: "Brandeis's theory reflects the belief, then current, that monopoly is ubiquitous and easily spread by the simple device of contracts tying monopoly to nonmonopoly products. It also reveals the period's deep distrust of patents" (2005, 33).[9] From 1939 to 1947, in nearly a dozen antitrust cases, the Supreme Court condemned the use of patents to monopolize industry or stifle competition.[10] About one-third of those cases involved patent

[8] *Motion Picture Patents Co. v. Universal Films Mfg. Co.*, 243 U.S. 502 (1917)

[9] *Cabrice Corp. v. American Patents Corp.*, 283 U.S. 27 (1931)

[10] See: *Ethyl Gasoline Corp. v. United States*, 309 U.S. 436 (1940), *Morton Salt Co. v. G. S. Suppiger Co.*, 314 U.S. 488 (1942), *B. B. Chemical Co. v. Ellis*, 314 U.S. 495 (1942), *United States v. Univis Lens Co.*, 316 U.S. 241 (1942), *United States v. Masonite Corp.*, 316 U.S. 265 (1942), *Mercoid Corp. v. Mid-Continental Investment Co.*, 320 U.S. 661 (1944), *Mercoid*

tie-ins. In one of the patent tie-in cases, in 1947, the Supreme Court ruled in *International Salt* that all tying arrangements that involved a product in which a seller has a monopoly, such as a patent, were per se illegal.[11] In sum, in the 1940s, the U.S. courts tended to believe that a tying arrangement was destructive and that a patent presumed the existence of economic power.

Echoing the anti-patent concerns of U.S. political leaders and the U.S. Supreme Court were two future European members of the Mont Pèlerin Society, Arnold Plant[12] and Michael Polanyi.[13] Plant maintained that patents, like all forms of monopoly, were deleterious to society because they diverted resources from other forms of production that might be more beneficial to society. According to Plant, with a patent system in place, a certain combination of output would result – say, Combination A. With an open market price system in place and without a patent system, another combination of output would result – say, Combination B. Which combination was more generally useful? According to Plant, this could not be determined by any system of economic analysis. Thus, he trenchantly stated, "the science of economics as it stands to-day furnishes no basis of justification for this enormous experiment in the encouragement of a particular activity by enabling monopolistic price control" (51). In lamenting the economic troubles of England, Plant asked: "Can it be that the patent system is in part responsible for our present economic troubles?" (51)[14]

Corp. v. Minneapolis-Honeywell Regulator Co., 320 U.S. 680 (1944), *Hartford-Empire Co. v. U.S.*, 323 U.S. 386, 392 (1945), *United States v. National Lead Co.*, 332 U.S. 319 (1947), and *International Salt Co. v. United States*, 332 U.S. 392 (1947).

11 *International Salt Co. v. United States*, 332 U.S. 392 (1947)

12 Plant, a professor at the London School of Economics (LSE), got his chair in the economics department in 1930. He received a Knighthood in the Birthday Honours in 1947, the same year he joined the Mont Pèlerin Society. In 1934, he published two articles, one on patents and the other on copyright.

13 Polanyi was a philosopher of science with the utmost concern about the social distribution of knowledge. He had fled from Berlin to Manchester when the Nazis came to power. His work exploring the nature, authority, and success of science won him acclaim and provided some foundational principles for the field of science studies. For more on Polanyi, refer to Mirowski (2004, 54).

14 In providing additional criticisms of the patent system, Plant's analysis included four noteworthy anti-patent claims. First, Plant observed that patents were unnecessary in some industries for the production of inventions. Without patents, the fashion industry burgeoned with a high rate of invention. Additionally, the creation of inventions in the field of medicine took place, partly due to altruistic motives and professional drive for repute. Second, according to Plant, the patent system only served the one who secured the patent, providing no financial reward to the numerous other participants in the invention process. Plant incisively stated, "Lotteries in open competition there may well be; but the lottery of the patent system awards but one prize, and that a monopoly, while those

For Polanyi, invention and research crucially depended on the vast, unrestricted network of human knowledge. Patent law primarily proved problematic because, according to Polanyi, "it aims for a purpose which cannot be rationally achieved. It tries to parcel up a stream of creative thought into a series of distinct claims, each of which is to constitute the basis of a separately owned monopoly. But the growth of human knowledge cannot be divided up into such sharply circumscribed phases" (1944, 70). In short, patents restricted knowledge and thus discouraged invention, thereby making society poorer. Additionally, in the spirit of leverage theory, Polanyi observed: "[Patents] have become the means for consolidating certain trade monopolies, the restrictive functions of which extend far beyond the exploitation of the patented inventions" (63). Seeing the manifold problems of the patent system, Polanyi proposed to overhaul the patent system in order to lessen the restrictions of knowledge this system caused. Polanyi suggested: "In order that inventions may be used by all, we must relieve inventors of the necessity of earning their rewards commercially, and must grant them instead the right to be rewarded from the public purse" (1944, 65).[15]

Across the Atlantic, Frank Knight and Henry Simons concurred with the anti-patent attitudes of Plant and Polanyi. Knight labeled the patent system "exceedingly crude" (1921, 372) and suggested that this system was an unfortunate vestige of a time when rulers "granted monopolies as gifts to favorites, or sold them to raise revenue" (1933, 93). Knight also called the patent system "wasteful" and "evil" (93). The artificially high price of a patented product excluded large numbers of would-be consumers from the market and thereby reduced the use of that good. In addition to these

who subscribe most of its value may be precluded from qualifying for the prize" (46). Third, Plant asserted that patents prevented future discoveries because an inventor, fearing that he or she would transgress another's patent, would be deterred. Plant observed, "competitors instead of helping to improve the best, are compelled in self-preservation to apply themselves to the devising of alternatives which, though possibly inferior, will circumvent the patent" (46). Thus, for Plant, the patent system caused a mal-distribution of resources. Fourth, the patent system was no longer necessary to ensure that businesses did not conceal their inventions. Although the patent system might have had a beneficial role to play in the eighteenth century, when numerous small businesses tended to be individually owned, the patent system, according to Plant, had no equivalent role to play in the early twentieth century, which depended on large scale manufacture. For Plant, because of large-scale manufacture, protracted secrecy tended to be infeasible. Even though there might be exceptions, such as a chemical process, Plant maintained, "such cases, if they indeed exist outside the pages of detective fiction and sensational literature, must surely be exceptional, and unlikely to be eradicated by the inducements of temporary patent production" (44).

15 For a more detailed look at Polanyi's position on patents, see Johns (2006).

would-be buyers, Knight, agreeing with Plant, also thought inventors themselves suffered:

> [I]t is undoubtedly a very rare and exceptional case where the really deserving inventor gets anything like a fair reward. If anyone gains, it is some purchaser of the invention or at best an inventor who adds a detail or finishing touch that makes an idea practicable where the real work of pioneering and exploration has been done by others. (1921, 372)

In short, the patent system misguided the rewards for invention. Knight, like Polanyi, advocated it would be politically intelligent to replace the patent system, which he called an "artificial monopoly," with "some direct method of stimulating and rewarding research" (372).

Simons, in the spirit of classical liberalism, condemned the patent system because it enabled firms to restrict competition, both actual and potential, and thereby augment their monopoly power. He observed, "It is shameful to have permitted … the gross abuse of patent privilege for extortion, exclusion, and output restriction" (1948, 130). Simons demanded, "we must … prevent their appropriating vast areas of the market by patent pooling and intimidation of infringement litigation" (248). Simons believed that large firms in particular had greater protection from infringement litigation. About small firms and startup firms, Simons observed, "The extreme vulnerability … to such litigation and the great advantages of combination and vast size on this score suggest perhaps the most serious indictment of our patent law" (319, fn 10).[16]

According to Simons, the economic ills stemming from patents went even deeper. Echoing Polanyi's position, Simons wrote, "Just as free trade requires free and equal access to markets, [industrial research] likewise requires equal and reasonable access, if not wholly free access, to technical knowledge and patentable devices" (248). Thus, Simons attacked means employed by firms, such as patent pooling, that facilitated differential access to knowledge.

Simons had nothing positive to say about patents or the patent system. Simons thought that U.S. patent law urgently needed "complete overhauling,"

[16] Concurring with Simons, Myron Watkins and George Stocking shed further light on Simons's concern: "A large company with a formidable collection of patents and ample financial resources can impose an insupportable burden on a small enterprise by forcing it to defend its right to use techniques or to manufacture products that, as it eventually turns out, may be entirely in the public domain. Even the most scrupulous care to avoid invasion of existing patent rights cannot render the small company immune from infringement litigation. For it costs as much – if not more – to defend an infringement suit as to prosecute it. A small competitor can stand the financial strain only so long before it succumbs to its more powerful rival" (1950, 741).

and that its problems could not be "resolved by simplistic devices" (248). In sum, the goals of patent reform needed to include the provision of reasonable or even complete access to technical knowledge and patentable devices; it likewise needed to address the problem of monopoly by preventing firms from using the intimidation of infringement litigation and seizing the market through patent pooling.

7.2. "Free" Enterprise or Competitive Order

In December 1946, just a few months before the first Mont Pèlerin Society meeting, Hayek handwrote a note to Director, which he included with Director's formal invitation to the meeting. Hayek penned, "May I add to this formal circular that I am especially counting on your interest and active support.... I am even hoping that you might be willing to join with me in opening the discussion on the [subject of "Free" Enterprise or Competitive Order]!"[17]

Director had the utmost respect for Hayek. In 1945, Director believed that Hayek's ideas should be propagated anywhere there was free discussion, especially the United States.[18] That same year, Director claimed in a book review of *The Road to Serfdom*: "There is no economist writing in English more eminently qualified to [explore the ultimate political implications of abandoning the competitive system]" (1945, 174). Therefore, it is not surprisingly that when Hayek and Director delivered their lectures at the opening session on "'Free' Enterprise or Competitive Order," they generally agreed with each other. They addressed the fundamental question of how the legal framework ought to be altered to make competition work effectively – that is, how to design a "competitive order" (Hayek 1948, 111). Both viewed this task to be of the utmost necessity and believed doing so would result in a robust liberal program to counter what they regarded as a pronounced trend toward collectivism.

Hayek and Director suggested that simply enforcing property rights and ensuring freedom of contract, the guiding lights of nineteenth-century liberalism, were not sufficient. Consequently, in each of their talks, they addressed a number of legal issues, of which the following three are particularly relevant to the analysis in this chapter: the law of property – particularly patents; the law dealing with "the problem of industrial monopoly" (i.e., antitrust law); and the law of corporations.

[17] DPRL, December 28, 1946, box 1, folder: "correspondence. 1946–1952."
[18] MPHI, Director to Croswell Bowen, July 12, 1945, box 43, folder 16.

Of the three, Hayek had the most to say about the law of property. For him, the fundamental problem was: "[What] ought to be the contents of property rights"? (1948, 113). Hayek believed that creating an effective competitive order crucially depended on answering this question.[19] Although Hayek did not offer a specific program of reform, he did point out what he believed to be a serious problem in the field of property law. He maintained, "Where the law of property is concerned, it is not difficult to see that the simple rules which are adequate to ordinary mobile 'things' or 'chattel' are not suitable for indefinite extension" (Hayek 1948, 113). Hayek had in mind the questionable extensions of trademarks, copyright, and patents for inventions. It was, according to Hayek, "beyond doubt that … a slavish application of the concept of property as it has been developed for material things has done a great deal to foster the growth of monopoly and that here drastic reforms may be required if competition is to be made to work" (Hayek 1948, 114).

Patent law particularly troubled Hayek. He believed it necessary to "seriously … examine whether the award of a monopoly privilege is really the most appropriate and effective form of reward" (114). Patent law, according to Hayek, provided "so clear an illustration" of why "ready-made" formulas should not be applied and why it was necessary "to go back to the rationale of the market system and to decide for each class what the precise rights are to be which the government ought to protect" (114). To illustrate his point, he quoted the then well-known U.S. Supreme Court opinion, *Continental Paper Bag Co. v. Eastern Paper Bag Co.*: "[A]s to the suggestion that the competitors were excluded from the use of the patent we answer that such exclusion may be said to be the very essence of the right conferred by the patent … as it is the privilege of any owner of property to use it or not use it without any question of motive" (quoted on 114).[20] The fact that the

[19] Here, Hayek quoted John Stuart Mill at length to show the importance of undertaking this endeavor: "The principle of private property has never yet had a fair trial in any country … The laws of property have never yet conformed to the principles on which the justification of private property rests. They have made property of things which never ought to be property, and absolute property where only a qualified property ought to exist … if the tendency of legislators had been to favour the diffusion, instead of the concentration of wealth, to encourage the subdivision of large units instead of striving to keep them together; the principle of private property would have been found to have no real connection with the physical and social evils which have made so many minds turn eagerly to any prospect of relief, however desperate" (quoted in 1948, 110).

[20] See *Continental Paper Bag Co. v. Eastern Paper Bag Co.*, 210 U.S. 405 (1909). According to Myron Watkins and George Stocking, this case was a "notorious example" of how, "armed with a patent," "a consolidation or restrictive trade pool was almost immune to antitrust action" (1950, 735). This case is also known for the following famous dictum: "… patents are

Court maintained that any owner of property had the right of use "without any question of motive" struck Hayek as "significant for the way in which a mechanical extension of the property concept by lawyers has done so much to create undesirable and harmful privilege" (114).

Although Director devoted relatively little time in his speech to the topic of property law, he did concur with Hayek's condemnation of patents as a means to extend monopoly power. In the spirit of the leverage argument, Director observed, "A study of the American antitrust cases discloses the crucial importance which patents on inventions have played in creating and maintaining industrial monopoly."[21] From 1939 to 1947, the Supreme Court condemned the use of patents to monopolize industry or stifle competition in nearly a dozen antitrust cases,[22] and about one-third of those cases concerned patent tie-ins. To begin to address the patent problem, according to Director, there had to be a "drastic reduction of the period of the monopoly grant by change of existing statutory rules and existing administrative procedure."[23]

Director's unqualified negative view of patents stemmed from his opposition to concentrated economic power. Director, like Simons, was convinced that the liberal doctrine needed, above all else, to champion freedom by "promoting the dispersion of power necessary for competitive order."[24] Simons, according to Coase (1998, 602), "had a very considerable influence" on Director's worldview. Indeed, Director (1948), in his "Prefatory Note" for Simons's posthumously published *Economic Policy for a Free Society*, expressed his disappointment that Simons's work had not been more widely read and discussed, both among the general educated public and among professional economists. It is thus not surprising that Director gave voice to Simons's ideas in his Mont Pèlerin address.

Although Director maintained that international trade provided a substantial check on industrial monopoly, he cautioned that this was not sufficient. Director blamed England's overconfidence in the ability of international trade to eliminate monopoly as a significant cause of the relatively large number of monopolies in England. Director expressed qualified praise for the enforcement of American antitrust law, but suggested that

property, and entitled to the same rights and sanctions as other property," which, according to the Supreme Court, even gave the patentee the right to suppress her invention if she wished. Surely this would have been one Supreme Court case that kindled Hayek's concern about the unwarranted extension of property rights into new domains.

21 MPS1947LA, 79.

22 For a list of the cases, see note 10 supra.

23 MPS1947LA, 79.

24 MPS1947LA, 77–78.

more vigorous antitrust was necessary to address the substantial amount of monopoly power in the American economy. Notably, Director, despite the reputation he would later gain as a fierce critic of established antitrust law, offered no criticisms of antitrust doctrine at this time; in fact, his lecture suggested that the problem was not with antitrust doctrine but with the lack of vigor in its enforcement.

Like Director, Hayek objected to the growth of monopoly. They both saw status quo corporate law as a cause of monopoly.[25] According to Hayek, "it was only because of special legislation conferring special rights … that size of enterprise has become an advantage beyond the point where it is justified by technological facts" (116). In the spirit of Simons, Director took a stronger line: "The unlimited power of corporations must be removed."[26] Director asserted that the antitrust laws were "mere stopgap measures,"[27] and suggested therefore that radical corporate reform was needed. Director advocated controlling combinations among businesses and reforming corporate law. He asserted:

> Excessive size can be challenged through the prohibition of corporate ownership of other corporations, through the elimination of interlocking directorates, through a limitation of the scope of activity of corporations, through increased control of enterprise by property owners and perhaps too through a direct limitation of the size of corporate enterprise.[28]

Although Hayek did not offer as many corporate reform recommendations as Director did, he concurred that it might be beneficial to "impede the indefinite growth of individual corporations" and suggested that it might also be beneficial to repeal legislation that recognized corporations as fictitious or legal persons (1948, 116).[29]

In sum, Hayek and Director advocated legal reform in order to create a competitive order. They objected to patent law because it undermined

[25] Hayek maintained, "I do not think that there can be much doubt that the particular form legislation has taken in [the law of corporations and particularly that concerning limited liability] has greatly assisted the growth of monopoly" (1948, 116).

[26] MPS1947LA, 80.

[27] MPS1947LA, 79.

[28] MPS1947LA, 80.

[29] Hayek stated, "It appears to me also as if historically in the field of the law of corporations we had a situation rather analogous to that in the field of the law of property to which I have already referred. As in the law of property the rules developed for ordinary mobile property were extended uncritically and without appropriate modifications to all sorts of new rights; thus the recognition of corporations as fictitious or legal persons has had the effect that all the rights of a natural person were automatically extended to corporations" (1948, 116).

effective competition and thereby contributed to the economic problems. Like Knight and Simons, they strongly challenged the status quo patent law. Like Plant and Polanyi, they attributed the problem of industrial monopoly to patents. And Director himself, like Polanyi and the New Dealers, suggested that patents could serve as a lever to allow a patent-holding firm to extend its monopoly power. Most notably, in their speeches, neither Hayek nor Director stated anything positive about patents.

7.3. Chicago Neoliberalism and the Shift on Patents

The negative attitude toward patents held by liberal Chicago economists did not go unnoticed at the University of Chicago. In 1948, Robert Hutchins, then President of the University of Chicago, stated, "Some of our professors criticize capitalism on the ground that … [it] has … too much governmental planning and control, as in the case of patents and tariffs" (quoted in the *New York Times*, 69). However, in the 1950s, during the Chicago-based effort to reformulate liberalism, the position on patents to which Hutchins had referred would be remarkably altered.

Of those present at the 1947 Mont Pèlerin meeting, it was predominantly the members of the Chicago School who later became known for their pro-patent position. Others – including Hayek, Fritz Machlup, and the ordoliberals – continued to display a negative attitude toward patents.[30,31] It is beyond the scope of this chapter to consider why others did not shift their patent position and how this reflects on the development of neoliberal doctrine overall. Instead, this section will trace the emergence of the Chicago School's pro-patent position and link this position shift to the Chicago-based effort to reconstitute the liberal doctrine. The views of Simons,

[30] Fritz Machlup (1962) argued, for example, that the patent system was superfluous for an industry comprised of large firms. Oligopolistic competition would ensure that R&D investment would be made because a firm would not want its rivals to surpass it in the technological race. Hayek also expressed a critical view of patents, claiming, in 1973, that patent laws facilitated the rise of monopoly, "It is probable, however, that in the field of enterprise monopoly would never have become a serious problem if government had not assisted its development … [with] the law of industrial patents" (http://www.angelfire.com/rebellion/oldwhig4ever/systematic.html Access date: 08/20/08).

[31] Two ordoliberals who were charter members of the Mont Pèlerin Society were Walter Eucken and Wilhem Roepke. Like Director in 1947, the ordoliberals, who staunchly objected to concentrated market power, advocated for patent reform to help to address this problem; they sought to prevent the further retardation of technological process and suggested obligation licenses as an alternative (Hanslowe 1960, 99). For more on the common ground between the Chicago School Mont Pelerin members and the ordoliberal Mont Pèlerin members at the start of the Mont Pèlerin Society, see Van Horn (2009).

Knight, and the pre-neoliberal Director, as well as those of Hayek, Plant, and Polanyi, will serve as useful foils to illustrate the significant extent of the shift at Chicago. To appreciate this shift, it is first necessary to understand some related developments in the Chicago School's effort to reformulate liberalism.

In October 1946, Director assumed leadership of the Volker-funded Free Market Study (henceforth, "the Study").[32] Director and the Study's members (Milton Friedman, Frank Knight, Edward Levi, Garfield Cox, and Wilbur Katz) convened regularly in order to discuss and debate. Like the Mont Pèlerin Society, the Study sought to understand the legal foundations necessary for an effective competitive order.[33] Director's "Free Market Study" outline, which served as the basis for the organization of the study, listed a number of legal and policy areas to investigate in order to move toward a competitive order. Included on his list were antitrust enforcement, corporation policy, and patent policy.[34] The Study's task had a sense of urgency because of the perceived strength of collectivist forces. Hayek conveyed this urgency when he wrote: "The intellectual revival of liberalism is already under way.... Will it be in time?" (1949, 433)

At the second meeting of the Study, Director distributed a research proposal entitled "A Program of Factual Research into Questions Basic to the Formulation of a Liberal Economic Policy." As Director's title suggests, the topics the Study decided to investigate were not chosen purely because of theoretical concerns: Political necessity was a factor. By empirically investigating the facts taken for granted by both liberals and their opponents, Director believed it would be possible to develop a more robust liberal policy to counter collectivism and thereby bring about policy changes in the United States.

The Study decided to concentrate its efforts mainly on issues concerning industrial monopoly and corporations. It hired researchers, Warren

[32] For more background information about the Study, see Van Horn and Mirowski (2009). For more information on the activites of the Study and the Antitrust Project, see Van Horn (2009).

[33] After the first Mont Pèlerin meeting, several charter members drew up a "Draft Statement of Aims" of the Mont Pèlerin Society. In the statement, point five further demonstrates the pivotal importance of the competitive order to its framers: "The preservation of an effective competitive order depends upon a proper legal and institutional framework. The existing framework must be considerably modified to make the operation of competition more efficient and beneficial. The precise character of the legal and institutional framework within which competition will work most effectively and which will supplement the working of competition is an urgent problem on which continued exchange of views is required" (quoted in Hartwell 1995, 49).

[34] TSPR, "Free Market Study," undated, box 39 (addenda), folder: Free Market Study.

Nutter for example (1951), to do empirical work on the issue of industrial monopoly and brought likeminded visiting scholars to Chicago. (For more on Nutter's analysis, see Van Horn, Chapter 10, this volume.) During the early years of the Study (1946–1949), Director, Friedman, and others were uncertain how to reconstitute liberalism in order to best combat socialism and other forms of collectivism. Like Director during his 1947 Mont Pèlerin address, they in many ways echoed the beliefs of classical liberals, expressing concerns about concentrations of power, including industrial monopoly.

The Study afforded its members the time to explore various ways to reformulate liberalism. Thus, the Study served as an incubator for a new form of liberalism, "Chicago neoliberalism." By the latter half of the project (1950–1952), Chicago neoliberal claims started to emerge. By 1950, industrial monopoly was no longer seen as a relatively omnipresent and powerful phenomenon in the United States; it was seen as relatively unpervasive and benign because the "corrosive effects" of competition would always eventually undermine it (Director 1950). By 1951, large corporations were no longer considered a threat to competition because of their concentrated power; they were considered another feature of a competitive market because they approximated the impersonal ideal of the market (Director 1951). Consequently, concentrated markets tended to be efficient, regardless of the size of the corporations.

As the Study ended, the Volker-funded Antitrust Project began (1952), and reconsiderations of liberalism proceeded apace. Director headed the project, Edward Levi assisted. The members included John McGee, William Letwin, Robert Bork, and Ward Bowman.[35] The Antitrust Project focused

[35] In their reminiscences, members of the Chicago School list John Jewkes as a member of the Antitrust Project (Kitch 1983). However, I have excluded him from this list for several reasons. First, unlike the other members, Jewkes did not come to Chicago until midway through the Antitrust Project, in 1954 (Jewkes, et al. 1958, 13). Second, unlike the other Antitrust Project members, Jewkes did not attribute a significant role to Director in the development of his ideas. In fact, in *The Sources of Invention*, which he started to write while at the University of Chicago Law School, Jewkes only thanks Edward Levi for encouraging him to persevere (Jewkes, et al. 1958, 13). (For analysis of Director's role as an immensely influential educator, see Van Horn [2011 forthcoming]). Third, in his correspondence with Jewkes, one can infer that Director asked Jewkes not to come to Chicago to participate in the Antitrust Project, but to participate in a yearlong seminar. Jewkes wrote: "You once suggested that during the year I am to spend at Chicago we might run jointly a seminar under some title as the 'Economics of Invention' or the 'Economics of Enterprise.' I am much interested in this subject" (DPRL, November 19, 1951, box: 1, file: Correspondence: 1946–1952). Moreover, unlike the other Antitrust Project members, Jewkes said nothing about this project in any of his acknowledgments. Lastly, and related the second claim, Jewkes belongs in the British industrialist tradition in the vein of Arnold Plant. In *The Sources of Invention* and in an earlier article (Jewkes 1953, 203),

on issues of monopoly, select areas of antitrust law, and the history of the Sherman Act.[36] It investigated these topics in the light of the conclusions of the Study. Moreover, in the spirit of the Study's attempt to influence policy, it investigated these topics with a critical eye toward U.S. antitrust law precedent, and many of the conclusions of the Antitrust Project contravened the conclusions of the courts. In 1954, for instance, Bork, in contrast to Director's classical-liberal concern in 1947 about the excessive size of corporations and their concentrated economic power, maintained that "[vertical mergers added] nothing to monopoly power" (195). This Chicago neoliberal position suggested, therefore, that vertical mergers should always be legal. Consequently, Bork suggested that one aspect of antitrust law precedent, which required an investigation of motives of a vertical merger in order to make a determination of its legality, was not only extraneous, but also erroneous.

Bork's article fell under the Antitrust Project's umbrella article and manifesto, "Trade Regulation," by Director and Levi, which they published in 1956.[37] In this article, Director and Levi demonstrated skepticism about the extension of monopoly power through the use of exclusionary practices such as tying arrangements and disdain for adjudication or legislation that regarded these practices as per se deleterious or as per se illegal (Packard 1963, 56). Director and Levi suggested that exclusionary practices were no worse than harmless price discrimination and served as either competitive tactics equally available to all businesses or as means of maximizing returns on an established market position.[38] Thus, Director and Levi maintained that when the courts deemed it necessary to consider the legality of an exclusionary practice, they should utilize a rule of reason analysis, not a per se approach.[39]

Jewkes praised Plant. Moreover, Jewkes took an approach similar to that of Plant in understanding economic issues, and Jewkes concurred for the most part with Plant's assessment of the patent system with the exception that Jewkes thought this system was necessary to protect the individual inventor (Jewkes, et al. 1958, 187–188).

[36] For a list of the articles and books that the Antitrust Project published and that it caused to be published, see Priest (2005, 353–354).

[37] Herbert Packard, a Stanford law professor who surveyed the state of research in antitrust law in the 1950s and early 1960s, commented: "[There] does appear in the work done [by the Antitrust Project] a common approach which, one gathers, derives importantly from the views of Professor Aaron Director who, together with Dean Levi, teaches antitrust at Chicago. If there is a 'Chicago school' of antitrust thought, its manifesto is presumably the article by Levi and Director on Trade Regulation" (1963, 55).

[38] Bork and Bowman (1965) concur with this description. They asserted, "Director's analysis indicates that absent special factors that have not been shown to exist, so-called exclusionary practices are not means of injuring the competitive process" (1965, 366).

[39] According to the rule of reason, "The courts were to determine reasonableness by considering the conditions leading to the adoption of the restraint, the effects of the restraint,

7.3.1. *The Incipience of the Chicago Neoliberal Pro-Patent Position*

In May of 1952, when it was Director's turn to speak at the "Conference on the Arts, Publishing, and the Law," he asserted that patents were "aberrations in the market." Although patents redirected resources in order to foster invention, it was unclear, according to Director, whether this allocation of resources was optimal. Director stated: "You realize, of course, these resources otherwise would be doing something else. In directing them to a particular field, such as inventing or writing, we feel we are promoting a desirable and social objective" (1952, 107). Thus, Director, like Plant, maintained that the economic foundations of patent law were "shaky" and that no solid basis existed for extending the scope of patent protection.

However, in contrast to his 1947 Mont Pèlerin address, Director did not stress that patents provided a means to expand and solidify industrial monopoly power. This position was no longer tenable, at least when considering the long-run effects of patents, because of his reformulated Chicago neoliberal attitude toward concentrations of power, especially large corporations and industrial monopoly. Director stressed that competition threatened to undermine all forms of monopoly and that monopoly did not threaten to permanently suppress competition; he stated, "there is no such thing as a monopoly which is automatically protected from rival activity" (1952, 108). Implying that both patent monopolies and industrial monopolies were transitory, Director, departing from his 1947 views, suggested that patents could not serve to make an industrial monopoly or a large corporation immune from competition. Thus, even though he regarded patents as "aberrations in the market," he no longer viewed them to be as great a threat as he previously did. In short, Director came to view patents and industrial monopoly like a self-limiting skin disease; although such a disease might be aggravating to a person in the short term, in the long term the body would heal itself. Attempts to alleviate the disease in the short term would prove iatrogenic.

7.3.2. *Patents and Tying Arrangements*

In the early 1950s, Director suggested that Myron Watkins's 1927 book, *Industrial Combinations and Public Policy*, reflected the "[representative] economic opinion on the methods which can be used by large firms to get larger, or to impede entry."[40] Like Simons, and like Director prior to 1950,

actual and probable, and the intentions of the participants, as indicated by their actions" (Dietz 1951, p. 8). In contrast to a per se approach, under the rule of reason, the courts had to determine on a case-by-case basis whether an unreasonable restraint of trade occurred.

40 DPRL, undated document, box 3, folder 18. It is reasonable to infer that Director wrote this very short analysis of Watkins and wrote it no earlier than the 1950s. This document

Watkins feared the power of large corporations: "When size gives power there is generally some temptation to exercise that power" (66). In the spirit of Simons, he further added, "In business, as in warfare, whatever furthers the ends of victory is defensible.... [T]here are business leaders, just as there are military commanders, who prefer an assured victory achieved by questionable means to a dubious victory gained by well-approved means" (66–67). Watkins classified patent tie-ins among the "questionable means." They merely served to extend the reach of already established monopoly power (76).

Director sharply criticized Watkins for providing "no analysis whatever" of his claim that patent tie-ins created and extended monopoly power.[41] During the Antitrust Project, Director provided his own analysis of the issue of patent tie-ins, thereby further developing the Chicago pro-patent position.

Unlike Watkins and the U.S. Supreme Court in the 1950s, Director and Levi did not view tying a patented product to an unpatented product as anticompetitive. To Director and Levi a tying arrangement (like other "exclusionary practices"), even if it involved a patent, was essentially a competitive tactic and a benign form of price discrimination (1956, 292). In their view, this tended to be the case regardless of the extent of monopoly power held by the firm engaging in a tying arrangement. Thus, they implicitly rejected not only the leverage theory of the Supreme Court, but also Director's 1947 position that industrial monopolies utilized patents to augment their market power. Furthermore, Director and Levi implied that an industrial monopoly holding a patent monopoly was not necessarily problematic – a Chicago neoliberal development that was contrary to the classical liberal concern about concentrations of economic power.

In 1957, Director further demonstrated his departure from his pre-1950 views on patents and concentrations of corporate power in his review of Carl Kaysen's *United States v. United Shoe Machinery Corporation*. Kaysen, an economist trained in the Harvard School tradition, had clerked for Judge Charles Wyzanski in the early 1950s on the *United Shoe* case ("Economist to Assist Judge" 1950).[42] Based on this experience, Kaysen published a book-length study of the problem of monopoly and the methods of dealing with it. Kaysen condemned United as a monopoly and claimed that United maintained its monopoly power partly through abusive exclusionary

refers to many of the issues addressed by the Antitrust Project and uses conclusions of the Antitrust Project to criticize Watkins.

[41] DPRL, undated document, box 3, folder 18.

[42] *United States v. United Shoe Machinery Co.*, 110 F. Supp. 295 (D. Mass. 1953).

practices (Kaysen 1956). Director, contrary to Kaysen, maintained that United was not an illegal monopoly. Monopoly was "thrust upon" United; it merely took advantage of vast economies of scale. According to Director, United passed the "test of survival," a test used "as a means of identifying the presence or absence of economies of scale" (1957, 608). Director claimed that the fact that United survived for roughly fifty years with an unchanged market share indicated the competitive success of United in availing itself of economies of scale. Director thus suggested that patents, which were crucial to the formation of United Shoe in 1899, in no way entrenched United's monopoly power. Director also observed that the 1922 ruling against United that prohibited it from using certain patent tie-ins arrangements did not in any way lessen United's market share (609); thus, Director maintained that historical evidence suggested patent tie-ins were not problematic. Clearly, Director no longer held his sweeping suspicion that patents created and extended monopoly power; he expressed no concern about the fact that United had an industrial monopoly coupled with a patent monopoly. Furthermore, contrary to his 1952 conference statement, Director, now when referring to patents, no longer expressed reservations.

Director's endorsement of the "survival test" not only indicated his pro-patent position, but also his approval of concentrations of power in the market. By 1957, Director, contrary to Simons, had come to believe that large corporations tended to represent economic efficiency rather than entrenched political power.[43] Director also rejected Simons's suspicion of large firms. Unlike Simons, Director dismissed the notion that large firms used spurious lawsuits involving patents to cripple smaller firms: "There is no evidence that this is a characteristic of large firms."[44]

In his article, "Tying Arrangements and the Leverage Problem," Bowman (1957) provided an in-depth analysis of patent tie-ins, thereby expounding on Director and Levi's 1956 analysis. Bowman regarded patents as an institution that performed some "useful public services" and stated nothing negative about patents. Like Director and Levi, he suggested that a tying sale that involved a patented product could merely be a means of effectively utilizing monopoly power that was already possessed, not a means of extending

[43] In 1943, Henry Simons stated, "The efficiency of gigantic corporations is usually a vestigial reputation earned during early, rapid growth – a memory of youth rather than an attribute of maturity. Grown large, they become essentially political bodies, run by lawyers, bankers, and specialized politicians, and persisting mainly to preserve the power of control groups and to reward unnaturally an admittedly rare talent for holding together enterprise aggregations which ought to collapse from excessive size" (1948, 246).

[44] DPRL, undated document, box 3, folder 18.

that monopoly power. A firm with a patent monopoly could not maximize its monopoly revenue and concomitantly impose a tying arrangement to extend its monopoly power. An example based on the *International Salt* case best illustrates his point. Assume that a food canner would pay at most \$1,000 in order to lease a salt-dispensing machine (a patented product) and that salt was competitively priced at P_c. If the International Salt company would like to lease the food canner its machine and require the food canner to purchase only its salt, could the lessor charge \$1,000 for the machine and \$5 more than the competitive price of salt (P_c +\$5)? If the lessor did this, the lessee would end up paying [\$1,000 + (P_c + \$5)] or (\$1,005 +P_c). Because \$1,005 was greater than the maximum the food canner was willing to pay for the machine, the food canner would not lease the machine. In general, therefore, two monopoly profits could not be gained from one monopoly – hence, the name, "Single Monopoly Profit Theorem."[45]

For Bowman, the key to determining if an existing patent monopoly had extended its monopoly power through a tying arrangement was observing changes in the level of output. If a seller maximized his returns of the patented product (the tying product) and the same level of output of the unpatented product (the tied product) was produced, then the seller had not extended his monopoly power. Consequently, who was producing the output was unimportant; only the level of output mattered. In Bowman's words: "The imposition of a tie-in under these circumstances determines the identity of the seller, but the amount of the tied product actually sold will not differ at all from that which could be sold if the optimum price for the tying product were set" (23). Thus, if the industry became more concentrated as a result, this would be irrelevant; the restriction of supply mattered, not the change in the percentage of market share. In 1947, Director certainly would have objected to those cases in which a patent-tie increased market concentration on the grounds that the patent tie-in increased corporate power. Thus, the reconstituted liberal attitude toward concentrations of power that came out the Study made possible the conclusion that patent-ties were not problematic. In sum, the Chicago neoliberal conclusions of the Study led to the more limited vision for antitrust held by the postwar Chicago School.

The emergence of Chicago neoliberalism radically changed how the Chicago School regarded both concentrations of market power and patents. Unlike Simons in 1934, the Chicago neoliberals regarded neither as a great threat to effective competition and hence democracy. Indeed, the postwar

[45] See Bowman's article for a few exceptions he gives to this general case.

Chicago School became known for defending large corporations and for upholding a pro-patent position.

7.4. Conclusion

In 1958, just two years after the Antitrust Project ended, Justice Black stated the following about tying arrangements in the *Northern Pacific Railway Company v. United States* decision:

> [Tying arrangements] deny competitors free access to the market for the tied product, not because the party imposing the tying requirements has a better product or a lower price but because of his power or leverage in another market.... They are unreasonable in and of themselves whenever a party has sufficient economic power with respect to the tying product to appreciably restrain free competition in the market for this tied product.[46]

Because a patent by definition conferred monopoly power, the Court thus suggested that firms that utilized a patent tie-in committed a violation of the antitrust laws. In *Northern Pacific Railway Company*, the Court thus reinforced its 1947 ruling in *International Salt* that patent tie-ins were per se illegal in spite of the recent publications of the Antitrust Project.

In 1973, in his book *Patent and Antitrust Law*, Ward Bowman, the then former Antitrust Project member, listed *Northern Pacific Railway Company* as one case among many that applied wrongheaded analysis to tie-ins. Bowen based his book largely on the conclusions of the Antitrust Project, and his analysis exemplifies the Chicago School's shift in attitude toward patents. In his preface, Bowman reported, "The analysis on which the conclusions of this work are based is derived from years of association with colleagues, from whose oral and written contributions I have long borrowed heavily.... I am especially indebted to professors Aaron Director, Robert H. Bork, [and] John S. McGee" (1973, vii). Moreover, Bork, himself also a previous Antitrust Project member, extolled and agreed with Bowman's analysis (Bork [1978] 1993, xvi). Furthermore, George Priest, a member of the Chicago School, claims that the Antitrust Project inspired Bowman's book (2005, 353). Thus, Bowman's book may be taken as a culminating intellectual effort of the Antitrust Project.

In contrast to Simons and the pre-neoliberal Director, Bowman expressed broad approval of patents. He considered a patent to be a "justified" and "desirable" temporary monopoly essential for discovery and technological development, and he claimed that the patent system was market oriented

[46] *Northern Pacific Railway Company v. United States* 356 U.S. 1 (1958).

in that its functioning depended on commercial reward. Because of his broad acceptance of patents, Bowman criticized key arguments of Plant and Knight. Bowman challenged Plant's 1934 argument that patents divert resources from what may very well be more productive activity. It is worth recalling here that Director had echoed Plant's argument in 1952. In challenging Plant's and thereby also Director's original contention, Bowman claimed that Plant failed to appreciate that some inventions would not have occurred except for the patent system. Bowman stated: "But for the patent system ... there would not be the products of invention – which reflect opportunity costs – restrictions on whose use, however certain, could never outweigh the greater restriction of not having them at all" (20). In criticizing Knight's 1921 analysis of patents, Bowman especially targeted Knight's claim that the patent system should be replaced with a better alternative that directly stimulated research and reward. Bowman sharply criticized Knight for not proposing a better alternative. Bowman claimed that a "direct" method of providing a reward implied that it had to be done through a "rewarder" rather than through a market-oriented reward system. Bowman objected: "An alternative reward system to supplant consumer judgment as the ultimate determinant of value of patentable invention is not necessarily superior merely because a patent provides some monopoly power" (31).

Bowman directed his most significant criticism toward supporters of leveraging theory: "[T]he antitrust/patent conflict ... is to a large extent illusory. It is based on a long-accepted but mistaken notion that a legal monopoly, a patent, may be used as a lever to monopolize the unpatented" (ix). Bowman's argument against leveraging echoed the one in his 1957 paper. He maintained that a patent tie-in was not a device to illegally extend monopoly power, but a legitimate device to maximize profit from the patent. As Bowman tersely put it: "Patent leveraging, in a word, is no more plausible than lifting oneself by one's bootstraps" (55).

Bowman singled out *Motion Picture Patents* as the source of the bad precedent that led to a host of rulings that followed and strengthened the "leverage fallacy."[47] Of the cases that followed the train of *Motion Picture Patents*' fallacious reasoning, the Court issued rulings on five of them: *Morton Salt*, *B. B. Chemical*, the *Mercoid* cases, and *International Salt* occurred from 1942

[47] Bowman observed: "The development of the law with respect to tying practice has been a one-way street. Its signpost was misdirected by Justice White in *Motion Picture Patents* in 1917. His leveraging fallacy was received as gospel.... [T]he Court has since 1917 consistently applied faulty economics leading to the wrong answers to the questions it has asked" (182).

to 1947. It is notable that when Director blamed patents without qualification in his 1947 Mont Pèlerin speech, he surely had these Supreme Court decisions in mind. Ironically, immediately after his 1947 speech, Director spearheaded the effort to reconstitute liberalism at Chicago, which would ultimately lead to conclusions that undermined his 1947 ideas about patents. Indeed, Bowman suggested that Director dispelled the leveraging theory that he had previously endorsed: "Leveraging a legitimate patent monopoly into an additional or broader monopoly, the basis of much if not most of patent misuse doctrine, is a mythology derived directly from erroneous antitrust doctrine long familiar to students of Aaron Director" (1973, 57).

The neoliberal developments of the Study led to the reconsideration of Director's 1947 support of leveraging theory. By the early 1950s, the Study had reached the conclusion that concentrations of industrial power – large corporations or industrial monopoly – would eventually always be supplanted by the forces of competition. No longer seeing concentrations of power as a grave threat that had to be reckoned with, Director, Levi, and Bowman regarded patent tie-ins as a competitive tactic – even though patent tie-ins could very well result in an increased concentration of market power in the market of the tied product (or the market of the unpatented product). A patent tie-in became regarded as a means for the patent-holding firm to recoup its investment in the patented product.

Additionally, with the neoliberal developments during the Study and the Antitrust Project, the Chicago School adopted a sanguine attitude toward large corporations and their business practices. Contrary to the claims of Simons and those of Director and Hayek in 1947, Director and the other members of these investigations no longer considered limiting the size of corporations and other radical forms of corporate reform, and they no longer viewed business practices, such as vertical integration, with suspicion. With this shift in attitude toward corporations and their practices came a shift in perception of patents. Director ended his broad hostility toward patents and his of view patents as frequently misused by corporations. Instead, he adopted an attitude of broad acceptance of patents and began to regard them as infrequently misused.

It would be many years before the United States courts and legal community would take the work of Director and the Antitrust Project seriously. With hindsight, Friedman suggested that it was unrealistic to expect immediate change. He saw his work as well as that of his colleagues to be that of "[developing] alternatives to existing policies, to keep them alive and available until the politically impossible becomes the politically inevitable" (1982, xiv). Here, Friedman echoed Hayek's 1947 Mont Pèlerin address. Hayek had stated:

> Public opinion … is the work of men like ourselves, the economists and political philosophers of the past few generations, who have created the political climate in which the politicians of our time must move.… It is from [a] long-run point of view that we must look at our task. It is the beliefs which must spread, if a free society is to be preserved, or restored, not what is practicable at the moment, which must be our concern. (1948, 108)

In a way, therefore, the Study, the Antitrust Project, and later the Law and Economics Program acted as incubators for Chicago neoliberlaism and thereby kept its core insights "alive and available" for later use.

The impact of this later use should not be underestimated. About thirty years after the emergence of Chicago neoliberalism, the Reagan Administration's appointees to the Antitrust Division of the Department of Justice echoed the arguments in Bowman's *Patent and Antitrust Law*, including his analysis of patent tie-ins.[48] The Antitrust Division staked out a broad area in which it would not challenge patent licensing agreements, including patent tie-ins. Thus, firms, without fear of prosecution, used patent tie-ins. More recently, in 2007, the U.S. Department of Justice and the Federal Trade Commission (the two federal agencies that enforce antitrust laws in the United States) as well as the Antitrust Modernization Commission endorsed a fundamental idea of the Antitrust Project: The federal agencies and the commission espoused a rule of reason approach in those cases in which patent rights conflicted with the objectives of antitrust law. Thus, all three opposed the per se illegality of patent tie-ins, and all three suggested that the claim that patents created and extended business monopoly should be viewed with skepticism.

We have come a long way from pronounced hostility toward patents as instruments used to undermine effective competition by the liberals of the 1930s and 1940s to the broad acceptance and defense of patents as key building blocks of the competitive order of a market-based society by the Chicago neoliberals. As this chapter has argued, the pro-patent position of the Chicago School emerged during the Free Market Study and the Antitrust Project and marked an important step in the overall effort of Director and his colleagues to reconstitute liberalism and understand the competitive order.

[48] This paragraph draws from Scherer (2008, 37–39).

Bibliography

Archival Sources

DPRL	Aaron Director Papers, Regenstein Library, University of Chicago.
GSRL	George Stigler Papers, Regenstein Library, University of Chicago.
MPHI	Fritz Machlup Papers, Hoover Institution, Stanford University
MPS1947LA	Records of the 1947 meeting, Mont Pèlerin Society, Liberaal Archief, Ghent Belgium
TSPR	Theodore Schultz Papers, Regenstein Library, University of Chicago.

References

Areeda, Philip, Louis Kaplow, and Aaron Edlin. 2004. *Antitrust Analysis*. 6th edition. New York: Aspen Publishers.

Arnold, Thurman. 1942a. "The Abuse of Patents." *The Atlantic Monthly* (July): 14–20.

1942b. "We Must Reform the Patent Law." *The Atlantic Monthly* (September): 47–54.

Bork, Robert. 1954. "Vertical Integration and the Sherman Act: The Legal History of an Economic Misconception." *University of Chicago Law Review* 22: 157–201.

Bork, Robert H. [1978] 1993. *The Antitrust Paradox*. New York: Basic Books.

Bork, Robert and Ward Bowman. 1965. "The Crisis in Antitrust." *Columbia Law Review* 65(3): 363–376.

Bowman, Ward S. 1957. "Tying Arrangements and the Leverage Problem." *Yale Law Review* 67: 19.

1973. *Patent and Antitrust Law*. Chicago: University of Chicago Press.

Campbell, D. and Klaes, M. 2008. "The Principle of Institutional Direction: Coase's Regulatory Critique of Intervention." *Cambridge Journal of Economics* 29(2): 263–288.

Cheung, S.N.S. 1977. Property Rights and Invention. In S.N.S. Cheung ed. 2005 *Economic Explanation*. Hong Kong: Arcadia Press, pp. 547–599.

Coase, Ronald. 1998. "Aaron Director." in *The New Palgrave Dictionary of Economics and the Law*. ed. Paul Newman. New York: Macmillan.

De Long, J. Bradford. 1990. "In Defense of Henry Simons' Standing as a Classical Liberal," *Cato Journal* 9: 601–618.

Dietz, Arthur T. 1951. *An Introduction to the Antitrust Laws*. New York: Bookman Associates.

Director, Aaron. 1945. "Review of 'The Road to Serfdom' by Friedrich A. Hayek." *The American Economic Review* 35: 173–175.

1948. "Prefatory Note." In *Economic Policy for a Free Society*. Chicago: University of Chicago Press, pp. v–vii.

1950. Review of Charles E. Lindblom, *Unions and Capitalism*. *University of Chicago Law Review* 18: 164–167.

1951. "Conference on Corporation Law and Finance." *University of Chicago Law School* v. 8.

1952. "Conference on Arts, Publishing, and the Law." *University of Chicago Law School* pp. 106–108.

1957. Review of Carl Kaysen, *United States v. United Shoe Machinery Corporation: An Economic Analysis of an Antitrust Case. University of Chicago Law Review* 24: 606–611.

Director, Aaron and Edward Levi. 1956. "Trade Regulation." *Northwestern University Law Review* 51: 281–296.

Epstein, R. 2006. "What's Good for Pharma Is Good For America." *The Boston Globe*. Dec 3.

Friedman, Milton. [1982] 2002. "Preface, 1982." In *Capitalism and Freedom*. Chicago: University of Chicago Press.

Hartwell, R. Max. 1995. *A History of the Mont Pelerin Society*. Indianapolis: Liberty Fund.

Hayek, F. A. 1949. "The Intellectuals and Socialism." *The University of Chicago Law Review* 16(3): 417–433.

1948. "Free" Enterprise and Competitive Order. In F. A. Hayek ed. *Individualism and Economic Order*. Chicago: University of Chicago Press, pp. 107–118.

Hovenkamp, Herbert. 2005. *The Antitrust Enterprise*. Cambridge: Harvard University Press.

Jewkes, John. 1953. "Monopoly and Economic Progress." *Economica* 20(New Series) (79): 197–214.

Jewkes, John, David Sawers, and Richard Stillerman. 1958. *The Sources of Invention*. New York: St. Martin's Press.

Johns, Adrian. 2006. "Intellectual Property and the Nature of Science." *Cultural Studies* 20(2): 145–164.

Kaysen, Karl. 1956. *United States v. United Shoe Machinery Corporation*. Cambridge: Harvard University Press.

Kitch, Edmund W. (ed.). 1983. "The Fire of Truth: A Remembrance of Law and Economics at Chicago, 1932–1970." *Journal of Law & Econ* 26: 163–234.

Knight, Frank. 1921. *Risk, Uncertainty, and Profit*. New York: Houghton Mifflin Company.

[1933] 1951. *The Economic Organization*. New York: Augustus M. Kelly, Inc.

Machlup, Fritz. 1962. *The Production and Distribution of Knowledge in the United States*. Princeton NJ: Princeton University Press.

May, Christopher and Susan K. Sell. 2006. *Intellectual Property Rights: A Critical History*. London: Lynne Rienner Publishers.

Mirowski, Philip. 2004. *The Effortless Economy of Science?* Durham: Duke University Press.

2009. "Postface: Defining Neoliberalism." In *The Road from Mont Pelerin*, edited by, P. Mirowski and D. Plehwe. Cambridge: Harvard University Press.

New York Times 1948. "Freedom to Think Urged by Hutchins." November 7, 1948, p. 69.

"Economist to Assist Judge in Trust Case." 1950. *The New York Times*. December 20th, p. 23.

Nik-Khah, Edward. 2010. Working Paper: "Getting Hooked on Drugs: The Chicago School, the Pharmaceutical Project, and the Construction of Medical Neoliberalism."

Nutter, G. Warren. 1951. *The Extent of Enterprise Monopoly in the United States, 1899–1939*. Chicago: University of Chicago Press.

Packard, Herbert L. 1963. *The State of Research in Antitrust Law*. New Haven, CT: Walter E. Meyer Research Institute of Law.

Plant, Arnold. 1934. "The Economic Theory Concerning Patents for Inventions." *Economica* 1(1): 30–51.

1974. *Selected Essays and Addresses*. New York: Routledge Press.

Polanyi, Michael. 1944. "Patent Reform." *The Review of Economic Studies* 11(2): 61–76.

Priest, George L. 2005. "The Rise of Law and Economics: A Memoir of the Early Years." In F. Parisi and C. K. Rowley, eds., *The Origins of Law and Economics*. Northampton, MA: Locke Institute.

Ptak, Ralf. 2009. "Neoliberalism in Germany." In *The Road from Mont Pelerin*, edited by, P. Mirowski and D. Plehwe. Cambridge, MA: Harvard University Press.

Simons, Henry C. 1948. *Economic Policy for a Free Society*. Chicago: University of Chicago Press.

Scherer, F. M. 2008. "Conservative Economics and Antitrust: A Variety of Influences." In *How the Chicago School Overshot the Mark*, edited by Robert Pitofsky. New York: Oxford University Press.

Van Horn, Robert. 2009. "Reinventing Monopoly and the Role of Corporations." In *The Road from Mont Pelerin*, edited by, P. Mirowski and D. Plehwe. Cambridge, MA: Harvard University Press.

2010 forthcoming. "Harry Aaron Director: The Coming of Age of a Reformer Skeptic." *History of Political Economy*.

Van Horn, Robert and Philip Mirowski. 2009. "The Rise of the Chicago School of Economics and the Birth of Neoliberalism." In *The Road from Mont Pelerin*, edited by, P. Mirowski and D. Plehwe. Cambridge, MA: Harvard University Press.

Waller, Spencer Weber. 2005. *Thurman Arnold: A Biography*. New York: New York University Press.

Watkins, Myron W. 1927. *Industrial Combinations and Public Policy*. New York: Houghton Mifflin Company.

Watkins, Myron W. and George W. Stocking. 1950. "Patent Monopolies and Free Enterprise." *Vanderbilt Law Review* 3: 729–765.

EIGHT

Allusions to Evolution

Edifying Evolutionary Biology rather than Economic Theory

Jack Vromen

The danger is that dabbling in sociobiology may prove to be more attractive to many economists than the use of sociobiological findings to improve our economics.
– Coase 1978, 245

8.1. Introduction

In some of their papers, the second generation Chicago economists Gordon Tullock, Gary S. Becker and Jack Hirshleifer explicitly forge a link with evolutionary biology. This chapter discusses these papers. I am interested mainly in two issues. One is whether these papers are in any way related to the so-called selection arguments that Alchian (1950) and Friedman (1953), as key exponents of the first generation of the Chicago School of economics, advanced earlier (Vromen 1995). Do the papers build on the selection arguments, for example, or are they completely unrelated? The second issue is what specific forms the links forged with evolutionary biology take in the papers. In particular, what purposes are these links meant to serve?[1] Are they meant to contribute to an improved economic theory, to an improved biological theory, or to both of them?

8.2. Alchian's (1950) and Friedman (1953)'s Selection Argument: From Leaves around a Tree to Businessmen and Back

A lot has been written about Friedman's (1953) selection argument. However, for the purpose of this paper we can be very short. The crucial

I want to thank Eric L. Charnov for providing helpful information (in private correspondence) about the history of optimality models in evolutionary biology (and in behavioral ecology in particular).

[1] In this paper, I will look at theoretical purposes only. See Mirowski (this volume) for a discussion of the political purpose that these links allegedly served.

passage reads, "given natural selection, acceptance of the hypothesis [viz. the maximization-of-returns hypothesis] can be based largely on the judgment that it summarizes appropriately the conditions for survival" (Friedman 1953, 22). Friedman argues that economists can confide in their maximization-of-returns hypothesis because it accurately describes the behavior of surviving firms.[2] Unlike Alchian, who, as we shall see, warned economists not to be overconfident about the applicability of the hypothesis on selectionist grounds, Friedman apparently did not see any reason for economists not to base their confidence in the hypothesis on such grounds. Friedman's main reason for forwarding his selection argument clearly was to restore or boost confidence in the maximization-of-returns hypothesis (or, more broadly, marginal analysis). As we shall see in the next sections, second-generation Chicago economists such as Tullock and Becker take the validity of this argument for granted not so much as a justification for their continued use of marginalist analysis in economics, but in their excursions into evolutionary biology. After all, Friedman's argument seems to imply that maximization hypotheses accurately describes or predicts the outcomes of selection processes not only in the economic realm, but in any realm. In fact, in developing his argument that the maximization-of-returns hypothesis accurately describes the outcome of economic market selection, Friedman discusses the potential usefulness of a maximization hypothesis to predict behavior in the biological realm. What is interesting is that Friedman himself recoiled from urging biologists (and more broadly, evolutionary theorists) to accept maximization hypotheses.

Based on a study of earlier drafts of Friedman's (1953) essay, Hammond (2004) convincingly argues that Alchian and Friedman arrived at the idea to provide a selection argument independently from one another. It is clear that even though Alchian (1950) predates Friedman (1953), earlier drafts of Friedman, written before Friedman read (earlier drafts of) Alchian's paper, already contained roughly the same formulation of the selection argument as the one that finally made it to print. What is less clear is whether or not there has been a reverse influence of Friedman on Alchian. Based on a letter that Alchian sent to Friedman in 1949 (that accompanied the revision of his 1950 paper, which Friedman – in his position of editor of *The Journal of Political Economy (JPE)* – demanded from Alchian), Philip Mirowski (this volume) suggests that Friedman used his power as

[2] Vromen (2009) contains a more elaborate discussion of Friedman's selection argument, of the argument's place in Friedman's methodology, and of recent insights about the argument's validity.

JPE editor to make Alchian rewrite his paper more clearly in line with Friedman's own unflinching defense of neoclassical economics. Whether or not Alchian's earlier version was more critical of neoclassical economics than the published (1950) version, we cannot tell on the available evidence. We would at any rate need to see earlier drafts of Alchian's paper to find out what changes he made in subsequent versions. What might support Mirowski's reading, however, is that Alchian's (alleged) friend and RAND colleague Stephen Enke took the main message of Alchian's (1950) allusions to market selection to be rather different than what Friedman wanted to read into it: Rather than providing marginal analysis with a more secure theoretical foundation, marginal analysis should be superseded by what Enke (1951) calls "viability analysis." Instead of continuing with marginal analyses, economic analysis should try to find out what sort of firm behavior is viable under various conditions. Enke's main reason for pleading for a replacement of marginal by viability analysis is that he is not confident that marginal analysis and viability analysis lead to the same predictions under a wide set of conditions. As we will see, Alchian himself was indeed also far from perfectly confident about that.

Alchian's stance toward marginal analysis is somewhat ambivalent, even in the final published (1950) version. In the marginalism controversy (cf. also Mirowski's discussion of the Full Cost Pricing Debate in Chapter 9 of this volume), he clearly sides with the marginalists. The counterevidence amassed by the anti-marginalists, Alchian argues, need not and does not invalidate marginal analysis. Empirical investigations via questionnaire methods are incapable of evaluating the validity of marginal productivity analysis. If there is one thing Alchian sets out to do in the paper, it is to show that "individual motivation and foresight, while sufficient, are not necessary" (ibid, 217) for marginal analysis to be useful in making predictions about industry behavior. Marginal analysis can be useful even if businessmen do not pursue profits, or (in the more likely situation) if businessmen do try to attain maximum profits but lack the foresight that would guarantee success in such attempts. As Alchian himself puts it in a footnote, "This approach reveals how the 'facts' of Lester's dispute with Machlup can be handled with standard economic tools" (ibid., 217).

Thus Alchian is squarely in the marginalist's camp.[3] However, there are also statements suggesting that economists should not lean back and rest

[3] Thus I am in broad agreement with Mirowski's assertion (this volume) that the resort to biological language in the immediate postwar period was part of a defence of the newly established neoclassical orthodoxy rather than a rallying cry for those dissatisfied with that orthodoxy.

content with marginal analysis. He argues for example, that "Most conventional economic tools and concepts are still useful, although in a vastly different analytical framework – one which is closely akin to the theory of biological evolution" (Alchian 1950, 219–220), and "The formalization of this approach awaits the marriage of the theory of stochastic processes and economics" (ibid., 221). Apparently there is still some theoretical work to do for economists. Far from telling economists that they can marvel at and acquiesce in the undiminished predictive powers of marginal analysis, Alchian here seems to envisage the development of a new analytical framework or approach.

Even though Alchian does not exhibit a more thoroughgoing understanding of evolutionary biology than Friedman, he at least engages in an attempt to think things through in more depth and detail. Unlike Friedman, who simply does not go into this, Alchian asks himself what would or could be plausible counterparts of key biological concepts in economics: "The economic counterparts of genetic heredity, mutations, and natural selection are imitation, innovation, and positive profits" (ibid., 220). This answer can be said to present the point of departure for Nelson and Winter's (1982) attempt to develop an explicit evolutionary alternative for "orthodox economics." Alchian furthermore displays a more profound understanding than Friedman of the fact that evolutionary theorizing entails population thinking (Mayr 1982, Metcalfe 1989). Contrary to Friedman, who argues that every surviving firm cannot be but maximizing its returns, Alchian more cautiously argues that the only thing that can be predicted is that there is a tendency in the behavior of firms in some industries to go in this direction: "The prediction will not assert that every – or, indeed, any – firm necessarily changes its characteristics. It asserts, instead, that the characteristics of the new *set* of firms, or possibly a set of new firms, will change" (ibid, 216). Finally, and most importantly, Alchian shows a greater awareness than Friedman of the fact that evolutionary processes produce the outcomes that marginal analysis predicts only if certain conditions are met. Alchian notes correctly, for example, that "unfortunately" (ibid., 219) trial-and-error processes (in firm behavior) need not converge on a "profit maximizing" equilibrium. In particular, if the environment changes, the comparability of the actual results of the trials is destroyed. Alchian also rightly draws attention to the fact that "what really counts is the various actions actually tried" (Alchian 1950, 220). There is no guarantee that the best (or optimum) action is among the set of various actions actually tried. For reasons like this, Alchian concludes: "The economist may be pushing his luck too far in arguing that actions in response to changes in environment and changes in satisfaction with the existing states of affairs will converge as a result of adaptation or adoption toward the optimum action that should have been selected, if foresight had been perfect" (ibid, 220).

All these finesses and subtleties were lost on Friedman. It seems Friedman did not really make an effort to get the similarities and dissimilarities between biological and economic processes right. As remarked earlier, the only thing Friedman seemed to be interested in was to restore and boost confidence in maximization hypotheses and marginal analyses in economics. However, unlike later followers of Friedman's selection argument, who thought that Friedman's selection argument could be generalized so that maximization hypotheses could be applied also to predict outcomes of selection processes in the biological realm, Friedman recoiled from advocating maximization hypotheses in the biological realm. This is remarkable, because in his essay Friedman does argue that maximization hypotheses can accurately predict surviving behavior in the biological realm as well.

In preparing the ground for his argument that only those businessmen who behave as if they are maximizing returns survive market selection, Friedman discusses not just the example of the expert billiard player, but also (before that) the "largely parallel" example of trees having a greater density of leaves on the sunny south side than on other sides (Friedman 1953, 19–20).[4] This typical behavior of leaves, Friedman argues, can be predicted on the basis of the hypothesis that leaves are positioned as if each leaf deliberately sought to maximize the amount of sunlight it receives. The main point Friedman wants to make here of course is once again that the objection that leaves do not really seek in any meaningful sense – they do not deliberate where to be positioned and lack the competences to calculate the "optimum" position – does not invalidate the hypothesis. Properly understood, Friedman's hypothesis does not imply that leaves actually do these things (they only behave as if they did these things). Thus the objection is misdirected and irrelevant. What the hypothesis does imply is clearly consistent with observations about the differential positioning of leaves on trees and *this* is what is relevant.

So far so good. But the interesting thing is that Friedman does not go so far as to suggest that his contrived "maximization-of-sunlight" hypothesis should be seriously entertained. Why not? Friedman does argue that the "largely parallel" maximization-of-returns hypothesis should be seriously entertained. The arguments that he brings to the fore to support the

[4] Whether these two examples are really largely parallel remains to be seen. In the example of the expert billiard player, Friedman simply takes for granted that the playing of the expert billiard player is perfect (or approximates perfection). No allusion is made to some sort of selection process (such as tough competition) responsible for this.

maximization-of-returns hypothesis seem to carry over immediately to the maximization-of-sunlight hypothesis. We have already seen that Friedman does not regard the objection that businessmen lack the information or competence to really calculate maximum profits as a sound counterargument. It is clear that leaves lack such a competence. Yet if such a lack (on the part of businessmen) does not undermine the maximization-of-returns hypothesis, then the fact that leaves do not have such a competence does not undermine the maximization-of-sunlight hypothesis either. The same reasoning applies to the incapability of leaves to seek and to deliberate, as Friedman himself argues. This too does not undermine the maximization-of-sunlight hypothesis. Furthermore, in his selection argument Friedman argues that confidence in the maximization-of-returns hypothesis is based on the fact that there is a selection process going on in markets and that the hypothesis accurately predicts the behavior of surviving firms. It is clear that Friedman believes that similar selection processes see to it that leaves behave as if they maximize sunlight: "[T]he result achieved by purely passive adaptation to external circumstances is the same as the result that would be achieved by deliberate accommodation to them" (ibid., 20).[5] Thus virtually all the arguments that Friedman amasses in support of the maximization-of-returns hypothesis seem to apply with equal force in support of the maximization-of-sunlight hypothesis.

What prevents Friedman from concluding that the maximization-of-sunlight hypothesis is as valid and useful as the maximization-of-returns hypothesis is that there is an alternative hypothesis (which "explains" and predicts the differential density of leaves around trees as a result achieved by purely passive adaptation to external circumstances; let's call this an adaptationist hypothesis)[6] available that is to be preferred on both theoretical and empirical grounds:

> This alternative hypothesis is more attractive than the constructed hypothesis not because its "assumptions" are more "realistic" but rather because it is part of a more

[5] In footnote 14 on page 19, Friedman rightly observes that this example is similar to and in much the same spirit ("… though independent in origin") as an example given in Alchian (1950). Alchian discusses the example to underscore one of his main points, namely that what looks like the result of motivational individual adapting sometimes actually is the result of environmental adoption.

[6] Friedman does not display a thorough understanding of evolutionary theory in these passages. It is true that environmental factors (such as the exposure to sunlight) determine the position and differential density of leaves around trees. But this is not a selection, but a developmental process. It might be the case that natural selection has favored trees in which the positioning of leaves responds to the relative availability of sunlight. But how the leaves are positioned for each individual tree is a matter of how the tree, given the tree's genetic material, responds to environmental circumstances in its developmental growth process.

general theory that applies to a wider variety of phenomena, of which the position of leaves around a tree is a special case, has more implications capable of being contradicted, and has failed to be contradicted under a wider variety of circumstances. The direct evidence for the growth of leaves is in this way strengthened by the indirect evidence from the other phenomena to which the more general theory applies. (Friedman 1953, 20)

Apparently Friedman believes that the alternative adaptationist hypothesis is part of a more general selection (or evolutionary) theory than the maximization-of-sunlight hypothesis and that this more general theory has more implications capable of being contradicted. Friedman does not tell us why the maximization-of-sunlight hypothesis could not be part of an equally (or even more) general maximization theory than selection (or evolutionary) theory that is equally (or even more) capable of being contradicted and that will fail to be contradicted under an equally wide (or even wider) variety of circumstances. Why couldn't the economic maximization framework be applied beyond the economic realm? That would make for a very general theory indeed. It seems that the real argument for Friedman not to propose this is a theoretically conservative one: General selection theory has already proven its worth and value in the respects mentioned, and it is because of this that it is more attractive than Friedman's constructed hypothesis.

This impression, that it is for theoretically conservative reasons that Friedman recoils from proposing to use maximization hypotheses across the board, is strengthened by the "even more important body of evidence" (ibid, 22) that Friedman brings to the fore to support the maximization-of-returns hypothesis immediately after his exposition of his selection argument. There too we find references to the generality of the hypothesis (this time the maximization-of-returns hypothesis) as a major theoretical virtue of the hypothesis, as well as to direct and indirect evidence for the repeated failure of the hypothesis's implications to be contradicted (as empirical support). What Friedman here adds to the story, however, is that "the continued use and acceptance of the hypothesis over a long period, and the failure of any coherent, self-consistent alternative to be developed and be widely accepted, is strong indirect testimony to its worth" (ibid, 23). So the fact that the maximization-of-returns hypothesis de facto is widely accepted in the economics discipline and has been the only game in town for quite a while is taken as evidence for the acceptability of the hypothesis in economics.

Whether or not this is a sound argument,[7] it seems it is this argument that is decisive for Friedman as to why biologists should stick to their

[7] Note that, thus formulated, Friedman's argument here comes close to (if it is not identical to) the notorious naturalistic fallacy.

well-entrenched adaptationist hypotheses.[8] Apart from this argument, it is hard to see why biologists (or evolutionary theorists in general) should not entertain maximization hypotheses such as the maximization-of-sunlight hypothesis seriously. Just think of what Friedman could have argued were it not for this theoretical conservative stand. He could have argued that because maximization hypotheses accurately describe (or predict) the outcomes of selection processes, maximization hypotheses can also be usefully deployed outside of what is traditionally considered to be the economic domain, in particular in the biological domain. However, he could also have argued for the opposite claim that adaptationist hypotheses can also be usefully deployed outside what is traditionally considered to be the biological domain, in particular in the economic domain. This is not what Friedman argues. The uses of adaptationist hypotheses and maximization hypotheses should be kept to their own traditional domains. Thus Friedman arguably shows some respect for what practitioners in other disciplines have done and achieved in their own domain.

Friedman recoils from urging biologists (and more broadly, evolutionary theorists) to accept maximization hypotheses instead of their familiar adaptationist hypotheses. As we shall see, the second generation proved considerably less reticent when it comes to promoting maximization hypotheses in evolutionary biology.

8.3. Gordon Tullock's Excursions into Evolutionary Biology

Gordon Tullock sees absolutely no reason not to apply maximization hypotheses in studying the behavior of nonhuman animals. On the contrary, Tullock's version of *bioeconomics* is one in which the use of the constrained maximization framework of standard economic theory in evolutionary biology is demonstrated and actively promoted (Vromen 2007).[9] Occasional rhetorical allusions to bioeconomics being a two-way transfer of ideas, concepts, and techniques between economics and biology

[8] As Steven Medema points out in his contribution to this volume, Friedman might also have taken over Frank Knight's view that the applicability of economic theory is quite limited. The fact that Friedman's 1976 edition of *Price Theory* mentions Becker's work on the economics of the household and human capital only in passing speaks in favor of this view.

[9] Gordon Tullock was one of the Founders (together with Jack Hirshleifer) of the International Society for Bioeconomics. The Society sponsors the *The Journal of Bioeconomics*, which was launched in 1999. As Landa and Ghiselin (1999) officially declare in the first issue of the *Journal*, bioeconomics encourages a mutually beneficial two-way transfer of ideas, concepts, and techniques between biology and economics.

notwithstanding, if Tullock's own work is to exemplify bioeconomics, then bioeconomics essentially is a one-way transfer of modeling techniques from economics to biology. There is nothing really in Tullock's writings suggesting that economics could learn something from (or could be enriched by) biology.[10] As Tullock remarks about his own "biological" articles, "indeed, it could be argued that I have never left economics, that all of my 'biological' articles are simply economics articles in which I have rather unusual sets of entities maximizing a rather unusual utility function" (Tullock 1979, 2).

Looking back on his own early excursions into biology, Tullock (1999) points out that Malthus's views on population growth and the (natural and artificial) checks on it had a great impact on the evolutionary thinking of both Darwin and Wallace. In fact, Malthus's gloomy views had a greater, more lasting impact on biology than it had on economics. Tullock suggests that there are good reasons for this. Nonhuman animals lack the sophisticated cognitive capacities that humans exercise to reverse the trend of rate of growth in resources lagging behind the natural rate of growth of the human population: "[N]on-humans do not make technological progress. They do not practice artificial birth control" (Tullock 1999, 14). In other words, the economic "constrained maximization" framework might be more suitable to describe and predict nonhuman behavior than it is to describe and predict human (economic) behavior, not despite, but rather precisely because of the fact that nonhumans are less clever than humans.

After observing that it is no coincidence that in the first six decades of the twentieth century, biology and economics proceeded more or less independently, Tullock argues that it could not remain unnoticed that "structurally the two fields had much in common. In both cases the basic problem was maximizing subject to a constraints" (Tullock 1999, 15).[11] The suggestion is that economists just were earlier than biologists to discover that this is the basic problem in their field. It took biologists more time to find this out. Actually, some economists too pointed out that constrained maximization is the basic problem also in biology before this dawned on biologists. One of these economists was (not surprisingly) Tullock himself.

One of Tullock's earliest excursions into biology, Tullock (1971a), is an illustration of standard economic analysis's fruitfulness for the study of biological phenomena (in this specific case the consumption of the eucosmid moth *Ernarmonia conicolana* by coal tits). Tullock shows that the existing

[10] See, e.g., "Unfortunately, I cannot claim that reading the book will add anything more to the usual economists' tool kit" (Tullock 1994, 4).

[11] I guess the "... a" before "... constraints" here is a typo.

explanation of the coal tits' consumption behavior in biology can be greatly simplified by treating coal tits as careful optimizing shoppers.[12] This analogical treatment of the coal tits' consumption behavior is warranted, Tullock argues, because it makes sense to assume that coal tits have inherited reasonably efficient patterns of behavior. After all, if their ancestors did not evolve such patterns, they would not have survived and have left offspring. This clearly echoes Friedman's assurance that maximization hypotheses accurately describe the behavior of individuals that survive selection processes. There is nothing that economists learn from this transfer of their constrained maximization framework to biology, it seems, or it should be that economic analysis can also be fruitfully applied in the biological realm. Economic analysis itself, whether it is applied in the (traditional) economic realm or elsewhere, is not enriched or improved by it.[13]

Roughly the same picture resurfaces in Tullock (1994), aptly called *The Economics of Non-Human Societies*. Although this little book is published a few decades after Tullock's earliest excursions into biology, it actually is based on an unpublished book manuscript (called *Coordination without Command: The Organization of Insect Societies*, "which was an effort to use economic tools to analyze the internal social structure of ants and termites and a few other species"; Tullock 1994, vii) that Tullock put together in the 1970s. Here, too, Tullock engages in economic analyses of the nests of ants (and of other social insects). To Tullock, this means first and foremost that *preference functions* are ascribed to animals: "I assume that the animals, plants, ameboid single-cells of the sponges, and the 'individual' cells of the slime molds all have something which is functionally equivalent to the preference function that we find in human beings" (ibid., 72). Tullock points out that in nonhuman societies cooperation is induced by a preference function and environmental coordination. It is to be noted that Tullock does not postulate the existence of markets in nonhuman societies. It is only in human societies that we have both hierarchies and the market, he argues; in most nonhuman societies we have neither of them. However, Tullock does argue that in human and nonhuman societies alike, central command is not necessary to get cooperation off the ground.[14]

[12] Note that Tullock is not arguing here that application of standard economic theory's constrained maximization framework in biology necessarily leads to different results or insights. The main gain envisioned is increased simplicity in explanation.

[13] Tullock (1979) argues that there is not much for economists to learn about human society from sociobiological studies of animal societies.

[14] Tullock adds: "I do not want my fellow members of the Mont Pèlerin Society to feel that I have forgotten the possibility of coordinating activity by market arrangements" (Tullock 1994, 23).

Tullock (1999) reports that he contributed more or less accidentally to biology. Tullock recalls that while reading Lack (1966) on birds, he expected, but didn't find, an exposition in terms of demand and supply curves. It was obvious to Tullock not only that Lack's account of the birds' behavior lent itself to an exposition in terms of demand and supply curves, but also that such an exposition would make Lack's account much simpler and clearer. Indeed, Tullock thought this was so obvious that he had to be persuaded to work it out in a paper for a renowned biological journal.[15] It was not his deepest paper, Tullock wryly remarks, but he was prepared to render this service to biologists: "Biologists were looking around for something like this, and I provided it" (Tullock 1999, 16). Tullock (1999) still shows amazement about the success the paper had in terms of citations and quotations biologists subsequently made to the paper.[16]

Does Tullock really believe that there was no one before him to notice the usefulness of the "economic" constrained maximization framework for studying animal behavior? Presumably he does, but the belief is clearly false. Levins (1968) and MacArthur (1965) predated Tullock (1971a), for example. Biologists did not have to wait for Tullock to show them "the way." What is more, some of the papers that made the connection earlier have been quoted more often than Tullock's own 1971a paper. And there surely are many papers published after Tullock (1971a) that exploited the constrained maximization framework in studying animal behavior and that are quoted much more often than Tullock (1971a).[17] In Parker's (2006) recent overview of the history of behavioral ecology, Tullock is not even mentioned once.[18] Thus Tullock seems to overrate the impact his own work had on biology. Presumably, Tullock simply is unaware of all the other attempts to get the constrained maximization framework accepted in the biology profession. Tullock clearly did not read very extensively and deeply into the biological literature. This in turn suggests that he was not really interested in acquiring a profound understanding of biology. What he was really interested in, it

[15] Note how similar this narrative is to Alchian's (1982) narrative about the history of his own 1950 paper.

[16] But note also that at other places Tullock reveals his disappointment about the fact that biologists did not seem to be interested in some of his other work ("Unfortunately, no biologist, not even Wilson, was interested" Tullock 1994, viii).

[17] As Eric L. Charnov writes: "his [Tullock 1971a] paper, known to me while still in grad school, (though published in the worlds top ecol/evol journal) has only been cited ~60 times; influential optimal foraging papers from the same era[+/– 5 yrs] are at ~500–1500 citations, and owe nothing to Tullock even for inspiration" (personal communication).

[18] Becker and Hirshleifer are not mentioned either. By contrast, the work of John Nash and Peter Hammerstein is referred to.

seems, is in demonstrating the vast potential of the constrained maximization framework for studying behavior not only within but also outside the economic realm.

8.4. Gary S. Becker's Rotten Kid

There is no doubt that Becker subscribes to Tullock's view that "the economic toolkit," which for Becker mainly implies the assumption of three things – constrained maximization for individual behavior, equilibrium for social, aggregate behavior, and stable preferences – is preeminently suited to describe and predict outcomes of evolutionary processes. In fact, Becker (1962) was evidently inspired by and wrote in the same spirit as Friedman's (1953) selection argument. The great achievement of this argument, Becker argues, is that it shows that the decisions of irrational firms are limited by a budget constraint. Firms that continually fail to make positive profits will eventually "run out of gas." This is why market responses tend to be rational even in the face of irrational firm behavior.

In Becker (1976), however, Becker seems to want to go beyond this. There he argues that evolution should mean more to economists than just "an occasional appendage" to the main body of economic analysis (Becker 1976, 818). There is more to learn for economists from evolution than that maximizers tend to be selected both in economic and biological systems (ibid.). Evolution does not merely support economic analysis, it can also, and more importantly, add something to economic analysis. Becker argues that economics would gain from combining the techniques in population genetics, entomology, and other biological foundations of sociobiology with the analytical techniques of economists (ibid., 826). More specifically, what economics could gain from taking the techniques from the biological foundations of sociobiology into account is that it could help economists with specifying what tastes or preferences people have. Economists generally take preferences as given; sociobiology holds out the promise of explaining not only what preferences people have, but also why they have them.

Apparently, Becker is looking for how economists can incorporate into their theories and analyses insights into how preferences evolved genetically. Several statements in Becker (1976) indicate that Becker takes sociobiology (and the analytical techniques developed in the subdisciplines in biology underlying sociobiology) to be the main source or supplier of these insights. Upon closer inspection, however, it turns out that this is not the case. The official rhetoric in Becker (1976) is one of economics and sociobiology mutually informing and enriching each other. Yet what is actually argued for is that Becker's own economic model of altruism is superior to and improves on existing sociobiologists' "group selectionist" accounts of altruism. Rather than pleading for a two-way transfer of techniques and insights from biology to economics, the main message is that biologists have something to learn from economic analysis rather than the other way around.

Let us have a closer look at the central argument in Becker's paper. What Becker sets out to show is that an altruistic individual (call him "Big Daddy") can attain higher personal fitness than an (otherwise equally able) egoistic individual, despite the fact that the altruistic individual is willing to increase the fitness of another individual (call him "Rotten Kid") at the expense of his own personal fitness.[19] Becker shows that the direct fitness disadvantages of Big Daddy's altruism may be more than compensated for by the beneficial indirect effects on the behavior of Rotten Kid (ibid, 820). If Rotten Kid knows about Big Daddy's altruism (and can correctly anticipate Big Daddy's reactions), then this knowledge might entice Rotten Kid to behave differently than how Kid would behave if he had an egoistic Daddy (or if he lacked this knowledge). If indeed Rotten Kid is induced to behave differently (more "cooperatively") then Big Daddy, even if he forgoes some of his own personal fitness to raise the personal fitness of Rotten Kid, can end up having a fitness that exceeds that of an (equally able) egoistic individual.

Thus Becker's (1974) so-called Rotten-Kid Theorem is a crucial part of the argument here: Egoistic Rotten Kid behaves as if he too were altruistic because it is in his own interest to do so. Egoistic Rotten Kid figures out that he is eventually better off if he does not settle immediately for the seemingly best possible outcome but instead leaves something to altruistic Big Daddy, for he correctly anticipates that this initial loss is more than offset by Big Daddy transferring part of the income left to him to Rotten Kid. This is why Rotten Kid behaves *as if* he, like Big Daddy, were also altruistic. It seems that Rotten Kid, like Big Daddy, is concerned about social income (or about "group fitness"), whereas all he is really concerned with is his own interest (its own personal fitness). It is the special configuration of *social interaction* that makes Rotten Kid behave as if he were altruistic.

What exactly is the contribution of sociobiology to this argument? Nothing at all! As Becker himself remarks, Becker's model is a purely economic one (Becker 1976, 818, 825), uncontaminated by alien elements from

[19] "Rotten Kid" is named after Becker's (1974) Rotten-Kid Theorem. The persona of "Big Daddy" was introduced in Hirshleifer's (1976) commentary on Becker (1976).

other disciplines. Instead of adopting one of the sociobiological models or explanations of altruism, Becker develops his own economic model. Becker presents sociobiological accounts of the evolution of altruism not as supplements or complements to economic analysis, but as unnecessary (ibid, 818) and incomplete (ibid., 819) accounts that are to be superseded by his own superior, more parsimonious, and fuller economic model.

In fact, as already noted and as Becker himself does not conceal, Becker's economic model of altruism is a variant of Becker (1974). Becker (1974) is an attempt to use simple tools of economic theory to analyze social interactions in general and intrafamily behavior in particular. The only differences with the model presented in Becker (1974) are that the arguments in the utility functions posited in Becker (1974) – consumption of the acting agent and possibly also of another agent – are substituted by fitness and that "shadow prices" are posited instead of market prices. Becker argues that, suitably reinterpreted, all the results obtained in Becker (1974) (such as the result that "the existence of a head economizes on the amount of true love required in a family," Becker 1974, 1091) carry over to the evolution of altruism: "The important point is that all the earlier results on the consumption of goods apply equally to this analysis of fitness" (Becker 1976, 823).

Does Becker seriously think that his economic model of altruism tells us something about how our altruistic impulses and preferences (if any) actually evolved way back in history? This is hard to tell. Becker's model seems to presuppose that individuals are endowed with quite sophisticated cognitive capacities. How else could Rotten Kid correctly anticipate what Big Daddy is going to do? As we have just seen, it is a crucial part in Becker's argument that Rotten Kid is capable of doing this. Is it reasonable to assume that during the time that our basic preferences evolved, our ancestors were already equipped with such cognitive capacities? Perhaps it is telling that Becker does not go into this.

Becker wants to contribute to solving what Wilson called "the central theoretical problem of sociobiology: how can altruism, which by definition reduces personal fitness, possibly evolve by natural selection?" (Wilson 1975, 12; quoted in Becker 1976, 818). Indeed, Becker treats this problem not as an empirical but as a theoretical problem that calls for a theoretical solution that has to meet certain desiderata (i.e., that has to display certain theoretical virtues). If possible, reference to dubious notions such as "group selection" is to be avoided, for example. One of the things Becker argues is that sociobiological models of "group" selection are unnecessary. He wants to point out that economic models of individual rationality (constrained maximization) in elementary situations of physical and social interaction suffice to explain altruism. Furthermore, if possible the theoretical solution should be general. Becker argues that his model is more general than kinship models because the individuals in his models need not have genes in common with one another. Becker's own analysis extends beyond kin toward unrelated neighbors and coworkers. It is on these *theoretical grounds* that Becker believes his economic model is superior to existing sociobiological models. Whether his model also gives a more realistic representation of how altruism actually evolved is an altogether different matter.

Thus Becker does not seem to be very interested in how altruism actually evolved. He does not seem to be very interested in what actually is done in sociobiology either.[20] Becker argues that the well-known kin selection model in sociobiology is a variant of a wider set of group selection models (Becker 1976, 818). If Becker had read the relevant literature more extensively and more carefully, he would have noticed that evolutionary biologists treat kin selection and group selection as perfect opposites of each other! Kin selection models are seen and were also originally presented by Hamilton as explanations of how altruism and cooperation could evolve without group selection. The idea is that individuals can enhance their "inclusive fitness" by helping their genetic relatives (where the degree of "sacrifice" should be proportional to the degree of genetic relatedness). There is no group selection going on here in any meaningful sense.[21] Indeed, kin selection models were among the models that prompted Richard Dawkins (1976) to single out the gene (and certainly not the group!) as the unit of selection in Darwinian biological evolution.

Or take the very notion of altruism itself. Becker criticizes Wilson for confusing two notions of altruism (Becker 1976, 824). The one notion is that altruism by definition reduces personal fitness, the other is that an act is altruistic when a person (or animal) increases the fitness of another at the expense of his own fitness. Becker claims that he has shown that the latter notion does not imply the former: "Using the latter definition, I have shown that altruism may actually increase personal fitness because of its effect on the behavior of others" (ibid., 824). Becker is right that he has shown that the personal fitness of an individual may increase (via indirect beneficial effects) even if the individual increases the fitness of another at the expense of his own personal fitness. However, Becker is wrong in asserting that he

[20] Only the usual suspects (Trivers 1974 and Wilson 1975) are referred to in the references.

[21] This was at least how it was generally conceived of by biologists by the time Becker wrote his paper. Recently, Sober and Wilson (1998) have argued that there is group selection in kin selection models, but this argument is contested in the community of evolutionary scholars.

uses the latter definition of "altruism" in showing this. Note that the second (latter) definition is purely in terms of behavior and its actual fitness consequences. It is completely silent on what motivates the person to engage in an altruistic act. This is the form of (evolutionary) altruism evolutionary biologists are interested in. By contrast, in his own economic model of altruism Becker defines an altruist in terms of a particular sort of motivation (or "willingness"): "By definition, an altruist is willing to reduce his own consumption in order to increase the consumption of others" (ibid., 818). In Becker's model, neither acts nor behavior are altruistic (or not), but persons, or more precisely, the preferences of persons (on which they are assumed to act). This is a form of (psychological) altruism that most social scientists are interested in. If Becker had taken the trouble to look carefully into sociobiology, if he had noticed the difference between Wilson's second definition of altruism and his own, then he should have seen that in his own model Rotten Kid does not merely behave as if it were altruistic, as Becker himself argues, but he behaves genuinely altruistically (on Wilson's second definition). If the behavior of Big Daddy is truly altruistic on the ground that he forgoes personal fitness and increases Rotten Kid's personal fitness (and despite the fact that, ultimately, his personal fitness increases), then Rotten Kid's behavior is equally truly altruistic. Rotten Kid also forgoes personal fitness and increases Big Daddy's personal fitness.

That Becker failed to see the latter can be called a serious omission. As one of Becker's compatriots, Jack Hirshleifer, never got tired of reminding us, behavior is never the outcome of preferences alone; behavior is always the outcome of preferences in combination with constraints (or opportunities). Indeed, this seems to be one of the main lessons of the Rotten-Kid Theorem: Given the right circumstances, Rotten Kid can be induced to behave altruistically (or as if he were altruistic, depending on what definition one adopts). Just as selfish Rotten Kid can be induced to behave as if he were altruistic, altruistic Big Daddy can in principle be induced to behave as if he were selfish (i.e., increasing his own personal fitness and decreasing personal fitness of Rotten Kid). But before we turn to Hirshleifer, let us first take stock.

Despite his statements to the effect that *both* economics and sociobiology are to benefit from the combination of their respective analytical frameworks, what Becker really argues for is that sociobiological analyses of altruism can benefit from taking the constrained maximization framework from economics on board. What is sold as a mutually beneficial two-way transfer of analytical frameworks turns out to be a one-way transfer of the analytical framework from economics to sociobiology from which only sociobiology is to benefit. Becker does not seriously take recourse to existing sociobiological studies or analyses in order to find out what arguments to posit in utility functions. In fact, Becker does not show a real interest in what (socio)biology could offer economists at all. Instead, what he is mostly interested in is in showing how standard economic analysis can improve on sociobiological analyses of the evolution of altruism.

8.5. Jack Hirshleifer's Interests in Evolutionary Biology

Things are surely different with Hirshleifer. Unlike Tullock and Becker, who did not take a great interest in evolutionary biology and whose understanding of evolutionary biology was accordingly poor, Jack Hirshleifer undeniably displayed a greater interest in evolutionary biology and also had a deeper understanding of it. A cursory glance at Hirshleifer's lengthy and insightful early papers (Hirshleifer 1977, 1982) suffices to see that Hirshleifer read much more of evolutionary biology than Tullock and Becker presumably ever did. There is a much richer and better-informed discussion of relevant literature in evolutionary biology than one can find in Tullock's and Becker's writings. Although the selection of biological papers and books listed in the references section in Hirshleifer's papers is once again skewed toward the "adaptationist" and sociobiological camp in evolutionary biology (such as the work of Alexander, Hamilton, Maynard Smith, Charnov, Lotka, Trivers, and Ghiselin; there is no single reference to Gould and Lewontin 1979, for example),[22] one can also find sympathetic discussions of (and references to) works such as Nelson and Winter (1982) and Boyd and Richerson (1985).

Hirshleifer displays a serious interest – in a much more profound way and in much greater detail than Tullock and Becker ever did – in what possibly could be credible economic analogs and counterparts of key concepts and notions in (evolutionary) biology. In Hirshleifer (1977), one of the issues Hirshleifer struggles with is whether organisms or genes in biological systems should be viewed as the proper analogs of the fundamental acting unit in economic systems, the individual. If genes are the proper analogs, then firms in economic systems are perhaps the proper analogs of organisms in the biological system. Issues like these have also been occupying economists who, like Richard Nelson and Sidney Winter (and,

[22] Only in Hirshleifer (1985) do we find a reference to Lewontin (1979), and a few statements that assuming that surviving organisms behave *as if* they maximize fitness is somewhat controversial in evolutionary biology.

more recently, Geoff Hodgson), tried to find out to what extent processes of economic evolution can be seen as analogous to processes of biological evolution.

There is also a lot Hirshleifer has in common with Tullock and especially with Becker, however. Just like Tullock and Becker, Hirshleifer more or less takes for granted that a generalized version of the thrust of Friedman's selection argument holds true:

> What happens in the biological realm is that, given a sufficiently long run, *natural selection under Malthusian competition* allows survival only of the most successful among the possible strategies. So the result ends up almost *as if* baboons or rats or crabgrass plants were consciously optimizing. (Hirshleifer 1987b, 171–172)

Like Tullock and Becker, but unlike Friedman himself, Hirshleifer has not the slightest reservation or hesitation to use the constrained maximization framework of economic theory to describe the behavior of surviving organisms. What biologists can learn from economic theory in particular, Hirshleifer consistently argues, is that behavior is never fully determined by an organism's "preferences" (or instincts, drives, or dispositions) alone, but always also by the prevailing constraints and opportunities.

What Hirshleifer additionally shares with Tullock and Becker is nicely illustrated in Hirshleifer (1978). Hirshleifer (1978) elaborates on Ghiselin's (1978) proposal to regard biology as natural economy, the social sciences (and economics in particular) as political economy, and both as branches of general economy. Hirshleifer agrees with Ghiselin that the existence of institutions such as law, government, and property in political economy marks a crucial difference with natural economy (in which there are no such institutions). Note that this was one of the reasons for Tullock to argue that there is not much that economists can learn from biologists. Hirshleifer also agrees with Ghiselin, however, that the underlying realities of natural economy always shine through in political economy. What Hirshleifer seems to have in mind when talking of the underlying realities of natural economy are the preferences (such as innate benevolence or malevolence) that are adaptive rather than arbitrary. Note that this is reminiscent of Becker's (1976) avowal that what economists can learn from (socio)biology is what preferences have (or have had) survival value.

We also saw, however, that Becker does not really make an attempt to learn something from (socio)biology. Instead, Becker argues that in their attempts to show how altruism could have evolved, (socio)biologists can learn something from economic models of socially interacting constrained maximizing individuals. How serious is Hirshleifer in arguing that economic models, and the model of "economic man" in particular, can and should be enriched and broadened by evolutionary biology? The "programmatic contention" (as Hirshleifer himself calls it) here is that "preference patterns, despite seemingly arbitrary elements, have survived because they are mainly adaptive to environmental conditions" (Hirshleifer 1977a, 18).[23] Hirshleifer consistently argued that insights about the evolution of our own species help to go beyond the narrow conception of "economic man". The insights suggest that economic conception of man and of human behavior should be enriched But who are to provide these insights? How much can and should economics rely on biology to find out what preference patterns are adaptive to environmental conditions?

Once again, closer inspection reveals that also Hirshleifer holds that economic rather than biological analysis is supposed to do the job. Hirshleifer's work sheds more light on what preferences (or, more broadly, what proximate causes) are (or have been) adaptive. His work owes a lot to and is written in very much the same spirit as Becker (1976).[24] In fact, Hirshleifer's own contributions on this front started with a comment on Becker (1976). The main point in his comment (Hirshleifer 1976) is that Becker's argument that the fitness of altruistic Big Daddy can exceed that of an equally able nonaltruistic father crucially depends on Big Daddy having the last word. If Rotten Kid and Big Daddy are to make their decisions simultaneously, or if Rotten Kid has the last word, the argument falters. Especially if Rotten Kid has the last word, Big Daddy's fitness will be lower than that of an equally able nonaltruistic father.

One of Hirshleifer's more influential papers in this area of research,[25] Hirshleifer (1987a), can be seen as a follow-up and generalization of Becker

[23] See also: "[W]here standard economics takes the satisfaction of preferences as the primitive objective or 'utility function' of the acting individuals, biological theory suggests that what seems like mere preference or taste evolves out of the objective dictates of reproductive survival" (Hirshleifer 1977a, 50).

Philosopher John Dupré (2001) fears the "imperialist" combination of neoclassical economics with evolutionary psychology (and with evolutionary cognitive science), whereas philosopher (and economist) Don Ross (2005) welcomes it.

[24] Unlike Becker, Hirshleifer never presented a clear thesis or research program of his own (or it should be the economics of conflict and of conflict resolution as his own field). Instead, what we find in Hirshleifer's writings is a host of suggestions waiting to be worked out.

[25] This is part of what might be called Hirshleifer's tragedy of life (as a professional economist): Hirshleifer (1987) clearly predates Robert Frank's (1988) idea of emotions as commitment devices (as Frank 1988 observes), but it was Frank and not Hirschleifer who got the credit for it. A similar thing seems to have happened with Axelrod's (1984) account of the evolution of cooperation: Here, too, Hirshleifer's earlier work on the evolution of various strategies of reciprocity (cf. Hirshleifer 1982) seems to have predated Axelrod (1984),

(1976) and Hirshleifer (1976). What Hirshleifer wants to show here is that particular forms of "irrational" emotional behavior exist because they somewhat paradoxically enable the individuals exhibiting the forms of behavior to out-compete those that display rational behavior: "The economist must go beyond the assumption of "economic man" precisely because of the economic advantage of *not* behaving like economic man – an advantage that presumably explains why the world is not populated solely by economic men" (Hirshleifer 1987a, 322).[26] This phrasing might suggest that standard economic analysis, with its assumption of "economic man," is ill-suited to explain how people that do not behave like economic man can attain economic advantage. Yet Hirshleifer is clearly of a different opinion: Following up on his Hirshleifer (1976) he puts standard economic analysis to creative use to show how this is possible. "My discussion follows a lead by Becker (1976), who demonstrated how "altruism" can, in effect, force cooperation upon a completely selfish partner (the 'Rotten-Kid Theorem'). I shall try to show more generally here how, and up to what limits, positive or negative emotions can serve a constructive role as guarantors of threats or promises in social interactions" (Hirshleifer 1987a, 308).[27]

Hirshleifer (1987a) starts by discussing the well-known problem that making promises or threats only seemingly offers an easy escape from concluding that individuals get stuck in mutually harmful inefficient defection or cheating equilibria in mixed-motive games. The problem is that talk is cheap; when the time arrives to fulfill (or live up to) promises and threats, it is no longer in the interest of those that made the promises and threats to fulfill the promises and threats. Knowing this, the other party (or player) will not find the promises and threats credible – unless, that is, the promises and threats are backed up by something that make promises and threats credible.

Hirshleifer goes on to argue that emotions can play this role; emotions can serve as guarantors of threats and promises. If a person is benevolent toward a particular other person, for example, and if having this emotion makes the person cooperate, then this could back up the person's promise

but Axelrod got all the credit. See Demsetz (2005) for a short but informative overview of the work of Hirshleifer.

26 See also: "The thrust of the argument here has been that certain patterns of emotional payoffs to interpersonal cooperative opportunities can make retention of a capacity for emotion materially profitable" (Hirshleifer 1987, 321).

27 Hirshleifer's discussion draws our attention to the interesting possibility that standard economic theory's constrained maximization framework might do a better job in describing the outcomes of evolutionary processes than in explaining human behavior. See Vromen (2003) for further discussion.

sufficiently. Hirshleifer discusses benevolence and malevolence as action-independent emotions, and anger and gratitude as action-dependent emotions. The underlying idea with the latter is that people become so angry about an action undertaken by another person that the angry person loses control over his actions. The anger could make the person act "irrationally" against what, rationally speaking, would be in his best "objective" interest to do. The general point Hirshleifer wants to make is that people acting on their emotions might be better off in terms of material gains actually reaped (i.e. the personal income they actually enjoy) than people lacking these emotions, not despite but precisely because of their "irrational" emotions.

How precisely this could work is illustrated visually by Hirshleifer with the aid of standard indifference curve analysis. Although the analysis itself is familiar and standard among economists, the use to which Hirshleifer puts it is creative.[28] Instead of putting different goods and services that some consumer might want to have on the axes, the axes now stand for the incomes that the benevolent person and some other (possibly receiving) person might enjoy. A benevolent person will have the usual convex difference curves, whereas the opposite malevolent person will have concave difference curves. Next to the indifference curves, Hirshleifer also plots (135-degree) income transfer lines for benevolent persons and (45-degree) income deprivation lines on the assumption that benevolent/malevolent persons can choose to transfer/deprive part of his income on a 1:1 basis. Finally, a productive opportunity curve is plotted.

With the aid of this analytical apparatus, Hirshleifer is able to derive several results. One of them is once again a demonstration of the Rotten-Kid Theorem. The idea is that the game is played sequentially. Self-interested Rotten Kid is the first mover ("First") and benevolent Big Daddy is the second mover ("Second"). Rotten Kid first can choose what point on (or within) the productive opportunity curve to pick. After this, Big Daddy decides what part of his personal income to transfer to Rotten Kid (based on his indifference curves). With all of these assumptions in place, Hirshleifer is able to show that if Rotten Kid is farsighted (i.e., is able to anticipate the subsequent income-transferring behavior of Big Daddy correctly), Rotten Kid will choose another point on the productive opportunity curve than if Big Daddy weren't (and if this were known by Rotten Kid) benevolent. As Hirshleifer himself observes, the important part of his result is not that farsighted, selfish Rotten Kid can be induced (enticed) by benevolent (or "hard altruistic") Big Daddy to act as if he too were altruistic ("soft altruism") so

[28] This creative use of indifference curve analysis is foreshadowed in Hirshleifer (1976).

that he is better off. The important part is rather that Big Daddy is better off as well (than he would be if he were not benevolent or altruistic; the implicit assumption is that if Big Daddy were a self-interested economic man, point M would be the end result – which is worse for both than A).

Thus the crux of the matter here is the same as it is in Becker (1976) and in Frank (1988): "Irrational" emotions can only have survival value if the person acting on his emotions (such as altruistic Big Daddy) somehow is able to reliably *signal* his emotions and if the other individual(s) (such as egoistic Rotten Kid) is able to notice the signal (and what it stands for). Only then will the other individual(s) act in such a way that the fitness of the person having the emotions is enhanced rather than diminished.

To cut things short, what Hirshleifer contributes to the nascent field of bioeconomics is not so different from what Tullock and Becker contribute to it: demonstrations that the constrained maximization framework of standard economic theory can be fruitfully deployed to study processes of biological evolution and their outcomes. Hirshleifer's writings undoubtedly display a more profound understanding of work done in evolutionary biology than Tullock's and Becker's writings. In his informed overviews (Hirshleifer 1977, 1982), Hirshleifer introduced the economics profession to what was going on in substantial parts of biological literature in an accessible way. However, despite declamations to the effect that connecting biology and economics implies (and should imply) a two-way transfer of ideas and concepts between biology and economics from which both biology and economics are to benefit, in the end his own contributions entail a one-way transfer of the constrained maximization framework from economics to biology from which biological analyses of selection processes are to benefit.

8.6. The Self-Sufficiency of Economic analysis and Economic(s) Imperialism

Becker (1976) and Hirshleifer (1987) suggest that economic analysis is in a way *self-sufficient*: Economic analysis does not need any input from other disciplines. The constrained maximization framework of economic analysis is suited not only to study current behavior on the basis of given preferences, but also to identify what these "given" preferences are! Economic analysis can tell us what preferences have (or had) survival value as well as what behavior people display given these preferences. Earlier economists such as Robbins might have thought that economics depends on psychology for identifying preferences. Sociobiologists and evolutionary psychologists might think that it is rather evolutionary biology that economists have to rely on for this purpose. But if we are to believe Becker and Hirshleifer, the fact of the matter is that economic analysis can do all these things on its own. Economics can render this service to itself. There is no need, it seems, for economists to take recourse to any other discipline.

Or so it seems. Note that neither Becker nor Hirshleifer deploys economic analysis to discover what (basic) preferences survived (or possibly could have survived) selection processes. Instead, they deploy economic analysis to show that already identified (or suggested) preferences such as altruism and benevolence could have survived selection processes. In other words, they deploy economic analysis to find out whether an evolutionary rationale can be provided for preferences for which they (or others) have independent reason to believe (or assume) they exist and exert influence on behavior.

Becker and Hirshleifer do not engage in a grand attempt to identify all the basic preferences people have. They do not show a great interest in embarking on such an ambitious project. They seem to show even less interest in *revising* existing economic analysis on the basis of a full specification of all the arguments in the utility functions. In this, they differ markedly from economists who have started doing this. I am thinking here in particular of so-called *social preferences* models (cf. Güth and Yaari 1992, Fehr and Schmidt 1999, Bolton and Ockenfels 2000).

What Becker (1976) and Hirshleifer (1987) seem to be really interested in, it seems, is rather in showing the usefulness and fruitfulness of the constrained maximization framework of economic analysis in shedding light on how altruistic (and other non-self-interested) preferences and the like could have evolved. Like Tullock, they are in the business of promoting the use of the constrained maximization framework outside the traditional boundaries of economics as a discipline. It is no coincidence that Tullock (McKenzie and Tullock 1975, Tullock 1987) and Hirshleifer (1985, 1987b) have been actively advancing *economic imperialism* (or economics imperialism; Mäki 2002) and that Becker is usually seen as economic imperialism's leading protagonist.[29] All three believe that economics (constrained maximization at the individual level and equilibrium at the social level of analysis) provides "the universal grammar of social science" (Hirshleifer 1985, 52). Indeed, as we have seen in this paper, they believe the scope of economics is not limited to social science, but extends to evolutionary biology:

[29] Interestingly, though, Tullock's, Becker's, and Hirshleifer's inroads into evolutionary biology are not even mentioned in Lazear (2000).

"Economic imperialism – the use of economic analytical models to study all forms of social relations rather than only the market interactions of 'rational' decision makers – is similarly entirely consonant with the evolutionary approach" (Hirshleifer 1982, 52).[30]

In calling Tullock, Becker, and Hirshleifer economic imperialists some clarification might be in order. It is not necessarily the case that those inroads into other disciplines are aggressive, hostile intrusions meant to conquer the disciplines. Such inroads can be made with the best intentions. They may be inspired by the (in itself) noble intention to contribute to the growth of knowledge in the other disciplines. It is not necessarily the case either that there is disdain for what practitioners in other disciplines have accomplished in their own domain either. Typically, however, it is the case that there is not much understanding and appreciation of what is going on (and of what has been going on) in those other disciplines. No serious attempts are made to acquaint oneself with the history and tradition of the other disciplines, to get a feel for the specific sort of problems that occupy the practitioners of the other disciplines and for the specific *couleur locale* in the other disciplines' culture.

This is exactly what seems to have happened with Tullock's, Becker's, and Hirshleifer's inroads into evolutionary biology. If the relevant criterion is whether or not they contributed to the spread of the constrained maximization framework in evolutionary biology, their inroads were not very successful. To be sure, the constrained maximization framework has been used and applied more often in evolutionary biology (and especially in subbranches such as behavioral ecology) after Tullock, Becker, and Hirshleifer wrote their papers. Yet it is highly questionable that their papers contributed much to this. As already indicated earlier, there were already papers using the constrained maximization framework before Tullock, Becker, and Hirshleifer wrote theirs.[31] It is telling that (with the possible exception of Hirshleifer) they were largely unaware of that. Attempts to estimate impact factors (such as in Parker 2006) suggest that other papers were far more instrumental in having the constrained maximization framework spread in evolutionary biology than Tullock's, Becker's, and Hirshleifer's. As Eric L.

[30] The similarity adduced is with "economic man." Following Ghiselin (1978), Hirshleifer also argues that economics and biology should be seen as one (or united) rather than as two competing imperialisms: "In short, these two colliding imperialisms can say, with the comic-strip character Pogo, 'We have seen the enemy, and he is us!'" (Hirshleifer 1985, 65).

[31] It is always good (and for some economists, sobering) to keep in mind also that optimality principles and optimality analysis did not originate from within economics (Schoemaker 1982, 1991).

Charnov has suggested to me, part of the reason for this might well be that that the three did not try to find out what specific sorts of problems evolutionary biologists were struggling with (or were interested in). By contrast, Charnov surmises, economist Colin W. Clark (cf. Mangel and Clark 1988) succeeded in attracting the attention and interest of behavioral ecologists because he did try to link up with the biologist's interests. This, of course, only further strengthens the idea that the three were simply not very interested in what was actually going on in evolutionary biology.

8.7. Conclusions

Both Alchian's (1950) and Friedman's (1953) selection arguments were clearly meant to defend marginal analysis against (what both Alchian and Friedman took to be) misguided antimarginalist critiques. Both argued that even if businessmen do not literally do the things that marginalist analysis seemingly ascribe to them, a selection mechanism in markets akin to natural selection in evolutionary biology would see to it that the predictions of marginal analysis tend to hold. However, whereas Alchian's text contains various reservations and qualifications and also suggestions as to how processes of economic evolution, analogous to processes of biological evolution, could be studied further, Friedman simply boldly declares that the maximization-of-returns hypothesis summarizes appropriately the conditions for survival. Friedman's version won the day in Chicago. Apparently without reckoning with the possibility that they might be "pushing their luck too far" (Alchian 1950, 220), the second generation Chicago School economists Tullock, Becker, and Hirshleifer simply take for granted that constrained maximization hypotheses accurately describe the behavior of individuals surviving selection processes.

In fact, the second-generation Chicago economists took Friedman's selection argument further than Friedman himself ever wanted to take it. In preparing the ground for his selection argument, Friedman discusses the parallel example of the positioning of leaves around trees. Friedman argues that the hypothesis that leaves maximize exposure to sunlight would do a good job in predicting the positioning of leaves around trees. What prevents Friedman from seriously proposing maximization hypothesis like this one in evolutionary biology is the fact that there is already a well-entrenched and successful program of putting forward adaptationist hypotheses in evolutionary biology. Thus Friedman showed some respect for traditional disciplinary boundaries and for established traditions of theorizing in other disciplines. This is different with the second-generation Chicago School economists. Tullock, Becker, and Hirshleifer were considerably less reticent in crossing disciplinary boundaries. What they have in common is their belief in the usefulness and fruitfulness of applying the constrained maximization framework of standard economic theory in studying processes of biological evolution and their outcomes.

Officially, the credo of the bioeconomics of Tullock, Becker, and Hirshleifer is to promote and contribute to a mutually beneficial two-way transfer of ideas, concepts, and approaches between biology and economics. Becker and especially Hirshleifer suggest that evolutionary biology can enrich economics by providing a fuller view of human motivation than the narrow-minded model of economic man. However, here too Becker and Hirshleifer seem to be more interested in showing that the constrained maximization framework of economists can complement, if not supersede existing (socio)biological accounts of the evolution of non-self-interested motives and preferences than in looking at what economists can learn from existing (socio)biological accounts. Thus Tullock-, Becker-, and Hirshleifer-type bioeconomics turns out to be a one-way transfer of the constrained maximization framework of economic theory to evolutionary biology from which evolutionary biology is to benefit. This economic imperialist project does not seem to have been particularly successful. The constrained maximization framework did gain more ground in evolutionary biology in the last few decades, but the papers of Tullock, Becker, and Hirshleifer did not seem to have contributed much to this.

References

Alchian, Armen A. 1950. "Uncertainty, Evolution and Economic Theory." *Journal of Political Economy* 58: 211–222.

1982. "Intervention (on p. 149)." In R.O. Zerbe Jr. (ed.), *Research in Laws and Economics* 4. Greenwich (etc.): JAI Press Inc.

Axelrod, Robert. 1984. *The Evolution of Cooperation*. New York: Basic Books.

Becker, Gary S. 1962. "Irrational Behavior and Economic Theory." *Journal of Political Economy* 70: 1–13.

1974. "A Theory of Social Interactions." *Journal of Political Economy* 82: 1032–1093.

1976. "Altruism, Egoism, and Genetic Fitness: Economics and Sociobiology." *Journal of Economic Literature* 14(3): 817–826.

Bolton, Gary E. and Axel Ockenfels. 2000. "ERC: A Theory of Equity, Reciprocity and Competition." *American Economic Review* 90: 166–193.

Boyd, Richard and Peter Richerson. 1985. *Culture and the Evolutionary Process*. Chicago: University of Chicago Press.

Buchanan, James M. and Gordon Tullock. 1962. *The Calculus of Consent: Logical Foundations of Constitutional Democracy*. Ann Arbor: University of Michigan Press.

Coase, Ronald. 1978. "Discussion (of Ghiselin 1978)." *American Economic Review (Papers and Proceedings)* 68: 244–245.

Dawkins, Richard. 1976. *The Selfish Gene*. Oxford: Oxford University Press.

Demsetz, Harold. 2005. "Professor Jack Hirshleifer (1925–2005): A Life Remembered." *Journal of Bioeconomics* 7: 209–214.

Dupré, John. 2001. *Human Nature and the Limits of Science*. Oxford: Oxford University Press.

Enke, Stephen. 1951. "On Maximizing Profits: A Distinction Between Chamberlain and Robinson." *American Economic Review* 41: 566–578.

Fehr, Ernst and Klaus Schmidt. 1999. "A Theory of Fairness, Competition, and Cooperation." *Quarterly Journal of Economics* 114: 817–868.

Frank, Robert H. 1988. *Passions within Reason*. New York: W.W. Norton & Company.

Friedman, Milton. 1953. *Essays in Positive Economics*. Chicago: University of Chicago Press.

Ghiselin, Michael T. 1974. *The Economy of Nature and the Evolution of Sex*. Berkeley and Los Angeles, CA: University of California Press.

1978. "The Economy of the Body." *American Economic Review (Papers and Proceedings)* 68: 233–237.

Gould, Stephen Jay and Richard Lewontin. 1979. "The Spandrels of San Marco and the Panglossian Paradigm: A Critique of the Adaptationist Programme." *Proceedings of the Royal Society London* 205: 581–598.

Güth, Werner and Menahem E. Yaari. 1991. "Explaining Reciprocal Behavior in Simple Strategic Games: An Evolutionary Approach." In U. Witt, ed., *Explaining Process and Change: Approaches to Evolutionary Economics*. Ann Arbor: University of Michigan, pp. 23–34.

Hammond, J. Dan. 2004. "Early Drafts of Friedman's Methodology Essay." In Uskali Mäki, ed., *The Methodology of Positive Economics: Reflections on the Milton Friedman Legacy*, Cambridge University Press, 2009, pp. 68–89.

Hirshleifer, Jack. 1976. "Shakespeare vs. Becker on Altruism: The Importance of Having the Last Word." *Journal of Economic Literature* 15(2): 500–502.

1977. "Economics from a Biological Viewpoint." *Journal of Law and Economics* 20(1): 1–52.

1978. "Competition, Cooperation, and Conflict in Economics and Biology." *American Economic Review (Papers and Proceedings)* 68: 238–243.

1982. "Evolutionary Models in Economics and Law: Cooperation versus Conflict Strategies." In R.O. Zerbe Jr., ed., *Research in Laws and Economics* 4. Greenwich (etc.): JAI Press Inc., pp. 1–60.

1985. "The Expanding Domain of Economics." *American Economic Review* 75: 53–68.

1987a. "On the Emotions as Guarantors of Threats and Promises." In John Dupré, ed., *The Latest on the Best: Essays on Evolution and Optimality*. Cambridge, MA: MIT Press, pp. 307–326.

1987b. "The Economic Approach to Conflict." In Radnitzky and Bernholz, pp. 335–364.

Lack, David. 1966. *Population Studies of Birds*. Clarendon Press: London.

Landa, Janet T. and Michael T. Ghiselin. 1999. "The Emerging Discipline of Bioeconomics: Aims and Scope of the Journal of Bioeconomics." *Journal of Bioeconomics* 1: 5–12.

Lazear, Edward P. 2000. "Economic Imperialism." *Quarterly Journal of Economics* 115(1): 99–146.

Levins, Richard. 1968. *Evolution in Changing Environments*. Princeton: Princeton University Press.

MacArthur, Robert H. 1965. "Patterns of species diversity." *Biological Review* 40: 510–533.

Mäki, Uskali. 2002. "Explanatory Ecumenism and Economics Imperialism." *Economics and Philosophy* 18(2): 235–257.

Mangel, Mark and Colin W. Clark. 1988. *Dynamic Modeling in Behavioral Ecology*. Princeton: Princeton University Press.

Mayr, Ernst. 1982. *The Growth of Biological Thought*. Cambridge, MA: Harvard University Press.

McKenzie, Richard B. and Gordon Tullock. 1975. *The New World of Economics: Exploration into the Human Experience*. Homewood, IL.: R.D. Irwin.

Metcalfe, J. Stanley. 1989. "Evolution and Economic Change." In A. Silberston, ed., *Technology and Economic Progress*. Basingstone, Hampshire: Macmillan Press.

Mirowski, Phil. 2007. "On the Origins (in Chicago) of Some Species of Neoliberal Evolutionary Economics (this volume).

Nelson, Richard R. and Sidney Winter. 1982. *An Evolutionary Theory of Economic Change*. Cambridge, MA: Harvard University Press.

Parker, Geoff A. 2006. "Behavioural Ecology: The Science of Natural History." In J.R. Lucas and L.W. Simmons, eds., *Essays on Animal Behaviour: Celebrating 50 years of Animal Behaviour*. Burlington, MA: Elsevier, pp. 23–56.

Radnitzky, Gerard and Peter Bernholz (eds.). 1987. *Economic Imperialism: The Economic Method Applied Outside the Field of Economics*. New York: Paragon House.

Ross, Don. 2005. *Economic Theory and Cognitive Science: Microexplanation*. Cambridge, MA: MIT Press.

Schoemaker, Paul J.H. 1982. "Optimality Principles in Science: Some Epistemological Issues." In J.H.P. Paelinck and P.H. Vossen, eds., *The Quest for Optimality*. Brookfield, VT: Gower, pp. 5–31.

1991. "The Quest for Optimality: A Positive Heuristic of Science?" *Behavioral and Brain Sciences* 14: 205–245.

Sober, Elliott and David S. Wilson. 1998. *Unto Others: The Evolution and Psychology of Unselfish Behavior*. Cambridge, MA: Harvard University Press.

Trivers, Robert. 1971. "The Evolution of Reciprocal Altruism." *Quarterly Review of Biology* 46: 35–57.

Tullock, Gordon. 1971a. "The Coal Tit as a Careful Shopper." *The American Naturalist* 105: 77–80.

1971b. "Biological Externalities." *Journal of Theoretical Biology* 33: 379–392.

1979. "Sociobiology and Economics." *Atlantic Economic Journal* 7: 1–10.

1987. "Autocracy." In Radnitzky, Gerard and Peter Bernholz, eds., *Economic Imperialism: The Economic Method Applied Outside the Field of Economics*. New York: Paragon House, pp. 365–381.

1994. *The Economics of Non-Human Societies*. Tucson, AZ: Pallas Press.

1999. "Some Personal Reflections on the History of Bioeconomics." *Journal of Bioeconomics* 1: 13–18.

Vromen, Jack. 1995. *Economic Evolution: An Enquiry into the Foundations of "New Institutional Economics"*. London: Routledge.

2003. "Why the Economic Conception of Human Behaviour Might Lack a Biological Basis." *Theoria* 18(48): 297–323.

2007. "Neuroeconomics as a Natural Extension of Bioeconomics: The Shifting Scope of Standard Economic Theory." *Journal of Bioeconomics* 9(2): 145–167.

2009. "Friedman's Selection Argument Revisited." In Uskali Mäki, ed., *The Methodology of Economics. Milton Friedman's Essay at 50*. Cambridge, MA: Cambridge University Press.

Wilson, Edward O. 1975. *Sociobiology: The New Synthesis*. Cambridge, MA: The Belknap Press of Harvard University Press.

NINE

On the Origins (at Chicago) of Some Species of Neoliberal Evolutionary Economics

Philip Mirowski

What a book a Devil's Chaplain might write on the clumsy, wasteful, blunderingly low & horridly cruel works of nature!
– Charles Darwin
Quoted in (Desmond and Moore 1991, 449)

These days, you would probably have to search far and wide to find an economist who scorns the siren song of an "evolutionary economics." Many seem to think that the immanent prospect of a concertedly "Darwinian" bioeconomics is laden with promise, thoroughly exhilarating, and a glorious liberation from the more buttoned-down methodology of science that had dominated the previous generation of economic orthodoxy, itself sometimes characterized by the disparaging term "physics envy."[1] More often than not, they also seem to approach evolution as a phenomenon that is intrinsically upbeat and edifying, forgetting that Darwin himself struggled with a rather darker view of Nature and man's place within it (as in our epigraph). Sometimes the terminology of evolution designates nothing more precise than nonspecific pervasive change versus the supposed stasis of neoclassical theory: "Always history is being made; opinions, attitudes and institutions change, and there is evolution in the nature of capitalism"

I want to thank Dan Hammond for sharing the Alchian-Friedman correspondence, Mie Augier for providing a copy of the Alchian interview, Eddie Nik-Khah for pointing to some sources in the Stigler papers, and Geoff Hodgson for permission to reproduce Figure 9.1. I am beholden to Jack Vromen and the participants at the Notre Dame Conference on the Chicago School for comments. The late lamented Department of Economics and Policy Studies provided support for the Conference. Also, an earlier version of this paper was produced well before (Levallois 2009), and that author was provided with a version of it in 2007 prior to his own publication.

[1] Not infrequently, reference is made to my own early work (1989) as supporting such a position. See, for instance, (Hodgson 1993, 21; Witt 1999; Dopfer 2001, 75). My own position is that it is unclear the extent to which modern biology itself has successfully escaped physics envy.

(Knight, 1935, 184). Furthermore, economists have had recourse to the most amazingly diverse range of supposed progenitors of their evolutionary brand of economics, from Alfred Marshall to Thorstein Veblen to Joseph Schumpeter to Carl Menger to Herbert Spencer to Kenneth Boulding to Albert Schäffle to Sidney Winter to John Nash, and so on. The mere fact that no two of these candidates would have deigned to wholeheartedly endorse each other's version of economics, much less provide any single coherent intellectual framework that might encompass the other, reveals the extent to which "evolutionary economics" has been a leaky portmanteau bucket, temporarily confining whatever the individual theorist wished to put in it, at least until anything potent drained away of its own accord.

Of course, not everyone has coquetted with evolution in economics in so blasé or cavalier a fashion. A special dispensation must be issued to Geoffrey Hodgson, who, from his *Economics and Evolution* (1993) onward, has thrashed against the prevailing current to nail down precisely what many historical thinkers actually meant when they ventured to implement their evocative summons of biology into economics, hoping to bend Nature to their own purposes. Of late, Hodgson has been concerned, however, to sift out what he deems to be illegitimate appeals to biology from the version of evolution he himself favors, which he has called "Universal Darwinism" (2002; Hodgson and Knudsen, 2006; Nelson, 2007). Adopting a stance nominally opposed to those who deal in metaphors and analogies, he currently advocates instead a regulatory ontological principle of natural selection that he claims transcends academic disciplines, physical organisms, or empirical detail. For someone unusually sensitive to the diverse variant referents of the evolution concept throughout the history of biology, his current quest to hold all economic discourse up to a single timeless evolutionary benchmark runs the risk of obscuring the multifarious uses of bioeconomics language by economists; it may end up providing unintended cover for those earlier economists whom he formerly indicted as innocent of any deep understanding of biology. Fervent invocations of a unified Theory of Everything risks peremptorily banishing "The Social," along with blurring the alternative meanings of "The Natural" in economics and social theory in general. Not everyone regards the theory of evolution, as it is currently understood, as the ideal vehicle to deliver economics from the happy valley of conceptual complacency, or even the postcrisis discombobulation it now occupies.[2]

[2] On recent reactions of economists to the Great Recession which began in 2007, see (Mirowski 2010).

Indeed, one purpose of this paper is to argue that resort to biological language in the immediate postwar period in America happened to be much more a characteristic trope of those hard at work constructing neoliberalism and defending the newly established neoclassical orthodoxy than it was a rallying cry for those dissatisfied with that orthodoxy. I want to dispel the impression that resort to evolutionary ideas was "radical" in the American context. Although one disputes the pronouncements of the distinguished historian Carl Degler with trepidation, he is simply historically mistaken when he asserts, "Frequent as the charge of a conservative bias to biological explanations may have been, it was both inaccurate and irrelevant" (1991, 319), at least when it comes to economics. Heterodox economists pining for a different style of economics have also done their bit to erase this history: "[E]volutionary strands and concepts … seemed to vanish in the early postwar period" (Nelson and Winter, 2002, 24). The narrative I present here inverts the standard story I myself heard so often as a tyro economist back in the 1970s: People then said that being favorably inclined toward evolutionary economics meant that one nurtured a sensitive warm regard for prewar Institutionalist economics, or that one apprehended the need for a truly dynamic analysis missing in conventional optimization theory, or that one aspired to be a Big Thinker unfettered by narrow parochial disciplinary concerns, or perhaps that one realized that textbook microeconomics missed out on everything that made capitalism a successful economic formation.[3] Only now in retrospect can we come to appreciate that substantial attempts to import evolutionary language into economics in the 1950s and 1960s were mainly the province of thinkers associated with the right, and not so much that of the political left. Hodgson himself (2004, 262) has pointed out that the heirs to pre–World War I Institutionalism (such as they were) had largely abandoned biological evolution as a theoretical organizing principle in the 1930s; and as for microeconomics, the vectors of influence were becoming oriented in the opposite direction, as it was being projected back onto the behavior of animals in that period. At the end of this chapter, we will briefly entertain the unusual proposition that it was the revanchist Chicago economics version of evolution that has colored the vernacular perception of *biological* evolution in the popular culture, rather than vice versa.

[3] Hodgson (1994, 426) has sometimes engaged in this rhetoric that evolution would just naturally accompany heterodox inclinations: "Strangely, the invocation of the natural selection argument by Friedman and others is not used to bolster an evolutionary approach to the understanding of economic problems, but of profit maximization along traditional lines." There would be nothing "strange" about it if we approached evolution as primarily a neoliberal trope in economics and elsewhere, as we do in this paper.

Jack Vromen has argued in a number of texts (1994, 1995, this volume) that defense of neoclassical microeconomics was a major motivation of some of the figures we shall discuss; what has been missing so far from his account are the added considerations that (1) most of these protagonists were united by the fact that they belonged to the premier postwar debating society of the neoliberal project, the Mont Pèlerin Society, and (2) most of the protagonists were demonstrably innocent of the ferment in modern biology that was taking place all around them. Thus we conclude that the impetus to rethink evolution at mid-century in economics *did not come from within biology itself*. This should signal that there was something else eminently political about this particular recourse to Nature in the 1950s and beyond, something rather specific to the history of economics at that juncture. Hence, rather than approach each individual postwar contribution to discussion of evolution in splendid isolation, as has previously tended to be the habit in the history of economic thought, it will alter our perspective to consider them as a group engaged in dialogue with one another, especially (but not exclusively) at the University of Chicago.

Chicago has not conventionally been considered a hotbed of evolutionary economics.[4] The joke has gone that, if anything, they were more Spencerian than Darwinian: "Chicago has been accused of being a school that not only believes in the survival of the fittest, it practices it" (Van Overtveldt, 2007, 41). The joke, however, masks a rather tough-minded fact about the self-conception of Chicago economics, made manifest in an unpublished overview of the Chicago School by George Stigler in 1977:

> The extension of economic logic to all purposive human action, *and to its deep affinity with the theory of biological survival*, is the arch on which the vast program of research rests. The theme is hardly unique or original to Chicago – Wicksteed himself has large claims – but nowhere else is it applied with the comprehensiveness and the lack of self-consciousness with which it is pursued in Chicago. It will form the cutting edge of the Chicago School in the decade ahead.[5] (emphasis added)

I think we should take this claim very seriously (though perhaps resort to some metaphor more foundational and less wobbly than an arch). Although there exists a literature that explores the use and/or abuse of evolutionary metaphor by particular individuals in the Chicago Pantheon in isolation,

4 The exception was in an aside made by Armen Alchian in his interview with Mie Augier in February 28, 2000, which prompted the composition of the current paper. From now on, this unpublished interview will be cited as (Alchian interview 2000).

5 George Stigler, "Schools in Science," 21; Box 20, Stigler Papers, Regenstein Library, University of Chicago.

no one approaches this phenomenon as a *systemic intellectual hallmark* of postwar Chicago economics. Indeed, building on a case made by Rob Van Horn and myself elsewhere[6] that Chicago should be considered not in isolation, but rather as an arm of the Neoliberal Thought Collective, then recourse to biological evolution after World War II could be approached as a trademark move of neoliberal thinkers more generally. It is symptomatic of many things, but especially their deep uneasiness about the role of science in their own social theories.

Indeed, a favorable stance toward evolution is not often associated with modern neoliberalism, because that stance is often confused/conflated with creationist paleoconservatism, which treats Darwin himself as the Devil's Chaplain. The fact that the connection has languished overlooked is testimony to the numerous misunderstandings of evolution that persist in the economics discipline down to the present. Identifying the precise characteristics of the Chicago School of Evolutionary Economics would thus go some distance in fostering a better understanding the allure of bioeconomics, sociobiology, and their mutant offspring for many economists in the era of the triumph of neoliberalism, and would serve to illuminate the pitfalls encountered by those (say, at the Santa Fe Institute[7]) who believe evolution should constitute the basis of an alternative to the modern economic orthodoxy.

9.1. Prelude to Some Serious Predators

If we were told that a man lived a long and prosperous life in the world of Chicago gangsters, we would be entitled to make some guesses as to the sort of man he was. Like successful Chicago gangsters, our genes have survived, in some cases for millions of years, in a highly competitive world (Dawkins, 1976, 2).

A few preliminaries need to be gotten out of the way before to begin to track the trajectory of evolution at Chicago. The economics department at Chicago had suffered the depredations of wartime mobilization, and by 1945 it could claim very little of the commitments or personnel that would later qualify it as exemplifying the "Chicago School of Economics."

6 See the paper in (Mirowski and Plehwe 2009).

7 See, for instance, (Gintis 2007, 4): "Economic and biological theory therefore have a natural affinity: The choice consistency on which the rational actor model depends is rendered plausible by biological evolutionary theory." It seems there are few better examples of supposedly progressive thinkers retailing lightly reprocessed neoliberal doctrine than this.

In another publication (Mirowski and Van Horn, 2009; this volume), we have explained how the quest by Henry Simons to reconstitute the economics faculty with the help of Friedrich Hayek and the financial support of the Volker Fund led to the hiring of most of the personnel who would put the school on the map in the period 1946–1950.[8] In effect, Hayek served as the impresario of the debut of the Chicago School, even though he was not physically present at the time. At the very same time, Hayek first convened his closed international debating society at Mont Pèlerin in 1947, which would subsequently be situated at the very core of the construction of neoliberalism in the postwar period (Mirowski and Plehwe, 2009), and would provide the first international platform for Chicago political economy. Thus, for purposes of this paper, there is no need to search for obscure "precursors" of the discussion of evolution in economics at Chicago prior to 1946, because by and large, they were irrelevant to the constitution of Chicago as a proponent of neoclassical economics with its characteristic postwar conservative flavor. This is particularly true when it comes to Frank Knight, often mistakenly saddled with paternity of the school. As Hodgson (2004, 334) correctly notes, Knight was in any event acridly hostile to importation of any ideas from biology into economics.

The prelude to the libretto entitled "Evolution at Chicago" did not take place geographically on the shores of Lake Michigan but, incongruously, rather mostly in Britain, in the circles surrounding Hayek just before and after the publication of his notorious *Road to Serfdom* (1945). The countertenors include early Mont Pèlerin members Fritz Machlup and Karl Popper; Aaron Director was a bit player. The prelude was divided into two movements: the first, the "Full-Cost Pricing Debate," and the other, the Popper-Hayek dialogue on the "Poverty of Historicism." Because both have been covered extensively in the literature, we shall only briefly touch upon each, stressing the ways that they came to bear on the subsequent question of evolution in economics.

The Full-Cost Pricing Debate was initiated by the Oxford Economists Research Group in the late 1930s calling into question the empirical cogency of Marshallian price theory.[9] By interviewing various corporate figures, members of this group such as R. L. Hall and C. J. Hitch (1939) thought that they had discovered that the businesses did not adhere to

[8] "From 1945 to 1946, the landscape [at Chicago] changed dramatically" (Van Overtveldt 2007, 26).

[9] This paragraph is based upon the following primary (Lester 1946; Hitch and Hall, 1966; Machlup 1946) and secondary literature: (Lee 1981; Lee and Lessman 1992; Mongin 1981; Vromen 1994).

marginalist principles of optimization, but instead tended to set prices by adding up prime costs at a target level of output and imposing a fixed profit markup. This explained, in their view, why prices were sticky when demand contracted, and thus economic variables subsisted far from market-clearing equilibrium. The resonance with the new-fangled Keynesian theory was fully intentional. Roy Harrod, also a member of the Oxford group, sought to rationalize this finding by suggesting that "certain procedures, of which the full cost principle is one example, are thrown up purely by chance and survive by a process akin to natural selection in biology" (1939, 7). This notion that full cost pricing was commonplace, and therefore required a different explanation, was also picked up by Richard Lester (1946) in the United States. At this juncture, future Mont Pèlerin Society (MPS) member Fritz Machlup entered the fray, stepping up to defend what appeared at the time as a very damaging attack on the cogency of neoclassical microeconomics. Machlup's (1946) defense reprised the predicament of Molière's *Bourgeois Gentilhomme*, in that he maintained that the businessmen could be in fact conforming to the precepts of neoclassical maximization without realizing it. Whereas Machlup was concerned to stress the Austrian fascination with subjectivity in personal experience and contrast it with how things seemed to an outside observer, this did not seem an especially compelling mode of defense in the United States, particularly for one of our major protagonists (and later MPS member), Armen Alchian. Subtlety in standpoint epistemology was never a strong suit in America. Patently, the overriding concern was how to reconcile the seeming empirical weakness of the neoclassical price theory with the growing conviction that it represented the most promising scientific approach to economics, just in the period it was coming to displace all other schools of economics in the United States.

An entirely parallel but distinct overture was emerging stage right in London, where Friedrich Hayek was busy rescuing Karl Popper from antipodal oblivion in New Zealand.[10] Popper had come to Hayek's attention as a scholar attempting to diagnose the political disease they both believed had beset the social sciences in the 1930s. Popper had taken to denouncing something he called "historicism," which turned out to be a messy amalgam of Marxism, ideas ascribed to Otto Neurath and Karl Mannheim, and the social ideas of some Marxist biologists like C. H. Waddington, Joseph Needham, J. D. Bernal, and a cast of thousands. Although there was substantial overlap in the roster, the list of culprits on Hayek's rap sheet were not identical with those on Popper's; and indeed,

[10] The main sources for this paragraph are (Hacohen 2000; Mirowski 2002b; Uebel 2000).

Hayek had been flirting with the idea that it was "scientism" that was the real danger in the 1930s and early 1940s, something that would have been an anathema to Popper. Thankfully, we need not address all their repressed contradictions here; all we need to do is foreshadow the ways in which their discussions would subsequently play out in the context of Mont Pèlerin and Chicago. (We shall return to the issue of Hayek's changing relationship to the natural sciences in Section 4, concentrating on the period after he moved to Chicago; but for the present, we simply want to highlight the role of Popper in foregrounding the issue of evolution for early Mont Pèlerin.)

According to Hacohen, in 1939 Popper set out to attack the Marxian dialectic and replace it with what he considered his own epistemology of "trial and error." Popper then conceived of a philosophical ambition to reform and fortify all social science, even though at that juncture he knew very little about any particular social science (Hacohen, 2000, 374). In the manuscript that eventually became *The Poverty of Historicism* (first published in Hayek's London School of Economics [LSE] house journal in 1944–1945), Popper then decided that his dismissal of "historicism" would imply that he should indict the theory of evolution as well, essentially denying that any laws of evolution did or could exist. "The evolution of life on earth is not a law, but only a singular historical statement. Universal laws make assertions concerning some invariant order" (1957, 108). In his endearingly idiosyncratic fashion, he proceeded to confuse and conflate "historicism" with the theory of evolution. "The recent vogue of historicism might be regarded as merely part of the vogue of evolutionism" (1957, 106). Never a serious historian of ideas, nor indeed much of an empiricist, Popper had gotten that part of the story wrong. As Carl Degler (1991) has argued, by the 1930s biological metaphors and concepts had been widely routed from the Anglophone social sciences, for reasons ranging from revulsion toward the Nazi regime, to shifts in the ethnic makeup of the academic community, to a predilection to treat Culture as a separate powerful buffer against Nature, and much else besides. Yet that did not make a dent in Popper's popularity at the time, because he was interpreted as raising the issue of whether evolutionary theory could plausibly be conscripted into a conservative political movement, or whether it was all just a bunch of pseudoscience palaver. "In many historicist and evolutionist writings it is impossible to discover where the metaphor ends and the serious theory begins" (1957, 119fn). Even at this early stage, "serious theory" for Popper looked a lot like neoclassical economics. By contrast, corrupted social science looked like Marxism, and more pointedly, history with nomothetic ambitions.

It is important here to notice that Popper was most emphatically *not* making reference to biological evolution in order to invest the social sciences with the patina of scientific credibility (the usual indictment of evolutionary economics) through imitation of biology; rather, he was suggesting instead that there was something unhealthy about the commonplace conviction that evolution was an established physical law, and that this pathology was exacerbated when evolution was imported into social science. In part because he changed his tune on this later in life,[11] the fact that he was pivotal in raising the issue of evolution for the Mont Pèlerin crowd in the later 1940s has been egregiously overlooked.

Another possible reason this bit of evidence has been neglected is the long (some might say interminable) controversy over the exact meaning and significance of Milton Friedman's infamous essay on the "Methodology of Positive Economics."[12] Methodologists have incessantly wrangled over whether Friedman was a good and faithful Popperian, or perhaps a lapsed Popperian instrumentalist, or an unwitting Deweyan, a garbled positivist, or else maybe none of these. Again, we are fortunate in not having to take a position on this issue, because what matters in the present context is that Friedman himself has repeatedly admitted he cared little for philosophy, read next to none of it, but that right around the time of the composition of the essay, was nonetheless deeply influenced by Popper's discussions at Mont Pèlerin:

> Shortly after I had completed a first draft, George Stigler and I had long discussions with Karl Popper in 1947 at the founding meeting of the Mont Pèlerin Society. The part of the discussions I remember best had to do with scientific methodology.... These discussions at Mont Pèlerin were my first exposure to his views. I found them highly compatible with the views I had independently come to, though far more sophisticated and more fully developed. That conversation had a good deal of influence on the final version of the essay. (Friedman and Friedman, 1998, 215)

Although most historians have taken this to imply that Friedman derived his infamous methodological prescriptions that "assumptions don't matter"

[11] Essentially the later Popper still maintained the theory of evolution was untestable, but was nevertheless a metaphysical research program that qualified as science because it resembled "situational logic," his neologism for rational choice theory. On this see (Popper 1976, 167–178). Significantly, this resembles the later position of the Chicago School figures such as Gary Becker, Gordon Tullock, and Jack Hirshleifer.

[12] The first chapter in (Friedman 1953), which will be our source in this paper. On the debate, see (Hirsch and de Marchi 1990; Boland 1997; Maki 2009). My feeling is that Boland (1997, 42) gets it just right: "Friedman's essay is not very philosophically minded – it is a rejection of any need to deal with most of the questions with which philosophically minded economists have been so concerned."

and "only predictions count" from a superficial grasp of Popper's position, from our current perspective we want to open up the possibility that Friedman also first encountered Popper's disdain for historicism and the weaknesses of contemporary social science at Mont Pèlerin. Indeed, one thing they would share from thenceforward was the precept that there was essentially no relevant distinction between the natural and social sciences: They were all party to the same methodological strictures. Because Popper had been holding forth on the status of evolutionary theory at that juncture, it would have been a part of the bequest.

Evolutionary theory bears, in itself, no necessary or intrinsic political or social valence. That is why it is critical for this paper to foreground the extent to which the economists in this account came to the issue of evolution in the 1940s and 1950s largely through Mont Pèlerin and the project to construct a neoliberal political economy. Most of our protagonists first encountered the topic equipped with no special expertise or avid interest in biology. (Jack Vromen documents this characterization in his contribution to this volume.) Their concerns encompassed rather *economic* issues such as the presumed legitimacy of neoclassical price theory, the meaning of competition in economics, the (ir)relevance of history to analysis, and the best way to argue against socialism. At no time did they display any sense that they had been living through a watershed period of the revival within biology of *Darwinian* evolutionary theory after a long stretch in the late nineteenth century of dominance of non-Darwinian theories and approaches.[13] There was little in the way of acknowledgment of the then-recent integration of Mendelism and Darwinism in the first third of the century, nor any familiarity with the work of figures such as T. H. Morgan, William Bateson, and J. B. S. Haldane. More to the point, there is no evidence they were aware of the work of Sewall Wright at the University of Chicago, where early glimmers of what would later be called "the modern synthesis" was beginning to attack the simple conflation of natural selection with pure maximization on the fitness surface (Depew and Weber, 1995, chapter 11). Indeed, to a man they seemed totally oblivious to the research happening all around them just after the events that would catapult biology to the status of *primus inter pares* of all the sciences, namely the discovery of DNA in 1953.

Thus the neoliberal assignation with evolution around mid-century recounted later owed nearly nothing to the ways in which biologists had been framing evolutionary theory in the first half of the twentieth century.

[13] This revival of Darwin in the early twentieth century is stressed by, among others, (Bowler, 1988; Depew and Weber 1995; Smocovitis 2005).

Realizing that conditions within economics have done little to clarify the referents of "evolution" presupposed by the participants, Hodgson (1998) has sought to provide a taxonomy of the primary issues that seemed to cause the most dissention within postwar "evolutionary economics" as opposed to the state of play in biology. There he suggests that the binaries that capture the widest distribution of positions are four-fold: evolution treated as a generator of novelty (or not), genetic explanation as reductionist (or not), change as gradual (or saltationist), and appeal made to explicit biological theory (or not). The participants at Mont Pèlerin were not able to come to complete consensus on each of these binaries. The Chicago contingent did tend to favor reductionist and gradualist versions of evolution, but sought to avoid serious consideration of the generation of novelty and to generally renounce any methodological commitment to appeal to actual contemporary biology. The reason that this is at all significant is that it remains the rough characterization of what passes today as evolutionary economics within the orthodox profession, something I will be calling "thin evolution." In that sense, the orthodoxy is beholden to Chicago for pioneering a distinctly "neoclassical" economistic theory of evolution, which now has found its popularizers in ever-wider arenas in such figures as Daniel Dennett (1995) and Richard Dawkins (1976).

9.2. Survival of the Fatuous

The saga of evolution at Chicago begins with Armen Alchian (1914– ; Ph.D. Stanford 1944; RAND employee 1949–1960, consultant 1946–1949; Professor UCLA 1946–1995). Although he received both undergraduate and graduate training at Stanford, the Chicago connection was initially forged through Allen Wallis, who served as his thesis advisor just before moving to Chicago. The MPS connection was guaranteed through Wallis and Machlup, whom he had known at Stanford: He was an early admirer of their politics. He was the first economist hired at RAND, the famous think tank that played such a significant role in postwar neoclassical economics (Mirowski, 2002). He became the conduit through which many Chicago stalwarts such as Ronald Coase, Gary Becker, and others received lucrative consultancies from RAND.[14] Indeed the RAND connection will prove just as significant as the Chicago link and the British prelude, although that

14 "John Williams had known Hitch from Oxford and we invited him out here ... when Hitch stayed, he became the chief and he did the recruiting and I helped with the recruiting. We got a group primarily from Harvard and Chicago" (Alchian interview, 2000).

is not the way Alchian (2006, xxii–xxiii) himself tells the story for public consumption:

> In my early years of teaching, a pair of confrontational articles by Richard Lester and Fritz Machlup, published in the leading journal, the *American Economic Review*, were dutifully studied with disappointment and distress. Current readers will be astonished to know that the debate was about whether business people "really" used marginal productivity and profit maximization analysis in making decisions! Lester said "no"; Machlup said "yes."... If that was the quality of analysis passing for economics, I should have stayed in the military I thought. So one day in class I explained what I had read. Then a bit testily, I complained about the quality of the articles, all in the privacy of the classroom. I then explained what I thought the two economists should have said. They should have said, "Read Darwin! It's not what you think you are doing or how you rationalize your choice of that action. It's whether that action has survival value. And if outside analysts can identify the reasons the chosen action had survival value, and the direction changes in the environment (constraints) affect survival conditions, economists don't have to worry about how people discover by thought or luck what are the new best conditions. Competitive trial and error will evolve toward the fittest – whom economists characterize as profit maximizers." Word of my comments passed to my colleague Professor Stephen Enke.... He remarked the comments would make a publishable article. I scoffed it was all too obvious and trivial.... To my genuine surprise, a very encouraging letter was quickly (by current standards) received from a Professor Milton Friedman, of whom I had heard. The paper would be published if a few suggested extrapolations and minor modifications were made. The article quickly appeared. It was my first article.

Although this rings true, it is at best only a partial account. The omitted aspect is hinted at in the Alchian interview, 2000: "[I]t was done on RAND time, but it was mostly developed outside of RAND." What did RAND have to do with evolution? The relevant considerations were, first, Alchian had been involved in hiring Charles Hitch of the Full Cost Controversy fame at RAND; and second, a controversy over weapons procurement at RAND had pushed him in the direction of the "as-if" story presented in the 1950 evolution paper, cleansed and vetted, in good Cold War fashion, of any reference to weapons.

Charles Johnston Hitch (1910–1995) was an American who had been a member of the Oxford Economists Research Group until 1948, at which point he was recruited at RAND to become head of the Economics Section. Interestingly, Alchian never once cites Hitch nor mentions his work; but it beggars credulity not to see that some of Alchian's emotions about the profit maximization controversy in 1949, right after the appearance of Hitch on the scene, had absolutely nothing to do with his situation at RAND. Hitch cut a dashing figure by all accounts, seconded to the OSS during the war, and rapidly rose through the RAND ranks, later becoming Assistant Secretary of Defense under Robert McNamara, and later still, President of the University of California system. It seems safe to say that Hitch was successful to a degree that Alchian was not. But to top it off, RAND was roiled by an important controversy in the late 1940s, to which both were party, having to do with weapons procurement.

In the late 1940s, the military had yet to be convinced that economists had anything interesting to say about how to conduct war, or even concerning how best to pursue technological improvement of weapons systems.[15] Although the points of contention were many, the short version is that Alchian became the champion of the position of "letting the market handle it," as pitched against the "systems analysts" at RAND, who were convinced that there was no way the United States would get a fully operational nuclear capacity by letting private defense contractors handle the details:

> We made no attempt to tell them at that time that they should be doing more economics – "them" being the engineering people who were mostly physicists – until we had a group there.... They were primarily concerned about the technical features.... But they were doing that for the defense, so there had to be a choice of weapons and of how much they would cost.... That was one of the first things I did for the economics division at RAND – to work on the idea that costs were important. It was a hard battle, a very hard battle ... and for that it took more than one of two economists ... we were discussing the allocation of nuclear material between the army and the navy and the air force and each one of them wanted more bombs, more materiel, and the problem was, how do you allocate it? Well, there is a very simple rule in economics that you have a scarce resource – you allocate to each person and you will soon find out that there is a trade basically. And through trade you get the best outcome. (Alchian interview 2000)

The armed services brass and the scientist/engineers, who fancied themselves experts in rational planning, thought this was one of the stupidest things they had ever heard. The prospect of some colonels sitting in a bunker bidding on nukes for use struck them as preposterous; but worse, they felt that almost every aspect of nuclear weapons were so beset with uncertainty that it would have been dereliction of duty to pretend the costs and consequences of any particular program were sufficiently well known or even well defined enough to conduct cost-benefit calculations on them. But Alchian's cadre at RAND became famous for their brazen attempts to "calculate the incalculable" while thinking the unthinkable, by maintaining that "The actually procured and operated weapon is what identifies

[15] The following paragraph is based on (Hounshell 2000; Jardini 1996; Mirowski, 2002a 397–402).

the ultimate realized costs of our military strength" (Alchian, 1953b, 5). Not only did they apply this to existing weapons, but also to weapons that were as yet only a gleam in some colonel's eye, such as the ICBM. The systems analysts preached that the only way the United States would beat the Russians to such a mission-critical weapons system would be to plan the entire process top-down, from the earliest phase of basic scientific research to the later phases of manufacturing of components. The Alchian group vehemently disagreed, proposing instead to fund numerous private firms to conduct the early-stage R&D on missile systems, with each embarking on multiple alternative design concepts, and then let market competition decide which was the best technological path to support (Hounshell, 2000). Needless to say, in the end the Alchian position lost out when it came to building the actual ICBM; but that did not prevent the RAND analysts from blasting ahead with the beginnings of an "economics of technological innovation" predicated on neoclassical market concepts.[16] These weapons disputes were concerned with the "survival of the fittest" and produced some of the most bellicose versions of competition ever imagined; yet in the face of looming Armageddon, Alchian insisted that the market would nonetheless successfully unearth the correct path to pursue, even in the face of utter ignorance, paralyzing terror, and uncertainty.

The presence of Hitch at RAND and the concurrent weapons debate were the major conditioning factors and repressed subtext behind Alchian's paper "Uncertainty, Evolution and Economic Theory," which appeared in the 1950 *Journal of Political Economy*. Of course, none of this made any appearance in the published version. Instead, Alchian framed his analysis as constituting a continuation of basic neoclassical theory as found in Alfred Marshall: "[W]e shall be reverting to a Marshallian type of analysis combined with the essentials of Darwinian evolutionary natural selection" (1950, 19n). The paper begins with a critique of profit maximization as a general explanatory principle under uncertainty: "[W]here foresight is uncertain, 'profit maximization' is meaningless as a guide to specifiable action" (1950, 19).[17]

[16] Hounshell (2000) describes how much of the economics of science and technology began with the weapons controversy at RAND. It included such figures as Richard Nelson, Burton Klein, Kenneth Arrow, and Sidney Winter, who not accidentally became the strongest critic of Alchian and Friedman's Chicago-style evolutionary economics. Unfortunately, we cannot pursue this fascinating development in the current paper, but see (Hodgson 1994).

[17] That point is echoed a few years later at RAND in the discussions about the validity of system analysis: Because of uncertainty, "the consequences of a specified action cannot be uniquely identified in advance, [and] there is not available any generally accepted rule for rational behavior." Therefore, "it is difficult to tell whether a successful person – one

Although the paper claims its motives as essentially conservative, namely, to bring economics back to "a Marshallian type of analysis," what is noteworthy is the relative dearth of any citations to Darwin or, indeed, to Marshall. "Biology" is discussed only in the most cursorily superficial terms, absent even the bare bones of the by-then conventional litany of variation, inheritance, and specification of selection mechanisms, except in a final passage in the conclusion: "The economic counterparts of genetic heredity, mutations and natural selection are imitation, innovation and positive profits" (1950, 220). However, what is being imitated is left wholly without specification, later sowing doubt as to whether it exhibited sufficient invariance and persistence required for evolution; variation is likewise left unexplained. Even the selection mechanisms are left unspecified, with everything nominally collapsed to a single undefined profit index. We shall return to this problem in our discussion of what we shall characterize as "thin evolution."

The basic message is this: Economic theory will still be able to validate neoclassical outcomes if the market mechanism is understood to be functioning as a selection mechanism, selecting over different manifestations of firm (or individual) behavior with profit as the motive underlying the evolutionary process. This is asserted to lead to the conclusion that economic success is not based on motivation, but rather on results; individual behavior without "rationality, motivation and foresight" is said by Alchian to be perfectly consistent with aggregate neoclassical predictions (21). How this was to be squared with what one found actually written in Marshall was left unexplored.[18] The one characteristic Alchian did share with Marshall, however, was a relative disconnect from anything actually found in Darwin (Groenewegen in Laurent and Nightingale, 2001; Vromen, this volume). Whether evolution would actually attain a maximum was never demonstrated; it was simply presumed. Uncertainty precludes individual

who has a good record of making good decisions – owes his success to blind chance, or to excellent forecasting ability, or to excellent analytic ability which enables him to maximize for specified forecasts.... [I]f our difficulty lies in poor forecasting ability, the impact of system analysis is reduced" (Alchian and Kessel 1954, 5). See also Alchian (1953b): "We cannot estimate what the most efficient kind of weapon will be.... We cannot sensibly choose to do research in order to later be able to develop and produce the 'optimum' weapon system. We simply do not have the required degree of foresight nor the ability to determine what we shall be able to learn and know" (5–6).

[18] An example of non-Marshallianism; Marshall (1920, 5) clearly thought that individual motivation and foresight made an important difference to what he regarded as an evolutionary process, and identified "self-reliance, independence, deliberate choice and forethought," rather than competition, as the "fundamental characteristics of modern industrial life." In Alchian's disdain for the historical text we also discover a nascent Chicago practice.

intentional maximization, but is claimed to be consistent with different forms of learning through imitation of successful rules or individual trial-and-error learning. Alchian motivated his claim, not by evidence or a mathematical model, but by a thought experiment:

> Assume that thousands of travelers set out from Chicago, selecting their roads completely at random and without foresight. Only our "economist" knows that on but one road are there any gasoline stations. He can state categorically that travelers will *continue* to travel only on that road; those on other roads will soon run out of gas.... The correct direction of travel will be established. As circumstances (economic environment) change, the analyst (economist) can select the type of participants (firms) that will now become successful; he may also be able to diagnose the conditions most conducive to a greater probability of survival." (1950, 22) ...
>
> There is an alternative method which treats the decisions and criteria dictated by the economic system as more important than those made by the individuals in it. By backing away from the trees – the optimization calculus of individual units – we can better discern the forest of impersonal market forces. (1950, 19)

The fact that it was not so much biology per se as Alchian's image of physics (actually, thermodynamics)[19] that seemed to inspire his vision of uncertainty was revealed in his footnote 12: "The atoms and electrons do not know the laws of nature; the physicist does not impart to each atom a willful scheme based upon the laws [sic] of conservation of energy, etc.... The similarity between this argument and Gibbsean statistical mechanics, as well as biological evolution, is *not* mere coincidence." Grave hints concerning the Unity of Science abound; but the promissory note is never cashed. Of course, neither Alchian nor anyone else in economics seemed aware of the vast neo-Kantian literature in the philosophy of science that had argued that optimization principles and conservation laws were themselves mere artifacts of a certain modality of formulating a closed deterministic argument in mathematical format, and were not actually to be found anywhere in Nature (Mirowski, 1989, chapter 2). What mattered to Alchian and apparently captivated his audience was that the neoclassical model be deemed approximately "correct," even though its key assumptions bore no relationship to the underlying phenomenon. "[O]nly the method of use, rather than the usefulness, of economic tools and concepts is affected by the approach suggested here" (1950). It was this claim, in particular, that was soon to become Chicago economics house doctrine.

If Alchian deserves credit for anything, it is for pioneering the version of thin evolution that later took hold in Chicago. The confusion starts with

[19] This point was made in a 2007 version of this paper, and at the Notre Dame conference well before (Levallois 2009).

the notion of "selection," a term that too readily conjures up connotations of one-shot selection of elements from a given set, resembling the selection of commodities in a marketplace (Knudsen, 2002). That is emphatically *not* the meaning it betokens in biological evolutionary theory, where it denotes a winnowing down of differential replication of descent through modification. Alchian omits a number of important components of Darwinian evolution, including: (1) specification of the relative stability of the firms vis-à-vis their environment; (2) restrictions on the complete plasticity of the firm in its reactions to the environment, through his confusion of genetic transfer with imitation; (3) provision of any guarantee of the maintained identity of either the replicator or the interactor (by suppressing the distinction); and (4) an account of the emergence and operation of the selection rules. Because of this sloppiness, Alchian seems not to appreciate that natural selection per se does not constitute the sum total of evolutionary dynamics, but serves as only one component (others include drift, neutral mutation, frequency dependence of co-evolution, etc.). In thin evolution, both descent and differential replication are treated as mere secondary considerations, and the phenotype/genotype distinction is suppressed as a prelude to neglecting or ignoring them completely, producing an entirely "ahistorical" travesty of evolution. It is no accident this ends up looking more like extremum models in physics. Thus, in thin evolution, there is no real evolutionary change, as understood by sophisticated proponents of Darwinism.[20] "Thick evolution," here equated with the elaborate literature in biology that takes account of the numerous interacting mechanisms of change, from evo-devo to "spandrels" to group selection to genetic drift and beyond, was nowhere taken seriously.

Edith Penrose (1952) quickly took Alchian to task for his misuse of the biological analogy of evolution; although we cannot go into the substance of her critique here,[21] it is worthwhile to note that she and other sophisticated

[20] As long ago as 1984, I insisted that there was no serious theory of evolution in Nelson and Winter (see Mirowski 1988, 166–167). That case was made with much greater specificity for both Alchian and Nelson and Winter by (Knudsen 2002). The fact such critiques have been repeatedly ignored suggests that it is not the logic of evolutionary explanation that is the major motivation for the appeal to evolution.

[21] Penrose, in (1952) "Biological Analogies in the Theory of the Firm," opposed uncritical adaptations of biological reasoning without warnings about the negative analogies between biological and firm evolution. The most important problem for Penrose was that biological analogies abstracted from *intentionality* – not blind evolution. This reflects probably the influence of Fritz Machlup who was a strong advocate of methodological dualism. Penrose was at the time engaged in a research project on patents under Machlup and did her Ph.D. with him. She warns that economic systems are not replicas of biological systems. Neglect of intentionality implied according to Penrose:

contemporary readers flagged Alchian's cavalier references to evolution for the caricature and misrepresentation that they surely were back in that era. This resulted in yet another practice resorted to with alacrity in neoliberal evolutionary economics: Backpedaling with regard to metaphoric isomorphisms when the going got tough (1953a): "The theory I presented stands independent of the biological analogy. Criticisms of the latter are irrelevant to the theory ... every reference to the biological analogy was merely expository."

Alchian's riposte (1953a) to Penrose further shrugged off the imperatives of biology, conjured in Alchian (1950), by equating evolutionary outcomes as efficient equilibria (1953a, 600). Compared to the original article, Alchian in his response came closer to baldly identifying "surviving" firms as profit maximizing firms (602). Part of the background for Alchian's more radical response was probably the prompting of his friend and RAND colleague, Stephen Enke (1951), where the bridge between surviving firms and profit maximizing firms becomes clearer. Enke (1953) also kept the controversy alive by producing a response to Penrose's (1953) rejoinder: "It is within the wit of man to describe in aggregate terms some of the qualitative characteristics of surviving firms – but not to prescribe quantitatively the measures that will maximize the profits of an individual firm" (1953, 603).

9.3. Friedman's Ice-9

It might seem pedantic and superfluous to devote an entire section of our inquiry to an author who only referred to evolution in one paragraph of one paper; except, of course, when that author is Milton Friedman and the paper is "The Methodology of Positive Economics." The reaction to this single paragraph, which has launched Hellenic-style the entire careers of certain economists, makes one quake at the power that an off-hand comment can

First, the analogy between innovations and mutations breaks down since mutations in biology are not correlated with the environment. Mutation in biology is not explained but in economics it is possible to relate innovative activity to the wish for more profit (Penrose 1952, 815). Second, it becomes impossible to understand competition if we cannot rely on intentional behavior: If there is no conscious competition in the market, competition is alone a question of entry of new firms and there is nothing "in the reproductive process of firms that would ensure that more firms would constantly be created that can survive" (1952, 812). Third, it becomes impossible to understand how firms instead of being selected by the environment seek to change these – to actively create barriers to entry. For Penrose, one can't assume lack of motivation, because in response to uncertainty firms will consciously try to change their environment. Such patterns of reactions makes prediction possible. (Penrose 1952, 816)

exert on an audience poised and ready to receive it. Like Kurt Vonnegut's Ice-9, it crystallized the attitudes of a whole generation. The secondary literature on this paper is massively daunting,[22] and shows no sign of tapering off fifty years later, probably because this paper set the tone and content of the scientific aspirations of the Chicago School in certain key respects, just one of which is the association of the School with a very particular doctrine of the place of evolution in social life. The truncated exposition helped promote the thin conception of evolution, a case of life imitating art. We shall severely limit our considerations here to the question of evolution, although much else rides on the acceptance or rejection of Friedman's gambit.

We reproduce here most of the earth-shaking paragraph, with the proviso that Friedman felt he had to replace the term "profits" with the rather more anodyne term "returns" (Vromen, 1994, 37–39):

> Confidence in the maximization-of-returns hypothesis is justified ... unless the behavior of businessmen in some way or other approximated behavior consistent with the maximization of returns, it seems unlikely that they would remain in business for long. Let the apparent immediate determinant of business behavior be anything at all – habitual reaction, random chance, or whatnot. Whenever this determinant happens to lead to behavior consistent with rational and informed maximization of returns, the business will prosper and acquire resources with which to expand; whenever it does not, the business will tend to lose resources and can be kept in existence only by the addition of resources from the outside. The process of "natural selection" thus helps to validate the hypothesis – or rather, given natural selection, acceptance of the hypothesis can be based largely on the judgment that it summarizes appropriately the conditions for survival. (Friedman, 1953, 22)

That is that: Just a paragraph used to support Friedman's larger theses, which we state here in truncated form as "assumptions don't matter, only predictions"; that everything sensible has been said already in Marshall; and that the Full Cost Controversy has been a waste of time and can safely be ignored by economists. Richard Lester, Roy Harrod, Charles Hitch, the Cowles Commission, and even Thorstein Veblen (1953, 30) are all reprimanded by name. The latter is especially interesting, because by explicitly quoting Veblen's famous "Why is Economics Not an Evolutionary Science?" Friedman seems to suggest that neoclassical economics has (inadvertently?) been an evolutionary science all along, and that the Institutionalists who inhabited Chicago at the beginning of the century had been safely consigned to the obsolescence of the horse-and-buggy era.

[22] See, for a sampling: (Boland 1997; Hirsch and de Marchi 1990; Vromen 1994; Nelson and Winter 2002; Winter 1964; Hammond 2004; Walters 1987; McCloskey 1985; Schaffer 1989; Maki 2009).

Now, this sounds a lot like Alchian (although I will not be the first to argue they are not really conceptually identical). Friedman thought so too, because just before the magic paragraph, his footnote 14 admits: "This example, and some of the subsequent discussion, though independent in origin, is similar to and in much the same spirit" as Alchian (1950). What he doesn't tell us is that he was the *JPE* editor who accepted the paper for publication after making Alchian revise his original version. There is something curious about his insistence that he had anticipated or independently re-created Alchian's thesis, given that it is difficult to escape the conclusion that his argument is orders of magnitude sketchier and less substantial than that found in a paper that had been published three years before his own. The situation is partially clarified by the correspondence between the two concerning Alchian's paper.[23] In an early draft of the "Methodology" paper written in 1948, apparently Friedman was already arguing his thesis that businessmen acted "as if" they were profit maximizers. Most of the argument happens at the individual level, but Dan Hammond (forthcoming) reports there was also a sentence claiming if firms chose their output randomly but all funding was from profits, then the result via selection would be the same as profit maximization. Soon thereafter Alchian's manuscript arrived on his desk. We do not have his original referee report, but in the letter to Friedman dated November 10, 1949, that accompanied his revision Alchian wrote:

> I was particularly distressed at your charge of methodological naiveté – not because I resent criticism, but instead because I completely agree with your argument and was upset that the earlier version should have given the contrary impression.... On the other hand I was encouraged by your recommendation that I revise and resubmit the paper by your reference to similar developments in your own work. Fundamentally the paper seems to represent an attempt to integrate into economic analysis those methods used in other sciences (statistical mechanics and evolutionary biology) in an effort to explain and predict the apparent order in economic behavior despite uncertainty and diversity of motivation. While I should hasten to say that was not the original attitude one could explain the outcome as if it were.

We can deduce from this that (1) their arguments started out looking quite different; (2) that Alchian's version paid substantially more attention to the natural sciences than Friedman (with his fanciful pseudo-theory "examples" of billiard players, leaves on trees, and balls dropped from airplanes); and

[23] I am very grateful to Dan Hammond for supplying copies of the correspondence from the Friedman papers, Hoover Institution, Box 4, as well as a draft of Hammond (forthcoming), especially given that Dan takes the position that Friedman had arrived at the evolution argument before Alchian.

(3) Friedman used his position as gatekeeper to force Alchian to bring his account closer to Friedman's own. Absent Alchian's actual drafts, we will never know the exact nature of the editorial exactions,[24] but it is hard to accept that Friedman was ever a very avid advocate of the importance of Darwinian evolution as a theoretical principle. This is reinforced by the point first made in Section 1, that Friedman's philosophical inspiration can be traced back to Karl Popper, who had been warning of the dubious historicist character of any law of evolution. Yet with Alchian achieving priority in print, it nevertheless was Friedman's bulimic appeal to natural selection without conceptual substance that carried the day at Chicago, provoking wave after wave of conjectures, refutations, and responses and setting the tone for the Chicago School of evolutionary economics.

Even after the revisions, Alchian's version still made a modicum more sense than Friedman's truncated pharisaical account.[25] A few examples: Alchian was careful to insist that his story worked in terms of *ex post* realized profits, whereas Friedman thought he could get away with "expected maximization of returns" (1953, 21fn16). Friedman just presumed the extremum would ensue, whereas Alchian was careful to notice that this would depend crucially on "correct" behaviors falling within the candidate set of actions actually found among the existing set of firms. Friedman wrote as though each individual firm would be pushed toward a maximum, whereas Alchian wrote about distributions of aggregate behaviors. Friedman wrote "A fundamental hypothesis of science is that appearances are deceptive" (33), but it was Alchian who extended this precept symmetrically to become incorporated into the economic agent as well. Friedman's contempt for the realism of assumptions tended to bleed over into his disdain for taking the details of evolution seriously, which is why he became such a juicy target for subsequent economists like Sidney Winter, whose formal modeling activities ended up looking quite a bit like Alchian (but, we hasten to add, not like Darwin).[26] But all those attempts to list and codify the circumstances under which it would look "as if" maximizing firms were being selected and others weeded out – the guarantee of sufficient variation among firms to cover the fitness landscape, the specification of adequate firm inertia and invariance of behavior to present something to be selected, the stipulation that profits need not necessarily be ploughed back

[24] And thus we find ourselves unable to answer how much of the thin conception of evolution to apportion to Friedman, and how much to Alchian.

[25] "Alchian is more careful than Friedman" (Vromen 1994, 39). Vromen seems to have changed his mind in this volume.

[26] For more on this, see (Mirowski 1988, chap. 9; Knudsen 2002).

into the "successful" activities, frequency dependence of selection has to be neutralized, and the travesty that firms could be treated as self-contained sums of capital in the face of an intricate web of flows of funds between firms – none of this seemed to matter much at Chicago. The interesting question is therefore: Why all this enthusiasm for the Friedmanite version of evolution, given that no one at Chicago felt compelled to actually parse out the dynamic mechanism lying behind their unstinting confidence in the "truth" of neoclassical theory?

The short sharp initial answer is that Chicago has always loved arguments where it is asserted that things that seem important to mere mortals don't matter for market success. Think of the Modigliani-Miller theorem, the Coase theorem, the denial of the relevance of income effects in price theory, the belief in the neutrality of money, and so on. The sheer inevitability of these invariance propositions became central to the rhetoric of Chicago in the postwar era.

It is hard to escape the conclusion that the overarching objective circa 1953 was to keep doggedly repeating that *nothing* could impugn the truth of the Chicago version of neoclassical price theory – not the reports of the agents, not statistical empiricism concerning firm profits and behavior, not demonstrations of logical infelicities within the model, not getting the history of doctrines right, not reasoned arguments about the pros and cons of specific assumptions – nothing. This turned out to be the Big Kahuna of "don't matter" doctrines and became a nonnegotiable precept of Chicago research. Friedman's acolytes fervently pledged their troth to "science," but it all boiled down in practice to local chauvinism. Simple static partial equilibrium exercises became the Hyde Park technique of choice until well into the 1980s, irrespective of anything going on in and around biology: This became conflated with a legend about something they called "natural selection." It also became the easy two-sentence put-down of any obstreperous Doubting Thomas in microeconomics courses across the nation.

So that's one part of the answer; but it is not the whole story. There is also the consideration that over the course of the 1950s and 1960s, appeals to evolution progressively became associated with the development of neoliberal politics, both at Chicago and Mont Pèlerin. One can observe this in Popper's role reversal on evolution, retracting his earlier denunciation and elevating evolutionary epistemology into the centerpiece of his system. It became the underpinning of Richard Posner's quest to present the common law as "naturally efficient." It was incorporated into Peter Bauer's critique of development economics, and became part of Herbert Giersch's attempt to revive and co-opt a Schumpeterian theory of growth. As Vromen explains in this volume, Gordon Tullock began to explore how much he might blur the boundaries between animal ethology and public choice theory. Gary Becker and Vernon Smith started to claim they had things to say about evolution. Friedrich Hayek turned evolution into the basis of a whole neoliberal political philosophy. Time and again, neoliberals recovered their Spencerian "red in tooth and claw" roots, but expressed them in the language of current biological analogies. Not each and every neoliberal at Mont Pèlerin was concerned to deploy evolution to defend the neoclassical orthodoxy in economics (as we shall observe with Hayek in the next section); but for Chicago, Friedmanite methodological evolutionism and evolution construed as political doctrine resonated and reinforced one another. Over time, it became easier to reconcile their methodological preferences with their political affiliations because both could be expressed in the same idiom. The convergence, although in no way necessary, was no coincidence either: It had been hashed out over decades of Mont Pèlerin–sponsored conclaves.

There is a third reason Chicago learned to love a thin version of evolution in the later 1950s and 1960s. This was the period in which the Cowles Commission had become infatuated with recasting their version of neoclassical theory as an "economics of information" (Mirowski, 2002, 370 et seq.). They had been exploring various ways to model the neoclassical agent as an "information processor," using resources from Shannon information theory, Blackwell state-space theory, and von Neumann's computational enthusiasms. Indeed, this was an era in which the newfangled theories of information and computation were thought to have the possibility of revolutionizing all the sciences, including biology (Kay, 2000; Segal, 2003). Chicago knew about this due to the presence of Arrow, Marschak, Hurwicz, and others, but also because Friedman's collaborator Leonard Savage was a regular participant at the Macy Cybernetics conferences. The Chicago group around Friedman was hostile to these forays for an array of reasons. First, if you were an advocate of the position that assumptions didn't matter (especially when it came to utility theory), then equipping the neoclassical agent with all sorts of information-processing abilities would appear a nonstarter. Second, it seems Savage, who was employed in the Chicago Institute of Radiology and Biophysics as well as the department of statistics from 1946 to 1960 (Wallis, 1991), had become skeptical of these developments within biology, believing that his version of subjectivist probability was more than sufficient to deal with such issues. Relationships with the Argonne Labs at Chicago, which had become a hotbed of the information-theory version of natural selection around Henry Quastler (Kay, 2000,. 116

et seq.), were less than collegial. This all panned out as Chicago economists coming to believe that a thin version of evolution could in effect substitute for the then-fashionable economics of information: One could avoid all the baroque mathematical models and troublesome cognitive considerations and simply assert that evolution guaranteed that the market conveyed all the relevant information to all the critical parties whenever they needed it. It became almost a tautology: If you had missed out on some crucial information, than natural selection would remove you from the thought community. This transmutation of thin evolution into the "efficient markets hypothesis" became another hallmark of the Chicago School.

9.4. The Evolution of Hayek

Even though Friedman's version of thin evolution became house doctrine at Chicago in the 1950s, there was at least one more postwar Chicago economist who shared the neoliberal ambitions but felt that the solid intellectual foundations for an economics of evolution had yet to be laid. Not every single Chicago neoliberal bought into the shibboleth of thin evolution: the signal exception was Friedrich Hayek. His forays into evolutionary theory have also become the subject of a massive secondary literature, perhaps second only in size to that devoted to Friedman's "Methodology" essay.[27] For that very reason, there appears little that can be added to what is already widely known – except, possibly, the project of situating him more concertedly within the Chicago context and further explicating his relationship to natural science metaphors.[28] Bruce Caldwell, the best of the Hayek scholars, notes that Hayek's considerations on evolution really dated after his arrival in Chicago in 1950. This, we now know, is right when Friedman and Alchian were hashing out their various positions, and just after the first few meetings of Mont Pèlerin. Differences with Friedman were already beginning to surface, starting with the refusal of the economics department to offer him an affiliation. So this turned out to be a pivotal period, one where Hayek conceived of a project to provide an alternative neoliberal version of evolutionary economics different from the thin version taking root in the economics department and the Law School after his arrival.

Hayek's relationship to work in the natural sciences is rather unusual in that it seems to fall into three relatively distinct phases. In his early career in

[27] See, for example (Caldwell 2000, 2001 2002, 2004a; Hodgson 1994; Angner 2002, 2004; De Vlieghere 1994; Shearmur 1996; Vanberg 1994; Whitman 1998; Kerstenetzky 2000; Ebenstein, 2003; Beck 2009).

[28] Parts of this section are taken from (Mirowski 2008).

Austria, he did enjoy some background in biology and psychology, although these did not seem to inform his work on economics. After his move to the LSE in 1931, however, he began to advocate a position that asserted that "scientism" was the root of political confusion in political economy, in what he himself called his "Abuse of Reason" project. This, by the way, was the era of his first encounters with Popper covered in Section 1. Under the influence of the neo-Kantian school of Rickert, Windelband, and Dilthey, he preached that the social sciences were fundamentally different from the natural sciences, both in terms of their objects and methods. Somehow this resulted in a joint condemnation of historicism and scientism, a position that may have made some sense in German, but did not translate well into the Anglo context. The move from the LSE to Chicago roughly marks the boundary of this third period, where evolution loomed ever larger in his theoretical prognostications.

It was sometime after 1945 (Caldwell, 2000, 9) that Hayek set aside his other projects and took up an old student manuscript that he eventually worked up as *The Sensory Order* (1952). Although he once admitted this was an attempt to translate his Austrian capital theory into the neurons of the brain (in Weimer and Palermo, 1982, 291), it also became the first salvo in a thesis about the natural limitations of what a mind could "know." As he later wrote, "My conception of evolution, of a spontaneous order and of the methods and limits of our endeavors to explain complex phenomena have been formed largely in the course of working on that book" (Hayek, 1979b, 199).

It seems that in Chicago Hayek finally decided that he would employ a biological version of natural science to "naturalize" the Market and therefore portray the socialist planning ambition as "unnatural." By jumping on someone else's Natural Science bandwagon rather than demonizing scientism, he was finally conceding that all his earlier attempts at refutation of socialists had been for naught. Yet it was also an implicit critique of Friedman's thin evolutionism. I think this Chicago transformation was composed of at least three components:

(1) Hayek would now concede the portrait of a single "unified science" that he had been resisting for at least a decade or more. There was no open renunciation of his prior position, no *mea culpa*; instead, he simply began to rely on Karl Popper to inform people on what "real science" looked like (Hacohen, 2000).

(2) Hayek began to endorse various aspects of the "cybernetics" project that sought to reduce thought to mechanism. This was the source of his embrace of the "sciences of complexity," which he derived from Warren Weaver (Mirowski, 2002a, 175). This happened right when Chicago economics was distancing itself from it.

(3) With a lag, Hayek began to appeal to "evolution" to explain how an ineffable complex order, which he simply equated with the Market, could have come about. The onus for ineffability was thus shifted from Germanic philosophy to biologistic metaphor.

To put the matter with a certain crude concision, for Hayek, the proposition that "Markets do the thinking that people cannot" was extricated from its relatively mysterious status in his "Abuse of Reason" project at the LSE to assume its more concertedly Naturalistic status in Chicago by means of an endorsement of the proposition that "Matter can think." Although this move was forward looking (and became the hallmark of the neoclassical orthodoxy in the later twentieth century: Mirowski 2002a), it was not particularly original with Hayek. The ontological flattening of the "Thing that thinks" allowed him to blur the level that his analysis operated on, be it brains or individuals or groups. "It is more than a metaphor to describe the price system as a kind of machinery for registering change, or a system of telecommunications" (1972, 87). The reason that he could distribute cognition in this manner was that he was concurrently describing the individual mind equally as a machine for registering change. Thus I cannot accept Caldwell's assertion that, at least in phase (3), Hayek's "agent is a real human being who inhabits a specific social space, not some atomistic and asocial automaton" (2004a, 286).

It seems that Hayek was much more serious about making some connections with contemporary biology than any of his colleagues in the economics department, the Business School, or the Law School. Some of his later claims that the theory of evolution could already be found in eighteenth-century Scots thinkers like Smith and Hume proved a bit of an embarrassment, and his attempt to downgrade Darwin's importance for evolution appeared downright bizarre, but at least he appears to have read and cited a number of biologists. He convened a seminar on the "Scientific Method and the Study of Society" in 1952 and managed to get a number of Chicago natural science faculty to attend, including Sewall Wright (who, however, left the University in 1955). He struggled with Popper's denunciations of evolution by claiming that, although it could not predict, the law of evolution could at least provide generic "explanations of the principle"; and maybe that was the best we could hope from economics as well.

The response to Popper's denunciations of evolution at the MPS, the escalating need to come to terms with the natural sciences, and Hayek' position that economists were impotent to plan the economy all came together in his 1955 paper, "Degrees of Explanation" (reprinted in Hayek, 1967). Whereas Popper had claimed the theory of evolution was not *falsifiable*,

Hayek morphed this proposition into an assertion that it was exemplary of "pattern prediction," which "doesn't aim at specific predictions of particular events, nor is [it] ... expected to be confirmed or refuted by observation" (1967, 12). The point was to situate economics and evolutionary theory on the same epistemic footing, dealing with more "complex" phenomena than generally were the subject of physics, not accidentally the science then beloved of the technical left-leaning theorists housed at the Cowles Commission. Hayek then tied the supposed shared nature of evolution and economics to the impossibility of planning, because "explanation of the principle allows creation of favourable circumstances not favourable control of outcomes.... Such activities in which we are guided by a knowledge merely of the principle of the thing should perhaps better be described by the term *cultivation* than by the familiar term 'control' – cultivation in the sense in which the farmer and gardener cultivates his plants" (1967, 19). Here Hayek attempted to counterpose the machine rationality of postwar neoclassical theory with a "green" and earthy Austrian-inflected science, which maintained a harmony with Nature by acknowledging one could not subjugate it.

Hayek also participated in the Darwin Centennial Celebration held at Chicago in November 1959, and thus was exposed to a wide range of positions concerning the extension of evolutionary theory to the mind and social and cultural formations (Caldwell, 2000, 12; Tax, 1960). There is no evidence of which I am aware of any of the conventional Chicago School protagonists taking part. The usual suspects apparently felt no need to catch up on what had been happening with Darwin. The centennial has been described by historians like Smocovitis (2005) as the first realization outside of the small circle of core biologists that the "modern synthesis" had once more reevaluated the contribution of Darwin in the history of evolutionary theory: "The 1959 Darwin centenary was indeed the pivotal moment in the emergence of histories of 'Darwin and the Darwinian Revolution ... [it] led ultimately to the writing and rewriting of the history and philosophy of biology by Ernst Mayr and others that evolved into the 'Darwin Industry' by the 1980s" (2005, 46–47).

In light of the this periodization, some of Geoffrey Hodgson's strictures on Hayek begin to make more sense than Caldwell has been willing to concede (Caldwell, 2001; Hodgson, 2004b). The conviction that a "non-Darwinian evolution" could still support a Naturalistic defense of the market was a precept more or less lifted from some of the cyberneticists. Angner (2002) argues that this was linked up with the ideas about group selection Hayek had encountered back at the LSE. The notion that evolution displays an unambiguous "arrow of time" in the direction of greater complexity was another favored doctrine of cyberneticians, though it effectively revealed the suppressed heritage of Spencer. By the late 1960s, Hayek had found an accommodation between theories of knowledge and his own understanding of biology. At that point, Hayek sought to package together this ontology of cybernetics with his own special version of evolution so as to maintain that not only were markets adaptive, but that "it is impossible, not only to replace spontaneous order by organization and at the same time utilize as much of the dispersed knowledge in all of its members as possible, but also to improve or correct this order by interfering in it by direct commands. Such a combination of spontaneous order and organization can never be rational to adopt" (1973, 51).

Here Hayek's thesis that the brain will never fully comprehend itself became wedded to the parallel thesis that Science informs us that we will never fully comprehend the evolved Natural Order.[29] Finally we observe that Hayek at Chicago sought to naturalize the Market and thus refute socialists by committing something very akin to the "Naturalistic Fallacy" (Angner, 2004).[30] As he wrote in his final book, "the extended order is perfectly natural: in the sense that it has itself, like similar biological phenomena, evolved naturally in the cause of natural selection" (1988, 19). Hence we cannot accept Caldwell's assertion that Hayek's "evolutionary thought had no teleology attached to it" (2004a, 357). It may not be nice to "fool Mother Nature," but how would we know that we had transgressed, except through a self-referential tissue of natural science metaphors?

Whatever one thinks of the validity of the components of the argument, it should be clear that Hayek developed a sophisticated neoliberal position with respect to evolutionary economics in reaction to the thin evolutionism favored in the Chicago economics department. One thing that this history problematizes is that, although skirmishes between the Friedmanite and

[29] Hayek tended to make misleading citations to Gödel's Theorems late in his career, probably because he had come to depend on the proposition that science itself can inform us of the "limits to science." I cannot explore here how this position links up with his late-career hostility to democracy, but see (Mirowski 2004).

[30] Again, space considerations preclude giving this claim the attention it would require. For instance, there is much dispute over what would constitute the commission of the fallacy (Wilson, Dietrich, and Clark, 2003). Angner (2004) seeks to absolve Hayek of the fallacy by imagining that Hayek consciously inserted a normative premise in his reasoning, but just never fleshed out the case for why spontaneous orders were "desirable." I find this last interpretation unpersuasive, because the missing premise was always the undesirability of socialism. Caldwell and Reiss (2006) stridently deny Hayek ever committed anything approaching the fallacy, whereas Angner (2006) finds this unpersuasive.

Hayekian wings of the neoliberal movement flared up with some frequency toward the end of the millennium, there has as yet been no instance of an acolyte of the former criticizing the evolutionary doctrines of the latter. The reasons for this are obscure. As we shall argue in the last section, it is in fact the thin Chicago version of evolution that has come to triumph within the economics profession and in the popular culture, and not Hayek's. Contemporary economists persist in making all manner of superficial appeals to biological evolution, claiming that it sweetly resonates with orthodox neoclassical theory, all the while absolving themselves of actually confronting important contemporary arguments over the shape and structure of evolutionary theory.[31] Partly, no doubt, this is due to the headway that the neoclassical model has made in certain areas of biology (such as sociobiology) and philosophy (Dan Dennett and his "memes").

Yet in the final analysis, all the sound and fury over natural philosophy was not the most important legacy of Hayek's Chicago period. That instead came with his project to mobilize a cadre of scholars to come up with a New- or Neo-Liberalism to rally the antisocialist cause at its post–World War II nadir. The organization Hayek first convened in Mont Pèlerin April 1–10, 1947, became by all accounts the effective zero point from which the Neoliberal Thought Collective was born.[32] It was the *institutional* resolution to the failures that had plagued Hayek's quest in the first two periods of his life. It also served as the debating society for the different fledgling variants of neoliberal evolution in their nascent period.

It is a shame that Caldwell and other Hayek commentators so tend to neglect the MPS (see Caldwell, this volume), because it became the culmination of Hayek's own third period prognostications, the obverse face of his late-period works on law and the state. No single mind could comprehend itself, therefore no single mind could oppose the antimarket *Weltanschauung* that so oppressed Hayek and his comrades in the 1940s. To oppose those despised "second-hand dealers in ideas," he realized one had to nurture his own battalion of dealers as well as some of the ideas they would retail. Hayek realized that one had to embrace and revel in the contradiction of an "organized" spontaneous order and create an *entire set of institutions* to generate and promote the sort of social science (and even natural science!) he

[31] This argument is made in some detail in (Mirowski 2007). (Klaes 2004) is a symptom of current practice. Some interesting recent work that questions the simple conflation of natural selection with maximization on a fitness surface is (Fontana 2005; Pigliucci and Kaplan 2006; Dupré 1987; Ariew and Lewontin 2004; Moss 2004).

[32] This set of events have been described by many historians: (Cockett 1995; Hartwell 1995; Plehwe and Walpen 2004; Mirowski and Plehwe 2009).

felt would stand as a bulwark against creeping totalitarianism. No conventional "intellectual history" can begin to do justice to the extent to which his vision has been successful at the dawn of the twenty-first century – which is why his name continues to live on when those of other economists rapidly slide into oblivion.

9.5. Chicago: Doin' Things They Won't Do on Broadway

The number of Chicago School economists who have taken it upon themselves to pronounce their economic blessing upon the place of evolution in the grand scheme of things is quite striking once one begins to gather them together in one place. Beyond those cited in previous sections of this paper, some more recent and rather high-profile examples have been Gary Becker (1976), Robert Lucas, Jack Hirshleifer (1977; 1978), Gordon Tullock (1979), and Arthur Robson (2001). As Jack Vromen argues, the second generation tended to assert that the validity of neoclassical economics carried over into the biological domain rather than actually appropriate anything from biology. The time has come to approach this as a structural phenomenon requiring explanation, and not some artifact of the enthusiasms of this or that isolated individual thinker. It is apparent from perusing their writings that they have come to regard thin evolution as intellectually sanctioned from within their own tradition. Richard Posner nicely captures this sense of *entitlement*:

> "Economic theory is closely related to the theory of evolution.... Evolution deals with unconscious maximizers; economics with conscious maximizers, persons." ... "Politics is about enmity," he says. "It's about getting together with your friends and knocking off your enemies. The basic fallacy of liberalism is the idea that if we get together with reasonable people we can agree on everything. But you can't agree: strife is ineradicable, a fundamental part of nature, in storms and in human relations." (Posner quoted in MacFarquhar, 2001)

This doctrine has now spread as a commonplace among economists who would otherwise not be caught dead being labeled as neoliberals. Here is just one example: "What should be recognized is that evolution is bigger than either biology or economics. It is a pervasive property of all systems that have a history, a budget constraint, and in which the process that generates innovation is stochastic" (Mokyr, 2006, 1009). Though this might have held water back in the days of R. A. Fisher, it is far from the actual state of play in biology today. We should now recognize this as the characteristic thin doctrine of evolution, whose history was described earlier, and which now can be found well removed from the watershed of Lake Michigan.

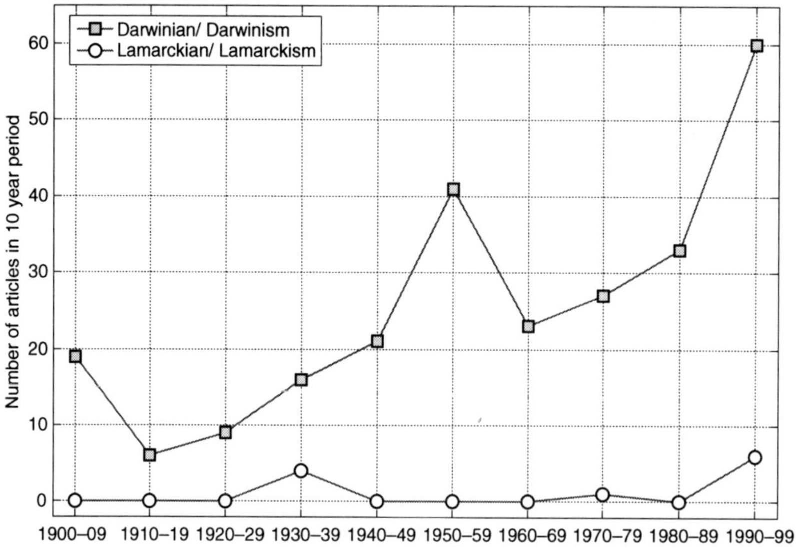

Figure 9.1. Articles mentioning Darwinism and Lamarckism in twenty-seven economics journals, 1900–1999. (From Hodgson and Knudsen 2007, 355. With permission.)

At least within the precincts of orthodox economics, the neoliberal conception of thin evolution has swept the field. The historical timing recounted in this paper explains the unusual pattern of citations of Darwin in major economics journals, as revealed in Figure 9.1.

The noticeable bump in the decade of the 1950s with regard to mentions of Darwin in twenty-seven economics journals archived in JSTOR, juxtaposed with the absence of any commensurate surge in mentions of Lamarck (the fallback position of those who claim that sociocultural evolution is intrinsically "different" from biology), testifies to the central role of the Chicago School in framing the discussion of evolution in postwar economics. Although we cannot dig deeper here, we might hypothesize that it was Chicago economists who also deserve credit for the upward trend since the 1940s, and not, as many would have it, the heterodox avant garde. If we entertain this larger hypothesis, then a number of questions suddenly become more salient. They include:

1. What were the main forces acting to spread thin evolutionism outside the narrow orbit of Chicago?
2. What functions does thin evolutionism perform in the contemporary cultural setting?

3. Why don't contemporary "evolutionary economists" appreciate the extent to which their ambitions are hampered and undermined by the prevalence of the doctrine of thin evolution (sometimes even in their own work)?
4. Why don't repeated critiques in economics that thin evolution has no corresponding place in biology have any effect on its continued success?

Starting with the last two questions first, I have only encountered one plausible answer: "It is no small irony that the neo-Schumpeterians and paleo-institutionalists use [the term] 'evolutionary' to signal 'not neoclassical,' when the evolutionary theory most influencing mainstream economics itself resembles neoclassical economics. This may be evidence not of Darwin in evolutionary economics, but of neoclassical economics in contemporary Darwinian theory" (Leonard, 2003, 353). Although one might quibble with the exact designations "most" and "Darwinian," it is indisputable that a neoclassical version of thin evolutionism has made profound inroads in various sectors of biology in the last decades of the twentieth century. It started back in the 1970s with the sociobiology phenomenon; continued with the importation of Nash game theory into animal ethology in the 1980s (Smith 1982); and exfoliated outward with evolutionary psychology and neuroeconomics in the 1990s. The reasons for this seemingly retrograde phenomenon cannot be discussed here,[33] and in any event it is only just beginning to attract the attention of serious philosophers and historians of science. There is no question that this development has further insulated the thin version of evolution from critique, because the practice of the second generation of Chicago-style economists has been to apply simple neoclassical models to animals, and not import Darwinian evolutionary considerations into economics.

This, in turn, raises the question of the current status of research in just those sectors of biology where thin evolution has made inroads. Just because a class of models becomes popular in a natural science need not imply this was solely attributable to predictive success, analytical cogency, or any of the other candidates so often proposed by philosophers of science. Indeed, molecular biologists have recently been engaged in undermining the beanbag notion of the gene that seems to underlie so many importations of neoclassical models; so the status of evolutionary theory is still in flux, and many of those models may still fall prey to the advances elsewhere in biology. Nevertheless, the fact that thin evolution spread from

[33] But see (Vromen 2005; Palladino 1991). Vromen points out that Richard Dawkins was popularizing Hamilton, Trivers, and Maynard Smith among others; what would be required is a history that would subject their influences to critical scrutiny.

Chicago economics to the larger culture with relative alacrity hints at other conditioning factors.

This paper documents the close historical connection between the rise of thin evolution within Chicago economics and the project of the construction of a neoliberal political doctrine that would underwrite a conservative approach not just to economics, but to all areas of life. The Mont Pèlerin Society early on abjured a narrow disciplinary approach in favor of a broad transdisciplinary philosophy that would unite Nature and Society under a single comprehensive set of concepts. The writings of Friedrich Hayek surveyed previously provide one very perspicuous instance of these broad ambitions. The success of those ambitions are exemplified in recent claims to turn a thin version of evolution into a "Universal Darwinism," a doctrine so unspecific and all-encompassing that the neoliberal rallying cry of "There is no alternative" would become inescapable. One cannot read the work of Daniel Dennett, for instance, without grasping the nettle that the plan has been to project Friedman's doctrine of the "as if" onto the entirety of phenomenological reality. The more such a project became dominant in the culture, the easier it has become to export Chicago economics into various "under-formalized" and mathematically light areas of biology.

Hence the success of the neoliberal political movement has had curious feedback onto the subsequent trajectories of the theory of evolution in biology and, consequently, on the longevity of thin evolution in economics. What this really turns out to be in practice is each new improved version of Alchian (or Friedman or Winter) denying that they need be held to any intellectual standards found within biological science or within formalized theories of evolution. Indeed, some of these figures have explicitly said that they bear no allegiance to any specific models from biology, and can bend words to mean anything they find convenient or salutary. These theorists seek to enjoy the metaphorical warm glow that derives from biology occupying the envious position of the best funded and apparently most progressive of all the natural sciences at the turn of the millennium, while abjuring any requirement to understand how and why biology has been bequeathed that status. Perhaps this is not so very different from the stumbling attempts of the early neoclassicals in the last decades of the nineteenth century to piggyback onto the Energetics movement in physics without understanding its consequences or implications (Mirowski, 1989). Although hardly conducive to clarity in thought, history teaches the practice is rarely fatal.

The real lessons, I think, are to be learned by those who thought that appeals to evolution might provide a prophylactic against the encroachment of the neoclassical orthodoxy in economics. There is no such thing as a Grand Theory of Evolution above and beyond the particular formats it assumes in any particular discipline, be it molecular genetics, animal ethology, cultural anthropology, or neoclassical economics, pace Daniel Dennett and his memetic hordes. Theories of evolution in biology have undergone repeated revision and transformation over the last 150 years (Depew and Weber, 1995); and given some recent arguments, there is no reason to think that we have yet arrived at some "final" version of the theory that can account for the dizzying array of biological organisms and their molecular peccadilloes, much less social and cultural phenomena. Some reputable philosophers (Beatty, 1995) have even claimed that there are no general laws of evolution, because every generalization has uncovered telling counterexamples. As I write this, I open the newspaper to read that an entirely fallacious theory of the gene has underwritten the supposed biotech gold rush, with the consequence that mistaken impositions of intellectual property (justified by Chicago School theories) are now coming to threaten the very integrity of the scientific research process (Caruso, 2007). Maybe, just maybe, the clash of politics and science will provoke a further revision of the theory of evolution, and the End of History will once again be postponed.

References

Alchian, Armen. 1950. "Uncertainty, Evolution and Economic Theory." *Journal of Political Economy* (58):211–221.

1953a. "Biological Analogies in the Theory of the Firm: Comment." *American Economic Review* (43):600–603.

1953b. "Systems Analysis – Friend or Foe?" RAND D-1778.

2006. *The Collected Works of Armen Alchian, vol. 1*. Indianapolis: Liberty Fund.

Alchian, Armen and Reuben Kessell. 1954. "A Proper Role for Systems Analysis." RAND D-2057.

Alchian, A., G.D. Bodenhord, S. Enke, C.J Hitch, J. Hirschleifer and A. Marshall. 1951. "What is the best system?" RAND D-860.

Angner, Erik. 2002. "The History of Hayek's Theory of Cultural Evolution." *Studies in the History and Philosophy of the Biological Sciences* (33):695–718.

2004. "Did Hayek Commit the Naturalistic Fallacy?" *Journal of the History of Economic Thought*, (26):349–361.

Angner, Eric. 2006. "Response to Caldwell and Reiss." *Journal of the History of Economic Thought* (28):371–373.

Ariew, Andre and Richard Lewontin. 2004. "The Confusions of Fitness." *British Journal for the Philosophy of Science* (55):347–363.

Beatty, John. 1995. "The Evolutionary Contingency Thesis." In G. Wolters and J. Lennox, eds., *Concepts, Theories and Rationality in the Biological Sciences*. Pittsburgh: University of Pittsburgh Press.

Beck, Naomi. 2009. "In Search of the Proper Scientific Approach: Hayek's Views on Biology, Methodology and the Nature of Economics." *Science in Context*, (22):567–585.

Becker, Gary. 1962. "Irrational Behavior and Economic Theory." *Journal of Political Economy*, (70):1–13.

1976. "Altruism, Egotism and Genetic Fitness: Economics and Sociobiology," *Journal of Economic Literature* (14):817–826.

Boland, Lawrence. 1997. *Critical Economic Methodology: A Personal Odyssey*. London: Routledge.

Bowler, Peter. 1988. *The Non-Darwinian Revolution*. Baltimore: Johns Hopkins Press.

Caldwell, Bruce. 2000. "The Emergence of Hayek's Ideas on Cultural Evolution." *Review of Austrian Economics* (13):5–22.

2001. "Hodgson on Hayek : A Critique." *Cambridge Journal of Economics* (25):539–553.

2004a. *Hayek's Challenge*. Chicago: University of Chicago Press.

2004b. "Some Reflections on F.A. Hayek's Sensory Order." *Journal of Bioeconomics* (6):239–254.

Caldwell, Bruce and Julien Reiss. 2006. "Did Hayek Commit the Naturalistic Fallacy?" *Journal of the History of Economic Thought* (28):359–370.

Carnap, Rudolf. 1963. "Intellectual Autobiography." In *The Philosophy of Rudolf Carnap*. Ed. Paul Schlipp. La Salle: Open Court.

Caruso, Denise. 2007. "A Tougher Look at Gene Theory, and a Challenge to Bioindustry," *New York Times*, July 1.

Cockett, Richard. 1995. *Thinking the Unthinkable: Think Tanks and the Economic Counter-Revolution, 1931–83*. London: Fontana.

Cordes, Christian. 2006. "Darwinism in Economics: From Analogy to Continuity." *Journal of Evolutionary Economics* (16):529–541.

2007. "Turning Economics into an Evolutionary Science: Veblen, the Selection Metaphor, and Analogical Thinking." *Journal of Economic Issues* (41):135–154.

Dawkins, Richard. 1976. *The Selfish Gene*. Oxford: Oxford University Press.

Degler, Carl. 1991. *In Search of Human Nature: The Decline and Revival of Darwinism in American Social Thought*. New York: Oxford University Press.

Dennett, Daniel. 1995. *Darwin's Dangerous Idea*. New York: Simon & Schuster.

Depew, David and Bruce Weber. 1995. *Darwinism Evolving*. Cambridge: MIT Press.

Desmond, Adrian and James Moore. 1991. *Darwin*. London: Michael Joseph.

Dopfer, Kurt, ed. 2001. *Evolutionary Economics: Program and Scope*. Boston: Kluwer.

Dupré, John, ed. 1987. *The Latest on the Best: Essays on Evolution and Optimality*. Cambridge: MIT Press.

Ebenstein, Alan. 2001. *Friedrich Hayek: A Biography*. New York: Palgrave.

Enke, Stephen. 1949. "Economic Life Formulae for Air Force Equipment." RAND D-672.

1951. "On Maximizing Profits: A Distinction Between Chamberlin and Robinson." *American Economic Review* 41 (4): 566–578.

1953. "Biological Analogies in the Theory of the Firm: Comment." *American Economic Review* 43: 603.

Fontana, Walter. 2005. "The Topology of the Possible." In A. Wimmer and R. Koessler, eds., *Paradigms of Change*.

Friedman, Milton. 1953. *Essays in Positive Economics*. Chicago: University of Chicago Press.

Friedman, Milton and Rose Friedman. 1998. *Two Lucky People*. Chicago: University of Chicago Press.

Giere, Ronald and Alan Richardson, eds. 1996. *Origins of Logical Empiricism*. Minnesota: University of Minnesota Press.

Gintis, Herbert. 2007. "A Framework for the Unification of the Behavioral Sciences." *Behavioral and Brain Science* (30):1–61.

Hacohen, Malachi. 2000. *Karl Popper: The Formative Years, 1902–45*. New York: Cambridge University Press.

Hammond, J. Dan. 2004. Early Drafts of Friedman's Methodology Essay," unpub. Ms.

Harrod, Roy. 1939. "Price and Cost in Entrepreneur's Policy." *Oxford Economic Studies* (2): 1–11.

Hartwell, R. Max. 1995. *A History of the Mont Pèlerin Society*. Indianapolis: Liberty Fund.

Hayek, Friedrich. 1962. Preface to English Language Edition of Heinrich Rickert, *Science and History*. New York: Van Nostrand.

1967. *Studies in Philosophy, Politics and Economics*. New York: Simon & Schuster.

1972. *Individualism and Economic Order*. Chicago: Gateway.

1973. *Law, Legislation and Liberty. Vol. 1* London: Routledge and Kegan Paul.

1979a [1952]. *The Counter-Revolution of Science*. Indianapolis: Liberty Press.

1979b. *Law, Legislation and Liberty. Vol. 3* Chicago: University of Chicago Press.

1982. "The Sensory Order after 25 Years." In W. Weimer & D. Palermo, eds., *Cognition and the Symbolic Process*. Hillsdale: Erlbaum.

1988. *The Fatal Conceit*. Chicago: University of Chicago Press.

Hirsch, Abraham and Neil de Marchi. 1990. *Milton Friedman: Economics in Theory and Practice*. Ann Arbor: University of Michigan Press.

Hirshleifer, Jack. 1977. "Economics from a Biological Viewpoint." *Journal of Law and Economics* (20):1–52.

Hodgson, Geoffrey. 1993. *Economics and Evolution*. Ann Arbor: University of Michigan Press.

1994. "Optimization and Evolution: Winter's Critique of Friedman Revisited." *Cambridge Journal of Economics* (18):413–430.

1998. Entries for "Evolutionary Economics" and "Selectionist Arguments." In J.B. Davis, D.W. Hands & U. Maki, eds. *The Handbook of Economic Methodology*. Cheltenham: Elgar.

2002. "Darwinism in Economics: From Analogy to Ontology." *Journal of Evolutionary Economics*. (12):259–281.

2004a. *The Evolution of Institutional Economics*. London: Routledge.

2004b. "Hayekian Evolution Reconsidered: A Response to Caldwell." *Cambridge Journal of Economics* 28:291–300.

Hodgson, Geoffrey and Thorbjorn Knudsen. 2006. "Why We Need a Generalized Darwinism, and Why a Generalized Darwinism is Not Enough." *Journal of Economic Behavior and Organization* (61):1–19.

2007. "Evolutionary Theory Beyond Lamarckism." *Journal of Evolutionary Economics* (17):353–359.

Hounshell, David. 2000. "The Medium is the Message" In T. Hughes and A. Hughes, eds., *Systems, Experts and Computers*. Cambridge: MIT Press.

Houthakker, Hendrik. 1956. "Economics and Biology: Specialization and Speciation." ONR Technical Report 30. Stanford University.

Jardini, David. 1996. *Out of the Blue Yonder*. Ph.D. thesis, history, Carnegie-Mellon.

Kay, Lily. 2000. *Who Wrote the Book of Life?* Stanford: Stanford University Press.

Kerstenetzky, Celia. 2000. "Hayek: The Evolutionary and the Evolutionist." *Rationality and Society* (12):163–184.

Klaes, Matthias. 2004. "Evolutionary Economics: In Defense of Vagueness." *Journal of Economic Methodology* 11:359–376.

Knight, Frank. 1935. *The Ethics of Competition*. New York: Harper.

Knudsen, Thorbjorn. 2002. "Economic Selection Theory." *Journal of Evolutionary Economics* (12):443–470.

Laurent, John and John Nightingale, eds. 2001. *Darwinism and Evolutionary Economics*. Cheltenham: Elgar.

Lee, F.S. 1981. "The Oxford Challenge to Marshallian Supply and Demand." *Oxford Economic Papers* (33):339–351.

Lee, F.S. and J. Lessman. 1992. "The Fate of an Errant Hypothesis: The Doctrine of Normal Cost Prices." *History of Political Economy* (24):273–310.

Leonard, Thomas. 2003. Review of (Laurent & Nightingale, 2001). *History of Political Economy* (35):350–353.

Lester, R.A. 1946. "Shortcomings of Marginal Analysis for Wage-Employment Problems." *American Economic Review* (36):63–82.

Levallois, Clement. 2009. "One Analogy Can Hide Another: Physics and Biology in Alchian's Economic Natural Selection." *History of Political Economy* (41):163–181.

Lewontin, Richard. 1987. "The Shape of Optimality." In J. Dupré, ed., *The Latest on the Best*. Cambridge: MIT Press.

MacFarquhar, Larissa. 2001. "The Bench Burner." *New Yorker* December 10: (77):78–89.

Machlup, Fritz. 1946. "Marginal Analysis and Empirical Research." *American Economic Review* (36): 519–554.

Mailath, George. 1998. "Do People Play Nash Equilibrium?" *Journal of Economic Literature* (36):1347–1374.

Maki, Uskali, ed. 2009. *The Methodology of Positive Economics*. London: Routledge.

McCloskey, Donald. 1985. *The Rhetoric of Economics*. Madison: University of Wisconsin Press.

McGuckin, William. 1984. *Scientists, Society and the State*. Columbus: Ohio State University Press.

Mirowski, Philip. 1988. *Against Mechanism*. Totawa: Rowman & Littlefield.

1989. *More Heat than Light*. New York: Cambridge University Press.

2002a. *Machine Dreams*. New York: Cambridge University Press.

2002b. Review of Malachi Hacohen's *Karl Popper. Isis* June: 324–325.

2004. "The Scientific Dimensions of Social Thought and their Distant Echoes in American 20th Century Philosophy of Science." *Studies in the History and Philosophy of Science*.

2007. "Markets Come to Bits: Markomata and the Future of Computational Evolutionary Economics." *Journal of Economic Behavior and Organizatio*, (63):209–242.

2008. "Naturalizing the Market on the Road to Revisionism." *Journal of Institutional Economics* (3):351–372.

2010. "The Great Mortification." *Hedgehog Review*, Fall.

Mirowski, Philip and Wade Hands, eds. 2006. *Agreement on Demand*. Durham: Duke University Press.

Mirowski, Philip and Dieter Plehwe, eds. 2009. *The Road from Mont Pèlerin: the Making of the Neoliberal Thought Collective*. Cambridge: Harvard University Press.
Mokyr, Joel. 2006. "Economics and the Biologists: A Review of Geerat Vermeij's *Nature: An Economic History*." *Journal of Economic Literature* (44):1005–1013.
Mongin, Philippe. 1982. "The Full Cost Controversy in the 1940s and 1950s." *History of Political Economy* (24):311–56.
Moss, Lenny. 2004. *What Genes Can't Do*. Cambridge: MIT Press.
Nelson, Richard. 1957. "Invention, Research and Development: A Survey" RAND D-4739.
1995. "Recent Evolutionary Theorizing about Economic Change." *Journal of Economic Literature* (33):48–90.
2007. "Universal Darwinism and Evolutionary Social Science." *Biology and Philosophy* (22):73–94.
Nelson, Richard and Sidney Winter. 1982. *An Evolutionary Theory of Economic Change* Cambridge: Harvard University Press.
2002. "Evolutionary Theorizing in Economics." *Journal of Economic Perspectives* (16):23–46.
O'Neill, John. 2003. "Socialism, Associations and the Market." *Economy and Society* (32): 184–206.
Palladino, Paolo. 1991. "Defining Ecology: Ecological Theories, Mathematical Models, and Applied Biology in the 1960s and 1970s." *Journal of the History of Biology* (24):223–41.
Penrose, E. 1952: "Biological Analogies in the Theory of the Firm." *American Economics Review* 42 (5): 804–819.
1953. "Biological Analogies in the Theory of the Firm: Rejoinder." *American Economic Review* 43(4):603–609.
Pickering, Mary. 1993. *Auguste Comte*. New York: Cambridge University Press.
Pigliucci, Massimo and Kaplan, Jonathan. 2006. *Making Sense of Evolution*. Chicago: University of Chicago Press.
Popper, Karl. 1957. *The Poverty of Historicism*. Boston: Beacon.
1976. *Unended Quest*. London: Fontana.
Robson, Arthur. 2001. "Why Would Nature Give Individuals Utility Functions?" *Journal of Political Economy* (109):900–914.
Samuelson, Larry. 1997. *Evolutionary Games and Equilibrium Selection*. Cambridge: MIT Press.
Schafer, Mark E. 1989. "Are Profit-Maximizers the Best Survivors? A Darwinian Model of Natural Selection." *Journal of Economic Behavior and Organization* (12):29–45.
Segal, Jerome. 2003. "The Use of Information Theory in Biology: A Historical Perspective." *History and Philosophy of the Life Sciences* (25):275–281.
Shearmur, Jeremy. 1994. "Hayek and the Case for the Market." In Jack Birner and Rudy van Zijp, eds., *Hayek, Coordination and Evolution*. London: Routledge.
1996. *Hayek and After*. London: Routledge.
Smith, John Maynard. 1982. *Evolution and the Theory of Games*. Cambridge: Cambridge University Press.
Smith, Vernon. 1982. "Markets as Economizers of Information: Experimental Examination of the Hayek Hypothesis." *Economic Inquiry* (20): 165–79.
2003. "Constructivist and Ecological Rationality in Economics." *American Economic Review* (93):465–508.

Smocovitis, Vassili. 2005. "It Ain't Over till its Over: Rethinking the Darwinian Revolution." *Journal of the History of Biology* (38):33–49.

Tax, Sol, ed. 1960. *Evolution after Darwin. Vol.3 Issues in Evolution.* Chicago: University of Chicago Press.

Tullock, Gordon. 1979. "Sociobiology and Economics." *Atlantic Economic Journal,* (7):1–10.

Uebel, Thomas. 1995. "Otto Neurath's Idealist Inheritance." *Synthese* (103):87–121.

2000. "Some Scientism, Some Historicism, Some Critics: Hayek's and Popper's Critiques Revisited." In M. Stone and J. Wolff, eds., *The Proper Ambition of Science.* London: Routledge.

Valdes, Juan. 1995. *Pinochet's Economists: The Chicago Boys in Chile.* New York: Cambridge University Press.

Van Overtveldt, Johan. 2007. *The Chicago School.* Chicago: Agate.

von Neumann, John. 1966. *The Theory of Self-Reproducing Automata.* Urbana: University of Illinois Press.

Vromen, Jack. 1994. *Evolution and Efficiency.* Delft: Eburon.

1995. *Evolution in Economics.* London: Routledge.

2005. "Neuroeconomics as a Natural Extension of Bioeconomics" unpub ms.

2010. "Allusions to Evolution: Edifying Evolutionary Biology rather than Economic Theory" (this volume).

Wallis, Allen. 1991. "Leonard Jimmie Savage." In Edward Shils, ed., *Remembering the University of Chicago.* Chicago: University of Chicago Press.

Walters, Alan. 1987. "Milton Friedman." In *New Palgrave.* London: Macmillan.

Weimer, W. and D. Palermo, eds. 1982. *Cognition and Symbolic Processes, vol. 2.* Hillsdale: Erlbaum.

Wilson, David, Eric Dietrich, and Anne Clark. 2003. "On the Inappropriate Use of the Naturalistic Fallacy in Evolutionary Psychology." *Biology and Philosophy* (18):669–682.

Winter, Sidney. 1961. "The Sources of Economic Collapse." RAND D-8662.

1964. "Economics, Natural Selection, and the Theory of the Firm." *Yale Economic Essays* (4):225–274.

1987. "Natural Selection and Evolution." In *New Palgrave.* London: Macmillan.

Witt, Ulrich. 1999. "Bioeconomics as Economics from a Darwinian Perspective." *Journal of Bioeconomics* (1):19–34.

PART FOUR

DEBATING “CHICAGO NEOLIBERALISM”

TEN

Jacob Viner's Critique of Chicago Neoliberalism

Robert Van Horn

> [M]ay I suggest that no greater damage can be done to the interests of American "Big Business" than to give them the impression that any substantial fraction of the free members (i.e., not in the way of government, or of special economic interests) of the American economic profession believes that the present role of "Big Business" in the American economy is a healthy or durable one.[1]
>
> – Jacob Viner

While at the University of Chicago from 1916 to 1917 and from 1919 to 1946, Jacob Viner became famous for his teaching of "Economics 301," a price theory course, which, as Paul Samuelson (1972, 6) remembered it, was "celebrated for Viner's ferocious manhandling of students, in which he not only reduced women to tears but on his good days drove returned paratroopers into hysteria and paralysis." The folklore of the Chicago School claims that through this course Viner enlightened and inspired future Chicago economists, such as Milton Friedman, George Stigler, and Aaron Director. For example, about Director, Ronald Coase states that Jacob Viner's price theory course "swept away like chaff in a windstorm the nebulous idealism … of [Director's youth]" (1998, 602).[2]

I am indebted to the Center for the History of Political Economy at Duke University and the University of Rhode Island Seed Grant Fund for research support. I would like to thank Thomas Stapleford and Edward Nik-Khah for thoughtful and useful comments and Monica Van Horn and David DeLong for helpful editorial comments on multiple drafts. Archival material quoted from the Jacob Viner Papers, Public Policy Papers, Department of Rare Books and Special Collections, Princeton University Mudd Library quoted with permission; archival material quoted from the Mont Pèlerin Society Records, Liberaal Archief Ghent quoted with permission; and archival material quoted from Henry Simons Papers, Regenstein Library, University of Chicago quoted with permission.

1 VPML, letter, Viner to Clark, November 8, 1948, box 26, folder 15.

2 Also, about Stigler, Gary Becker (1993, 761) claims that Viner substantially influenced his thinking.

Although Viner may have initially inspired the leaders of the postwar Chicago School, it would be a mistake to assume that Viner was in full agreement with or closely tied to this school. About twenty years after he left the University of Chicago, Viner recalled that he had heard "rumors about a 'Chicago School'" that was engaged in an "organized battle" against collectivism.[3] Viner stated that he "remained skeptical" about this until he attended a 1951 conference at the Chicago Law School, which Aaron Director and Edward Levi headed and the Volker Fund financed. "From then on," Viner wrote, "I was willing to consider the existence of a 'Chicago School,' (but one not confined to the economics department and not embracing all of the department)."[4] Viner added that: "But at no time was I consciously a member of it, and it is my vague impression that if there was such a school it did not regard me as a member, or at least a loyal and qualified member."[5]

Nineteen forty-six not only marks the year Viner left the University of Chicago for Princeton University, but also the year that the Chicago-based effort to reconstitute liberalism began (see Peck and Van Horn and Klaes, both in this volume). By the early fall of that year, Aaron Director led the Free Market Study (1946–1952) in its examination of the legal foundations of capitalism in order to create a more robust form of liberalism to countervail collectivism. By the 1950s, as Chapter 7 of this volume details, a "new liberalism" or "Chicago neoliberalism" began to emerge.

Even though Viner had taught Director and Friedman, he was not in any way involved with the efforts to reformulate liberalism based in the Chicago Law School. Indeed, the combination of his surprise at the formation of a "Chicago School" and his firm claim the he was not affiliated with this School in the early 1950s suggests not only that he did not keep in close touch with his former pupils during the period 1946–1950, but also that the views of his former students had substantially evolved since the time he had left. Consequently, through the examination of Viner, we can gain an understanding of how someone who was part of the pre-1946 tradition of Chicago economics would view the rise of Chicago neoliberalism, particularly the Chicago neoliberal claims about business monopoly, antitrust law, and corporations. This chapter specifically focuses on how Viner might have responded to the Chicago neoliberal developments of the Free Market Study and its sister project, the Antitrust Project (1952–1956), both of which played a crucial role in laying the foundations of Chicago neoliberalism.

[3] VPML, letter, November 24, 1969, Viner to Don Patinkin, Box 21, folder: 10.

[4] Ibid.

[5] Ibid.

Three sections follow. Section one argues that prior to 1950 a group of Chicago economists, which included Henry Simons and Viner, strongly opposed concentrated business power, rooting their opposition in classical liberalism. I refer to this group as the "Chicago classical liberals." This section mainly focuses on Simons as a representative of this cohort and draws on some unexploited archival material to do so. By examining the opposition of Chicago classical liberals to concentrations of business power, it will be possible to appreciate the radical nature of the departures from classical liberalism during the Free Market Study in the early 1950s.

Section two contrasts two contemporaneous studies of business monopoly and corporations that reached disparate conclusions: the Chicago Law School–based Free Market Study and the Twentieth Century Fund investigation on monopoly and free enterprise. The Twentieth Century Fund investigation, led by classical liberals George Stocking and Myron Watkins, is significant because Viner served on its Advisory Committee and applauded its efforts. In this respect, the Fund's investigation reveals how Viner and other researchers committed to classical liberalism assessed the threat of business monopoly in the early postwar era. Consequently, it offers a useful counterpoint to Chicago's contemporaneous Free Market Study.

Section three focuses on Viner's 1959 Chicago Law School address, where he adhered to the Chicago classical liberal notion that concentrations of business power were deleterious to the economy and society. Based on this address, section three argues that Viner should be viewed a severe critic of not only the Chicago neoliberal conclusions of the Free Market Study and the Antitrust Project, but also of Friedman's understanding of competition and business monopoly in *Capitalism and Freedom*.

10.1. Opposing Concentrations of Economic Power: The Chicago Classical Liberals

From the mid-1930s through the mid-1940s, among the economists (and economists in training) associated with the University of Chicago, there was a cohort of economists – which included Viner, Simons, Aaron Director, Milton Friedman, and George Stigler – who opposed concentrations of economic power on the basis of the classical liberal doctrine.[6] Simons was

6 Frank Knight is not included in this list because I could not find evidence in his writings that he opposed concentrations of power on the basis of the classical liberal doctrine. Although Knight recognized monopoly as both a "major mechanical weakness" and a

the public face of this group. According to the preeminent historian Ellis Hawley ([1966] 1995, 292), Simons's "widely read" 1934 pamphlet, *A Positive Program for Laissez Faire*, was at the vanguard of a barrage of arguments against increased concentration in industry. According the University of Chicago Press, by November of 1949, Simons's pamphlet had sold nearly 24,000 copies.[7] Simons is also significant because, as we will see, he inspired some of the leaders of the later Chicago neoliberal movement with his pamphlet, which many of his colleagues considered the pinnacle of his scholarly work.[8] Consequently, to appreciate the Chicago classical liberals, it is useful to closely look at Simons's opposition to concentrations of business power in his *Positive Program*.

Simons squarely located his own work within the classical liberal tradition. In the opening line of his *Positive Program*, Simons asserted: "This is frankly a propagandist tract – a defense of the thesis that traditional liberalism offers ... the best basis ... for a program of economic reconstruction" (1948, 40). Indeed, Simons staunchly opposed the New Deal in his *Positive Program* precisely because it ignored the insights of Adam Smith, a point he made forcefully in 1933 when he addressed the Social Workers Discussion Group at the University of Chicago. Simons opened his talk with invective directed toward the Roosevelt Administration: "We have called up all the expletives in condemning the policies of Mr. Hoover; and we need them all and more to express our feelings with regard to the present administration.... We now feel obliged to condemn [Roosevelt] for the opposite kind of error – for the willingness to tinker foolhardily with every exposed part of the economic machine.... [T]he so-called brain-trust ... needs nothing so badly as an understanding of Adam Smith."[9]

For Simons, understanding Adam Smith entailed understanding the deleterious consequences of concentrations of power in the market. In the spirit of classical liberalism, Simons observed: "The great enemy of democracy is monopoly, in all its forms: gigantic corporations, trade associations and other agencies for price control, trade-unions – or, in general, organization and concentration of power within functional classes" (43).

"real evil in many cases," he, as far as I can tell, did not consider business monopoly to be a concentration of power that undermined freedom or liberty (1946, 85). Moreover, contrary to the Chicago economists examined in this section, Knight maintained, "most monopolies are in fact relatively temporary" (1946, 85).

7 UCPP, "Stock Short Report," 11/1/49, box 422, folder 1.

8 For evidence that Simons's *Positive Program* was the pinnacle of his work, see SPRL, box 13, folder 1 and see Director (1948).

9 SPRL, "Notes from talk given June 7, 1933 at the Harmony Cafeteria Social Workers Discussion Group on The New Deal," box 13, folder 2.

Concentrations of power posed a threat to the price system, the *sine qua non* of freedom.[10] Thus, a monopolist was like a thief because its monopoly power led to the trade of commodities at prices that failed to reflect underlying social scarcities. Simons believed that the proliferation of monopoly had led to the Depression and the dissolution of economic efficiency.[11] Because a monopoly could exert a tremendous power in order to exploit society and sabotage the economy, the state must, as Simons put it, "destroy" that monopoly (43). If the state acted otherwise, the consequence, according to Simons, would be "a usurpation of sovereignty" by the monopolists and, perhaps even, "a domination of the state by them" (43).

The societal ramifications of monopoly, according to Simons, were deplorable: "The gains from monopoly organization in general are likely, of course, to accrue predominantly to the strong and to be derived at the expense of the weak" (49). As a result, monopoly power, especially in the hands of large corporations, tended to create gross inequality, both in terms of power and income. Simons maintained:

> An important factor in existing inequality … is the gigantic corporation. We may recognize, in the almost unlimited grants of powers to corporate bodies, one of the greatest sins of government against the free-enterprise system. There is … no reasonable excuse … for hundred-million-dollar corporations, no matter what form their property may take. Even if the much advertised economies of gigantic financial combinations were real, sound policy would wisely sacrifice these economies to preservation of more economic freedom and equality. (52)

Further, Simons derided anyone who supported the status quo, with its great concentrations of power and gross income inequality: "Surely there is something unlovely, to modern as against medieval minds, about marked inequality of either kind" (51).

[10] It is worth noting that Simons continued to oppose concentrations of business power and adhere to the policy recommendations about corporations that he had made in his *Positive Program* well after writing it. For example, in his 1941 article entitled "For a Free-Market Liberalism," Simons still endorsed his policy recommendations for corporate reform that he had advanced in his *Positive Program* (Simons 1948, 101). And in 1943, Simons still maintained a strongly negative view of corporations: "The efficiency of gigantic corporations is usually a vestigial reputation earned during early, rapid growth – a memory of youth rather than an attribute of maturity. Grown large, they become essentially political bodies, run by lawyers, bankers, and specialized politicians, and persisting mainly to preserve the power of control groups and to reward unnaturally an admittedly rare talent for holding together enterprise aggregations which ought to collapse from excessive size" (1948, 246).

[11] Simons defined "economic efficiency" as: "an allocation such that units of every kind of productive service make equally important contributions to the social product in all the different uses among which they are transferable" (47).

Simons called for an "outright dismantling of … gigantic corporations" and "persistent prosecution" of producers who organized to restrict output or maintain price. He championed "unqualified repudiation of the so-called 'rule of reason,'" which he claimed granted absurd powers to corporations. He warned of the dangers of private mergers that resulted in monopoly power, "regardless of how reasonably that power may appear to be exercised," and recommended that vertical integration be permitted only when it did not harm the maintenance of effective competition. Simons demanded vigorous antitrust enforcement, maintaining that an antitrust violation ought to be considered "a major crime" and "prosecuted unremittingly by a vigilant administrative body" (Simons recommended the Federal Trade Commission).[12] In sum, according to Simons, "*there must be a complete 'new deal' with respect to the private corporation….* [The] corporation is simply running away with our economic (and political) system" (58).

Even though Simons acknowledged that the corporate firm served a useful social function by pooling resources in order to take advantage of otherwise unattainable economies of scale, corporate power needed to be checked by clearly established rules of the game. Simons's specific recommendations for corporate reform included: (1) the federal government, not states, should charter corporations, and the existing state-granted charters should be annulled; (2) a corporation that manufactures or sells goods and services should not have an ownership interest in another corporation; and (3) all corporations should have the amount of property they own limited, which should ensure that no single corporation dominates an industry.

As for Simons's policy recommendations that run counter to those typically supported by a proponent of classical liberalism, such as his call to gradually nationalize all industries for which competition could not serve as an effective regulatory agency (1948, 57), they should be understood not as an admission that classical liberalism was obsolete but – as Viner (1960) himself later argued – as an attempt to address exceptional economics circumstances in the inspiration of classical liberalism. (In Simons's case, the exceptional circumstance was the Great Depression.) It is worth noting that Simons himself privately confessed to using a "low, debating trick" when he

[12] In the mid-1940s, Simons also demonstrated his opposition to concentrations of business power when he approved of the role antitrust law played in preventing business monopoly. Indeed, Simons praised the antitrust crusade of Thurman Arnold, head of the United States Antitrust Division in the Department of Justice from 1937 to 1943. Simons had great admiration for Arnold: "One cannot deny that Arnold has done a magnificent job. The record is impressive, even when one makes every allowance for the favorable circumstances which he faced" (1948, 100).

called for the nationalization of certain industries.[13] Shortly after the publication of his pamphlet, Simons wrote to F. A. Hayek:

> Most of our so-called "liberals" and "New-Dealers" are really asking us to adopt for all industry a scheme of things closely comparable in essentials to that which we have been practicing in the case of the railroads. And I am willing to prostitute my judgment somewhat, in advocating government ownership, in order to vent my spleen fully as to the merit of a grand system of private monopoly with government regulation of prices and wages.[14]

In the conclusion of his pamphlet, Simons emphasized that his antimonopoly, anti-gigantic-corporation proposals would not only serve to help to maintain liberty, but also to prevent another Depression from happening in the future. In closing his *Positive Program*, Simons called for "the custodians of the great liberal traditions" to join him in order to stop the movement toward collectivism in the United States (1948, 77). Two young scholars swiftly responded to Simons's call. George Stigler and Allen Wallis, both graduate students at the University of Chicago at that time, wrote an editorial in the *New York Times* entitled "Problems of Competition." In it, they criticized a previously published editorial, written by a layperson. In doing so, they demonstrated their antimonopoly bias. For example, they stated: "It is … not correct to say that imperfect competition might by chance 'work out well for the common good,'" because convincing evidence demonstrated that "monopolization reduces the national income" (Wallis and Stigler 1934b).

In another editorial, Stigler and Wallis (1934) adduced Simons's *Positive Program* as an exemplar of great scholarship. They stated: "[E]conomics enables us to formulate … concrete and practical proposals for social policies, such, for example, as that contained in Professor Henry Simons's brilliant and suggestive 'A Positive Program for Laissez Faire.'" Indeed, Stigler himself later acknowledged in his *Memoirs* that Simons's *Positive Program* deeply influenced him (Stigler 1988); until the 1950s, he believed in the need for robust antimonopoly policies to safeguard competition. (For Stigler and Wallis's role in the rise of Chicago neoliberlism, see Nik-Khah, Chapter 5, this volume.)

Besides Stigler and Wallis, President Robert Hutchins and Milton Friedman were among the admirers of Simons's *Positive Program* affiliated with the University of Chicago. Because opposition to concentrations of business power was a central theme of Simons's pamphlet, this

[13] SPRL, December 18, 1934, box 3, file 40.
[14] Ibid.

suggests that they too adhered to Simons's classical liberal view on this matter, which further indicates that Simons's views were relatively pervasive at Chicago. Shortly after its publication, Hutchins distributed copies of Simons's *Positive Program* to prominent Washington officials, including the Secretary of the Interior Harold Ickes and the Secretary of the Treasury Henry Morgenthau.[15] Friedman later stated, "I thought at the time that [Simons's pamphlet] was strongly pro-free market in orientation" (quoted in Kitch 1983); for Friedman, calling a work "strongly pro-free market" amounted to high praise.

Aaron Director also concurred with Simons's views. In 1947, one year after Simons's untimely death, Director gave voice to Chicago classical liberalism in his Mont Pèlerin Society address.[16] Director echoed in many ways Simons's grave concern about concentrations of power. Director blamed the existing inequality of income and inequality of wealth on monopoly power in industry[17]; he condemned patents without qualification as a means to extend monopoly power and strongly criticized corporate law for the growth of monopoly; and he called for radical corporate reforms and basically gave voice to Simons's policy recommendations for corporate reform in the *Positive Program*.[18] Director also advocated that even more vigorous antitrust enforcement was necessary.

Director's critical attitude toward concentrations of power and his resultant policy advice were not surprising given that, according to Coase (1998, 602), Director considered Simons his "best friend" and mentor. Indeed, Director highly praised Simons's pamphlet just one year after his Mont Pèlerin address.[19] In fact, after he had befriended Simons, Director, in 1933, displayed for the first time strong skepticism toward concentrated business power. When commenting on business power, Director said: "Adam Smith said all that needs to be said on this point: 'People of the same trade seldom

[15] HPRL, box 72, folder 7.

[16] For background information on the Mont Pèlerin Society, see Peck; Van Horn and Klaes; and Nik-Khah, chapter 6, this volume.

[17] MPS1947LA, 84.

[18] Director stated: "The unlimited power of corporations must be removed. Excessive size can be challenged through the prohibition of corporate ownership of other corporations, through the elimination of interlocking directorates, through a limitation of the scope of activity of corporations, through increased control of enterprise by property owners and perhaps too through a direct limitation of the size of corporate enterprise" (MPS1947LA, 80).

[19] It is also not surprising that Director echoed Simons because Lloyd Mints, a colleague of Director and Simons, said in 1946 that Director was "in general agreement with [Simons's] position" SPRL, letter, Mints to Director, June 26, 1946, box 13, folder 1. For Director's praise of Simons's pamphlet in 1948, see Director (1948).

meet together, even for merriment and diversion, but the conversation ends in a conspiracy against the public, or in some contrivance to raise prices'" (1933, 24).

Notably, the later leaders of Chicago neoliberalism – Friedman, Director, Stigler, and Wallis – all extolled Simons's *Positive Program* and held Simons in high esteem. Simons himself attributed his strong skepticism of concentrations of power partly to Jacob Viner. Simons wrote: "A distinctive feature of 'Chicago economics,' as represented ... by Viner, is its traditional-liberal political philosophy – its emphasis on the virtues of dispersion of economic power (free markets) and of political decentralization."[20]

Indeed, Viner was a forceful critic of concentrations of business power. Viner considered himself an "Old-English Liberal" and believed that opposition to monopoly power was a cornerstone of that faith.[21] This echoed Viner's understanding of Adam Smith. According to Viner (1927, 198–199), Smith believed that private monopoly corrupted the natural order on which all economic phenomena depended.

Viner's own views on business monopoly in the late 1930s can be gleaned from his correspondence with Laird Bell, a distinguished attorney and public benefactor of Chicago. In writing Bell, Viner acknowledged that big business had some benefits, but emphasized, "the mere *size* of business units tends almost inevitably to result in attempts to escape the impact of competition which have important – and in my opinion highly desirable – consequences for the operation of the economic system." Viner considered this to be "*the* most important economic issue of our day" because "'bigness' ... *is* the essential element in the faulty working ... of our economic system."[22]

10.2. The Twentieth-Century Fund Project versus the Free Market Study

In 1948, Evens Clark of the Twentieth Century Fund (now called The Century Foundation)[23] wrote Viner and asked him to participate on an

[20] SPRL, undated, box 8, file 9. Although this file is undated, its contents suggest that Simons wrote it in the mid-1940s.

[21] VPML, letter, Viner to Douglas, June 3, 1945, box 9, folder 4.

[22] VPML, November 16, 1937, box 3, folder 33.

[23] During the 1940s and 1950s, the Twentieth Century Fund published reports (primarily focused on the United States) on various pressing social and economic issues – including labor, agriculture, international affairs, taxation, and electric power. Some examples of Twentieth Century Fund Studies from this time period include the following: Murray (1955), Burns and Caine (1948), Dewhurst et al. (1955), and Stewart and Dewhurst

Advisory Committee to evaluate the progress of a study by George Stocking and Myron Watkins, which would later be published as *Monopoly and Free Enterprise* (1951). Viner had recently commented on and praised two other Twentieth Century Fund studies, Stocking and Watkins's *Cartels or Competition?* and *Cartels in Action*,[24] both of which dealt with the issue of monopoly power.[25] Viner agreed to join the Advisory Committee, which also included James M. Landis (Chairman), A. S. Goss, Marion Hedges, Donald M. Nelson, J. Raymond Walsh, and Frank Surface.[26] Notably, Surface was an employee of the Standard Oil Company.[27]

In organizing the committee for the Stocking and Watkins investigation, the Twentieth Century Fund took pains to put together a committee that represented multiple perspectives with the hope that a higher quality manuscript would be produced. As Stocking and Watkins made progress on their manuscript, the Twentieth-Century Fund circulated portions of it among the committee members for commentary. The comments of the committee members would sometimes be circulated among the committee members as well as Stocking and Watkins. The committee members would also occasionally meet to discuss the manuscript and its progress in order to make recommendations. After the investigation was complete, the

(1939). The Twentieth Century Fund currently describes itself as an institution "committed to the belief that a mix of effective government, open democracy, and free markets is the most effective solution to the major challenges facing the United States." (See The Century Foundation. "The Century Foundation: An Overview." The Century Foundation Website. www.tcf.org/about.asp. Access date July 6, 2010.) Since its inception, part of the Fund's mission has included presenting academic research in language that the general public can understand. Evans Clark, the executive director of the fund in the immediate post–World War II period, wrote: "It is the Fund's hope that the educator, the clothing manufacturer, the cattle-man, the wheat farmer, the Federal Reserve Board member, the labor unionist, the senator from this state or that, the President himself, as well as the average citizen who wants to know what this economy of ours is all about – that each of them can find in this volume some of the basic facts he needs to do his job more intelligently" (Clark 1947, viii).

24 See Stocking and Watkins (1948) and Stocking and Watkins (1946).

25 VPML, letter, Viner to Clark, December 10, 1945, box 26, folder 15; VPML, letter, Viner to Clark, March 31, 1947, box 26, folder 15.

26 James M. Landis was the former Chairman of both the Civil Aeronautics Board and Securities and Exchange Commission, as well as the former Dean of Harvard Law School; A. S. Goss served as Master of The National Grange (Gross died before the manuscript was published); Marion Hedges was Special Assistant to the Labor Advisers, Economic Cooperation Administration; Donald M. Nelson was then the Chairman of Electronized Chemicals Cooperation and the former Chairman of the War Production Board; and J. Raymond Walsh was Director at Large, National Bureau of Economic Research.

27 In 1951, Surface was "Consultant to Management" for Standard Oil. In the mid-1940s, Surface headed the Sales Research office, coordinating sales research for both international and domestic subsidiaries (Chandler [1962], 221).

committee members produced a report, which was published as chapter 16, "A Program to Promote Competition," in *Monopoly and Free Enterprise.*

The conclusions and implications of *Monopoly and Free Enterprise* were twofold. First, Stocking and Watkins argued that the economic concentration in industry and the size of the business firm had greatly increased since the time of the Civil War and had reached the point that it was no longer justifiable on the basis of economies of scale. Second, they maintained that the increased concentration in each industry was likely to harm social welfare. The sellers in concentrated industries could utilize their power to control the market and could engage in concerted action without violating antitrust law.

Like the Chicago classical liberals, Stocking and Watkins opposed concentrations of business power and large corporations. Indeed, one reviewer of their manuscript, Neil Jacoby, said: "The Survey reflects a sound liberal (Manchester style) philosophy" (1951, 515). Like Simons, Stocking and Watkins advocated vigorous antitrust enforcement, maintained that much of advertising was wasteful, and claimed that the patent system needed to be overhauled. (See Van Horn and Klaes, this volume for Simons's views on patents.) Moreover, like Simons, Stocking and Watkins partly blamed corporate law for increased business concentration and suggested requiring federal incorporation to at least partly address the problem.

Surface, with the assistance of Courtney Brown, also an employee of Standard Oil, sharply criticized the classical-liberal bent of Stocking and Watkins. Surface claimed: "Certainly in the days of Adam Smith there was nothing like the modern corporation in existence. Yet we are trying to fit these concepts into the theories developed by Adam Smith."[28] Surface claimed that the study was essentially "a presentation of arguments designed to bolster preconceived theories of how our economic system should be organized."[29] In contrast to Stocking and Watkins as well as the Chicago classical liberals, Surface advanced the following contentions: (1) an industry of a few sellers was not necessarily an indication the industry probably lacked competition[30]; (2) a very large corporation was not incompatible with the public interest because of its size[31]; (3) business practices that might

[28] VPML, letter, Surface to Clark, September 30, 1949, box 26, folder 15.

[29] VPML, letter, Surface to Clark, August 26, 1948, box 26, folder 15.

[30] "It cannot be inferred that an industry is ineffectively competitive in the sense that public interest is not served, simply because it is characterized by a few large firms, or that the dissolution of such firms would necessarily make competition more effective" (VPML, letter, Brown to Clark, September 22, 1948, box 26, folder 15).

[31] "There is not too much evidence that the power of most corporations has been used to the disadvantage of the public" (VPML, letter, Surface to Clark, August 26, 1948, box 26, folder 15).

appear to be monopolistic practices were actually competitive tactics[32]; (4) it was doubtful whether there had been an increased concentration in many industries[33]; (5) the existence of monopoly power was not necessarily problematic[34]; and (6) the view that business monopoly should be destroyed or broken up into smaller units was pernicious.[35] Surface also faulted Stocking and Watkins for not examining the social and economic benefits of the corporation and strongly suggested that Stocking and Watkins insert a chapter to address this topic.

As he did for Stocking and Watkins, Surface suggested Viner used an outdated mode of economic analysis based on the economic philosophy of Adam Smith and criticized him for not being educated in modern business practices.[36] Surface's criticism of Viner is not at all surprising because Viner had no major criticisms of Stocking and Watkins's work. Indeed, Stocking considered Viner an ally and a proponent of deconcentration.[37] Like Stocking and Watkins, Viner believed business monopoly to be a pervasive and serious problem.[38] In a letter to Clark, Viner wrote:

> I perhaps should make it clear, as to my own position, that I have a bias … against monopoly as a method of economic organization, [and] have an overwhelming bias against it on moral and political grounds. Moreover, I think it is the major threat to the continuation of a free enterprise economy, pretty much regardless of its economic merits or demerits.[39]

The Committee Report, of which Viner approved, in many ways echoed Viner's grave concern about concentrations of power and his disdain for monopoly. To deal with the problem of concentrations of business power, the report, in a sense, offered a "positive program" for reform. It advocated vigorous antitrust enforcement and maintained that the Sherman Act should be amended to allow the government to prosecute big business solely on the grounds of its size. Although the report did not claim that concentrations of power should be unconditionally prosecuted, it maintained that concentrations of business power that harmed the public interest – which the report said would often be the case – should be broken up or regulated. Moreover,

32 VPML, letter, Brown to Clark, September 22, 1948, box 26, folder 15.

33 VPML, letter, Surface to Clark, April 25, 1949, box 26, folder 15.

34 Interestingly, in response to accusations along these lines, Surface said he liked to counter with the following analogy: "In a statement of this kind, I always like to refer back to the old illustration that you can use a brick to commit murder, but that hardly seems a reason to prohibit the manufacture of bricks" (Surface to Clark, April 25, 1949, box 26, folder 15).

35 VPML, letter, Surface to Clark, February 3, 1949, box 26, folder 15.

36 VPML, letter, Surface to Clark, September 30, 1949, box 26, folder 15.

37 VPML, letter, Stocking to J. Frederic Dewhurst, October 2, 1948, box 26, folder 15.

38 VPML, letter, Viner to Clark, November 8, 1948, box 26, folder 15.

39 VPML, letter, Viner to Clark, September 16, 1948, box 26, folder 15.

it maintained that the concentrations of power should be evaluated on the basis of both economic and noneconomic grounds and that the burden of proof should fall on the shoulders of business itself. Indeed, the report pointed out that even if a business could demonstrate that its concentration brought about increased economic efficiency, that business might still be found harmful to the public interest on noneconomic grounds. In order to increase antitrust enforcement, the report suggested that the appropriations to the Federal Trade Commission be increased and that the investigatory powers of the Federal Trade Commission be enhanced.[40] Like Simons's *Positive Program*, the report claimed that dispersing concentrations of industrial power would safeguard freedom, and if deleterious concentrations of power were not adequately dealt with, collectivism would be the very likely logical outcome. Indeed, as the epigraph by Viner suggests, big business needed to be protected from itself.

The members of the committee had the option to insert footnotes in the Committee Report to voice disagreement with its claims. Viner had very few objections; he only opted to insert a few short footnotes. Surface, however, peppered the Committee Report with footnotes that objected to the report's stern treatment of concentrations of business power. Nonetheless, Viner sincerely welcomed Surface's participation: "I am glad that we … have on the Committee vigorous and articulate apologists for monopoly."[41]

Surface primarily demonstrated his dissatisfaction with the Committee Report in its "Supplementary Comment," which was appended to the end of the Report. Surface maintained:

> [I]ndiscriminate attacks are being directed against large industry, apparently based on the specious theory that bigness is inherently bad and big companies are guilty

[40] In 1952, Stephen Spingarn of the Federal Trade Commission used the Committee Report as evidence that funds to the Federal Trade Commission should be increased (SSTL, "General Statement in Support of Federal Trade Commission Request to the Bureau of the Budget for More Adequate Appropriations for the Fiscal Year 1954," October 14, 1952, box 49, file: "Federal Trade Commission File Anti-Monopoly Conference").

[41] VPML, letter, Viner to Clark, November 8, 1948, box 26, folder 15. Interestingly, contrary to Surface's claim that Stocking and Watkins should extract all traces of opinion from their investigation and thereby make their investigation objective, Viner maintained, "I find it hard to imagine how the monopoly problem can be dealt with in significant terms if the rule of elimination of all expressions of opinion is strictly interpreted." Indeed, Viner stated:

> I do not think it is practical to write an elaborate work on the working of economic process in modern society on a completely "objective" basis.… Anyone who could do so would be pathological, and the pathology would be likely to extend to his selection of premises – it is always necessary to begin somewhere, but where one begins can have great influence on where one ends up – and on his decisions as to what are facts and what myths. In so far as is possible, value-judgments, should be labeled as such, but their systematic exclusion is, I am convinced, not in practice either possible or desirable. They should not be concealed, they should not be eccentric, and they should not be elaborated or didactically pressed.

of misuse of power until proved innocent. Such attacks are not in the public interest. They represent a purely negative approach to certain important questions about industrial concentration that call for constructive solutions. (Surface 1951, 570)

Surface claimed that big enterprise greatly contributed to the strength of the U.S. economy and maintained that the Committee Report, if its policy recommendations to crack down on concentrations of business power were put into practice, would significantly damage the U.S. economy.

While Viner participated on the Twentieth Century Fund Committee on monopoly and free enterprise, the Free Market Study, which began in the fall of 1946, was under way. Prior to 1950, members of the Free Market Study sounded very much like Henry Simons. Like Simons, they feared concentrations of power, wanted to implement radical reforms to address problems that stemmed from the modern corporation, criticized patents as means for firms to extend monopoly power, advocated vigorous antitrust enforcement, and believed the problem of industrial monopoly to be relatively widespread.[42] However, during the course of the Free Market Study's effort to reconstitute liberalism, its initial positions on concentrations of business power dramatically changed, signaling the birth and rise of Chicago neoliberalism. This change would at least in part be shaped by the Study's attempt to respond to collectivism.

At the second meeting of the study, in the fall of 1946, Director distributed a research proposal entitled: "A Program of Factual Research into Questions Basic to the Formulation of a Liberal Economic Policy." By empirically investigating the facts taken for granted by both liberals and their opponents, Director believed it would be possible to develop a robust liberal policy to counter collectivism and thereby bring about policy changes in the United States. In this spirit, the Free Market Study analyzed the topic of industrial monopoly. It sought to challenge its opponents on the Left, the "collectivists," who interpreted the rise of monopoly as inevitable, predicting that the forces of competition would prove ineffectual in the face of such growth and thus insisting that the only rational solution was socialist control of the economy.[43] In short, Director and the other members of the Free Market Study sought to challenge what might be called the "inevitability thesis," which, according to Director, gave rise to collectivism (1951, v).

Director believed that if an objective empirical study could demonstrate that competition prevailed over monopoly in the absence of government

[42] For the ways the Free Market Study during its early years tended to represent Simons, see Van Horn (2009).

[43] See, for example, Tarshis (1946).

support, then the position of the Left would be undermined.[44] The Free Market Study challenged the inevitability thesis through the doctoral work of Warren Nutter. Nutter, under the supervision of Director, O. H. Brownlee, and Milton Friedman, wrote his dissertation at the University of Chicago in association with the Study. Nutter completed his dissertation in 1949, and the University of Chicago Press published it two years later as *The Extent of Enterprise Monopoly in the United States, 1899–1939.*

Nutter undertook an empirical study on the extent of business monopoly in the United States and, contrary to what Stocking and Watkins's investigation suggested, found that there had been no significant increase in business monopoly since 1900. Because proponents of the inevitability thesis maintained that monopoly had been substantially increasing, Nutter's investigation dealt a sharp blow by suggesting that the Left had exaggerated the growth of monopoly and thus was mistaken about its inevitability.

Besides reconsidering its position that industrial monopoly was relatively prevalent, the Free Market Study and its sister project, the Antitrust Project (1952–1956), arrived at a host of claims that sharply diverged from its pre-1950 claims that had been inspired by the classical-liberal opposition to concentrations of power. By the mid-1950s, Director and other members of the Free Market Study no longer saw industrial monopoly as pervasive and threatening, no longer viewed large corporations as deleterious to competition, no longer maintained that corporate power had to be reigned in through legal reform, and no longer championed vigorous antitrust enforcement. The Free Market Study's position that concentrations of business power were relatively benign marked the rise of Chicago neoliberalism.

The neoliberal claims of the Free Market Study diverged sharply from those of the Stocking and Watkins investigation. Stocking and Watkins maintained that a concentrated industry was harmful to the economy and society because the firms in that industry would abuse their market power. The Free Market Study, on the other hand, maintained that firms in concentrated industries tended to act competitively as opposed to abusively. Additionally, unlike Stocking and Watkins, the Free Market Study adopted a relatively sanguine attitude toward large corporations and claimed they approximated the impersonal ideal of the market. The Free Market Study and the Antitrust Project also had a great deal more faith than Stocking and Watkins in the power of competition to undermine monopoly power and thus recommended lessening antitrust enforcement.

44 FPHI, October 30, 1946, box 79, folder 4.

Ironically, in their effort to reconstitute liberalism, Director and other members of the Free Market Study ended up sharply departing from Viner and Simons's forceful opposition to concentrations of power and thereby aligned themselves – albeit unwittingly – more closely with the views of Frank Surface of Standard Oil.

10.3. Jacob Viner's Critique of Chicago Neoliberalism

In 1958, Director invited Viner to give the second annual "Henry Simons Lecture."[45] In 1959, when Viner delivered his address, he again demonstrated his hostility toward big business and concentrations of power, and he rooted this hostility in the tradition of Adam Smith:

> The classical exponents of laissez faire always qualified their enthusiasm for the free market by the condition that it should be a competitive market. Adam Smith ... intensely disliked monopoly in all its forms. He regarded merchants as perpetual seekers of monopoly power. Also, because he thought that in all but routine activities they would inevitably be inefficient, he disliked all large-scale privately owned companies. (1960, 65)

In light of this classical liberal view of monopoly, Viner lamented the state of the contemporary market structure: "[M]onopoly is so prevalent in the markets of the western world today" (1960s, 66). Indeed, Viner claimed that anyone who championed the virtues of the competitive market as if it existed or would exist in the future egregiously overlooked the ubiquity of monopoly. Viner called for a challenge to monopoly practices: "[G]iven the prevalence or danger of substantial intrusion of monopoly into the market, the logic of the laissez-faire defense of the market against state-intervention collapses and there is called for instead, by its very logic, state-suppression or state-regulation of monopoly practices" (67).

Even though Viner advocated the suppression and regulation of monopoly, and thereby indicated that the government needed to adopt a positive role in the economy, he still considered himself a classical liberal. Viner indicated that classical liberals sometimes had to advocate a positive state role "in the case of emergency or abnormal conditions" (1960, 46) – in Viner's case, immense monopoly power. Likewise, Viner suggested that Simons's *Positive Program* was in the spirit of classical liberalism and was an attempt to use positive state action to address an economic emergency,

[45] VPML, October 27, 1958, Viner to Director, box 8, folder 21. The Chicago Law School established a lecture series in honor of Henry Simons, and George Stigler gave the premier lecture (VPML, October 22, 1958, Director to Viner, box 8, folder 21).

the Great Depression, which Simons had claimed stemmed to a large extent from large corporations and monopoly power.

Once we acknowledge that Viner and Simons were classical liberals and opposed all forms of concentrations of power, it is then possible to more fully appreciate the radical departure from classical liberalism in the early 1950s during the Free Market Study. Simons would have rejected the Chicago neoliberal claims of the Free Market Study, and Viner did reject them. Unlike the Free Market Study, which maintained that large corporations and industrial monopoly were relatively benign forces in the economy, Viner and Simons considered them relatively deleterious forces in the economy, and unlike the Free Market Study, which claimed that the prevalence of business monopoly and its power were grossly exaggerated, Viner and Simons claimed that business monopoly and its power was indeed prevalent as well as seriously problematic.

It is also then possible to appreciate that it is premature to claim that the Free Market Study adopted a far less critical attitude toward concentrations of business power solely because of its empirical investigations. Viner, as Gary Becker (1993, 761) points out, highly valued testing claims with empirical and historical evidence. Nonetheless, even though Nutter's empirical analysis indicated that the extent of industrial monopoly had changed little since 1900, and other related empirical studies by Chicago economists – such as Harberger (1954) – suggested that business monopoly was relatively benign, Viner still forcefully opposed concentrations of business power and claimed such concentrations of power were prevalent in his Chicago Law School address. Although it is beyond the scope of this chapter to examine why the members of the Free Market Study changed their views and why Viner did not, the analysis in this chapter suggests that Viner's continued opposition stemmed at least in part from his steadfast faith in classical liberalism and in part from the fact that he valued studies – for example, Stocking and Watkins's 1951 investigation – conducted in the spirit of classical liberalism.

Contrasting Viner's 1960 conception of concentrations of business power with Friedman's views in *Capitalism and Freedom* (1962) is also instructive. In his book, Friedman trumpeted the benefits of the competitive market and echoed the conclusion of the Free Market Study. Adducing the work of Warren Nutter, Friedman claimed that the extent of the industrial monopoly was not a serious problem. He maintained that because of this, and because he presumed that large corporations approximated the impersonal ideal of the market there was, in his words, "[a] wide … range of … industries for which it is appropriate to treat the economy as if it were competitive" ([1962], 120).

Just two years before the publication of Friedman's book, Viner, however, viewed proclamations of the benefits of free competitive markets and statements that concentrations of business power were not pervasive as pernicious. Commenting on the enormity of the concentration of power in the economy, Viner said: "[D]iscussion of the merits of the free competitive market as if that were what we were living with or were at all likely to have the good fortune to live with in the future seem to me academic in the only pejorative sense of that adjective" (1960, 66). The contrast between Viner's perception of business monopoly and Friedman's perception of it is stark because Viner remained rooted in the classical liberal tradition of Chicago economics and never adopted the Chicago neoliberal position that large corporations and industrial monopoly were relatively benign.

One might object that because Friedman's *Capitalism and Freedom* called for the elimination of all government support of business monopoly and for the enforcement of antitrust laws, suggesting that Friedman was pro-corporate relative to Viner would be inaccurate. However, Friedman's call to action, when considered in light of the findings of the Free Market Study and the Antitrust Project and when contrasted with Simons and Viner's call to action against concentrations of business power, essentially has little to no practical significance for industrial monopoly and large corporations per se. First of all, contrary to Simons and Viner, Friedman claimed that the extent of monopoly was greatly exaggerated and most markets should be treated "as if" they are competitive.[46] Second, the Antitrust Project found in the 1950s that a broad range of antitrust enforcement was unacceptable. For example, Robert Bork, contrary to Supreme Court precedent, claimed that all forms of vertical integration should be legal, and Ward Bowman, again contrary to Supreme Court precedent, found that tying arrangements should not be per se illegal. Furthermore, the Antitrust Project adopted a favorable attitude toward rule of reason analysis. Under the rule of reason, the courts had to determine whether an unreasonable restraint of trade occurred.[47] Simons, however, repudiated the use of the rule of reason by the courts because he believed that unambiguous and unequivocal rules of the game should guide antitrust enforcement: "[When] lawyers try to draw a line

[46] According to Friedman, "[As] I have studied economic activities in the United States, I have become increasingly impressed with how wide is the range of problems and industries for which it is appropriate to treat the economy as if it were competitive" (120).

[47] According to the rule of reason, "The courts were to determine reasonableness by considering the conditions leading to the adoption of the restraint, the effects of the restraint, actual and probable, and the intentions of the participants, as indicated by their actions" (Dietz 1951, 8).

between lawful and unlawful restraint of trade, they invariably end up with something that looks like the silhouette of a roller-coaster.... The purpose may be laudable; but the result is that few people get caught, rather fortuitously, and the growth of monopoly, with perhaps some formal modification, proceeds apace" (1948, 101). Simons also claimed that the rule of reason granted absurd powers to corporations (1948, 42–43). In light of the findings of the Antitrust Project, Friedman's call for antitrust enforcement is significantly limited in scope and vigor. Third, in contrast to Simons, Friedman never condemned corporations, except those that harmed the market due to government support. Friedman suggested that if a corporation did do wrong, then that action must have stemmed from some pernicious government policy – hence, Philip Mirowski's aphorism: "Corporations can do no wrong, or at least they are not to be blamed if they do" (Mirowski 2009, 438). Fourth, Friedman's *Capitalism and Freedom* offered no policy prescriptions to address corporate power tantamount to those found in Simons's *Positive Program* and Director's 1947 Mont Pèlerin address. Simons and Director in 1947 considered limiting the size of corporations, eliminating interlocking directorates, forbidding all forms of mergers, circumscribing the scope of corporate activities, and more (see Chapter 7 of this volume). In Friedman's work, there is nothing remotely close to Director's 1947 proclamation: "The unlimited power of corporations must be removed."[48] Friedman's call for antitrust enforcement is relatively limited in scope and without vigor – it is practically an empty call to action. (Indeed, Friedman condemns an instance of government antitrust action just a couple pages after his call for antitrust enforcement.) Additionally, Friedman's call for the elimination of the direct government support of business monopoly is essentially a condemnation of government. In sum, Friedman (and eventually Director, too) advocated strong pro-corporate policy prescriptions relative to the tradition of Simons and Viner.

Once we acknowledge that the classical liberal concern about concentrations of business power motivated the policy recommendations of Simons and Viner and that the emerging neoliberalism at Chicago was devoid of this motivation, this prompts the question: What other departures from the Chicago tradition of classical liberalism transpired? Although this chapter is too limited to address this question in full, Chapter 7 of this volume makes a contribution toward this end: The Chicago classical liberal tradition was broadly hostile to patents and condemned their monopoly increasing

[48] MPS1947LA, p.80.

capabilities, whereas Chicago neoliberalism broadly accepted patents and maintained that their monopoly-increasing capabilities were few.

10.4. Concluding Remarks

Viner believed a cornerstone of classical liberalism was the opposition to concentrations of business power. While some of his students once thought similarly, because of the rise of Chicago neoliberalism during the Free Market Study and the Antitrust Project, Viner, by the 1950s, found himself to be a critic of Director and his other former students. Contrary to Viner, as well as Simons, the Chicago neoliberals believed concentrations of power were relatively benign. Indeed, because Viner referred to Frank Surface of Standard Oil as an "apologist" for monopoly, and because the position of the Chicago neoliberals on concentrations of business power was similar to that of Surface, Viner most probably would have considered Director and other members of the Free Market Study and the Antitrust Project apologists for business monopoly as well.

About twenty years after Viner delivered his Chicago Law School speech, in 1983, Director, Friedman, Stigler, and other members of the Chicago School gathered to reflect on the rise of the postwar Chicago School.[49] During their colloquy, they conversed about Simons's *Positive Program*. Even though Director, Friedman, Stigler, and Wallis all had extolled Simons's pamphlet prior to the rise of Chicago neoliberalism, they offered Simons's work only faint applause – if any applause at all. If they had discussed Viner's Law School address, they, in all likelihood, would have frowned upon their former teacher's strong opposition to concentrations of power and his endorsement of Simons's *Positive Program*. Much had changed since the time that they were all Chicago classical liberals.

References

Archival Sources

FPHI	Milton Friedman Papers, Hoover Institution
HPRL	Robert Hutchins Papers, Regenstein Library, University of Chicago.
MPS1947LA	Records of the 1947 meeting, Mont Pèlerin Society, Liberaal Archief, Ghent Belgium
SPRL	Henry Simons Papers, Regenstein Library, University of Chicago
SSTL	Stephen Spingarn Papers, Harry Truman Presidential Library
UCPP	University of Chicago Press Papers, Regenstein Library, University of Chicago

[49] See Kitch (1983)

VPML Jacob Viner Papers, Public Policy Papers, Department of Rare Books and Special Collections, Princeton University Mudd Library.

Published Sources

Becker, Gary. 1993. "George Joseph Stigler." *Journal of Political Economy*. 101(5): 761–767.

Benedict, Murray R. 1955. *Can We Solve the Farm Problem? An Analysis of Federal Aid to Agriculture*. New York: Twentieth Century Fund.

Burns, Arthur R. and Caine, Walter E. 1948. *Electric Power and Government Policy*. New York: Twentieth Century Fund.

Chandler, Alfred D. [1962] 1990. *Strategy and Structure*. Cambridge, MA: Massachusetts Institute of Technology Press.

Clark, Evans. 1947. "Foreward." In *America's Needs and Resources*. By Dewhurst, J. Frederic and associates. New York: The Twentieth Century Fund.

Coase, Ronald. 1998. "Aaron Director." In *The New Palgrave Dictionary of Economics and the Law*. ed. Paul Newman. New York: Macmillan.

Dewhurst, J. Frederick and associates. 1955. *America's Needs and Resources: A New Survey*. New York: Twentieth Century Fund.

Dietz, Arthur T. 1951. *An Introduction to the Antitrust Laws*. New York: Bookman Associates.

Director, Aaron. 1933. *The Economics of Technocracy*. Chicago: University of Chicago Press.

1948. "Prefatory Note." In *Economic Policy for a Free Society*. Chicago: University of Chicago Press. Pp. v–vii.

Friedman, Milton. [1962] 2002. *Capitalism and Freedom*. Chicago: University of Chicago Press.

Harberger, Arnold. 1954. "Monopoly and Resource Allocation." *The American Economic Review*, 44(2), Papers and Proceedings of the Sixty-sixth Annual Meeting of the American Economic Association: 77–87.

Hawley, Ellis W. [1966] 1995. *The New Deal and the Problem of Monopoly*. New York: Fordham University Press.

Jacoby, Neil. 1951. "Perspectives on Monopoly." *Journal of Political Economy* 59(6): 514–527.

Kitch, Edmund W. (ed.). 1983. "The Fire of Truth: A Remembrance of Law and Economics at Chicago, 1932–1970." *Journal of Law & Econ*. 26: 163–234.

Knight, Frank H. 1946. "The Sickness of Liberal Society." *Ethics*. 56(2): 79–95.

Mirowski, Philip. 2009. "Postface: Defining Neoliberalism." In *The Road from Mont Pelerin*, ed. P. Mirowski and D. Plehwe. Cambridge: Harvard University Press.

Nutter, G. Warren. 1951. *The Extent of Enterprise Monopoly in the United States, 1899–1939*. Chicago: University of Chicago Press.

Samuelson, Paul A. 1972. "Economics in a Golden Age: A Personal Memoir." In *The Twentieth-Century Sciences: Studies in the Biography of Ideas*, ed. Gerald Holton, New York: W. W. Norton. Pp. 155–70.

Simons, Henry C. 1948. *Economic Policy for a Free Society*. Chicago: University of Chicago Press.

Stewart, Paul W. and Dewhurst , J. Frederic. 1939. *Does Distribution Cost Too Much?* New York: The Twentieth Century Fund.

Stigler, George. 1988. *Memoirs of an Unregulated Economist*. New York: Basic Books.

Stocking, George Ward and Watkins, Myron Webster. 1946. *Cartels in Action: Case Studies in International Business Diplomacy*. New York: The Twentieth Century Fund.

1948. *Cartels or Competition? The Economics of International Controls by Business and Government*. New York: The Twentieth Century Fund.

1951. *Monopoly and Free Enterprise*. New York: Twentieth Century Fund.

Surface, Frank M. 1951 "Supplementary Comment." In Stocking, George Ward and Watkins, Myron Webster, eds., *Monopoly and Free Enterprise*. New York: Twentieth Century Fund. Pp. 569–571.

Tarshis, Lorie. 1946. *The Elements of Economics*. Boston: Houghton Mifflins Co.

Van Horn, Robert. 2009. "Reinventing Monopoly and the Role of Corporations." In *The Road from Mont Pèlerin*, ed. P. Mirowski and D. Plehwe. Cambridge, MA: Harvard University Press.

forthcoming. "Comrades in Arms: An Exploration of the Political and Intellectual Relationship of F. A. Hayek and Aaron Director." *The Journal of the History of Economic Thought*.

Van Horn, Robert and Mirowski, Philip. 2009. "The Rise of the Chicago School of Economics and the Birth of Neoliberalism." In *The Road from Mont Pèlerin*, ed. P. Mirowski and D. Plehwe. Cambridge, MA: Harvard University Press.

Viner, Jacob. 1927. "Adam Smith and Laissez Faire." *The Journal of Political Economy* 35(2): 198–232.

1960. "The Intellectual History of Laissez Faire." *The Journal of Law and Economics* 3: 45–69.

Wallis, Allen and Stigler, George. 1934. "Professor Simons' Book." Letter to the Editor. *New York Times*. December 24, 1934.

1934b. "Problems of Competition." Letter to the Editor. *New York Times*. December 7, 1934.

ELEVEN

The Chicago School, Hayek, and Neoliberalism

Bruce Caldwell

The tracing of influences is the most treacherous ground in the history of thought.
– F.A. Hayek [1952] 1979, *The Counter-Revolution of Science*, 358.

Friedrich A. Hayek taught at the University of Chicago from the fall semester of 1950 through 1962, a period during which the second, or new, Chicago School of Economics was formed.[1] The question naturally arises: What was his role in its formation?

A quick look at the historical record, and common sense itself, suggests that it must have been close to nil. Milton Friedman, whom many would consider the central figure in the School, was hired in 1946, before Hayek had arrived. Hayek tried to get a job in the economics department in 1948, but they declined to make him an offer. He ended up instead on the Committee on Social Thought. During his time at Chicago (1950–1962)

I originally prepared a paper entitled "Hayek and the Chicago School" for the Conference on the Chicago School of Economics, held at Notre Dame University on September 14–16, 2007. This greatly revised, and retitled, paper draws only in part on the earlier one, and principally responds to two papers, listed in the bibliography as Van Horn-Mirowski 2008 and Van Horn 2008. The two papers that I was responding to were widely circulated before they ultimately were published as Van Horn-Mirowski 2009, Van Horn 2009, and part of one of them appeared in Mirowski 2009. Rather than trying to modify my page references from the original two papers to their subsequent publication in three, I have retained the page references from the original two papers.

All quotations from F. A. Hayek appear with the permission of the Estate of F. A. Hayek. I received useful comments on earlier drafts from Craufurd Goodwin, Wade Hands, and Roy Weintraub, as well as from members of the History of Political Economy workshop at Duke University, but all commentators are exempted from responsibility for any views expressed in the paper.

[1] As the definition of "the Chicago School" is evidently contestable and contested ground, I leave it undefined, and instead simply mention here some of the principals often associated with the term: Milton Friedman, Aaron Director, Gary Becker, and George Stigler – the last of whom did not arrive in Chicago until 1958.

Hayek worked principally on political philosophy rather than economics, with *The Constitution of Liberty* (1960) being the end result. And Hayek famously disagreed with the leader of the Chicago School, Milton Friedman, on monetary theory and methodology, two of the defining aspects of Friedman's legacy.

Consistent with the sentiments expressed by Hayek in the opening quotation, this paper will serve as a warning against *quick* looks at historical records (though I hope not against the use of common sense!) in untangling questions of influence. In a remarkable recent paper (henceforth VHM 2008), Rob Van Horn and Phil Mirowski offer a compelling revisionist account of the formation of the Chicago School(s), one that places Hayek, Henry Simons, and Aaron Director at the heart of the action.[2] Their paper is based on a meticulous investigation of the relevant archival documents. After briefly summarizing some of their most important findings, I will offer a few comments about their reading of the historical record. Most of these involve small quibbles. In general, I find their new interpretation quite convincing.

Unfortunately, that account is part of a larger narrative about the roles of the Chicago School and the Mont Pèlerin Society in the formation of what Van Horn and Mirowski term "neoliberalism." This larger narrative relies much less on archival material and contains claims (often in the form of hints and innuendoes) that have not been substantiated. In my opinion, the larger narrative is deeply flawed and should be kept separate from the fine archive-based research just mentioned. In later sections of the paper I will offer reasons for this judgment, and in the process offer alternative explanations to those provided by VHM about the relationship between Hayek, the Chicago School, and neoliberalism.

11.1. Hayek's "Indispensable and Pivotal Role" in Creating the School – The Van Horn–Mirowski Thesis

The salient details of VHM's account of the origins of the Chicago School may be quickly sketched. As background, the American edition of Hayek's book *The Road to Serfdom* was published in September, 1944. It sold fairly briskly, but was not a best-seller. Everything changed, however, when a *Reader's Digest* condensation by Max Eastman appeared in April 1945.

[2] I say School(s) because it is part of their thesis that, due to Director's influence, the Chicago School of Economics and the Law and Economics program at the Law School grew up together.

Counting the original article and a subsequent Book-of-the-Month Club reprint, nearly 10 million copies of the condensation were produced. The condensation came out while Hayek was in transit by ship to the United States – he was coming to do a speaking tour to promote the book. He had envisioned a rather low-key affair in which he would speak principally to a few academic audiences. By the time he had arrived, the tour had been handed over to a professional promotional agency and he ended up giving talks to all manner of groups (Caldwell, in Hayek 2007, 18–20).

One of these was the Detroit Economics Club, where he talked on April 23, 1945. Harold Luhnow, president of the Volker Fund, was in the audience, and he arranged a meeting with Hayek. Luhnow proposed that Hayek write an American *Road to Serfdom*, a project that the Volker Fund would underwrite. Hayek was not willing to undertake the project himself, but suggested in a letter sent from England on May 3 that Friedrich Lutz at Princeton might do it, or alternatively that "a number of people" at Chicago might be brought in (VHM 2008, 3). As the Chicago reference suggests, Hayek had discussed the Luhnow proposal with some Chicago academics, most importantly Henry Simons, an economist working at the Law School and author of *A Positive Program for Laissez Faire* ([1934] 1948).

For his part, Simons saw Luhnow's proposal as an opportunity for coaxing his friend Aaron Director back to Chicago from Washington, DC, where the latter had been working during the war in a government office. By June 1945, Simons had prepared a memorandum that proposed an institute, with Director as director, that would publish both "scholarly and semi-popular literature" concerned with "political philosophy and practical problems of economic policy" (VHM 2008, 10). The institute was to run for twenty years. (This was, of course, quite a different animal from what Luhnow had wanted.) A meeting was held in Washington later that month to discuss Simons's proposal, with Simons, Director, Friedman, Herbert Stein, Homer Jones, and Fritz Machlup in attendance. Alternative proposals with shorter time frames and a greater emphasis on empirical work were advanced by some of the discussants.[3] Perhaps most important, Director was not convinced that he should leave Washington to direct the institute, which must have been a real disappointment for Simons.

Both Director and Simons reported on the meeting to Hayek, who in July corresponded with Luhnow to tell him that although he had not identified

[3] Though no detailed account of the discussion at the meeting has surfaced, the proposed switch in emphasis away from philosophy and toward empirical work presumably reflected the influence of Milton Friedman.

anyone to do the American *Road to Serfdom*, he was willing to come to the States in 1946 to try again. In the meantime, he noted that there were other initiatives that Luhnow might want to support, and included Simons's memo about the Chicago institute as well as his own proposal for the formation of an international Acton-Tocqueville Society, an entity that would ultimately become the Mont Pèlerin Society. In his August reply, Luhnow did not bite; he wanted an American *Road to Serfdom*, not these other proposals.

The Volker Fund was, however, willing to finance Hayek's 1946 visits to Chicago and Stanford. By the time the trip took place, the Simons proposal had morphed into something closer to what Luhnow wanted: a Free Market Study, based in Chicago, again with Director at the head, and with various others (among them Milton Friedman, who would be joining the economics department faculty in the fall) contributing research. The study would produce, possibly within three years, a work of a semipopular character that detailed the role of a free market in the allocation of goods and in the promotion of political and economic freedom. A critical provision was that Director be offered a tenured position in the Law School following a Volker-funded five-year period that was to be devoted to research for and the writing of the book. Although the Law School agreed, the proposal to grant Director tenure automatically after five years was shot down by the Central Administration in a meeting in early June. Without Director, the project fell through. Shortly thereafter (June 19) Henry Simons died, having overdosed on sleeping pills. As VHM (19) note, "Given the precise timing, it is difficult not to imagine some connection between Simons' suicide and the Director snafu."

Although Simons's death was a both a tragedy in itself and seemingly disastrous in its consequences for the project, things were made even worse by the discovery that the rejection of Director may have rested on a misunderstanding. Soon after being notified of Simons's death, Director heard from the dean of the Law School that another plan, in which Director would come to the Law School on Volker money for five years, but without the subsequent guarantee of tenure, was on the table. Director wrote to Hayek to ask what he should do. Hayek urged him to accept, which Director did. Hayek's role in convincing Director to come to Chicago, according to VHM (20), "demonstrates Hayek's indispensable and pivotal role in the creation of the Chicago School."

Van Horn and Mirowski are to be commended for providing this new and, in its broad outline, compelling account of the origins of the Chicago School. Given the facts of the case, as summarized previously, it is clear that both Henry Simons and Friedrich Hayek played important parts in the construction of the Chicago School: As VHM put it, Hayek might be viewed as "the prime external contractor" and Simons as "the prime architect." At the end of the day, however, I think that Simons played the most important part – to change metaphors, he was the leading man. I would further add to their account that "chance" should be credited with playing an important supporting role – meaning that, as is often the case in historical episodes, the ultimate outcome had a lot to do with the unintended consequences of the actions of many unrelated individuals.

Let us turn first to the relative weights to be given to Simons versus Hayek. Though it was Hayek whom Luhnow in the first instance contacted, it was Simons who was keen to use the opportunity to draw Director back to Chicago. Had Simons not stepped in, Hayek doubtless would have pursued Friedrich Lutz at Princeton, who apparently was his first choice to write an American *Road to Serfdom*.[4] Note too that it was Simons who transformed Luhnow's invitation to write a book into a wholly different vision, the formation of an institute that would establish the University of Chicago as a base for the study of free market ideas. As Aaron Director would write in his 1947 "Prefatory Note" to Simons's posthumously published *Economic Policy for a Free Society*, "Through his writings and more especially through his teaching at the University of Chicago, he [Simons] was slowly establishing himself as the head of a 'school'" (Director, in Simons 1948, v). Hayek, of course, wanted to use Luhnow money for a very different purpose, namely helping to fund the Mont Pèlerin Society, a project that he had had in mind since at least 1944, and probably since 1938.[5] Hayek's 1946 trip was aimed at trying to get the American *Road to Serfdom* (now transformed to the Free Market Study) under way, but he was also trying to arrange funding and identify participants for the first meeting of the Society. In this he was successful: The meeting took place in April of the next year, and the Volker Fund sprang for the travel costs of the American contingent. All of this suggests that it was Simons who had the vision of creating a school in Chicago,

[4] Though in 1945 Hayek was not looking for a job in the States, two years later he was trying to get a job at Princeton. He may well have had in the back of his mind the possibility of a future job at Princeton when he thought of Lutz as a candidate for Luhnow's book project.

[5] Hayek delivered a paper at the Political Society at King's College, Cambridge, in February 1944 in which he called for the formation of an Acton Society which would be financed by private funds. See Hayek [1967] 1992, 203, 209 ff. In 1938 he participated in the Colloque Lippmann in Paris. In an interview on February 27, 1984, in which he was speaking about the beginnings of the Mont Pèlerin Society, Hayek said, "the origin of it all was really the conference of Walter Lippmann in 1938."

whereas Hayek's vision of creating an international society (though complementary, to be sure) was decidedly different.

I would also place less weight than do VHM on Hayek's letter of July 10, 1946, in which he urged Director to accept the new offer from the Law School.[6] It seems quite appropriate, given the death of Simons, that Director would first notify Hayek and, as it were, get his blessings on any new plan (it was, after all, frequently referred to by the principals as "the Hayek project") before accepting an offer. And, given Director's letter, *of course* Hayek was going to say that he thought that Director should accept. On this reading, what was said in the exchange between Director and Hayek was pro forma, and indeed almost obligatory on both sides. I think that it was Simons's death that convinced Director to take the job, not Hayek's letter.[7]

What about the chance elements? Simply put, they were everywhere in this story. Had there been no *Reader's Digest* condensation of *The Road to Serfdom*, Luhnow, who from VHM's account does not strike one as a deep reader, would probably never have heard of F. A. Hayek.[8] The story of how

6 VHM (2008, 20) note that the crucial line in Hayek's letter to Director read as follows: "I do want to say that in a sense it would seem to me even more important than before that you should accept...."

7 That Director would oversee the republication of Simons's works suggests that he felt some kind of obligation toward his recently deceased friend, if not some responsibility. This was in any event Hayek's own view, which he shared in an interview with Bill Bartley at the Hoover Institution in October, 1983: "[In 1946] I spent 6 weeks each in Chicago and Stanford, concentrating and trying to persuade Henry Simons at Chicago to do it. Simons consented on one condition, that Aaron Director (who is here [that is, at the Hoover Institution] now) was willing to collaborate with him. And Aaron Director refused to do that. He was then in Washington in government service. I'd hardly left Chicago when Henry Simons died. He killed himself with an overdose of sleeping pills, but some people said he had the habit, every time he woke up, to take more. This happens. The curious reaction of Aaron Director was that now he saw it as his duty to continue. This led to the appointment of Aaron Director at the Law School, with the aim that he should write an American *Road to Serfdom*, which he never did. But it initiated a lot of activity of Mr. Luhnow, and I think the man turned completely crazy in the end."

In their text, Van Horn and Mirowski repeatedly refer to Simons's death as a suicide. Unless there was a suicide note (and if there was, they offer no evidence of one), the possibility suggested by Hayek – that it was an accidental overdose – must be taken seriously. Without evidence, it seems to me in poor taste simply to label it a suicide. Nor is it necessary for the story: The *possibility* that it was a suicide would, I think, have been enough to convince Director to come back to Chicago to take up the work that his friend Simons had begun.

8 Like many others, presumably Luhnow only knew the condensation, not the book. According to VHM (2008, 14) Luhnow "suggested the book *How We Live* by Fred G. Clark (1944) as a stylistic model for the *American Road to Serfdom*. One doubts if Hayek had ever seen a copy, for if he had, he would have immediately soured on Luhnow. *How We Live* was a large print book, with didactic pictures facing each page of 'text,' which itself consisted of single sentence paragraphs written for people who still moved their lips as they read. The quality of argument resembled a fourth-grade civics textbook."

the condensation came to be is itself also rather remarkable: Apparently Harry Gideonse had a chance encounter with a press staffer on the train into Chicago one day, and suggested that a copy of *The Road to Serfdom* be sent to Max Eastman. Eastman, former editor of *The Masses* and enthusiast for the Russian Revolution, but by then a roving editor for *Reader's Digest*, was so impressed with the book that he offered to do a condensation. What if Gideonse had missed his train that morning? Note too that Hayek's manuscript had been offered to three other presses, all of which had turned him down, before it was sent to Chicago. It might well have been rejected by Chicago too, given the distinctly ambivalent first reader's report by Frank Knight. It was the second report by the socialist Jacob Marschak that convinced the press to take a chance on the manuscript (Caldwell, in Hayek 2007, 15–19). Thus the unlikely trio of Harry Gideonse, Max Eastman, and Jacob Marschak were in their own ways all bit players in the creation of the Chicago School, for without them Hayek would not have talked before the Detroit Economics Club on April 23, 1945. Finally, there is no discussion in VHM of how it was that Milton Friedman got the offer to come to Chicago, but clearly, whoever was instrumental in that decision should also be credited with helping to form the School.

11.2. The Larger Theme – Classical Liberalism, Neoliberalism, and Corporate Power

The VHM paper ultimately was published in a volume titled *The Road from Mont Pèlerin: The Making of the Neoliberal Thought Collective* (Mirowski and Plehwe, eds. 2009), which collects papers from a conference on that theme held at New York University in April 2005.[9] As the subtitle of the volume suggests, the purpose is to trace the development of neoliberalism, which VHM (29) define as follows: "Neoliberalism is a theory of how to

[9] The phrase "thought collective" will for some evoke the specter of totalitarian thought control; for others it will bring to mind Ludwik Fleck's idea that scientific facts depend on styles of thought unconsciously adopted by specific scientific communities but which nonetheless control their perception of the world (Fleck 1979; cf. Cohen and Schnelle, eds. 1986). Van Horn and Mirowski may also be commenting ironically on the idea of liberals organizing to defend the market system, rather than simply trusting to spontaneous orders, as they often urge others to do (note the VHM 2008, 27 comment about Friedman joking to Hayek about forming an organization, which VHM liken to "the oxymoron of an 'Anarchists' Convention'"). The comment by Friedman, and its repetition in VHM, shows that none of them seem to appreciate Hayek's clear distinction between organizations and orders. Hayek certainly understood that an organization is an effective way to pursue a well-defined goal. He simply did not think that it provided an effective way to organize a complex system like an economy. For a clear exposition of the distinction, see the chapter "Cosmos and Taxis" in Hayek 1973, 35–54.

re-engineer the state in order to guarantee the success of the market and its most important participants, modern corporations" (29).[10]

The term "neoliberalism" has many connotations. For some it means simply the movement toward "market deregulation, state decentralization, and reduced state intervention into economic affairs in general" that began to take hold in countries like the United States and Britain the late 1970s and that was given added impetus by the collapse of the Soviet Union (Campbell and Pedersen, eds., 2001, 1). For others the connotations are darker. One author presents it, for example, as in an "either-or" relationship with democracy (MacEwan 1999). Another takes Coalitional Provisional Authority chief Paul Bremer's edicts on how the Iraqi economy should be run as a paradigmatic example of how to create a neoliberal state:

> According to neoliberal theory, the sorts of measures that Bremer outlined were both necessary and sufficient for the creation of wealth and therefore for the improved well-being of the population at large.... What the US evidently sought to impose by main force on Iraq was a state apparatus whose fundamental mission was to facilitate conditions for profitable capital accumulation on the part of domestic and foreign capital. I call this kind of apparatus a *neoliberal state*. The freedoms it embodies reflect the interests of private property owners, businesses, multinational corporations, and financial capital. Bremer invited the Iraqis, in short, to ride their horse of freedom straight into the neoliberal corral. (Harvey 2005)

Even less flattering descriptions of neoliberalism may be found on the Internet.[11]

Neoliberalism, then, is not generally used as a term of approbation. The doctrine purportedly provides a rationale for powerful transnational corporations who wish to utilize the power of the state to advance their own

[10] The emphasis on corporations was even more evident in the original title of their paper, "The Road to a World Made Safe for Corporations: The Rise of the Chicago School of Economics."

[11] Two popular (they ranked first and fifth in a recent search on the word "neoliberalism") and representative sites are http://en.wikipedia.org/wiki/Neoliberalism, where neoliberalism is linked with an increase in human trafficking, the traumatization of the working classes, "belligerent capitalism," and high incarceration rates in the United States that aim at "keeping unemployment statistics low, and stimulating economic growth through maintaining a contemporary slave population within the U.S. and promoting prison construction and militarized policing," and http://www.globalexchange.org/campaigns/econ101/neoliberalDefined.html, where the neoliberal *modus operandi* is described as follows: "A memorable definition of this process came from Subcomandante Marcos at the Zapatista-sponsored Encuentro Intercontinental por la Humanidad y contra el Neoliberalismo (Inter-continental Encounter for Humanity and Against Neo-liberalism) of August 1996 in Chiapas when he said: 'what the Right offers is to turn the world into one big mall where they can buy Indians here, women there ...' and he might have added, children, immigrants, workers or even a whole country like Mexico."

interests. The chief desideratum of transnational capital is a stable global economy, which ensures both a steady supply of resources for the production process and a steady supply of consumers for the purchasing of goods. Corporations accordingly use international organizations like the World Bank, the WTO, and the IMF, as well as the military power of strong states (and in particular the United States) to enforce the ideology of the market and to spread Western (especially consumerist) values.

There are of course echoes here of the perennial socialist ideas that the principal aim of the liberal state is to protect the interests of the capital-owning class and that imperialism is a necessary consequence of the insatiable capitalist thirst for raw materials and vents for their goods, as well as the age-old disdain felt by many intellectuals of commerce and also of the very notion of American "culture," albeit suitably updated to reflect the current world scene.[12] What is more novel in the VHM account is the suggestion that certain intellectuals were not simply accomplices in the movement toward corporate global control of the economy, but they actually helped to engineer it. For the central claim of VHM is that neoliberalism finds its origins in the writings of the members of the Chicago School and the Mont Pèlerin Society.[13]

Neoliberalism is contrasted with classical liberalism, which preceded it. Though VHM recognize that the term "classical liberalism" is typically used to describe the views of earlier writers, for them Henry Simons, author of *A Positive Program for Laissez Faire*, is taken to be a representative modern classical liberal.[14] For those who might think that certain of Simons's policy recommendations (such as the nationalization of the railroads) sound more like socialism than liberalism, VHM counter by noting that all of Simons's proposed interventions were designed to fight concentrations of power in all of its forms, especially monopoly power.[15] Because the aim

[12] See, e.g., Markovits 2007, who explores the longevity among European elites of antipathy toward America, noting "how integral and ubiquitous the anti-American tropes about Americans' alleged venality, mediocrity, uncouthness, lack of culture, and above all inauthenticity have been to European elite opinion for well over two hundred years" (5).

[13] VHM (2008, 27): "The ultimate purpose of institutions such as the MPS and the Chicago School was not so much to revive a dormant classical liberalism, as it was to forge a neoliberalism better suited to modern conditions."

[14] VHM (2008, 5): "Simons' 'Positive Program' reads today more like a left-leaning attack on corporate prerogatives than anything we might today associate with a neo-conservative agenda; but in the 1930s it was situated well within the bounds of 'classical liberalism.'"

[15] Thus (VHM 2008, 5) approvingly cite Simon's claim that "… *the great enemy of democracy is monopoly, in all its forms*: gigantic corporations, trade associations and other agencies for price control, trade-unions or, in general, organization and concentration of power within functional classes" (Simons 1948, 43). They do not discuss a point frequently made

of such interventions was "to maintain a propitious market milieu ... where competition, the agency of control, can function effectively" (VHM 2008, 5), Simons counts as a classical liberal. As Van Horn (2008) demonstrates, in the 1930s and into the 1940s both Milton Friedman and Aaron Director appear to have held views quite similar to those of Simons regarding the dangers posed by corporations and monopoly. This was not to last, however. After Friedman and Director participated in the Free Market Study, their views began to change.[16] Their final position is summarized with the pithy line, "Corporations can do no wrong" (VHM 2008, 29).

Why did the change of views take place? Though VHM never quite come out and say it directly, the clear implication of their paper is that it was due to pressure from the Volker Fund, which financed Hayek's chair at the Committee on Social Thought, provided funds for the Free Market Study and the Antitrust Project that followed it, and often paid for American scholars to attend meetings of the Mont Pèlerin Society. It is worth quoting VHM at some length here:

> The politics of postwar America presumed not only a powerful state, but also a configuration of powerful corporations whose international competitors had mostly been reduced to shadows of their former selves. In promoting "freedom," they were primarily intent upon guaranteeing the freedom of corporations to conduct their affairs as they wished. Thus, the Volker Fund was not interested in bankrolling a classical liberal economic position resembling that of Henry Simons, for it did not adequately correspond to their objectives. American corporations did not fear concentrations of power, and generally favored the existence of a powerful Cold War state. It is our contention that the Volker Fund pushed for a reformulation of classic liberalism in the American context to conform to its Cold War anti-socialist agenda. The participants in the Free Market Study, and even eventually Hayek, would just have to learn to adjust to the emergent doctrines of Neoliberalism. (VHM 2008, 24)

VHM imply that both Hayek and Friedman ultimately gave in to the pressure to toe the Luhnow line. They suggest that personal financial exigencies help to explain Hayek's capitulation – after his move to Chicago, Hayek purportedly admitted to his secretary that he was forced "to do everything for money" (34). On the other hand, Friedman, whose *Capitalism and Freedom* they portray as providing the "corporate neoliberal version of *Road to Serfdom*" that Luhnow "had arguably paid for many times over,"

by Hayek that "Liberalism and democracy, although compatible, are not the same." See Hayek [1966] 1967, 161.

[16] This raises the question, unasked in VHM 2008, of whether had he lived Simons would also have changed his views.

is excoriated (36). His book is variously described as "a Volker product through and through," "low-balled towards *hoi polloi*," and a work filled with "confident bromides" that "wore its own provenance on its sleeve: it was *proud* to be the work of an intellectual for hire" (37–38).

To sum up: Henry Simons was a classical liberal because he opposed monopoly power in all its forms, which VHM take to be a defining characteristic of classical liberalism. In the years prior to the Free Market Study, both Friedman and Director shared at least some of Simons's suspicions about corporate power and the dangers of monopoly. Then they changed their minds. Although the start of the Cold War made such a move timely (a strong American state and powerful American corporations being viewed as the best safeguard against the spread of communism), the switch also involved a "follow the money" story. In short, Friedman and the others were turned by their corporate handlers. This then was the birth of the ideology that would later emerge in full force as neoliberalism, a term that some of the principals were using as far back as the 1930s. Another part of the larger narrative, evident in the book though not in the VHM paper about origins, is that the rapid ascendancy of neoliberal ideology in the 1990s was due in large part to the efforts of corporately financed think tanks that were inspired by, or were direct offshoots of, the Mont Pèlerin Society.

11.3. Some Problems with the VHM Theses

I wish to challenge certain of the VHM theses, but perhaps it is best to begin with certain areas of agreement. It is clearly true that free market ideology began to become more popular in the United States and Britain by the early 1980s, and worldwide after the collapse of the Soviet Union. It is also evident that individuals associated with both the Mont Pèlerin Society and the Chicago School are free market advocates, and that free market think tanks have grown rather dramatically in number worldwide, especially since the 1970s. Whether one views such developments with alarm, indifference, or enthusiasm evidently depends on one's views on the benefits and costs of the deregulation and extension of markets.

The fundamental question of how important think tank activities or the Chicago School free market ideology were to the adoption of market reforms in various countries is an open one, I think. Did the intellectual arguments lead to the changes, or would we agree with George Stigler's typically cynical (but nonetheless probably more often true than not) statement about the importance of economists: "[O]ur influence appears to be powerful only when we support policies ripe for adoption" (Stigler 1987, 11)?

My own priors are that in certain specific countries the influence of a think tank may have been quite important, but in general that it was the apparent manifest failures of communism that promoted a willingness to try new policies, just as the apparent manifest failures of capitalism had done in the 1930s.[17]

In any event, what is at issue here are certain specific claims made by Van Horn and Mirowski in their paper, claims that I wish to challenge. The first has to do with their portrayal of liberalism in the 1930s. I will argue that their claim that Henry Simons is best viewed as a classical liberal is unhelpful and potentially misleading, for it obscures the fact that the single most important unifying principle for 1930s liberals was their opposition to the doctrine of laissez-faire, a doctrine that all of them associated with classical liberalism. My second objection is to the insinuation that money was the motivating factor behind Director, Friedman, and others changing their opinions in the 1950s regarding monopoly. This will bring me to my final point of dissent, in which I will argue that, at least as they appear to define it, the term neoliberalism is not a doctrine that any of the principal actors promoted or defended.[18] I feel that none of the claims that I will criticize is well-defended, and that their presence in the VHM paper detracts from an otherwise creditable piece of scholarship.

11.3.1. *Liberalisms*

My first objection may well strike some as merely a verbal quibble, for words like "liberal" and "classical liberal" have certainly been used by many people in many different ways. Even so, there does exist a fair amount of consensus concerning the various historical stages of liberal thought, as a thumbnail sketch will reveal.[19]

The foundations of liberal thought may be found in the writings of such men as Locke, Montesquieu, the Scottish moral philosophers (especially

[17] Labour and socialist organizations produced scads of position papers in England in the 1930s, so a similar question about their influence on postwar Labour government policies might be asked. A nice starting point would be Elizabeth Durbin's important 1985 study, *New Jerusalems*.

[18] In this I echo Deepak Lal, who in the notes to the preface of his *Reviving the Invisible Hand* (which carries the subtitle *The Case for Classical Liberalism in the Twenty-First Century*) labels neoliberalism "a vile phrase" and "meaningless." Lal goes on favorably to quote Mario Vargas Llosa's assessment that the term was invented not "to express a conceptual reality, but rather as a corrosive weapon of derision … designed to semantically devalue the doctrine of liberalism" (Lal 2006, 237).

[19] For four assessments of liberalism from very different viewpoints, but which agree as to the major categories of liberal thought, see Hayek [1973] 1978, Hobhouse [1911] 1994, Holmes 1993, and Laski 1936.

Smith and Hume), and Kant, Madison, and J. S. Mill. The doctrine as it gradually emerged was associated with such ideas as the rule of law, and especially of equality before the law; the free exercise of religious expression; freedom of the press and of association; constitutionalism, the balance of powers, and free competitive elections; the protection of private property; and freedom of contract and of trade. As the nineteenth century progressed, British liberalism in particular came more and more to be identified with the idea of laissez-faire, of complete freedom of contract and of trade, sometimes labeled Manchesterism by its opponents, and associated most closely with Richard Cobden and John Bright, the leaders of the Anti-Corn-Law League. Hayek noted that this variant of liberalism embraced "a somewhat more extreme *laissez-faire* position than would have been required by the liberal principles of Adam Smith and the classical economists following him," but also noted:

> Their predominant free trade position was combined with a strong anti-imperialist, anti-interventionist and anti-militarist attitude and an aversion to all expansion of government powers; the increase of public expenditures was regarded by them as mainly due to undesirable intervention in overseas affairs. Their opposition was directed chiefly against the expansion of the powers of central government, and most improvements were expected from autonomous efforts either of local government or of voluntary organizations. (Hayek [1973] 1978, 129)[20]

Laissez faire was a *negative* doctrine – it limited government activity to the protection of life and property, the prosecution of fraud, and the enforcement of contracts. Derided by socialists like Ferdinand Lassalle as "the night-watchman state," this variant of liberalism was by the close of the nineteenth century viewed by many liberal social theorists to be inadequate. A "new" or "social" liberalism, associated in Britain with the philosopher T. H. Green and the journalist, politician, and social thinker L. T. Hobhouse, was born. One of the foundational principles of liberalism is that agents be allowed freely to contract. To this the social liberals added: so long as the

[20] I will simply note in passing that many self-described Austrians or Hayekians of my acquaintance would assent to everything that is said in this passage, which illustrates the difficulty of simplistic labels. Indeed, in the United States, the only principled prewar opposition to the preemptive attack on Iraq was, besides pacifists, to be found among libertarians, and their reasoning typically echoed the ideas and values articulated by Hayek in the quotation cited earlier.

Such views should not be confused with neoconservativism, which is very different. For example, while neoconservatives might consider the restriction of trade via embargoes as simply another political tool for accomplishing their *realpolitik* ends, libertarians tend to see free trade as an essential means to promote peace, and accordingly support the unilateral dropping of trade barriers and domestic subsidies.

agents are roughly comparable in bargaining strength. As Hobhouse put it in his chapter titled (and critical of) "*Laissez Faire*":

> True consent is free consent, and full freedom of consent implies equality on the part of both parties to the bargain. Just as the government first secured the elements of freedom for all when it prevented the physically stronger man from slaying, beating, despoiling his neighbors, so it secures a larger measure of freedom for all by every restriction which it imposes with a view to preventing one man from making use of his advantages to the disadvantage of others. (Hobhouse [1911] 1994, 43)

The new liberalism evidently opened up a much larger scope for government intervention to correct for inequalities in bargaining power.

By the 1930s liberalism in whatever form was widely considered a wholly bankrupt doctrine. It had not only failed to provide a bulwark against fascism on the continent or communism in Russia, it was held responsible for creating a depression in those countries that had not yet succumbed to totalitarianism. In the final chapter of his 1936 tome, *The Rise of Liberalism*, Harold Laski significantly wrote of liberalism in the past tense:

> The state, in fact, by reason of the interests which went into its making, had purposes more limited than the general well-being of the community. Its fundamental aim was to serve the owners of property ... given the nature of the liberal state, all questions had ultimately to be referred to the essential motive upon which the liberal state was built – the motive of profit-making....
>
> As an organized society, the liberal state, at bottom, had no defined object save the making of wealth ... so obsessed had it become by its material achievements that it was unable to think of success in any other terms. (Laski 1936, 298–299)[21]

Laski was making the case for socialism, and indeed in the midst of the Great Depression, an event that many had blamed on the rise of cartels and monopolies, many among the intelligentsia thought that some form of socialist planning was the only viable way forward, constituting as it were a "middle way" between a collapsed *laissez faire* capitalist system on the one hand, and totalitarianism of the communist and fascist varieties on the other. In such an environment, "letting things be" was a laughable nonstarter as a policy prescription, emblematic of the failed policies that in most people's minds had led to the current crisis. Those like Hayek who wanted to propose another sort of middle way, one that envisioned a revitalized liberalism, had to *distance* themselves from the older, *laissez faire* version of liberalism.

This is why in his 1933 inaugural lecture at the London School of Economics (LSE) Hayek faulted the classical economists for allowing "the impression to

[21] The subtitle of Laski's volume was *The Philosophy of a Business Civilization*, which echoes sentiments expressed in VHM.

gain ground that *laissez faire* was their ultimate and only conclusion," noting that "To remedy this deficiency must be one of the main tasks of the future" (Hayek [1933] 1991, 31). The next year Hayek would send Henry Simons a laudatory note on the publication of *A Positive Program for Laissez Faire*. Even though he disagreed with Simons's specific policy prescription concerning nationalizing certain types of monopolistic industries, Hayek welcomed Simons's book because it was exactly the sort of thing he had called for in his inaugural – a program that defended a liberal agenda, but one that would go beyond the simple idea of *laissez faire*.[22] Hayek would repeat his criticisms of *laissez faire* throughout the 1930s and 1940s, including in his opening address at the first Mont Pèlerin Society meeting.[23]

Hayek and Simons were not outliers among the small group of intellectuals who were still prepared to defend liberalism. Virtually all of the participants at the Colloque Lippmann, for example, shared their views (Mises appears to have been the only one willing to defend the old *laissez faire* doctrines).[24] Thus in the first paragraph of his opening address to the gathering, Louis Rougier took as a starting premise that the old "Manchesterian" doctrine of *laissez faire* should be abandoned (Rougier, 1938, 13). Where the participants differed was on the exact form that the new liberalism was to take. What changes in the institutional framework were necessary so that competition could again flourish? How far along the road from the old classical liberalism to the new more interventionist liberalism of Hobhouse and Green were they prepared to go?[25] Further discussion of such critical issues would be necessary. As noted in footnote 6, the Mont Pèlerin Society would eventually provide the venue for such discussions.

[22] It should perhaps be noted that though Hayek was critical of *laissez faire* and Simons an advocate of a positive program for it, they were essentially making the same point: that one must go beyond the simple invocation of *laissez faire* to articulate and put into place the institutional setting within which competition could work. As noted above, *laissez faire* was a negative doctrine. Simons was proposing a positive alternative formulation.

[23] See, e.g., Hayek, ed., [1935] 1975, 21–22; [1939] 1997, 194–195; [1944] 2007, 85–86; [1947] 1948, 109–111.

[24] In this regard, we might note Henry Simons's 1944 review of Mises's book, *Omnipotent Government*, where he labeled Mises "the toughest old liberal or Manchesterite of his time. Arch enemy of nazism, communism, socialism, syndicalism, protectionism, and all government interventionism, he is also perhaps the worst enemy of his own libertarian cause" (192).

[25] It is significant that in the book (Lippmann 1937) that gave rise to the Colloque, Walter Lippmann mentioned not just Hayek and Mises, but John Maynard Keynes and Graham Wallas as among the contemporary thinkers whose ideas had influenced him (vii). That such a diverse set of thinkers could be considered as members of the same camp shows the kind of world they lived in, and should serve as a reminder to readers of today just how much the world has changed since then.

We come at last to how best to label the views held by Hayek, Simons, the Colloque Lippmann participants, and men like Director and Friedman in the 1930s. This was, of course, a problem that the principals themselves wrestled with – that is why the term neoliberalism was discussed at the Colloque as a possible new label.[26] VHM chose "classical liberal" to describe them. However, for those who equate classical liberalism with the doctrine of *laissez faire*, this label is simply wrong, because as we have shown, all of them rejected *laissez faire*.[27] I think it is probably best to abandon any attempts at labeling and instead simply point out that the one idea that all of them (Mises excepted) accepted was that liberalism must move beyond the doctrine of *laissez faire*.

We may close this section by looking briefly at how Hayek, writing about liberalism some thirty-five years after the Colloque Lippmann, would characterize things. In a section on "Positive Tasks of Liberal Legislation" (note the word *positive*) he chastised "traditional liberal doctrine" for never developing "a legal framework designed to preserve an effective market order" (Hayek [1973] 1978, 145), and went on to say:

> If the free enterprise system is to work beneficially, it is not sufficient that the laws satisfy the negative criteria sketched earlier. It is also necessary that their positive content be such as to make the market mechanism operate satisfactorily. This requires in particular rules which favor the preservation of competition and restrain, so far as possible, the development of monopolistic positions. These problems were somewhat neglected by nineteenth-century liberal doctrine and were examined systematically only more recently by some of the "neo-liberal" groups.
>
> It is probable, however, that in the field of enterprise monopoly would never have become a serious problem if government had not assisted its development by tariffs, certain features of the law of corporations and of the law of industrial patents. (ibid., 145–146)[28]

[26] As Van Horn 2008, 15–16 documents, Friedman, who was not at the Colloque Lippmann, used the term "neoliberal" once in 1951 to describe his own views. He did so explicitly to distance himself from the *laissez faire* views typically associated with earlier forms of liberalism.

[27] Significantly Hayek [1973] 1978, 128–129, was one who identified "classical British liberalism" with *laissez faire*. Hayek despaired over finding a good label for his own views. He did not like the word "libertarian," and liberal standing alone was apt in America to be confused with "progressive" liberalism. For reasons evident from the text, classical liberal also would not work. His final solution was to refer to himself as an "old Whig," invoking the eighteenth-century liberal tradition that preceded the classical liberalism of Cobden and Bright.

[28] This is one of the only times that Hayek actually uses the word "neoliberal," and it is significant that, writing in 1973, he should associate it with the desire to limit monopoly power. At least in 1973, he seems to have been an unlikely architect of VHM's brand of "neoliberalism."

11.3.2. *Doing It for the Money*

The point of the Free Market Study (1946–1952) and the Antitrust Project (1953–1957) was to investigate exactly what sorts of legal and institutional changes might be necessary to create and maintain an effective competitive environment, to discover, in Hayek's words, that set of rules that would "favor the preservation of competition and restrain, so far as possible, the development of monopolistic positions" (Hayek [1973] 1978, 146). Van Horn 2008 details some of the specific issues that were examined, among them the effects of price discrimination, vertical integration, resale price maintenance agreements, and tying arrangements. A major finding of the studies was that the amounts and types of regulation of industry that had been envisioned in the 1930s and 1940s as necessary to control monopoly had been substantially overestimated. This conclusion was based in part on empirical studies by Warren Nutter (1951) and Fred Weston (1953), who had found that, contrary to the then popular wisdom, the extent of monopoly had not increased over the past fifty years, and that most of the growth in firm size that had occurred was due to internal growth rather than merger activity. These and other studies led them to recommend the use of an (implicit) rule of reason approach over the then predominant "per se" approach in assessing the merits of antitrust actions in which various exclusionary practices were at issue. Perhaps the most important change, however, was to embrace the general belief that market competition itself was the most effective limit to monopoly power. As Van Horn (2008, 16) puts it, "competition became Director's philosopher's stone, and the only way it would lose its prodigious powers was whenever government intervened." Van Horn contrasts this view with those held by the "Ordoliberals" of West Germany, who favored a more activist role for antitrust than did the Chicago School economists.

Van Horn has provided a carefully documented account of how the Free Market Study and the Antitrust Project led Director, Friedman, and others at Chicago to a more cautious view about the necessity of direct government intervention to create a competitive environment. My objection is not to Van Horn's study, but to the role it plays in the larger VHM thesis, and in particular to their suggestion there that the change in attitude toward monopoly occurred because Friedman et al. had become "intellectuals for hire." As noted, Van Horn and Mirowski never quite come out and say that money explains why Director and Friedman changed their views. One suspects that the main reason they do not is that, in contrast to the first part of their paper, where archival documentation of nearly every statement is provided, there appears to be little tangible evidence for the claim.[29] So what sorts of things *do* Van Horn and Mirowski mention to lend credibility to their suggestion?

The first is the simple fact that the Free Market Study and the Antitrust Project were both financed by the Volker Fund.[30] It is of course always fair to note when a study is funded by an agency that has a particular agenda. But without further supporting evidence it is a slender reed on which to hang the severe charge that one has altered one's results to satisfy those footing the bill.

A second piece of evidence is that Luhnow tried to control how his funds were used. As VHM (2008, 23) put it, "Luhnow and the Volker officers were not mere accessories to the rise of the Chicago school: they were hands-on players, determined and persistent in making every dollar count, supervising doctrine as well as organization." This fairly extravagant claim is supported by providing two examples of Luhnow's assertion of control. The first is that Luhnow wanted Hayek to put Loren Miller and Leonard Read on the Advisory Committee to the Free Market Study. The second is that he objected to Theodore Schultz being on the committee. Hayek went along with the first recommendation, but not with the second. This is not exactly conclusive evidence of undue influence. The fact that the Volker Fund never cut off funding for Director despite his failure to finish the promised book suggests that Luhnow's allegedly tight control of matters was perhaps somewhat less complete than VHM imagine.[31]

Additional supporting evidence is the claim that the very idea that the reemergence of competition could eliminate a monopoly was in the 1950s "an outrageous oxymoron" (Van Horn 2008, 14), an idea in which

[29] Their larger argument has all the trappings of a conspiracy theory. And of course, in the twisted world of conspiracy theory logic, the absence of evidence might well be taken as compelling evidence of the success of the conspiracy and of the thoroughness of the conspirators. Denials of any conspiracy by those accused can be similarly dismissed: *of course* they will deny it. Conspiracy theories are so long-lived precisely because they cannot be refuted: How does one prove a negative; how does one establish that one is *not* hiding something?

[30] In a footnote at the beginning of their paper, VHM (2008, 1) state, "This paper was not facilitated by any outside funding or support, a fact bearing some relevance to its thesis." I am not sure what the term "facilitated" means, but for the record, the conference at which the paper was presented was organized through the International Center for Advanced Studies at NYU, which over the years received support from the Ford, Rockefeller, and Mellon Foundations, as well as funding from the university itself.

[31] Ironically, one of the themes of Mirowski 2002 is that just because a certain funding agency "wants" a specific result does not mean it will get it – in that volume, Alfred Cowles and the U.S. military provided cases in point.

presumably no sane person could believe without financial persuasion. Now it is certainly true that in the 1950s the majority view favored activist intervention for the promotion of competition – as Van Horn demonstrates, per se rules were then the norm in antitrust matters. It was the validity of this majority opinion that the Chicago School economists were questioning.

It is not true, however, that the view that they eventually settled on was unprecedented. As might be expected, Ludwig von Mises (writing in 1927), like Carl Menger before him (writing in 1871), claimed that monopoly profits spur others to enter the market, thereby undercutting the monopolist position (Menger 1976, 216–218; Mises, 1985, 90–95). Mises added that this would happen either directly through entry or indirectly through the introduction of substitutes, and claimed further that this would occur unless the market was protected from competition by government through such devices as tariff protection, tax laws, licensing arrangements, and so forth.[32] Mises expressed similar views at the Colloque Lippmann (Mises, in Rougier 1938, 36–37).

Though anathema to VHM, this theme of a dynamic market process became a mainstay of the Austrian worldview.[33] From the Austrian perspective, the achievement of a monopoly position is often the reward of effective entrepreneurship, as the search for profits drives entrepreneurs to discover new products and processes. The same search for profits, however, also implies that bigness and market power are not *long run* problems, precisely because of constantly reemerging competition. To utilize a pithy metaphor – there will always been a Fortune 500, but its membership is constantly changing over time. In this view, monopoly power is always impermanent. It can only persist if it is sanctioned by government, a situation in which the control mechanism of rivalrous market competition is rendered ineffective by being declared illegal.

Mises was not alone in holding such opinions. Frank Knight, for example, wrote in 1941 (*nota bene*, well before the FMS!) that "It is needful to state that the role of 'monopoly' in actual economic life is enormously exaggerated in the popular mind and also that a large part of the monopoly which is real, and especially the worst part, is due to the activities of government" (Knight 1941, 103). Knight's example alone suggests at a minimum that one

[32] At one point in his discussion, Mises took as an example the railroad industry. Noting how there used to be much talk about the "transportation monopoly," he observed that now that competition from cars and trucks and planes was emerging, no one mentioned it anymore (Mises 1985, 94–95). It is ironic that the railroad industry was one of those that Simons, writing in 1934, claimed had become so monopolized that it required nationalization.

[33] Kirzner 1973 is still perhaps the clearest exposition of the view.

need not have been "on the take" to think that monopoly unsanctioned by government was only a minor problem.

There are additional reasons to reject the idea that Director and Friedman altered their ideas simply to please a donor. From what we know about their personalities (it is difficult to imagine anyone getting Milton Friedman to say something that he did not believe) and their actions (Director didn't even finish the book!), it is hard to credit any story that depends on their having capitulated to outside pressure. Such a story would also have to explain why they stuck with the new views once the money had stopped coming.

I have saved for last Van Horn and Mirowski's treatment of Hayek, which might be described as character assassination by innuendo. Here is what they say of Hayek, circa 1950:

> Even though Hayek had not received a position in the economics department, he still nonetheless was paraded as a figurehead of the New Chicago to business magnates, invited to Hutchins' house to dine and deipnosophize with them. The neoliberal project was in full swing at Chicago, and, at least initially, Hayek was its public face.[34] Later, in August, Hayek remarked to his private secretary Charlotte Cubitt that he was forced from now on "to do everything for money" (quoted in Hoover 2003, 195). But, in retrospect, what else could he have expected?

If one reads this straight through it would be easy to come to the conclusion that Hayek was indeed on the take, especially given his apparent contemporaneous confession to his secretary and its juxtaposition with reports of his dinner activities with corporate magnates. A closer look, however, reveals the passage to be a mistaken reading of a mistaken secondary source.

Charlotte Cubitt, the original source of the apparently damaging quote about Hayek having "to do everything for money," served as Hayek's secretary from 1977 until he died in 1992, and she wrote a book about her experiences that was based on diaries she kept during that time. Though hers is a fascinating document of the "chambermaid tells all" variety written by an obviously kindly soul, she is hardly an unimpeachable source.

[34] What follows is the footnote that VHM provided at this point:

The British Ambassador to the United States reported in March of 1945: "Wall Street looks on Hayek as the richest goldmine yet discovered and are peddling his views everywhere" (quoted in Hoover 2003, 184). For example, Hayek and Hutchins entertained "Laird Bell, Chairman of the Board of Trustees of the University [of Chicago]; John Ivy, an oil operator from Huston, Texas; Meyer Kestenbaum, President of Hart, Schaffner and Marx; William J. Kelly, President of Machinery and Allied Products Institute; Oscar Mayer, President of Oscar Mayer & Company, meat packers; John L. McCaffrey, President of International Harvester Company; and Hermon D. Smith, Vice-President of Marsh & McLennan, Insurance" (Hutchins to Hayek, January 12, 1950, F.A. Hayek Collection, Hoover Institution, box 55, folder 1).

In any event, Hayek's conversation with Cubitt did not take place in August 1950, which VHM imply.[35] Hayek's conversation with Cubitt in fact took place *at least twenty-seven years later*.[36] Furthermore, the context was not a discussion of his time at Chicago, but rather a reaction to the fact that in retirement Hayek received money (from which Cubitt's salary was paid) from a variety of foundations, and sometimes there were gaps in the flow of money, which forced him to ask for more:

> I once asked Hayek whether he did not mind having to beg for money so often. He just laughed, said that he did not mind in the least, that all his professional decisions had been based on financial considerations, and that he had accepted the Freiburg position because he had been offered half a professor's salary and a life pension. Yet, he added, he had never done anything for money that he did not actually want to do. As an example he told me that as a young man he had been offered the directorship of the Bank of Austria, but had not fancied the position despite the attractive salary. (Cubitt 2006, 10)

It seems clear that Hayek is talking about various employment decisions he had made when he talked about doing things for money. By juxtaposing his statement with the claim that Hayek had become the "public face" of neoliberalism, VHM make it appear that he was making a contemporaneous confession to something much more sinister.

The lengthy footnote (reproduced in note 35) in support of the claim that Hayek had become the public face of neoliberalism in Chicago also demands scrutiny. The British Ambassador's comment, reported on in the footnote, occurred in *1945*, soon after *The Road to Serfdom* had been published. It referred to the reception of Hayek's book by the business community in 1945, not to Hayek's activities in Chicago, and indeed was made before Hayek had even met Luhnow.[37] Furthermore, we are told nothing about the purpose of the dinner that Hayek attended that is reported on in the latter part of the footnote. Was it a board of trustees dinner? Was

[35] The fault here is mainly due to the exposition by Kenneth Hoover, VHM's source for the quote, who wrote, "In August 1950 Friedrich and Helene were married in Austria. Hayek's new wife had no financial resources. He was forced from this point forward, as he commented to his private secretary Charlotte Cubitt, 'to do everything for money,' though he claimed that he never did anything he would not have done otherwise" (Hoover 2003, 195). Hoover makes it seem that Cubitt had said that, after his divorce and remarriage in 1950, Hayek needed money. Cubitt did not say this; as I show in the text, the context for Hayek's comment about money was completely different from what Hoover asserts.

[36] I say "at least" twenty-seven years later because, though Cubitt tells the story in the chapter of the book devoted to 1977, her saying that "I once asked Hayek" may indicate that the conversation took place later in their relationship (Cubitt 2006, 10).

[37] For more on the reception of *The Road to Serfdom* in the United States, see Caldwell 2007, 18–23.

President Hutchins simply trolling for potential donors? Was Hayek paid to attend? Did he speak? Did he give the same sort of speech that he did on his book tour in 1945, when he caused horror among the assembled businessmen by calling for them to open their markets to foreign competition?[38] We do not know. And as for this serving as an example of his being the public face of neoliberalism at Chicago, it should simply be noted that the dinner occurred in January, 1950, that is, eight months *before* Hayek started teaching at the University.

I do not know why Hayek attended the dinner in January 1950, or what might have been said there. Yet it takes a considerable amount of creative interpretation to link this event with an offhand statement that he made almost three decades later in a private conversation with his secretary about employment decisions he had made over the years, a statement that made no reference at all to Chicago.

One can understand why VHM were so eager to use the quotation from Hoover's book: If one is trying to show that a group of people had become "intellectuals for hire," but have no real evidence, such a statement is just too good to give up. But their accusation is probably the most serious one that anyone can make about an intellectual. It need not be added that Hayek is a controversial figure, one with many enemies who will be happy to use such a claim, one now made by well respected scholars and in print, against him. One wishes that they would have simply gone back to read what Hayek had actually said. If they had, it is unlikely (or so one hopes) that they would have been party to this kind of character assassination.

I have argued that VHM have not offered much support for their suggestion that money was the motivating factor behind any change in views that may have taken place. If it wasn't Luhnow's money, what caused the Chicago economists to reach the conclusion by the 1950s that monopoly was not the great threat that it may earlier have seemed?

I suspect that one motivating factor was that, with the onset of the Cold War, the threat of wholesale nationalization of industry in the West had more or less disappeared, so there was less urgency to come up with proposed alternatives to central planning. Yet it may also have been that, after studying the matter intensively for a number of years, they simply came to believe that much of the popular wisdom concerning the dangers of monopoly were overblown. Van Horn mentions the empirical work by Weston and Nutter that showed that monopoly power had not grown over the past fifty years, and that increases in firm size were due to internal growth rather than

[38] Ibid., 20.

merger activity. Harberger's 1954 study on the deadweight welfare losses associated with monopoly also suggested that it was much less of a problem than had originally been thought. Another widely held view was that technological advance made the growth of monopoly inevitable. This was challenged, however, by a government study, undertaken by the Temporary National Economic Committee (TNEP) on the concentration of economic power. Noting that the committee could not be accused of having a classical liberal bias (it was set up by FDR), Hayek quoted some salient findings from the study in *The Road to Serfdom*:

> The superior efficiency of large establishments has not been demonstrated; the advantages that are supposed to destroy competition have failed to manifest themselves in many fields. Nor do economies of size, where they exist, invariably necessitate monopoly.... It should be noted, moreover, that monopoly is frequently the product of factors other than the lower costs of greater size. It is attained through collusive agreement and promoted by public policies. When these agreements are invalidated and when these policies are reversed, competitive conditions can be restored. (TNEP, quoted in Hayek [1944] 2007, 92–93)

The question of how much competition is necessary to restrain monopoly was another key issue. Of course, if one thought that markets must approximate the perfectly competitive market models of economic theory, few real-world markets would be deemed "competitive." However, as early as 1940 J. M. Clark had offered his theory of workable competition, one that provided empirical proxies to address just this question (Clark 1940). For his part, Hayek contributed an important piece, "The Meaning of Competition," in which he warned against the common view that "the so-called theory of 'perfect competition' provides the appropriate model for judging the effectiveness of competition in real life and that, to the extent that real competition differs from that model, it is undesirable and even harmful" (Hayek [1946] 1948, 92). He was certainly not alone in this view.[39]

Van Horn and Mirowski may think little of the empirical and theoretical studies that were produced during this time, and which appear to have

[39] Cf. Joseph Schumpeter's preface to the second edition of *Capitalism, Socialism and Democracy*: "The classical theory of monopolistic pricing (the Cournot-Marshall theory) is not entirely valueless.... But it works with assumptions that are so restrictive as to exclude its *direct* application to reality. In particular it cannot be used for what it *is* being used in current teaching, namely, for a comparison between the way in which a purely competitive economy functions and the way in which an economy functions that contains substantial elements of monopoly ... much more important than the manner in which capitalism administers given industrial structures is the manner in which it creates them.... And into this process of creation the monopoly element enters necessarily" (emphasis in the original) (Schumpeter [1942] 1950, x).

led Friedman, Director, and Hayek to worry less about monopoly in the 1950s than they had during the intense decade of the 1930s. They may disagree with the conclusions that were reached and wish to undercut them. To fail to deal with the arguments and instead simply to insinuate that anyone capable of holding such views must be on the take is not much of a response.

11.3.3. *What Is VHM's Version of Neoliberalism, and Did the Chicago School Create It?*

The central claim of the larger VHM thesis is that the doctrine called neoliberalism had its origins in the writings of the Hayek and the Chicago School economists and was subsequently spread by the activities of neoliberal think tanks. VHM (2008, 28–29) offer the following description of the major tenets of neoliberalism:

1. **Neoliberalism starts with a critique of state reason**. The limits of government are related to intrinsic limitations on a state's power to know, and hence to supervise. These limits are not fixed for all time, however. Nevertheless, the Market always surpasses the state's ability to process information.

2. **Neoclassical economics is a good representation of the capacities of the market as information processor**. Here the Chicago Program tended to diverge from the later Hayek himself. This is related to a profound change in neoclassical economics located just after World War II (Mirowski 2002).

3. **Politics *as if* it were a market, and an economic theory of "democracy."** This supports the application of neoclassical models to previously political topics; but it also explains why the neoliberal movement must seek and consolidate political power by operating from within the state. It also justifies alliances with the powerful in order to push the neoliberal agenda, and promotes a right-wing suspicion about the virtues of democracy.

4. **Government order predicated on appropriate government of the self**. Freedom is not the realization of any *telos*, but rather the positing of autonomous self-governed individuals, all naturally equipped with a neoclassical version of "rationality" and motives of self-interest. Yet neoclassical economics was not inherently neoliberal; Chicago strove to define it as such.

5. **Corporations can do no wrong**. This is one of the strongest areas of divergence from Classical Liberalism, with its ingrained suspicion of joint stock companies and monopoly. The internal workings of the corporation are instead presented as though they were themselves normally functioning markets. This underwrites a "degovernmentalization of the state" through privatization of education, health, and even portions of the military.

6. **Discipline of the nation-state through international initiatives**. This was initially implemented through neoliberal takeover of the IMF, WTO, the World Bank, and other previously classical liberal transnational institutions. It began as advocacy

of "free trade" and floating exchange rates, but rapidly became subordinate to the programs of transnational corporations, to whom it became attached.

7. The Market (suitably re-engineered and promoted) can always provide solutions to problems seemingly caused by The Market in the first place. Monopoly is eventually undone by "competition"; pollution is abated by the trading of "emissions permits"; even McCarthyism is thwarted by competition between employers (Friedman 1962, 20).

I have to confess that when I first read this list, I did not know exactly what to make of it. Number one seems to refer to Hayek's thesis that markets are able to coordinate dispersed information better than state planning can, and number three to public choice theory, though the characterization of the implications of public choice theory is suspect.[40] Number two refers to Mirowski's own writings about the market as an information processor, and four seems to combine the neoclassical version of methodological individualism with liberalism's insistence that the individual is the best judge of his or her own interests. Seven is the view that a competitive market environment makes it difficult to sustain a monopoly, and that market solutions when feasible are preferable to command and control solutions. Five and six seem to be about how corporations use the state to accomplish their own goals.

One reason it is difficult to come to grips with the list is evident: VHM offer only one reference to the writings of any of the protagonists, and in the one reference they do make – to Friedman and McCarthyism, a reference they repeat again elsewhere in the paper – they distort Friedman's views.[41] But let us accept for the moment that Hayek and the Chicago economists believed that markets help to coordinate dispersed knowledge, that public choice theory helps to explain some of the problems that are associated with democratic governance, that a competitive market environment makes it difficult to sustain a monopoly, and that market solutions when feasible

[40] Given their overriding concern about the ill effects of monopoly, one would think that VHM would embrace at least that portion of public choice analysis that deals with rent-seeking, which shows *inter alia* how powerful interests (among them corporations) use the power of the state to gain and maintain monopoly power.

[41] Friedman 1962, 20, characterized the Hollywood blacklist as "an unfree act that destroys freedom because it was a collusive arrangement that that used coercive means to prevent voluntary exchanges." He went on to contrast the fact that many people on the blacklist still were able to find employment with what the situation would have been had the state been the employer. In their second reference to Friedman's argument, VHM (2008, 36) deride him for having the "*chutzpah* to cite McCarthyism as 'another example of the market in promoting freedom,'" which rather astonishingly suggests that Friedman favored McCarthyism.

are preferable to command and control solutions.[42] These are not wildly controversial theses, at least among economists. The most important theses are not these, but points five and six about monopolies and organizations like the IMF, WTO, and World Bank. So we must ask: Where in the writings of Hayek and the Chicago economists is to be found any support for the theses that corporations can do no wrong or that international agencies overseeing trade should make themselves subservient to the wishes of transnational corporations? It is here that citations should have been provided, yet none are.

Of course, VHM do later in the paper take Friedman's 1962 book, *Capitalism and Freedom*, as fully representative of the new neoliberal outlook. Here is their paraphrase of Friedman's views (their parenthetical references are to pages in Friedman 1962):

> Monopoly, should it exist, is blamed on the government, and deemed relatively harmless. Patents are deemed not to be monopolies simply because they participate in the definition of property rights (p.127). There is no such thing as a social or political responsibility of corporations (p.133), and as a special bonus thrown to his patrons, he proposed that the corporate income tax be abolished (p.132). The education industry should be privatized, which includes spinning off ownership of those ridiculous state universities (p.99). (VHM 2008, 36–37)

This summary of Friedman's views is accurate enough, as far as it goes, though it should be added that they misrepresent his argument for eliminating the double taxation of corporate profits, which by eliminating the incentive for corporations to retain earnings would have as one of its effects a reduction in the advantage that established corporations have over new competitors (Friedman 1962, 130). Perhaps more egregious is that VHM neglect to include in their summary Friedman's own very clear statement about what he considers appropriate government policy regarding monopoly:

> The first and most urgent necessity in the area of government policy is the elimination of those measures which directly support monopoly, whether enterprise monopoly or labor monopoly, and an even-handed enforcement of the laws on enterprises and labor unions alike. Both should be subjected to the anti-trust laws; both should be treated alike with respect to laws about the destruction of property and about interference with private activities. (Friedman 1962, 132)

[42] I leave off reference to methodological individualism because I think that Hayek and the Chicago economists differed on this point, and to Mirowski's thesis about neoclassical economics in the postwar period because it involves Mirowski's views rather than views held by the protagonists.

I have a hard time finding anything at all objectionable in Friedman's statement. Given VHM's clear antipathy toward his writings, it would have been helpful had they provided an argument for what they find pernicious in this view.

I suspect that there are two things that critics like VHM find objectionable. The first is the claim it is very difficult to sustain a monopoly or cartel in the long run without government protection.[43] This makes corporations seem less powerful than such critics think that they are, and it places a considerable amount of blame on government, whose regulations such critics view as holding the solution to the problem of corporate monopoly power. If this is indeed one of the chief complaints, such critics must at a minimum respond to the fundamental libertarian/Chicago/Austrian critique of government intervention, namely the fear that powerful special interests (e.g., corporations) are typically the ones that are in the best position to use the legally sanctioned and enforced power of the state to further their own interests (e.g., by limiting foreign competition through tariffs; by bringing antitrust cases against their competition). VHM somehow manage to turn this fear into a desideratum of the people they describe as neoliberals: They argue that the Chicago neoliberals *want* to make such abuses easier for powerful corporations.

The second objection is to the claim that labor monopoly can be as bad or worse than enterprise monopoly.[44] This seems to favor powerful corporate

[43] As I tell my introductory classes, three conditions must be met for a cartel successfully to collude through time: They must control a large share of total output; there must be no close substitutes for their product; and they must be able easily to catch and sanction cheaters on the collusive agreement. It is possible, but difficult, for all three of these conditions to hold through time – unless, of course, the government makes it illegal or difficult (e.g., through erecting trade barriers) for new competitors to challenge the established firms.

[44] Interestingly, Friedman (1962, 121–125) thinks that the problems posed by both enterprise and labor monopoly are overestimated, because both comprise such a small part of the overall economy, whereas Simons (1948, 55) demurs:

"Industrial monopolies are not yet a serious evil.... In a community bent on preserving libertarian democracy, enterprise monopolies, standing alone, would be diagnosed as a simple skin disease and easily remedied.

The hard monopoly problem is labor organization. Here are monopolies, actual and imminent, with really great power, economic, political, and military. Once grown large, they cannot easily be taken apart like enterprise aggregations. Like corporations and up to about the same size or scale, unions have real social uses – which may outweigh abuses. But their size potentials and their appetites for power exceed even those of business corporations."

One is tempted to ask: Should we infer from this that Simons, whom VHM are so eager to praise, would favor a per se rule for the breaking up of unions that had gotten too big? Would they?

interests over those of the working man. It must be emphasized that neither Hayek nor Friedman thought that there was anything wrong with the voluntary association of labor. What they criticized, again, was the government granting unions legal protection from competition, such as when closed shop laws were passed that made it illegal for nonunion workers to be employed by a firm. Do VHM and other critics favor such state-granted and legally enforced monopoly privileges, and on what grounds?

On the most basic level, critics of neoliberalism seem not to understand that the greatest and most powerful monopoly is the government, precisely because it has the police power behind it. Hayek of course understood this, and restated for the twentieth century the liberal solution to the problem: The state is to be granted a monopoly over the powers of coercion, and then constitutionally limited in the use of its power to those instances where it is required to prevent coercion. For all their concern about monopoly, VHM are inexplicably sanguine about the one agency whose monopoly power is the most extensive.

To return to the main theme: VHM assert, but provide no evidence for, the claim that the Chicago School economists and Hayek supported neoliberalism. Yet if a key element of neoliberalism is to use the power of the state to do the bidding of big corporations, it is the exact opposite of the views that these economists have defended over the years. For them the state is something that must be limited precisely because of its own monopoly powers, and for its ability to grant its most powerful patrons legally enforceable monopoly power. The Chicago School economists favored free trade precisely because it limited the power of corporations.[45] In the topsy-turvy world of the larger VHM thesis, such men become neoliberals who favored free trade *and* a powerful state in order to *assist* large corporations.

Mario Vargas Llosa (2000, 16) was right: Neoliberalism appears to be simply a term of derision, one designed to devalue the doctrine of liberalism. It was not a doctrine cooked up by Hayek and the Chicago School

[45] I first saw Milton Friedman when he gave a talk at Duke University when I was in graduate school. By happenstance I ran into him as he was coming out a back exit after the talk. I identified myself as someone studying economics, and told him that I agreed with many of the things that he had said about the benefits of markets and about the unintended consequences of government interference – his talk had included the example of how government-mandated seat belts had increased highway fatalities – but that I worried about the market power of oligopolists. He responded by placing his hand on my shoulder and asking, "Now, what in your opinion would be the best thing we could do to reduce the power of large American corporations?" I ventured, "Open up their markets to foreign competition?" He patted me on the shoulder as if to say, "good boy," smiled his avuncular smile, and went on his way.

economists, but by opponents who wish to tar them with pernicious views in order to dismiss them. In this VHM appear to be participating in the latest instantiation of a long tradition of non-Marxist antiliberal thought.[46]

A much simpler, and more straightforward story may be told about Hayek and the Chicago School economists. In the 1930s the few remaining intellectuals who were prepared to defend liberalism were on the defensive. Their critics accused them of embracing a policy of pure *laissez faire*. In response, they insisted that there was a role for the state in creating an environment in which competition could flourish – and they sometimes used the term neoliberalism to distinguish their views from *laissez faire* liberalism. Many of them initially thought that promoting a competitive environment required fairly strict control of corporations, a view that was rampant in the 1930s. As they studied the matter more closely after the war, however, they came to the conclusion that the rule of reason should be used in deciding antitrust cases rather than a per se rule, which was hardly a radical finding. VHM take three of the facts just mentioned – that some of the principals sometimes used the word neoliberalism, that they favored a role for the state in setting up an institutional environment in which competition could work, and that they came to believe that this did not require per se rules for antitrust – to construct the case that they were the fathers of modern neoliberalism. They provide little evidence for this controversial claim, and nowhere do they acknowledge or respond to the argument that free trade is a major impediment to corporate control.

I will conclude by noting that there *is* one set of thinkers who could with some justice accuse Friedman and Hayek of being neoliberals. Anarcho-libertarians like Murray Rothbard believe that the state should be abolished, that all state activity should be replaced by private sector provision, including the court system, police, national defense, roads, and so on. Rothbard argued that the government should be subjected to the same moral and juridical calculus as an individual, and if it were, its true nature would be revealed: War (which is declared by states) is mass murder, conscription is slavery, and taxation is robbery (Rothbard 1973, 10). Rothbard also claimed

[46] Holmes 1993, 187 describes some of the tenets of the antiliberal tradition as follows: "… classical European liberals ignored the social constitution of the individual, were scornful of the common good, disparaged authority, sacrificed the public to the private, belittled political participation, neglected virtue, idolized economic man, declared values to be subjective, reduced man to a pleasure-pain machine, abolished self-restraint, placed excessive faith in Reason, and generally dissolved all nourishing bonds." He goes on to say, "This is a daunting list of allegations. When confronted one at a time with the claims actually defended in classic liberal texts, however, they either seem exaggerated or wrong." Precisely.

that big corporations were responsible for the growth of the state, so as better to utilize it for their own benefit.[47] From his perspective, people like Hayek and Friedman, who acknowledged a positive role for the state, fit the description of neoliberals.[48] VHM should be cautious, though, if they are tempted to join Rothbard in his condemnation of the Chicago School economists and Hayek: Rothbard's research was frequently funded by the Volker Fund (see Rothbard 1982, x)! So much for Luhnow using his money to make the world safe for corporations.

11.4. Epilogue – Why This Debate Will Never Go Away

I will close with a brief caricature of the monopoly power question, and then offer a personal reminiscence that ties it to the well-known Friedman-Hayek dispute over methodology. In broad outline, the two sides in the monopoly power debate – one that sees the world populated by huge corporations that are out of control and must be constrained by government, the other that sees bigness everywhere but, because above-normal profits provide incentives to entry or to produce substitutes, is not a problem to worry about – have existed side by side throughout the past century. One can see it in theoretical debates, with market and state socialists, Galbraith's theory of countervailing powers, and theories regarding imperfect competition and strategic trade on one side, and on the other, the Austrian view, Clark's idea of workable competition, Stigler's capture theory of regulation (the notion that firms seek to be regulated to avoid competition), and Baumol's contestable markets theory. Every generation of economists seemed to provide a slightly different theoretical gloss on it, but in its broadest outline, the debate did not change much over the century.

I suspect that Friedman, the great proponent of positive economics, thought that various types of empirical studies were going to be able to answer the question once and for all. And I presume that Hayek, the great critic of scientism, thought that, in principle, no amount of data was going to be able to answer it. As a graduate student, I took an industrial organization class because this was one of the questions I desperately wanted an answer to: It was the 1970s; getting an answer to the debate between

47 He put it this way: "... the *real* antipode to liberty today is the existing Corporate Monopoly Welfare-Warfare State.... it is precisely Big Business that is largely responsible for the twentieth century march into aggressive statism." (Rothbard 1973, 17).

48 In a recent biography of Ludwig von Mises written from an anarcho-libertarian perspective, Friedman, Hayek, and members of the Mont Pèlerin Society are indeed characterized as neoliberals. See Hülsmann 2007, 708–712, 842–843, 864–872.

capitalism and socialism was one of the reasons I was studying economics, and the tendency toward monopoly was (as always) a key question for that debate. Back in those days the study of industrial organization was highly empirical.[49] I can well remember the first day of class when the professor told us that though there had been many hundreds of empirical papers in all areas of industrial organization, as far as he could tell there were only two robust results. One of these was that there appeared to be some positive correlation between market share and profits. (I now forget the other one.) Clearly that result is consistent with the view that monopolies tend to make monopoly profits. On the other hand, it does not provide evidence against the Austrian counterargument that, over time, such profits cannot be sustained without government protection. I don't know of any way to test the latter claim other than to look at the makeup of the Fortune 500 to see what has changed, but even if that were done, how big of a change would count? It does not seem that the key question is decidable empirically.[50]

Anyway, I submit that the fact that when Rob Van Horn and Philip Mirowski look at the world and see one thing (a world dominated by big corporations), and I look at the world and see another (constantly rotating membership in the Fortune 500), and that the debate we are having is one that has existed for more than a century of careful and creative scientific work, one thing seems clear – in terms of the debates about methodology that they had, Hayek was right about the limits of knowledge in economics, and Friedman and other positivists who hoped that empirical studies would answer such questions were wrong. Or as Hayek often put it – "what we can know in the field of economics is so much less than what people aspire to" (Hayek, in Caldwell 2004, 373).

References

Caldwell, Bruce. 2004. *Hayek's Challenge: An Intellectual Biography of F.A. Hayek.* Chicago: University of Chicago Press.

2007. "Introduction." In F.A. Hayek, *The Road to Serfdom: Texts and Documents.* Bruce Caldwell, ed., vol. 2 of *The Collected Works of F.A. Hayek.* Chicago: University of Chicago Press, pp. 1 – 33.

Campbell, John and Pedersen, Ove, eds. 2001. *The Rise of Neoliberalism and Institutional Analysis.* Princeton: Princeton University Press.

[49] One of the only textbooks I ever bought without being required to was F. M. Scherer's classic 1980 text on industrial organization. Its footnotes basically provided a literature review of all the relevant empirical studies.

[50] I think that the failure to get empirical answers to the "big questions" is one reason that industrial organization has moved away from empirical studies and today is so dominated by game theory.

Clark, Fred G. 1944. *How We Live*. Princeton: Van Nostrand.

Clark, J.M. 1940. "Toward a Theory of Workable Competition," *American Economic Review*, vol. 30, June, pp. 241–256.

Cohen, Robert S. and Schnelle, Thomas, eds. 1986. *Cognition and Fact: Materials on Ludwik Fleck*, vol. 87 of *Boston Studies in the Philosophy of Science*. Dordrecht: D. Reidel.

Cubitt, C.E. 2006. *A Life of Friedrich August von Hayek*. Bedfordshire, UK: Authors Online Ltd.

Director, Aaron. 1948. "Prefatory Note." In *Economic Policy for a Free Society*. Chicago: University of Chicago Press, pp. v–vii.

Durbin, Elizabeth. 1985. *New Jerusalems: The Labour Party and the Economics of Democratic Socialism*. London: Routledge and Kegan Paul.

Fleck, Ludwik. 1979. *Genesis and Development of a Scientific Fact*. Translated by Fred Bradley and Thaddeus J. Trenn. Chicago: University of Chicago Press.

Friedman, Milton. 1962. *Capitalism and Freedom*. Chicago: University of Chicago Press.

Harberger, Arnold. 1954. "Monopoly and Resource Allocation," *American Economic Review Papers and Proceedings*, vol. 44, May, pp. 77–87.

Harvey, David. 2005. *A Brief History of Neoliberalism*. Oxford: Oxford University Press.

Hayek, F. A. [1933] 1991. "The Trend of Economic Thinking," in *The Trend of Economic Thinking*. W.W. Bartley, III and Stephen Kresge, eds., vol. 3 of *The Collected Works of F.A. Hayek*. Chicago: University of Chicago Press, pp. 17–34.

Hayek, F. A. ed. [1935] 1975. *Collectivist Economic Planning. Critical Studies on the Possibilities of Socialism*. Clifton, N.J.: Kelley.

[1944] 2007. *The Road to Serfdom: Texts and Documents*. Bruce Caldwell, ed., vol. 2 of *The Collected Works of F.A. Hayek*. Chicago: University of Chicago Press.

[1946] 1948. "The Meaning of Competition." In Hayek, ed. *Individualism and Economic Order*. Chicago: University of Chicago Press, pp. 92–106.

[1947] 1948. "'Free' Enterprise and the Competitive Order." In Hayek, ed. *Individualism and Economic Order*. Chicago: University of Chicago Press, pp. 107–118.

[1952] 1979. *The Counter-Revolution of Science*. Indianapolis, IN: Liberty Fund.

The Constitution of Liberty. Chicago: University of Chicago Press.

[1967] 1992. "Historians and the Future of Europe." In Peter Klein, ed. *The Fortunes of Liberalism*, vol. 4 of *The Collected Works of F.A. Hayek*. Chicago: University of Chicago Press, pp. 201–15.

[1966] 1967. "The Principles of a Liberal Social Order." In Hayek, ed. *Studies in Philosophy, Politics and Economics*. Chicago: University of Chicago Press, pp. 160–177.

1973. *Rules and Order*, vol. 1 of *Law, Legislation and Liberty*. Chicago: University of Chicago Press.

[1973] 1978. "Liberalism," in Hayek, ed. *New Studies in Philosophy, Politics, Economics and the History of Ideas*. Chicago: University of Chicago Press, pp. 119–51.

Holmes, Stephen. 1993. *The Anatomy of Antiliberalism*. Cambridge: Harvard University Press.

Hobhouse, L.T. [1911] 1994. "Liberalism." In James Meadowcroft, ed. *Liberalism and Other Writings*. Cambridge: Cambridge University Press, pp. 1–120.

Hoover, Kenneth. 2003. *Economics as Ideology: Keynes, Laski, Hayek, and the Creation of Contemporary Politics*. Lanham, MD: Rowman and Littlefield.

Hülsmann, Jörg Guido. 2007. *Mises: The Last Knight of Liberalism*. Auburn, AL: Ludwig von Mises Institute.

Kirzner, Israel. 1973. *Competition and Entrepreneurship*. Chicago and London: University of Chicago Press.

Knight, Frank H. 1941. "The Meaning of Freedom," *Ethics*, vol. 52, October, pp. 86–109.

Lal, Deepak. 2006. *Reviving the Invisible Hand: The Case for Classical Liberalism in the Twenty-First Century*. Princeton: Princeton University Press.

Laski, Harold. 1936. *The Rise of Liberalism: The Philosophy of a Business Civilization*. New York: Harper and Brothers.

Lippmann, Walter. 1937. *An Inquiry into the Principles of The Good Society*. Boston: Little, Brown and Co.

Markovits, Andrei. 2007. *Uncouth Nation: Why Europe Dislikes America*. Princeton: Princeton University Press.

MacEwan, Arthur. 1999. *Neo-Liberalism or Democracy? Economic Strategy, Markets, and Alternatives for the 21st Century*. London: Zed Books.

Menger, Carl. 1976. *Principles of Economics*. Translated by James Dingwall. New York: New York University Press.

Mirowski, Philip. 2002. *Machine Dreams: Economics Becomes a Cyborg Science*. Cambridge: Cambridge University Press.

2009. "Postface: Defining Neoliberalism." In Philip Mirowski and Dieter Plehwe, eds., *The Road from Mont Pèlerin: The Making of the Neoliberal Thought Collective*. Cambridge, MA: Harvard University Press, pp. 417–455.

Mises, Ludwig von. 1985. *Liberalism in the Classical Tradition*. Translated by Ralph Raico. Irvington-on-Hudson, N.Y.: Foundation for Economic Education.

Nutter, G. Warren. 1951. *The Extent of Enterprise Monopoly in the United States, 1899–1939*. Chicago: University of Chicago Press.

Rothbard, Murray. 1972. *For a New Liberty*. New York: Macmillan.

1982. *The Ethics of Liberty*. Atlantic Highlands, NJ : Humanities Press.

Rougier, Louis. 1938. *Compte-rendu des seances du colloque Walter Lippmann, 26–30 Aout 1938*. Paris: Librarie de Médicis.

Scherer, F.M. 1980. *Industrial Market Structure and Economic Performance*. 2nd ed. Chicago: Rand McNally.

Schumpeter, Joseph A. [1942] 1950. *Capitalism, Socialism and Democracy*, 3rd ed. New York: Harper and Row.

Simons, Henry. [1934] 1948. *A Positive Program for Laissez Faire*. In Simons, *Economic Policy for a Free Society*. Chicago: University of Chicago Press, pp. 40–77.

1944. "Review: Ludwig von Mises, *Omnipotent Government*," *Annals of the American Academy of Political and Social Science*, vol. 236, November, pp. 192–93.

1948. *Economic Policy for a Free Society*. Chicago: University of Chicago Press.

Stigler, George. 1987. "Bookshelf: Economic Thought Over 1000 Years," *The Wall Street Journal*. October 2. p. 1.

Van Horn, Rob. 2008. "Reinventing Monopoly and the Role of Corporations: The Roots of Chicago Law and Economics." Manuscript.

2009. "Reinventing Monopoly and the Role of Corporations: The Roots of Chicago Law and Economics." In Philip Mirowski and Dieter Plehwe, eds., *The Road to Mont Pèlerin: The Making of the Neoliberal Thought Collective*. Cambridge, MA: Harvard University Press, pp. 204–237.

Van Horn, Rob, and Mirowski, Philip. 2008. "The Rise of the Chicago School of Economics and the Birth of Neoliberalism." Manuscript.

2009. "The Rise of the Chicago School of Economics and the Birth of Neoliberalism." In Philip Mirowski and Dieter Plehwe, eds., *The Road to Mont Pèlerin: The Making of the Neoliberal Thought Collective*. Cambridge, MA: Harvard University Press, pp. 139–178.

Vargas Llosa, Mario. 2000. "Liberalism in the New Millennium." In I. Vasquez, ed. *Global Fortune*. Washington, DC: Cato Institute.

Weston, J. Fred. 1953. *The Role of Mergers in the Growth of Large Firms*. Berkeley and Los Angeles: University of California Press.

TWELVE

The Lucky Consistency of Milton Friedman's Science and Politics, 1933–1963

Béatrice Cherrier

> During my whole career, I have considered myself somewhat of a schizophrenic, which might be a universal characteristic. On the one hand, I was interested in science *qua* science, and I have tried – successfully I hope – not to let my ideological viewpoints contaminate my scientific work. On the other, I felt deeply concerned with the course of events and I wanted to influence them so as to enhance human freedom. Luckily, these two aspects of my interests appeared to me as perfectly compatible.
>
> – Milton Friedman 1993, 189

Like most of his peers, Milton Friedman (1953a, 4) confidently claimed that he was able to prevent his political beliefs from interfering with his scientific practice. In so doing, he indeed gained the respect of many including political adversaries: "Even those who, like myself, often find themselves in basic political disagreements with him, must greatly admire and indeed envy his fearless and penetrating insight of the deepest roots of economic issues. He has done more directly and indirectly, to train economists in rigorous thinking and in the uncovering of common prejudices than any

Correspondence may be addressed to Béatrice Cherrier, EconomiX-Cachan, Departement d'Economie, 61 av. President Wilson, 94235 Cachan Cedex, France; e-mail: beatrice.cherrier@gmail.com. This research was funded by an *Aires Culturelles* grant from the French Ministry of Research and the Dorothy Leet grant from the *Association Française des Femmes d'Université*. I am indebted to Carol Leadenham and her team at the Hoover Institution, Stanford, CA for their help with the Milton Friedman Papers, and to Augus Burgin for providing Mont Pèlerin archives. I am also very grateful to Phil Mirowski and Rob Van Horn for inviting me to participate to the conference on Rethinking the Chicago School of Economics, University of Notre Dame, September 2007, and helping me with several revisions of this paper. I also thank Philippe Fontaine, Tiago Mata, Roger Backhouse, Clément Levallois, Dan Hammond, David Teira, Ross Emmett, Warren Samuels, and participants at the first HISRECO conference in Nanterre in June 2007 for their very helpful comments. Finally, this paper has benefited from sustained debates with Jean Baptiste Fleury and Steven Medema. Any remaining errors are my own.

other teacher in many decades," wrote Keynesian economist Abba Lerner to the Nobel Prize committee in 1976.[1] This strict separation between science and politics was taken for granted by some historians of the Chicago School such as Van Overtveldt 2007, allowing them to focus exclusively on the internal reasons for the success of the Chicago School – excellence and debate culture, mastering of neoclassical price theory, and importance of empirical work.

Judging from the stir created by the reception of the Bank of Sweden Prize in Economic Science by Friedman, however, it seems that a number of economists were not convinced by Lerner's statement, nor would they agree with Van Overtveldt's history.[2] There was strong suspicion that the consistency between Friedman's market-oriented microeconomics and his antistatist political recommendations was not merely accidental.[3] His macroeconomic work has similarly been interpreted as an attempt to shatter the pillars of American Keynesianism, an attack realized at the expense of reliable theoretical and empirical foundations.[4] On the side of historians of economics and economic methodologists, Friedman's work has been described as an idealized view of the free-market system and as a positive rationalization of his political convictions (Samuels 1976, 7–13 and 363–395; Nelson 2001; Lavoie and Seccareccia 1993, 16). Familiar with the Marx-Mannheim critique of economics, those critics were concerned with hunting down the ideological dimension of economic science. Though the Marxist concept of "ideology" has gradually been replaced by references to vision, paradigms, ethics, or value judgments, the idea remains the same – the economist is influenced by his social status and his political beliefs, and economic theories are not only designed to explain the world, but also to support group interests and legitimize particular courses of actions (see, for instance, Amadae 2003). In this vein, Robert Van Horn and Philip Mirowski 2009, by uncovering the links between some Chicago projects, the establishment of the Mont Pèlerin Society (hereafter MPS), and their

1 Lerner to members of the Alfred Memorial Prize committee, undated (probably 1973), Abba Lerner Archives, Box10 folder 7.

2 See, for instance, Myrdal, (1977, 52) or Kaldor (1978, viii), and Rose Friedman (1977, 20) for an opposite version.

3 See, for instance, Bhagwati 1977's depiction of Friedman as an "ideologue" or Rapping in Klamer 1984.

4 For instance, Keynesian economist Franco Modigliani claimed that "Friedman is driven by the idea that whatever the government does is bad. He has a mission and seems to be willing to sacrifice some intellectual honesty for that" (Modigliani in Klamer 1984, 120), and Culbertson (quoted in Hammond 1996, 117) accused Friedman of a "deliberate misrepresentation of the truth" in his review of *A Monetary History*.

funding by conservative organizations, have recently argued that "the rise of the Chicago School must be understood as one component of a specific larger transnational project of innovating doctrines of neoliberalism for the postwar world" (140).

These narratives, however, provide no detailed account of the process whereby political values may have influenced Friedman's science.[5] Yet given that Friedman, as a statistician, subjected his hypotheses to a demanding process of confrontation with facts, the survival of some private beliefs in his science calls for further explanation. Likewise, Friedman's 1998 claim that it was his science that influenced his politics rather than the reverse is left unexplored. If it is now widely acknowledged that economic research is inescapably pervaded by ideology, then, says David Colander (2005, 11–12), the consideration must be shifted to "intentional ideological bias … that exceeds that ideological background level of ideology that affects us all."[6] Yet a framework in which persuasion (see McCloskey 1983), social control, and the ideological functions of economic theorizing is emphasized, and in which it is difficult to distinguish between the role of ideology in the *application* of a theory (a case well documented) and in its *formation* is not suited to the analysis of Friedman's "intentions."

Investigating how Friedman's ideas were initially formed requires a framework in which Friedman's beliefs can be disentangled from his propaganda strategies, and this paper is an attempt to provide one. To that end, we will consider economic research and political activity as just two ways of making sense of the world. Both activities rely on beliefs, views, and values built from private experience and from an understanding of the social environment, themselves deriving from religion, readings, professional training, encounters, and so on. These beliefs are ethical and political, but also positive (they amount to a view of the working of society and motivation of agents) and methodological (they assume certain methods to reach objective truths and a certain role of science in society). They tend to be combined in an "overview," an overarching picture of the world we will call a "worldview" in the tradition of phenomenology and hermeneutics; and in

[5] Warren Samuels (1976, 374) suggested that theories are value laden because Chicagoans assumed hypotheses taken from an a priori paradigm (the superiority of market solutions) and only paid attention to evidence consistent with these hypotheses. For Lepage 1977, both Chicago's science and ideology were rooted in the same representation of the human being as a rational maximizer.

[6] According to this principle, "it is Friedman, not Kenneth Arrow or Armatya Sen, who would, in my view, be far more likely to be described as crossing the ideological line," Colander (2005, 22) concluded.

the process, some beliefs are used outside their natural sphere.[7] They are neither necessarily conscious nor consistent with each other, and they are transformed, adjusted, and corrected throughout the economist's life. They form an interpretative framework that is used as a heuristic for the discovery of new facts and theories within science, and which may provide factual certainties on which to build a political ideology.

The thesis of this paper is that Friedman's scientific and political conclusions were consistent because they were jointly developed from a strong worldview, one that was framed during the 1930s and 1940s and were constantly reinforced afterward. This worldview was based on a vision of society composed of free, independent, self-interested individuals cooperating through market mechanisms to exchange goods, ideas, and values, resulting in mutual benefit and global stability. Individual freedom should therefore prevail over other values, Friedman claimed. This sanguine vision of society was paired with a distrust of collective action and a willingness to limit strictly (albeit not suppress) state intervention. The methodological belief that science helped reach consensus among citizens by producing objective knowledge through the confrontation with facts was another crucial feature of Friedman's worldview. Some of these beliefs developed from Friedman's private history and temperament, others from his training, professional encounters, and experiences. It is on these same core beliefs that Friedman simultaneously built a scientific and political system in the 1950s and 1960s.

Section 1 describes the origins and characteristics of Friedman's worldview, from his student days to the postwar years, when he was hired at Chicago, became interested in monetary economics, and participated in the founding of the MPS. Section 2 shows how Friedman's worldview informed his choice of hypotheses, his understanding of the "facts" (data series and historical evidence) he compared them to, and his econometrics. Section 3 examines the policy recommendations that Friedman produced *qua* scientist and *qua* political activist. In this in-between area where applied economics required reliance on private conceptions of the economic system

[7] We could alternatively have used the words cosmology, patterns, gestalts, world picture, or others. The purpose here is not to invoke such and such specific theory of understanding and of the possibility of objective knowledge. Nor is it to argue that this concept is systematically distinct from that of ideology; Schumpeter 1949 equated ideology with a "precognitive scheme" and a "vision" (see also Heilbroner 1990), and our definition of a worldview echoes Samuel's (1977, 470) definition of ideology. The somewhat artificial distinction between these two notions is meant to differentiate between an approach based on collective values, social control, and propaganda from one based on individual essential beliefs.

and where neoliberal doctrines were grounded in academic research, the boundaries of science and politics become blurred.

12.1. The Making of a Worldview, 1933–1948

Friedman's double connection with Chicago (where he studied economics with Jacob Viner, Frank Knight, and Henry Schultz) and the NBER (his study of income with Simon Kuznets in 1937–1941 would earn him a Ph.D. from Columbia) and his early practice as an economist (at the National Resource Committee in 1935–1937 and the Treasury in 1941–1943) and as a statistician (at the Statistical Research Group [SRG] in 1943–1945) is described in Jamie Peck, Tom Stapleford, and Dan Hammond's articles in this volume. From the variety of scientific practices and political perspectives he encountered in this formative period, Friedman fashioned the methodological, theoretical, and political beliefs that would form the basis of his worldview.

12.1.1. *How to Produce Scientific Knowledge Useful in a Free Society?*

Friedman's methodology was shaped gradually and pragmatically in reaction to the various scientific practices he encountered. His 1933 work on the estimation of demand curves, conducted under the leadership of Henry Schultz, plus his research on the National Resources Committee (see Stapleford, this volume) led to a rejection of rational choice–based microeconomics. Building indifference curves empirically was impossible, he argued, because agents rationalize or are confused, and are therefore not reliable (Friedman and Wallis 1942). His encounter with Keynesian theory, through the estimation of the tax rise necessary to curb inflation for the Treasury in 1942 and in the review of Oskar Lange's *Price Flexibility and Employment* in 1946 and Abba Lerner's *The Economic of Control* in 1947, caused him similar reservations. Friedman found the income-expenditure and the multiplier theories poor representations of the numerous channels whereby consumption behavior impacted prices and pointed to their lack of empirical content. His NBER study led to his encounter with the theory of imperfect competition, which the NBER director Reynold Noyes wanted him to adopt for the study of the medical profession because of differences in abilities and equipment. Instead, Friedman and Kuznets assumed that physicians competed freely, applied Marshallian price theory, and warned that the framework chosen should depend on the practical issue at hand (in their case, emphasizing the similarities *within* each medical profession to analyze income differences *between* them).[8] In fact, Friedman already believed that the perfect competition theory *always* proved "more useful for concrete analysis" (Friedman 1941, 390). By the end of the 1940s, he realized that these various theories he had challenged exhibited common characteristics: Their quest for descriptive accuracy ended up in a "retreat into purely formal theory." He collected them under the label "Walrassian economics" and lamented the "increasing prestige of speculative analysis" (Friedman to Ruggles 28/06/51, Box 32 Folder 16, MFA).

To this Walrassian economics, he opposed his own Marshallian approach, a policy-oriented and concrete problem-solving method he claimed to have found in his reading of Marshall's *Principles*, from which he borrowed his methodological catchphrase that science is "an engine for the discovery of concrete truth" (Friedman 1949, 469; 1953a, 35; see also Hammond, this volume). The economist should not strive to reach realistic statements valid in *all* circumstances, he explained, but theories "analytically relevant" for the issue at hand and judged by their predictive ability (Friedman 1940; 1953a, 9).[9] This policy-oriented approach, however, raised the threat that the economist, as a citizen personally involved in the issues he studied, might blend his positive analysis with ideological beliefs. Friedman had to face these very accusations in 1938, when the Board of Directors of the NBER opposed the publication of the income study on ground it was ideologically laden.[10] Friedman and Kuznets replied with a lengthy report adducing new empirical evidence and tests to their case, and concluded that "our interest in social problems (and who doesn't have such interests?) has stimulated us to make, rather than prevented us from making, an objective and tolerably thorough study of the facts of professional income."[11] Friedman's early confidence in the scientist's immunization from ideological bias was indeed firmly grounded in the empirical methodology he had inherited from his statistical training, his NBER affiliation, and his experience at the National Resources Committee, where despite the planning purpose of the institution and the left-wing ideology of most members, economists were committed to objectivity, empirical work, and cultivating relationships across the

[8] "Memorandum in reply to Noyes," 1941, p.7–8, Box 37 folder 24, MFA.

[9] The two drafts of Friedman's 1953 methodology essay are tellingly titled "Descriptive Validity vs. Analytical Relevance in Economic Theory" (1948) and "The Relevance of Economic Analysis to Prediction and Policy" (1952) (Hammond 2004).

[10] The main bone of contention was Friedman and Kuznets's explanation of the particularly high average income of physicians as compared with dentists by restrictions of entry in the medical profession.

[11] *Memorandum by Noyes*, undated; Crum to Carlson, 27/08/42; Memorandum to the Directors, by Friedman & Kuznets, undated 1943–1944, p25–26, Box 37 folder 24, MFA. See Also Friedman (1953, 4) especially the comparison with natural sciences.

political spectrum (Stapleford, this volume). It was therefore a pragmatic rather than philosophical stance, prompted by his observation that people from various political backgrounds (free-market oriented businessmen as well as public planners) would accept the same set of quantitative data as a basis for policy, and that he, as a neoliberal, could work with progressives such as Simon Kuznets and Wesley Mitchell.

A joint outgrowth of the Chicago Marshallian tradition and of his NBER affiliation, Friedman's methodology was also closely related to his vision of society and the role of the scientist within it. The preface of his work in professional incomes reveals that even before he became an activist, Friedman already envisioned American society as a combination of free, independent, self-reliant, and autonomous individuals seeking their material welfare and some agreement on common values through the exchange of goods and ideas: "[T]his approach treats professional activity as taking place in an economy best described as a free enterprise system in which the production of goods and distribution of incomes are regulated primarily by the impersonal mechanism of the market" (Friedman and Kuznets 1945, v). Such vision probably stemmed from his personal history: The survival of his parents, poor Jewish emigrants, he attributed to the American free enterprise system; and his ability to pay for his studies after his father's death by finding casual jobs in the midst of the Great Depression endowed him with a sanguine view of individuals. The preservation of a "free society in which voluntary cooperation is to be the foundation" required a "framework for settling differences of opinion by peaceful means." And in the wake of his encounter with Jimmy Savage in 1943 at the SRG, Friedman "ha[d] been led increasingly to regard scientific method as a set of conventions for resolving disagreements." As he later wrote to Friedrich Hayek: "I have been much influenced by the work of … James Savage … [who] claimed that probability judgments are judgments held by individuals separately, that there is nothing objective about any of these, and that the only way to define objective probability is in terms of agreement among different persons' subjective probabilities … [Savage] argues that the true function of statistics is not to discover knowledge but to resolve disagreement among people on subjective p," he explained. The kind of "true, though untestable, explanation" advocated by Hayek would however not help settling disagreements between free men "peacefully." Only the empirical confrontation with fact would convince them, he continued in the same letter.[12]

[12] Friedman to Hayek, 11/09/75, Box 20 folder 19, Hayek papers. Friedman's vision of the role of the scientist within society was also underpinned by his natural inclination for proselytizing and his faith in the power of ideas to change society (Nelson, 2001, 140).

12.1.2. *Market Efficiency and the "Competitive Order" as a Reality*

Friedman's personal vision of human motives and society was reinforced by his (selective) understanding of the philosophical framework Knight transmitted to him at Chicago. Knight's depiction of a society as a set of rational individuals endowed with diverging preferences and pursuing their welfare, as well as his claim that market-oriented systems should be favored because planning presupposed unattainable perfect information, struck a chord with the young student. Friedman's optimistic focus on the benefits of cooperation through markets nonetheless superseded his teacher's insistence on the pervasiveness of value conflicts and his warnings that the role of economic motives in human affairs should not be overlooked and that economic science should supplemented with an ethical reflection (see Emmett 2007 on the legacy of Knight). Although Friedman only used utility maximization as an "as if" hypothesis, in line with his 1942 rejection of rational choice theory, individual choices of the economic kind nonetheless formed a cornerstone of his worldview and acted as a heuristic for his research. For instance, his work on income distribution (Friedman 1953b) aimed at demonstrating that income inequality is not so much a product of institutional and legal constraints as it is the result of free individual choices and taste for risk (Hirsch and de Marchi 1990, 174). His vision of human motives have also overflowed the boundaries of the scientific sphere, so that his whole worldview can be characterized as essentially economic. As argued by Miller (1962, 68), "a major characteristic of the Chicagoans is their tendency to see and to apply economics all around them." This is illustrated, for instance, by Friedman and Stigler's early recreational talks of children as commodities and the associated calculation of "the cost of purchasing children in country and in city" to explain the birth-rate differential between countries and cities (Friedman to Stigler, 1952, quoted in Hammond and Hammond, 2006, 126). This also explains why economists renown for their forays in sociology, psychology, or political science, such as Gary Becker, emphasized the influence of Friedman on their intellectual development (see Becker 1993).[13]

According to Leonard Rapping (in Klamer 1984, 221), a former Chicago student, Friedman thought the coordination of these free autonomous individuals proceeded unimpeded: "[M]any Chicago people would argue that

[13] Friedman strongly supported the publication of Becker's thesis on *The Economics of Discrimination* (1957) against skeptics and admired his subsequent work on crime and punishment, family, and time allocation.

the world is, in fact, competitive," he remarked. Van Horn 2009 has extensively documented how this belief grew out of Friedman's participation in the Free Market Study (FMS), a project designed to demonstrate through objective and impartial empirical investigation that the American economy is competitive. Under the influence of its chairman, Aaron Director (Friedman's brother-in-law), Friedman endorsed the idea that the importance of monopolies in the American economy had been greatly overestimated; because economic forces tended to restore competition on markets, they could be considered minor and transitory. He tied his belief to compelling scientific evidence, to the empirical evaluation of the importance of monopolies within the United States provided by his student Warren Nutter, and to his personal observations during a 1950–1951 journey around Europe.[14] In a letter to colleague, close friend, and political ally George Stigler, in which we can consequently assume he dispensed with rhetorical flourish, he commented that "by comparison, America is perfectly competitive – you don't need to measure the degree of monopoly: it's zero").[15] Also, it was not only monopolies whose importance was overestimated, but also the other perceived obstacles to market adjustments, such as price rigidities (Friedman 1948) or unions, whose impact on wage he estimated as limited (Friedman, 1951a, 16).

Friedman's view of the economic system as free economic agents coordinating through competitive markets – a view he had built from a mix of private experiences, intellectual influences, and scientific evidence – gradually reinforced itself as Friedman shifted his attention back and forth between scientific and non-scientific spheres. It created lenses through which he interpreted new evidence, which he therefore saw as supporting his beliefs. For instance, Friedman (1958) retained from a trip to India and other developing countries during the 1950s the notion that economic development must rest primarily on the aspirations and actions of millions of individuals risking their own capital and seeking their own fortunes. His colleague Neil Jacoby, who supported a more active role of the government, made it perfectly clear that their disagreement was rooted in their diverging views of human nature: "I do not have the same faith that you do that there are in underdeveloped countries at the present time millions of 'able, active and

14 See also Schliesser, this volume, on the methodological ties between Nutter's dissertation and Friedman's methodology.

15 Friedman to Stigler, 15/01/50 [51], cited in Hammond and Hammond 2006. Friedman attributed the preservation of competition within the United States to America's culture and the Sherman antitrust law. (*Free Enterprise. An American View 1950*, Box 41 Folder 2, MFA).

vigorous people' who are motivated to engage in enterprise and who have the skills and capacities to do so."[16]

The consistency I have identified may seem overstated (see Hacohen 2007 on the danger of this widespread fault of historians). However, together with the process just described, I attribute the unusual stability of Friedman's vision to the protective and united Chicago intellectual environment in which he spent his remaining life. Friedman's closest colleagues, including Stigler, Wallis, and his wife Rose, exhibited similar scientific backgrounds (Chicago training with a NBER-style empirical practice). The cross-fertilization of their ideas produced a common paradigm that they succeeded in institutionalizing at the University of Chicago, one that is said to have grown largely out of Friedman's vision (Miller 1962; Reder 1982, 10, 32–33; Stigler 1963, 1988). The demanding Ph.D. program, which "inculcated distinctive habits of thought" in students (Reder 1982, 9; see also Emmett in this volume), and the constant financial backing of their research program enabled Friedman to transmit his vision through the price theory course he taught between 1946 and 1963 (see, for instance, the testimonies of Becker 1993, 32, and Lucas and Rapping in Klamer 1984); and some of their subsequent contributions (listed in Reder 1982, for instance) eventually came as a scientific legitimization of his worldview.

12.1.3. *A Liberalism Grounded in a Distrust of Government and Lobbies*

Like his positive beliefs, the political convictions of Friedman can be seen as a mix of intellectual influences and personal observations. The conservatism of his early mentors Homer Jones and Arthur Burns first oriented Friedman toward classical liberalism, a tendency then reinforced by Knight's teaching. His main source of inspiration, however, was Simons's *A Positive Programme for Laissez-Faire* (1934), especially its emphasis on freedom and on the need to organize a large sector of economic life competitively to preserve it (Friedman 1951c, 1955). Friedman found

[16] Jacoby to Friedman, 03/09/58, Box 28 folder 27, MFA. See also his report on a 1962–1963 world tour: "What impressed me most was the striking conflict between widely held beliefs and the empirical evidence. It is widely believed that economic progress in underdeveloped countries requires active governmental intervention in the form of central economic planning in order to assure the effective use of limited resources. Yet, if an observer who knew nothing about the ideological disputes on recent decades, or about current governmental policies, were asked to rank the various countries we visited according to the standards of living of ordinary people and the signs of material progress in their living conditions, there is little doubt that he would put the countries that have relied most heavily on central planning at the bottom and those that have relied on it least at the top"(Friedman to Anderson, 27/01/64, Box 23 Folder 3, MFA).

the book "strongly pro free market in orientation," and completely overlooked Simons's condemnation of concentration of economic power in unions, large corporations, and in the hands of government, a neglect he later attributed to the comparatively "strongly prosocialist" intellectual atmosphere of Chicago (Kitch 1983, 178–179). His permanent contacts with the little group mentioned earlier, in particular his marriage to Rose Director, who is credited with being the driving force behind Friedman's political zeal (Silk 1976, 68), explained why he remained remarkably immunized from the many progressive influences he encountered in his formative years – the teaching of Paul Douglas at Chicago, Mitchell and Kuznets at Columbia and NBER, the institutionalism of Wisconsin, and the Keynesian atmosphere of Washington administrations.[17]

The strength of Friedman's liberalism can also be explained by the several negative experiences of collective action, lobbies, and bureaucracy he went through in this formative period. Friedman interpreted the NBER controversy over his work with Kuznets as an excuse to defend the interests of medical lobbies (Friedman 1998, 74). In 1941, he was caught in the University of Wisconsin's internal department fights. Because he taught statistics and because he was Jewish, he was attacked by officials willing to merge the economic department with the business school (Lampman 1993, 118–121). From his stay at the Treasury, "[he] concluded that ... the frenctic atmosphere of a political capital, with its concentration of day-to-day issues ... renders a true scientific attitude almost untenable" (Friedman R. 1976a), Rose remembered. He interpreted a controversy between the Treasury and Leon Henderson and John Galbraith from the Office of Price Administration (OPA) over the estimation of the amount of additional taxes necessary to curb inflation as a deliberate strategy by the OPA to secure the legal authority over the determination of prices (Friedman 1998, 111). Finally, on publication of *Roofs or Ceilings* (1946), a pamphlet against rent controls, Friedman and Stigler were asked by Leonard Read and O. Watts, directors of the very conservative Foundation for Economic Education (FEE) who commissioned the book, to delete some paragraphs ironically considered as "collectivist propaganda" (Skousen 1998).[18] The two authors firmly refused to do so.[19]

[17] Rose later undertook the editorial work for *Capitalism and Freedom* 1962, coauthored the bestseller *Free to Choose* 1981, and insisted that her husband accept to write chronicles for *Newsweek* (Friedman 1998, 356).

[18] Friedman and Stigler's incriminated statement was that they, like most economists, were seeking the most efficient means to attain "even more equality than there is at present, not alone for housing but for all products" (Friedman and Stigler 1946, 6).

[19] Friedman to Read, undated 1946, Box 38 Folder 6, MFA.

These experiences made Friedman aware that public intervention was plagued by multiple biases and inefficiencies, but he was also conscious that in some cases government help was unavoidable.[20] The diagnosis that the expanding role of the state and the present-day social and economic issues required an in-depth modernization of the principles of liberalism was one that he shared with the other American and European intellectuals (including Director, Knight, and Stigler), businessmen, and journalists who gathered in 1947 at the initiative of Hayek to create the MPS.[21] Friedman's participation in the society identified him as a neoliberal (Mirowski 2009, 429), but whether MPS *influenced* Friedman's political thinking rather than *reflected* it is however difficult to document, for reasons touched upon in the last section. Whether Friedman's liberalism preexisted or not, it was nevertheless this founding meeting that initiated his activism.

That Friedman's positive, methodological, and political beliefs jointly developed from a range of private and scientific experiences explain why they were inextricably interwoven. This common set of beliefs built both his monetarism and his brand of neoliberalism in the following decades.

12.2. How Friedman's Beliefs Influenced His Science

Between 1948 and 1962, Friedman produced his major works, which include *The Theory of the Consumption Function* (1957), as well as his theoretical and empirical work on money found in *A Restatement of the Quantity Theory* (1956) and *A Monetary History of the United States* (1963) with Anna Schwartz. For both subjects, Friedman told a story of his intellectual development that emphasized that "the sequence of problems dealt with is determined by the internal structure of the work and not really by these kinds of external influences."[22] Still, his invariably anti-Keynesian and anti-interventionist conclusions suggest otherwise.

12.2.1. *The Underlying Quest for Stable Behaviors and Self-Stabilizing Mechanisms*

In 1967, Friedman claimed that "it was a sheer accident that led me to undertake as my first major project the study of incomes from independent

[20] "Even if we had completely free access to different employments and to capital, there would still be the problem of poverty," he remarked in his introduction to a 1947 MPS session on "taxation, poverty and income distribution" (Box 5, folder 12, MPS archives)

[21] On the history of the MPS, see among others Hartwell 1995 and Mirowski and Plehwe 2009.

[22] Friedman to Breit, 22/06/67, Box 21 folder 26, MFA.

professional practices. I was simply offered a job to work on that. It was there that the ideas about the importance of a regression toward the mean about the notions of permanent and transitory elements of income developed." Indeed, the Permanent Income Hypothesis is often described as the outgrowth of Kuznets's paradox – that the marginal propensity to consume remained stable across time despite steady increase in aggregate income, in contradiction with the Keynesian theory – and of the postwar attempts by several economists including Rose Friedman to explain current consumption by variables other than current income (see Hynes 1998). Thanks to his permanent-transitory income framework and ingenious identification hypotheses, Friedman was able to reconcile these opposing empirical conclusions within a single explanatory model. This model implied that the multiplier associated with government spending was very low unless the associated additional income was seen as permanent by households, thereby making stabilization policy inefficient.

This anti-interventionist conclusion, however, suggests that Friedman was influenced by more than just the technical developments in the field. Friedman's main motive for devising a new consumption theory was indeed to defeat the "secular stagnation thesis" and the idea that there could be long-run underemployment: "[T]he doubts about the adequacy of the Keynesian consumption function raised by the empirical evidence were reinforced by the theoretical controversy about Keynes's proposition that *there is no automatic force* in a monetary economy to assure the existence of a *full-employment equilibrium position*," Friedman (1957, 5; emphasis added) wrote in the introduction to his consumption book. Because the existence of a "full employment equilibrium," a consequence of the assumption that markets *are* competitive, was a cornerstone of the Chicago view (Reder 1982, 11–12), Friedman sought to build a dynamic theory that would supplement static Marshallian theory. His participation in a subgroup of the Committee on Public Issues of the American Economic Association devoted to the problem of economic instability in 1947–1949 and his 1948 reflection on monetary policy made him aware that the touchstone of his disagreement with Keynesians was the issue of stability. The long run stability and full employment that he believed characterized capitalist societies meant that the free coordination of self-seeking individuals through markets necessary embodied self-stabilizing mechanisms, such as the real balance effect (Friedman 1948). As a result, Friedman's consumption theory assumed a relation between consumption and wealth, both with stable characteristics: wealth consisted in the attribution of a constant annual income (except for a transitory component) on an infinite horizon, the so-called permanent income. Likewise, the consumer was said to consume his resources at a stable rate. Friedman's worldview therefore imposed preconceptions on what should be looked for in the data.

Friedman's account of his work on money is similarly thin and linear: "Once having started studying in the field of money, the internal logic of that development led a life of its own," he wrote to William Breit. His monetarism developed from the reexamination of the historical evidence for the 1929–1933 period, he claimed, and from the "Chicago Oral tradition" that made it natural for him to turn to the quantity theory as a theoretical framework (Friedman 1956, 3).[23] Yet the conclusions he had reached by 1963 – the stability of the velocity of circulation of money, the responsibility of the Federal Reserve in the worsening of the 1929 crisis, the variations in the stock of money as a major cause of business cycles, and the existence of "lags in transmission" prohibiting the use of discretionary policies – again sounded anti-Keynesian and fit perfectly with his neoliberal values. The coincidence was striking enough so that Hirsch and De Marchi (1990, 205) provided the following reconstruction of Friedman's intellectual development:

> In retrospect it looks as if he had seen by the late forties that he could not make an impression on the dominant Keynesian thinking merely by expressing methodological reservations about the system and its concepts. Something had to be offered in its place, an alternative that bypassed what he had long recognized as the key Keynesian element, the multiplier, and which performed better on the prediction front than it did. He chose the quantity theory as his candidate and probably began the NBER study with the aim of collecting data appropriate to testing the adequacy of a simple quantity theory hypothesis.

If not a deliberate strategy, Friedman's focus on a reformulated quantity theory may be explained again by his quest for stable behavior and self-stabilizing mechanisms. He came to the study of money with an a priori opposition to the Keynesian representation of the economic system, in which, according to Modigliani (1977, 27), "a private enterprise economy using an intangible money *needs* to be stabilized, *can* be stabilized, and therefore *should* be stabilized." For Keynesians, instability arose from the erratic move of interests rates, which in turn determine investment and the demand for money. Because of the possibility of liquidity traps caused by low interest rates, policy makers must resort to fiscal policy to restore equilibrium.

[23] The existence of a Chicago oral tradition has been one of the most debated claims by Friedman. The huge literature initiated by Patinkin's denial of such tradition is collected in Leeson 2003.

The hypotheses *a contrario* selected by Friedman (see Hammond 1996, 59–63 for details) – money is an asset used by households to adjust their portfolios, the velocity is a consequence of individual choices rather than technical factors – were consistent with his belief that economic outcomes resulted from the interactions of autonomous agents through competitive markets. His quest for stable behaviors influenced both the kind of data he collected and the pattern he found in them, for example, the procyclical and stable behavior of the velocity (Friedman 1952b, 621). He then explained it by a reformulation of the quantity theory where the demand for money was determined by permanent income (Friedman 1956) but not by interest rates (see Friedman's 1959 empirical study and Tobin's 1965 critique). Such reformulation allowed for a self-stabilizing mechanism through portfolio allocation, making government stabilization policy unnecessary (Modigliani 1977, 27). This framework in turn influenced Friedman and Schwartz's subsequent interpretation of new historical evidence. In the *Monetary History*, they explained the downward trend of velocity prior to World War II by the rise of income and the fact that money was a luxury good, and attributed the trend reversal after the war to enhanced expectations of economic stability, an explanation that their Keynesian opponents condemned as ad hoc (Tobin 1970).

However, it appears that Friedman's opponents were less critical of his theoretical hypotheses than of his empirical practice. At first, they called the latter "naïve" and "deceptively pretentious empiricism" (Culbertson, quoted in Hammond 1996, 115–118; Modigliani and Ando 1965; Kareken and Solow 1963), but when monetarism gradually came to be seen by economists and political figures as a valuable alternative to Keynesian economics, the tone hardened. Friedman was accused of "chicanery" and "charlatanism" (Johnson 1971; Kaldor 1982) and of distorting his results (Desai 1981; Hendry and Ericsson 1983). The violence of the attacks reached a climax when Frank Hahn (1984 1985, 326) derided the "sheer bravado of reducing the beautiful structure of general equilibrium theory to one or two log-linear equations" and compared Friedman's econometric methods to ancient Greek oracles. Friedman had succeeded in engaging his Keynesian opponents in an "econometric race," which eventually left the hegemony of the income-expenditure theory seriously undermined (see Leeson 2000, chapter 3). Yet the choice of econometric weapons by both sides was not merely driven by alleged technical superiority and scientific purity; it also indicated opposite visions of the usefulness of these results for the formation of economic policy.

12.2.2. *How Visions of Government Informed Econometric Choices*

The monetarist-Keynesian econometric race brought to the fore diverging conceptions of empirical work, epitomized by Tjalling Koopmans's famous "measurement without theory" critique of Burns and Mitchell's *Measuring Business Cycles* (1946).[24] Cowles researchers tried to model the economy as an exhaustive set of interdependent, simultaneous, and stochastic relationships of the Walrassian kind, and believed that the data would speak only once such exhaustive structural models were imposed on them.[25] Friedman found such undertaking unduly optimistic given their little of knowledge of economic behavior and saw it therefore as doomed to failure, as he explained to Joseph Willits from the Rockefeller Foundation in 1947.[26] Yet Cowles econometrics was also informed by the political agenda of its members. That Jacob Marschak, director of research between 1943 and 1947, titled the blueprint for his directorship "Statistical Foundations of Rational Economic Policy" is telling of what he believed was his and his fellow economists' social role: "I hope we can become 'social engineers,'" he had stated a few years earlier (Marschak 1941, 448). All this reflected the socialist background he shared with several other European émigrés from the Cowles Commission (see Mirowski 2002, chapter 5), or more precisely, their desire to ground government intervention/planning in scientific research. The specification-identification-estimation-testing procedure was designed with this purpose in mind, so that Cowles-style econometrics embodied a certain conception of the state from the beginning.

Friedman's econometrics belonged to a different tradition. The methodology of his study of the monetary history of the United States, including his emphasis on dynamics (understood as lags in adjustments [Friedman 1951b, 114]), his work with time rates of changes rather than variable levels, his first difference detrending technique, and his breaking up of times series in permanent and transitory components all bore the mark of the NBER; likewise, were his preference for single equation models owed to the NBER tradition and to his past work on alloys at the SRG (Friedman 1998, 143). Unlike Cowles econometrics, the NBER methods, created by progressive economists such as Mitchell and Kuznets, did not embody a distinctive

[24] Friedman helped Rutledge Vining's draft a reply to Koopmans, but he refused to be publicly acknowledged (Vining to Friedman, 01/11/48, MFA Box 34 Folder 33).

[25] For a detailed exposition of the Cowles method, see Christ 1994 and Epstein 1987.

[26] Friedman to Willits, 26/09/47, Box 35 Folder 16, MFA, see also Mirowski (2002, 215–220).

policy orientation and remained pragmatic and adaptable enough to accommodate Friedman's own worldview. His concern for self-stabilizing mechanisms and the disturbing effect of government intervention prompted him to borrow some mathematical patterns he had encountered years before in noneconomic work at the SRG. While preparing a report of shotgun errors in 1943, he was introduced to the nascent research on control engineering. In the models he studied, time lags and feedback loops implied that external action on systems can be destabilizing (Klein 2007, 22). The NBER tradition of looking for peaks and lags patterns in the data helped Friedman transplant these mathematical models into economics, thereby enabling him to highlight the potential destabilizing character of discretionary policies. Also, because he had no desire to improve government interventions he believed were inefficient, there was no need that the variables in his equations be controllable or that their endogeneity or exogeneity be precisely specified.

It was precisely these features of Friedman' s methods that drew fire from his Keynesian opponents. Nothing ensured that Friedman's variables, exogenous in his single equation models, would remain so in a model of a whole economy, Modigliani and Ando (1965, 693) complained. "The Friedman and Meiselman game of testing a one-equation one-variable model ... cannot be expected to throw any light on such basic issues as how to our economic systems work, or how it can be stabilized," they worried.[27] In the same vein, Karcken and Solow 1963 challenged the definition of money Friedman used in his 1961 estimation of the lags in monetary policy and recommended that the money variable be something that the Federal Reserve controlled directly. They insisted that *ceteris paribus* conditions be met and that the identification of money supply and demand factors be tackled. They also warned that a bare leading correlation between the peaks and troughs of monetary and income series could in no way stand for a demonstration that changes in the money supply *cause* business cycles (foreshadowing Tobin's 1970 famous *Post Hoc Ergo Propter Hoc* critique). As pointed out by Hammond 1996, Friedman was satisfied with a grey judgment on the "largely independent role of money" in lieu of the clear-cut causality Keynesians needed to implement their interventionist agenda.

[27] On the Friedman-Meiselman versus Ando-Modigliani controversy, Modigliani (1989, 578) later noted: "I must acknowledge that the difference in parameters is partly the results of prior beliefs of ideology.... There is obviously an ideological bias in assessing the values of the parameters ... we end up with somewhat different estimates of the same thing."

12.2.3. *The Crucial Role of Historical Evidence and its Dependence upon Private Beliefs*

Finally, Friedman's challengers reproached him with his inconsistent position toward econometrics. In a 1940 review of *Business Cycles in the United States of America*, Friedman had already faulted Jan Tinbergen for selecting the explanatory variables he knew would provide the highest correlation coefficient, thereby rendering the statistical tests of significance meaningless. Instead, he proposed to follow Mitchell's requirement that empirical work "must be judged, not by the coefficients of correlations obtained within the period for which they have manipulated the data, but by the coefficients which they get in earlier on later periods" (Friedman 1940, 660). Yet as pointed out by Mayer (1972, 59), in the *Theory of the Consumption Function* Friedman assumed the Permanent Income Hypothesis (PIH) was true and then adjusted the data to fit his hypothesis. Furthermore, the key prediction of the PIH – that the income elasticity is zero for transitory income and unity for permanent income, was never put to test. Diesing (1985, 65–69) also noted that, depending of the results of the tests for the PIH, Friedman resorted to a range of data-adjustments tactics. He sometimes exaggerated the fit with theory, invented ad hoc explanations for divergences, or rejected some data as unreliable or expressed puzzlement for the discrepancies. Several reviewers similarly pointed out the lack of modern tests other than on goodness of fit in his other works (see for instance Klein 1958, 543). When in 1951 Karl Christ used W. Marshall's new technique of out-of-samples testing to assess Lawrence Klein's macrostructural model of the U.S. economy, Friedman was one of the few in the profession to take notice in a review of Christ's paper (see Qin 1993, 138–139). It is therefore surprising that he did not subsequently make use of those tests that apparently fit his methodology perfectly.

These inconsistencies manifest Friedman's ambiguous position toward empirical work (exhaustively documented in Leeson 2000, chapter 2). In spite of his advanced statistical training and influential contributions to the field, he did not believe that econometrics could corroborate tentative hypotheses and yield causal relationships. Statistical evidence could be misleading, he warned, and high t statistics and R2 were "a test primarily of the skill and patience of the analyst" (Friedman 1951b, 108). Friedman's faith that the confrontation with fact brought scientific progress rather relied on the close analysis of historical evidence, and it was through historical narrative and counterfactual evidence rather than hypothesis testing that he intended to demonstrate the importance of money in business cycles. As he later put in a letter to Robert Leeson:

> I would never have been comfortable with the conclusions reached if the only basis for them had been the statistical correlations we were presenting. However ... I felt very confident in the evidence from history independently of the evidence from the statistical correlations, and hence regarded these as confirmatory rather than decisive evidence. (quoted in Leeson 2000, 38)

For Friedman, the varied character of economic history was a substitute for the lack of controlled experiments in economics: "[T]he student of economic change ... can observe monetary experience under sufficiently disparate conditions to sort out what is common from what is adventitious and to acquire considerable confidence that what is common can be counted to hold under still other circumstances" (Friedman and Schwartz 1963, 676). Hence his interest in wartime and depression periods – they provide "precisely the kind of evidence that we would like to get by 'critical' experiments if we conduct them" (Friedman 1952b, 612). In line with Mitchell's institutionalist vision (see Stapleford, this volume), Friedman ascribed a crucial role to historical evidence, proceedings of central banks meetings or events such as the 1928 death of the governor of the New York Federal Reserve. This reliance on historical episodes provided an ultimate channel whereby his distrust of the state informed his science. Indeed, his interpretation of such evidence was itself influenced by his worldview. For instance, the record shows that Friedman began his study of the monetary history of the United States with a clear picture of the role of the Federal Reserve in the Great Depression already in mind. During a 1947 Mont Pèlerin conference, Friedman approved a fellow economist's remark that "the history of the 1920s shows monetary discretion at its best" with an explicit statement: "I agree. The big error in Fed policy was that of 1931."[28] After spending the summer of 1948 reading monetary theory and history, he then wrote to Walter Stewart, chairman of the Rockefeller Foundation Board of trustees, saying, "the one general conclusion I came up with after going through this material and also some of the more recent material on the Federal Reserve, was the hunch that the Federal Reserve System had on the whole made matters worse rather than better. This is of course a pretty dogmatic statement, and I don't by any means feel utterly confident in it. It is also a statement entirely at variance with what I would have said in advance, so at least it derives from the evidence."[29] No wonder that Peter Temin, an economic historian and author of a history of the Great Depression, subsequently noted

[28] *Proceedings*, Box 87 Folder 10, MFA. This archive may have been misfiled and may be part of the proceedings of a 1948 conference organized within the Free Market Study.

[29] Friedman to Stewart, 12/01/49, Box 33 Folder 35, MFA.

that "their [Friedman and Schwartz's] narrative ... assumes the conclusion and describes the Depression in terms of it; it does not test it or prove it at all" (Temin, 1976, 15–16). Much later, in 1977, Modigliani also concurred that the source of his disagreement with Friedman ultimately was their different views on government intervention:

> Value judgments end up by playing a role in your assessment of parameters and of the evidence we consider ... And there is no question that Milton and I, looking at the same evidence, may reach different conclusions as to what it means. Because, to him, it is so clear that government intervention is bad that there cannot be an occasion where it was good! Whereas, to me, government discretion can be good or bad. (Modigliani, 1977, 10)

Not only were Friedman's theoretical hypotheses informed by a priori beliefs about the stability of the economic system and the harmful effects of government intervention, but the very process whereby he confronted these hypotheses with facts – the collection of data, the choice of discriminating historical events, the modeling, and the interpretation of tests – also appeared undetermined and inconclusive enough to allow Friedman's values to enter the inquiry.

12.3. Friedman's Policy Recommendations between Science and Politics

Friedman reflected on policy both as a scientist (see for instance Friedman 1948; 1952a; 1959), in line with his view that positive economics should comprise "the art of economics" (Friedman 1953a, 5; see Stapleford, this volume, for a discussion of the status of the "art of economics" in the 1953 essay), and as a political activist – such as in *Newsweek* chronicles, books like *Capitalism and Freedom* (1962), or his *Free to Choose* television show in the eighties. And it is when Friedman reflected on economic policy that the consistency between his science and politics was the most striking; whatever the sphere they belonged to, his proposals systematically favored free-market solutions over government intervention. If the boundaries between the two spheres become blurred in that in-between area, it is, we argue, both because the art of economics entailed the use of extra-scientific hypotheses and because Friedman sought to ground his neoliberalism in his scientific expertise.

12.3.1. *How Scientific Policy Discussions Make Room for Private Values*

Friedman considered the "art of economics" as directly deriving from positive analysis because he believed that the economist did not need to choose the social "ends" to be pursued and could therefore remain detached when discussing policy proposals: "[D]ifferences about economic policy among disinterested citizens derive predominantly from different predictions about the economic consequences of taking action … rather than from fundamental differences in basic values," he argued (Friedman 1953a, 5). He accordingly got into the habit of stating the "agreed ends" in the title or the first sentences of his articles. For instance, "A Monetary and Fiscal Framework for Economic Stability" (1948) began with the statement that: "[T]he basic long-run objectives, shared I am sure by most economists, are political freedom, economic efficiency, and substantial equality of economic power… I believe – and at this stage agreement will be far less widespread – that all three objectives can best be realized by relying, as far as possible, on a market mechanism within a 'competitive order' to organize the utilization of economic resources"(Friedman 1948, 246). Friedman seemingly saw no contradiction between ends such as price stability and employment and efficiency and equality, and his 1948 paper precisely aimed at showing that if price and wages were flexible, a policy proposal built for long-term stability *also* provided the best short-run regulation of the cycle.[30] Yet most of his colleagues found the idea of a general agreement on values extremely naïve. Albert Hart, a Columbia Keynesian economist trained at Chicago, remarked in a letter to Friedman that "giving priority to 'price flexibility' measures over employment strikes me as self-defeating through intensifying the forces which make prices misbehave." Possibly influenced by such comments and by Rose Friedman's (1976b, 22) opinion that "it is possible to predict an economist's positive view from my knowledge of his political orientation," Friedman later acknowledged a possible "inconsistency" between alternative ends and a "difference in time perspective" as regards their selection (Friedman 1977, 12, Friedman 1968). And his own preference for "the long view" over the short run undoubtedly rested on his belief in individual rationality and the system's stability.

Reflecting on his lifelong policy disagreement with Franco Modigliani, Friedman (1977, 12) also conceded a second source of disagreement: "our judgment of the way in which policy is formed, operates, and develops." Indeed, a policy proposal includes the choice of the institutional arrangement in which the causal sequence will take place, one that is rooted in the economist's vision of current institutions and the level of changes acceptable

[30] In a famous 1977 public debate with Modigliani again, he categorically refused to attribute their disagreement to the weight they respectively attached to inflation and unemployment (Friedman 1977, 12).

by public opinion. With regards to institutional matters, Friedman's position was ambiguous. In a 1953 rejoinder to Henry Oliver on *Economic Advice and Political Limitations*, he insisted that "economists should put politics aside in discussions of public policy" (see also Reder 1982, 26). As a matter of fact, the policy proposals outlined in his "Monetary Framework" were, by his own admission, designed as "a rational economic program for a free enterprise system" (1948, 254) in which prices and wages are flexible, a restriction his reviewer John Neff (1949, 947) saw as a major weakness. In the same vein, when Hart derided Friedman's 100 percent reserve proposal as "utopian blueprints," the latter replied that "one should set down the broad outline of the appropriate social framework without compromise. The compromise will come anyway." At the same time, Friedman (1953c, 252) also claimed that the economist should take into account "the realities of political life" because they "in part determine what the effects of a policy will be." His policy recommendations systematically took as a premise the belief that government intervention is an inefficient means to achieve whatever ends are considered, including employment and equality. Accordingly, the stumbling block of his disagreement with Neff on "The Monetary Framework" was "the relative merits of automatic and discretionary action" (Friedman 1949b, 942). Against the possibility of discretionary intervention, Friedman (1948, 255) held that government intervention was plagued by a recognition lag, an action lag, and an effect lag. Inspired by Simons (1934), he consequently advocated a system in which these lags would be reduced through the operation of automatic stabilizers – a predetermined countercyclical deficit funded by money creation coupled with a 100 percent reserve requirement in order to eliminate private creation of money and the discretionary control by the central bank. His opposition to fixed exchange rates was similarly underpinned by a wide range of anti-interventionists arguments. In 1948, he pointed to the possibility that the government makes larger mistakes with respect to the exchange rate level than private market operators, he also warned that government officials could display speculative tendencies. And he fought Lionel Robbins's skepticism toward free exchange rates with the observation that government would never "submit to the harsh discipline of any standard involving rigid exchange rates when it conflicts when the demand of full employment," because of the pressure of public opinion. [31]

[31] Hart to Friedman, Friedman to Hart, 4/08/1947, Box 38 Folder 13. MFA. "1947 Proceedings," Box 87 Folder10, Mont Pelerin Archives. Friedman to Robbins, 22/02/52, Box 32 folder 6. The comparison of these arguments with those given to Barry Goldwater, the Republican Party's nominee for the 1964 presidential election, illustrates how Friedman's scientific and political reflections eventually converge in the same policy proposals: "Such a measure is

The content of Friedman's proposals also derived from the influence of the zeitgeist of the neoliberal community. The sessions Friedman attended at the founding meeting of the MPS included one on "Contra-Cyclical Measures, Full Employment and Monetary Reform," another on "Free Enterprise or Competitive Order," and those devoted to the drafting of the "Statement of Aims." Its final version included the redefinition of the functions of the state with the underlying ideas that the conditions for the existence of a free society and a competitive order should be constructed; that government intervention should be limited by "the rule of law"; that it should be possible to establish minimum living standards by means not inimical to the functioning of markets; that the misuses of history for collectivist argumentation should be challenged; and that MPS members should work to design an international order safeguarding liberty (Harwell 1995, 49–50; Van Horn and Mirowski 2009, 159–160). Five months later, Friedman presented a draft of "A Monetary Framework" to the Econometric Society. The coincidence between it and the MPS manifesto is striking: "(1) Government must provide a monetary framework for a competitive order since the competitive order cannot provide one for itself. (2) This monetary framework should operate under the 'rule of law' rather than discretionary authority. (3) … general fiscal measures (as contrasted with specific intervention) are the most desirable non-free market means of decreasing inequality" (Friedman 1948, 246). The proximity in time suggests that Friedman's worldview was developed within the broader intellectual and political movement that gave birth to the MPS, but also makes it difficult to assess whether Friedman was influenced precisely by what he heard at the sessions.

In policy discussions as well, Friedman's worldview operated as a heuristic for the defense of new institutional arrangements, for the reshaping of the relationships between the state and economic individuals. However, the record of Friedman's participation to the rebirth of liberalism also suggest that, within the political sphere, his (and Chicago's) vision of the task specifically relied on scientific expertise, another characteristic shared by many MPS members.

12.3.2. *A Scientific Demonstration of the Superiority of Neoliberalism?*

From the beginning, the MPS was divided on what strategy to adopt to modernize and spread liberalism (Hartwell 1995, 103), an intellectual division

a direct restriction on individual freedom, no less so if done in the name of saving dollars than if done, as the Russians do, to keep their citizens from contract with the rest of the world … [it was] invented by Schacht and first introduced in Germany in 1934," Friedman wrote (Friedman to Goldwater, 12/12/60, Box 27 folder 24, MFA).

intensified by the cultural/geographical one (Mirowski 2009, 442). Whereas the old European guard – led by the Swiss businessman Albert Hunold, a financial benefactor of the society – saw the MPS as a platform for political lobbying, Friedman and the other Chicago economists involved in the society insisted that the defense of neoliberalism should be grounded in scientific analysis. Friedman's viewpoint largely contributed to the blurring of the boundaries between his science and politics.

The connection between science and neoliberalism was already implicit in his first talks on the subject, given in Paris and London during his journey around Europe in the early 1950s. In them, he explained that socialists and collectivists had failed on the means advocated rather than the ends pursued, on which there is wide agreement on ultimate values in Western societies:

> The major fault of the collectivist philosophy that has dominated the western world is not in its objectives – collectivists have wanted to do good, to maintain and extend freedom and democracy, and at the same time to improve the material welfare of the great masses of the people. The fault has rather been in the means. Failures to recognize the difficulty of the economic problem of efficiency coordinating the activities of millions of people led to readiness to discard the price system without an adequate substitute and to a belief that it would be easy to do much better by a central plan. Together with an overestimate of the extent of agreement on detailed objectives, it led to a belief that one could achieve widespread agreement on a "plan" couched in precise terms and hence avoid those conflicts of interests that could be resolved only by coercion. The means collectivists seek to employ are fundamentally inconsistent with the ends they seek to attain.[32]

If Friedman disagreed with socialists and interventionists about the means, then such disagreement could be solved through scientific inquiry. The opportunity to connect scientific research and political thinking more explicitly came in 1955 when John Van Sickle and Benjamin Rogge from Wabash College asked Friedman to give a series of conferences on the principles of economic liberalism and its policy applications. In reaction to the success of Kenneth Galbraith's *The Affluent Society*, Rose Friedman later gathered these lectures in a book: *Capitalism and Freedom* (hereafter *C&F*) would sell more than one million copies.[33] Unembarrassed with giving his thinking elaborated philosophical foundations, Friedman began his

[32] "Neoliberalism and its Prospects," Box 42 Folder 8, MFA, later published in the Mont Pèlerin's journal, *Farmand*.

[33] Friedman identified Galbraith as one of his main opponents and devoted much energy to counter his views. He wrote a pamphlet entitled *From Galbraith to Economic Freedom* (1977) and counterattacked Galbraith's 1977 television series *The Age of Uncertainty* with the *Free to Choose* show, broadcast in 1981.

opening lecture directly by setting the preservation of freedom as the main end for policies, one that, in accordance with his past experience of being part of a racial, intellectual, and political minority, he defined as "freedom from coercion."[34] This negative definition of freedom (see Smith 1988) received no further justification or elaboration. He then argued that the best protection from the coercion of the majority is the market, because it works as a "system of proportional representation" that provides coordination without standardization and a "check" to political power. He offered as an example the case of McCarthyism, where the academic market of labor had succeeded in protecting scientists against discrimination. However controversial, this example was more than a rhetorical device designed to shock the audience and genuinely reflected his understanding of the society he lived in. His choice seemingly derived from a lengthy private exchange with fellow economist, MPS member and friend Fritz Machlup. When the latter confessed his refusal to vote for Eisenhower because he received McCarthy's support, Friedman claimed Eisenhower's election would turn McCarthy into a "harmless snake."[35] By assigning a political function to the market, Friedman grounded his political analysis in his economic expertise. And by pointing out that "a necessary condition for individual freedom is the organization of the bulk of economic activity through private enterprise operating in a free market – a form of organization I shall refer to as competitive capitalism" (chapter 1 of *C&F*), he brought the debate into his area of expertise. In a last twist, he further narrowed his concern to the question of the redefinition of the role of the government in relation to markets (chapter 2 of *C&F*): "How can we keep the government we create from becoming a Frankenstein that will destroy the very freedom we establish it to protect?" (Friedman 1962, 2)

Turning the case for liberalism into a problem of weighing the benefits of markets against those of government intervention allowed Friedman to switch most of the argumentation from the political to the scientific level. In *C&F*, he first and foremost intended to restore "true facts" by relying on the evidence uncovered in his and his colleagues' empirical research and to derive policy proposal from this adequate representation of the economic world. Almost each chapter surveyed an issue previously dealt with in some academic articles. Friedman, for instance, used his monetary research to argue that "*the fact is* that that the Great Depression, like most other

[34] "All of us here are accustomed to being members of an intellectual minority, to being accused by fellow intellectuals of being reactionaries or apologists or just plain nuts," he characteristically emphasized in a 1976 MPS speech (quoted in Frazer 1988, 1972).

[35] Friedman to Machlup, 28/10/52, Box 38 Folder 25.

periods of severe unemployment, was produced by government mismanagement rather than by any inherent private instability of the private economy" (Friedman, 1962, 38, emphasis added), and then referred to his 1948 "Monetary Framework" article to support his proposal of a rule of action. The chapters on "international financial and trade arrangements," "fiscal policy," "occupational licensures," and "the distribution of income" echoed his work on floating exchange rates (1953d), excise and income tax (1942, 1952c), and incomes from independent professions (1945). The chapter "Monopoly and the Social Responsibility of Business and Labor" made extensive use of Nutter's 1951 study to insist that "*the most important fact* about enterprise monopoly is its relative unimportance from the point of view of the economy as a whole" (Friedman 1962, 121–25, emphasis added).

On the basis of the ideas that monopolies tend to be suppressed by competitive forces, that businessmen have no social responsibility, and that corporate income tax should be abolished, all contained in *C&F*, and on the basis of the Free Market Study and the funding of both projects by the Volker Fund, Van Horn 2009 and Mirowski and Van Horn 2010 assert that Friedman's (and Chicago) liberalism was "nominally anti-statist but in practice pro-corporate." Our impression is that, on the contrary, Friedman's stance was antistatist rather than pro-corporate, if only because Friedman's view of monopolies was paired with the symmetrical belief that the impact of unions on wages was overestimated. Also, although Friedman believed that public monopolies were more harmful than private ones, he harshly condemned both. It is indeed doubtful that Volker officials endorsed Friedman's denunciation of government support of the railroad, truck, gas, communication, radio and television, aeronautic, and building industries through regulations, subsidies, and tariffs (Friedman 1962, 123–129), or his recriminations against the New York Stock Exchange, AT&T, and American Oil companies in his *Newsweek* chronicles (Friedman 1972, 285; 308–310). As Samuelson remarked in a 1976 *Newsweek* column, "the adjective 'conservative' does not do proper justice to a thinker who would refuse the steel industry its import quotas, strip Texas of its oil subsidies, and deprive the railroads and the trucking interests of their protective regulations" (cited in Friedman, R. 1977, 27). As made clear by all his writings on the subject, Friedman had an interest in dealing with corporations and monopolies only inasmuch as they epitomized the drawbacks of government intervention. As for the repeated financial support of the Volker Fund, funding does not necessarily mean influence, and the *Roofs or Ceilings* dispute mentioned in previous sections fully testify to Friedman's intellectual independence with regard to funding bodies.

Friedman's political writings thus displayed a strong economic bent and a willingness to ground his arguments in scientific empirical research, one that can account for the consistency of his academic and political policy proposals. This scientific flavor was also apparent in subsequent projects and even became an asset for supporting funding bodies. To publicize their free society ideals, Friedman, Stigler, Hayek, Rogge, and Van Sickle created a collection of books entitled the Principles of Freedom series. With the help of journalist and petroleum consultant Ruth Sheldon Knowles, by 1963 they had secured funds from several big companies including Shell, the Continental and the New Jersey Oil companies, U.S. Steel, General Electric, DuPont, and Ford Motor, some of which Friedman had criticized in *C&F* and would later attack again in *Newsweek*. What appealed to these subscribers was that their ideological leanings could be supported by scientific expertise. The members of the advisory committee were recruited among well-known intellectual, including among others Maurice Allais, Knight, Gottfried Haberler, John Jewkes, Karl Popper, and L. Von Mises; and the brochure designed to raise funds, which Friedman extensively contributed to draft, emphasized scholarly orientation:

> We propose to enlist the collaboration of distinguished scholars in the preparation of a series of books dealing with important, controversial and misunderstood economic and political issues of the days.... The series will be designed for a number of audiences: young undergraduate students, businessmen, labor leaders, politicians, journalists, and the informed public. In order to reach these audiences, every volume should combine the highest quality of scholarship with lucidity and brevity. To this end we plan to bring together, when needed, the skills of scholars and professional writers.[36]

All the participants to the Principles of Freedom project except Knowles were MPS members. Yet the influence of the society of Friedman's political thinking is again difficult to assess. Friedman was a background character in the establishment of the society. He only intervened during general sessions to emphasize "that liberalism has a humanitarian aim and is a progressive philosophy,"[37] and he remained so in the first decade of existence of the MPS. He attended only three of the first ten meetings (the founding one, Bloemendaal 1950, and Princeton 1958), and only became a regular

36 RSK to Rogge, December 1963; RSK to Committee 04/03/64, Box 88 folder 5; RSK to Van Sickle, 08/08/65, Box 98 Folder 5, MFA. Knowles also characteristically remarked that "they [underwriters] feel our project is what should be done because of the scholars on the Committee."

37 "Statement of Aims; Monday April 7th" (Box 5, folder 12, MPS archives). See also "discussion of Agenda, April 4th" (Box 5, folder 13, MPS archives)

participant in 1960.[38] Friedman, Stigler, and others took over the leadership of the society in 1961 after the tumultuous resignation of Hunold and the withdrawal of Hayek (see Hartwell 1995). Admittedly, some of Friedman's political ideas matched those of the MPS, such as the insistence that the functions of the state should be redefined, not destroyed (Mirowski 2009, 436). However, some of his other political ideas, such as his exclusive focus on the economic dimension of political issues, conflicted with the Hayekian/Austrian wing of the society. In sum, I view MPS as a catalyst rather than a source of influence in Friedman's intellectual development.

12.4. Conclusion

This account shows that the consistency between Friedman's science and politics cannot be reduced to a deliberate or unconscious distortion of assumptions, models, results, and policy advice to fit one's political convictions. Our explanation highlights the complex interplay between the positive, ethical, and methodological beliefs that developed from Friedman's private experiences and observations, intellectual influences, and empirically tested scientific hypotheses. His faith in the benefits of a free individualistic society, in the stability of market-oriented systems, and his distrust of most forms of state intervention are the most salient features of his worldview. Although these beliefs provided *substantive* hypotheses on the world that influenced his research, his methodological choices, in particular his reliance on historical evidence rather than econometric procedures, shaped the *channels* whereby these hypotheses survived the confrontation with facts (on which he grounded his scientific objectivity). Friedman's worldview was in turn strengthened by these scientific confirmations; thus it appeared as a solid basis on which he could ground his neoliberal ideology, thereby blurring the boundaries between his scientific activity and his political propaganda.

References

Archival Sources

Milton Friedman Collection, Hoover Institution Archives, Stanford University.
Mont Pèlerin Archives, Hoover Institution Archives, Stanford University.
Hayek Collection, Hoover Institution Archives, Stanford University.
Abba Lerner Archives, Library of Congress, Washington.

[38] The triggering factor was Hunold's opposition to the membership of Seldon Harris and his discontent at the increasing role played by Harris's Institute of Economic Affairs in the management of the society.

Published Sources

Amadae, S. M. 2003. *Rationalizing Capitalist Democracy: The Cold War Origins of Rational Choice Liberalism*. Chicago: Chicago University Press.

Becker, Gary S. 1957. *The Economics of Discrimination*. Chicago, University of Chicago Press.

1993. "Milton Friedman." In Hammond, Dan, ed. *The Legacy of Milton Friedman as a Teacher*. Cheltenham: Edward Elgar.

Bhagwati, Jagdish. 1977. "Harry J. Johnson." *Journal of International Economics* 7: 221–9.

Christ, Carl F. 1994. "The Cowles Commission's Contributions to Econometrics at Chicago, 1939–1955." *Journal of Economic Literature* 32 (1): 30–59.

Colander, David. 2005. "Economics as an Ideologically Challenged Science." *Revue de Philosophie Economique* 11: 9–30.

Desai, Meghnad. 1981. *Testing Monetarism*. London: Frances Pinter.

Diesing, Paul. 1985. "Hypothesis Testing and Data Interpretation: the case of Milton Friedman." *Research in the History of Economic Thought and Methodology* 3: 61–89.

Emmett, Ross B. 2007. "Did the Chicago School Reject Frank Knight? Assessing Frank Knight's Place in the Chicago Economics Tradition." *Working paper*.

Epstein, R.J. 1987. *A History of Econometrics*. Amsterdam: North Holland.

Frazer, W. 1988. *Power and Ideas: Milton Friedman and the Big U-Turn*. Gainesville: Gulf Atlantic.

Friedman, Milton. 1940. Business Cycles in U.S.A., 1919–1932, II. *American Economic Review* 30: 657–660.

1941. "Triffin, Robert M., Monopolistic Competition and General Equilibrium Theory (Book Review)." *Journal of Farm Economics* 23(1): 389.

1942. "The Inflationary Gap: II. Discussion of the Inflationary Gap." *The American Economic Review* 32(2): 314–20.

1946. "Lange on Price Flexibility and Employment: A Methodological Criticism." *The Journal of Economic Review* 36(4): 613–631.

1947. "Lerner on the Economics of Control." *The Journal of Political Economy* 55(5): 405–416.

1948. "A Monetary and Fiscal Framework for Economic Stability." *The American Economic Review* 38(3): 245–264.

1949 "The Marshallian Demand Curve." *The Journal of Political Economy* 57(6): 463–495.

1949b. "Professor Friedman's Proposal: Rejoinder."*The American Economic Review* 39(5): 949–955

1951a. "Some Comments on the Significance of Labor Unions for Economic Policy." In *The Impact of the Union* edited by D Wright, New York: Harcourt Brace.

1951b. "Comment on 'A Test of an Econometric Model for the United-States, 1921–1947,' by C. Christ." In *Conference on Business Cycles*. New York: National Bureau of Economic Research.

1951c. "Neoliberalism and its Prospects." Milton Friedman Archives.

1952a. "The "Welfare" Effects of an Income Tax and an Excise Tax." *The Journal of Political Economy* 60(1): 25–33.

1952b "Price, Income, and Monetary Changes in Three Wartime Periods." *The American Economic Review* 42(2): 612–625.
1953a. "The Methodology of Positive Economics." In *Essays in Positive Economics.* London: Chicago University Press. *Check edition.*
1953b. "Choice, Chance, and the Personal Distribution of Income." *The Journal of Political Economy* 61(4): 277–290.
1953c. "Economic Advice and Political Limitations: Rejoinder." *The Review of Economic Statistics* 35(3): 252.
1953d. "The case for Flexible Exchange Rates." In *Essays in Positive Economics.* Chicago: Chicago University Press.
1955. "Liberalism Old Style," Milton Friedman Archives.
1956. "The Quantity Theory of Money – A Restatement." In *Studies in the Quantity Theory of Money*, edited by M. Friedman. Chicago: University of Chicago Press.
1957. *A Theory of the Consumption Function*; NBER General series 63. Princeton: Princeton University Press.
[1958] 1995. *Foreign Economic Aid: Means and Objectives. Yale Review.* Stanford: Hoover Institution Press.
1959. "The Demand for Money: Some Theoretical and Empirical Results." *The Journal of Political Economy* 67(4): 327–351.
1962. *Capitalism and Freedom.* Chicago: University of Chicago Press.
[1972] 1975. *An Economist's Protest.* 2nd ed. Glen Ridge, New Jersey: Thomas Horton and Daugthers.
1977. "Discussion." In Friedman, Milton, Modigliani, Franco, *The Monetarist Controversy: A Seminar Discussion.* University Press of the Pacific.
1993. "Postface." In Lavoie M., Seccareccia M.*Milton Friedman et son œuvre.* Montreal : Les presses de l'Université de Montréal.
Friedman, Milton and Friedman, Rose. 1981. *Free to Choose: A Personal Statement*; Ringwood, Vic.: Penguin Australia.
1998. *Two Lucky People.* Chicago: Chicago University Press.
Friedman, Milton and Kuznets, Simon. 1945. *Income From Independent Professional Practice.* NBER Publications 45. New York: National Bureau of Economic Research.
Friedman, Milton and Schwartz, Anna. J. 1963. *A Monetary History of the United States, 1867–1960.* NBER Studies in business cycles no. 12. Princeton: Princeton University Press.
Friedman, Milton and Stigler, George J. 1946. *Roofs or Ceilings? The Current Housing Problem.* Irvington-on-Hudson: Foundation for Economic Education.
Friedman, Milton and Allen, Wallis. 1942. "The Empirical Derivation of Indifference Functions." In Lange Oscar, McIntire Francis, Yntema Theordore eds., *Studies in Mathematical Economics and Econometrics, in Memory of Henry Schultz*, Chicago: University of Chicago Press, 775–89.
Friedman, Rose. 1976a. "Milton Friedman: Husband and Colleague – The Beginning of a Career." *Oriental Economist* 44 (June): 18–23.
1976b. "Milton Friedman: Husband and Colleague – A Spokesman for Libertarianism." *Oriental Economist* 44 (September): 22–27.
1977. "Milton Friedman: Husband and Colleague – The Nobel Award." *Oriental Economist* vol. 45 (February), 24–28.
Galbraith, John K. 1952. *A Theory of Price Control.* London: Geoffrey Cumberlege.

Hacohen, Malachi. 2007. "Rediscovering Intellectual Biography – and its Limits." *History of Political Economy* 39(Suppl 1): 9–29.

Hahn, Frank. 1984. "Why I am not a Monetarist." In *Equilibrium and Macroeconomics*. Cambridge, MA: M.I.T. Press.

1985. "Some Keynesian Reflections on Monetarism." In Vicarelli Fausto ed., *Keynes's Relevance Today*. London: Macmillan.

Hammond, Dan. 1996. *Theory and Measurement: Causality Issues in Milton Friedman's Monetary Economics*. Cambridge : Cambridge University Press.

2004. "Friedman's Methodology Essay in Context." working paper.

Hammond, Dan and Claire H., Hammond. 2006. *Making Chicago Price Theory: Friedman-Stigler Correspondance 1045–1957*. New-York: Routledge.

Hartwell, Ronald M. 1995. *A History of the Mont Pelerin Society*. Indiannapolis: Liberty Fund Inc.

Heilbroner, Robert. 1990. "Analysis and Vision in the History of Modern Economic Thought." *Journal of Economic Literature* 28: 1097–114.

Hendry, D.F. and Ericsson, N.R., 1983. "Assertion Without Empirical Basis: An Econometric Appraisal of 'Monetary Trends in … the United Kingdom' by Milton Friedman and Anna Schwartz." In Bank of England Panel of Academic Consultants, *Monetary Trends in the United Kingdom*, pp.45–101, Panel Paper no. 22.

Hirsch, A. and De Marchi, N. 1990. *Milton Friedman: Economics in Theory and in Practice*. Ann Arbor: University of Michigan Press.

Hynes, Allan J. 1998. "The Emergence of the Neoclassical Consumption Function: The Formative Years, 1940–1952." *Journal of the History of Economic Thought* 20 (1).

Johnson, Harry J. 1971. "The Keynesian Revolution and the Monetarist Counter-Revolution." *American Economic Review* 61(2): 91 106.

Kaldor, Nicholas. 1978. *Further Essays on Applied Economics*. London: Duckworth.

1982. *The Scourge of Monetarism*. Oxford: Oxford University Press.

Kareken, John, and Solow, Robert M. 1963. "Lags in Monetary Policy." In *Stabilization Policies*. Commission on Money and Credit. Englewood Cliffs, NJ: Prentice Hall.

Klein, Judy. 2007. "Post War Economics and Shotgun Weddings in Control Engineering." working paper.

Klein, Lawrence R. 1958. "The Friedman-Becker Illusion." *The Journal of Political Economy*, vol.66 no. 6, 539–545.

Kitch, Edmund. 1983. "The Fire of the Truth: A Remebrance of Law and Economics at Chicago, 1932–1970." *Journal of Law and Economics* 26 (1): 163 231.

Klamer, Arjo. 1984. *Conversations with Economists: New Classical Economists and Opponents Speak Out on the Current Controversy in Macroeconomics*. Rowman & Littlefield Publishers.

Lampman, Robert J. 1993. "Essay II. The Milton Friedman Affair at Wisconsin, 1940–41." In Lampman R. ed, *Economists at Wisconsin, 1892–1992*. Madison: The Board of Regents of the University of Wisconsin System

Lavoie, M. and Seccareccia, M. 1993. *Milton Friedman et Son Oeuvre*. Montreal : Les presses de l'Université de Montréal.

Leeson, Robert. 2000. *The Eclipse of Keynesianism: The Political Economy of the Chicago Counter-Revolution*.New York: Palgrave.

Leeson, Robert (ed). 2003. *Keynes, Chicago and Friedman*. London: Pickering and Chatto.

Lepage, H. 1977. "Les 'Nouveaux Economistes' américains : une révolution scientifique et idéologique." *Diogène* (100): 231–251.

Marschak, Jacob. 1941. "A Discussion on Methods in Economics." *Journal of Political Economy* 49(3), 441–448.

Mayer, Thomas. 1972. *Permanent Income, Wleath, and Consumption*. Berkeley: University of California Press.

McCloskey, Donald N. 1983 "The Rhetoric of Economics." *Journal of Economic Literature* 31(2), 481–517.

Miller, H. 1962. "On the Chicago School of Economics." *The Journal of Political Economy* 70: 100–123.

Mirowski, P. 2002. *Machine Dreams: Economics Becomes a Cyborg Science*. Cambridge: Cambridge University Press.

Mirowski, Philip. 2009. "Postface: Defining Neoliberalism." In Philip Mirowski and Deiter Plehwe, eds., *The Road from Mont Pèlerin: The Making of the Neoliberal Thought Collective*. Cambridge, MA: Harvard University Press,

Modigliani, Franco and Ando, Albert. 1965. "The Relative Stability of Monetary Stability and the Investment Multiplier." *The American Economic Review* 55(4): 693–728.

Modigliani, Franco. 1977. "Should We Forsake Stabilization Policies." Reprinted in Friedman, Milton, Modigliani, Franco, *The Monetarist Controversy: A Seminar Discussion*. University Press of the Pacific.

1989. "An Interview." In *The Economic of Imperfect Competition and Employment: Joan Robinson and Beyond*, edited by Feiwel G.R. London: Macmillan.

Myrdal, Gunnar. 1977. "The Nobel Prize in Economic Science." *Challenge* 50 (March-April).

Neff, John U. 1949. "Professor Friedman's Proposal: A Comment." *American Economic Review* 39(5): 946–949.

Nelson, Robert. 2001. *Economics as Religion: From Samuelson to Chicago and Beyond*. University Park: Pennsylvania State University Press.

Qin, Duo. 1993. *The Formation of Econometrics: An Historical Perspective*. Oxford: Clarendon Press.

Reder, Melvin R. 1982. "Chicago Economics: Permanence and Change." *Journal of Economic Litterature* 20 (1): 1–38.

Samuels, Warren J., ed. [1976] 1993. *The Chicago School of Political Economy*. New Brunswick: Transaction Publishers.

Samuels, Warren, J. 1977. "Ideology in Economics." In Weintraub S. (ed) *Modern Economic Thought*, Oxford: Blackwell.

Schumpeter, Joseph A. 1949. "Science and Ideology." *American Economic Review* 39: 345:59.

Silk, L. 1976. *Five Economists*. New-York: Basic Books, Inc. Publishers.

Simons, Henry. 1934. *A Positive Program for Laissez-Faire: Some Proposals for a Liberal Economic Policy*. Chicago: Chicago University Press.

Skousen, Mark. 1998. "Vienna and Chicago: A Tale of Two Schools." *The Freeman* 48(2).

Smith, Vardaman. 1998. "Friedman, Liberalism, and the Meaning of Negative Freedom." *Economics and Philosophy*, (14): 75–94.

Stigler, Georges J. [1988] 2003. *Memoirs of an Unregulated Economist*. Chicago: university of Chicago Press.

Temin, Peter. 1976. *Did Monetary Force Cause the Great Depression?* New York: Norton.

Tobin, James. 1965. "The Monetary Interpretation of History." *American Economic Review* 55: 464–485.

1970. "Money and Income: Post Hoc Ergo Propter Hoc?" *Quaterly Journal of Economics* 84: 301–317.

Van Horn, Robert. 2009. "Reinventing Monopoly and the Role of Corporations: the Roots of Chicago Law and Economics." In Philip Mirowski and Deiter Plehwe, eds., *The Road from Mont Pèlerin: The Making of the Neoliberal Thought Collective*. Cambridge, MA: Harvard University Press.

Van Horn, Robert and Mirowski, Philip. 2009. "The rise of the Chicago School of Economics and the birth of neoliberalism." In Philip Mirowski and Deiter Plehwe, eds., *The Road from Mont Pèlerin: The Making of the Neoliberal Thought Collective*. Cambridge, MA: Harvard University Press, 139–178.

2010. "Chicago and Neoliberalism." in Ross Emmett ed., *The Elgar Companion to the Chicago School of Economics*, Northampton, MA:Edward Elgar.

Van Overtveldt, Johan. 2007. *The Chicago School: How the University of Chicago Assembled the Thinkers Who Revolutionized Economic and Business*. Chicago: Agate.

THIRTEEN

Chicago Neoliberalism and the Genesis of the Milton Friedman Institute (2006–2009)

Edward Nik-Khah

13.1. Introduction

The year is 2011. With the Great Recession approaching its fourth birthday, and economists still struggling to make sense of what markets have wrought, it is no surprise that the reputations of some celebrated economists have taken a hit. In some cases, the reappraisal was dramatic and probably decisive. (Will it ever again be possible to call Alan Greenspan the "Maestro" with a straight face?) In other cases, the crisis has served less to settle matters than to inflame ongoing disputes. So it is with Milton Friedman.

Friedman is probably best known outside of academic economics for his championing of promarket views (and his aggressive attacks on opposing views) in his widely read books like *Capitalism and Freedom*, his PBS series *Free to Choose*, and his recurring *Newsweek* column. In 2008 (in what now looks like a case of catastrophically bad timing) the administration of the University of Chicago decided it would be an opportune time to "honor Friedman's legacy" and announced it planned to establish a privately funded $200 million research institute. It did not take long for University of Chicago professors numbering more than one hundred in total from fields as disparate as anthropology, political science, and statistics to express their displeasure. Presently, the dispute broke out of the confines of the university and spilled onto the pages of the *New York Times* and the *Wall Street Journal*.

Much of the dispute turned on what one understood Friedman's legacy to be.[1] Critics argued that because Friedman's most obvious legacy was his

Author's note: I am grateful to Rob Van Horn for his extensive comments on this chapter and to Tom Scheiding for his comments on an earlier draft. I acknowledge the research assistance of Samantha Sterba.

[1] A sample of newspaper headlines provides some indication of how focused the protagonists were on Friedman's legacy: "University of Chicago's New Institute Honors Milton

promarket politics, naming an institute after Friedman – particularly one with a $200 million war chest – amounted to an official endorsement of his politics. Friedman's political beliefs were beside the point, countered supporters of the institute. In their view, his most important legacy was a commitment to empiricism and analytical rigor. In this way, the controversy over the Milton Friedman Institute (MFI) resembled a referendum on the career of Milton Friedman himself. Supporters reminded us of his Nobel Prize; critics reminded us of his interactions with Augusto Pinochet. Both argued that the reputation of the University of Chicago hung in the balance. The disagreement intensified with the arrival of the current crisis. Critics charged that Friedman's ideas caused it; Mark Hansen, Dean of Social Sciences and member of the MFI administrative oversight committee, shot back, "How do you know?" and suggested that such questions are best left for Friedman Institute economists to sort out.[2]

Yet what if all the heated rhetoric about Friedman's career misses the crucial point? After all, one doesn't spend $200 million merely to "celebrate a legacy." This chapter argues that one learns more about the activities of the MFI, and thereby the present day Chicago School, by viewing the MFI through the lens of the history of "Chicago neoliberalism." Compelling circumstantial reasons suggest the potential for this approach to be fruitful: Milton Friedman was a former president of the central organizational hub for neoliberal activities, the Mont Pèlerin Society (MPS), and, with the establishment of the MFI, Chicago now has a high profile institute or center named for each of its former MPS presidents (the others being the Stigler Center for the Study of the Economy and the State and the Becker Center on Chicago Price Theory). Additionally, there are better reasons: A former president of the MPS (Gary Becker) plays a prominent role within the MFI, and members of the MFI board have participated in neoliberal think tanks. This chapter

Friedman"; "University of Chicago Economists to Focus their Pioneering Research in New Institute Honoring Memory of Milton Friedman"; "Protests Grow over Friedman Honour"; "Debate Rages over Legacy of a Free-market Icon"; "On Chicago Campus, Milton Friedman's Legacy of Controversy Continues"; "As Wall Street Collapses, So Does Milton Friedman's Legacy." Gary Becker interprets most of the controversy as pertaining to Friedman's legacy, which he defends in his blog at http://www.becker-posner-blog.com/archives/2008/10/observations_on.html; Yali Amit, a leader of the petitioners opposed to the institute, mostly agrees: Adrian Florido and Michael Lipkin 2008, "Faculty Senate Meets to Discuss Friedman Issue" (available: http://www.chicagomaroon.com/2008/10/17/faculty-senate-meets-to-discuss-friedman-institute).

2 Hansen quoted in Amy Braverman Puma, "What's in a Name?" *University of Chicago Magazine*. Available: http://magazine.uchicago.edu/0811/chicago_journal/whats_in_a_name.shtml

does indeed reveal that the MFI employs a method of knowledge production that fits the Chicago neoliberal script: the construction of doctrines with the express purpose of influencing policy, the employment of a fine-grained intellectual division of labor to do so, and the financing of these activities by powerful economic elites.

To directly address a potential misunderstanding up front, the rationale for examining the controversial MFI is not because it is interesting in its own right, nor is it to pronounce which side of the debate is "right"; but instead, it is because the controversy furthers our understanding of the present-day Chicago School. The controversy provides evidence about how the Chicago School organizes itself and to what ends; it also reveals the level of knowledge about the Chicago School held by those who are critical of it. There is evidently a great deal of interest about the present-day operations of the Chicago School. Given this interest, the reader might feel justified asking how the rich histories contained in the previous chapters may be used to understand the Chicago School today. This chapter provides an answer: It builds on existing histories of Chicago neoliberalism by bringing the account of the Chicago School up to the present day and uses the MFI as a proxy to do so.

To develop its account of present-day Chicago, this chapter examines a nontraditional assortment of materials – the unpublished work of the MFI steering committee, as well as their public statements as reported in newspapers and on blogs.[3] It focuses, first, on the original proposal drafted by the MFI steering committee, and augments this reading by considering themes that emerged from this book as well as studies of Chicago neoliberalism beyond this volume. Next, this chapter focuses on the petition presented against the MFI and argues that viewing the MFI through the lens of Chicago neoliberalism can better structure the concerns expressed in this petition.

13.2. What the History of Chicago Neoliberalism Can Tell Us about the MFI

Shortly after the November 2006 death of Milton Friedman, a handful of professors at Chicago began conversations with Chicago President Robert Zimmer on the possibility of organizing an institute to be named after

[3] Of course, examining sources from the press and from blogs carries with it a risk of devaluing the kind of archival work undertaken by serious historians of thought. But the intended lesson of this chapter is precisely the opposite: It is only by coming to terms with the historical evidence that one can get beneath surface appearances.

Friedman.[4] In May 2007, president Zimmer convened an ad hoc committee of prominent professors from economics, business, and law to study the possibility of forming an institute. He named Lars Hansen chair, and placed Gary Becker, John Cochrane, James Heckman, Robert Lucas, Kevin Murphy, and Eric Posner on the steering committee. The committee submitted a report (Hansen et al. 2008) in January 2008 that called for the establishment of a Milton Friedman Institute (MFI), and presented it to the Council of the Faculty Senate in February, at which time the president and provost, Thomas Rosenbaum, approved the plan. The MFI began limited operation in July 2008, and by February 2009 the MFI was fully operational, with a slight name change (the "Milton Friedman Institute for Research in Economics"). The steering committee remained the same, and Lars Hansen assumed its directorship. Because the members who drafted the initial report remain in charge of the MFI, the report provides a peek into the activities of the Chicago School.

As one might expect, the authors of the MFI proposal framed its activities in terms of the legacy of Milton Friedman. However, one does not learn much from the proposal about what this legacy is:

> Milton Friedman typified and became emblematic of the "Chicago School" of economics until his death one year ago.... The institute that the committee is proposing would build upon this important tradition by investigating research questions related to economic policy through the use of formal economic models with explicit empirical underpinnings. Following Friedman's lead, the design and evaluation of economic policy requires analyses that respect the incentives of individuals and the essential role of markets in allocating goods and services. As Friedman and others continually demonstrated, design of public policy without regard to market alternatives has adverse social consequences. (Hansen et al. 2008, 2)

Although the proposal includes items that are somewhat "Friedman-esque," the list it provides does seem a bit short, at least as far as celebrations of legacies go. Although some of the more concrete examples of projects offered in the proposal do connect more directly to Friedman's work (the proposal does mention monetary policy), others have little to do with Friedman (the proposal also calls for developing dynamic stochastic equilibrium models).[5]

4 The timeline is cribbed from (Hansen 2008).

5 There is some disagreement between members about the MFI about how to conceive of Friedman's legacy. In the immediate aftermath of Milton Friedman's death, prominent members of the Chicago School – including MFI committee members Gary Becker, Robert Lucas, and James Heckman – gathered for a roundtable celebrating his legacy. Heckman recalls that it quickly became apparent that there was considerable disagreement about just what Friedman's legacy was:

> When Friedman died, a couple of years ago, we had a symposium for the alumni devoted to Friedman's legacy. I was talking about the permanent income hypothesis; Lucas

If one wants to learn more about the inspiration behind the MFI proposal, one is probably better off comparing it with the activities of centers at the Chicago School that are already in operation – the Becker Center on Chicago Price Theory and the Stigler Center for the Study of the Economy and the State. The Becker Center mission statement reads as follows: "The [Becker] Center builds on the rich tradition of Chicago Price Theory that emphasizes the fundamental role of markets and incentives in understanding and improving all aspects of modern life."[6] Steven Levitt, founding director of the Becker Center, explains: "Our goal [is] … to further the rich tradition of Chicago economics that emphasizes answering real-world questions through a combination of rigorous models and careful data analysis."[7] The Stigler Center's mission statement reads as follows:

> [T]he Stigler Center seeks to … make a unique contribution to the field through the application of "Chicago-style" analysis to issues confronting economic policy markers at all levels of government. That analysis is marked by an effort to verify theoretical predictions of behavior through a careful analysis of data and evidence. Known worldwide, the "Chicago School" of Economics views theory not as an end but as a tool to assist in understanding the real world. It also is noted for a deep appreciation of the ability of private markets to allocate scarce resources efficiently.

When considered alongside the Becker and Stigler centers, the mission of the MFI, as articulated within the proposal, does not appear especially novel. One repeatedly encounters references to "Chicago-style" analysis, "Chicago Price Theory," an "appreciation of markets," the "fundamental role of markets," the "essential role of markets," the importance of "incentives," the need to connect somehow to the "real world," and need for "empirical underpinnings" or "data." Although the institutions have different emphases (the Becker Center emphasizes study of all areas of human behavior; the Stigler Center focuses on the relationship between the economy and

was talking about rational expectations. We have some bright alums. One woman got up and said, "Look at the evidence on 401k plans and how people misuse them, or don't use them. Are you really saying that people look ahead and plan rationally?" And Lucas said, "Yes, that's what the theory of rational expectations says, and that's part of Friedman's legacy." I said, "No, it isn't. He was much more empirically minded than that. They moved too far away from the data."

John Cassady, "Interview with James Heckman." Available: http://www.newyorker.com/online/blogs/johncassidy/2010/01/interview-with-james-heckman.html.

6 The statement can be found at the Web site for the Becker Center on Chicago Price Theory, available at: http://research.chicagobooth.edu/pricetheory/about/index.aspx (accessed 5/24/2010).

7 Steven Levitt, "Becoming the Becker Center on Chicago Price Theory," available at: http://www.chicagobooth.edu/capideas/may07/intro.aspx.

the state), there are large areas of overlap, not only in mission, but also in directorship and membership: Gary Becker serves as director of the Becker Center and on the executive committee of the Stigler Center; Kevin Murphy serves as a director of the Becker Center and as a research faculty member of the Stigler Center. Given the similarity in missions and the interlocking directorates of these institutions, one can generalize from the activities of one across the rest of these institutions; to the extent that the MFI proposal reveals something about the beliefs, values, and goals of its members, one can then learn something important about the Chicago School today.

The proposal of the MFI committee reveals that today's Chicago School resembles that of the previous generation with respect to the themes developed in the introduction to this volume and pursued throughout by its authors: The Chicago School's view of the aims of economic science distinguishes it from other academic institutions; concerns about building an economics for policy assume paramount importance; and Chicago scholars are "empire builders" who seek to forge relations with economic elites for the purpose of creating and promoting their ideas. Therefore, like the previous generation of the Chicago School, examining the proposal through a neoliberal lens offers a valuable perspective on these themes. The remainder of this section draws on ideas developed within the literature on Chicago neoliberalism to address these three historical themes. First, Chicago scholars believe they possess a comparative advantage in the construction of an economics for policy, differentiating them from other schools such as MIT or Yale. Philip Mirowski (2009) has previously identified the construction of an economics built for policy as a hallmark neoliberal position. Second, the Chicago School relies on a fine-grained intellectual division of labor to promote their ideas about policy. Dieter Plehwe (2009) has previously noted that neoliberals rely on both academic and nonacademic institutions to influence ideas and policy. Third, Chicago's empire-building activities are often grounded in beliefs about the operation of the marketplace of ideas. Elite scientists define their efforts in such a way as to secure the support of economic elites for the purpose of combating undesirable approaches to policy, an observation about neoliberals made by Mirowski (2009) and developed for the specific case of Stigler in (Nik-Khah this volume).

13.2.1. *Competition in the Marketplace of Ideas*

The first theme relates to the mechanisms and aims of intellectual competition. In addressing the mechanisms of intellectual competition, the MFI proposal indicates a need to keep Chicago competitive by attracting high-quality scholars in various stages of their careers, retaining the ones they already have, and attracting good students. The MFI committee is clearly concerned with maintaining competitiveness vis-à-vis other top programs:

> Some of the most outstanding economics departments, business schools, and law schools that we compete with are housed in universities making substantial investments in infrastructure to support economic research. Chicago economics requires at least comparable resources to those of our top competitors. (Hansen et al. 2008, 3)

MFI committee members have often individually echoed this reasoning. For example, Gary Becker argued that the MFI would allow Chicago to "compete much more effectively against Princeton, Harvard, and Stanford – schools much better endowed than we are"[8]; Lars Hansen asserted, "The economics department is small, compared to some of its rivals."[9] The proposal attributes much of the infrastructural advantages of the other institutions to the presence of institutes on their campuses: Yale has the Cowles Commission; MIT and Harvard have the NBER. This narrower form of competition – competition for talent – is pretty ordinary: Every school and institute faces the same issue, and each must marshal resources to address it. These kinds of "nuts and bolts" activities – recruiting and retaining faculty – though undoubtedly important, do not seem, however, like the sort that could inspire hundreds of millions in donations.

Donors are likely to want to know why someone should fund this institute as opposed to one at, say, Columbia. Chicago scholars have a ready answer:

> Relative to … other top schools, the Chicago economics department is small both in terms of size and resources. The Friedman Institute will increase the scale at which Chicago economics will operate, giving us a better chance of competing with the other top schools for faculty and students. The Friedman Institute will help us *compete in the marketplace for ideas*. [Emphasis added][10]

Although Steven Levitt is not himself a member of the MFI steering committee, his reasoning echoes that provided by the MFI steering committee. Here we have reference to two types of competition – the narrower competition for resources, and the more significant competition in the arena of ideas. Chicago has its comparative advantage in the latter. As Levitt put it: "The Chicago economics department views the world differently than anyone

[8] Becker quoted in Kari Lydersen, "University's Plans for Milton Friedman Institute Spark Outcry," Washington Post August 29, 2008, A03.

[9] Hansen quoted in Kurt Jacobsen, "Milton Friedman Gives Chicago a Headache," *The Guardian* August 26, 2008.

[10] Steven Levitt on his blog: http://freakonomics.blogs.nytimes.com/2008/06/23/david-warsh-on-the-new-milton-friedman-institute/.

else, even other economics departments."[11] As pointed out elsewhere in this volume (Peck; Nik-Khah), the Chicago School has often viewed itself as engaged in opposition to the "East-coast establishment." Likewise, one does get the sense from the MFI proposal that a selling point of the institute is not merely its aspiration to assemble a good academic group, but also to promote a distinct set of ideas about the economy and the best way to do economics: "We see the Milton Friedman Institute as critical for preserving and fostering the strong tradition of Chicago economics" (2). Although it would be incorrect to suggest that there is universal agreement on precisely what distinguishes "Chicago economics" from its competitors in the marketplace of ideas, nevertheless there is, even among MFI committee members, broad agreement that one crucial difference pertains to its orientation toward policy. One of its members, John Cochrane, observes that Chicago economists "view free markets as a good place to start"; Gary Becker sums up the perspective in the form of two propositions: "The first proposition of Chicago economics [is] that free markets generally do a good job ... and the second proposition of Chicago economics [is] that governments don't do a good job."[12] In placing such emphasis on policy, the MFI proposal is in step with the other Chicago centers, enabling the MFI to take advantage of the same kind of generosity expressed in the recent past by a primary donor for the Becker Center (formerly known as the Initiative on Chicago Price Theory):

> I support the Initiative on Chicago Price Theory for a variety of reasons.... I have always had a great respect for the marketplace and the price incentive system.... I was fortunate to have a career during a time and place that provided me the opportunity to observe firsthand how the price incentive system could work for the benefit of society.... As in agriculture, which I have personally witnessed, the social and economic benefits of this kind of research can be enormous.[13]

[11] Steven Levitt on his blog: http://freakonomics.blogs.nytimes.com/2008/06/23/david-warsh-on-the-new-milton-friedman-institute/.

[12] Some stress Chicago's methodological approach: Kevin Murphy argues that Chicago economics is "based on the belief that the tools of economic analysis are really useful for explaining things in the real world," whereas James Heckman argues that Chicago is defined by the belief that "people react to incentives, and that incentives are important" and "linking empirical work to theory." John Cassady, "Interview with Kevin Murphy" (available: http://www.newyorker.com/online/blogs/johncassidy/2010/01/interview-with-kevin-murphy.html) and "Interview with James Heckman" (available: http://www.newyorker.com/online/blogs/johncassidy/2010/01/interview-with-james-heckman.html). Elsewhere, Heckman does acknowledge the relationship between economics and ideology: Sara Jerome, "Rifts Develop within MFI Committee," Available: www.chicagomaroon.com/2008/10/17/rifts-develop-within-mfi-committee.

[13] Remarks of Richard O. Ryan at the Inaugural Initiative on Chicago Price Theory Conference, available: http://research.chicagobooth.edu/pricetheory/events/conferences/2006conference.aspx.

13.2.2. *Building an Economics for Policy*

It is possible to glean from the MFI proposal a bit about how figures at Chicago conceive the relationship between academics and policy:

> The intellectual focus of the institute would reflect the traditions of the Chicago School and typify some of Milton Friedman's most interesting academic work, including his seminal work on the permanent income theory of consumption, his critical analysis of monetary policy, and his advocacy for market alternatives to ill conceived policy initiatives.... We recommend naming the institute the Milton Friedman Institute to honor Friedman's legacy and to indicate how the work of the Institute will, like the work of Friedman, have a deep influence on economic theory and policy around the globe. (Hansen et al. 2008, 2)

The proposal clearly reserves a large role for policy in the activities of the MFI, as do the Becker and Stigler centers. Given the central role of policy in the Chicago approach promoted within the MFI proposal, one would expect some evidence of a sophisticated appreciation of the role of the scholar in the policy-making process. Although this role is not fully spelled out, a close reading of the proposal sheds some light on the Chicago perspective. It is noteworthy that the proposal celebrates Friedman's "advocacy for market alternatives to ill conceived policy initiatives" not because it signals a judgment that only promarket policies are not inherently "ill conceived" (a fair-minded reader can reasonably interpret the formulation as announcing a critical perspective toward all sorts of policies), but instead because it calls for "advocacy," a role that one does not usually associate with academic work. Becker provided some indication of his view about the appropriate relationship between academics and advocacy for policies during an exchange with Eugene Fama at a Chicago GSB roundtable celebrating the life of Milton Friedman:

> Becker: [Friedman] was willing to go a little bit into the argumentation stage. Not everybody can do that well. There's a kind of division of labor between having the ideas and being able to promote them. He was good at both. And he went into the argumentation stage and was a tremendous arguer, and usually on the right positions.... [Chicago economists] taught you something about the division of labor, right? Some people do one thing well, and other people do other things well. He happened to be somebody that did a bunch of things well.... There are some good public intellectuals now, but the correlation between that and being good academic [economists] is weak....
>
> Fama: You have to have the interest, too. Most of us are happy just convincing our colleagues. Milton wanted to convince the whole world.
>
> Becker: Well, I wouldn't mind doing it if I could.[14]

[14] Gary Becker, in "Recalling Milton Friedman, Colleague and Teacher," audio available at http://www.chicagobooth.edu/news/2006-11-30_friedman.aspx. The quoted material appears between 36:00 and 40:45.

Although the significance that Becker assigns the activity of advocacy is unsurprising in light of his authorship of a column for *Business Week* and his popular blog site with Richard Posner,[15] one should note well that he repeatedly speaks of an intellectual "division of labor" consisting of two "stages," an academic stage and an advocacy stage. Although it is tempting to view references to the division of labor in the marketplace for ideas as mere figures of speech, such references should be taken seriously when emitted from a member of the Chicago School, particularly a former president of the MPS. This form of intellectual division of labor across various academic and nonacademic knowledge-producing institutions is a characteristic feature of neoliberalism (Plehwe 2009, 6), as is the imperative for academic work to have a "deep influence" on economics policies "around the globe." Therefore, to understand the significance of activities undertaken by the MFI, one must look beyond Hyde Park and consider the activities of closely related academic and nonacademic institutions.

Whereas sometimes both stages take place within the university (e.g., the MFI hosts several workshops for the purpose of disseminating its message to opinion makers, policy makers, and the public), other times, each stage in this division of labor has had its own supporting institution: Universities produce the academic work, and think tanks (e.g., the American Enterprise Institute or the Cato Institute) reprocess it into a more easily digestible form. Of course, Adam Smith's argument for the advantages of the division of labor really only supports the separation of tasks and not occupations (Marglin 1974). Members of the MFI steering committee have often participated in both academics and advocacy (Gary Becker and Kevin Murphy are affiliated with the American Enterprise Institute, whereas John Cochrane holds a position as an adjunct researcher at the Cato Institute), a fact that underscores the significance the need to have an impact on policy has in shaping the academic work produced. One can expect this pattern to be maintained at Chicago.

13.2.3. *Empire Building and the Governance of Research*

A third theme emerging from the MFI proposal pertains to the organization and direction – the "governance" – of research. Academics cherish their independence to conduct research, and yet it is inevitable that decisions about which research to support must be made. The MFI proposal provides some indication of the Chicago perspective on how best to make these decisions. It places the authority for recruitment and the selection of

[15] Becker's columns are reproduced in (Becker and Becker 1998) and his blog exchanges with Posner are reproduced in (Becker and Posner 2009).

themes within the hands of a committee well steeped in the Chicago neoliberal tradition; if the past year is to provide any indication, the themes closely (though not perfectly) correspond to the research interests of the committee members – for example, there has been a good deal of work on human capital theory.[16] The proposal also calls for visitors to lead some of the themed workshops and programs, and therefore the MFI relies to a large extent on faculty untenured at Chicago, a position compatible with Friedman's own views, as he opposed tenure (Peck, this volume). Finally, it places short- to medium-term visitors within a "research institute," a decision that calls for a bit of explanation because it is not clear why a normal departmental structure would be inconsistent with constructing a policy science. Could not expanding the economics program, hiring more professors in complementary schools such as business and law, or proposing an entirely new interdisciplinary graduate program accomplish the same thing? According to Robert Lucas, the answer was no:

> A department has broad teaching and research responsibilities, all of which must be met if first-rate status is to be maintained.... Promoting and hiring decisions are democratic, and new additions must bring something of fairly general interest to the table.
>
> In a research institute, strong leaders ... can place bets boldly. They do not need to campaign for votes. They are free to identify talent that the world has not yet certified and to recruit with the promise of freedom and good colleagues. (Lucas 2008)

The explicit distinction made between the departmental and research-institute method of organization in terms of democracy and leadership is significant. It suggests that the MFI would be structured to empower its committee to "place bets boldly" – something like department chairs without the inconvenience of normal tenure and hiring decisions. It calls to mind George Stigler's views as discussed in Chapter 5 of this volume; he believed that a strong leader was necessary to overcome the stultifying views of professional consensus, and that normal department structures would just get in the way. Although we have nothing close to the kind of comprehensive argument presented by Stigler by the present group of leaders at Chicago, one does find traces of this perspective in Lucas[17]; one also finds a compatible view expressed by Levitt: "If there was ever a time when it made sense for economics professors to be given tenure, that time has

[16] The original MFI proposal included as possibilities the design of monetary and tax policy in an uncertain environment, the interaction of decentralized markets for credit and insurance and the design of public policy, and the study of how legal traditions can influence economic growth.

[17] As discussed in Chapter 6, Stigler was instrumental in recruiting Lucas from Carnegie.

surely passed. The same is likely true of other university disciplines."[18] One of the advantages attributed to the research institute was that it would allow the director to circumnavigate normal academic channels and thereby improve the production of research. Such a method of organization is designed to empower those running the research institute and therefore calls attention to the increasing influence of the members of the MFI committee. One can view some of the initial activities of the MFI as early confirmation of the empowerment of committee members: the focus on human capital, theories of the family, and finance. This method of constructing institutions to develop and transmit ideas about the best way to do social science is another characteristic feature of neoliberalism.

Of course, it would require enormous resources for the Institute to operate at the scale envisioned by the MFI steering committee. To "provide financial support at a level that would ensure the long-term success of the Institute," the proposal recommended the establishment of a "Milton Friedman Institute Founder's Society," composed of the "most generous friends and supporters of the Institute" (Hansen et al. 2008, 8). This group would enjoy privileged access to MFI events.[19] The proposal also called for this group to participate in a more substantive fashion:

> The Institute would be served by establishing a visiting committee comprised of leading scholars, policy experts, and friends of the Institute. This group, which would meet no more than once or twice a year, would offer suggestions for new directions for the Institute to explore and offer high level guidance on the operations of the Institute. (8)

Given that the suggestion for establishing the Founder's Society was included in a section entitled "Governance and Administration of the Institute," and given the way the term "friends of the Institute" is used, one might reasonably conclude that the intention of the proposal was to involve donors in substantive discussions about the direction of research undertaken at the MFI. Indeed, many have arrived at this conclusion, prompting a handful of denials and protestations of shocked disbelief that anyone could possibly call the motives of MFI board members into question: "[T]his Institute cannot be research for hire whereby conclusions are pre-ordained and

[18] Levitt, "Let's just get rid of tenure (including mine)," available: http://freaknomics.blogs.nytimes.com/2007/03/03/lets-just-get-rid-of-tenure/. Apparently, being a "rogue economist" never carries any uncompensated risk to one's career.

[19] Included in the description of benefits are "discussions with the Director of the Institute," "Conversations with faculty, students, and visiting fellows in the Institute," and "a keynote address by a leading economist." The description is available on the MFI Web site, http://mfi.uchicago.edu/giving/

economists simply provide supporting evidence. We have no interest in such an institute" (Hansen 2008, 6). Such a response precludes consideration of some of the most interesting connections between economics and scientific knowledge creation.

More reflective of the historical position of the Chicago School is the reaction of James Heckman:

> I doubt there is a truly unbiased academic.... If you think the [Chicago] GSB is an unbiased environment, think again. They are recruited for their views. I wonder how many free marketers would get jobs in anthropology or sociology.... It's true of any institute. You state a mission, attract funders. They expect the mission to be fulfilled. Very rarely do people fund pure knowledge. (Heckman in Jerome 2008)

One might raise questions about the independence of an institute that relies on private funding. Such questions are perhaps understandable, but, according to Heckman, they are unfortunately misinformed and perhaps a bit naïve about how good science gets produced because all environments are biased in their own way. Moreover, the fact that all environments are biased is no cause for concern: The Chicago School is biased, but so too is the Chicago anthropology department, and so is Harvard economics, albeit in a different way. Members of the Chicago School view themselves as competing furiously in the marketplace of ideas against a handful of megaliths, not only against other well-funded economics departments, but also other disciplines that hold distinct views about markets and society.[20] Funding increases competition in the marketplace of ideas. Although this marketplace of ideas might not be "perfectly competitive," funding such initiatives as the MFI will improve outcomes in the marketplace of ideas. In this way a certain type of intellectual diversity within a department or a unit is regarded negatively, and a certain type of bias introduced by funding by economic elites is viewed positively.[21] What one wants are strong units with a common sense of purpose (defined by a strong program-building scientist), placed on financial foundations secure enough to allow it to

[20] The antagonism of Chicago to other disciplines immediately brings to mind "economics imperialism," a program often associated with Chicago School economists. For an explication of economics imperialism as an imperative of Chicago neoliberalism, see (Nik-Khah and Van Horn 2010).

[21] This position is important to bear in mind when interpreting the well-publicized dispute that broke out between Heckman and fellow MFI member John Cochrane over whether they should accede to a name change for the institute. This dispute did not so much concern the nature of bias, but whether it would be worth it to risk losing a handful of donations to lessen the perception of bias. See: Sara Jerome, "Rifts Develop within MFI Committee," available: http://www.chicagomaroon.com/2008/10/17/rifts-develop-within-mfi-committee.

out-compete other such units (or disciplines). As discussed in Chapter 5 of this volume, Stigler shared this goal.

If the circumstance that initiated discussions of the MFI was unique (the death of Friedman), viewing the MFI through the lens of Chicago neoliberalism drives home the point that the result of these discussions was not unique at Chicago. The MFI proposal calls for similar methods used at previously established centers at Chicago: workshops to organize research, the recruiting of young scholars, and the retaining of scholars already at Chicago. Animating all these activities were several beliefs: The Chicago School took a distinct approach toward economics and toward policy; this school pays special attention to promoting its doctrines outside traditional academic channels; and it views its bias as either no problem or perhaps even a virtue in that it might serve to counteract a stultified professional consensus.

What is novel about the MFI is the method it uses to promote the "Chicago approach." The MFI intends to run several short-term research projects, each run by visiting scholars and linked to workshops organized around specific themes (e.g., drug policy, education, monetary theory, property rights, development, and economics of the family). This feature represents something of a departure for the Chicago School, which in the past has organized research into "general purpose" workshops (Emmett, this volume).[22] These workshops would address specific policy-oriented areas and devote themselves to "both conceptual issues and practical issues of implementation," ultimately "to have an impact" (Hansen et al. 2008, 5). The use of short-term workshops is not unique to Chicago – the MFI proposal states that it is making use of methods of organizing research at central banks – but the incorporation of this method at such a large scale is noteworthy.

13.3. What CORES Gets Wrong about Chicago

Following the announcement of President Zimmer of the intention to establish the MFI, a group of concerned University of Chicago faculty responded with a June 2008 letter to Zimmer and Provost Thomas Rosenbaum, detailing several concerns about the plans to establish the new institute. These faculty members based their concerns expressed in this letter on their interpretation of the legacy of Milton Friedman and the announced plans contained within the "Proposal to Establish the Milton Friedman Institute."

[22] However, the Stigler Center has also sponsored visiting faculty.

This letter led immediately to several exchanges over the summer of that year and ultimately to a great deal of media attention. During this time, Professor of Computer Science and Statistics Yali Amit and Professor of History of Religions Bruce Lincoln formed with other concerned faculty the Committee for Open Research on Economy and Society (CORES), the main organization for those opposed in one form or another to the MFI. CORES then circulated a petition expressing opposition to the MFI. (Since that time it gathered 181 signatures from Chicago faculty and 1,517 from students, alumni, and those unaffiliated with Chicago.[23])

As a direct response to the petition, a meeting of the faculty senate was convened in October (the first such meeting of university-wide import in more than two decades). This meeting led directly to renaming the institute "Milton Friedman Institute for Research In Economics" instead of the "Milton Friedman Institute," a response to concerns that it would otherwise be difficult to separate Friedman's scholarly legacy from his ideological legacy. Lincoln praised the name change: "I think it's wonderful. Taking our views into account established them as caring administrators, seeing as their previous postures were ill-conceived. It restores my faith in them." Yali Amit said, mostly in agreement, "I don't want his name anywhere, but I think this is a reasonable compromise because it presents the Institute as an initiative of the economics department."[24] It is therefore reasonable to interpret much of the opposition to the MFI as rooted in beliefs about Friedman's legacy, an interpretation given some degree of corroboration by the inclusion of this concern as first among those listed in the CORES petition, as well as the public statements of CORES members.[25] Although petitioners were not in the position to make demands, the acquiescence to the name change reflects how large the symbolic importance of Friedman loomed in their minds, to the detriment of considering the present-day operation of the Chicago School.

Petitioners held strong opinions about the Chicago School, and they were sufficiently motivated by these opinions to voice an opposition to the MFI. The ideas circulated by petitioners therefore can be regarded as a good gauge of the state of non-economists' knowledge about the Chicago

[23] The text of the CORES petition is available online at: http://www.miltonfriedmancores.org/cores/petition/.

[24] Michael Lipkin, "Econ institute retains augmented Friedman moniker," The Chicago Maroon, October 31, 2008. Available: http://www.chicagomaroon.com/2008/10/31/econ-institute-retains-augmented-friedman-moniker.

[25] Yali Amit in Adrian Florido and Michael Lipkin 2008, "Faculty Senate Meets to Discuss Friedman Issue" (available: http://www.chicagomaroon.com/2008/10/17/faculty-senate-meets-to-discuss-friedman-institute).

School. No one disputes that the Chicago School has exerted a great deal of intellectual influence outside the confines of economics; therefore the impressions of non-economists about Chicago are worthy of our attention. We will indeed find that the petitioners do raise interesting and important issues pertaining to the MFI and the Chicago School, and ask questions that one generally does not find posed by academic economists. That said, I will argue that viewing the MFI through the lens of Chicago neoliberalism reveals a handful of blind spots about the Chicago School in the written protests of the petitioners.

Although the concerns raised by CORES about the MFI are varied (as one might expect, given the provenance of the petition), it is possible to organize them into a handful of themes – concerns about the legacy of Friedman, political bias, academic integrity, and the corporatization and privatization of the university. Petitioners have raised concerns that the university was celebrating the legacy of Milton Friedman. The first reason cited by the CORES opposition to the MFI is that it "threatens to be a flagship that will define the way our University is perceived by the public at large." The petition expresses concern that most people identify Friedman with his political positions and therefore will attribute to Chicago the intention of promoting those same political positions, claiming in particular, "It is not credible to claim that the MFI bears Mr. Friedman's name only in recognition of his technical accomplishments as an economist. Rather, it will be widely understood that his political positions are also being celebrated." It views this celebration as worrisome not only because of the perceived endorsement of a specific political view, but also because this view has had a negative influence: "[S]tate terror, crony capitalism, declining life expectancy, food shortages... have arisen where he and his disciples implemented these views." One gets the sense from the petitioners that they viewed the decision to name an institute after Friedman the tawdry outcome of trading off reputation for resources.

Second, petitioners expressed concern that research produced at the MFI will carry a political bias. The CORES petition charged that the "MFI's stated intention [is] to follow Friedman's lead in advocating market solutions to policy questions." The petition is certainly referring to the section of the MFI proposal that calls for an institute to "typify some of Milton Friedman's most interesting academic work, including... his advocacy for market alternatives to ill conceived policy initiatives" (Hansen et al. 2008, 2). A related complaint voiced in the petition is that the MFI will "engage in issues of policy and not limit itself to academic theory." It draws an analogy with the Hoover Institution at Stanford University, which housed Milton Friedman upon his retirement from Chicago as well as many other professors of the Chicago School for stays of varying lengths, including Gary Becker.

Third, petitioners raised concerns about the commercialization and privatization of the university. The petition charged, "The level of donor/corporate control over this Institute seems unprecedented in University history or policy." Here the petitioners singled out the establishment of the Milton Friedman Institute Founders Society, which they were concerned would tie special access to the size of contributions. In expanding on the previous point, the petition continues:

> Such arrangements also suggest increased privatization of the university and the cultivation of a symbiosis between scholars whose theories produce profits for a set of donors who then reinvest in those theories.... The analogy of research sponsored by drug and tobacco companies is not exact, but is too close for comfort.

In raising concerns about political bias, the independence of research, and the corporatization of the university, the CORES petitioners do touch upon issues of enduring significance not only for Chicago, but for all universities. However, one problem evident in the petition is a tendency to overstate the uniqueness and newness of features of the MFI. It is clear that the petitioners are unaware of many of the activities that have taken place at Chicago:

> Consider the following thought experiment. Would the Economics Department or the University imagine it could raise $200 million by founding a George Stigler Institute? George Stigler was a longtime colleague of Friedman's in the Economics Department, was also an unambiguous supporter of pure laissez-faire economics and, like Friedman, was a truly distinguished scholar who won a Noble Prize. But because he limited his publications to scholarly venues, rather than supplementing his scholarship with a free-market ideological crusade, his name would have considerably less value.[26]

The petitioners commit a rather revealing error here, because the Stigler Center for the Study of the Economy and the State has operated at Chicago for over three decades and is therefore much more than a mere "thought experiment" (and although it has not raised anywhere near $200 million, it has nevertheless proven quite successful in attracting contributions). As has been made clear by a number of this volume's authors (Van Horn and Mirowski; Nik-Khah; Emmett), a hallmark of the Chicago approach has been the construction of novel institutions supported by private funding.

One finds a similar blind spot in the petitioners' knowledge of the Chicago School in another charge: "The analogy of research sponsored by drug and

[26] CORES petition accessed on 11/5/08 at www.miltonfriedmancores.org/cores/petition

tobacco companies is not exact, but is too close for comfort." In light of the role of Proctor and Gamble in the establishment of the Stigler Center, and of Pfizer's continuing sponsorship of the Stigler Center, "analogy" would seem to be the wrong word: Drug companies *have* sponsored units that perform economic studies of regulation and government at Chicago. In light of the work on Chicago neoliberalism in this volume and elsewhere, the charge that donor control at the MFI is "unprecedented" betrays a profound ignorance about the operation of the Chicago School. Van Horn and Mirowski (2009) have revealed the role of the Volker Fund in the Free Market Study, pointing out in particular how Harold Luhnow, head of the Volker Fund, was able to "maintain control" over the project; Nik-Khah (in Chapter 5) reveals the role played by Charles Walgreen, Jr. in influencing the activities of the Walgreen Foundation. One of Chicago's distinguishing features is a willingness to tolerate – even celebrate – donor participation in its activities.

Finally, in concluding from the wording of MFI proposal that there is "no other unit of the University whose research findings are as predetermined as this one's apparently are," the petitioners reveal an unawareness of the operations of the Becker and Stigler Centers, both of which have similar mission statements. Although petitioners do raise some important issues, the petition provides some evidence of an unawareness of the history of the Chicago School.

Perhaps most importantly, examining the charge of political bias together with the charge of corporatization reveals a degree of incoherence in the CORES position. The first complaint expresses concern that the MFI will be engaged in an ideological war – a "free market ideological crusade" – whereas the second expresses concern that the MFI will focus on producing theories that "produce profits for a set of donors." Yet it is clear from the historical record both that Friedman and other members of the Chicago School have been motivated by their idea of the good society and that Chicago School members have developed their academic work in very close consultation with patrons.

One advantage of the neoliberalism account is that it offers a way to incorporate both observations without succumbing to incoherence. Chicago neoliberals did consider their beliefs about markets to be important. At the same time, they often carried out their academic work with one eye on the wants and needs of economic elites powerful enough to provide the muscle to advance the agenda: "For advocacy of capitalism to mean anything, the proponents must be able to finance their cause.… Radical movements in capitalist societies … have typically been supported by a few wealthy individuals … a role of inequality in wealth in preserving political freedom that is seldom noted" (Friedman, quoted in Van Horn and Mirowski [2009]). Or, to cite another Chicago neoliberal with special relevance to the present crisis:

> As political advisors [we can] say, "Look, the industry structure is changing." Like the banking industry has been undergoing important changes.… Whenever that's on the horizon … as it has been in banking for five or seven years … that's a great area to start deregulation. (Stigler in Hazlett 1984, 45)

However, neoliberals have never uncritically promoted the ideas of corporations or powerful patrons. As Dieter Plehwe (2009, 6–7) points out, neoliberal intellectuals were "deeply suspicious of the opportunistic pragmatism of postwar business leaders, many of whom had embraced corporatism and planning." Although economic elites did matter to neoliberal efforts, to characterize neoliberals' efforts as merely profit driven makes precisely the same kind of mistake made by those employing models of scientists as maximizing agents.

Overall, one gets the impression that petitioners are both behind and myopic in their analysis of the activities of the Chicago School and too fragmented in their understanding of how it operates. Focus on Friedman and the events in Chile, China, and the former Soviet Union has distracted attention from analysis of activities far more important to the present-day Chicago School, and far closer to home. Petitioners have failed to note that current members of the Chicago School, including those on the MFI committee, have actively participated in the kind of policy advocacy that has made petitioners uncomfortable; they have been unconvincing in challenging the relationship between funding and economic ideas produced at Chicago.

13.4. Conclusion

In the epilogue of his recently published book on the Chicago School, Johan Van Overtveldt asks: "Will the successful 20th century be followed by an equally successful 21st century at Chicago's department of economics?" He answers that this will depend on "whether or not the Chicago Tradition survives" (359–360). In discussing one of the institutions devised to ensure that the "Chicago Tradition" survives, this chapter has illuminated what crucial figures at Chicago deem this tradition to be and how they seek to preserve it; it thereby gives some hint of what one can expect of the Chicago School in the future. Given the launch of the MFI, along with the participation of several luminaries of the Chicago School in it, one fully expects the next generation of Chicago Scholars to observe some aspects of the Chicago Tradition.[27] Of course, they will inevitably depart from previous generations in other ways – the present generation certainly does – but one of the benefits of viewing this scholarship through the lens of Chicago neoliberalism is to draw attention to the most significant aspects of this tradition.

Petitioners have raised some interesting issues of global concern and have taken some steps to connecting these issues to the operation of the MFI, in the process providing some indication of the value of examining the activities of the Chicago School from an interdisciplinary perspective. They have raised important questions about the organization of research that do not usually occupy economists, even those specializing in the "economics of science." However, one gets the strong sense that a lack of knowledge about the operation of the Chicago School, as well as a lack of an overarching framework to give structure to their observations, has seriously hindered the petitioners' effectiveness in speaking to their concerns.

This chapter has argued that viewing Chicago through the lens of the history of Chicago neoliberalism provides just such an overarching framework. It meets the interdisciplinary and "theme-oriented" approach characteristic of this newest version of the Chicago School, with an interdisciplinary rather than a parochial sensibility. At the same time, this approach carries a commitment to pay close attention to economic theory, because Chicago neoliberals have crafted their form of neoclassical economics as a means to advancing on other domains of thought. The framework encourages one to attend to the role of purpose-built institutions in the propagation of knowledge about the economy, with the effect of sensitizing one to the relationship between these institutions and the nature of the knowledge produced.

Recent years have brought a burgeoning of interest about the impact of academic economics on the economy, with Chicago economists receiving a good deal of this attention. The onset of the Great Recession has bolstered interest in the impact of academic economics in general and Chicago economics in particular, with this interest now shaped by the widely shared impression that economists had a hand in bringing about the present economic crisis. Arriving at correct judgments about how economics actually matters in the world, and to what end, calls for careful analysis of academic

[27] Suffice it to say that it is premature to heed Richard Posner's call and give up using the term "The Chicago School." Posner in John Cassady, "Interview with Richard Posner." Available: http://www.newyorker.com/online/blogs/johncassidy/2010/01/interview-with-richard-posner.html.

papers, policy briefs, and the public docket, but also unpublished manuscripts and correspondences. In other words, it calls for the kinds of skills regularly employed by serious historians of economic thought. Given the importance of this issue not only for the economics profession, but also for society as a whole, one hopes historians of economic thought will heed the call.

References

Becker, Gary and Guity Becker. 1998. *The Economics of Life*. New York: McGraw-Hill.

Becker, Gary and Richard Posner. 2009. *Uncommon Sense*. Chicago: University of Chicago Press.

Hansen, Lars. 2008. "On the Milton Friedman Institute." Address delivered to the Chicago Faculty Senate.

Hansen, Lars, Gary Becker, John Cochrane, James Heckman, Robert Lucas, Kevin Murphy, and Eric Posner. 2008. "A Proposal to Establish The Milton Friedman Institute." Unpublished Report, University of Chicago.

Hazlett, Thomas. 1984. "Interview with George Stigler." *Reason* January: 44–48.

Lincoln, Bruce. 2008. "Address to the University Senate, 15 October 2008." Address delivered to the Chicago Faculty Senate.

Marglin, Stephen. 1974. "What Do Bosses Do?" *Review of Radical Political Economics* 6(2): 60–112.

Mirowski, Philip. 2009. "Postface: Defining Neoliberalism." In Philip Mirowski and Dieter Plehwe (eds.), *The Road from Mont Pèlerin: The Making of the Neoliberal Thought Collective*. Cambridge, MA: Harvard University Press.

Nik-Khah, Edward and Robert Van Horn. 2010. "Inland Empire: Economics Imperialism as an Imperative of Chicago Neoliberalism." Paper presented at the symposium: *Economics Made Fun in the Face of the Economic Crisis*, Erasmus Institute for Philosophy and Economics, Erasmus University Rotterdam.

Plehwe, Dieter. 2009. "Introduction." In Philip Mirowski and Dieter Plehwe (eds.), *The Road from Mont Pèlerin: The Making of the Neoliberal Thought Collective*. Cambridge, MA: Harvard University Press.

Stigler, George. 1963. *The Intellectual and the Market Place*. New York: Free Press of Glencoe.

Van Horn, Robert and Philip Mirowski. 2009. "The Rise of the Chicago School of Economics and the Birth of Neoliberalism." In *The Road from Mont Pèlerin*, edited by, P. Mirowski and D. Plehwe. Cambridge, MA: Harvard University Press.

Van Overtveldt, Johan. 2007. *The Chicago School: How the University of Chicago Assembled the Thinkers Who Revolutionized Economics and Business*. Chicago: Agate.

Index

Other books in the series (*continued from page iii*)

Lightning Source UK Ltd.
Milton Keynes UK
UKOW05f1209151113

221147UK00001B/52/P

9 781107 616431